Schools That Learn

PETER SENGE

NELDA CAMBRON-McCABE

TIMOTHY LUCAS

BRYAN SMITH

JANIS DUTTON

ART KLEINER

CROWN
BUSINESS

NEW YORK

Schools That Learn

A Fifth Discipline Fieldbook for Educators, Parents, and Everyone Who Cares About Education

Published in the United States by Crown Business, an imprint of the Crown Publishing Group, a division of Random House, Inc., New York. www.crownpublishing.com

Originally published in hardcover in slightly different form in the United States by Doubleday, a division of Random House, Inc., New York, in 2000.

Crown Business books are available at special discounts for bulk purchases for sales promotions or corporate use. Special editions, including personalized covers, excerpts of existing books, or books with corporate logos, can be created in large quantities for special needs. For more information, contact Premium Sales at (212) 572-2232 or e-mail specialmarkets@randomhouse.com.

Library of Congress Cataloging-in-Publication Data is available upon request.

ISBN 978-0-385-51822-2
eISBN 978-0-385-52186-4

Printed in the United States of America

Book design by Chris Welsh
Cover design by Jean Traina

10 9 8 7 6 5 4 3 2

First Revised Edition

Contents

Classroom

Getting Started

~~~~~~~~~~

I. Orientation

1. The Remembered Moment

There was once a young boy who was curious and bright; he had his own way of thinking about things and his own pace for caring about them. School didn't hold much relevance for him because he had other plans, and he was always busy learning. For instance, he collected medallions from every place he visited. Each day, he wore a different one to school around his neck.

One day his teacher said, "Matthew, tomorrow we are going to conduct a science experiment with metals. I bet we could learn something interesting about one of your necklaces." He could hardly wait to tell his parents, and much of the evening was spent discussing which medallion to take to school the next day. Finally he picked one laced with silver, from a trip he had taken with his grandfather. In the morning he was in a hurry to get to school. Returning home that evening, he shared his new scientific knowledge with his parents: metals all transmit electricity differently, and the silver in his medallion made it highly conductive.

The boy is much older now, but he still remembers that day, and he remembers what he learned about electricity. He also remembers the feelings he had—of his personal passions being genuinely interesting to others, of helping others learn, of being seen. The teacher may not remember that particular lesson, but she remembers other times when she made a special connection—sometimes with a student, other times with a mentor, a parent, another educator, or someone else—and came away changed.

Everyone reading this book, no doubt, has had similar experiences—when someone fired your imagination with new knowledge or touched a deep chord in you that opened doorways you didn't know existed. Why do

The Drive to Learn: An Interview with Edward T. Hall," *Santa Fe Lifestyle*, (Spring 1988), pp. 12–14.

experiences like these hold so much power? Perhaps it's because they are part of our most common birthright as human beings: our entry into life as eager and natural learners. "The drive to learn is as strong as the sexual drive," writes anthropologist Edward T. Hall. "It begins earlier and lasts longer."

Learning is at once deeply personal and inherently social; it connects us not just to knowledge in the abstract, but to each other. Why else would it matter so much when a teacher notices something special about a student? Throughout our lives, as we move from setting to setting, we encounter novelty and new challenges, small and large. If we are ready for them, living and learning become inseparable.

What if all communities were dedicated, first and foremost, to fostering this connection between living and learning? Such a world might feel very different from our own. There would be no boundaries between "school" and "work" and "life." Skillful people, from groundskeepers to accountants to scientists to artisans, would have a steady stream of apprentices, both children and adults. People of every age would continually embark on new endeavors and enterprises, taking failure in stride, readily seeking one another's help. Teenagers would spend most of their learning time outside school walls (as Hall puts it, "with all that energy, they shouldn't be in school"), working on projects with real meaning for them. And children would be everywhere, in civic meetings and business conferences, just as they are present in significant meetings among many indigenous peoples. An innate communitywide culture of learning would lead to fewer quick fixes that seem to work at first but then backfire. The children, the culture, and all everyday practices would continually remind people of the real purpose of our endeavors: to look out for the long term.

Arguably, with the pace of social, economic, and technological change continuing to accelerate, we are already moving into such a world, whether we are ready for it or not. Some critics say that this will make schools irrelevant. We feel exactly the opposite is true. No matter how technologically advanced our world becomes—no matter how many tablet computers they own or how many functions their smartphones perform—children will always need safe places for learning. They will always need launching pads from which to follow their curiosity into the larger world. And they will always need places to make the transition from their childhood homes to the larger society of peers and adults.

That is why a culture dedicated to learning would devote its resources to those institutions that most shape our development as learners. They might or might not resemble the schools we have today. But they would be places where everyone, young and old, would continuously develop and grow in each other's company; they would be incubation sites for continuous change and growth. If we want the world to improve, in other words, then we need schools that learn.

2. The Idea of a School That Learns

Schools that learn are everywhere, at least in people's imaginations. The core idea that has inspired this book—both in its first edition, published in the year 2000, and now in this second edition of 2012—is simple: institutions of learning can be designed and run as learning organizations. In other words, schools can be made sustainably vital and creative, not by fiat or command or by regulation or forced rankings, but by adopting a learning orientation. This means involving everyone in the system in expressing their aspirations, building their awareness, and developing their capabilities together. In a school that learns, people who traditionally may have been suspicious of one another—parents and teachers, educators and local businesspeople, administrators and union members, people inside and outside the school walls, students and adults—recognize their common stake in each other's future and the future of their community.

By now thousands of people in hundreds of schools have accumulated more than three decades' worth of experience in the practice of schools that learn. Much of this experience has taken place under other names: "school reform," "effective schools," "educational renewal," "systems thinking in the classroom," and even in some aspects of "no child left behind." The experimentation continues, and the resulting understanding of the relationship among educators, schools, learners, and communities continues to deepen.

Much of this activity—though by no means all—is grounded in the explicit work with learning organizations that was explored in the *Fifth Discipline* series of books. The seven Fifth Discipline volumes (counting second editions, including this one) are all based on a single core idea: that it is possible to create organizations that learn through the ongoing practice of five "learning disciplines" for changing the way people think and act together. These disciplines—systems thinking, personal mastery, working with mental models, building shared vision, and team learning—provide a great deal of leverage for those who want to foster and build better organizations and communities.

The six other volumes of the Fifth Discipline series (in order of publication, most recent first) are: Peter Senge, Bryan Smith, Nina Kruschwitz, Joe Laur, and Sara Schley, *The Necessary Revolution: How Individuals and Organizations Are Working Together to Create a Sustainable World* (2008); Peter Senge, *The Fifth Discipline: The Art and Practice of the Learning Organization* (revised and updated edition, 2006); Peter Senge, Nelda Cambron-McCabe, Timothy Lucas, Bryan Smith, Janis Dutton, and Art Kleiner, *Schools That Learn: A Fifth Discipline Fieldbook for Educators, Parents, and Everyone Who Cares About Education* (original edition, 2000); Peter Senge, Art Kleiner, Charlotte Roberts, Richard Ross, George Roth, and Bryan Smith, *The Dance of Change: The Challenges of Sustaining Momentum in Learning Organizations* (1999); Peter Senge, Art Kleiner, Charlotte Roberts, Richard Ross, and Bryan Smith, *The Fifth Discipline Fieldbook: Strategies and Tools for Building a Learning Organization* (1994); Peter Senge,

The Fifth Discipline: The Art and Practice of the Learning Organization (original edition, 1990).

All from Currency/Doubleday (a division of Random House).

For more on leverage and Buckminster Fuller's trim tab example, see *The Fifth Discipline*, (second edition, 2006), pp. 63–65.

LEVERAGE

Small, relatively inexpensive, well-focused actions can sometimes produce significant, enduring improvements, if they're in the right place. Systems thinkers refer to this principle as leverage. Tackling a difficult problem is often a matter of seeing where the high leverage lies. Leverage often comes from new ways of thinking. Human systems (such as schools) are particularly prone to being affected in large ways by small changes that are not obvious to most people—because they do not fully understand why the system operates the way it does.

~~~

The genesis for the first edition of *Schools That Learn* was the discovery that this overall approach seems to resonate with educators because it brings together two goals that often seem in conflict: to realize people's deepest aspirations and to foster better long-term educational performance. The results include noticeable improvements in test scores and other extrinsic measures, but, more importantly, they include breakthroughs of the mind and heart.

Whether you are a teacher, an administrator, a parent, or even a student, this book will help you achieve the same in your own school. The volume contains more than 170 pieces of writing by 67 authors. They include tools and methods, stories and reflections, guiding ideas, exercises, and resources that people have adopted to help make institutions of learning more like learning organizations. Many of the articles are intensely pragmatic, geared toward helping teachers, school administrators, or parents solve particular problems. Many of them are deeply reflective, aimed at helping you see the school world as you haven't seen it before, so you can operate within it, or change it, in more effective ways. These articles are not meant to be prescriptive or restrictive—they are easily adapted to a wide variety of circumstances, including higher education and lifelong learning. There are no "top-ten learning schools" in this book; we don't offer profiles of exemplary cases where star educators have figured out their problems in ways that the rest of us can simply copy. Indeed, no school's experience can be applied to another's situation wholesale. All schools, and their situations, are unique and require their own unique combination of theories, tools, and methods for learning.

We call this book *Schools That Learn*, but we are not limiting our vision to improving single schools or colleges as self-contained individual entities. That's because schools don't exist in isolation; instead they have the potential to be fulcrum points for learning in the communities around them. Sustainable communities need viable schools for all their children and learning opportunities for all their adults. In our view, a learning school is not so much a distinct and discrete place (for it may not stay in one building or facility) as a living system for learning—one dedicated to the idea that all those involved with it, individually and together, will be continually enhancing and expanding their awareness and capabilities.

Introducing the Five Learning Disciplines

PM   MM
SV ST TL

Schools that train people only to obey authority and follow the rules unquestioningly have poorly prepared their students for our increasingly complex and interdependent world. Today, people in all walks of life are called upon to act with greater autonomy, to lead as well as follow, to question difficult issues in a safe manner, and to become more conscious of the habits of thought that govern our behavior and shape our prospects.

The five disciplines of organizational learning are ongoing bodies of study and practice that help develop this type of perspective and skill. As many teachers and administrators have noted, the learning disciplines also offer effective ways to deal with the dilemmas and pressures of educational institutions.

Two of the disciplines represent ways of **articulating individual and collective aspirations**—and using those to set a direction.

- **Personal Mastery:** Personal mastery is the practice of developing a coherent image of your personal vision—the results you most want to create in your life—alongside a realistic assessment of the current reality of your life today. This produces an innate tension that, when cultivated, can expand your capacity to make better choices and to achieve more of the results that you have chosen.
- **Shared Vision:** This collective discipline establishes a focus on mutual purpose. People with a common purpose (e.g., the teachers, administrators, and staff in a school) can learn to nourish a sense of commitment in a group or organization by developing shared images of the future they seek to create and the strategies, principles, and guiding practices by which they hope to get there. A school or community that hopes to live by learning needs a common shared vision process.

Two of the disciplines involve the practice of **reflective thinking and generative conversation:**

- **Mental Models:** This discipline of reflection and inquiry skills is focused around developing awareness of attitudes and perceptions—your own and those of others around you. Working with mental models can also help you more clearly and honestly define current reality. Since most mental models in education are often "undiscussable" and hidden from view, one of the critical acts for a learning school is to develop the capability to talk safely and productively about dangerous and discomfiting subjects.
- **Team Learning:** This is a discipline of group interaction. Through such techniques as dialogue and skillful discussion, small groups of people transform their collective thinking, learning to mobilize their energies and actions to achieve common goals and draw forth an intelligence and ability greater than the sum of individual members' talents. Team learning can be fostered inside classrooms, between parents and teachers, among members of the community, and in the "pilot groups" that pursue successful school change.

And the final discipline (the "fifth" discipline of the original book) is an extensive body of knowledge and practice for **recognizing and managing complexity** in the world at large.

- **Systems Thinking:** In this discipline, people learn to better understand interdependency and change and thereby are able to deal more effectively with the forces that shape the consequences of their actions. Systems thinking is based on a growing body of theory about the behavior of feedback and complexity—the innate tendencies of a system that lead to growth or stability over time. Tools and techniques such as stock-and-flow diagrams, system archetypes, and various types of learning labs and simulations help students gain a broader and deeper understanding of the subjects they study. Systems thinking is a powerful practice for finding the leverage needed to achieve the most constructive change.

⟩⟩ Part II of this book, starting page 70, is an in-depth primer on the five disciplines.

Educators have told us that the learning disciplines sound great, and then they asked, "But what do we do Monday morning? How do we create a sense of systemic awareness or personal mastery within our staff? Is it worth even trying with students? How can we integrate these skills and practices with our existing curriculum and all the changes imposed on us? How do we discover exactly what type of learning classroom or school we wish to create? What do we do about the pressures coming from outside? How do we get started?"

Parents who are familiar with the learning disciplines have similar questions: "How do we use these disciplines to deal with problems like homework or disputes with other children? How do we use them in working with our children's teachers? What kind of relationship can we build between the school and the workplace or other places in the community?"

No book can provide the complete answers to these questions. But a book like this can introduce you to effective ways of approaching the problems. It can offer strategies that are grounded in the collective experience of people in a wide variety of public and private schools, colleges, and universities. And it can show you how to start developing your own strategies. In all, thousands of people, including parents, teachers, administrators, experts, politicians, and students themselves, are evolving together into a worldwide community of organizational learners in education. Those who take on the methods and tools of organizational learning, and who seek to understand the theories that underlie them, typically find they have a huge amount of leverage for change and influence that they did not recognize before and a far better awareness of what changes to push for. And that is fortunate, because together we face an extraordinarily difficult but vital and crucial task: re-creating schools to serve students who will come of age in a postindustrial and increasingly connected world.

The Current Reality of Schooling

During the fifteen years since we first started working on this book, we have often heard people voice the opinion that American schools are falling behind—that industrial-age schools are hopelessly failing. This perception dates back at least to 1983, when the U.S. government report, *A Nation at Risk*, argued that the country's population was too poorly educated to compete in the global marketplace. While many of the broad accusations of that report have since been proven false, the perception of schools in crisis remained strong and in recent years has only been exacerbated by reports of American test scores lagging far behind those in other nations, such as Finland and Singapore. Other countries have had their own bouts of collective anxiety about schools and their own frustration at not feeling able to improve. In addition to the stress this has placed on educators, many students feel extraordinary pressure to compete because of the pervasive fear that they will be shut out of a suc-

A Nation at Risk, National Commission on Excellence Report (U.S. Department of Education, 1983). The crisis assumptions of the report are questioned in David C. Berliner and Bruce J. Biddle, *The Manufactured Crisis: Myths, Fraud, and the Attack on America's Public Schools* (Basic Books, 1996).

cessful life unless they excel in school.

The causes of these pressures on schools are far more complex than many people realize. In the nineteenth-century industrial world, a one-size-fits-all educational system was a boon that reduced the abusiveness of child labor and brought opportunity to the world. By 1950, half of the eighteen year olds in industrialized nations expected to graduate secondary school; many of these people got relatively good jobs even though they had little more than sixth-grade-level math and reading skills.

Today, by any objective measure, when you take into account the full range of the school population, educators in the United States (and probably around the world) are much better at teaching basic skills than they were thirty or fifty years ago. After all, much has been learned about teaching and learning during those years, and much of that knowledge is now part of the typical teachers' training in any industrialized nation.

But at the same time, the bar has been raised dramatically. Just in the twelve years since the first edition of this book was published, the context of education—in the United States and elsewhere around the world—has subtly but irrevocably changed in several important ways:

For more on the educational needs of manufacturing, see Arvind Kaushal, Tom Mayor, and Patricia Riedl, "Manufacturing's Wake-Up Call," *strategy+business*, Autumn 2011, and the sidebar, "Revitalizing Education for Manufacturing," by Wallace Hopp and Roman Kapuscinski of the University of Michigan Tauber Institute for Global Operations, www.strategy-business.com/article/11306.

- **The pace of knowledge:** In the United States and many industrialized countries, the jobs available to people without much education continue to diminish, both in quality and relative quantity. There are still plenty of factory jobs available, but only for people who have basic computer literacy, a twelfth-grade reading level (for complex, ever-changing machine instructions), a grasp of statistics (for quality control), a basic background in physics, a little programming knowledge, and possibly proficiency in a foreign language (to telecommunicate with their counterparts in, say, Brazil or China). Emerging nations have their own unprecedented challenges for educational achievement, particularly as they make the transition to more middle-class economies and to more democratic and decentralized governments. Thus, countries and communities everywhere in the world see the quality of schools as a major factor—maybe the single greatest factor—in their ability to prosper and provide for their people.
- **Worldwide interdependence:** The emergence of successful enterprise and self-determination around the world is usually called "globalization," and it is enabled by universal factors such as communications links, social media, and trade, but its greatest effect has been local. People in nearly every local community, everywhere, feel their fate connected to others in a way they never have before. This has affected every nation's view of its schools.

For example, the Chinese national government mandated compulsory nine-year schooling in 1986; in the 2000s, free elementary school education spread throughout the country. There is an enormous emphasis on science and mathematics education in many Asian nations, aimed at producing graduates capable in technology. And yet there is also a perceived dearth of creativity. A Chinese postdoctoral student whom we know has studied the proficiency of Chinese school graduates who are now in their twenties. By and large, they know how to prepare diligently for formal exams, but comparatively few of them know how to take the kind of creative leap that leads to technological breakthroughs.

Meanwhile, in the United States, the system produces a fair number of creative innovators but is also perceived as failing to produce a broad base of graduates with basic science and math skills. As students from these two cultures continue to encounter each other, they will have a choice: to work together and combine their skills or to compete destructively against each other. Their ability to choose productively will depend, in part, on how well their schools have equipped them for the interdependent world they live in.

■ **Economic stress and social uncertainty:** The "have and have-not" economy, in which there is a widening gap between the quality of life and opportunity available to the rich and poor, has enormous effects on educational institutions. So does the diverse and unpredictable social and domestic landscape of many cultures today. Schools are expected to compensate for many social and economic factors that affect children: changes in family structure, rapidly shifting trends in television and popular culture, commercialism without end, poverty (and the inadequate nutrition and healthcare that often go with it), violence, child abuse, teenage pregnancy, substance abuse, and incessant social upheaval. Schools are now routinely charged with educating children from single-parent homes, children with mental and physical disabilities, children who are very poor/ homeless, and children who do not speak the dominant language.

Struggling to keep up with these kinds of demands, school leaders continually place their institutions on the frontier of change. (The perennial whirlwind of educational fads and fashions is a symptom of this struggle.) Yet schools also face intense pressure to slow down change, to be conservative, to reinforce traditional practices, and not to leave anyone behind. Finally, they must face these pressures, in many countries, under severe financial pressure as the impact of the global financial crisis continues to be felt.

■ **Technological change** directly raises pressure on schools today. Some experts blithely (and short-sightedly) predict that public schooling itself will die soon, "done in" by its inability to keep up with the pace of this change. That won't happen, but schools are being transformed. Already, many students from second grade onward are used to carrying their own smartphones and tablets and logging onto websites. Many of the most critical learning conversations for many students don't take place in class, or even at recess—they now take place online, at eight or ten o'clock at night, with people who live hundreds or thousands of miles away.

Technology is also dramatically changing the ways in which students access knowledge. In 1999, when we were writing the first edition of this book, Apple had not yet produced the first iPhone, iPod, or iPad; the World Wide Web was only a few years old; the eChalk company (whose technology platform is now prevalent in many schools) was just being founded; the Google search engine barely existed; and Wikipedia and Facebook were not even conceived of. Today, students of all ages and grade levels take all of these and more for granted and use them, sometimes counterproductively, as tools for their education. Meanwhile, teachers have also changed their habits accordingly—for example, posting and receiving assignments online, letting students critique each other's schoolwork, and using search engines to check for plagiarism.

All of this creates great opportunities for more engaged learning. For example, the conventional printed textbook is being replaced by electronic counterparts, some of which are assembled on the fly in school-specific or even classroom-specific versions, often with multimedia segments. When students are dissatisfied with the textbook or with a teacher's explanation, they can find alternatives in the form of interactive exercises and videos, delivered through self-tutoring services like the Khan Academy. New platforms like Twitter and YouTube have also made it easier to see how information is related across disciplines, by allowing independent creators to distribute work where the links among math, science, social sciences, music, and the humanities are brought to the foreground. These links are vital to understanding any of these disciplines today and tend to be inadequately covered by the ways that educational subjects (and the examinations that cover them) are organized.

But at the same time, the ubiquity of technology in schools creates new challenges and amplifies others that previously existed. For example, it can exacerbate the gap between haves (who come to school with their own computers) and have-nots (who must use institutional

As we were editing the second edition in 2011, the Khan Academy (www.khanacademy.org), a nonprofit compendium of videos and interactive exercises for PK–12 education, had just become prominent.

or shared computers); it can drown students and educators in poorly presented and misguided information; it can augment real-world bullying with cyberbullying; and it adds levels of complexity to the learning process that schools have never had to cope with before.

Nor is it clear that many educators are prepared for these technological opportunities and challenges. Just as the continued evolution of the Internet, of social media, and of mobile telephones has diminished the ability of authoritarian governments to maintain control, these technologies have also made it harder for educators to control the information students take in. Students are now learning on their own that any source of information, including the school, teacher, media, government, and each other, can be legitimately questioned. They are putting themselves forward on sites like Facebook and YouTube, making them more visible, more connected—and more vulnerable.

■ **Frustrations with the quality of education:** While schools have been charged with fixing many social problems they didn't create, they have been increasingly perceived as failing at their primary mission, which in itself creates a whole new set of problems.

The first is the fact that parents are often dissatisfied with the education their children receive. All six authors of this book are parents and educators, and all of us—and many of the people we know—have been so frustrated with the public school options available to our children at times that we have either placed our children in private school or seriously considered doing so. Nor have private schools been much better; in our experience, the task of being a parent means constantly being challenged by the shortfalls and learning disabilities of schools as a system. And we know we are not unusual.

Moreover, employers are frustrated with the skill levels of the people they hire. The constant refrain that schools are failing to equip students for the global economy is so ingrained that it has set the tone of dismal school-business relationships for at least four decades.

Students themselves are frustrated with the sheer time-wasting, numbing quality of so many hours that they spend at school, including many of their social hours. For proof, you need only think back to your own school years or see any popular movie about school life.

See "The Great Game of School," page 380.

And some communities are frustrated with the way school systems are governed, in which a small group of people on a school board—often elected with the support of only part of the community—can change a school system's direction abruptly and almost at whim.

To respond to all of these forces effectively will take a great deal of perspective, thought, and experimentation. No one really knows what the working world or, indeed, what civilization and culture worldwide will be like when today's kindergartners graduate from college. All we know is that those realities will be very different than the world most educators and parents knew when they were growing up. As *Fifth Discipline Fieldbook* coauthor Charlotte Roberts notes, "Do we really want to re-create the schools we remember from our own childhoods? Do we want to stop the flow of change and create stagnant pools of schooling because that's what educators were molded to fit into?"

Educators thus face an unprecedented set of challenges, but also a tremendous opportunity that they can't ignore: to broaden their students' horizons, catalyze innovation, incorporate systems thinking into the curriculum, and open themselves to the world outside. Unfortunately, many of the solutions that have been put in place so far are quick fixes, addressing only symptoms instead of underlying causes and therefore producing unintended consequences. If you are troubled by a mouse under a carpet and deal with the lump by stamping it down, the mouse will simply run to another part of the carpet.

One very prominent quick fix—the use of standardized tests to track and enforce educational quality—has led to a number of well-known "mouse trails": attempts to generate higher scores for schools even if that has to be done without real increases in learning or student capability. Schools have promoted prescription medication to help students focus, encouraged failing students to drop out so scores won't be counted, covered up or fudged test results, classified students as disabled (and thus exempt from some testing), or, most commonly, set up classrooms and curricula to "teach to the test": to focus on drill and practice for exams. Meanwhile, the ways in which the scores are often measured—for example, in comparisons of students from different ethnic backgrounds—make it look like the tests are helping close the "achievement gap," when actually the various groups are still as far apart as they have ever been (they're just getting better scores in aggregate, with the same disparities among them). These effects are, at best, counterproductive and sometimes downright harmful.

Worse still, the mechanistic solutions often replace classroom creativity and overwhelm the power of a student-teacher connection. Students who spend the bulk of their classroom time learning to pass tests lose opportunities to gain the many other skills they might find valuable as whole, competent, and generous human beings who contribute to the larger community around them. In other words, as educator and staff development expert Edward Joyner puts it, they learn to "pass the test but fail at life."

On the side effects of testing and school choice, see Diane Ravitch, *The Death and Life of the Great American School System: How Testing and Choice are Undermining Education* (Basic Books, 2010), reviewed on page 329.

Another quick fix is the idea of school choice: giving parents and students more options to attend different types of schools without extra cost. This type of solution takes many forms—magnet schools, home schooling, charter schools, vouchers, and policies allowing parents to apply to any elementary school in the city—but in all cases, the schools compete for applicants. Each of these approaches has been criticized, and a systemic view of them suggests that each has complex ramifications and consequences. Vouchers, for instance, are based on taking the responsibility for schools out of the public arena: a prospect mistrusted by most people in democratic societies. Charter schools often divert funds to schools with questionable management—or drain the best students and a disproportionate share of a community's education budget to one or two schools and leave the others bereft.

Though the principles of better accountability and of school choice seem undeniably valuable to many, experience has now shown that these principles do not automatically make things better when they are put in place. The potential of these solutions is only realized when they are implemented with care, attention, and perspective. As with any complex problem, the only viable sustainable solution to the problems facing our nation's schools is to adopt a learning orientation. This means recognizing that an institution of learning can also be a learning organization—in other words not thinking of the school as an isolated entity but as an interconnected set of processes and practices, linked by its nature both to the community around it and to the classrooms and individual learning experiences within it. It means fostering open dialogue and public engagement of the sort that makes the perspectives and underlying assumptions of various factions clear.

And that, in turn, is where the disciplines of organizational learning will help us overcome these challenges—from globalization to technological change to economic instability—and breathe new life into our educational system so that we can better prepare our children to thrive in a postindustrial world.

LEARNING

LEXICON

In the Chinese language, two characters represent the word "learning." The first character means "to study." It is composed of two parts: a symbol that means "to accumulate knowledge" is placed above a symbol for a child in a doorway. The second character means "to practice constantly," and it shows a bird developing the ability to leave the nest. The upper symbol represents flying;

the lower symbol, youth. For the Asian mind, learning is ongoing. "Study" and "practice constantly," together, suggest that learning should mean: "mastery of the way of self-improvement." —Peter Senge

Three Nested Systems of Activity

Good connections start with recognition. One of the most consistent themes underlying this book project is the need for a clear expression of "I See You": the ability to recognize each other's identity and value, particularly if one or both of us have been invisible to the other before now. The phrase comes from the opening of *The Fifth Discipline Fieldbook*:

> Among the tribes of northern Natal in South Africa, the most common greeting, equivalent to "hello" in English, is the expression: *Sawu bona*. It literally means, "I see you." If you are a member of the tribe, you might reply by saying *Sikhona*, "I am here." The order of the exchange is important: until you see me, I do not exist. It's as if, when you see me, you bring me into existence.
>
> This meaning, implicit in the language, is part of the spirit of *ubuntu*, a frame of mind prevalent among native people in Africa below the Sahara. The word "ubuntu" stems from the folk saying *Umuntu ngumuntu ngabantu*, which, from Zulu, literally translates as: "A person is a person because of other people." If you grow up with this perspective, your identity is based on the fact that you are seen—that the people around you respect and acknowledge you as a person.

From *The Fifth Discipline Fieldbook*, p. 3. Our understanding of the meaning of sawu bona and ubuntu derives from conversation with Louis van der Merwe and his colleagues James Nkosi and Andrew Mariti.

Who, then, are the participants in any effort to create a school that learns? Whether the school is public or private, urban or rural, large or small, there are three nested systems at play, interdependent with one another, and all with interwoven patterns of influence. These systems— the classroom, the school, and the community—interact in ways that are sometimes hard to see but that shape the priorities and needs of people at all levels. In any effort to foster schools that learn, changes will make a difference only if they take place at all three levels.

THE LEARNING CLASSROOM

At its core is the classroom—an ongoing gathering of students and teachers whose purpose is learning. Parents are not included within the boundary of the classroom because they are not residents there—they do not appear in class every day. Yet their presence is always felt. Their involvement is crucial to the functioning of the classroom (and the larger school as well). The three prime components of the classroom, therefore, exist in a cycle of mutual influence.

■ **Teachers:** There is no experience like a great teaching moment, which is why many teachers join the profession. Charlotte Roberts recalls the magic she experienced when she taught beginning reading as a first-grade teacher. "If you don't know how to read, the letters in a book are nothing more than squiggles on a page. The teacher's job is to help students unlock the squiggles. Then the day comes when the child proudly walks out of the classroom, a pre-primer under her arm like it's the *Wall Street Journal*. You can see it in her body language. 'Look at me! I'm going home to read to…' Mom and Dad, big brother, Grandma, or whoever's at home. There's nothing like the magic of that. Teachers know that magic and never lose sight of it."

  Three attitudes about teachers permeate this book. First, every school must have, as part of its core purpose, the promotion and development, the care and security—a recognition of the importance—of its teachers. Second, teachers must act as stewards for all students, fostering their relationships with each other and with the base of knowledge. Stewardship means holding a commitment to the entire learning community of the school, not just "my classroom" and "my students." Third, good teachers themselves are continuous and lifelong learners, with their knowledge of their subject—and of the craft of teaching—evolving throughout their lifetimes.

  In the last decade in particular, many teachers have found themselves drawn to reflect on their methods and to look for more innovative teaching approaches. It's either that or devote themselves to rote drill and command-and-control tactics in classrooms designed on the industrial factory model, with less and less effectiveness for their students. We hope this book will be useful for teachers who instead take on the role of learning professionals.

■ **Students:** Students are the only players who see all sides of the nested systems of education, yet they are typically the people who have the least influence on its design. In that sense, they are often (especially as they move on to middle school and high school) like drivers in a long traffic jam. They feel blocked by something they can't quite see, tempted to swarm past each other competitively, and unable to do anything about the problem.

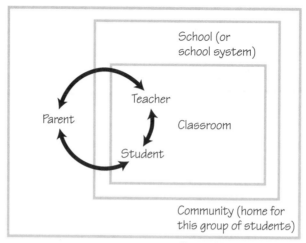

School (or school system)

Teacher

Parent

Classroom

Student

Community (home for this group of students)

The world at large (beyond the community)

In this book we see students not just as passive recipients of information but as cocreators of knowledge and participants in the evolution of the school. We acknowledge that most schoolchildren are still developing the cognitive and emotional capabilities for dealing with complex disciplines such as personal mastery and systems thinking. We also believe they are capable of creating a vision for their own lifelong learning and that to do so they need to be part of a system that nurtures all their capabilities and awareness. If you are a student coming to this book, we hope you will gain a better sense of how to take full membership in the systems in which you learn, from classroom to school to community.

■ **Parents:** One unfortunate mental model among educators is that parents are no longer interested in becoming involved in schools. Another mental model sees parents as the obstacles: source of demands that make the educator's job more difficult. Meanwhile, parents have negative mental models of their own about education. Some associate the school building with their own past history of uncomfortable learning. Others may hold back from getting involved in organizational learning for lack of time or lack of encouragement. Attitudes like these are pervasive, and they unnecessarily diminish children's learning.

We insist on writing for parents as well as for educators in this book because we know how much they need each other to establish learning classrooms and schools. If you are a parent reading this, we assume that you are a highly committed partner in the learning process of your children. We hope to show exactly how the development of children depends on the development of all the adults in the system, including yourself.

Part III of this book (pages 159–175, after the orientation and the primer on the learning disciplines), concerns the *learning classroom*. In five topics, ranging from theories about learning to teaching practices to systems thinking in the classroom, we investigate the current knowledge needed to re-create any classroom into a more sustained, successful, and purposeful collaborative environment.

THE LEARNING SCHOOL

Classrooms require an organizational infrastructure to sustain them. In this book, we consider schools, school systems, and systems of higher education as formal organizations—with a hierarchical structure, a key set of core constituents, and a board of directors elected (or appointed) by the school's community. To be sure, different communities organize their schools and universities in different ways—some school systems have only one school, while others have hundreds. But they all have the same basic mission: ensuring that classrooms exist to provide the highest quality learning experiences for all the students they serve.

The school is also a social system (a source of friendship and social status for most of the students attending), a source of ongoing development and training for its staff, and (in many places) a unionized workplace—all of which adds additional levels of complexity. Finally, some school leaders have learned that the school can be a very effective initial source for catalyzing change and innovation—in classrooms, in the school's own practices, and in the surrounding community.

Thus, we hope this book's readers will include many people who are primarily active at the school—not the classroom—level, such as:

■ **Superintendents:** Organizationally, superintendents possess more formal authority than anyone else in a school system. Yet the average tenure for a school district superintendent in the United States is less than three years. If you are a superintendent, one of the first steps in any learning initiative is recognizing the power that you do—and do not—have. As an executive leader of the school system, you are capable of setting an example of highly effective behavior and enabling the creation of a learning school system. But you cannot, alone, mandate reform or direct a reform effort. We hope this book will provide both the perspective and the tools you need to galvanize people in a way that will spark change throughout the school system, at an appropriate pace.

⟩⟩ For more about leadership of a school system, see page 414.

■ **Principals, school leaders, and higher education administrators:** In our experience, the impetus for change and reform often comes first from the principals, deans, and other administrators of individual schools. These are the instructional leaders for teachers—the people who set a tone for learning within the school. As a principal or school administrator, you may feel caught in the middle between parents, teachers, higher administrators and governing bodies and your own sense of what the students need. As you get involved in organizational learning at your school, you become even more of a fulcrum point—not just a supervisor of teachers but a "lead teacher and lead learner" and steward of the learning process as a whole.

■ **School board members, trustees, and university regents:** Oftentimes, school board members and trustees are seen as overseers, comptrollers, and policy setters rather than as learners with a direct impact on the children and students of the system. A board that models organizational learning in its own practices can make an enormous difference to the school system and to its members. If you are a member of such a board, we hope this book will help you see the limits that you set and possibilities that you bring forth as a steward of the system.

Part IV of this book (pages 176–208) concerns the learning school. We look at the development of the process and practice of school change, including the establishment of a collective vision, building awareness of current reality, the generation of effective leadership, and the task of scaling up pilot projects to involve an entire school or university system.

THE LEARNING COMMUNITY

The third, and by far the most complex level, is the community. More broadly, the community is the learning environment within which the school or college operates. As every parent knows, the school classroom provides only a small part of what a child, teenager, or college student learns during the course of a week. The rest comes from a range of activities and interests: from the media (television, magazines, popular music, and the Internet) and from friends and other peers. All of these influences, in turn, draw from the character of the community—local, regional, and international.

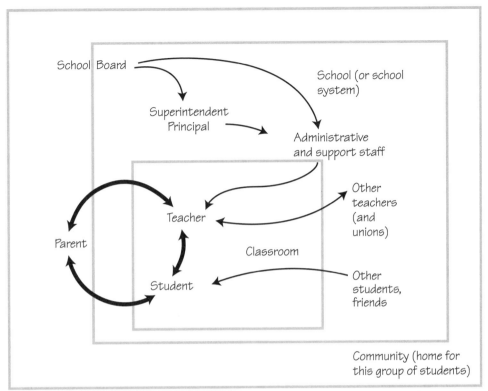

In the first edition of this book, we wrote about the importance of the school-community relationship, and we tried to offer tools and approaches for making that relationship stronger and more beneficial. Since then, we have seen even more dramatic evidence of its importance. In our increasingly interdependent world, no one can truly create a "school that learns" without engaging and changing the community that surrounds it. And whenever that engagement is incomplete, school reform efforts fail.

We have also seen how vulnerable innovative school leaders can be when they do not have full community support. Indeed, of the nine superintendents who wrote articles in the first edition of *Schools That Learn* (including coauthor Tim Lucas), not one is still in office in the same district. Some have moved to other districts; others have gone on to teach in higher education or work for other types of educational institutions. This statistic, while it may seem disheartening, doesn't mean that their ideas were wrong or their efforts were futile. Indeed, all of them achieved remarkable results. But it does suggest that an organizational learning initiative in schools cannot rely on any single leader, no matter how effective or charismatic; such learning needs to be grounded in a community of leaders.

}} See, for example, "'Lone Ranger to Lead Learner," by Peter Negroni, page 428; and "Creating }} a Core Learning Group," by Les Omotani, page 445.

Today, many communities are taking on a renewed involvement in the local school system—in part as a response to the new pressures they feel from economic stress or demographic change, and in part as a response to the growing number of children in many locales. Some old ideas, like "service learning," in which community members played a role in mentoring students, have become far more sophisticated. The idea of "community engagement"—establishing mutual reflection and joint learning initiatives among school leaders, students and, community members—has become increasingly prominent. This is probably the most effective way that a school system leader can redefine the school's relationship with the people outside its walls.

Three groups located primarily in the community system were often in our minds as we created the book:

- **Community members:** If you are a community member, then you may not be used to thinking of yourself as an educator or a learner. You may not have worked closely with schools in the past. But community leaders, businesspeople, people who work in community organizations, and educators are becoming more aware that they cannot operate in isolation from one another. Thus, a recurring theme in this book concerns school-community interdependence, even at the classroom level. We hope you will find a variety of ideas, methods, and resources for understanding, reforming, and improving those interrelationships for the sake of all the community's children and for the community's own sustainability.
- **Lifelong learners:** School, we've been told, is the place for learning, and adult life is the place for knowing. In this book, we consider ways to challenge that assumption in practice—both by making schools more of an environment that promotes learning for teachers and administrators as well as for students and by developing communities that support learning at all ages.
- **Educational professionals:** The first edition of this book found one of its most enduring audiences in the faculty and students of teacher education and educational leadership departments. But as people start talking more seriously about the purpose of schools, that dialogue will extend to other education professionals as well: to the writers

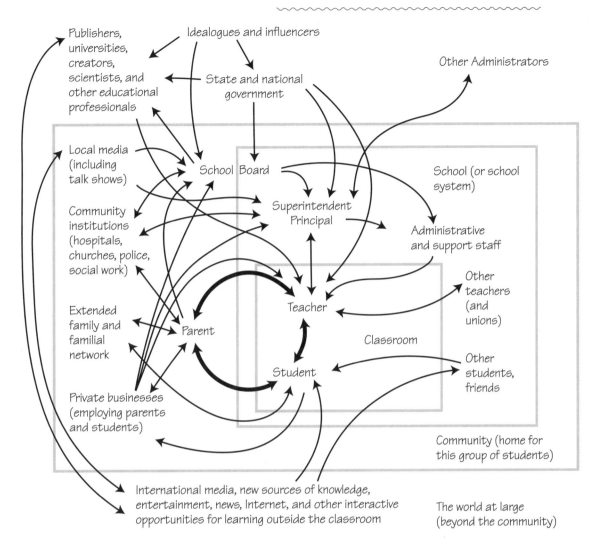

Publishers, universities, creators, scientists, and other educational professionals

Idealogues and influencers

Other Administrators

State and national government

Local media (including talk shows)

School Board

School (or school system)

Superintendent Principal

Community institutions (hospitals, churches, police, social work)

Administrative and support staff

Other teachers (and unions)

Extended family and familial network

Teacher

Parent

Classroom

Other students, friends

Student

Private businesses (employing parents and students)

Community (home for this group of students)

International media, new sources of knowledge, entertainment, news, Internet, and other interactive opportunities for learning outside the classroom

The world at large (beyond the community)

and editors of textbooks (which are rapidly losing quality and appeal as they get adapted to the immediate priorities set by standardized test committees or abandoned for more up-to-date and less expensive web-based resources); to the leaders of organizations like the Educational Testing Service, which have greater influence in schooling than ever before; and to professional researchers, writers, and theorists of the process of learning, who are changing their views in light of findings from cognitive neuroscience and brain research.

The most notable feature of the community level is its complexity. You might map your community's elements, and those of the world around it, a bit differently from the diagram shown here—but any realistic diagram would be just as complex. The patterns of influence (represented by the thin arrows of the diagram) flow among nearly all the elements. Some have direct influence on schools; with others, the influence is less direct—but there is always interaction. If you try to "fix" this system by intervening only to change the formal structures (the gray boxes), your efforts will backfire. Indeed, an effectively operating community (or classroom or school) is one where people recognize the webs of invisible influence, seek to strengthen them, and feel responsible to everyone connected to them. When that web breaks down, children fall through the cracks and are lost.

This map of a typical community is much like a longstanding systems thinking exercise called "The Wall." In this exercise, facilitators ask a group of people to name all the elements involved in a chronic, large-scale problem—such as world hunger, destruction of the rainforests, human rights violations, or a flailing economy. Gradually, people call out factors and their influence on other factors ("Population grows! Which increases the poverty rate!"). A facilitator faithfully records them, until a wall-full of white paper is covered with scribbled notations and lines of influence. Faced with this kind of complexity, many people throw up their hands in despair. It will never be possible to fix such a system, especially since it's obvious that no one is in charge! And if creating schools that learn depends on fostering learning at the community level, then at first glance it will seem as if this represents such an impossible problem.

But there is leverage available. It comes from recognizing the recurring patterns of systemic behavior and the simpler interrelationships that cause those patterns to exist. There is also leverage in fostering regular productive conversations and in inviting people at the community level to think through their futures together—what they want from each other, and from their schools.

In Part V of this book (pages 209–257), we consider the techniques and conceptual approaches that have proven effective in helping communities and schools learn from each other: creating a sense of community identity, making connections among diverse community leaders, and providing the infrastructure for sustainable communitywide learning.

PUTTING THE PIECES TOGETHER

With all of these constituents and levels, the movement for creating schools that learn is itself a kind of crossroads. People come to it from a wide variety of circumstances and with only a few things in common. They all have a commitment to the children of their communities. They know that each community's future is its children. They know that schools need to change—and that change happens sometimes incrementally and sometimes in big leaps, but it never happens without commitment from the people involved. Learners retain only that which they truly want to learn.

Unless you're willing to talk openly and honestly and risk the "sacred cows" of your classroom, school system, and community, you won't be able to achieve the goal of a learning organization. But if you've gone so far as to open this book, you've already taken the first step. We can't afford to stand still. There is too much at stake—for the children themselves, and for the rest of us.

3. Core Concepts About Learning in Organizations

The formal practice of organizational learning is relatively new, and many people are coming to it from a variety of backgrounds, disciplines, and orientations. Therefore, right at the beginning, we feel it is important to articulate the core guiding ideas that we have found to be at the heart of a learning organization. In other words, we hold these truths to be self-evident.

EVERY ORGANIZATION IS A PRODUCT OF HOW ITS MEMBERS THINK AND INTERACT

Organizations work the way they work because of the ways that people think. Policies and rules did not create the problems in classrooms or schools today, nor will they eliminate them. The true source of these problems is the mental models and relationships at every level of the system, from the teacher and students in a classroom to the national political governing bodies that oversee all schools. If you want to improve a school system, before you change the rules, you must look first to the ways that people think and interact together. Otherwise, the new policies and organizational structures will simply fade away, and the organization will revert, over time, to the way it was before.

This may be what Seymour Sarason meant when he wrote, "The more things change, the more they will remain the same." Sarason argues that effective school reform cannot happen until people move beyond superficial conceptions of educational systems and recognize the unseen values and attitudes about power, privilege, and knowledge that keep existing structures, regulations, and authority relationships in place. If there aren't fundamental shifts in how people think and interact, as well

Credit for articulating this idea belongs to Karl Weick, in *The Social Psychology of Organizing* (Addison-Wesley, 1969). Also see *The Fifth Discipline Fieldbook*, p. 48.

See Seymour B. Sarason, *The Predictable Failure of Educational Reform* (Jossey-Bass, 1990).

as in how they explore new ideas, then all the reorganizing, fads, and strategies in the world won't add up to much sustained improvement.

Changing the way we think means continually shifting our point of orientation. We must make time to look inward: to become aware of, and study, the tacit "truths" that we take for granted; the ways we create knowledge and make meaning in our lives; and the aspirations and expectations that govern what we choose from life. But we must also look outward, by exploring new ideas and different ways of thinking and interacting, connecting to multiple processes and relationships outside ourselves and clarifying our shared visions for the organization and the larger community. Changing the way we interact means redesigning not just the formal structures of the organization but the hard-to-see patterns of relationships among people and other aspects of the system, including the systems of knowledge.

How do people think and interact in your school system? Can they hold productive conversations, or do they advocate their views so strongly that others cannot be heard? Do they blame others for problems, or do they look at problems from the perspective of the system as a whole, recognizing that no one is individually to blame because all actions are interrelated? Do they assume that their view is the only plausible view, or do they inquire into different perspectives? Are they open to talking about the differences and similarities in the hopes and aspirations they (and others) hold? Are they genuinely interested in creating something new for their future and the future of the community's children?

See Paulo Freire, *Pedagogy of the Oppressed* (Continuum, 1975, 1995) p. 52ff; Fritjof Capra, *The Web of Life* (Doubleday, 1996), p. 272.

LEARNING IS CONNECTION

"One of the hardest parts of my job is to get teachers to understand there is someone else in the classroom with them," says an educator who works with PK–12 and university teachers to improve their teaching. "Too many have forgotten that they are teaching students as well as a subject." In many schools, knowledge is treated as a thing—objectified, disconnected from other forms of knowledge and from the knower. "Banking education," as the educator Paulo Freire has called it, is their dominant model for teaching and learning—teachers are supposed to "deposit" tokens of codified knowledge, discrete pieces of information, into students' heads.

But information, as author Fritjof Capra has noted, is not a thing that can be deposited. Instead, it is "a quantity, name, or short statement that we have abstracted from a whole network of relationships—a context, in which [the information] is embedded and which gives it meaning. We are so used to the abstractions that we tend to believe that meaning resides in the piece of information rather than in the context from which it has been abstracted."

Fields of knowledge do not exist separately from each other, nor do they exist separately from the people who study them. They are living systems made up of often invisible networks and interrelationships. Indeed, they may be among the most complex of living systems. The ideology of the nature of knowledge and knowing, the teachers' and learners' underlying beliefs and values about the nature of schooling, and social interactions in learning environments are all part of those living systems—and all affect the ability of individuals and groups to learn.

Furthermore, all learners construct knowledge from an inner scaffolding made up of their individual and social experiences, emotions, will, aptitudes, beliefs, values, self-awareness, purpose, and more. In other words, if you are learning in a classroom, what you understand is determined by how you understand things, who you are, and what you already know, as much as by what is covered and how and by whom it is delivered. To increase awareness of these factors is to strengthen the process of learning.

Too often, classrooms, professional development in schools and other organizations, parenting classes, and teacher or school leadership preparation programs focus only on two factors in learning—what is covered and how it is delivered. Sadly, educators are making their jobs not only more difficult but probably less effective as well. "Good teachers bring students into living communion with the subjects they teach," says Parker Palmer. "They also bring students into community with themselves and with each other."

Parker Palmer, *To Know as We Are Known: Education as a Spiritual Journey* (Harper, 1993), p. xvii.

LEARNING IS DRIVEN BY VISION

Too many organizations, including schools, ignore this precept, but it may be the most critical to their success. It can provide the power for people to learn and grow even when their situations or environments are disempowering.

When children are very young, they learn rapidly, in a way tied tightly to their purpose and vision. They learn to crawl and then to walk because they want to move on their own. They learn to ride a bike because they want to play with their friends who have bikes. Years later, they learn to drive because they want independence and mobility at a correspondingly greater range. Children learn all these new skills and more, from throwing a football to mastering a video game, because they *want* them. The same is true for adults. A ninety-one-year-old African American woman, who raised four children and helped raise their children, learns to read because this has been her lifelong vision. A college professor retires to Florida and learns to build his own sailboat because sailing is his passion. Grandparents who have shied away from new technology buy computers and learn to hook into the Internet because they want to exchange email

For research on student complaints about irrelevance, see Shirley M. Hord and Harvetta M. Robertson, "Listening to Students," *Journal of Staff Development* (Summer 1999), pp. 38–39. They suggest that students, especially in high school, hunger for learning and challenge. This hunger is communicated in their behavior, if not their words.

with their grandchildren. Lifelong learning, then, is the fundamental means by which people engage with life and create their desired futures.

But when children enter schools, the system often presents them with new goals unrelated to their own desires and aspirations—to please teachers, to get good marks on assignments, to receive awards and honors, and to be ranked high. This only gets worse over the years, as the increasing importance of grades, test scores, and other external motivators have the effect of further disconnecting students from their own visions. Listen to what children tell you (and tell researchers). While preschoolers may articulate their vision for "when I get bigger" quite clearly, older children complain about the irrelevance of schoolwork to their lives and their futures. They say they learn more outside of school than in, and they don't understand why most of the information they hear in class is supposed to be either interesting or important. What they don't, or can't, communicate in words, students often communicate through disruptive or disengaged behavior.

Some may fear that allowing students—or teachers for that matter—to pursue their "vision" in schools means letting people do whatever they want, abandoning rigor and lowering educational standards. Nothing could be further from the truth. When administrators and teachers focus on narrow and pragmatic questions, such as classroom management, increasing attendance and graduation rates, and improving test scores, then students may internalize those diminished visions and live with unnecessarily low horizons. Improving the numbers and providing safe learning spaces are legitimate goals, but they can't replace the power of a larger vision, personal and shared, as the driving force behind improving schools.

For material on building personal and shared vision, see pages 76, 209, and 341.

4. How to Read This Book

START ANYWHERE; GO ANYWHERE

We have designed the book to reward browsing. Cross-references embedded in the text, for example, allow you to jump from one topic to the next and point out meaningful links to follow.

MAKE THE BOOK YOUR OWN

Mark up the pages. Write answers to the solo exercises in the margins.

Draw. Scribble. Daydream. Note the results of what you have tried and ideas of what you would like to try. Over time, as your field notes accumulate, they will become a record of effective practices—and a tool for reflecting on designing the next stage of your change initiative.

USE THE EXERCISES AND TECHNIQUES

Exercises and techniques produce a different kind of learning from that which develops simply by reading about the work. If you feel "I already know that," ask yourself honestly whether your knowledge about these skills and methods shows up in your performance. If not, then try the approaches, techniques, and exercises that seem useful. Educators who use the exercises often tell us that although some may appear simple, they are powerful in practice.

ENGAGE OTHERS IN THINKING ABOUT CHANGE

Organizations, like all human groups, operate through conversation. That is especially true for classrooms, schools, and communities, the organizations to which this book is dedicated. The ideas in the book gain most of their value as starting points for conversation with others.

FOCUS ON CAPABILITIES, NOT ANSWERS

We think it is important to provide specific tools, techniques, and stories—but not as prescriptions or recipes to follow. In fact, if you look only for answers here, you may become frustrated; each coauthor and contributor has his or her own point of view, and they often disagree. Instead, by taking on the practices in this book (and others) and by exploring the results, you and your school or community can learn to create your own future, your own way.

MARGIN ICONS

To make browsing through the book easier, we use icons (small graphic symbols) to indicate different types of material. The following icons will appear in the margins regularly:

■ **Learning Disciplines:** This icon indicates a direct reference to one or more of the five main bodies of method and practice of this book. The appropriate acronyms are highlighted. The left leg of the stool shows Personal Mastery (PM) and Shared Vision (SV), the disciplines related to articulating individual and collective aspirations. The right leg shows Mental Models (MM) and Team Learning (TL), the disciplines of reflective thinking and generative conversation. And the middle leg shows Systems Thinking (ST), the discipline for recognizing and managing complexity.

}} For more on the "three-legged stool," see page 74.

- **Solo exercise:** An exercise that you practice alone—to deepen your understanding and capability, to set personal direction, or to provoke an "aha!" These also include exercises for students to practice alone in a classroom.

- **Team exercise:** An exercise for a group of people working together, sometimes in a classroom (with the teacher or a student as facilitator) and sometimes in a school or community team (conducted by a facilitator or team leader). Remember that classroom exercises can be adapted easily for schoolwide or community use (and vice versa).

- **Lexicon:** Guides to the roots of the words we use and the way we use them now. Articulating the precise meaning of words is important in a field like education, where so much jargon is used loosely.

- **Resource:** Recommendations of books, articles, videotapes, and websites that we and many practitioners have found valuable.

- **Toolkit:** A practical device or technique, such as a template or diagram, that you can use in the learning disciplines.

- **Guiding idea:** A principle (or set of principles) that we find meaningful as a philosophical source of light and direction.

5. What's New in the New Edition

In putting together this new edition, we have gone through the book with an eye toward the ideas, exercises, and tools that educators, parents, and others will find most useful—*now*. Many articles are timeless, and we have left them as is. Others have been updated, and there are a number of completely new articles, including one essay by Peter Senge, "The Systems Citizen," on page 558.

We have updated resources and references to reflect all new editions, beginning with *The Fifth Discipline,* for which a revised edition was released in 2006. We have also included many reviews of new books and resources.

In addition, we have added new tools and exercises in this volume, including many that were developed and tested in response to feedback from people who used the first edition. Some sections in the "Systems Thinking in the Classroom" section (page 268) have been brought up to date, and the primer on using the five disciplines (page 70) is completely revised and expanded. You will also find new stories and articles that reflect ongoing recent work and research in creating learning organizations.

We have resisted the temptation, however, to be overly topical. The previous edition lasted twelve years, and we hope this new edition will remain relevant and useful for a long time. Thus, while we mention new phenomena like Facebook, we have tried to avoid highlighting phenomena that may prove transient, such as (for example) the debates over strict achievement-oriented parenting styles that were sparked by the book *Battle Hymn of the Tiger Mother* in 2011. And while many ideas about education are interesting and worthwhile, we have limited our coverage to areas where we perceive a direct link to the work at the core of this book: the practice of building learning organizations in schools and education.

Amy Chua, *Battle Hymn of the Tiger Mother* (Penguin, 2011).

SOCIETY FOR ORGANIZATION LEARNING

New initiatives are continually emerging among educators, community leaders, and individuals—looking to combine insights from research and experience around systems thinking, schools that learn, large-scale change (using the "presencing" model developed by Otto Scharmer), and community growth and learning. One place to keep up is the Society for Organizational Learning, an international community composed of organizations and individuals, formed in 1997. The SoL website, at http://www.solonline.org, contains links to the evolving SoL Education Partnership. SoL also cosponsors (with the Presencing Institute) a website called The Academy for Systemic Change, at http://keli-yen.ning.com. It contains blog entries by Peter Senge and others and links to groups and schools that are experimenting intensively with the systems citizen concept. —Art Kleiner

 Also see The Systems Citizen, page 558; the Roca Foundation, page 525; and Education for Sustainability, page 537.

6. The Industrial Age System of Education

Peter Senge

We are all products of our age and, in turn, act in ways that re-create that age. As an old joke goes, it is difficult to know what fish talk about, but you can be sure it's not water. It is difficult for any of us in "advanced" societies to overestimate how much the effects of the industrial age have shaped the way we see the world. This "water"—our culturally embedded assumptions and habitual ways of operating—comes back to haunt us when we try to fundamentally rethink and reinvent the industrial-age institution we call school.

But how can we "see" assumptions that are so taken for granted? Start by looking at the artifacts of our educational culture, the way an anthropologist might. For example, stand outside a school and watch the children and adolescents entering. Notice the way they walk—stooped over, bearing their backpacks full of books and papers. The typical schoolchild's backpack can weigh anywhere from twenty to forty pounds. Pick up one of these packs and see how heavy it feels. To be sure, this is changing, because many students are starting to carry their textbooks in tablet computers. But though the backpacks will be physically lighter, the metaphorical load will be just as heavy—probably even heavier, since there will be one less visible sign of the load and thus one less restraint. This weight is an artifact of the industrial-age system of education.

In most secondary schools, where children start between the ages of ten and twelve, teachers are limited to one group of subjects each. They don't work together or coordinate their day-to-day efforts, and thus they often don't even know the total workload assigned to all students. Would they advocate that sixty-pound children carry the equivalent of twenty-five pounds of books home each night? Probably not. But the question is moot, because they have no way of knowing how much stress the system as a whole is piling onto these students.

Nor do the parents necessarily fully recognize the weight placed on their children. They are dealing with their own stress levels in the high-pressure workplaces of contemporary Western society. I have heard parents say that they approve of their children's heavy workloads: "It's preparing them to deal with the stress of the real world." Metaphorically, the parents are carrying the same backpack themselves. They have to-do lists that they'll never finish, and many feel pressed to respond to emails and text messages around the clock. Faced with literally never-ending work pressure, they think it's perfectly appropriate that their kids learn to endure the same kinds of pressures.

High-achieving children often seem deeply aware of the consequences of this loss of balance. "We were very surprised to find," said cognitive scientist Howard Gardner about a study of highly talented children that he conducted in the late 1990s, "that by the age of eleven or twelve, many children would talk about the importance of balance in their lives. This included kids who were skaters, actors, musicians, and people seriously involved in community service. They love their work and their activity. But they observed their parents and said to themselves, 'This is not the kind of life I want to lead.'"

These pressures were evident twelve years ago, when the first edition of this book was published. Schools and teachers found themselves forced to boost workloads continually at that time, while also taking more and more class time to prepare students for the tests on whose outcomes their budgets, and even positions, may depend. "There are many ways to measure a successful school," wrote New York Times education reporter Michael Winerip in 1999. But the only measure that matters to commentators and politicians, he added, "is performance on standardized tests. As long as that is true, those backpacks are likely to be full each night starting in grade one and maybe earlier."

Twelve years later, the pressure—on students, teachers, and schools—has only intensified. It is exacerbated, of course, by years of mandated performance increases on standardized tests in the U.S. and by federal programs (including, but not limited to, "No Child Left Behind") that focus on the symptoms of poor school performance without addressing—or even considering—the underlying causes. Indeed, few school leaders anywhere seem to recognize what they can do to address the deeper causes of their school's problems.

This situation leaves over-pressured students with two basic alternatives: cope or disengage. More and more of them disengage. The system then tracks them into classes for underachievers where they no longer will be challenged. Others try to cope, trapped in the conflict between competing against their peers (and pleasing their parents and teachers) versus being true to their own well-being. The end result is a lack of motivation and engagement, waste of their potential, and a diminishing of the contribution that they could make to society.

This quote came from a conversation between Gardner and Peter Senge in December 1999. Other parts of that conversation were published in the original version of *Schools That Learn*, p. 555. The study (and others) were conducted under the name "Good Work" at the Harvard Graduate School of Education, launched in 1995 by Howard Gardner, William Damon, and Mihaly Csikszentmihalyi. See their 15-year commemorative volume, published online: Howard Gardner (editor), *Good Work: Theory and Practice*, (GoodWork Project, 2010), www.goodworkproject.org.

Michael Winerip, "Homework Bound," *New York Times*, January 3, 1999.

Several popular films have emerged recently as signs of growing recognition and concern among many parents and educators around the world that the industrial model of schooling is destructive and that we have lost our way. See Vicki Abeles, producer and codirector/writer, *The Race to Nowhere* (Reel Link Films, 2010), www.racetonowhere.com and Davis Guggenheim, director/writer, *Waiting for Superman* (Paramount Vintage, 2010), www.waitingforsuperman.com.

See Daniel Boorstin, *The Discoverers* (Harry N. Abrams, 1983, 1991), pp. 108–109; also Arthur A. Koestler, *The Sleepwalkers* (Hutchinson/Penguin, 1959), p. 536.

Russel Ackoff, *Creating the Corporate Future*, (John Wiley and Sons, 1981), p. 6; and Lewis Mumford, *Technics and Human Development*, (Harcourt Brace Jovanovich, 1967).

THE INDUSTRIAL-AGE HERITAGE OF SCHOOLS

How did this situation arise? A little history helps to see a fuller picture.

In many ways, the industrial age had its roots in the fascination of Kepler, Descartes, Newton, and other seventeenth-century scientists with the clock as a model for the cosmos. "My aim," wrote Johannes Kepler in 1605, "is to show that the celestial machine is to be likened not to a divine organism but rather to a clockwork." According to historian Daniel Boorstin, "Descartes made the clock his prototypical machine." Isaac Newton, says Arthur Koestler, assigned to God a twofold function "as Creator of the universal clockwork and as its Supervisor for maintenance and repair."

For these scientists, it became natural to conceive of the world as made up of discrete components that fit together like the parts in a machine. This offered the beguiling promise that ultimately the universe could be understood completely. If the behavior of atoms, conceived as tiny bouncing billiard balls, could be predicted, so could the behavior of more complex objects assembled from them. A worldview emerged that became the foundation for 350 years of scientific progress: Once you analyze the parts, the world can be predicted and controlled, as a machine is controlled. As Russell Ackoff puts it, "The universe was believed to be a machine that was created by God to do his work. Man, as part of that machine, was expected to serve God's purposes…It obviously followed that man ought to be creating machines to do his work." So powerful was the machine metaphor that writers like Ackoff, borrowing from historians like Lewis Mumford, dubbed the industrial age the "Machine Age."

Machine-age thinking became the foundation for organizations and management when Frederick the Great, the eighteenth-century Prussian ruler, achieved military successes by instituting standardization, uniformity, and drill training. Before then, as management writer Gareth Morgan notes, armies had been unruly mobs of "criminals, paupers, foreign mercenaries, and unwilling conscripts." Now they became great machines, with interchangeable parts (intensely drilled men who could replace one another easily), standardized equipment, and strict regulations. Not surprisingly, Frederick devised many of his techniques by studying machines. He was "fascinated," writes Morgan, "by the workings of automated toys such as mechanical men, and in his quest to shape the army into a reliable and efficient instrument, he introduced many reforms that actually served to reduce his soldiers to automata."

Inspired by progress in Newtonian science, industrialists of the nineteenth century patterned their organizations directly after Frederick the Great's army, including such mechanistic structures as the "chain of command," the "line" and "staff" organizations, and the "training and development" approach to learning. The organization as machine eventually found its prototypical embodiment in the assembly line. The assembly line produced an unparalleled number of uniform manufactured objects more reliably and efficiently than ever before. As scientific progress manifested itself in new and increasingly powerful technologies, these were incorporated into the assembly line, enabling previously unimaginable increases in labor productivity. From 1770 to 1812, labor productivity increased 120 times in the British textile industry. By 1880, according to business historian Alfred Chandler, Jr., "four-fifths of the people working on the production of goods were working in mechanized factories." The assembly line also transformed the conditions of work: interchangeable, trained workers doing precisely designed repetitive tasks, orchestrated by a rhythm set by external bosses.

It is little surprise that educators of the mid-nineteenth century explicitly borrowed their new designs from the factory builders they admired. The result was an industrial-age school system fashioned in the image of the assembly line, the icon of the booming industrial age. In fact, school may be the starkest example in modern society of an entire institution modeled after the assembly line. Like any assembly line, the system was organized in discrete stages. Called grades, they segregated children by age (just as an assembly line grouped products according to their stage of completion). Everyone was supposed to move from stage to stage together. Each stage had local supervisors—the teachers responsible for it. Classes of twenty to forty students met for specified periods in a scheduled day to drill for tests. The whole school was designed to run at a uniform speed, complete with bells on the walls and rigid daily time schedules. Each teacher knew what had to be covered in order to keep the whole line moving, even though he or she had little influence on its preset speed, which was determined by the "bosses"—the state requirements, school boards, administration, and standardized curricula.

Although few of us today appreciate how deeply assembly-line concepts are embedded in the modern school, nineteenth-century writers spoke admiringly of schools as analogues to machines and factories. According to historian David Tyack, "As eighteenth-century theologians could think of God as a clock-maker without derogation, so [too] the social engineers searching for new organizational forms used the words 'machine' or 'factory' without investing them with the negative associations they evoke today." For example, machine concepts like standardization played a role in creating unified school systems. In 1844 Samuel Gridley Howe, a newly elected Massachusetts Board of Education

For more about Frederick the Great and his influence on the modern organization, see Gareth Morgan, *Images of Organization* (Sage Publications, 1969), pp. 22–25. This link between Frederick's army and schools is also mentioned in "The Drive to Learn: An Interview with Edward T. Hall," *Santa Fe Lifestyle* (Spring 1988), pp. 12–14.

The figures on labor productivity come from Paul Hawken, Amory Lovins, and L. Hunter Lovins, *Natural Capitalism: Creating the Next Industrial Revolution* (Little, Brown and Company, 1990), p. 170; they in turn are quoting Natalie McPherson, *Machines and Economic Growth* (Greenwood Press, 1994). The Chandler quote is from Alfred Chandler, Jr., *The Visible Hand: The Managerial Revolution in American Business* (Harvard University Press, 1977), pp. 245–246.

David B. Tyack, *The One Best System: A History of American Urban Education* (Harvard University Press, 1974), p. 42.

member, implemented a standardized test and used the dismal results to galvanize public outrage about the decentralized Boston schools, leading to their consolidation as a single, citywide system, an approach that ultimately influenced schools throughout North America and the rest of the world.

The result of this machine-age thinking was a model of school as something separate from daily life, something governed in an authoritarian manner, oriented above all else to producing, as efficiently as possible, a standardized product. It was a model demanding the same type of routinized labor input needed for the rapidly growing industrial-age factory workplace—and was as dependent on maintaining rigid control as were the armies of Frederick the Great.

While the assembly-line school system dramatically increased educational productivity, it also created many of the most intractable problems with which students, teachers, and parents struggle to this day. It operationally grouped kids into two categories: smart kids and dumb kids. Those who did not learn at the speed of the assembly line either fell off or were forced to struggle continually to keep pace; they were labeled "slow" or, in today's more fashionable jargon, "learning disabled." It established uniformity of product and process as norms, thereby naïvely assuming that all children learn in the same way. It made educators into controllers and inspectors, thereby transforming the traditional mentor-mentee relationship and establishing teacher-centered rather than learner-centered learning. Motivation became the teacher's responsibility rather than the learner's. Discipline became adherence to rules set by the teacher rather than the self. Assessment centered on gaining the teacher's approval rather than objectively gauging one's own capabilities. Finally, the assembly-line model tacitly identified students as the product rather than the creators of learning, passive objects being shaped by an educational process beyond their influence.

Today, however, the assembly-line education system is under stress. Its products are no longer judged adequate by society. Its productivity is questioned. And it is responding in the only way the system knows how to respond: by doing what it has always done, but harder. Workloads increase. Standardized testing is intensified. Space for teachers to be innovative and adapt to learners' idiosyncratic needs is reduced. And the children's backpacks grow heavier and heavier.

Among neurophysiologists there is a common expression: "The brain downshifts under stress." When we are fearful, we revert to our most habitual behaviors. Larger human systems are no different. Whether it espouses behavior or not, the educational system is responding to the pressure to perform by trying to turn up the speed of the assembly line. While this might get more students to the graduation point, all of us—students, teachers, and parents—should be asking whether it produces more learning. Or are we running harder and faster to get to a place that feels less and less relevant: a place where no one really wants to go?

A SYSTEM TRAPPED

Many have argued that the industrial age ended decades ago, as the world of smoke stacks and mass production was replaced by that of bits and bytes. But this confuses shifts in dominant technologies with shifts in the underlying values and processes that defined the industrial age. More steel is produced in the world today than ever before. So, too, are more automobiles produced and more coal burned. The dominant technologies may shift, but the industrial-age mentality remains, with our institutions still stuck in it.

Businesses, for example, are still trying to apply industrial-age solutions to twenty-first century problems. They respond to increasing pressures for performance and profit while reducing headcount and standardizing their products and processes; they manage employees from the top down rather than fostering the participation and commitment of employees at all levels; and they are less concerned with social and environmental impacts than financial results. This has contributed to a wide range of problems, from faulty product designs to deteriorating ecosystems around the world and the global economic recession.

Yet, as someone who spends considerable time with both educators and businesspeople, it is my judgment that educators feel even more trapped and less able to innovate than do their business counterparts. A number of years ago, I asked a group of educators a question I have often asked of business groups: "Do you believe that significant change occurs only as a result of a crisis?" In business groups, typically three-quarters will respond affirmatively. But, then, others will tell stories of significant changes that arose without a crisis, from passion and imagination, from leaders of many types willing to take risks in favor of something in which they believed. The group of educators responded differently. Very few raised their hands at my first question. Puzzled, I asked, "Does that mean that you believe that significant innovation can occur without crises?" Again, no one raised a hand. Now really puzzled, I asked, "Well, if change doesn't occur in response to a crisis, and it doesn't occur in the absence of a crisis, what other possibilities are there?" A soft voice from the audience responded, "I guess we don't believe significant change can occur under any circumstances." Those who have not worked within the institutions of education often do not appreciate just how disempowered most educators feel.

Most businesspeople believe that the reason educational institutions do not innovate is the lack of competition. Feeling pressed themselves to innovate or die, they see this sense of urgency missing in education. While I believe there is some validity to this view, I also believe it is too simplistic. It implies that all that is needed is more competition in education. While movements like charter schools have created more choice, there is little evidence they are leading fundamental innovation on any meaningful scale. Education writer and leader Michael Fullan notes that there are many good examples of "raising the bar" and "lowering the gap" in student achievement for basic skills, "but we have not accomplished much in terms of higher-order skills." But it is exactly innovation for higher-order skills—like critical thinking, self-directed learning, communication, and collaboration—that is most needed to prepare students for a world of growing interdependence and change.

Where real innovation occurs, it rarely lasts or spreads. There have always been small numbers of highly innovative public schools, often inspired by new insights into child development or learning theory or bold visions for how a school could truly serve kids. Yet few can sustain their innovations beyond the tenure of a few innovators. Once a key principal or superintendent or a few highly capable teachers leave, everything returns to the norm.

The reason for this, I believe, is that there exist distinctive industrial-age features of schools that make sustained innovation more challenging than in business. Until these are recognized, simplistic strategies like increasing competition are likely to lead to disappointing long-term results.

The first distinctive feature is that while business *adopted* machine-age ideas such as the assembly line, it was not born with these ideas. Businesses have been significant social institutions for thousands of years. The corporation as a legal entity dates in some forms to the Middle Ages and, before that, to the Roman Empire. The very word "company" has roots that reach back at least a thousand years, deriving from the same roots as "companion"—literally a sharing of bread (*compania*—com and panis) in Latin. By comparison, the modern education system is new. Starting with one-room schoolhouses in farming communities in the seventeenth and eighteenth centuries, it expanded to reach all children only with the urban school systems of the nineteenth century. As a result, the vast majority of assumptions and practices of schools are inseparable from the machine-age view of the world.

The quote from Michael Fullan comes from a conversation conducted with Peter Senge in 2011.

See Fernand Braudel, *The Wheels of Commerce* (University of California Press, 1992), p. 572ff; and Tyack, *The One Best System*, p. 37.

Second, as it evolved, the school system became far more tightly embedded in larger social systems than did business. Individual schools sit within local school districts, which in turn nest within state departments of education that set policy and standards. Consequently, schools are buffeted by many shifts in the political winds that pass companies by (as we see with pressures for increased standardized testing, for example). Moreover, schools are a part of a community in ways that businesses are not. In particular, businesses do not have parents as part of their system of governance. Businesses have investors and customers, but their concerns are relatively narrow. Investors will basically let the business run its affairs any way it wants, so long as it achieves an adequate financial return. Customers care about the quality of the product but (with some exceptions) are generally indifferent to how the business operates. Parents not only have goals for what their children learn but very definite ideas about how that learning should occur, ideas strongly anchored in their own experiences as schoolchildren.

Herein lies probably the most problematic distinction of the education system when viewed from the standpoint of innovation and adaptation. We all went to school together! In other words, we are all products of the industrial-age school. Of all institutions, school sits most "upstream" in people's minds. It was our first and most formative introduction to what Dr. W. Edwards Deming called "the prevailing system of management"—the machine world of teachers in control, students dependent on teachers' approval, and learning defined as getting an A on the test. Most of us developed our survival skills for industrial-age institutions in first and second grade. We learned how to please the teacher, as we would later try to please our boss. We learned how to avoid wrong answers and raise our hand when we knew the right answer, habits that would later shape the ongoing workplace dance of avoiding blame and seeking credit for successes. We learned how to be quiet when we felt lost, which is why no one questions the boss in the official meeting, even when he or she makes no sense.

Coming to recognize how much the industrial-age school lives in each of us can be sobering. But it is also enabling, especially when we recognize that the industrial-age education system that has spread around the world in the past 150 years will inevitably change in the coming decades. This will not happen because such change is easy. Indeed, as most educators know only too well, few institutions are more resistant to innovation and change than primary and secondary education. It will happen because fundamental change is necessary if human society is to survive and thrive in the world in which we now live. Continuing industrial expansion has created such social and ecological imbalances that it cannot continue as is. And the coming changes will not be possible without re-creating the two central institutions—business and education—that have been the primary propagators of the industrial-age worldview and skill set.

Just as school has been the generative institution for machine-age thinking, so too could it be a pivot for creating more learning-oriented and systemically intelligent societies. In truth, the time to inculcate systems thinking is when we are young: when innate intuitions about interdependency are still alive and before fragmented academic subjects transform us into master reductionists. The time to develop inquiry and reflection skills, likewise, is when we are young, not after thirty years of institutional conditioning aimed at learning to impress people with how smart we are. It is a tragedy that, for most of us, school is not a place for deepening our sense of who we are and what we are committed to. If it were, think of the lasting impact it would have.

Such changes are unlikely to happen until we understand more deeply the core assumptions upon which the industrial-age school is based. This is the DNA of our contemporary school system, and it will continue to exert its iron grip on any efforts at fundamental change until it is recognized and understood.

For more about theories-in-use, see Peter Senge, *The Fifth Discipline* (second edition, 2006), p. 176ff; Art Kleiner, *The Age of Heretics: A History of the Radical Thinkers Who Reinvented Corporate Management* (Jossey-Bass, 2008), p. 215ff.; and the original source, Chris Argyris and Donald Schön, *Organizational Learning: A Theory of Action Perspective* (Addison-Wesley, 1978).

Industrial-Age Assumptions About Learning

It is important to note at the outset that most educators would probably disagree in principle with these assumptions. By most educators, I mean everyone from school board members to administrators to teachers. Parents often disagree with them as well. And yet the system seems to embody these assumptions, and everyone acts as if they were correct—even if they would prefer to act differently. Such is the power of unexamined shared mental models—or, as social scientist Chris Argyris calls them, "theories-in-use"—that often are 180 degrees at odds with theories and beliefs that people espouse.

1. CHILDREN ARE DEFICIENT AND SCHOOLS FIX THEM

Years ago I heard an educator say something that I have not forgotten: "We have no idea the trauma the young child suffers at school." What trauma was she talking about?

How many of us learned in school that we could not paint? How many of us remember the teacher telling us not to sing with the other children because we were so out of tune? Or perhaps we learned that we were not good at math? Or English? I believe that few of us escaped this self-labeling. Even though we may have long since stopped recalling them, we carry these assessments of ourselves inside, often accompanied by strategies of avoidance to disguise our deficiencies.

These traumas occur because conformity is a core value of the industrial age. An assembly line that produces continual and unpredictable variety would not be considered efficient. But that is exactly what nature does: it generates infinite variety. The high regard for standardization that is built into assembly-line thinking leads naturally to seeing children as poorly formed "raw materials" from which the school system produces educated final products. Outside the school, learning is active and natural for people—we engage in learning constantly through day-to-day living. But within the school, learning is viewed in a different way. Edward Joyner, a former director of the Comer Project at Yale and an expert on staff development, calls this the "deficit perspective" of learning—an attitude held among educators and parents alike who believe that the job of schools is to make up for innate failings in the students themselves.

Edward Joyner, "To Ask the Best of Children, We Must Ask the Best of Ourselves," in James P. Comer, Michael Ben-Avie, Norris M. Haynes, and Edward T. Joyner, *Child by Child* (Columbia Teachers College Press, 1999), p. 278.

See "No More Drive-By Staff Development," page 396.

Educators don't give speeches advocating the deficit perspective, but every school child knows its sting, which naturally extends from specific to general self-assessments. Young children who get Cs or Ds on their first math test are very likely to conclude not only that their answers are wrong but that they themselves are "wrong." Before long, schoolroom evaluations become sweeping self-assessments: "I'm not all right. There's something wrong with me. I don't have what I need to succeed in life." These fears are reinforced by a management system that vests unilateral power in the educational "system" and that determines what is studied, how it is to be studied, and who has power to declare success or failure. It is no wonder that most kids internalize a simple conclusion, "I am not respected here."

The deficit perspective is especially pernicious because it is undiscussable. It is difficult for children to articulate to an adult that they do not feel respected when the adult feels this is normal because he or she experienced the same disrespect as a child. When they see their peers treated with similar disrespect, the topic is even harder to discuss. Moreover, as Chris Argyris says, "the undiscussability is undiscussable." This is the mark of all self-sealing cultural dysfunctions, and it is worst of all when children are involved. They learn that they cannot talk about the fact that they cannot talk about the disrespect they feel.

For more about undiscussable topics see: Chris Argyris, *Flawed Advice and the Management Trap* (Oxford University Press, 2000); and William R. Noonan, *Discussing the Undiscussable: A Guide to Overcoming Defensive Routines in the Workplace* (Jossey-Bass, 2007).

Parents experience their own form of the deficit perspective; when their kids' performance does not measure up, they conclude that they have failed as parents. Moreover, the experience of watching their kids struggle to perform often brings back the parents' own performance anxiety from when they were in school. Their natural concern for their children gets mixed with their own internalized traumas from long ago. Many relive their own school anxieties every time their kid takes a test or brings home a report card.

The deficit perspective has precursors that predate the industrial era, including some religious attitudes that children are born wicked. But it is interesting that the industrial age emerged at a time in which child-rearing experts, beginning in Europe, made the deficit perspective a core of parental practice. As German psychologist Alice Miller has shown, many nineteenth-century popular books on child rearing spoke of the need to "break the child's spirit and willfulness," so that he or she would become compliant. Dr. Schreber, a popular 1850s writer, admonished parents to regard an infant's screaming or crying as a test of wills and instructed them to employ "stern words, threatening gestures, rapping on the bed…or if none of this helps…mild corporeal admonitions." Such methods would be necessary only a few times, Schreber insisted to worried parents, "and then you will be master of the child forever." Miller quotes another writer's instructions on "abolishing" willfulness in the child's first year. Here the machine metaphors of control and order are even more explicit. The parent is instructed "to labor over them" to implant a strict "love of order," which can "come about only in quite a mechanical way. Everything must follow the rules of orderliness. Food and drink, clothing, sleep, and indeed the child's entire little household must be orderly and must never be altered in the least to accommodate their willfulness or whim."

The irony of the deficit view is that it shifts the burden of developing self-control from the child's own emerging capabilities to a perceived need for control and intervention by adults—first the parent, then the teacher. Rather than cultivating a child's sense of personal responsibility through awareness of the consequences of her or his own choices, it can actually foster a deep sense of victimization and lack of responsibility. (Interestingly, Miller observes that Schreber's son was treated by Sigmund Freud for paranoia.)

The deficit perspective assumes that something is broken and needs to be fixed. It is a reasonable way to think about machines, because machines cannot fix themselves. But it is a poor fit for living systems like children, which grow and evolve of their own accord.

See Alice Miller, *For Your Own Good: Hidden Cruelty in Child-Rearing and the Roots of Violence*, trans. Hunter Hannum and Hildegarde Hannum (Noonday Press, 1990), pp. 5, 11–12.

2. LEARNING TAKES PLACE IN THE HEAD, NOT IN THE BODY AS A WHOLE

"In the Western tradition," write philosophers George Lakoff and Mark Johnson, "the autonomous capacity of reason is regarded as what makes us essentially human, distinguishing us from all other animals." The prevailing Western theory sees reason as independent of perception, motion, emotion, or any other aspect of the body. But, as the authors show, recent evidence from cognitive science (the systematic study of mental operations in humans and computers) has challenged this premise. This evidence tells us "that human reason is a form of animal reason, a reason inextricably tied to our bodies and the peculiarities of our brains."

In other words, human cognitive development involves just as much "body knowledge" as it does "mind knowledge." Learning is inseparable from action. "All doing is knowing, and all knowing is doing," as Chilean biologists and cognitive scientists Humberto Maturana and Francisco Varela put it. Knowledge, in this context, does not mean only a mental storehouse of facts and theories, accumulated in memory, but the capacity to do something with this information. Indeed, the facts and theories may be stored not in our conscious reasoning and memory but literally in our bodies. Most of us know how to ride a bicycle but very few understand intellectually how we do it—that is, the laws of gyroscopic motion whereby the bicycle works. Similarly, we know how to talk, but we probably don't know all the rules and structures of language in any conscious way. Even something as simple as dialing telephone numbers shows the whole body nature of knowing: I often have trouble remembering many numbers, but if my fingers are on a phone key pad, they know where to go. (This body memory is gradually being displaced by the automatically stored numbers on modern phones, with their own version of body memory—nudging a list of names with my fingertip just long enough to land on the one I want.)

But while learning occurs in the whole body, the traditional classroom is based on the assumption that learning is a purely intellectual affair. Only the head is required; the rest of the body can be checked at the door. This is painfully obvious for those children who need to move to be alert and engaged and for whom having to sit in a chair and not move for an hour can be torture. The result is a passive rather than an active learning environment. Book-learning and lectures reign supreme. Students are receivers of so-called knowledge—mostly facts and predetermined answers to set puzzles they must solve.

This over-intellectualized notion of learning also accounts for why traditional schooling emphasizes mathematical and verbal development over other types. This is tragic, because, as Howard Gardner and others have shown, there is a spectrum of intelligences involved in learning,

George Lakoff and Mark Johnson, *Philosophy in the Flesh: The Embodied Mind and its Challenge to Western Thought* (Basic Books, 1999), p. 17.

Humberto Maturana and Francisco Varela, *The Tree of Knowledge: The Biological Roots of Human Understanding*, trans. Robert Paolucci (Shambhala Publications, 1997), p. 27.

including musical, kinesthetic, spatial, interpersonal, and emotional capabilities as well as the abstract symbolic reasoning of the intellect. Each person has different talents and propensities, but we all have the potential to embrace the full spectrum of intelligences in our personal development, and the more modalities of learning we engage, the broader and deeper is our growth.

⧘⧘ See resources and guides to multiple intelligence and learning styles beginning on page 181.

The notion of whole-body learning has been devalued in the modern schoolroom, with tragic consequences. I will never forget a beautiful story told by Victor Weisskopf, the retired chairman of the Physics Department at MIT, and a member of the famed Manhattan Project that developed the atomic bomb. He talked of vivid memories of sitting underneath the piano, at age three or four, while his grandmother played Bach. He could still feel the sensation of the music washing over him. "That is when I became a physicist," he said. When we assume that learning takes place only in the head, we deny much of what makes us human.

3. EVERYONE LEARNS, OR SHOULD LEARN, IN THE SAME WAY

Many years ago, in a kids' dialogue circle, I heard one fifth-grade boy ask another, "What would be the perfect school?" Without hesitating, the second replied, "One student, one teacher."

For many people in school, the sense of each child as a unique learner seems a far off aspiration. The assembly-line schools of the industrial age treat all children as the same, unshaped clay to be molded to the needs of the society and the specs of the curriculum. Many teachers know a good deal about multiple intelligences, the stages of child development, and the many ways that different children learn. But they struggle to implement their understanding, given the pressures they face. Some educators estimate that most teachers spend up to one month out of the year teaching test-taking skills, so students can meet standardized test performance goals.

It is time we took seriously the vision articulated by that fifth grader. Just as there is extraordinary variety in types of intelligence, so too is there extraordinary variety in how people learn. The past sixty years have seen groundbreaking research on child development, on learning styles, and on the nature of the learning process. All of this work points in the direction of appreciating variety. Some children can learn only when they are moving their bodies. Others need quiet, while still others thrive on constant activity. Some kids are natural experimenters, always pushing themselves. Others need to be challenged.

Despite growing theory and evidence of different learning styles, these ideas pose almost insurmountable hurdles for the assembly-line, teacher-centered schoolroom. Individual teachers, even with a teacher's aide, cannot possibly accommodate the variety of learners with whom they are confronted. They end up in interminable struggles to maintain classroom order. They try as best they can to make the same subject engaging for different learners. They make themselves available to talk with unhappy parents. But they are trapped between a rigid educational process on one hand and the variety of human beings sitting in front of them on the other. The tragic outcome is frustration on all sides: teachers who either give up or get burned out and a great many kids who either get cast aside or forced to learn in ways that significantly compromise their learning potential.

A teacher once commented to me that she had eighteen kids in her class, and fifteen had different sorts of "learning problems." What is the real meaning of this comment? For the teacher, I believe it was an expression of frustration, a plaintive acknowledgment that she could not provide all that her kids required. But what does it mean when five-sixths of the kids in a class are "abnormal"? Does it not say something about how normal is defined?

Similarly, what should we make of the plethora of "learning disabilities" that has become so widespread in recent years? Is this group of labels really a means of understanding children's problems—or a sign of increasing pressure from the assembly line to force nature's variety to match *its* requirements? As educators become increasingly sophisticated in diagnosing different shades of "disability," are we not just making them more and more sophisticated "inspectors," able to detect increasing numbers of raw materials that do not fit the needs of the machine? I understand that the intent among many educators is to do more to help different kids who learn in different ways. But isn't the real help needed a fundamental redesign of the industrial-age classroom? Can't we aspire to help all students by creating schools that are truly learner-centered, where teachers become designers and catalysts rather than centers of attention and fonts of knowledge?

Here too the deficit model casts a long shadow, leading subtly to seeing difference as a problem to be fixed rather than variety to be celebrated and accommodated. What we call "disability" is in truth a description of mismatch between educational process and person. Why not label the educational process as "disabled," instead of the person?

Moreover, what does it mean to an individual to be labeled as having "a disability"? How does that label shape an individual's sense of self through his or her lifetime? Are we losing our ability to distinguish between appreciating our differences versus seeing ourselves, and each other, as disabled?

The identification of learning disabilities is closely related to the use of drugs prescribed to treat these different disabilities. For example, no one knows exactly how many school kids in America are taking methylphenidate (Ritalin) or similar drugs today, but this has been arguably the nation's largest drug problem for many years. Methylphenidate, which is chemically similar to cocaine and amphetamines, is typically prescribed for children diagnosed with "attention deficit hyperactivity disorder" (ADHD). In 2007, 5.4 million U.S. children, age six through seventeen, had been diagnosed with ADHD at some point during their lives; that number had risen about 5 percent per year in the U.S. since 1997. A very high percentage of them are taking Ritalin regularly. I have heard many teachers estimate that between 10 and 20 percent of the students in their classrooms are on the drug. It has become so normalized that many college students take it, with or without a prescription. And Ritalin use among preschoolers in daycare programs, starting as young as age two, has been commonplace since the mid-1990s, usually in violation of the warnings from the drug manufacturer.

Is Ritalin a boon for frustrated educators and parents and poorly performing students, as is often claimed, or is it one more sign of the ongoing clash between nature's variety and schools' drive for conformity and performance? ADHD is a typical diagnosis for children having trouble concentrating in school. Typically, the child shows signs of not being able to keep pace with the demands of the classroom. A teacher alerts the parents that their child is having difficulties, the parents confer with a physician, and the drug is prescribed.

But much of the research on ADHD suggests that its symptoms may be characteristic not of "disability" but of high creativity. A good friend and MIT colleague was once told by his child's teacher that the child probably had ADHD and should be put on Ritalin. Unpersuaded, he and his wife did some reading and discovered a book written by two MDs, both of whom would be diagnosed with ADHD were they school-children today. My MIT friend concluded from reading the book that he too probably has ADHD. He discovered, for example, that people with ADHD tend to excel at "parallel processing"—doing two or more things simultaneously. This is one reason that such children often have difficulty with schoolrooms that force them to do one thing at a time. He and his wife concluded that rather than putting their child on drugs, he should be allowed to develop his gifts, and they as parents needed to

These statistics come from P.N. Pastor and C.A. Reuben, *Diagnosed Attention Deficit Hyperactivity Disorder and Learning Disability: United States, 2004–2006* (National Center for Health Statistics, U.S. Centers for Disease Control and Prevention, 2008) http://www.cdc.gov/nchs/data/series/sr_10/Sr10_237.pdf.

Sources on Ritalin use among very young children include: Joseph T. Coyle, "Psychotropic Drug Use in Very Young Children," *Journal of the American Medical Association*, vol. 280, no. 8 (February 23, 2000), p. 1059; and Julie Magno Zito, Daniel J. Safer, MD, Susan dos Reis, James F. Gardner, Myde Boles, and Frances Lynch, "Trends in the Prescribing of Psychotropic Medications to Preschoolers," *Journal of the American Medical Association*, vol. 280, no. 8 (February 23, 2000), p. 1025.

The book was almost certainly Edward Hallowell and John Ratey, *Driven to Distraction: Recognizing and Coping with Attention Deficit Disorder from Childhood to Adulthood* (Touchstone, 1994).

find a way to make the child's education more compatible with the type of person he was.

This story also illustrates the immense practical challenges posed by the mismatch between assembly-line schools and the variety of children's ways of learning. One wonders why the epidemic in Ritalin and other doctor-prescribed drugs for young children has not been met with outrage by parents. The answer is probably that most parents today do not have the time to be outraged. They are stressed and overworked and may be coping with their own stress through drugs. They are worried that their child will fall behind in school and not get into a good college. Most feel trapped, with few options—just as most teachers feel trapped, doing their best to maintain control in a classroom full of very different learners.

Finally, the "one-size-fits-all" classroom probably also accounts for why, for many students, motivation for school learning drops off within a few years of starting formal schooling. Their initial excitement wanes when they sense that they are not the favored ones in this environment. They are not highly verbal or do not think quickly or do not excel at presenting their thoughts in a crisp, linear fashion. Perhaps they rebel at competing against their peers for grades. Whatever the source of disconnect, they are not among those who fit in the machine-age classroom.

Our assembly line thinking forces us to treat the natural variety of human beings as somehow aberrant because they do not fit the needs of the machine. "Those of us who have taught," says Edward Joyner, "know that you can know the subject matter well and not be able to deliver it *if you don't know the children well.*" (italics added)

4. LEARNING TAKES PLACE IN THE CLASSROOM, NOT IN THE WORLD

The industrial-age school puts the classroom at the center of the learning process. Yet genuine learning occurs in the context of our lives, and the long-term impact of any new learning depends on its relationship to the world around us. For example, in difficult times, painful though they may be, we often come to understandings that would not otherwise be possible. Because the classroom-centered model dominates, the many places where learning occurs in a child's life—playgrounds, home, theater and sports teams, and (for many) the streets—are discounted. Every relationship in a child's life carries a dimension of potential learning; everything she or he does can be done in a spirit of learning. These learning places are all, by and large, invisible from the classroom viewpoint.

Of course, most educators understand this and appreciate the many contexts in which learning occurs. They know the importance of athletics, music, art, and theater. But when there are problems, the tyranny of the classroom model comes to the surface. When there are budget pressures, the arts and electives budgets are often the first to be cut. If classroom budgets are cut, teachers may lose supplies or be forced to squeeze in more children, but no one thinks of eliminating classrooms altogether. "Oh, no, you could never do that," people say. "Because where would children learn?"

Even in an age when networked computers and social media are available to anyone, anywhere, at increasingly lower costs, and where they shape the way many young people communicate and live, the traditional classroom is still somehow unquestioned. I do not suggest that we should become uncritical boosters of electronic media—including the Internet, multi-player games, and Facebook—as a panacea for disengaged learners. Rather, I think it is important to ask what might a classroom full of kids and adults be like if it were truly designed for learning and seen as only one of many settings in which learning occurs.

5. THERE ARE SMART KIDS AND DUMB KIDS

The cumulative effect of these four assumptions is seen in arguably the deepest and most pernicious assumption of the machine-age school: that there are only two kinds of kids—smart kids and dumb kids. The smart kids are those who excel in school. The dumb ones are those who do not.

There are two distinct issues inherent in this assumption: school performance and the variety of human beings' innate capacities. We have been conditioned to think in terms of static categories, so it is natural to label kids in terms of where we see they fit. But labels quickly become self-fulfilling prophecies. When a teacher sees a student as a poor performer and treats the student as such, the student becomes disengaged and indeed performs poorly. This is the famous "self-fulfilling prophecy," as defined by sociologist Robert Merton in the late 1940s. It became known as the "Pygmalion effect" in the mid-1960s, when psychologist Robert Rosenthal and school principal Lenore Jacobson applied the insight to schools. In a series of research studies at Jacobson's school, they discovered that teachers' labels for kids shaped their performance, which in turn reinforced the labels. Though first studied long ago, the dynamic is no less pernicious in today's world of "high-stakes testing" and pressures for schools and students to perform.

See Robert Merton, *Social Theory and Social Structure* (Free Press, 1968) and Robert Rosenthal and Lenore Jacobson, *Pygmalion in the Classroom: Teacher Expectation and Pupils' Intellectual Development*, (Irvington Publishers, 1968, 1992).

Reversing this vicious self-fulfilling cycle is the key to many of the most successful programs for disengaged learners. They are typically based on action-learning principles, connecting learners to nature and community. One example is the alternative high school program at Maritime Gloucester (formerly known as the Maritime Heritage Center) in Gloucester, Massachusetts. It engages students in hands-on, experiential work, where they conduct marine biology experiments or build water wheels and solar distillation units. This learning is real to them in ways that their classroom learning is not—disengagement turns to engagement, they tend to stay in school rather than drop out, and their academic performance improves as well. The goal of the program is to make learning relevant. As David Brown, one of the instructors in the program, puts it, "When they first come in, they're closed down. By the time they're halfway through this program, they're open and paying attention; they can take on a real-life or an academic problem, apply what they know to learn what they don't, and solve it themselves."

This assumption about smart and dumb kids is so deeply ingrained in our society that it is hard to imagine an alternative. But the alternative is right before us: All human beings are born with unique gifts. The healthy functioning of any community depends on its capacity to develop each person's gift. When we hold a newborn, we do not see a smart or dumb kid. We see the miracle of life creating itself. The loss of that awareness is the greatest toll exacted by our prevailing system of education, in and out of school.

This is an extension of the Compass Program, an alternative high school program in Gloucester; for more information see http://www.gloucestermaritimecenter.org. For another example, see The Urban Ecology Center in Milwaukee, WI: www.urbanecologycenter.org.

Industrial-Age Assumptions About School

There exists another set of underlying assumptions embodied in the institution of the industrial-age school regarding the way the school itself is organized and sees its task. Like the assumptions about learning, these assumptions are very difficult for us to see and often contrary to what people consciously espouse. We take them for granted because we have lived in an industrial-era school for a good part of our lives—most educators have been there for most of their lives. Moreover, those of us who are not educators work in industrial-era organizations organized along similar principles.

1. SCHOOLS ARE RUN BY SPECIALISTS WHO MAINTAIN CONTROL

As in all industrial-age organizations, the tasks of an industrial-age school are broken into discrete pieces called "jobs." The industrial-age management model breaks the system into pieces, creates specialists, lets everybody do his or her piece, and assumes that someone else makes sure the whole system works. In schools, one person is a principal; another is a teacher; someone else is a superintendent. We assume that this sort of division of labor is an obvious necessity of working together. We often see no compelling need to build partnership or teams among those people or a sense of collective responsibility. Instead, it is assumed that if each person does his or her highly specialized job, then things will work out. In fact, there are few more individualistic professions today than teaching, typically with each teacher doing his or her work almost in complete isolation.

But what children experience is a highly fragmented system that is the antithesis of a team. It's as if basketball players decided never to pass the ball, or if everyone in an orchestra decided to play only solos. "One of the most important, and challenging, things that you can possibly do in a school system," says former Corvallis, Oregon, superintendent Jim Ford, "is to break down the walls that separate teachers, administrators, parents, and kids—to help people see the school as a community and that the community is the school."

In this fragmented system, the unilateralness of adult authority creates little if any voice for student leadership. Indeed, the very term is an oxymoron beyond adult-sanctioned corrals, like "the Student Council." The idea that the students should have a say, for example, in what is taught and how it is taught is anathema in most schools. As highly successful superintendent Les Omotani says, "If you would just ask the kids, they would've told you right away what was working and what wasn't working." But the authority of adults to run the school generally remains unquestioned.

See "Creating a Core Learning Group" by Les Omotani, page 445.

As one high school principal commented, "As I reflect on my work, and indeed my career as an educator, I realize that my number-one concern has been control. This is the heart of what our system is all about." In a system based on maintaining control, it is the job of the teachers to control the students, the administrators to control the teachers, and the school board to maintain control over the system as a whole.

Control is not an inherently dysfunctional concept—all viable living systems have evolved capabilities for control or balance. The problem lies in the industrial-age notion of control. A living system controls itself. A machine is controlled by its operator. Teachers, administrators, and boards can easily become the operators of the machine called school.

Moreover, any system of hierarchical control, even if it has very good people, is subject to abuse. Many years ago, I knew a sixth grader who had been accused of cheating on a multiple-choice test. He was new to his school. The teacher humiliated him—giving him an F and calling his parents. The boy was devastated. "I didn't look at anybody's paper!" he said. But the teacher refused to believe him because he had seen the boy's head moving. Of course, no one except the boy actually could know what he saw, as opposed to where his face was pointed. But the teacher remained resolute in his assessment. He ended the meeting with the child's parents by saying, "Look, I don't believe in holding grudges against kids. If he recognizes that he shouldn't do this again, it will not count against him."

The teacher clearly felt he was being generous—even magnanimous. But he never questioned the subjective sense he made of what he observed. He alone, not the child, had the power to define "cheating." It was part of his role as a teacher as he saw it.

For the child, now a young man, the experience reinforced his awareness of where control really lay. He felt profoundly disrespected. He remains angry at traditional schools and teachers to this day.

The teacher's actions, though extreme, were completely consistent with the assembly-line model of control: Just as an inspector has power over whether a product on an assembly line is acceptable, the teacher has power to judge unilaterally a child's behavior.

2. KNOWLEDGE IS INHERENTLY FRAGMENTED

Control based on fragmented specialization appears to be a logical way to organize schools because of another industrial-age assumption—the assumption that knowledge itself is fragmented, that knowledge arises in discrete categories. Literature, art, and the humanities are separate from mathematics, which is distinct from biology and earth science, which in turn are distinct from history, geography, and psychology. From this fragmented perspective, it is easy to ignore the fact that life isn't quite like that, that life presents itself to us whole, that challenging problems are challenging because they have many interdependent facets. When was the last time you encountered a problem that was purely a math problem? Or purely an interpersonal problem? Or a problem where you only had to figure out the technically correct solution and then people would automatically do what was needed? Life's interdependencies tend to remain invisible to the fragmented academic theory of knowledge. Given this theory of knowledge, it comes as no surprise that the further an individual progresses in the formal system of education, the narrower and narrower his or her knowledge becomes.

This fragmented theory of knowledge is antithetical to a systems view of reality: that reality is composed fundamentally of relationships, not things. The systems view recognizes the interrelatedness of subject matter. But industrial-age schools find it very difficult to recognize those interrelationships; instead, they implicitly tell students that what matters most in life are narrow piles of knowledge.

"The fragmentation of knowledge is the saddest irony of our business," says Tim Lucas. "Here we have all of this incredible life-nourishing material—literature, mathematics, and on and on. It's unending. Kids recognize its vitality when they start out, and yet, somewhere along the line, it becomes dead for so many of them. And the institutions are often dead too. There may be little spots of light, but it is so sad, because what could be more exciting than the knowledge of civilization?"

3. SCHOOLS COMMUNICATE "THE TRUTH"

Our system of education is based on an implicit theory that philosophers call "naïve realism." Naïve realists are people who think that "what they see is." We all live most of our lives as naïve realists because the data of our senses presents itself to us with such compelling force. We then tend to treat our perceptions as absolute fact, like the teacher who "saw" the young boy cheat.

That we move quickly from sense data to interpretations is not a problem per se; it is a characteristic of human perception. The problem arises when we fail to recognize that it is happening.

In the traditional industrial-age schoolroom, teachers do not teach as if they are communicating socially constructed views or interpretations. They teach as if they are communicating truth. Kids learn "what happened" in history, not an accepted story about what happened. Kids learn scientific truths, not models of reality that have proven useful. They learn the one right way to solve a particular problem, not the complexities of different perspectives on the same phenomenon. As a consequence, students' tolerance for ambiguity and conflict is diminished, and their critical thinking skills fail to develop. They fail to see the contingency of human understanding. Instead, they become habituated to sanitized, politically correct bits of knowledge, only to eventually find themselves deeply frustrated and disoriented by life's complexities.

Humberto Maturana and Francisco Varela have developed a pioneering theory of the biological bases of cognition—the Santiago theory of cognition. A synthesis of biological and cognitive science, the implications of this theory for human beings can be summarized in the simple statement: "Everything said is said by somebody." No human being ever produces a definitive statement about reality. It's not biologically possible to do so. This fact does not invalidate science or history, any more than it does literature or art. But it does invite us

The Tree of Knowledge, pp. 27, 34, and 206ff.

to consider science or history as social phenomenon, created by communities of people who agree to certain standards and procedures and thereby advance a shared understanding, which understanding is always imperfect. Nor does the Santiago theory imply that there is no reality independent of human observation (a philosophical view called solipsism). It simply states that human beings cannot make absolute statements about reality.

What does this mean for schools? Consider the teachers who touched you as a student, not because they knew the answer but precisely because they didn't know. Their curiosity inspired you, and their passion fired your imagination. They were so excited about what you might learn together that you loved them as teachers. You valued their experience. You knew they had thought about their subject a lot, and you were interested in their thoughts, but they didn't give you "the answers" in any absolute sense. When they told you "This is what happened," they were really saying "This is one view of what happened; here is something to think about." Your questions were regarded as a valid way to link established ideas to your own understanding. In fact, they had their own questions, and it was this common questioning that made the two of you, ultimately, equals.

By contrast, naïve realism fits neatly with and subtly reinforces the deficit perspective of learning. It reifies the view that children are deficient by establishing a caste of experts—teachers—who hold the answers. Because their answers are unquestionable, the superiority of the teacher's knowledge, and the inferiority of the student's, is institutionally established.

4. LEARNING IS PRIMARILY INDIVIDUALISTIC AND COMPETITION ACCELERATES LEARNING

Because we see knowledge as something that teachers have and students are supposed to get, we see it as possessed by individuals, and we tend to see the learning process as being similarly individualistic. But this is a dangerous oversimplification.

Consider something as basic as walking. Learning to walk appears to be a prototypical individual learning process. But is it really? Consider the importance of having the examples of parents, siblings, and other children to emulate. In fact, what it means to learn to walk is to join a community of walkers, just as mastering natural language brings us membership in a community of talkers. When we think in this way, we come to realize that all learning is social as well as individual.

Yet the traditional schoolroom focuses almost exclusively on the individual perspective. Individual learners are supposed to master subject matter. Individuals are tested for their comprehension, and individuals compete with one another to determine how well they do.

I do not believe that competition is inherently bad. I am the type of person who enjoys competition and have always loved competitive sports. I believe that under the right circumstances, competition can enhance learning. But I also believe that many of our modern societies, such as the United States, have lost appreciation for the healthy balance between competition and collaboration. The two can coexist. Indeed, they do so in most healthy living systems. Nature exhibits competition when different animals compete for the same food, but it also exhibits collaboration, as when packs of animals hunt together or when one species creates conditions that aid another's survival. In fact, the whole idea of individual competition at the heart of evolution today seems like a curious nineteenth-century oversimplification, as we better understand the ways that entire ecosystems survive or die out. "Living beings…are no more inherently bloodthirsty, competitive, and carnivorous than they are peaceful, cooperative, and languid," wrote microbiologist Lynn Margulis (co-developer of the Gaia hypothesis). "Among the most successful—that is, abundant—living beings on the planet are ones that have teamed up." Plants and fungi, animals and bacteria, for example, exist in continual ongoing symbiosis.

Ultimately, the consequences of excessive competitiveness go beyond who wins and who loses to affect us all. We internalize competitiveness as a basic ingredient of any organizational setting. In business, this results in people often expending as much of their energies competing against one another as in competing against their external "competitors." In all settings, we come to see ourselves in a never-ending struggle to win, or at least to avoid losing. This situation affects winners as much as losers and stamps all of us with habits of thought and action that shape our behavior for a lifetime—what Chris Argyris calls "defensive routines." His research has shown why "smart people don't learn" in many work settings, because they have so much invested in proving what they know and avoiding being seen as not knowing, poignant examples of Alfie Kohn's famous phrase, "punished by rewards."

To be sure, many educators today have concerns about excessive competition and value collaboration and cooperative work. Group projects are more and more common; in some schools, complex subjects are routinely taught by pairs of teachers, who can strengthen each other's perspectives and work more closely with different students. Encouraging schools and school systems to collaborate in improving educational outcomes is a cornerstone of Michael Fullan's widely recognized work on system change in education. "We try to get principals focused on the

Lynn Margulis and Dorion Sagan, *What is Life?* (Simon & Schuster, 1995) p. 192. We are grateful to Elaine Johnson for reminding us of this book's statements about cooperation.

Chris Argyris, "Teaching Smart People How to Learn," *Harvard Business Review* (May–June 1991), HBR Reprint #91301; and *Flawed Advice and the Management Trap: How Managers Can Know When They're Getting Good Advice and When They're Not* (Oxford University Press, 2000); and Alfie Kohn, *Punished by Rewards: The Trouble with Gold Stars, Incentive Plans, A's, Praise, and Other Bribes* (Houghton Mifflin, 1999).

performance of other schools, just as we get superintendents to focus on the performance of other systems," says Fullan.

But educational practices still remain highly ambivalent on the subject. It often appears that educators fail to see just how thoroughly competition is designed into schools. Many teachers lament that "students focus too much on grades," ignoring the signals those students have received their entire school career that grades are the key to success in school and getting into college.

In the early 1990s, I participated in a meeting of state school department heads, at the outset of interest in "quality management in education." Dr. W. Edwards Deming was the keynote speaker. He began his presentation by saying "We've been sold down the river by competition," and proceeded to talk about the experience of leading firms around the world in fostering teams, collaboration, and shared responsibility. When he was done, one of the state leaders said, "Dr. Deming, obviously you don't know that we educators also value collaboration. Cooperative learning strategies are being used in many schoolrooms in America today. And I don't see anything wrong with rewarding those schools who do it best." Apparently, for this educational leader, collaboration was great for kids but not for adults; he had seemingly discounted the idea of teachers, administrators, and schools collaborating to build common knowledge.

Moving Beyond the Industrial-Age Model

All of these industrial-age assumptions—about the learner and the school—come together in the critical issue of assessment: deciding how to assess performance in and of schools. Few subjects have been more divisive in public education over the past decades, with strong external pressures to increase accountability colliding against the concerns of educators about the negative effects of performance pressure on teachers and students alike.

Again, a bit of historical perspective is helpful—both to appreciate why we have followed the path we have followed and to begin to imagine how an alternative path might unfold. This alternative path could support the innovation truly needed today if we are to have schools capable of preparing students to face the challenges of today's world.

Viewed from the standpoint of the innovation that is needed, the testing movements of the past two decades—both the first phase in the 1990s and the high-stakes testing of the 2000s—stand out as a sort of last gasp of the industrial-age school.

See Michael Fullan, *Motion Leadership: The Skinny on Becoming Change Savvy* (School Improvement Network, 2009). Also see Michael Fullan, *All Systems Go: The Change Imperative for Whole System Reform* (Corwin Press, 2010). Fullan's website is www.michaelfullan.ca.

Assessing performance has always been a source of contradictory aims in traditional schools. For example, a cornerstone of lifelong learning, and one key to success in higher education, is the capacity to set learning goals and effectively assess one's own progress. But traditional schools have relied on a teacher-centered assessment process where the teacher is the authority, choosing and controlling the child's grade and ability to proceed. The contradiction is present no matter how skilled, competent, and well-meaning the individual teacher is. If a child's primary orientation in school becomes pleasing a teacher, then the teacher and student are, in effect, colluding in shifting the developmental burden away from objective self-assessment: the ability to judge for yourself how well you are doing. The result can be adults who spend their careers currying favor rather than doing something they truly regard as meaningful. Few educators would espouse this result, but the system of specialization and control consistently produces it.

See Bena Kallick, "Assessment as Learning," page 221.

This reliance on external evaluation has cast a long shadow over efforts to improve schools based on concerns over their performance. Starting in the 1980s, reports like *A Nation at Risk* raised great doubts about American schools' effectiveness, historically a source of pride among Americans. By the early 1990s, a growing movement had developed among businesses concerned about the consequences for U.S. competitiveness, which resulted in a series of significant gatherings organized by business groups like The Conference Board and The Business Roundtable. Ironically, many turned to the burgeoning "quality movement" for the solution—even though the movement's most popular recommendations contradicted its own fundamental insights.

By the mid-1990s, a new consensus had started to form, strongly rooted in the mainstream U.S. business community: The way to turn around failing schools was to set targets, make them measurable, and make educators accountable for hitting those targets. The measures, in the form of standardized tests, started to be administered uniformly—starting with early grades in primary school and then performance-tracked on up through secondary school. For the first time, differences in performance among schools were publicly visible, creating pressures on lower-performing schools to close the gap.

Though this approach was championed in the name of quality, the basic management philosophy underlying it was anathema to many pioneers of the quality movement. Dr. W. Edwards Deming, considered by many the philosophical leader of the movement, derided any form of management based on rating and ranking people. He said that the standardized test approach was like "management by objectives," a business goal-tracking method that, according to Deming, had been a primary reason for the demise of the U.S. manufacturing industry. Indeed, I heard Deming make that statement at a major gathering of state education department heads in New York in the early 1990s. But the train was pulling out of the station, and a nation desperate for a fix to its broken schools had an answer and vigorous champions for that answer.

To many businesspeople involved in these school reform efforts, the problem was not unlike one they had faced in business: there were good performers and poor performers, and they had to push the poor performers—the bad teachers—out of the system. It was easy to overlook the fact that "rank and yank" systems had rarely, if ever, worked effectively in business. In truth, there rarely are that many poor performers in a professional environment; the problem is that there are so many hurdles that make it difficult to perform well. Rather than creating a hostile climate for low performers, the way to raise teacher quality is to create an environment more conducive to continual learning and development for the teachers.

The testing movement became even more intensive with the Bush Administration's "No Child Left Behind" program. High-stakes testing became the new norm, where students were unable to graduate from high school if they did not pass key tests. Before long it was common for newspapers to publish the test score results for different schools and school systems. In many cases, the results did improve—but often with significant unintended side effects. For example, a longitudinal study of the students who graduated from Boston public schools in 2000 found that 65 percent went on to post-secondary schools, an impressive improvement relative to 50 percent in 1985. However, by 2007, only 35 percent of those graduates from 2000 had completed a post-secondary degree program. The rest had apparently been given a credential but were not prepared for the challenge.

See Andrew Sum, et al., *Getting to the Finish Line: College Enrollment and Graduation, A Seven-Year Longitudinal Study of the Boston Public Schools Class of 2000*, (Center for Labor Market Studies, Northeastern University and Boston Private Industry Council, November 2008). Available at http://www.bostonpic.org/sites/default/files/resources/BPS%20college%20graduation%20study.pdf.

Two aspects of this recent history are particularly noteworthy. First, much of the energy for reform came from the business community. The views of business had great political clout, as they have since educators began training students for factory jobs at the outset of the industrial era. Second, the business voice that was the loudest did not come from innovators but from mainstream managers. The management-by-objectives paradigm was in line with the way they felt management should work. Those with alternative business perspectives, who would be more likely to champion Deming's quality management and more learning-oriented corporate cultures or to support innovation and continual improvement, did not have much influence in the school debates. The debates were about performance, not innovation.

I believe the times are now right for the voices for innovation to join in the discussions on school reform. While there is no one simple way to summarize the alternative management paradigm, it starts with focusing on deeper understanding of the actual processes needed to produce results and to continually innovate and improve and a much stronger emphasis on building individual and collective capacity to achieve this. The management-by-objectives view believes you can improve things through measures and incentives; the learning-oriented view believes that incentives cannot cause people to accomplish things that they are not capable of accomplishing. The management-by-objectives view is purely top down. The learning-oriented view believes overarching aims are crucial, but so too is genuine commitment from the people who must achieve those aims. The management-by-objectives view tends to focus on quick improvements like higher scores, the learning-oriented view on deeper changes that may take longer but also last longer—though it also values setting interim targets to gauge progress and adapt strategies.

Obviously, I have a bias, but it is one that I think appropriate for the realities of change in schools. The businessperson who thinks that schools should be managed like businesses often ignores the many features that truly are different about schools. For example, imagine that you're manufacturing something and you receive shipments of defective parts that will compromise the quality of your product. When asked what they would do in this situation, the businessperson says, "Obviously, we'd find a different supplier." But, this is not really an option for the public schools. Kids come into our schools from broken homes, often woefully unprepared and disadvantaged academically. Should we send them back?

This is just one of many fundamental differences between business and education realities. They all point to the same conclusion. We need a system of management that can deal with the realities on the ground of schools, that is deeply immersed in studying and improving the actual processes that support learning, and that continually builds the capacities of all concerned to improve performance in the short term and to innovate and continue to improve over the long term.

None of this should imply that tools like standardized tests are unimportant. They can provide meaningful information to educators and students alike. But they need to be used for improvement, not punishment. And they do *not* constitute a change strategy.

For a genuine change strategy, we need to think more clearly about

The point about suppliers is taken from Larry Cuban, *The Blackboard and the Bottom Line* (Harvard University Press, 2004).

our aims for education. Only then can we have solid foundation for knowing what sort of performance we are seeking and how best to assess and move toward it. We need innovation, but innovation for what?

Conditions for Innovation

Despite the many difficulties that exist today, conditions are ripe for basic innovation in schools.

First, there are unprecedented signs of breakdown in the assembly-line school concept and process. Extraordinary stress is one symptom of breakdown. Another is the increasing separation of "haves" and "have-nots." Those who can afford it increasingly put their children in private school, where they purchase smaller class sizes, the opportunity to be surrounded by other elite students, and access to teachers who are more satisfied with their working conditions. Others opt for home schooling, by some accounts the fastest growing segment of precollege education, estimated to involve more than two million children in the United States as of 2010. Charter schools also create a space of innovation. But neither private nor home schooling nor charters are options for the majority of families, and those in public school are being increasingly shut out of society's best opportunities. As a result of growing inequity, social unrest and disturbance are growing. Moreover, I believe concern over education seems to be growing throughout the industrialized world at levels that would have seemed almost unimaginable a few years ago.

See Bryan D. Ray, "2.04 Million Homeschool Students in the United States in 2010," (National Home Education Research Institute, January 3, 2011) http://www.nheri.org/HomeschoolPopulationReport2010.html.

Second, many of the historic social conditions upon which the industrial-age school relied no longer exist. Part of this is due to demographic changes. The captive female labor market that schools depended on to draw the majority of teachers has disappeared, as women now pursue a much broader range of professions. More problematic, traditional schools depended on traditional family and community structures that no longer exist. In the United States, the traditional family structure whereby one parent worked and one parent remained at home to raise kids ceased to be a social norm during the 1960s and 1970s. Today families with two working parents or a single parent are the norm. The breakdown of the traditional parent-child-school relationship has left schools taking on more of a childcare role, and conversations between parents and teachers often are more focused on easing parents' stresses than on helping the children academically. In that context, standardization of academics is even more difficult.

Perhaps as historic is the elimination of the school's monopoly on the provision of information, due to the growth in communication and media technology. One hundred years ago, children knew little of what was going on in the larger world beyond what they were explicitly told at home or at school. Today, the typical teenager has at least as much access to knowledge about the world as parents and teachers have. Moreover, social media and mobile computer technologies provide a mix of fun and learning in ways that schoolrooms cannot match: they are controlled by the learner, available when the learner is ready, and embedded in networks of mutual interests among peers. Changes in family structure have rendered these media technologies especially influential, since they often fill the gap as substitute parents.

Last, even if these multiple symptoms of profound change were ignored, the simple fact is that the working world is no longer looking for "industrial workers." Authors like Daniel Pink document the ongoing shift in the workplace from "algorithmic tasks" (following a preordained path) to "heuristic tasks" (working effectively in contexts needing experimentation and innovative thinking). A 2005 McKinsey & Company study estimated that 30 percent of current job growth is from jobs with algorithmic tasks, while 70 percent of job growth is from heuristic ones. Similarly, Jonathan Spector, CEO of The Conference Board, testified to the House Appropriations Committee in 2008 that survey information from more than one thousand U.S. business executives stressed the need for "creativity, innovation, critical thinking, and problem-solving" in schools. (These results were summarized in a 2006 report from the Conference Board called *Are They Really Ready to Work?*)

The former dean of MIT's engineering school, Gordon Brown, used to say, "To be a teacher you must be a prophet—because you are trying to prepare people for a world thirty to fifty years into the future." By continuing to prop up the industrial-age concept of schools through teacher-centered instruction, learning as memorizing, and extrinsic control, we are preparing students for a world that is ceasing to exist.

I believe we are seeing the beginnings of a new consensus on the basic aims of education. Studies like *Are They Really Ready to Work?* show the need for new non-machine-age skills for the global knowledge workplace: higher-order capacities like understanding complex issues, collaborating, producing outcomes in the face of uncertainty and ambiguity, and being self-motivated and community-oriented. Though formative, I believe this consensus will grow, especially as more evidence becomes available that we can achieve such goals in public schools.

⟩⟩ Also see "Context and Engagement," page 293.

See Daniel Pink, *Drive* (Riverhead Books, 2009), p. 29; "The Next Revolution in Interaction," *McKinsey Quarterly 4* (2005), p. 25–26; Jonathan Spector, "Written Testimony to the House Appropriations Subcommittee on Interior, Environment & Related Agencies Hearing on the 'Role of the Arts in Creativity and Innovation,'" (April 1, 2008); The Conference Board, Corporate Voices for Working Families, Partnership for 21st Century Skills, and Society for Human Resource Management, *Are They Really Ready to Work? Employers' Perspectives on the Basic Knowledge and Applied Skills of New Entrants to the 21st Century U.S. Workforce,* (The Conference Board, 2006).

Still, it is easy to be daunted by the challenge of transforming industrial-age schools, especially considering that their underlying assumptions still match the thinking of most people and most of society's institutions. But such reactions miss an important point. The challenge is not to come up with a simple set of fixes. Indeed, the machine-age concept of "fixes" itself is part of the problem. Many historians of school reform, from Seymour Sarason to Diane Ravitch to David Tyack and Larry Cuban, have noted the ways in which well-intentioned "fixes" have made problems worse. Schools are not "broken" and in need of fixing. They are social institutions under stress that need to evolve.

Similarly, we don't need "the answer"—in the sense of a single blueprint for the school of the future. In fact, that may be exactly what is *not* needed. Instead, we need growing awareness of the nature of the underlying problems that schools face and willingness to experiment from many quarters and many philosophical perspectives. Studies show that the basic innovation that creates new industries typically involves a combination of several new technologies. For example, the birth of the commercial airline industry involved many innovations in aircraft design and technologies, from engines to wing flaps, in the first decades of the twentieth century; but it also required the development of jet engines and radar in the 1940s. Like technological innovation, institutional innovation usually arises only as multiple new component innovations come together to create ensembles of new ideas and approaches that can support widespread application. Many of those innovations are here now, as you'll learn throughout this book.

But what will cause the diverse innovations needed to cohere together, leading to a new overall movement of deep change? I believe that the answer lies in a new guiding metaphor. Just as the machine metaphor shaped the thinking that created schools in the industrial age, the emerging understanding of living systems can guide thinking for the future.

See Seymour Sarason, *The Predictable Failure of School Reform* (Jossey-Bass, 1990); Diane Ravitch, *The Troubled Crusade: American Education 1945–1980* (Basic Books, 1983); and David Tyack and Larry Cuban, *Tinkering Toward Utopia: A Century of Public School Reform* (Harvard University Press, 1995).

The School as a Living System

Over the past hundred years, a revolution has been occurring in our scientific view of the world: a "systems revolution" characterized by the study and appreciation of living systems and by their ability to explain behavior that can't be understood in purely mechanistic terms. The systems revolution started in physics and moved gradually into biology. It also has roots in engineering, especially the understanding of dynamic feedback systems. It is penetrating gradually into the cognitive sciences and the social sciences. But the process is just at its outset. (Even though the beginnings of the systems view date to 1900 or so, it takes a very long time for a fundamental shift in scientific worldview to work its way into society; those who favor this worldview have learned to be patient.)

See the primer on Systems Thinking, page 123.

What is this revolutionary living systems view all about? It starts with the assertion that the fundamental nature of reality is relationships, not things. Newtonian culture tells us that the world is composed of things. Newton's atoms were like tiny billiard balls colliding and transferring energy. But the science of the last hundred years tells us that more than 99 percent of everything is empty space! Even the remaining 1 percent is not just "very little things" such as protons and electrons, but a kind of probability that tangible properties will manifest themselves in that subatomic space.

At a more human scale, this "thing" that we call a body is, in fact, not nearly so material as it appears to us. The inventor Buckminster Fuller used to hold up his hand and ask, "What is this?"

Most everyone answered, "It's a hand."

"No," he would say, "it is a patterned integrity. It is the capacity to produce hands, a structure of relationships which continues to manifest itself as a hand."

Fuller was pointing to what biologists now call "autopoiesis," or the self-producing character of the living. Our hand is continually replacing itself as old cells die and new ones are born. It takes a few months to replace all the cells in the hand, but we get a completely new pancreas every day, and the entire body replaces itself in a few years. In that sense, your body does not "have" a hand or a foot or any other particular body part, so much as it has the capacity to produce all of these continually. This is a stunning statement of fact for those of us used to thinking that "We are our bodies." But this is the nature of living systems. The body is more like a river, with new substance flowing through and being organized continually, just as the banks of the river organize the water flowing through. Seeds do not produce trees. They organize the process of creating trees.

See Fritjof Capra, *The Web of Life: A New Scientific Understanding of Living Systems* (Anchor Books, 1996) and Margulis and Sagan, *What is Life?*

In this revolutionary new understanding of living systems, some scientists also believe that living systems are distinctly characterized by emergent self-organization (behaviors and structures that cannot be predicted based on past behaviors and structures) and cognition, the ability to "make sense" of their environment. Although the new science of living systems is in its infancy, we are clearly learning that we have treated much that surrounds us like lifeless things—trees, planets, even social systems like schools—because we have not understood deeply enough the properties associated with life. Living systems are not made of things; they do not have "thingness." Rather, things themselves are the results of living systems, arising out of a fundamental reality of relationships.

A living system thus has the capacity to create itself. Herein lies a fundamental distinction between living systems and machines: living systems are self-made while machines are made by others.

The more we understand living systems in this way, the more aware we become of the mental conditioning inherent in the industrial age. Unlike machines, living systems continually grow and evolve, form new relationships, and have innate goals to exist and to re-create themselves. Although living systems are like machines in some ways—they have recurring behavior and their future development can be influenced—they are neither predictable nor controllable. Moreover, living systems create machines, starting with the simple tools used by birds and other mammals, right up to our most sophisticated technologies. In a sense, the living systems view subsumes the machine view rather than opposing it. When relativity theory gradually became accepted, it was said that, "Einstein replanted Newton's plant in a larger pot." The same could be said of the living systems age relative to the machine age. The problem is not machine-age thinking per se but the dysfunctional habit of seeing everything through that lens.

A VISION FOR A LIVING SCHOOL

What would happen if school was organized with an appreciation of the value of living systems rather than machines? In effect, the rest of this book addresses this question. But we can begin with a few ruminations.

First, if the material to be learned was treated less like a stable fact to be memorized and more like a living, changing being, the learning process would come alive. Consider, for example, the subject of biology. Ironically, the study of life is for most students a dead, boring subject. I was shocked to discover, in talking with my oldest son, that he had been taught high school biology in the 1990s exactly as I had learned it many years earlier: endless disconnected facts to memorize about cell walls and nuclei, ectoplasm and endoplasm, then more facts about blood cells and muscle tissue cells, and so on and so on. Biology becomes a completely different subject when the learner starts with understanding how a living cell functions, creates itself, and interacts with its environment to maintain internal balances conducive to the dynamic processes continually unfolding within it.

Moreover, instead of learning about these ideas as scientific facts to be memorized, what if learners themselves could discover them through interacting with computer simulations that let them create cells and experiment with how they would survive and adapt under different circumstances? They could then, for example, explore the nature of cancer. At one level, cancer is nothing but uncontrolled cell division—mitosis run amuck. Could learners create conditions in their simulations that would cause the signals from surrounding tissues that normally limit cell division to fail? All of a sudden, students could discover for themselves the many lives of the cell, the prototypical living system. When you consider the contrast between biology under the machine learning model and the living system model, which do you think would be more captivating and fulfilling?

Learning the humanities could also be dramatically different. Years ago I met a woman who taught English literature in a high school in a high-poverty neighborhood in Tucson. She had to teach Shakespeare to Hispanic and Native American kids who were wondering how they would eat the next day. The industrial model made the story of Hamlet into a static thing—a set of character names and plot lines to be memorized. But her boyfriend, who taught science in another school, had been using computer simulation models like that of the way cells worked. So she decided to build a simulation of Hamlet. It traced the growth of Hamlet's anger and resentment and the way that this, in turn, made the king and queen misunderstand him, with tragic results.

Suddenly Hamlet came alive. The kids could ask questions like "What if Polonius hadn't hidden behind the curtain? What if Hamlet hadn't slain him? What if he had done something else? What might have happened?" A static tableau became a living tapestry of people interacting with one another, brought alive because the learners could themselves interact with Hamlet through translating their what-if questions into simulation experiments.

I will never forget sitting around with some of those kids two years later and listening to one boy, Raphael, a Hispanic student who had been thinking of dropping out of school before encountering this teacher's class. I asked him to tell me what that computer simulation model of Hamlet had meant to him. "My brain popped open," he said. He got reconnected to school, his grades improved, and he graduated. He also rediscovered his love for music. As we talked about the career he was making for himself as a musician, he spontaneously started drawing system causal loop diagrams (a systems learning exercise described on page 140) with the other kids—to discuss his music!

Clearly, there is something significantly different about studying subjects as if they were alive. Such an educational process rests on:

■ Learner-centered learning rather than teacher-centered learning;
■ Encouraging variety, not homogeneity—embracing multiple intelligences and diverse learning styles; and
■ Understanding a world of interdependency and change rather than memorizing facts and striving for right answers.

Similarly, if we began treating schools as living systems instead of as machines, we would:

■ Constantly reflect on the theories-in-use of everyone involved in the education process;
■ Continually explore how to integrate diverse academic subjects into meaningful learning experiences for children and adults; and
■ View those who make a school—teachers, students, parents—as a community and begin to reintegrate education within webs of social relationships that link friends, families, and diverse institutions to build healthy communities.

When we inhabit a school as a living system, we discover that it is always evolving. We participate in that evolution by asking questions like "Why is the system this way? Why do these rules exist? How do they help and how to they impede achieving our aims? What is the purpose of this practice?" We are not willing to settle for explanations meant to pacify or disable us, such as, "The people who have the power make it that way." Since we are part of the system ourselves, we are drawn to inquire more deeply, to look for ways that our own assumptions and habitual actions are integral to creating the system as it operates today. Constant questioning becomes a way of life for students, teachers, parents, and administrators.

The assumptions identified here can provide a starting point. They are generic, not specific. Each will be more influential in some settings than in others. What is important is for all concerned to think for themselves, and to talk together, about how these and other assumptions play out in their own school setting and to see where their energies for innovation really lead. Only then will the idea of school as a living system actually come alive.

The aim of this questioning is not criticism but learning—making the school environment about learning for everyone concerned. I remember asking a principal of a very innovative school how she defined her job. She answered, "My job is creating an environment where teachers continually learn." She believed that teachers being deeply engaged in their own learning process would inevitably enable them to create a better learning environment for students.

Finally, school can reestablish its place as a social institution by making children's lives, not the classroom, once again the center of their learning. There are many examples of such schools, and often they draw in people from the surrounding community, who begin to see themselves as part of the school. For example, at Creswell Middle School in Oregon, monthly "kid days" have been conducted for years. These were organized days on which school was officially closed so that students, educators, and community members could get together in informal dialogues and look at the self-creating social networks that were in fact making the school possible.

"There were people in my dialogue group whom I wasn't particularly fond of," one student recalled later. "I didn't dislike them, but I didn't see them as people I could relate to. Then we started talking; they shared their views, and I listened to what they had to say. Now, when I pass that group in the hall, I have less reason to think that they dislike me. The dialogue gave at least one person in each of the different cliques in our school a thought: Maybe this person isn't so different, and we should probably treat him or her with some respect."

When the learning process is truly oriented around the lives and learning of the students, the boundary of "the school" becomes more open to the larger community, and education becomes a social rather than mechanistic process. At one school in New Mexico, it took a remarkably simple curriculum innovation to connect the school and community. In tenth grade, the students could declare one thing they wanted to learn from someone in the community, find a mentor to teach them, and make that into one of their classes. It might be carpentry, desktop publishing, or cooking. It was up to the student (and a simple screening process the school used to assess mentors). Not only did this put students in charge of their own learning; it situated that learning within the community where they lived and, over time, resulted in a network of adult mentors who became closely connected with the school.

Drawing teachers and learners from the community can also have an impact within the school walls. For example, one school found an ingenious method for helping fourth graders struggling with fractions, a very common problem. They put them to work in the school kitchen for a few days. Suddenly fractions became very practical as they had to scale recipes up and down—and the young cooks became teachers for their classmates.

Another school invited a community organization called the Waters Foundation to help them deal with violence between cliques—a problem that many schools struggle with. One widely viewed video, produced by the Foundation, shows three six-year-old boys talking about a system map they drew to understand why they are having fights on the playground. Sitting around a library table, they describe the ways that "mean words" and "hurt feelings" can reinforce each other and then the "different ways we can intervene in the system." Says one child, "We tried saying I'm sorry, but that didn't really work." He then proceeds to describe some of the things they will try next time when they find themselves "stuck in the loop." Their search for an alternative offers a beautiful lesson in "life as learning." At a recent gathering, one of them, now all of seven years old, reported that, "We are now best friends."

T.A. Benson, *First Grade Problem-Solving*, (The Waters Foundation, 2011) http://www.watersfoundation.org/index.cfm?fuseaction=whatsnew.website:first-grade problem-solving.

Over the years, I have seen many stories like these, and they have taught me an important lesson. I believe there exists a deep hunger among most adults to be more connected to the lives of children. The fragmentation of adults from the lives of children is a deep source of loss in our society. Even if we are not parents or educators ourselves, we cannot walk away from children and let them be the responsibility of a professional elite. Human beings are deeply, innately connected to the lives of children. Caring for children is rooted deeply in us. It is part of our biological heritage.

Rethinking schools as living organisms more like a tree than a car part, and education as a social process more resembling a community than a factory, may seem idealistic or even quixotic. Yet it is worth noting that this was the nature of schools for the vast majority of our collective history. Human societies have educated their young for tens of thousands of years, long before industrial-age schools. In Daniel Quinn's novel *My Ishmael*, he describes the typical tribal educational system:

"Youngsters 'graduate' from childhood at age thirteen or fourteen and by this age have basically learned all they need in order to function as adults in their community. They've learned so much, in fact, that if the rest of the community were simply to vanish overnight, they'd be able to survive without the least difficulty. They'd know how to make the tools needed for hunting and fishing. They'd know how to shelter and clothe themselves." They have done all this without any schools, simply by doing what all children do: by watching members of the community and spending time with the people who know something about what they want to learn. "Graduation" from the tribal system inevitably in-

The description of schooling is in Daniel Quinn, *My Ishmael* (Bantam, 1997); p. 126ff. The quote is from page 129. These insights into rites of passage come, in part, from conversations with Louis van der Merwe.

volves a rite of passage, where people are tutored in the tribe's heritage and traditions and learn the importance of enduring suffering and facing a challenge on their own. After this graduation, they are welcomed into an adult community to which they now are expected to contribute. We should remember this when we look at today's high school students struggling to find their place as a "community contributor" without the benefit of any such formal rite.

Of course, life does not move backward. We will not go back to living in tribes. But any approach to education that has been around for many thousands of years warrants being taken seriously—that we would look to understand how it works. And if we look closely, we see that it embodies several characteristics that may now seem familiar: children are continually learning, learning occurs in day-to-day situations of living, and the institutions that support learning are integrated into the workings of society.

Learning is supported by our nature; it is a manifestation of the search for development in all living beings. It can be diverted or blocked, but it can't be prevented from occurring. The core educational task in our time is to evolve institutions and practices that assist, not supplant, that natural learning process.

Who Will Lead the Change?

One last comment on why schools seem remarkably difficult institutions to change and where the most significant source of leverage may lie. Industrial-age schools have a structural blind spot unlike almost any other contemporary institution. This blind spot arises because the only person who could in fact reflect on how the system as a whole is functioning is the one person who has no voice in the system and usually no power to provide meaningful feedback that could guide change. This person is the student.

The student is the one person who sees the whole picture: all the classes, the challenges on the playground and streets, all the stress at home, the multiple conflicting messages from media—the total environment. Kids know when the overall workload is too big or small, when the stress level is too high or the level of respect too low. But they have no power or standing in the system. Their opinions are discounted. They are, after all, just kids—in a system run by adults supposedly for their benefit.

To see the folly of this, imagine that we enforced a rule on a company's workers: under no circumstances are you to talk to customers. We would not expect that company to survive for long. If anything, silencing the voice of the students is even more limiting. Unlike customers who passively purchase what a company produces, students co-produce the results achieved by schools. Where there is no student engagement, there is no learning.

I thus have come to believe that the real hope for deep and enduring processes of evolution in schools lies with students. They have a deep passion for making schools work. They are connected to the future in ways that no adult is—and in many ways today more connected to the larger world and its challenges. They have imagination and ways of seeing things that have not yet been reshaped by the formal education process. And they are crying out to be involved, to become more responsible for their environment.

This does not mean that all that is needed is student leadership. But it does mean that without the leadership of students, there is little hope. The rest of us have been in the system of education for our entire lives. We are truly the fish in the water of industrial-age assumptions. Young people are acutely aware of how dramatically our world is evolving away from those assumptions. And young people are still new enough to the system that they can see the tacit rules and assumptions and help the rest of us see them as well.

⟩⟩ See, for example, "The Youth Leadership Forum," page 389.

We do not need to have all the answers worked out in advance. But we need to have the capacity as communities to prioritize new thinking and new practice and to persist in supporting it. We need diverse leaders of all ages and from all sectors willing to travel together into a future we can only begin to imagine. Education for a post-industrial age world requires realizing that humans will be living together differently in the coming decades—or they will not be living well at all—and that young people often have deeper intuitions than do adults regarding the changes ahead.

II. A Primer on the Five Disciplines

1. Creating a Context for Organizational Learning

Are you a teacher and constantly exhausted from dealing with unexpected problems? Or maybe you're an administrator and feel that you can't accomplish enough? If you're a parent, when you see something wrong in your child's report card, do you feel as if there is no recourse? And if you are a student, do you feel that the school is mismatched with your world, your life, and your goals?

A learning discipline provides an answer to these kinds of problems and more—an answer in the form of changes in your day-to-day practice. As you regularly think about your problems and work a bit differently, you gradually build your capacity to produce desired results. To make that easier, the disciplines incorporate tools and techniques: guided methods that lead naturally to new kinds of capabilities. (Buckminster Fuller used to say that if you want to teach people a new way of thinking, don't bother trying to teach that way of thinking directly. Instead, give them a tool, the use of which will lead to new ways of thinking.)

Many educators are familiar with a variety of tools and techniques to enable learning. The craft of teaching is often built around them, starting with the thousands of rubrics and lesson plans developed by classroom teachers and shared with others. The learning disciplines of this book are a set of equally useful methods and techniques, developed and refined to enable learning at a team and organizational level.

If you don't know what to do first in this book, here is the place to start. There is no simple recipe, because everyone's needs are different. But there is a conceptual underpinning to the material throughout

Schools That Learn, and it starts here—where we lay out the tools of the five learning disciplines and theories and principles behind them.

The Deep Learning Cycle

As educators and people who care about schools, we are keenly aware of the personal impact the process of learning can have. We may remember in our own lives what it was like to learn to read, drive a car, play a musical instrument, take up a new sport, or operate skillfully in our profession. Indeed, most people are changed, often profoundly, by intensive learning experiences. This is not just a matter of feeling proud, happy, or emotionally affected. It is a process that takes place, often unseen, within people, and it's one that makes it easier to act in new ways over time.

You can often trigger this process through a new tool or technique. For example, you might use the "iceberg" model (page 126) or a systems-oriented simulation like FishBanks (page 541) to look more closely at a problem affecting your school—perhaps a problem around bullying or academic performance or the management of a forest near the school grounds. As you use these tools, you develop new skills and capabilities, such as the ability to chart and interpret causal relationships between seemingly unrelated symptoms of a problem. This affects your awareness and sensibility: you begin to see some aspects of the problem in a different way than you did before. Over time, as you talk more openly about these issues, new beliefs and assumptions begin to form. Solutions that once seemed viable no longer work; others, that seemed impractical, now hold out real possibility. This enables further development of your skills and capabilities.

The system shown in the diagram on page 72 constitutes the essence of the practice by which a learning organization is built. In the background panel at the upper right is the "deep learning cycle"—the interrelated capacity for change inside individuals and embodied in group cultures. Learning takes place when new skills and capabilities (such as skills in productive conversation or systems thinking), new awarenesses and sensibilities (awareness of our aspirations, current reality, and mental models), and new attitudes and beliefs (values and assumptions about the world) reinforce each other.

Changes in the deep learning cycle can be profound and even irreversible, but they are difficult to initiate. Hence the less enduring but more tangible "domain of action," shown at lower left. Teams and lead-

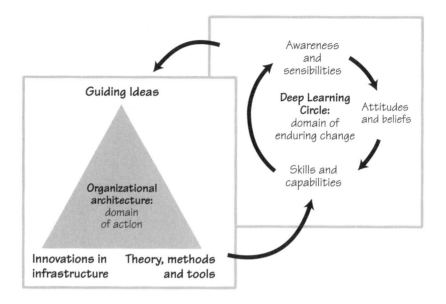

ers, at any level, can act by articulating guiding ideas (and holding conversations about them), by creating innovations in infrastructure, and by instituting regular practice in new methods and techniques, based on a consistent set of underlying theories about building human capabilities.

The key focus for activity is in the triangle, but the core of sustainable change lies in the circle. Both continuously reinforce each other—indeed, all the elements, as they increase in strength and quality, also strengthen each other. (In systems thinking, as we'll see later in this book, these would be called reinforcing cycles.)

Thus, as you consciously recognize that you can't solve this complex problem alone, you may increase the time you spend reflecting on it with others, talking together about the deep assumptions and patterns of behavior that drive results in your school. These conversations, in turn, may lead you all to see aspects of your own collective behavior more clearly. You may see, for example, how some people are continually stuck in particular roles in the conversation; how time and time again they raise objections half-heartedly, only to be shouted down; or how others cut off discussion of difficult issues, even when everyone else is ready to talk about them. This new level of awareness and sensitivity allows you to detect places where you can improve the conversation simply by interjecting a comment: "I think there's something being said here that we may have overlooked…"

And it may also adjust your views of human nature. Perhaps you harbored the assumption that many students (or parents, or teachers, or administrators) are simply "tough to deal with." And as a result, in subsequent conversations with those individuals, you never actually heard the words they said; you only heard the reactions that they triggered in you. But once your awareness grows, your attitudes and beliefs about people may well change. You may now come to realize that these students aren't difficult; rather, they're innately shy and need to be drawn out, or they feel no close connection with the educators in the school.

That new set of attitudes and beliefs, in turn, will make it easier to talk reflectively with those individuals—which, in turn, will build your awareness even further and then lead to greater opportunities for new understanding. And the deep learning cycle—the learning cycle within you—will take on a momentum of its own.

To be sure, a deep learning cycle is difficult to initiate. Skills involving fundamental new ways of thinking and interacting require years to master—ask anyone who has studied a martial art or a musical instrument. New sensibilities and perceptions of our world are a byproduct of long-term growth and change. Deep beliefs and assumptions are not like light switches that can be turned on and off.

Thus we need to construct a shared environment, designed to help these changes occur readily and naturally. This is not unlike the building of a school itself: a place where learning is fostered. However, we're not putting a physical building together; we're building the organizational elements that foster learning throughout the system.

THREE ELEMENTS OF ORGANIZATIONAL LEARNING

There seem to be three basic organizational elements that can be put in place to allow the deep learning cycle to kick in:

- **Guiding ideas:** Deliberately articulated, profound statements that provide a philosophical underpinning for organizational change (like the ideas about liberty and law embodied in the United States Constitution). There is enormous leverage, for either school or community leaders, in articulating the future direction of the school. On pages 319 and 354 we explore some of the guiding ideas that school leaders can develop to inspire people to take steps together.
- **Innovations in infrastructure:** Just as there is a physical infrastructure (roads, corridors, bridges, walkways, energy links) in a community or building, there is also an established set of organizational practices that have just as much impact on determining behavior. These include the marked-out channels of information and communication, including the decision rights and reporting arrangements

Ronald Heifetz. *Leadership Without Easy Answers* (Harvard University Press, 1994), p. 253.

The idea of the deep learning cycle, and its relationship to the five learning disciplines, is covered in more detail in "Moving Forward: Thinking Strategically About Building Learning Organizations," by Peter Senge, in *The Fifth Discipline Fieldbook* (Doubleday, 1994) p. 15.

through which authority and accountability are established. They also include schedules, tax policies, salaries, and many other ingrained relationships and practices. All of these can be redesigned through innovation to lead to better learning; for example, a better design for in-service days, a greater level of autonomy granted to teachers, or a professional learning community where teachers benefit from each other's guidance are all innovations in infrastructure.

■ **Theories, tools, and methods:** In his writing about adaptive leadership, Ronald Heifetz uses the metaphor of a balcony overlooking a dance floor. Most of us spend the bulk of our work time enmeshed in the "dance" of day-to-day urgencies and tasks. But the most gifted leaders, according to Heifetz, can (seemingly without difficulty) step away from the dance and observe the patterns and dynamics as if from above. We don't have to literally climb to a balcony, but we can gain that type of perspective with practice, especially with the help of trusted colleagues who can use inquiry and other techniques to push our thinking further. When we go back on the dance floor, our time spent away makes us more successful, more likely to love our job and less likely to burn out.

To help people develop that kind of perspective, we rely on tools and methods that are buttressed by theory. The credibility of the five learning disciplines is derived from their underpinnings in the intensive study of group dynamics, systems, and the creative process, dating back a hundred years or more. In the margins of this book, we credit the sources of the tools and methods we recommend.

This "three legged stool" shows the way the learning disciplines fit together.

Teams and the "Three-Legged Stool"

At some time or another, most of us have been members of a "great team." It might have been in sports or the performing arts, perhaps in our work or on occasion in a school. Regardless of the setting, we probably remember the trust, the relationships, the acceptance, the synergy—and the results that we achieved. But we often forget that great teams rarely start off as great. Often, they don't start as teams at all. Usually, they start as a group of individuals. It takes time to learn to work as a whole group, just as it takes time to develop the knowledge of walking or riding a bicycle. In other words, great teams are learning organizations—groups of people who, over time, enhance their ability to create what they truly desire in their lives.

People often think of education as an individual endeavor. Teachers go into their classrooms, close the door, and teach alone; students are supposed to demonstrate their expertise alone, or they are considered to be "cheaters." But in an Internet- and social-media-enabled world, where students regularly connect on Facebook from their laptops during class, and where education practices have moved increasingly toward teacher collaboration during the past forty years, that mental model of the profession is long overdue for change. Learning disciplines involve teams of people seeking to improve their classrooms, schools, and communities through collective action, where the group is stronger, not weaker, than the individuals would be if they acted alone.

The five learning disciplines can be easily grouped into the three basic types of skills and capabilities they help develop for individuals and, especially, for teams. We sometimes depict them as three "legs of a stool":

- **Articulating individual and collective aspirations:** This is the ability to focus on what you truly care about and to change because you want to, not just because you need to. All of the learning disciplines, but particularly the practice of personal mastery and building shared vision, can help you develop these capabilities.
- **Recognizing and managing complexity:** This is the ability to see larger systems and forces at play, especially where complex and "messy" problems are concerned, and to construct public, testable ways of expressing those interrelationships. Constructing coherent descriptions of whole systems requires sophisticated conceptualization skills. The discipline of systems thinking is vital for developing these skills, especially in concert with the discipline of working with mental models.
- **Reflective thinking and generative conversation:** This is the ability to use in-depth contemplation, discussion and dialogue to raise awareness of one's own deeply held assumptions and patterns of behavior, both individual and collectively. Developing the capability for meaningful conversation may mean changing the rhythm and tone of typical conversations. Many people have grown used to preparing their response before they have even heard the other person's view; talking with them can feel like being in a tennis game in which each person "takes a shot" before he or she has even received the other's ball. A generative conversation, by contrast, is one which naturally leads people to reflect on their own (and each other's) thinking. These skills emerge especially strongly in the disciplines of working with mental models and team learning.

These three competencies—articulating aspiration, recognizing and managing complexity, and generative conversations—are far more effective when combined. In our experience, proficiency in one reinforces skill in the others. Hence the metaphor we use of a three-legged stool—no leg can be removed if you want to use the whole.

PM

2. Personal Mastery

A boy of five, on the first day of kindergarten, asked his teacher, "When am I going to learn to read?"

She said, a bit absently (for there was a lot going on), "Oh, that won't happen until next year, in first grade."

He didn't say anything, but an hour or so later, she noticed that he had slipped away when no one was looking. He walked out of the room and continued home (which fortunately was only a few blocks away). He went up to his startled mother and said, "I'll go back next year...when they're ready to teach me to read."

Stories like this show the extent to which aspiration and learning are linked. Learning does not occur in any enduring fashion unless it is sparked by the learner's own intrinsic interest and curiosity.

Personal mastery is a set of practices that support people—children and adults—in keeping their dreams whole while cultivating an awareness of the current reality around them. The resulting tension is a powerful force that can enable you to move your reality closer to your aspiration.

The practice of personal mastery is an individual matter. It is typically conducted through solo reflection. As with all disciplines, it is a lifelong process. Your personal vision and current reality will change as you move through life: growing up, graduating from school, forming relationships, starting a family, entering a career, buying your first home, choosing how and where to live, creating your family life, designing a retirement—all involve making choices, and all lead to opportunities for new choices.

Schools and other organizations have a key role to play in this discipline: by setting a context where people have time to reflect on their vision, by establishing an organizational commitment to the truth wherever possible, and by avoiding taking a position (explicit or implicit) about what other people (including children) *should* want or how they should view the world.

We first heard this story from Leonard Burrello, Professor Emeritus, Indiana University.

When people in the education field first begin to learn about the five disciplines, they are often drawn to helping children achieve personal mastery. Perhaps it's because the need for it is so evident. Schools are full of students who have no goals for themselves and don't see school as worthwhile. To fill that vacuum, they ask questions like: "What does the teacher want? How do I please the teacher?" Or later, "What do I have to do to get the grade I want?" Teachers, meanwhile, all too often give up their own aspirations and attune themselves to following the dictates of school administrators. With the industrial model of schooling reinforcing this type of dependency, the spark of learning soon flickers out. But with attention and deliberate effort, the discipline of personal mastery can help rekindle it.

See "The Industrial Age System of Education," page 32.

MASTERY

The term "mastery" descends from the Sanskrit root *mah*, meaning "greater." In Latin and Old English, it meant domination over something else ("I am your master"). But a variation evolved in medieval French: maître, or "master," meaning someone who was exceptionally proficient and skilled—a master of a craft.

The discipline of personal mastery reflects this second meaning. It refers not just to the ability to produce results but also to "master" the principles underlying the way you produce results.

Vision, Current Reality, and Commitment

Aspiration doesn't come naturally in most school settings. It must be deliberately cultivated. That cultivation, in oneself and in others, is the heart of this discipline. Many of the concepts that we have found valuable for this practice were developed and codified by the composer and educator Robert Fritz. He designed a three-stage process for adopting a "creative orientation" to life.

First, you articulate a personal vision: a clear view of the cherished aspirations that you want to create in your life. You make it as rich as possible: "Here's where I want to be."

VISION

CURRENT
REALITY

The creative tension of personal mastery is symbolized by this diagram of a rubber band. As you refine your vision and get a clearer awareness of current reality, the tension grows stronger between them. Like a rubber band seeking equilibrium, this system will pull to resolve the tension—one end of the rubber band will naturally move toward the other. If you can keep your vision high and the tension taut, even when the gap between your vision and current reality feels threatening or discomfiting, then current reality will move toward your vision.

Second, you focus on seeing current reality clearly, including the aspects of your vision that are far from realized. "Here's where I am—and where we are as an organization."

The gap between "where I want to be" and "where I am" inevitably produces a kind of tension, which Fritz calls "structural" tension (and which the Fifth Discipline books call "creative" tension.) Tension, by its nature, seeks resolution. It is as if there is a rubber band set up between the two poles of your vision and current reality: the band is stretched, and as it pulls back to its normal shape, it will pull reality and the vision closer together. This does not happen purely on a conscious level; nor is it entirely intuitive. The process integrates the two. By cultivating the ability to hold both your vision and your current reality in mind, you become attuned to the path between them. You become aware of opportunities you might otherwise have missed; you form an affinity with others who are moving in the same direction; you learn to look at challenges more dispassionately and find better ways of overcoming them.

To accentuate all of this, the practice of personal mastery includes a third step: making a conscious commitment to create the results that are most desired. Some frame this as "Here are the actions I must take." But it is more effective to say, "Here is the choice I make." You may never realize the exact details of your vision, but you will realize something powerful because you hold it. There are many stories of people who achieve extraordinary results with extraordinary visions—where the results happen to be different from their original intent. As Fritz says, "It's not what the vision is; it's what the vision does."

In our experience, people who are convinced that a vision or result is important, who can see clearly that they must change their life to reach that result, and who commit themselves to that result, do indeed feel compelled. They assimilate the vision not just consciously but unconsciously, at a level where it changes more of their behavior. They are more patient with themselves and with the world and more attentive to what is going on around them. All of this produces a sustained sense of energy and enthusiasm, which eventually produces tangible results, making the energy and enthusiasm stronger. And as they practice this way of thinking, they feel more competent and confident, and the tension pulls them forward through life.

For many people in schools today, the gap between vision and current reality is significant and will take some time to resolve. Meanwhile, the tension feels unfamiliar (and sometimes uncomfortable); Fritz calls the resulting feelings "emotional tension": basic beliefs that you are unworthy or powerless to obtain your deepest aspirations. You may be drawn to lessen these feelings by trying to narrow the gap in the easiest, fastest way—by letting your goals erode. Instead of seeking your true aspiration, you convince yourself you must be satisfied with less, because you will never succeed in getting what you want. Or you come to feel that you must wait until things get really bad, and then you'll force yourself to rise toward your vision. Or you decide that it's up to you to push ahead against all obstacles through sheer willpower, no matter what the cost. These coping strategies may feel right, but they do not move you closer to your aspiration in any unsustainable way.

Emotional tension also affects leaders at an institutional level. Instead of holding a full vision for your school ("a place where every child learns"), you may phrase it in a weaker way ("a place where motivated children may learn") that seems more realistic. At least this way you and your colleagues won't have the risk of failure. Or you may decide to hold off until things become intolerable, because only a crisis can galvanize change. Or you may choose to push ahead toward stretch goals, without worrying about the toll that this effort might take on your staff, your students, or yourself.

How then does one cope effectively with emotional tension? Not by denying it exists but by trying to see it more clearly and understanding why it is part of our current reality. This is only possible if you are willing to live in a continual learning mode, where you never "arrive," but you are always aware, as a Chinese proverb puts it, that the "journey is the reward."

Fostering Personal Mastery with Children

Children are particularly susceptible to emotional tension and lowered visions; they may believe adults who tell them that they can never have what they truly want. But they are also tuned in to creative tension: they know how to focus their own attention on achieving what they want. That is why, for a parent or a school, helping a child learn to cultivate personal mastery is one of the greatest possible gifts.

Indeed, if you deal with children regularly, you are *always* engaging with the discipline of personal mastery, whether you know it or not. You become, in the course of the day, coaches in personal mastery for these children.

This coaching starts with the way that you look at them. Are you open to their potential? Do you see how they can achieve their aspirations, no matter what their limits, their family background, or the obstacles before them? Can you set an example of personal mastery yourself? Can you be seen holding the kind of reflective conversation with yourself in which you dream of what you want for the future, then cast a clear eye on the world around you, and then accept the mission of creating your chosen future? Children and students who see adults doing this are more likely to learn to do it themselves.

See Robert Fritz' article, "Teaching Structural Tension," page 209.

Unfortunately, most schools do not provide enough of these examples. Their leaders tend to respond to pressures reactively, rather than moving proactively toward a vision for the school. Each new problem—from academic achievement gaps to bullying to budget crises to violence—must be responded to immediately. There is little time for thinking about what the school needs for the future, let alone what the individuals within that school want.

And yet schools have a key role to play in the discipline of personal mastery, by providing an environment where people have time to reflect on their vision, by establishing an organizational commitment to the truth wherever possible, and by avoiding taking a position (explicit or implicit) about what other people (including children) should want or how they should view the world.

See Charlotte Danielson, *Enhancing Professional Practice: A Framework for Teaching* (Association for Supervision and Curriculum Development, 2007).

For example, Charlotte Danielson, author of the widely used Praxis framework for teacher evaluation, argues that supervisors should not use any framework, like a checklist, that turns evaluation into a pure catch-and-punish process. In other words, educators should avoid evaluations where goals are split from the teacher's own aspirations and the job of the supervisor is primarily to catch those who don't meet some rigid, predetermined set of criteria.

Instead of policing, supervisors should use their time with a teacher to talk about vision, current reality, and choice: "What were you trying to achieve with this lesson? How would you have liked the lesson to go? How did it go? And what actions do you choose to take to make it better next time?" Then, the supervisor can go a step further: "What actions do we have to work on together? How can I be a resource to you, to better help you reach your own aspirations?"

This approach then ripples out into a variety of decisions at a broader, even district-wide level: What development courses get offered? What conferences get endorsed? Some districts foster this kind of communication by investing in teaching-mentorship programs in which teachers directly learn from others. Other districts set up book groups, with readings that relate to aspirations that teachers have identified. And others recast their supervision process around meaningful conversations, so that being supervised is not seen primarily as being judged; instead it is seen as one more opportunity to create a desired future.

Drawing Forth Personal Vision

This exercise begins informally. Write a few statements about your aspirations (the things you want to create in every aspect of your life). No one else need ever see them. There is no "proper" way to answer and no measurable way to win or lose. Playfulness, inventiveness, and spiritedness are all helpful in identifying your aspirations—imagine yourself as the child you once were, who might once have asked, "What do I want to be, to experience, to do when I grow up?"

Pick a place where you can sit in privacy, a quiet and relaxed space with comfortable furniture and no glaring lights or other visual distractions. Give yourself a block of time for this exercise—at least an hour, on a day relatively free of hassle. Hold your phone calls, shut down your computer, and don't see visitors.

1. YOUR FIRST ROUND OF VISION ARTICULATION

Begin by bringing yourself to a reflective frame of mind. Take a few deep breaths and let go of any tension as you exhale, so that you are relaxed, comfortable, and centered. If it is helpful, begin by recalling a meaningful image or memory—a favorite spot in nature, an encounter with a valued person, the image of an animal, or anytime where you felt something special was happening. Shut your eyes for a moment and try to stay with that image; then open your eyes and begin the following.

Imagine achieving a result in your life that you deeply desire. For the sake of this exercise, assume that any result you want is possible—even if you have no idea right now how to get there. It need not have to do directly with education, schools, or children; it could involve learning something you want to learn, improving a relationship that is less than perfect, or obtaining something that you dearly want. Or it could have to do directly with your classroom, your school, or your community.

Imagine yourself accepting into your life the full manifestation of this result. Describe in writing (or sketch) the experience you have imagined, using the present tense, as if it is happening now.

- What does it look like?
- What does it feel like?
- What words would you use to describe it?

Purpose:

To define your personal vision: the results you want most from life and the person you want to be. For educators, parents, students, or anyone, this exercise may bring forth deeply held aspirations around your purpose and wishes as a teacher and a learner.

This exercise is based upon the exercise "Drawing Forth Personal Vision," by Charlotte Roberts, Bryan Smith, and Rick Ross, in *The Fifth Discipline Fieldbook*, p. 201, that in turn was adapted in part from the Innovation Associates exercises "vision escalation" and "power of choice."

Your answers to these questions may depend, in part, on your role within the complex system of a school. If you're a parent, you may want your child to graduate with honors, to be a good person—or simply to learn to read this year. If you're a teacher, you may want to create a terrific curriculum, encompassing not just intellectual capability but athletic, musical, artistic, and social skills—or, perhaps, just to have a class that experiences the joy of learning. As an administrator, you may strive to be the best in the district—or you may simply be concerned about meeting state mandates. If you are a member of the community, you may care about attracting new parents so that real estate prices keep rising. And a student wants to learn what the student wants to learn—whether it's to read right now, to dive off the high board, to build things, to play music, to make friends, or simply to be yourself.

So answer those questions in any way you feel appropriate—and then pause to reconsider your answer. Did you articulate a vision that is close enough to what you actually want?

Perhaps you found this hard to do. Emotional tension may take many forms. You may have worried that your vision is not practical enough; that it's not achievable; that it doesn't fit what other people (a parent, a supervisor, a spouse) wants for you. You may worry that a vision would lead to upheaval—you are afraid of being like the teacher who, after this exercise, quit to become a forest ranger. Or like the supervisor who realized that he wanted to go back to teaching, took a pay cut, and returned to the classroom.

All of these concerns may be valid, but suspend them just for the moment, at least long enough to discern more clearly what your deepest wishes are. This is your articulation of your vision, and no one else will hear it. This exercise can't "run away" with you; it can only increase your awareness. Nonetheless, we suggest that you set your own limits on this exercise. If a subject seems potentially unsettling, do not focus on it. At the same time, the fact that you feel uneasy about something may be a clue to potential learning. Later, you may want to come back to that subject—at your discretion.

2. ADDING CONTEXT AND BREADTH

Having articulated one element of your personal vision, now add other components to that. Write out responses to the following questions, using the present tense as if your desired future had already come to pass. (This makes it easier to imagine.)

- In your ideal future, you are exactly the kind of person you want to be. What are your qualities?

- What material things do you own? Describe your ideal living environment.

- What have you achieved around health, fitness, athletics, and anything to do with your body?

- What types of relationships do you have with friends, family, romantic partners, and others?

- What is your ideal professional or vocational situation? If you are teaching, in what environment are you teaching; if not, what are you doing, and where?

- For teachers: What kind of teacher are you in your most desired future? How do your students see you? What impact do your efforts have? What are your personal goals for your job, your students, your curriculum? How do you interact with other teachers and with administrators?

- For parents: In your ideal future, how has your child realized his or her own aspirations—and yours? When you send your child to school, what do they experience there? What is your role as a parent? Are you a good provider? A model for behavior? Are you actively monitoring and mentoring, helping with homework? Or do you play a different kind of role with them? How does your parenting style change as your kids get older? What changes do you see as they grow up?

- For administrators: In your most desired future, how do you interact with other educators? How do you supervise other educators? What is the curriculum you are involved with and what qualities does it have? What is the tone, the feeling, the ambiance, and the structure of the school you have helped to create? What kind of leader are you and what kind of leaders do you work among?

- For students: What are you now able to do? What do you learn about? How are you recognized? Where do you go? What kinds of people are you with? What do you become?

- For everyone: What are you creating for yourself in the arena of individual learning, travel, reading, or other activities? What kind of community or society do you live in? What else, in any other arena of your life, represents the fulfillment of your most-desired results?

3. REFINING YOUR VISION

If you're like most people, the images you put down are a mixture of selfless and self-centered elements. People sometimes ask, "Is it all right to want to be covered in diamonds or to own a luxury sports car?" Yes—if these are the things you really want. But you need to ask yourself if you really want them or if they are manifestations of some other, more profound, desire. Part of the purpose of this exercise is to probe more deeply: Which aspect of these visions is closest to your primary desires, the ones you want the most?

Go down the list of elements of your personal vision, and, for each item, ask yourself the following two questions:

■ First, if you could have it right now, would you actually take it?

Some elements of your vision may not make it past this question. Others pass the test conditionally: "Yes, I would want it, but only if…" For others, you will realize that you do, in fact, want this very much.

If you are a teacher or parent, for instance, you may have written that you would like to own your own school. But if someone actually gave you a school, with all the responsibilities of managing it, your life might change for the worse. After imagining yourself responsible for a school, would you still take it? Or would you amend your desire: "I want an opportunity to experiment with new forms of teaching and learning, in a structure where I feel comfortable with the administration." You might not need your own school to have that.

■ Next, assume that you have your vision now. What does it bring you?

This question catapults you into a richer image of your vision, so you can see its underlying implications more clearly. For example, maybe you wrote down that you want a sports car. Why do you want it? What would it allow you to create? "I want it," you might say, "for the sense of freedom." But why do you want the sense of freedom?

The point is not to denigrate your vision thus far—it's fine to want a sports car—but to expand it. If a sense of freedom is truly important to you, how else could you create it? And if a sense of freedom is important because it might bring you something else, what is that deeper motivation?

Upon reflection, you might discover you want other forms of freedom, such as the freedom that comes from having a healthy physique (like the freedom to run outside with your children or learn a new sport). And why, in turn, would you want a well-toned body? To play tennis better? To attract admiration? Or just because…you want it for its own sake? All those reasons are valid, if they're your reasons.

Divining all the aspects of your personal vision takes time. It feels a bit like peeling back the layers of an onion, except that every layer remains valuable. At each layer, you ask again: If I could have it, would I take it? And if I had it, what would that bring me?

This exercise can be very effective when practiced with a trustworthy partner or coach. Taking turns, each leads the other through the questions, gently prompting each to understand: "If you could have it, would you take it? What would it bring you?" We have found that this exercise tends to lead people to feel a sense of mutual respect and even kinship—an inevitable byproduct, perhaps, of hearing someone else's deepest wishes.

Seeing Current Reality

The discipline of personal mastery does not stop with vision. Looking closely and clearly at current reality can be difficult, and there are many ways to begin.

Current reality includes every aspect of your life, but as a reader of this book, you may particularly want to consider these aspects of your current reality: the state of your community; the condition of your school; the environment of your classroom; the quality of learning that takes place in these systems; the demographics and family situations of the children involved; the level of organizational change taking place now; the challenges (or resistance) faced by the people involved and the quality of the changes; the number of kids failing or dropping out and the observable reasons why they seem to be failing; the resources available to you; the isolation or connectedness that you feel; the amount of blame in the air, aimed at you or other people; your own capabilities and concerns as a teacher, an administrator, a parent, a student, or a community member; the support shown to the school by the community.

The Process of Choice

The discipline of personal mastery calls on us to make choices. Picking the results and actions that you will stand behind is a significant act. And your choice, if made honestly and as part of a full-fledged personal mastery effort, will tend to inspire and strengthen the moves you make thereafter.

You do not need a formal "choosing" exercise. Make the choices in whatever manner, with whatever rituals, suit you best. You can do it facing a group, another person, or merely a mirror. It may be as simple as returning to the notes where you have written elements of your vision and actively choosing those for which you are ready. Simply say the words, formally, to yourself: "I choose…" and then complete the sentence. Having made that choice, the vision will become part of you—wherever it may lead.

Some of the practices in this book have proven particularly good for seeing current reality. For example, "Seeing the Learner" (p.176), "Assessment as Learning" (p. 221), "The Great Game of High School" (p. 380), and "Predetermined Uncertainty" (p. 360).

The practice of personal mastery is based on research on the creative process by Robert Fritz, described in his books *The Path of Least Resistance* (Fawcett-Columbine, 1989) and *Creating* (Fawcett-Columbine, 1991). The concept of creative tension was also articulated by Kurt Lewin, the founder of modern group dynamics research. See, for example, Art Kleiner, *The Age of Heretics* (Jossey-Bass, 2008), pp. 21–24, and Albert Marrow, *The Practical Theorist* (Basic Books, 1969), pp. 30–32. Other guiding ideas that underlie this discipline can be traced back to antiquity. Management writer Philip Mirvis suggests that a full survey of the field should include the work of psychologists Carl Rogers, Jean Piaget, Abraham Maslow, and Milton Erickson; management writers Frank Barron, Jay Ogilvy, Robert Quinn, Tim Gallwey, Jane Loevinger, and William Torbert; and concepts from both Eastern and Western spiritual disciplines.

Making a choice is much more powerful than saying, "I want…" even when the vision itself is exactly the same. Any life-changing choice—a marriage, the decision to bring a child into the world, a new job, or the choice of a personal vision—invokes a custodial sense. You become a servant to the vision you have chosen: a partner in the process of making it come to life.

When you consciously make a choice you are more attuned, on every level, to the opportunities that come your way. You are more willing to take risks and more clear in judging those risks. And you are more determined to get closer to your vision.

As you move closer to your chosen vision, both as an individual and in a school, community, or organization larger than yourself, the practice of personal mastery keeps engaging you to set your standards higher. You keep expanding and deepening your vision, and you challenge yourself further.

3. Shared Vision
Fostering Commitment to Common Purpose

It's the first day of school in September. Parents of kindergarteners are tentatively wondering which door to walk their children through. Seasoned high-schoolers are showing off the new clothes or the car that they paid for with their summer jobs. A rookie teacher nervously checks a lesson plan; an experienced administrator thinks, "Two more years and then I can retire."

There are three new school board members this fall: one representing a faith-based community, one voted in mostly by professional parents, and one representing the long-established population of the area, most of whose children have long since left home. The chamber of commerce is preparing to sponsor an open house, where hundreds of parents will descend upon the school, each with their own priorities and goals for their children.

As we saw in the discipline of personal mastery, all of these individuals have aspirations of their own—or they would if you asked them to think about it—and they all have their own ways of expressing them. The discipline of shared vision is the set of tools and techniques for bringing all of these disparate goals and statements into alignment. They already have one major element in common: their connection to a particular school or school system. But they do not yet know what other qualities they might share. And without the guidance of a shared vision, decision makers in a school system revert under pressure to expediency and habit, and no one will get what they want.

In building a shared vision, you will lead (or take part in) a group effort to develop images of "the future we want to create together," along with the values that will be important in getting there, the goals we hope to achieve along the way, and the principles and guiding practices we expect to employ. This generally involves a formal process, in which people committed to the future of the school meet regularly to chart a path together.

Not all shared visions are equal. Visions that tap into a school system's deeper sense of purpose have unique power to engender aspiration. The practical goal of such visions is to invite people to continuously renew their commitment to the people of the school, particularly the children and students. Many educators enter their careers with a strong sense of commitment to learning and teaching; but over time, it's easy for that commitment to atrophy. It gradually gets replaced with a sense of compliance—of being a "good soldier," perhaps, or going along with commands for the sake of the salary or reward. Compliance is not bad in itself; organizations depend on the activities of many people who are simply complying with the requirements of their job. But remember that a great school system (or any great organization) is a living system; it takes its vitality and energy from the commitments that people make to a common vision, into which they invest their thinking and emotions.

One might assume that "vision" is solely the top leader's job. In schools, the "vision" task generally falls to the superintendent, the principal, and the school board. Within a classroom, it may fall to a teacher. But visions based on authority alone are not sustainable. They may succeed in carrying a school or a school system through a crisis—"the superintendent wants us all to pull together to get through this budget crunch." But when the crisis is over, people will fall apart, back to their fractionalized and disparate hopes and dreams. They will never know what they can achieve by creating a shared vision of what their school, their classroom, and their community might be.

A vision is not really shared unless it has staying power and an evolving life force that lasts for years, propelling people through a continuous cycle of action, learning, and reflection. This in turn requires communication strategies—shared visions have a way of spreading through personal contact. To link multiple communities together, the school system depends on its informal networks—communication channels where people talk easily and freely, meeting at potluck suppers, participative

Margaret Wheatley wrote that "we need to be able to trust that something as simple as a clear core of values and vision, kept in motion through dialogue, can lead to order." They provide the "shape" for the organization, and within that context organizational members must be given significant freedom to create. See Margaret J. Wheatley, *Leadership and the New Science* (Berrett-Koehler, 1992), p. 147.

events, and other informal gatherings. Email, Skype, Facebook, or other online social networks can also support such collaboration. Still, while the Internet today is a more valuable communication tool than ever, as members of a community, we often still need to meet in person when we talk about what we really care about.

Also see shared vision processes for classrooms (page 216) or school and community (page 341).

Shared visions are often thought of on an organizational level, appropriate for schools and school systems. But they also play a significant role in classrooms and communities. In the classroom, shared experiences and conversations set a tone that allows every student to have a stake in everyone else's success, rather than seeing achievement as a zero-sum game, where one can only succeed if others fail. A vision of mutual reward can carry a group of students, including the conventional "winners" of the group, much farther than they could travel alone. Similarly, a community that devotes time and effort to building a shared vision is far more prepared to get the most from its schools and other institutions—and to get past the dissension and vested interests that impede progress.

In all cases—classroom, school, and community—the shared vision is most effective when it incorporates the three elements of creative tension from personal mastery: a clear picture of current reality, a clear statement of the desired outcomes ("what we want to create together"), and a collective choice about how to proceed.

Building Shared Vision in Schools

Shared vision strategies should be developmental. As interventions in a living system, all stages of the process should help build the leadership capacity of everyone in the system: the people at the top of the school system hierarchy (who must convene and foster a generative conversation) and the rest of the participants (whose commitment will make all the difference to realizing this vision).

The first step is to objectively diagnose your starting point. Every school system is in one of five potential states of readiness for shared vision. In this diagram, they are arranged in developmental order. The further to the left, the more the organization depends on a strong leader to "tell" everyone what the shared vision should be. The further to the right, the more leadership, direction-setting, and learning capacity the organization as a whole must have. In the state with the greatest amount

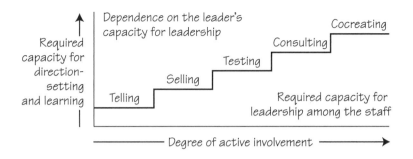

This sequence of stages was adapted from "Building Shared Vision: How to Begin," by Bryan Smith in *The Fifth Discipline Fieldbook* (p. 312). The visual diagram and some of the points along the continuum are influenced by "How to Choose a Leadership Pattern," by Robert Tannenbaum and Warren Schmidt, *Harvard Business Review*, (March/April 1958). Rick Ross also influenced the conceptual framework underlying this article.

of active involvement and collaboration, called co-creating, the superintendent or principal is less "the person with the answers," and more "the convener of a robust process."

STAGE 1: "TELLING"

Much of what passes for education is actually "telling:" homework given with no ability to question it, rules laid down for schedules and discipline with no opportunities for input, and an inexhaustible supply of rubrics that reduce learning to a set of directives: "If you want extra credit, complete questions 12, 13, and 14." Teachers are given their own equivalent: "Cover sections 1 to 30 in the syllabus, and you'll fulfill the requirements." Telling, in short, is an authority-driven transaction in which the instructions are clear and following them is mandatory.

In day-to-day school settings, "telling" is often most appropriate during a crisis, where everyone perceives that a dramatic change is necessary. When safety is an issue, the principal is expected to issue commands, and teachers and students don't get to vote. Nor should they expect to. The most effective way to set a vision for safety, if you're a principal, is to call a faculty meeting and say something like this: "We have some issues with unauthorized people entering the building. We have to keep more doors locked, and I want each teacher to do a stint on the outside. We're putting a policy of name tags in place. This is a critical change for us, but there's no avoiding it. Everyone must be on board."

Some school systems are only responsive to the "telling" approach, no matter what the circumstance. The superintendent (or principal) may have set the direction so completely, for such a long time, that the organization's will and ability to question it has atrophied.

In such a case, the leader might hold a "visioning" meeting, laying out a course of action on a curriculum change or other policy and presenting a rationale for it. He or she might ask for discussion or alternative views, but this is meaningless if everyone knows that the leader's view will prevail. To an outsider, the resulting vision might appear to have been ratified by everyone present; but very few people will be as committed to it as the superintendent is. When push comes to shove, people will balk—or, worse still, passive-aggressively undermine the vision. Then the superintendent might be heard saying, "Once again, we've just proved that people in this district spend all their time complaining. They're obviously not responsible. I'll just have to tell them what we're going to do from now on." Meanwhile, subordinates will say, "It's obvious now that this school system has no interest in our input about the direction of the future."

And yet a "told" vision, when executed effectively, is still better than no vision at all. We have seen top-down messages from superintendents that clearly and honestly describe a vision and sense of current reality in positive terms. Similarly, in the classroom, there are times when a student wants or needs a teacher to issue a clear directive for learning, with a concrete set of tasks to follow.

Here are some tips for mastering the telling mode: Inform people directly, clearly, and consistently. Substantiate what you've got to say. Tell the truth about current reality, even if it's difficult to hear; that way, you can generate the "pull" that comes from creative tension. For the same reason, be careful to build your message on a positive vision. Instead of saying, "Our vision is to avoid having bad test scores," say, "Our vision is to find a way to bring all students across a genuine threshold of learning, visible to everyone." There is a profound difference between "vision by desperation" and "vision by aspiration." Finally, don't fill in too many details of the vision, because putting it into practice may be the only opportunity that people have to make the vision their own. They need to fill in the details themselves.

⟩⟩ See "Personal Mastery," page 76.

However well it is communicated and executed, there are limits to a "telling" strategy. Research on verbal communications shows that people remember only about 25 percent of a message told to them. That percentage may be even less in a classroom. And each individual may remember a different 25 percent. Furthermore, if the message is a "told" vision, people may comply and do the bare minimum, but few will feel any reason to commit themselves to it. Leaders who rely on "telling" others often end up frustrated with what they perceive as poor communication: "I spelled out our direction, but people still don't seem to get it."

Also, a strategy of "telling" trains people to expect more telling—and to act accordingly. Teachers will balk when asked for their opinions or creativity, if only because they assume, based on past experience, that their responses won't make any difference. Students, similarly, will learn to avoid pressure by doing the minimum needed to score a grade. Community members will learn that their ideas aren't valued, and therefore they should take those ideas (and any other contributions of time or energy) elsewhere. A school system which sets its vision at the "telling" end of the spectrum will typically do so primarily because its leaders don't yet have the capability to do anything else. Nor will passive recipients of a vision be driven to develop their own capabilities. The most effective strategy, for those in authority, is to begin moving along the continuum, to engage people a little bit more—by "selling."

STAGE 2: "SELLING"

In this stage, the leader attempts to enroll people in something new, enlisting as much commitment as possible. In the classroom, you will often see teachers use "selling" as an approach to engage students as a means to an end. "If you really want to do AP Math, you'll need to learn this type of calculus." Or, "This summer's reading list will really help you when you get to sixth grade."

Selling is a very useful stance for leaders to take in an authoritarian system, because it makes clear that they want more than simple compliance. The system needs commitment. A principal might say to teachers, for example, "I'd like you to try something new—and I think you'll see it's practical. Between classes, you should stand out in the hallway and say hello to kids as they're walking by." The principal might go on to say, "Contractually, I can't mandate you to be out there. But I've noticed that there are fewer discipline and safety problems in those hallways where kids see teachers standing near their classroom doors. You know how easy it is for classes to get disrupted by incidents in the hall. This approach will work; I think you'll agree if you try it." That argument, if well-designed, will have some effect: It may draw in people who otherwise would not take part.

To master the selling mode, keep channels open for responses. Follow up your speeches with working sessions, so you can find out how many people are convinced. Selling, when executed well, is not manipulation. It is enrollment: giving people the opportunity to choose to follow a vision. If people see the vision is good for them, even if it takes a leap of faith, they will tend to sign on. The leader, in turn, makes the leap of faith that people will be responsive.

If you are a leader, your ability to sell this vision depends on your relationship with the people you are trying to reach. Implicitly, the act of selling tells them that you value your relationship with them and that you will not force them to do something they really don't want to do. If that's not true, then you may find it difficult to sell. One easy way to keep the message clean: instead of using the royal "we" ("This is the vision we endorse as a school system"), stick to the first person singular ("This is the vision I wish to put forth for the school"). Speak about why this change is important to you personally, what special value that you feel it will have for everyone, and why you hope they will make a commitment to it.

Selling can be a powerful process for leaders, but it too has limits. In many cases, the recipients of the sales pitch, be they administrators, teachers, students, or others, want to know that they will be rewarded (or at least not punished). A compliant "yes" often seems like the safest course for all. "I can go along with that," people say. "I'll give it a try." If the speaker wants to believe that people will sign on, he or she will accept the "yes," however half-hearted. If you need more commitment than that to make this vision work, then you will probably need to move forward to the next stage of a shared vision path: Testing.

STAGE 3: "TESTING"

In this stage, the leader lays out the vision for consideration—not just to find out whether people will support it but how enthusiastically they will endorse it and what aspects of the vision matter to them. The results are used to refine and redesign the next steps. The process of testing can in itself galvanize response; having been asked their opinion, people feel more compelled to discuss and consider the proposed vision. But the test must be sincere; the act of asking implies that the answers will be heeded. A shared vision which gains no support will, by implication, be sent back for revision and rethinking.

Experienced classroom teachers know how to use this type of test to spark interest. "We're looking at U.S. geography this month," a teacher might say, "and we usually look at it state by state. This year, I thought we'd do it differently—to focus on regions and river valleys. What do you think—and why?"

Similarly, an assistant superintendent of curriculum might say, "We want to change the fifth-grade approach to geography. Here are three proposed textbooks and a set of sample lesson plans for each. Which do you think is best, and why?" Or a school board member might ask people in a community group, "Which of these fundraising methods do you think will be most effective?" Note that the larger group has specifically been asked only for their opinion of the choices provided to them and not to offer other suggestions. But if other ideas come forth in a testing process, there is an implicit assumption that the leaders will pay attention to them.

To improve the quality of responses, provide as much information as possible. Present the options with all their ramifications spelled out, particularly any difficulties you see. Make the test clean and unbiased. Don't set it up intending them to choose option A and think it's their idea—they'll see through it, and you will lose your opportunity to learn what they think. For the same reason, protect people's privacy. Design the test so they can answer anonymously or at least without repercussion for negative answers. You can almost guarantee, in a testing process, that you will hear unexpected responses or that you will be alerted to problems that had never emerged before—but these could be immensely valuable to you as you move forward.

You will face the limits of testing when you discover that teachers, students, and staff all have a wide range of ideas and concerns that the choices you provide don't address. To compensate, you can add questions about the test itself: "How do you feel about these questions?" When people start to use these questions to talk about their own opinions in more depth, then you are no longer in the testing phase. The school system has moved on to consulting.

STAGE 4: "CONSULTING"

Consulting is the preferred stage for educators and school system leaders who recognize that they cannot possibly have *all* the answers. These leaders use this phase to invite the members of the classroom, the school, or the community to become the system's consultant.

Here, instead of asking for feedback on a set of options, you pose open-ended questions. In a classroom: "We're going to study Asia this month. Which countries do you think we should focus on?" In a school system: "We're initiating a new safety policy. What do you think are the right five steps? Everybody give me your suggestions, and I'll devise a policy."

The group of people canvassed might even extend beyond school system employees to parents, students, community members, and even the world at large through the Internet. But the control is still in place: The leader of the school system (or the teacher in the classroom) will make the final decision.

To master the consulting mode, bring together small teams of ten to fifteen people, ideally those with natural working relationships (like teachers at a similar grade level or people who work together regularly). In a large system, teams of people can split up to canvass others and then return to the first team to report back what they have found (this is called the "cascade" process). Collect anonymous written comments from participants; this ensures that people who do not wish to speak openly can also be heard. Finally, don't try to tell and consult simultaneously. If you tell them the "right" vision, as you see it, and then ask, "What do you think about this?" you will get a ho-hum response. Instead, to keep suggestions in reasonable territory, you can lay out boundaries: "Bear in mind that any vision should deal with our current problems around safety and should assume that we will not get any increase in our budget."

The "consulting" mode (like "telling," "selling," and "testing"), is limited by a tacit, usually unquestioned assumption: That the objective of the process is to create one vision for the entire school system. But experience suggests that this is a faulty premise, that visions are almost always anchored to a particular school or classroom. Yet a shared vision is strongest when it breaks through those walls and combines individual visions into a coherent whole. This can be achieved through the fifth stage of the process.

STAGE 5: "CO-CREATING"

When people are working for a set of goals that they have helped to create—rather than goals they set to please someone else—you can feel the difference. School leaders, educators, students, and staff members who understand this are ready to benefit from a "co-creating" shared vision process. This type of process places everyone in the school system in a creative orientation, where every individual makes choices about their desired future.

Consider, for example, a co-created classroom lesson. The teacher writes a single word on the board. It might be, "oceanography." Now everyone in the room walks up and maps the topics that they find interesting within oceanography; the links among the topics are the structure of the syllabus. "What do you know about the ocean?" asks the teacher. "What have you studied in the past? What do you want to learn?" The students write notes about fish, sharks, scuba diving, sunken wrecks, the effects of algae on global climate, the gulfstream, sailing ships, whales, the making of SpongeBob SquarePants, submarines, bathyspheres, the life of Jacques Cousteau, and much more. Then the teacher asks, "How can we organize this so we can each study things we're interested in—but also learn about oceans as a whole?" Together, they design the four-week coursework, list assignments, and take them on individually. They'll make presentations and teach each other. They'll use computers and libraries, interview knowledgeable people in the area, and perhaps take a field trip to a local aquarium or beach. Everything they do will feel like their choice, because it will be based on their collective thinking and design.

To make this kind of learning work (and, not coincidentally, meet the school's curriculum requirements) requires a great degree of involvement and skill—for both the teachers and the students. A similar level of skill is needed when visions are co-created at the school system or community level.

Consider, for example, a school safety problem approached through co-creating. A recognized leader in the school system convenes a group of educators, parents, community members, and students to solve the issue together. There may be some criteria the solution must meet—for example, it must fit within the budget and address any urgent concerns; it must also produce reasonable expectations of meeting the ultimate goal. But the leader does not come in with options or suggestions. The group develops those. Members consider difficult questions: "What do we know about safety? What are we overlooking? What will these solutions look like for each of our constituencies?" The end result is typically a better solution than anyone would have come up with on their own.

To master a co-creating shared vision process, start with personal vision. Give people time to think about (and articulate) the vision they would truly want to create, for themselves and the district. You may be afraid that this will lead to anarchy and disarray, but most people in a school system are eager to contribute and to link their personal vision to that of the larger system. Similarly, seek alignment, not agreement. People need to know that they have real freedom to speak their mind and lay out their true aspirations (and concerns), with no limits, encumbrances, or reprisals, and in an atmosphere of respect for everyone in the room. School administrators and community leaders must put aside their fear that "we must set limits on the vision or this will run out of control." The temptation will be strong to paper over differences for the sake of reaching a quick resolution. Discourage this; instead, use the disciplines of productive conversation (mental models and team learning, pages 97and 115) to talk openly about the assumptions and interpretations that have led to any irreconcilable views.

It takes time to become skilled at co-creating. A teacher or student who has only experienced "telling" or "selling" in the past may feel unprepared for it. Co-creating can be difficult (particularly for students attending classes in a language they don't know very well), because it depends on meaningful, in-depth conversations. That's why we often advocate stepping through the path deliberately and slowly, from telling all the way to co-creating, building your capacity at each step. In this way, a shared vision process provides a developmental path for those who wish to become leaders—in the classroom, the school, or the community.

The practice of shared vision has its roots in the "preferred vision" exercises developed by Ronald Lippitt in consultation with the Michigan YMCA, and later at the National Training Laboratories, during the 1950s and 1960s. See Art Kleiner, *The Age of Heretics: A History of the Radical Thinkers Who Reinvented Corporate Management* (Jossey-Bass, 2008), p. 21ff. Charlie Kiefer, Bryan Smith, and others at Innovation Associates developed the practice that we describe here.

Key Questions for a Shared Vision

This exercise came to our attention via a group of school superintendents in Florida. They talked eloquently about the way their school systems had responded to the devastation wrought by the 2004 hurricanes in that state. The schools became shelters. Some of the people preparing food for those shelters had lost their own houses. The community made it through, in part, by talking through a vision—not just of recovery but of their renewed aspirations for their homes and their children.

These questions are derived from the work of Rick DuFour and from a set of questions developed by Disney for evaluating the effectiveness of emergency preparedness systems.

1. Do we have a clear idea of the results we are creating through this vision?
2. Are we doing everything possible to achieve these results?
3. Do we align with critical stakeholders at local, regional, and state levels?
4. Does every teacher and staff member know their role in creating this vision?
5. What is the established standard for schools, and how does this vision surpass it?
6. What is the school culture like, and how does it reinforce this vision?
7. Who "owns" the vision in our school system?
8. Does our vision reflect the views of all stakeholders, internal and external?
9. Is our vision proactive or reactive?
10. What resources do we bring to bear in implementing this vision?

This framework isn't limited to use in crises; it can help you tackle a wide range of challenges. For example, if your vision involves an end to bullying:

1. Do you have a clear understanding of what that "end to bullying" looks like?
2. Are you doing everything possible—bringing everyone together, thinking through the results?
3. Does your vision align with others (such as the DARE program used in many states)? If you're in a middle school, does it align with visions put forth by the high school and elementary schools?
4. Have you engaged everyone who might want or need to be involved? What about coaches? Or the little league program? The Girl Scouts, and the faith-based communities?
5. What is the best material on bullying available right now? Can you visit schools with great programs?

6. Does your culture reflect the new attitudes about bullying?
7. If you create a plan and three members of your team leave, who's going to make sure this is sustained?
8. Every time you hire a new group of teachers, will this become part of their new teacher orientation? Do you have steps in place so you know what to do if a child continues to bully another child?
9. Are you just raising the penalty for bullying, or have you thought through the underlying causes of the problem?
10. What has to be noted in the budget to really make this work?

Notice how specific these questions can become, focused simultaneously on the broad overall direction and the specifics of implementation. That is one hallmark of a great shared vision: It conveys what you, as a large system, are committed to creating, and it puts both the forest and the trees into perspective, in service of that commitment.

4. Mental Models

Becoming More Aware of the Sources of Our Thinking

MM

Imagine the baseball field near your school is being upgraded one day (courtesy of a donation from a local construction company), and the workmen strike a patch of sandstone with fossils embedded in it. As they sweep the stone, students excitedly gather around, and they see what appears to be a set of dinosaur footprints that look something like this (see Exhibit 1, below):

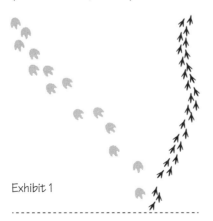

Exhibit 1

"What do you think happened here?" asks a teacher. All the students jump in with guesses. There were two different dinosaurs, they say, one with big feet and one with smaller feet. The big one's feet get farther apart, so it must have been running. Maybe it was chasing the smaller one; maybe it was hungry.

The workers dig up a little more stone, and now we see a

The dinosaur footprint puzzle dates back to the mid-1960s; it was published in the science text *Investigating the Earth*, by the American Geological Institute Earth Science Curriculum Project (Houghton-Mifflin, 1967). Interestingly, the tracks were based on real fossil footprints, the Paluxy dinosaur tracks found in rocks in Texas. See Jack Hassard, "The Dinosaur Footprint Puzzle: A Content or Process Approach?," *The Art of Teaching Science Blog*, November 2, 2010, http://www.artofteachingscience.org/?p=3081.

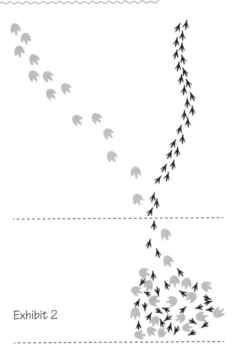

Exhibit 2

more complete image, as illustrated here (see Exhibit 2, left):

"The two of them got in a fight," says one student. "No, they're drinking from the same water hole," says another.

And then the workers clear the rest of the sandstone, producing a picture something like the one on the next page (see Exhibit 3).

"Hey," complains a student. "What happened to the little one?" By now, the site has attracted a large number of students from all grade levels. The middle school students have a theory: The big dinosaur ate the little one and walked away. But a third-grader says, "No, they're friends. The little one is riding on the big one's back." Someone else argues that it's a backwards-footed prehistoric animal, giving birth. Or was it a courtship? Hardly—the smaller one flew away and survived ("See where it jumped off?"). Or a pterodactyl swooped down and carried it away. An exchange student suggests that the two animals never met; the smaller one found food and flew away, and the larger one came fifteen minutes later, found nothing and stalked off. And then a canny high school student says, "Wait a minute. They probably lived thousands of years apart and just happened to be imprinted in the same piece of rock."

Find a picture or image of a set of dinosaur footprints and try this exercise yourself with a group of kids, gradually uncovering the full image, just as the imaginary workmen did. You'll find no shortage of widely varying interpretations, and many participants will be convinced that their interpretation must be right.

We sometimes use this exercise to open meetings of faculty or community groups. Then we turn to talk about whatever relevant events or issues are at hand—say a disciplinary problem or a budget dispute. "What happened here?" we ask, just as we did with the dinosaur exercise at the outset. Once again, everyone unveils their assumptions and attitudes. The first-year teacher who has just transferred from a different district has a very different mental model from the veteran teacher of 25 years; the secretary who has seen three superintendents come and go outside her office has yet another view, the custodian has another. The women who work in the lunch line describe one thing; the classroom teacher who walks through the cafeteria every day disagrees. And because they have safely explored their different perspectives for a story about dinosaurs, they are now ready to hear each other on a potentially more volatile real-world issue.

The point of this exercise is to demonstrate that human beings are creatures of interpretation. Our behavior and our attitudes are shaped by our mental models: the images, assumptions, and stories that we carry in our minds of ourselves, other people, institutions, and every aspect of the world.

Exhibit 3

Because mental models are usually tacit, existing below the level of awareness, they are often untested and unexamined. They are generally invisible to us—until we look for them. Thus, reading this passage, you may have easily made your own interpretations of the dinosaur tracks, but you may or may not have noticed the other assumptions you implicitly read into this passage: that the school can't afford to pay for its landscaping, that landscaping workers are male, that the students play baseball (instead of, say, cricket), that the students of all grades use the same field, that the fossils would naturally show dinosaurs (instead of a prehistoric mammal and bird), and that only children, as opposed to adults, would want to guess at the meaning of the footprints.

Differences between mental models explain why two people can observe the same event and describe it differently: They are paying attention to different details. The core task of the discipline of mental models is to bring tacit assumptions and attitudes to the surface so people can explore and talk about their differences and misunderstandings with minimal de-

Also see *The Danger of a Single Story,* a TedTalk video by Chimamanda Adichie. This can be helpful in engaging a group in the exploration of mental models and the consequences of not questioning the images and stories that different people hold. See http://www.ted.com/talks/lang/eng/chimamanda_adichie_the_danger_of_a_single_story.html.

fensiveness. This process is crucial for people who want to understand their world, or their school, more completely—because, like a pane of glass framing and subtly distorting our vision, our mental models determine what we see. In any new experience, most people are drawn to take in and remember only the information that reinforces their existing mental models.

Though at first glance, working with mental models may seem to be an intellectual exercise with little relevance to the "real world," it is probably the most practical of the five disciplines. It has direct relevance for a surprising number of seemingly intractable challenges in schools. That's because unexamined mental models limit people's ability to change. A group of superintendents and school board members may tacitly believe that the only way to improve the schools is to invest more money; therefore, they don't consider other possible approaches. A teacher may assume that students from the "wrong side of the tracks" don't care about school, so he subtly dismisses them out of hand. An administrator may assume that the local teachers' union will block all innovation, so she approaches the unions defensively, holding back as much information as possible—which in turn makes the union leaders more defensive and confirms their belief that administrators cannot be trusted. The leaders of a school reform effort may assume, without even being fully aware of it, that parents don't really know much about their children's needs. Therefore, they inadvertently alienate parent groups, without ever understanding why. A forty-five-year-old laborer who never earned a high school diploma may assume that his children's teachers look down on him, so he never summons the courage to come in to school for meetings, and the teachers think he doesn't care. A local community member may assume that, because many schoolteachers are women, they do not need to be paid as much—and vote down the school referendum for a pay raise.

The consequences of untested and unsurfaced mental models can be tragic for children. Statistics suggest that bullying is a lifelong trait; a middle-school child who is recognized by teachers as a bully has a 69 percent chance of having a felony record as an adult. But could that be because the teachers and administrators have a mental model of that child as a bully and treat the child accordingly? Or because the child holds an unseen, unspoken mental model that bullying is the most effective way to solve problems—and never finds a mentor who can safely and persuasively challenge that assumption?

The practice of "working with mental models" helps us see the metaphorical pane of glass we look through and helps us re-form the glass by creating new mental models that serve us better. Two types of skills are central to this practice: reflection (slowing down our thinking processes

The practice of working with mental models emerged from "action science," a field of inquiry developed by the theorists and educators Chris Argyris and Donald Schön. Their work, in turn, is grounded in the "double-bind" theory of anthropologist Gregory Bateson and the semantic work of linguist S. I. Hayakawa. See *The Fifth Discipline*, p. 172ff, and *The Fifth Discipline Fieldbook*, p. 264, for more about the roots of this work, and Art Kleiner, *The Age of Heretics*, p. 186ff, for the story of Chris Argyris's work. Also see Argyris, "Teaching Smart People How to Learn," in *Harvard Business Review* (May–June 1991, reprint #91301), and *Organizational Traps: Leadership, Culture, Organizational Design* (Oxford University Press, 2010).

to become aware of how we form our mental models) and inquiry (holding conversations where we openly share views and develop knowledge about each other's assumptions).

Inquiry may be a particularly novel skill for some educators. There is an unwritten rule in many organizations, including many schools, that people should not ask questions unless they already have the answer to offer. The discipline of mental models flies in the face of that idea. People ask questions in the practice of this discipline because they are trying to learn more about their own, and each other's, most deeply held attitudes and beliefs. It takes reflection and conversational practice to learn to do this well. The exercises and conversational tools described here have proven effective in a variety of venues, including many school systems and government agencies, precisely because they teach people not just to ask questions but to learn from the answers.

The Ladder of Inference

We live in a world of self-generating beliefs that remain largely untested. We adopt those beliefs because they are based on conclusions, which are inferred from what we observe, plus our past experience. Our ability to achieve the results we truly desire is eroded by our feelings that:

- Our beliefs are the truth.
- The truth is obvious.
- Our beliefs are based on real data.
- The data we select is the real data.

For example: Let's say I am a teacher presenting a proposed change in the science curriculum at a faculty meeting. Doris, an experienced teacher and department chair, sitting at the end of the table, seems bored out of her mind. She turns her dark, morose eyes away from me and puts her hand to her mouth, barely stifling a yawn. She doesn't ask any questions until I'm almost done, when she breaks in: "I think we should wait until next year." In this school, that typically means "Let's forget about this and move on." Everyone starts to shuffle papers and put notes away. Doris obviously thinks that I'm incompetent—which is a shame, because these ideas are exactly what she needs. Now that I think of it, she's never liked my ideas. Clearly, Doris is a power-hungry jerk. By the time I take my seat, I've made a decision: I'm not going to propose anything again to any group that includes Doris. She will always undermine me. It's too bad I have an enemy

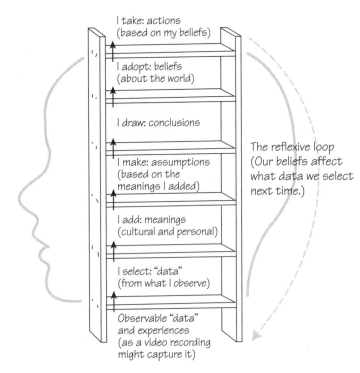

I take: actions
(based on my beliefs)

I adopt: beliefs
(about the world)

I draw: conclusions

I make: assumptions
(based on the
meanings I added)

I add: meanings
(cultural and personal)

I select: "data"
(from what I observe)

Observable "data"
and experiences
(as a video recording
might capture it)

The reflexive loop
(Our beliefs affect
what data we select
next time.)

This article is derived in part from "The Ladder of Inference," by Rick Ross, *Fifth Discipline Fieldbook*, p. 242.

who's so prominent in the school system.

During the space of a few minutes (or less), I have climbed up a mental "ladder of inference"—a common mental pathway of increasing abstraction, often leading to misguided beliefs:

- I started with the observable data: Doris's comment, which is a part of common experience.
- I selected some details about Doris's behavior: her glance away from me and apparent yawn. (I didn't notice her listening intently one moment before.)
- I added some interpretations of those details. (Doris wanted me to hurry up and finish).
- I moved rapidly up to assumptions about Doris's current state. (She's bored.)
- I concluded that Doris, in general, thinks I'm incompetent. In fact, I now believe that Doris (and probably everyone whom I associate with her) is opposed to me.

Thus, as I reach the top of the ladder, I've concluded that my belief is the truth, that the truth is obvious, and that it is based on real data. It all seems so reasonable, and it happens so quickly, that I'm not even aware I've done it. Moreover, all the rungs of the ladder take place in my head. The only part visible to anyone else is the directly observable data at the bottom and my own decision to take action at the top. The rest of my trip up the ladder is unseen, unquestioned, not considered fit for discussion, and enormously abstract. (These leaps up the ladder are sometimes called "leaps of abstraction.")

I've probably leapt up that ladder of inference many times before. The more I believe that Doris dislikes me, the more I reinforce my tendency to notice her malevolent behavior in the future. This phenomenon is known as the "reflexive loop": Our beliefs influence what data we focus on next time. And there is a counterpart to this reflexive loop in Doris's mind: As she reacts to my strangely antagonistic behavior, she's probably jumping up some rungs on her own ladder and forming certain conclusions about me. For no apparent reason, before too long, we could find ourselves becoming bitter enemies.

Now imagine me, Doris, and three others are on, say, a school curriculum committee, and we have these untested assumptions and beliefs. When we meet to deal with a concrete problem, the air is filled with misunderstandings, communication breakdowns, and feeble compromises.

Doris might indeed have been bored by my presentation—or she might have simply been eager to read the report on paper. She might think I'm incompetent, she might have other things on her mind, or she might be afraid to embarrass me. More likely than not, *she* has inferred that *I* think *she's* incompetent. We can't know, until we find a way to check our conclusions.

Unfortunately, assumptions and conclusions are difficult to test. For instance, suppose I wanted to find out if Doris really thought I was incompetent. I would have to pull her aside and ask her, "Doris, do you think I'm an idiot?" Even if I could find a way to phrase the question, would I believe her if she answered no? And would I forgive her if she answered yes?

You can't live your life without adding meaning or drawing conclusions. It would be an inefficient, tedious way to live. But you can improve your communications through reflection and by using the ladder of inference. For instance, once Doris and I understand the concepts behind the ladder of inference, we have a safe way to stop a conversation in its tracks and ask several questions:

- What is the observable data—that anyone would agree is real—that has led you to make that statement?
- Does everyone agree about the nature of the data?
- Can you run me through your reasoning?
- How did we get from that observable data to these abstract assumptions?

I can ask for data in an open-ended way: "Doris, what was your reaction to this presentation?" Or I can simply test the observable data by making a comment like this one: "You've been quiet, Doris." To which she might reply: "I'm taking notes; I think there's a lot of potential here."

Note that I don't say "Doris, I think you've moved way up the ladder of inference. Here's what you need to do to get down." The point of this method is not to diagnose Doris's attitude but to make everyone's thinking processes visible, to see what the differences are in our perceptions and what we have in common. (You might say, "I notice I'm moving up the ladder of inference, and maybe we all are. What is the data here?")

The ladder can be used in staff development, in the classroom, and

I won't propose new ideas to Doris; she'd use them against me.

Doris is a power-hungry jerk.

Doris has never liked my ideas, even when they're right for her.

Doris isn't listening to me.

Doris put her hand to her mouth while I was speaking.

We've either got to find a way to motivate Jean or ask her to leave.

Jean's not really interested in working with us.

She's probably been forced to show up, but she leaves as soon as she can.

She must not really be interested in the committee.

Jean, one of the teachers on our joint parent-teacher committee, left early today.

"Martin, you're not trying hard enough. You're going to fail."

Martin is always a problem case.

Martin fidgets whenever I call on him.

Martin is fidgety today.

Martin jumped in his chair when I called on him.

in a variety of school and community meetings. When teaching, for example, instead of letting arguments among students escalate, you can ask: "What did you actually hear or see that led you to this conclusion?"

The ladder of inference can often be used to resolve seemingly irreconcilable differences within school districts and among educators. For example, there are three pervasive mental models held by educators and experts in education today:

1. Each student is an individual, and education is most effective when it takes into account those individual differences ("there are all kinds of minds").
2. Schools are responsible to educate everyone within their reach ("no child should be left behind").
3. Schools are high-leverage institutions: The quality of a nation's democracy, culture, and economy all depend on the quality of its public schools.

These are all three reasonable statements in themselves; but when combined without examination, they can lead to difficult and polarizing conclusions. Much of the debate about education takes place through leaps up the ladder of inference related to these three statements. Education is most effective when it takes account of individual differences; therefore, any kind of standardized "drill and practice" is valueless. Many young people are illiterate or inadequately educated; therefore, schools are failing. Critics of public school overlook their obvious value to democracy; therefore, they must have a hidden agenda.

Any or all of these conclusions may be true; the point of the exercise is not to debunk them. Rather, the point of the exercise is to bring to light our thinking so that we can consider them objectively and dispassionately, often in the company of people who hold the opposite view.

Balancing Advocacy and Inquiry

Adapted from "Balancing Advocacy and Inquiry," by Rick Ross, Charlotte Roberts, and Art Kleiner, in *The Fifth Discipline Fieldbook*, p. 253.

Conducting a conversation that leads to greater collaborative insight, like many other skills, seems easy—until you try it. But a little bit of practice yields great results, and that practice can be incorporated into existing discussions.

The basic technique is simple to describe: Balance advocacy for your view against inquiry into others' views. Lay out your reasoning, and then encourage others to challenge it. "Here is my view, and here is how I have arrived at it. How does it sound to you? What makes sense to you and what doesn't? Do you see any ways I can improve it?" The payoff is the more creative and insightful realizations that occur when people combine multiple perspectives.

Inquiry (asking about the reasoning and assumptions behind other people's statements) is more powerful when you explain the reasoning and assumptions behind your own statements. Chances are, generally you will have a viewpoint of your own to express, and it is important to express it—in a context that allows you to learn more about others' views while they learn more about yours. This kind of advocacy can be thought of as "walking up the ladder of inference slowly": making your own thinking process visible.

Nor do we recommend that you switch in rote fashion from an adamant assertion ("Here's what I say") to a question ("Now what do you say?") and back again. Balancing inquiry and advocacy means developing a variety of ways of advocating and inquiring and integrating them together.

Here, then, are some conversational recipes that may help you, as a teacher or student, learn the skills of balancing inquiry and advocacy. Use them whenever a conversation offers an opportunity to learn—for example, when a group of students is considering a difficult point that requires information and participation from everyone on the team.

| PROTOCOLS FOR IMPROVED ADVOCACY | |
What to do	What to say
State your assumptions, and describe the data that led to them.	"Here's what I think, and here's how I got there."
Make your reasoning explicit.	"I came to this conclusion because . . ."
Explain the context of your point of view. Who will be affected by what you propose? How will they be affected, and why? Give examples, even if they're hypothetical or metaphorical.	"Imagine that you're a student coming into this school. (...or a small business person in this community, or a teacher approaching retirement, etc.) Here's how this idea would affect you."
As you speak, try to picture the other people's perspectives on what you are saying.	
Openly test your conclusions and assumptions.	"I am proposing this because (your observations or data) have led me to believe that (your conclusions). Is this a fair conclusion.
Encourage others to explore your model, your assumptions, and your data.	"What do you think about what I just said?" Or, "Do you see any flaws in my reasoning?"
Reveal where you are least clear in your thinking. Rather than making you vulnerable, this defuses the force of advocates who are opposed to you, and invites improvement.	"Here's one aspect which you might help me think through..."
Even when advocating: listen, stay open, and encourage others to provide different views.	"Do you see it differently?"

PROTOCOLS FOR IMPROVED INQUIRY
Ask others to make their thinking process visible

What to do	What to say
Gently walk people down the ladder of inference and find out what data they are operating from.	"What data do you have for that statement?" Or, more simply: "What leads you to say that?"
Use unaggressive language, particularly with people who are not familiar with these skills.	Instead of "What do you mean?" or "What's your proof?" say, "Can you help me understand your thinking here?"
Draw out their reasoning. Find out as much as you can about why they are saying what they are saying.	"What is the significance of that?" Or, "How does this relate to your other concerns?"
Explain your reasons for inquiring, and how your inquiry relates to your own concerns, hopes, and needs.	"I'm asking you about your assumptions here because..."

PROTOCOLS FOR FACING A POINT OF VIEW WITH WHICH YOU DISAGREE

What to do	What to say
Make sure you truly understand the other person's view.	"If I follow you correctly, you're saying that . . ."
Explore, listen, and offer your own views in an open way.	Ask, "Have you considered..." and then raise your concerns and state what is leading you to have them.

PROTOCOLS FOR WHEN YOU'RE AT AN IMPASSE

What to do	What to say
Embrace the impasse, and tease apart the current thinking on both sides.	"What do we both know to be true?" Or, "What do we both sense is true, but have no data for yet?"
Look for information that will help people move forward.	"What do we agree on, and what do we disagree on?"
Ask if there is any way you might together design an experiment or inquiry which could provide new information.	
Consider each person's mental model as a piece of a larger puzzle.	"Are we starting from two very different sets of assumptions here? Where do they come from?"
Ask what data or logic might change their views.	"What, then, would have to happen before you would consider the alternative?"
Ask for the group's help in redesigning the situation.	"It feels like we're getting into an impasse and I'm afraid we might walk away without any better understanding. Have you got any ideas that will help us clarify our thinking?"
Don't let conversation stop with an "agreement to disagree."	"I don't understand the assumptions underlying our disagreement."

The Advocacy/Inquiry Palette

We know a university faculty member who (at her students' suggestion) reproduced this chart at poster size and hung it on her classroom wall. Thereafter, in the final few minutes of each class, the students looked up at the wall chart and asked, "Where were we today? Were we in skillful discussion? Or were we simply asserting and withdrawing?"

During discussions, having the palette nearby fosters awareness: "I'd like to test something now," or "I realize I've just been politicking." This makes follow-through possible in a way that a mere lecture could never accomplish.

The advocacy/inquiry palette, by Charlotte Roberts and Rick Ross, originally appeared in *The Fifth Discipline Fieldbook*, p. 254. The innovator of this approach is Judy Rogers, professor of educational leadership, Miami University of Ohio.

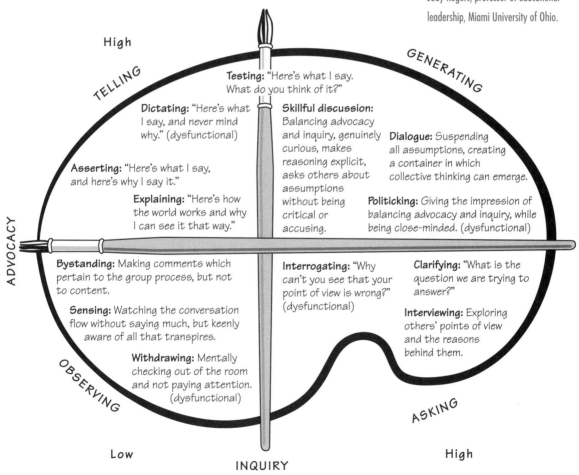

High

TELLING

GENERATING

Testing: "Here's what I say. What do you think of it?"

Dictating: "Here's what I say, and never mind why." (dysfunctional)

Skillful discussion: Balancing advocacy and inquiry, genuinely curious, makes reasoning explicit, asks others about assumptions without being critical or accusing.

Dialogue: Suspending all assumptions, creating a container in which collective thinking can emerge.

Asserting: "Here's what I say, and here's why I say it."

Explaining: "Here's how the world works and why I can see it that way."

Politicking: Giving the impression of balancing advocacy and inquiry, while being close-minded. (dysfunctional)

ADVOCACY

Bystanding: Making comments which pertain to the group process, but not to content.

Sensing: Watching the conversation flow without saying much, but keenly aware of all that transpires.

Withdrawing: Mentally checking out of the room and not paying attention. (dysfunctional)

Interrogating: "Why can't you see that your point of view is wrong?" (dysfunctional)

Clarifying: "What is the question we are trying to answer?"

Interviewing: Exploring others' points of view and the reasons behind them.

OBSERVING

ASKING

Low

INQUIRY

High

Cue Lines   Phil McArthur, Nelda Cambron-McCabe, Art Kleiner

Adapted in part from "Opening Lines" in *The Fifth Discipline Fieldbook*, p. 263.

Like actors who haven't learned their lines or have forgotten them in the heat of the moment, teachers and students sometimes wish there was someone they could turn to and say, as actors do on a movie set, "Give me the next line, please." You may feel this way, for instance, when the conversation is unfocused, people are digging in their heels, or tempers are rising. While you may see the problem, you may not know how to be helpful. Here are some conversational lines to use in impasses and other difficult situations, inside or outside of schools.

When...	You might say...
Strong views are expressed without any reasoning or illustrations...	"You may be right, but I'd like to understand more about what leads you to believe...?"
The discussion goes off on an apparent tangent...	"I'm unclear how that connects to what we've been saying. Can you say how you see it as relevant?"
You doubt the relevance of your own thoughts...	"This may not be relevant now. If so, let me know and I will think about it some more..."
Several views are advocated at once...	"We now have three ideas on the table." (Say what they are). I suggest we address them one at a time..."
You perceive a negative reaction in others...	"When you said (give illustration), I had the impression you were feeling (fill in the emotion). If so, I'd like to understand what I said that led to this."
People take positions but don't identify their concerns...	"I understand that is your position. I would like to understand the concerns you have. How do you see your position as the best way to resolve your concerns?"
An assertion is made but its point is not clear...	"What I understand you to be saying is (fill in the possible interpretation). Is that accurate?"
When it seems like a definition, phrase, or "loaded term" is leading to an impasse...	"When you said, (fill in term), I typically use that to mean (fill in connotation). What do you mean to say?"

Leading With Inquiry

Questions to reflect on	What to say in a live situation:
When advocating something, do I reveal my own thinking and assumptions? Do I make my reasoning explicit? (Do I walk up my ladder of inference slowly for other people?)	"Here's what I think, and here's how I came to that conclusion."

Questions to reflect on	What to say in a live situation:
Do I share observable data separate from my conclusions and test that data against others' perceptions?	"Here are some things we can all agree are happening because we see them—don't we?"
Do I encourage others to explore my model and assumptions?	"What do you think about what I just said?" "Do you see any flaws in my reasoning?" "What am I missing?"
Do I listen and stay open?	"Do you see it differently?" "How would you be affected by this?"
When faced with another person's view, do I ask them to make their thinking process visible, without assuming that I know what they'll say?	"Can you help me understand your thinking here?"
Do I gently walk others down the ladder of inference to find out what data they are operating from?	"What leads you to say that?" "Can you walk me through your reasoning?"
Do I explore others' reasoning in an open way, finding out as much as I can about why they are saying what they are saying?	"What is the significance of that?" "How does this relate to your other concerns?" "I'm not sure I understand your point."
Do I listen for larger meanings and concepts that may merge with my own views or provide a larger context?	"I'm asking you about your assumptions here because..." "How would your proposal affect...?" "Is this similar to...?" "Can you describe a typical example...?"
Do I check my understanding of their view?	"Am I correct that you're saying...?"
When at an impasse, do I look for the information that will help us move forward?	"What do we agree upon, and what do we disagree on—and why?"
Do I consider each person's mental model as part of a larger puzzle?	"Are we starting from two very different sets of assumptions here?" Or, "What's the source of our disagreement?"
Do I ask if there is any way we can design an experiment or inquiry to test our assumptions together?	"If we try to look into it together, perhaps we'll be able to calm my concern—or confirm it."
Do I ask for the group's help in redesigning the situation?	"It feels like we're getting to an impasse, and I'm afraid we're going to walk away without any better understanding. Do you have any ideas that will help us clarify our thinking?"
Do I ask guiding questions that move people into dialogue and deeper conversation?	"If we step back and look, what are the things we care most about in this debate?"
Am I willing to be influenced? Am I open to new learning?	"I think I might conceivably be convinced, but here's what I would need to understand..."

Purpose:

One of the most valuable skills in working with mental models is the ability to balance advocacy with inquiry—and, in many cases, to lead with inquiry first. Here are some conversational "recipes" that can help you move into deeper conversations and dialogue.

This exercise is derived in part from "Balancing Inquiry and Advocacy," by Charlotte Roberts and Rick Ross in *The Fifth Discipline Fieldbook*, p. 253.

The Left-Hand Column

STEP 1: CHOOSING A PROBLEM

The conversations conducted in schools—at administrative meetings, among teachers and administrators, between educators and parents, between students and everyone else, or among community members— often have difficult moments. Replaying those moments, and thinking carefully about how to respond to similar moments in the future, can be a powerful tool for learning to work with mental models. Select a difficult problem you've been involved with during the last month or two, the kind of tough, interpersonal one many of us try to ignore.

STEP 2: THE RIGHT-HAND COLUMN (WHAT WAS SAID)

Now think about the worst meeting you had this week, related to that issue.

Take several pieces of paper and draw a line down the center of each. (Or use the table feature in a word processing program to simulate two columns.) In the right hand column, write out the dialogue that actually occurred. The dialogue may go on for several pages. Leave the left-hand column blank until you're finished.

STEP 3: THE LEFT-HAND COLUMN (WHAT YOU WERE THINKING)

Now in the left-hand column, write down what you were thinking and feeling but not saying.

A Sample Case

A teacher (Jim Procter) is confronted by a parent (Jane) who feels that he is grading her child unfairly. In the right-hand column, Jim writes down his last conversation with Jane. In the left, Jim recalls his own thoughts. As you read through this, remember that Jane has her memory of this incident, with potentially her own "left-hand column," and her own assumptions and opportunities for inquiry.

What I was thinking	What was said
This is sixth grade. Why isn't Susan coming to see me herself?	JANE: Mr. Procter, you gave Susan a C in the class, and I don't think it's fair. I think she's doing A work, and I think you're giving her too much homework."

Purpose:

To become more aware of the tacit assumptions that govern many conversations and block success and to develop a way of talking about those tacit assumptions more effectively.

Overview:

Reflection on a transcript of a real exchange, developing skills for responding more effectively in the future.

This exercise is based upon the two-column research method developed by Chris Argyris and Donald A. Schön. The research method was first presented in their book, *Theory in Practice* (Jossey-Bass, 1974).

Some of the insights and approaches here were suggested by Robert Putnam.

For more about the left-hand column, see *The Fifth Discipline*, p. 195, and *The Fifth Discipline Fieldbook*, p. 246.

What I was thinking	What was said
I have had four parents question my grading this quarter. It must be a trend.	ME: Well, I tried to grade the papers accurately, and her skills are just not up to the same level as the "A" students in this class.
I don't recall what her last teacher said about Susan, but I doubt it was all that different.	JANE: That's not what her last teacher said. And I know for a fact that she's working as hard as she can.
This is going to take more time than I thought.	ME: This isn't just one assignment. I'm happy to look at it, but I don't think my view is going to change. She really isn't applying herself.
I treat all my students fairly.	JANE: Are you sure you're treating her fairly? She's always been considered gifted in the past.
Perhaps I can recommend some remedial steps for Jane. I should have paid attention earlier. Maybe there's something wrong at home.	ME: I didn't say I wouldn't work with Jane. I'm happy to work with her, if she's willing to sit down and improve. But why didn't she come to see me herself?
This is a kind of blackmail. I should really talk to the assistant principal about this before it escalates. But I can't let her know I'm concerned.	JANE: That's very nice, but I don't think she'll come and talk to you unless you change the grade first. Because she thinks the grade is unfair. And I agree.
	ME: Let me think about what to do, and I'll get back to you.

STEP 4: REFLECTION: USING YOUR LEFT-HAND COLUMN AS A RESOURCE

You can learn a great deal just from the act of writing out a case, putting it away for a week, and then looking at it again. The case becomes an artifact through which you can examine your own thinking as if you were looking at the thinking of someone else.

As you reflect, ask yourself:

■ What was my intention? What was I trying to accomplish?
■ Did I achieve the results I intended?
■ How might my comments have contributed to the difficulties?
■ What led me to make those comments?
■ How can I change the conversation for next time?
■ Why didn't I say what was in my left-hand column?
■ What assumptions am I making about the other person or people?
■ What were the benefits of operating this way? What were the risks?
■ What prevented me from acting differently?

In group meetings, when you feel angry or frustrated, the left-hand column is a valuable resource. If you focus your attention on your own thoughts and recognize what has perturbed you, you can then calmly stop the action and say, "I realize we've got important work to do, *but* once again I don't think we're focusing on the real issue. Let me tell you what I have been thinking but not saying..."

In other cases, leverage lies in the conversation itself. Begin by re-writing the previous conversation as you *might* have held it. How could you have revealed your thoughts in a way that would contributed to a more productive conversation, with better results for everyone involved? What could you have said that would let you see what was in the other person's left-hand column?

In particular, what questions could you ask that would have taken the conversation in a different direction? How could you lead with inquiry at each stage?

For example, when the parent says, "I know for a fact she's working as hard as she can," you might ask, "What do you see that leads you to say that?"

For a reality check, show the revised case to a third party (such as a trustworthy and open-minded colleague.)

You can also use this exercise to anticipate conversations you might have soon: writing down what you would be thinking, what you would say, what the other person might say—and what that might lead you to think. This can help you prepare for difficult conversations in advance, by recognizing some of the mental models that you hold and examining them ahead of time.

Amplification

The king had been betrayed. Henry II, twelfth-century ruler of England, had arranged for his bosom friend, fellow *bon vivant* and military partner, the archdeacon Thomas à Becket, to become Archbishop of Canterbury. Henry assumed that, this way, he could better control the Church. But the new Archbishop suddenly shifted allegiance; he broke contact with the King, gave up his palace and rich clothing, and refused to agree to Henry's demand to have clergy tried in the royal courts. When Becket excommunicated some of the bishops who were loyal to the King, they went to Henry to complain. At dinner one evening in 1169, the King was overheard grumbling, "Shall a man who has eaten my bread [meaning Becket] insult me and all the kingdom and not one of the lazy servants whom I nourish at my table [meaning his knights and courtiers] help me fix this affront?"

Four of the knights took Henry's offhand and frustrated remark as a command. They slipped out, rode to Canterbury, and killed the Archbishop. This murder, which the King apparently never intended, cost him nearly everything he valued: his former friend (with whom he had hoped to reconcile and whom he missed terribly); his standing with the Church (he was immediately excommunicated); the love of the people of England (despite humbling himself in his own pilgrimage to Canterbury); the political concessions Becket had spent years demanding from him (which he now granted with no further argument); and the respect of his own sons, who fought him in a series of wars that lasted the rest of his life. (And the hapless knights? Henry imprisoned them.)

Organizational theorist Charles Hampden-Turner calls this kind of phenomenon "amplification." People take action on what they perceive (or guess) that the person in a position of power wants to happen. A principal mentions a project he'd like to see someone start someday, even though he doesn't feel that strongly about it, and discovers three weeks later that someone has stayed up all night three nights in a row to put it on his desk. After a superintendent remarks that *The Fifth Discipline* by Peter Senge informs her thinking about schools, she notices copies of his books on people's desks and the frequent insertion of phrases such as mental models and systems thinking in conversations.

These responses occur because people don't know what those in the upper echelons really want. And, for various reasons, they do not ask or are afraid to ask for clarification. This means they are limited to the signals they pick up in meetings and chance encounters—signals that only represent a fraction of any leader's actual intentions. Faced with this lack of knowledge about the decisions they need to make, people tend to compensate by guessing—and often by guessing wrongly. Or they hedge their bets by making so many half-hearted, contradictory decisions that they get nowhere.

The consequence of guesswork? Sometimes it's simply wasted effort and miscued performance. But sometimes it's far worse. If a student in your class, or a teacher in your school, goes out on a limb and tries something with the hope that you'll like it, but it represents in fact a misreading of your intentions and you react, even kindly, with disapproval—then that individual will never take initiative again. Neither will anyone who was nearby when you reacted. (Nor, most likely, did any of Henry II's knights after that Becket episode, which probably explains why the rest of his military campaigns went so poorly.) From now on, people will wait for you to spell out assignments completely, volunteering nothing, because they have lost confidence in their ability to guess

Purpose:

To better understand mental models that can lead to miscues in communication between individuals in the core power group and others and to explore ways to clarify expectations. This exercise can be used for solo reflection or with breakout groups of four or five teachers or administrators. We have found it particularly helpful when both teachers and administrators are in the conversation together.

This passage and exercise were adapted from Art Kleiner, *Who Really Matters: The Core Group Theory of Power, Privilege and Success* (Doubleday, 2003), p. 74ff. The description of "amplification" comes from conversation with Charles Hampden-Turner.

your needs. Over time you will come to believe that no one who works for you is capable of thinking for themselves. Everyone else will come to believe that you are self-centered, arbitrary, and oblivious.

If you really want to break the guesswork cycle, you have to reduce the level of distortion in the signals that are amplified. Politicians, diplomats, and psychiatrists have long been aware that they have to be exceedingly careful with even their most casual remarks, because these can have huge effects on their listeners. As a teacher, or a school leader, you have to do something similar. This means knowing what messages you unconsciously convey and communicating them more consciously, setting an example yourself of the new behavior you want to promote.

This exercise can help you, on your own or in a group, explore the misunderstandings around you and find ways to avoid potentially disruptive efforts by well-intentioned individuals.

1. Have your comments ever been amplified?
    a. What was your intent?
    b. How did you communicate that intent?
    c. What did others perceive your intent to be?
    d. How did you learn about the misperception?
    e. What were the consequences?
    f. What would you have wanted to learn early about people's perception that you didn't find out until later?
2. Have you been in the position of "guessing" what someone wanted you to do?
    a. What did you perceive the leader's intent to be?
    b. What did you see or hear that led to this conclusion?
    c. How did you know whether this was important to the leader? What did he or she do that led you to this conclusion?
    d. How did you act differently after this communication?
    e. If you could be absolutely anonymous, what would you want to tell the leader about your response?
3. Whose voice is most likely to be amplified in your school—and why?
4. What strategies can be used to diminish the "guesswork" that occurs in amplification?

If you are conducting this exercise with breakout groups, then compare the responses. Ask each group to highlight the major points raised in their conversation. Record these on a Smart Board, flip chart, or overhead projector. Reviewing the recorded points, ask the group to prioritize a list of strategies that can be used in their setting.

5. Team Learning

TL

At its core, team learning is a discipline of practices designed, over time, to get the people on a team thinking and acting together. The team members do not need to think *alike*—indeed, it's unlikely that they ever will, and there's no reason that they should. But through regular practice, they can learn to be effective in concert.

Schools are rife with team activity. A classroom is a team of people who need each other to accomplish their mutual purpose: to develop competence together. This team implicitly includes people who are not thought of as being members: the writers of key books and resources used in the classroom, the staff whose work makes the learning possible, the administrators who provide the resources and support the classroom needs, and the parents whose participation gives the classroom some of its power. The *core* team, however, consists of the people who return to the classroom day after day—the teachers and students.

When you move up the nested systems into the school and community levels, teams conduct the bulk of work. Policies are set by an elected team known as the school board; the board, superintendent, and top administrators form a team of their own. Curriculum teams, site teams, and staff development teams all set the tone for innovation in schools. Intramural teams have become increasingly influential: for example, the National Superintendent's Roundtable has instigated meetings among a national group of superintendents who compare notes and build capabilities for organizational learning in their school systems. These capabilities have begun to filter out into their administrative teams; school boards in the individual school systems often practice such skills as working with mental models.

For more about the National Superintendent's Roundtable, see www.superintendentsforum.org.

Because of many schools' experience with team teaching, team building, and group dynamics, educators often believe that they have been practicing a version of this discipline for years. However, most team building involves separate "retreat-like" sessions for improving communications skills. Afterwards, the team returns and conducts its regular business in the same old counterproductive ways. Team learning, by contrast, is a discipline of *regularly* transforming day-to-day communication skills, in teacher meetings, staff development, and the classroom itself.

The heart of team learning is regular willingness, as a recurring group of people, to think and act together as a living system. This does not merely mean making one-time decisions or setting static roles and following through with discrete tasks. It means continuously talking, with respect and deliberation, about the issues that must be understood and resolved.

This discipline often involves going back to core questions: What has brought us to education as a profession—and what has kept us here? What do we fundamentally believe about children and their backgrounds? What aspects of our school need to change, and what needs to stay the same? There will be many perspectives, and the team does not have to agree on everything. But the team does have to be aligned.

Alignment

Team learning is based on the concept of alignment—as distinct from agreement. Derived from the French *aligner* ("to put in line"), alignment has the connotation of arranging a group of scattered elements so they function as a whole, by orienting them all to a common awareness of each other, their purpose, and their current reality. Even though people retain their individuality, their efforts will naturally move in a common direction. They waste less time and effort reaching common goals because they understand one another more completely. Even if they don't agree, they know each other well enough so that any of them can speak for the group as a whole, on many subjects, without having to check in first.

In a classroom, alignment develops when students all feel involved in their common learning endeavor, not just individual learning. In a school or community, alignment starts with the ability to see and respect each other and to establish some common mental models about reality.

This section is adapted, in part, from several articles on Dialogue in *The Fifth Discipline Fieldbook*, particularly "Dialogue," by William Isaacs (p. 357), "Designing a Dialogue Session," by William Isaacs and Bryan Smith (p. 374). Also see William Isaacs, *Dialogue: The Art of Thinking Together* (Doubleday, 1999).

Dialogue in Schools

The most effective practice we know for team learning emerges from the conversational form known as dialogue. William Isaacs, founder and director of the MIT Dialogue Project and the DiaLogos Institute, defines dialogue as a sustained collective inquiry into everyday experience and what we take for granted. The goal of dialogue is to open new ground by establishing a "container" or "field" for inquiry: a setting where people can become more aware of the context around their experience and of the processes of thought and feeling that created that experience.

In the practice of dialogue, we pay attention not only to the words, but to the spaces between the words; not only to the result of an action, but to its timing; not only to the things people say, but to the timbre and tone of their voices. We listen for the meaning of the field of inquiry, not only its discrete elements. During the dialogue process, people learn how to think together—not just in the sense of analyzing a shared problem or creating new pieces of shared knowledge, but in the sense of occupying a collective sensibility, in which the thoughts, emotions, and resulting actions belong not to one individual but to all of them together

Dialogue is an old practice. It may seem unfamiliar at first, but it feels very natural to most people once they start. That may explain why it seems to flourish in modern settings, despite a range of institutionalized barriers.

In your own school or school system, fostering a series of dialogues on important subjects can gradually establish a container in which people experience the primacy of the whole. You will be able to talk safely about controversial issues, such as union rules or disagreements about the curriculum, in a dispassionate space where people are encouraged to raise questions without having to leap to resolution. When you understand each other's thinking better, you can then begin to move into coordinated patterns of action, without the same artificial, tedious processes of decision making. You can start to act in an aligned way. In many cases, you will not need to work out an action plan for what everyone should do, any more than a flock of birds taking flight from a tree in perfectly natural order requires planning.

Dialogue is valuable as a kind of antidote to the fragmentation and isolation of modern life. People tend to divide the world into categories and then treat the categories as sacrosanct, forgetting that these categories are dynamic and ever-evolving. Disputes between business people and educators, labor and management, leftists and rightists, and members of the same family are all symptoms of this kind of hypnosis; they can't be "solved" through increased discussion or debate. They can only be resolved through a conversation where people are drawn to see past the blinders that they have put upon themselves.

The modern-day practice of dialogue draws deeply on the work of physicist David Bohm. Bohm pointed out that when the roots of thoughts are observed, thought itself seems to change for the better. See David Bohm, *Unfolding Meaning* (Foundation House, 1995). Also see www.david-bohm.net.

DESIGN FOR DIALOGUE

A skilled facilitator can help the group evolve to see the flow of energy and meaning among them becoming tangible and compelling. Outside facilitation is also valuable for maintaining perspective; it's easy to get sidetracked into debate, argument, or manipulative "consensus-building" unless someone keeps drawing the group back to its true purpose. But even without a facilitator, people can develop deeper, more dialogue-like conversations by following a few ground rules:

■ Begin with an invitation. People must be given the choice to participate.

- Practice suspending assumptions and beliefs when they come up—in other words, explore them from a variety of angles, make them explicit, give them considerable weight, and try to understand where they came from. The word "suspend" means "to hang in front." Hanging your assumptions in front of you so that you and others can reflect on them is a delicate and powerful art. The assumptions should be visible in the midst of the room, as if on a string, available for all (including the person who holds them) to question and explore.

- Open with a "check-in" at the beginning of every session and a "check-out" at the end. This means giving every participant an opportunity to simply speak for a moment about what he or she is thinking, is feeling, or has noticed. Stress the value of speaking from personal experience. When everyone knows that they will have some air time, people tend to relax.

For more about check-in, see page 258.

- Avoid agendas and elaborate preparations; these inhibit the free flow of conversation.

- While meeting over a meal may break the ice, we recommend that you avoid the temptation; restaurant service and eating can be distracting.

- Agree, as a group, to hold three meetings before you decide whether to continue or disband. Anything less may not be a fair experiment; it can take time to grow into the dialogue form of conversation.

- Speak to the center of the group, not to each other. Create a pool of common meaning. If two people start to argue with each other, or if the group's intent is hijacked in other ways, gently bring people's attention to the fact that you are off track, and move back toward the full group's desired direction.

- Let each person finish, and pause a beat before the next person speaks. Suggest that people base their comments on what the whole group needs to hear next—not on their own need to speak.

When these techniques are made part of an ongoing series of conversations, and when people have no agenda other than to establish deeper connection with those who are important to them, then something very powerful happens. One dialogue session, for example, covered the question of how much attention and money should be drawn away from the rest of the school budget for special education. The dialogue included teachers, administrators, parents, social workers, and community advocates. Everyone in the room had an entrenched attitude, grounded in personal experience with people with disabilities, experience as teachers, and feelings about state budgets and state legislatures. But once everyone spoke from the heart, everyone came to recognize the reasons why the others had come to their views. The problem took on a meaning that it had not had before, as if the great possibility of special education itself hung in the air before the group. Nothing was resolved; no policies were decided upon. But after these dialogues, the contentiousness of the issue seemed to disappear, as if people recognized that they had no choice but to approach this problem as members of one body. Later, in other meetings, decisions were made. People said they were far happier with the decisions and had a deeper understanding of what was at stake than they would have had if dialogue had never taken place.

Team Learning in Education

Many good teachers instinctively practice team learning already. Cooperative learning, for example, as researched and developed by David and Roger Johnson of the University of Minnesota, is an effective method of team learning used in many schools. This is when students take on tasks together, in groups of two or more, and the teacher trains them to facilitate, brainstorm, summarize each other's ideas, and even to "take on" particular points of view in dialogue, then switch roles so that they can see their previous assumptions suspended before the group.

See David Johnson and Roger Johnson, *Learning Together and Alone: Cooperative, Competitive, and Individualistic Learning* (Allyn and Bacon, 1999). Also see the University of Minnesota cooperative learning website at http://www.co-operation.org/.

Team learning methods have particular value in certain school structures. For example, in multi-age classrooms students greatly benefit from a collective knowledge base. At the start of a unit on history in a room of fourth and fifth graders, for instance, the teacher might ask, "What do we already know about the explorers of the New World?" and map the facts that students call out on the board. Fifth graders might remember facts from previous years that the third graders haven't yet learned, while a fourth grader who is fascinated by sailing ships might know many things that nobody else knows. But for this to work, younger students, who are physically smaller and perhaps intimidated, need the formal recognition that everyone has something to offer; and older students need to see that they will be treated as part of a whole group, not as dominators of the group.

Team learning techniques can be useful outside the classroom, as well. For example, it can be vital for school committees, especially when they have student representatives. Staff development, too, is a natural vehicle for team learning. The widespread use of professional learning communities provides an important practice arena where teachers learn from each other. You can open a dialogue about core values and beliefs: "Why are we here? What has brought us to education as a profession? What has kept us here?" Surprisingly few teachers have ever had that conversation in a large group of their peers, and it makes a difference.

See "No More Drive-By Staff Development," page 396.

More general forums are also valuable contexts for dialogue. One opening question for a schoolwide dialogue is: "If we could change anything we wanted about education—not about this school per se, but about the context of education in general—what would it be?" When the faculty and students at Miami University's Department of Educational Leadership asked themselves that question, they ended up talking about the deep need for learning about interdisciplinary humanities, especially for people in authority.

This all happened in the midst of an explosive disagreement about the direction of the department. The dialogue involved people from all conceivable points of view, from extremely conservative to Marxist; no one changed their opinions, but they did come face-to-face with the stake they all had, together, in the future of educating leaders *and* in the value of well-prepared leadership. This dialogue led to the development of an interdisciplinary curriculum on leadership that ultimately became widely recognized in the field.

For more about the Miami Educational Leadership program, see page 350.

Another valuable opening point for dialogue is simply: "What do teachers think about kids? What mental models do we hold, as educators, about the children of our district? And where do those mental models come from?" Some educators believe, at heart, that the ultimate responsibility for a child's learning lies with the school, and particularly with the school's leader—the superintendent. Others look squarely at the parents as the ultimate source of responsibility, others at the teacher, and others at the children themselves. An in-depth dialogue can help people see the policy implications of these divergent attitudes and where their attitudes come from.

Mapping Exercises for Team Learning

One of the biggest challenges teams face is setting a context of mutual understanding. Mind-mapping techniques, also known as associative conceptual diagrams, can help a great deal. These diagrams get everyone's assumptions, and the relationships among them, out in the open

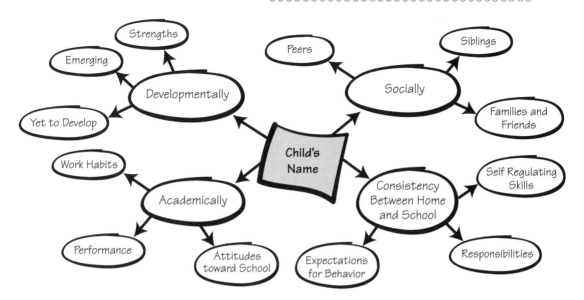

where the group can see and talk about them collectively. The map also helps capture the thinking of a group in an intensely visual way that prevents the conversation from bogging down.

For example, if you are an administrator and you have to decide whether to suspend a student, you can call the parents of the students involved, and any teachers who were involved, into a meeting. Start with a map showing the student's name and four different dimensions: His or her academic performance, developmental progress, social network, and the consistency between home and school life.

Ask everyone in the room to help fill in the circles. Ask the parents, for example, to talk about the child's relationships with brothers, sisters, and other children. "In the neighborhood, does he play with children who are older or younger?" Ask the teachers to describe what they have seen in unstructured situations, such as lunch and recess, as well as in class.

Then look at the student developmentally, particularly in terms of strengths, or what Robert Brooks calls their "islands of competence"— emerging possible talents and qualities that have not yet developed. "I know your child is the youngest male in our grade level," you might say. "How does that affect him?" Consider academic issues: work habits, performance, and attitudes towards school. "Does your child like school? How have his grades, scores, and reports fluctuated?"

Then consider the consistency between home and school. "Would it make sense," you might ask, "to try to document this troubling behavior in both home and school? And how do we do that?" As you talk, keep posting notes in the relevant places on the diagram. By the time you

See, for example, Robert Brooks and Sam Goldstein, *Raising Resilient Children: Fostering Strength, Hope and Optimism in Your Child* (McGraw-Hill, 2001), p. 135ff.

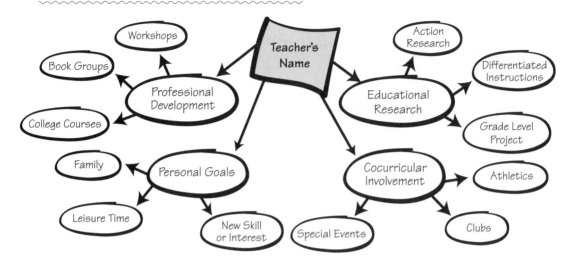

are done, the diagram will show how the child might be at risk, without blaming the child, the parents, or anyone else.

Mind-mapping has the same effect in other contexts. You can ask teachers to map each child in their class with a similar diagram, charting the traits they most appreciate about this student—along with the single trait (or perhaps two) that they would most want to change. Remind them to add themselves to the chart, for they too are an influence. Once those students' strengths and weaknesses are identified on the page, then teachers are more attuned to them and more responsive. This can be a useful diagram to show parents in conferences; it makes it easier for teachers to check their assumptions and raise difficult questions.

Teachers can create similar maps to track their own professional development. This is a useful document to talk over with supervisors. It can include such specific details as the names of courses they've taken but in context of the greater issue: their personal goals and the fit with the school's and community's vision. This map can build from year to year.

The World Café Nelda Cambron-McCabe

Juanita Brown with David Isaacs and The World Café Community, *The World Café: Shaping Our Futures Through Conversations That Matter* (Berrett-Koehler Publishers, 2005); *The World Café: A Resource Guide for Hosting Conversations That Matter* (PDF) (2009, Pegasus Communications, http://www.pegasus.com); World Café website, www.theworldcafe.com.

I experienced a World Café for the first time at a conference on systems thinking. Juanita Brown, who designed the process, set up provocative questions for a large group dialogue (several thousand people in all). The topic: building collaborations to change our organizations and the world. When I walked into the hotel ballroom, hundreds of small café tables with checkered tablecloths and flowers greeted me. I knew this would be an extraordinary experience. During the course of the next two hours, many people moved from table to table, while others stayed, taking their ideas and observations to a new level every time the conversation shifted. Two hours later, I left the session feeling an incredible connection to everyone in the room. Watching the evolving dialogue and collective intelligence build as we moved about the room gave me hope that such conversations could change the world.

Through Juanita Brown's publications and website, you can learn the basics of holding Café conversations. I've used the process in my work with school systems as well as with higher education faculty members at conferences. The Resource Guide electronic book succinctly lays out the guiding principles for holding a meaningful dialogue in this format; it covers everything from the development of your questions to the physical setting. *The World Café: Shaping Our Futures Through Conversations That Matter* is a book-length treatment of the process, providing a theoretical and philosophical grounding along with numerous examples of the World Café across diverse organizations. I found this book particularly critical in creating my Café designs. The World Café website offers further guidance and tools, many of which are free. Each time I've facilitated a session, I see the essential role of conversation in shaping our lives.

6. Systems Thinking

Many school administrators are drowning in crises. It's amazing to sit in a superintendent's office and listen to incoming phone calls—and equally amazing, in a sense, that he or she doesn't unplug the phone. Each event seems to require an immediate response. A child is hurt on school grounds, so additional supervisors must be assigned to the playgrounds. A bill before the state legislature would cut off revenue for some school programs; a trip is planned to the state capital. A parent is concerned about a child's performance, so a meeting is scheduled for that week. Whatever the problem, each time the superintendent (or another staff member) is tasked with making the fastest possible diagnosis and finding the most immediate solution.

But there's a very real chance some of these quick fixes will do more harm than good in the long run. Moreover, reacting to each event immediately and solving problems as they come up helps develop a kind of "attention-deficit culture" in the school system. Moving rapidly from one issue to the next, people grow highly skilled at solving crises instead of looking for ways to prevent them.

The discipline of systems thinking provides a different way of looking at problems and goals—not as isolated events but as components of larger but less visible structures that affect each other. To understand a system is to understand those interrelationships and how they recur and change over time. A school district is a system with many interrelated components: everything from the design of the buildings to the habits and attitudes of the people who work there to the policies and procedures imposed by the state and the community, as well as such implacable forces as available money and student population growth or decline. When you see how these affect each other, you can act far more effectively.

LEXICON

The phrase "systems thinking" has been used in different contexts to refer to other concepts. For more about this, see "Five Kinds of Systems Thinking," by Charlotte Roberts, in *The Dance of Change* (Crown Business, 1999) p. 137. We also recommend, for an in-depth look at the evolution of the understanding of open systems theory and system dynamics in particular, George P. Richardson, *Feedback Thought in Social Science and Systems Theory*, (University of Pennsylvania Press, 1991). For the history of several of these threads, see Art Kleiner, *The Age of Heretics* (Jossey-Bass, 2008).

SYSTEM/SYSTEMS THINKING

A system is any perceived structure whose elements "hang together" because they continually affect each other over time. The word "system" derives from the Greek verb *sunistanai*, which originally meant "to cause to stand together." As this origin suggests, the nature of a system includes the perception with which you observe it. Examples of systems (besides the school district) include biological organisms (including human bodies), the atmosphere, diseases, ecological niches, factories, chemical reactions, political entities, industries, families, teams—and all organizations. Within every school district, community, or classroom, there might be dozens of different systems worthy of notice: the governing process of the district, the impact of particular policies, the labor-management relationship, the curriculum development, the approaches to disciplining students, and the prevailing modes of staff behavior. Every child's life is a system. Every educational practice is a system.

The discipline of systems thinking is the study of system structure and behavior; and it is enriched by a set of tools and techniques that have developed over the past fifty years, particularly since the advent of powerful computers. Some of the tools and techniques are fairly simple; some require computer models (and the training to use them). All of them are accessible, however, and as you use them over time, you learn to recognize and respond to the "non-linear" aspects of everyday life, those situations in which cause and effect do not occur in the way that most people expect them to. You develop awareness of the complexity, interdependencies, change, and leverage—the ability to get maximum results with minimal expense and effort—of that system. And you learn more about the unintended consequences of your own life choices.

The tools and techniques of systems thinking may seem unfamiliar at first, but (as you'll see), the basic concepts may also resonate deeply within you. We have found that most children, for example, are natural systems thinkers, highly attuned to the interrelationships among nature, other people, emotions, thoughts, and themselves.

~~~

Systems Thinking in Education

Systems thinking is particularly relevant to education because of the types of problems that are prevalent in school systems. In *Leadership Without Easy Answers*, Ron Heifetz calls them "adaptive" problems, meaning that they cannot be solved with purely technical or specific responses. For example, a simple infection is a technical problem; it's curable with an antibiotic or other simple treatment, and conventional medical expertise is good enough to solve it. But a complex disease, like cancer or diabetes, requires much more than a technical solution or simple treatment. The diagnosis is uncertain, the outcome is more of a guess than a certainty, and the patient must be engaged to learn and change behaviors if the solution is to take hold. To Heifetz, this complexity and uncertainty qualifies a problem as adaptive.

Education issues can be even more complex and uncertain than healthcare issues for a number of reasons. The timeframes are longer—a child begins school at age three or four in many countries and may not leave school until age twenty-two or later. Knowledge and expertise are more fragmented and distributed than in medicine—though a general understanding of what makes effective schools is emerging, there is still far less consensus than there is in most biological fields. Teachers, administrators, and parents all bring some knowledge that the others lack; curriculums and other priorities are set outside the walls of the district; and in a sense, the student is the most expert of all, because only the student sees the entire system all the way through. Finally, like quality medicine, quality education hinges on a whole suite of life choices and a way of learning how to make them.

Ronald Heifetz, *Leadership Without Easy Answers* (Harvard University Press, 1994), p. 31ff.

Systems thinking can therefore make an enormous contribution in education. But it should not be treated as a solitary discipline. No one person's perspective is likely to be complete. Instead of working alone, gather a pilot group of committed people together to talk about a common situation. Consider it through various systems tools. Map the forces at play; look for similarities in the archetypes and systemic structures that you see. But also look for differences; there may be critical clues to the system in the gap between different people's perceptions of the problem.

Pay particular attention to the ways in which your own actions are part of the system at large. If you're prone to blaming someone else—the teachers, the parents, the school, the government, the local community, the businesses—ask yourself what part you have in that system that might have created that condition. What are you doing, specifically, that makes it difficult for the situation to improve.

Finally, try to identify leverage: the places where relatively small actions can produce relatively large results. Then experiment on a small scale, see the results, and talk about your experiments (and their results) with colleagues and other partners. In this way, your group's efforts become a natural part of the system, a form of feedback for the system as a whole, and a catalyst through which the system can improve itself.

The Iceberg

When the transatlantic ship Titanic approached an iceberg on its maiden voyage, the greatest threat to the ship was not the ice people could see above or at the water line but far below where the shape and structure, indeed most of the iceberg, would be difficult to see even in broad daylight. Most people are familiar with the phrase "tip of the iceberg," to indicate that there is more going on under the surface than we can easily see or describe. In other words, events on the surface are usually symptoms of something bigger.

Despite the murkiness of the water, the real leverage for change is found beneath the surface. From a systems perspective, focusing on a specific event—the tip of the iceberg—will prevent you from seeing the complexity of the school organization. The Iceberg Activity focuses a group's attention on understanding the problem. Though this exercise often helps people eventually come up with solutions to problems they have identified, it is better to think of it first as a way to understand the problem.

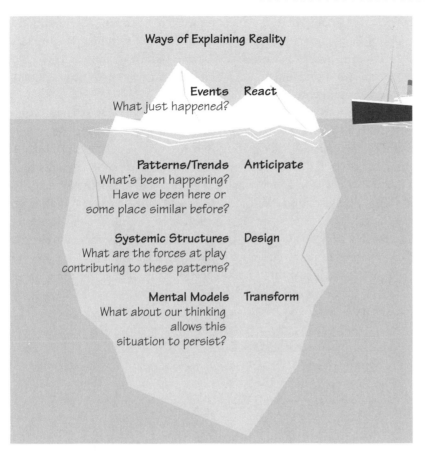

Ways of Explaining Reality

Events   **React**
What just happened?

Patterns/Trends   **Anticipate**
What's been happening?
Have we been here or
some place similar before?

Systemic Structures   **Design**
What are the forces at play
contributing to these patterns?

Mental Models   **Transform**
What about our thinking
allows this
situation to persist?

Purpose:

This activity can help you move from dealing with isolated events to seeing the interconnectedness of multiple events that may be widely separated in time and space. Instead of reacting to events or seeking a culprit to blame, your team can gain deeper insights into the structures and thinking underlying the challenges you face. The reflection and inquiry processes embedded in this exercise can help illustrate how the disciplines of systems thinking and mental models are intricately intertwined.

STEP 1: EVENTS

Name a critical event or issue that has emerged in your classroom, school, or community. Spend 15 or 20 minutes reflecting on the event and why it remains a problem. How have you and others responded to the event? How have you tried to solve it?

For example, not long ago, in the Crossroads Public School District, the state report card showed that the district had only a 78 percent graduation rate the previous year. Although the completion rate had been dropping over the past few years, no one was prepared for the most recent drop, particularly since districts in the state with similar demographics were experiencing 95 percent rates or higher. Moreover, just a few years before, they had seemed to be making progress.

This was upsetting news. Parents contacted school board members demanding that some action be taken. Factions blamed each other—teachers and administrators claimed parents and kids simply didn't care;

parents replied angrily that educators were not teaching their children; community members remained silent but vowed to remember the statistic the next time they were asked to vote on an operating levy; elected leaders began discussing new accountability measures to ensure a quick response from the district.

Such responses are typical and understandable. As the diagram suggests, people tend to respond to events by reacting—treating each event as a separate incident and tailoring your response accordingly. But while this reaction is understandable and common, it isn't generally effective. What if you saw your event (whatever it might be) as simply the tip of an iceberg? The visible part of the iceberg looks massive and threatening, but the most dangerous part of it is hidden by the surface of the ocean. You cannot navigate around it unless you can somehow penetrate the dark ocean and see the structure supporting the visible tip.

So what was below the tip of the iceberg?

STEP 2: PATTERNS AND TRENDS

Start with two questions: What's been happening? Have we been here or someplace similar before?

Explore the history of the event you have described in step one. Chart the course of related events over time on a graph. What patterns do you see emerging?

Crossroads is a fictional school district, but the events and analysis here are based on several true stories.

In the Crossroads Public School District, staff compiled data related to student characteristics, mobility in the district, and other events that seemed related to the graduation rate. They came up with a chart looking something like this:

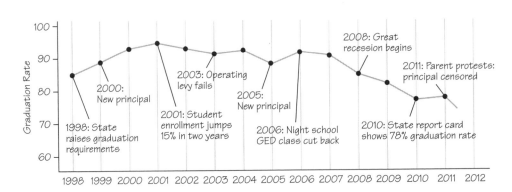

Systems specialists refer to these diagrams as behavior-over-time diagrams. The behavior depicted in these diagrams is not human activity but the behavior of the system: the patterns of rising and falling key variables. As patterns emerge, it is clear that most of them have been seen before. Rarely are patterns completely new. They may not look exactly the same, but they will certainly look similar to patterns that appeared two, five, or ten years earlier.

Looking at patterns of behavior might seem depressing at first; these patterns make it seem as if fate is inexorable. No matter what you do, you'll fall into that pattern. But that attitude is based on the false assumption that history will repeat itself. No major driving force affecting education, from the economy to government policies to demographics to trends in education, is predictable today. Thus patterns of behavior, while they reveal trends, are inadequate for making decisions. To look more deeply, you need to consider the root causes of the pattern—the interrelated forces that have brought you here.

STEP 3: SYSTEMIC STRUCTURE

What forces seem to create the pattern of behavior you described in Step 2? How do these systemic elements seem to influence each other? What fundamental aspects of the school must be changed, if you want to change the patterns?

Behind each pattern of behavior is a systemic structure—a set of seemingly unrelated factors that interact, even though they may be widely separated in time and place, and even though their relationships may be difficult to recognize. When studied, these structures reveal the points of greatest leverage. These are not necessarily the points of highest authority; they are the places where the ingrained channels of cause and effect are most susceptible to influence.

Many of these systems have developed over time as the result of habitual approaches to chronic problems. To redesign the system requires an understanding of existing structures and practices. For example, in the Crossroads Public School District's declining graduation rate, perhaps there is a combination of an increasingly diverse student population and low support for staff development to work with students who are experiencing academic difficulties. With a past reputation for academic excellence, the school system has attracted parents who want to give their children the best possible school experience. Many school administrators continue to make decisions based on their perception of their school as an elite college prep high. But the community has grown, with many parents who don't speak English as their first language or other educational needs that the school is unprepared for.

As economics forced the district to make cuts, this has exacerbated the problem of the graduation rate. But one major factor was often overlooked: turnover in school leadership. The principal who served from 2000 until 2005 had developed and promoted an alternative evening program that students were required to attend before being allowed to drop out. The program served GED students as well as those needing adult literacy classes, and like many programs it struggled with funding. Nonetheless, it provided a warm, individualized opportunity for student learning and was led by an energetic, supportive, and kind teacher. After the principal retired, the program was discontinued. Subsequently, the district attempted to enroll the students in an alternative high school nearby and created more reading and math remedial courses. But their success rates were much lower than the original evening program's had been.

You could try to describe these patterns of cause and effect in words, but it would be much more effective to map them out, using arrows to indicate cause and effect. The resulting "causal loop" diagram might look something like this:

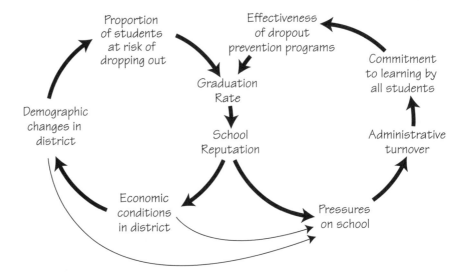

Note the number of factors that interrelate and the ways in which they combine to create a rise or fall in graduation rates. Notice also that there are few "pure" beginnings or endings—every factor influences some other factor, and is influenced by others. That's how the system evolves over time. When the graduation rate goes up, that affects the school's reputation and (eventually) the economic conditions of the community. These, in turn, affect the school's effectiveness and, ultimately, the graduation rate.

For more on causal loop diagrams, see page 140.

Throughout this book, we'll use a variety of tools—including causal loop diagrams and structural modeling—to help clarify and articulate the patterns of interrelationships that make up a system. We'll also see how different types of recurring patterns lead to predictable effects and point the way to understanding where your leverage might lie. We'll also show you how to begin developing computer models that can help you understand the systems with still more accuracy, detail, and potential for learning and understanding.

But there is always this critical step: to focus your attention on the systemic structures that matter most in your system and the ways they influence each other. In short, to look for elements that influence other elements.

Where do you need to focus to see your systemic structures more clearly?

STEP 4: MENTAL MODELS

Though the systemic structure can reveal very deep causal interrelationships that affect the problems you are trying to solve, there is still a deeper level: the mental models that engendered these systemic relationships in the first place. Systems often take their shape from the values, attitudes, and beliefs of the people in them. That's because our mental models, our theories about the way the world works, influence our actions, which in turn influence the interactions of the system.

Consider, for example, the mental models that give rise to students dropping out of school. Do people in the school district believe that the principal must be a superhero? Do they feel that any visible flaw is a sign that they have chosen the wrong person? Do they expect him or her to be thoroughly political and not ruffle any feathers or disturb any sacred cows?

What mental models, in turn, does the principal have about the community? About the teachers? About the teachers' unions? About the students and how many of them are capable of learning enough to graduate? About the best model for learning? And about him- or herself? Many administrators, as successful and well-educated people, have learned the power of advocacy but are not skilled in inquiry. They tend to hold the mental model that, when faced with a conflict, they can win by arguing more avidly and debating most fervently. In this way, they perpetuate the cycle of recurrent misunderstandings between themselves and teachers or parents.

This is a "limits to growth" archetype—see *The Fifth Discipline* by Peter Senge (Doubleday, 2006), p. 94.

Now consider the problem that you have been charting. Behind each element of the systemic structure is a set of attitudes and beliefs, some of which have been unchallenged, even though they are misleading or counterproductive, because they are unseen. Can you safely bring them to the surface and inquire about them? Only by surfacing these beliefs and assumptions can the system be transformed.

USING THE ICEBERG

This group exercise can be conducted about any major problem. As you move through the four steps, the conversation moves to a higher order: away from "quick fix" solutions and closer to a genuine understanding of the attitudes that have created the problem. At the beginning of each stage, lead with inquiry: ask people not to offer interpretations but to start by asking questions. Remember as you go through the next three steps: You are not looking for solutions—you are generating a better understanding of the situation. From that deeper understanding, sustainable solutions will emerge.

The Phantom Traffic Jam

Art Kleiner

Have you ever been stuck in a phantom traffic jam?

This is a traffic jam with no discernable cause—no highway construction, no accident obstructing the flow of cars and trucks, not even merging lanes. But all of a sudden traffic slows down to a near-standstill. You crawl along with the rest of the cars, and then, again for no discernible reason, the flow picks up again.

The phantom traffic jam is a systemic structure. It may not seem like one, because it has no formal relationship; it's just a bunch of cars, each apparently autonomous in their travels on the highway. But something has linked them together. Clearly it's not a random relationship, because phantom traffic jams recur continuously on high-speed roadways around the world.

The cause is always the same: Rubbernecking. Tailgating. Following too closely. When people leave too little space between their car and the car in front of them, a wave-frequency oscillation pattern ensues. The driver in front need only tap his or her brakes and slow down for a moment, and the next driver will overreact, braking more than necessary. The third driver will slam on the brakes even harder. Every car, overreacting a bit, is forced to slow down further, and the traffic flow ultimately stops.

See Robert Holmes: "When shock waves hit traffic: What turns a fast-moving stream of cars into a stagnant pool of frustrated motorists?" *New Scientist* (June 25, 1994).

As with many systemic structures, the critical interrelationships only become clear when you reflect on the following facts about the phantom traffic jam:

- Time is an important factor; the delay between one car braking and the next can make all the difference. Some structures have a lot of elements (or, as systems experts put it, they have "detail complexity"); but the most pernicious problems also tend to have "dynamic complexity." Their nature isn't understandable until you can see the elements interact over time.
- People's attitudes are part of the system as well. Countries where drivers don't follow too closely (either because of law or custom) tend not to have phantom traffic jams.
- It's very difficult for an individual to solve the problem unilaterally. Now that you know the cause of phantom traffic jams, you can try leaving more space between you and the next car when you drive on highways. But chances are, another driver will simply pull in front of you. Other capacity limits—like the number of lanes on the road— are probably beyond your ability to change.
- The most intuitively comforting solutions (such as following too closely when you're in a hurry) turn out to make the problem worse.
- Few people have much information about the problem. While you're in the traffic jam, you don't know how long it will last or what its cause has been. You won't know until you leave—or rather are propelled out the other end like a ball shot from a pitching machine.
- Finally, the system innately resists our motivation to change it. Imagine being in a hurry, stuck in a phantom traffic jam. During those 10 to 15 minutes of stop-and-go driving, you may care passionately about the causes of the problem. You might imagine how the highway could be better designed; you might fantasize about building a new lane or about legislating new restrictions on tailgating. But as soon as you leave the system, most likely you'll forget all about it.

In many ways, phantom traffic jams are much like school systems. Problems are complex, with few people having complete information about their causes, effects, and durations. The people stuck in them— students—often feel powerless to change anything significant. They can only endure and imagine how it might be different. As soon as they leave the school, however, they'll stop caring nearly so much—unless they become teachers themselves or have children of their own. Even then, they won't care in the same way.

To actually change the system causing the phantom traffic jams and eliminate them in the future, what would you do? One would have to consider changing a variety of factors, from highway designs to laws and policies to customs and values. There would be no clear or simple answers, and a large number of actions by many different people would be involved.

The dynamic of the phantom traffic jam—the emergent relationship among the cars on the road—is a structure. And in any complex system—whether it's a traffic jam or a classroom or a school district—it's the nature of the structures at play that most determine the behavior of the people within it.

STRUCTURES IN SCHOOL

What are the structures that most affect your school? They might include taken-for-granted hierarchical relationships, such as the division into elementary school, middle school, and high school. This is a structure. The social relationships into which students fall is a critically important structure (see "The Great Game of High School," page 380). The fact that English and Math have different intellectual heritages is a structure.

Another structure has to do with the relative shortage of qualified school leaders in many regions. It, in turn, is fueled by other structures which have to do with retirement ages, school budgets, and systems for training administrators.

Not all structures are that formal. Maybe there's a longstanding disagreement between two members of the board, both of whom have strong constituencies in town, and it's virtually impossible to get along with both of them—that's a structure.

It's easy to blame people for problems—to accuse people of being difficult or misguided. But when you see the structure behind the problem, you realize that just about anybody placed in that position in the structure would feel immense pressure to do the same thing.

Sometimes, if you want to change behavior, it's enough to raise awareness of the structures at play. Sometimes you have to enlist people in trying to change the structure. And sometimes you can figure out new structures to put in place to establish new behavior—if you recognize the feedback-related forces at play.

Systems Basics: The Nature of Feedback

Systems continually send signals to themselves, through circular loops of cause-and-effect relationships. Systems thinkers call this "feedback," because the effect of the system "feeds back," often after one or two intermediate stages, to influence itself. Since the mid-1950s, beginning with the work of Jay Forrester at the Massachusetts Institute of Technology, the behavior of feedback has been studied in depth through mathematical modeling, through computer simulations, and through the observation of systems in the real world. The result is a set of tools for mapping and charting systems that Forrester calls "system dynamics."

ST

Familiarity with system dynamics gives you a language for talking about complex events. Today, more and more people, in schools and elsewhere, understand that language. Its grammar starts here.

There are two basic kinds of feedback mechanisms. When you understand them, and how they operate separately and together, you gain a great awareness of the systems around you. They are both reinforcing processes, which accelerate and provide growth, and balancing processes, which oscillate and provide stability.

This section and the section that follows were adapted in part from the article "Systems Thinking in the Classroom," by Nina Kruschwitz, Debra Lyneis, and Lees Stuntz in the first edition of *Schools That Learn*.

REINFORCING PROCESSES: WHEN SMALL CHANGES BECOME BIG

Reinforcing processes are a form of feedback that leads to exponential growth or decline—either in nature or in human affairs. When a plant or animal is born, it begins to voraciously consume whatever it needs. The more it consumes, the faster it grows. The faster it grows, the faster it continues to consume. Its growth accelerates, faster and faster, until it runs up against other forces that begin to slow it down. In all reinforcing processes, small changes become larger. High birth rates lead to higher birth rates; industrial growth begets more industrial growth.

To grasp the often-surprising ramifications of exponential growth, consider an interest-bearing bank account. At first, an interest rate of, say, 5 percent per year, would generates only a few extra dollars each time it accrued. But if you left the interest in the account, the rate of growth would increase as interest began to accumulate on the old interest. After fifty years of depositing $1000 per year (at 5 percent interest), you'd have more than $231,000, more than four times as much as you would have gotten from depositing the same amounts in a piggy bank year after year. That is a virtuous spiral—albeit one that takes a long time to show its virtue.

But you'd be caught in a vicious spiral instead if, instead of investing money, you went into a growing spiral of debt. At first it would seem as if you were paying only small sums in interest. But over time, the balance you owed would grow with increasing speed, especially if the interest rate was more like 15 percent than 5 percent.

Don't underestimate the explosive power of reinforcing processes:

in their presence, linear thinking can always get us into trouble. For example, schools often assume that they will face steady, incremental growth in their need for increasing classroom space. They are startled to discover that when their new facilities arrive, the demand has already overshot the new supply of desks. It almost seems that the increased availability of space is creating a surge in the school population—and, in fact, that may be happening, by drawing people into the school system.

When someone remarks that "The sky's the limit," or "We're on a roll," or "This is our ticket to heaven," you can bet there's a reinforcing process nearby, headed in the "virtuous" direction the person prefers. When people say, "We're going to hell in a handbasket," or "We're taking a bobsled ride down the chute," or "We're spiraling to oblivion," you know they're caught in the other kind of reinforcing process—the vicious cycle.

The snowball at the center of this causal loop diagram represents a reinforcing process. As the school expands capacity to keep up with its growing student population, the community becomes more attractive, and more families seek to live there—putting accelerating pressure on the school for yet more expansion. Until some limit is reached, expansion in the district will not just continue but accelerate.

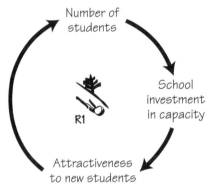

Number of students

School investment in capacity

R1

Attractiveness to new students

Often the critical factor that determines how the reinforcing process will go is the availability of information. Systems expert David Kreutzer points out that the number of supporters of Mahatma Gandhi's protest against the British continued to grow exponentially because there were well-established channels of communication among the Hindus who protested with him. Their practice of nonviolent resistance gave them an ongoing forum within which to keep meeting and planning new actions. By contrast, the spontaneous uprising in China's Tiananmen Square in 1989 had no underlying feedback loop, no structure for communication. The people gathering in the square did not know enough about each other to keep meeting after the tanks rolled toward the protest. In 2011, access to information through social media created a powerful feedback loop that generated sustained political uprisings in Tunisia, Egypt, Libya, and Syria.

A reinforcing process, by definition, is going to end. Whether virtuous or vicious, a cycle cannot grow forever. Somewhere, sometime, it will run up against at least one roadblock. For example, the burgeoning population of a school district eventually reaches a limit on the availability of room or else on the supply of new people eager to settle there. The interest-bearing savings account can reach a limit as well—sooner or later you'll need to spend that money, perhaps on a child's college education. Some limits may not appear in our lifetime, but you can rest assured that they will appear. There is no such thing as infinite growth.

BALANCING PROCESSES: PUSHING STABILITY AND RESISTANCE

Balancing processes ensure that every system never strays far from its "natural" operating range. Whether it's a human body's homeostatic cravings, an ecosystem's balance of predator and prey, or a company's "natural" expenses, you'll find that, no matter how you try to shift or change them, they'll tend to revert back to the way they were.

Balancing processes are often found in situations that seem to be self-correcting and self-regulating, whether the participants like it or not. If people talk about "being on a roller coaster" or "being flung up and down like a yo-yo," then they are caught in one type of balancing structure. If caught in another type, they may say, "We're running into walls," or "We can't break through the barrier," or "It's like a whack-a-mole; we deal with the problem in one place, and it pops up somewhere else." Despite the frustration they often engender, balancing processes aren't innately bad: They ensure, for example, that there is usually some way to stop a runaway vicious reinforcing spiral. Our survival depends on the many balancing processes that regulate Earth, the climate, and our bodies. The balancing process often represents a built-in intelligence to the system—something that keeps it moving toward the same stable goal, no matter how it is perturbed. It's as if the system itself "knows" "how things ought to be" and will do everything in its power to return to that state.

Balancing processes are always bound to a target—a point or goal for which the forces of the system are implicitly set. Whenever current reality doesn't match the target of a balancing process, the resulting gap (between the target and the system's actual performance) generates the kind of pressure that the system cannot ignore. The greater the gap, the greater the pressure. Until you recognize the gap and identify the goal or constraint that drives it, you won't understand the behavior of the balancing process.

Thus, causal loop diagrams for balancing processes don't show just the activity around the cycle but the external "goal" that influences it (usually drawn inside a box). They may also include a visible "delay," which generally changes the behavior of the system.

One common example of balancing processes in education is the perennial tension around grades. Everyone understands that there are severe problems in grading—the imprecision of having students' work reduced to numbers, the initiative-sapping impact of grade inflation, and the numbing effort that teachers must make to grade students and track their progress numerically. Every once in a while, discontent about grades rises high enough that a reform is initiated. But then the balancing processes of the system kick in. Students and parents alike need evaluation of their work. College and job applications require grades. And human competitiveness, whether natural or socially conditioned, comes into play. In a vacuum, with all these balancing forces arrayed against it, a grading reform effort will shut down. The problems of grading will return. Any serious reform effort would have to address the forces that keep this balancing loop in place.

DELAYS: WHEN THINGS HAPPEN…EVENTUALLY

There are often points in both reinforcing and balancing processes where a chain of influence takes a particularly long time to play out. Delays are caused because change often takes place in a flow. For instance, if a school system has a twelfth-grade class of 300 students and a kindergarten class of 800 students, the high school administrators can count on the fact that they will need to hire more teachers and expand facilities—but perhaps not right away. It could take eight years for that larger cohort to arrive at the door.

Delays can have enormous influence in the system, frequently accentuating the impact of other forces. This happens because delays are subtle: usually taken for granted, often ignored altogether, nearly always underestimated. In reinforcing processes, delays can shake our confidence, because growth doesn't come as quickly as expected. In balancing processes, delays can dramatically change the behavior of the system. When unacknowledged delays occur, people tend to react impatiently, usually redoubling their efforts to get what they want. This results in unnecessarily violent oscillations.

When trying to understand a system, it is very helpful to identify the most significant delays in the system. For example, consider the time it takes to find a new administrator. This is a time of paralysis for the system. Administrative capabilities drain out quickly. Yet the impact on performance may be

A simple balancing loop with delay diagram of a system with high administration turnover. It starts with the existence of a gap between the school system's "results" (the performance and learning of its children) and the public expectations held by parents in the district. If the gap is too great, public reaction leads administrators to quit or be fired, leading to an increase in turnover. This changes administrator effectiveness (often for the worse but always in a perceptible way), leading to a change (after a delay) in the school system results. Focusing on developing administrators' leadership capability and skills (through mentoring, training, and having them teach in the schools) would be much more productive. It would also be less costly to talk openly about the public's expectations for the schools.

School system results

Public expectations

Administration effectiveness

Public reaction

B1

Administration turnover in district

slow, because performance takes time to deplete. Therefore, a perceived crisis in performance may occur after a new administrator is already in place. That may lead to public disappointment, months before the new administrator's practices have had time to show any effect.

Using Behavior-Over-Time Diagrams

Diagramming the pattern of system behavior over time can help you see, very quickly, what types of systemic processes are probably at work. There's a lot of power in sharing perceptions about the system's current and past performance this way. It helps you move back from your assumptions about the problem to the actual data, by asking: "What are some important graphs about this problem?" Finally, since many classic systems stories (the archetypes that we describe later in this section) display their own distinctive patterns of behavior, behavior-over-time diagrams can be terrific diagnostic tools. Behavior-over-time graphs have an X and a Y axis, and the X (horizontal) axis always represents time. The Y shows whatever variable is changing over time.

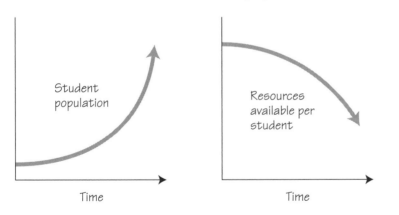

Reinforcing process: These behavior-over-time diagrams show the apparent pattern of behavior from the reinforcing process on page 136. The school population starts small but begins to grow dramatically, while the resources available for each student, after a modest decline at first, drop off precipitously. These diagrams show evidence that at least one reinforcing process is operating.

In classroom teaching, behavior-over-time graphs can enhance any curriculum, at any grade level, and don't require any special equipment. Most students already have seen graphs in some form, and that familiarity provides a good foundation for an introduction to systems thinking skills. Behavior-over-time graphs can be a first step to using more advanced tools—or they can be used alone to help students think about patterns of change over time.

For example, third-grade students in Carlisle, Massachusetts, were introduced to the "Mammoth Extinction Game," a curriculum-based activity, as part of their learning about the ice ages in social studies. They

This represents the visible system behavior for a balancing process common in schools: the inability to raise test scores. As the pressure for academic performance becomes stronger, courses and grading become tougher. Students' scores go up in the first flush of attention, then down as students and teachers get used to the new system, and then up again, more gently, with each new big push for performance. The oscillation continues until the district hits some "natural" level of expected performance.

For more examples and guidance, see Gene Stamell with Debra Lyneis, *Everyday Behavior-Over-Time Graphs* (Creative Learning Exchange, 2001); http://www.clexchange.org/ftp/documents/x-curricular/CC2001-11EverydayBOTGs.pdf. We also drew heavily on a previous paper, "Getting Started with BOTGs: Four Curriculum Examples," by Gayle Richardson and Debra Lyneis. There is also a short guide to common patterns of behavior in *The Fifth Discipline Fieldbook*, page 122.

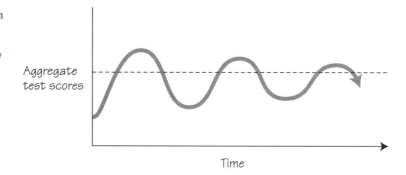

rolled dice to represent births and deaths of mammoths; with each round of the game, the group's herd declined. Although all the graphs showed the same general downward trend, each group's graph was different—demonstrating the variability inherent in living systems.

⟩⟩ The Mammoth Game and its use in the classroom is described in more detail on page 279.

Similarly, in a tenth-grade English class in Portland, Oregon, students reading *Lord of the Flies* by William Golding worked in groups to graph how the characters' level of power changed as the events of each chapter unfolded. "Their task was to trace the thread of the characters over the course of the book," said Tim Joy, their teacher. "They finished at home and when they came in the next day, I could barely get through attendance. They were showing each other their graphs, and their arguments were already unfolding. Even in the best of circumstances in honors classes, we'd never had such animated discussions. I had them get together and do graphs representing their consensus viewpoint. That was a stroke of dumb luck, because it led to homework where they chose a graph they disagreed with and stated their cases in a brief paper. Once I saw the students' responses—the degree of participation, the level of thinking and conversation—I knew this was a tool I wanted to keep using."

Working with Causal Loops

Ordinary spoken and written language is linear. We speak of one factor "causing" another: "A causes B." But systems are circular. Factor A never causes factor B; factors A and B continually influence each other. "Causal loop" diagrams (CLD) show that influence as arrows, from one element to another and back again. The symbol at the center shows what kind of feedback is involved. For reinforcing processes, we use a "snowball" and/or the letter R. For balancing processes, we use a "balance beam" and/or the letter B.

In the classroom, many teachers are drawn to causal loops and develop an intuitive feel for mapping out cause and effect. The diagrams can be useful in providing a quick visual that shows how different elements in a system influence one another. And they identify circular feedback: As different parts of a system affect each other, causes become effects which in turn become causes. For this reason, while behavior-over-time graphs describe "what" happens in a system, causal loops are particularly valuable in describing "why" a change takes place.

CLDs can depict fairly sophisticated and complex systems, but it's best to keep them simple at first. In talking with younger students about causal loop diagrams, you may need to read "around" the loop several times before they understand the idea that the original cause influences the effect and the original effect influences the cause, again and again. In loops that have more than two variables, reading around the loop starting from each variable will help reinforce the idea that each arrow represents a causal relationship. Since all variables in a causal loop diagram must be able to increase or decrease, choosing the right language is critical. Guide students to choose variables that are nouns, and talk about each element. What does it mean to say it's increasing? What does it mean to say it's decreasing?

Causal loop diagrams may come across, at first, as very abstract. Elementary school students will be able to understand one drawn and explained to them but probably won't be able to create one themselves. Even in sixth-grade classrooms, some teachers have found that only about half of the students, if given enough information about a system, could create a correct feedback loop from it. But students could add to or refine an existing causal loop diagram.

Reading comprehension becomes very important in using this tool, and if you're using non-curricular sources—newspapers, magazines, or research students conduct themselves—the information needed to complete a feedback loop is often difficult to find. In a unit on the American Revolution, for example, students in Brunswick, Georgia, spent several weeks reading, discussing, watching videos, and doing hands-on activities before they drew a causal loop as a class.

Finally, despite their seeming complexity, causal loop diagrams represent an oversimplified view of a situation and should never be mistaken for a complete analysis. They were originally developed solely as a communication tool, a simple visual way to show the basic dynamics of a system to others. They can be a wonderful way to begin a conversation,

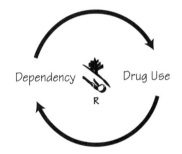

In this simple reinforcing causal loop diagram, as drug use increases, dependency on the drug increases, which in turn increases drug use, and so on.

A group of middle school students (part of the GIST program in Brunswick, GA) studying the American Revolution came to understand the role of escalating action and reaction when they developed a causal loop diagram that illustrated how colonists' anger at acts passed by the British Parliament served only to prompt the British to pass even more restrictive acts.

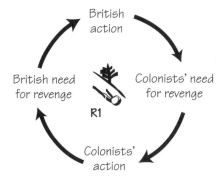

British action

Colonists' need for revenge

R1

British need for revenge

Colonists' action

but they don't necessarily lead students to understand a system in depth. For that type of exercise, being more specific about the rate of change and the subtle impact of one change on another, many systems experts turn to stock-and-flow diagrams.

Drawing Your Own Loops

If you are new to systems thinking, you may feel intimidated by these diagrams. The best way to deal with that is to draw some reinforcing and balancing loops of your own. Don't try to be "right" in your diagnosis, but try to provoke your own (and your team's) consideration of the same old problems from a new, unfamiliar perspective.

Pick a situation in your own school (or elsewhere) that accelerates. What are the factors that reinforce each other? Make a loop. Then try a balancing loop, or a system that promotes stability. Here are some guidelines for drawing the diagrams:

- Start with one key variable—a noun describing some element that you know is involved in the system. Then ask: "What are the other elements that affect that variable?" Work backward around the structure. About each element, ask: "What is causing changes in this element? What influences it to vary?"
- If you get stuck, try working forward: "What is the effect when this variable changes?" "What other elements must change?"
- Draw arrows to show the direction of movement. It doesn't matter if the loops go clockwise or counterclockwise but try to set them up so you (and other people) can easily follow the story.
- Put an R or snowball in the center of the diagram if the system tends toward runaway growth or decline and a B or balance beam in the center if it oscillates toward some kind of target or stability.
- Keep the loops simple. Draw as few elements as possible and label each element as simply and concisely as possible, aiming for clear forces that can be easily recognized. Use terms like "Student population," "Test scores," "Public response," instead of "Demographic trends," "Evaluations and metrics," or "Empathy and reaction."
- Give your variable elements generic names that don't predetermine

movement in any one direction, even if you anticipate only one type of change. For example, you may expect a burgeoning student population, but "Number of students" is a better label than "More students every year," because it will still apply no matter what happens.

- It's particularly valuable to include elements that are at least partly under your influence. "Amount of money invested in staff development" may be a factor that influences teacher turnover. If so, and if you control the staff development budget, this may help you recognize some of the leverage in the system.

- Use the loops as the starting point for conversations. After drawing a system diagram, show it to other people. Talk them through the story by starting at one element and describing a typical chain of causality. ("Public reaction leads to higher levels of administrator turnover. This in turn causes quality to go down, leading to poorer results and more public reaction.") Ask their opinion about what elements have been left out and whether the story, as a whole, rings true to them. Invite them to make up their own causal loops.

System Archetypes

System archetypes use causal loop diagrams to show generic stories in systems thinking—common patterns or structures that show up again and again in different settings. About a dozen of these have been identified and documented over the years. They can often be used to quickly reach a potential solution for a systemic problem.

These archetypes are invaluable for communicating about simple structures, but they do have one danger: they also easily lead people to overconfidence. Jeff Potash, the associate director of the Waters Center for System Dynamics at Trinity College of Vermont, cautions that people who are predisposed to want an easy answer will fall back on an archetype without even asking the right questions. Students who have spent years in a school system that values answers over questions might well be tempted to short-circuit their exploration in favor of being "right."

But allowing for that problem, the archetypes make it easy to recognize recurring systemic patterns that crop up in different situations—including the students' own lives. As students notice the similarities in these diagrams, a conversation about generic structures can emerge naturally. A middle school boy, talking to an administrator about his problems with a teacher, was reminded of the "Escalation" archetype he had studied the year before. Escalation is the archetype of arms races and advertising wars, one in which both sides get trapped in costly rivalry. He realized that he and the teacher kept trading comments that made both of them more and more unhappy; they were in effect stockpiling a nuclear arsenal of hurt and misunderstanding.

An Index to System Archetypes

- **Fixes That Fail:** A quick solution with unexpected long-term consequences—this page
- **Limits to Growth:** Improvement accelerates, seemingly unstoppable—and then suddenly stalls—covered in *The Fifth Discipline* page 94 and *The Fifth Discipline* page 129
- **Success to the Successful:** Things get better for "winners" and worse for "losers"—page 372
- **Shifting the Burden:** Systems unconsciously favor short-term, problematic, addictive solutions—page 375
- **Tragedy of the Commons:** An unmanaged, shared resource is overtaken and collapses—page 545

Fixes That Fail: The Forced Change

One of the most prevalent archetypes is called "Fixes That Fail." In short, this is when a quick fix applied to a complex problem ends up having long-term consequences. It shows up throughout history and literature—for example, in the Trojan Horse story, in Romeo and Juliet, and in the causes of the American Revolution and The Great Depression. And it probably shows up in your school system as well.

A well-meaning and talented principal initiates curriculum reform, the teachers come on board because they have no choice, and the principal micromanages the effort. Implicitly he says: "We're going to move forward, whether you like it or not." On the surface these efforts look successful because of the good things that happen. Change occurs, sometimes very quickly, and teachers admit that they learned something. But because the change is mandated, the teachers don't feel they own it; it isn't theirs. There is thus a tremendous cost. Teachers begin to teach "to the principal"; they prepare lessons they think the principal wants to see instead of what the students need. As the teachers close their doors, morale and innovation decline along with communication. Ironically, some of these principals are great educators in their own right, but their forceful influence as managers leads to the opposite of good education.

With the "Fixes That Fail" archetype in mind, a principal might approach curriculum reform differently. One strategy for dealing with this archetype is to increase awareness of the unintended consequences—to acknowledge openly that the "fix" is just the first effort to alleviate the symptom (and perhaps to meet state guidelines). This could be followed, in short order, by a sincere effort to create a teacher-designed curriculum, ideally in a team-based process that draws forth teachers' creativity and passion. Another strategy is to cut back on the severity and intensity of the fix: to set up curriculum reform in stages, so that people can adapt to it and make it their own. Finally, the most effective curriculum reform initiatives avoid this "fix" entirely. They start an open inquiry on the problems with the curriculum. Maybe the real problem has to do not with the subject matter but the way it is taught, and training in new classroom techniques (such as the use of simulations or team projects alongside lectures) will lead to better results.

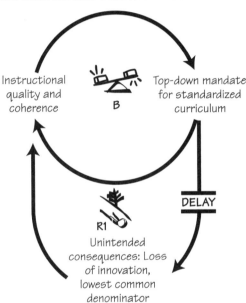

A "Fixes That Fail" archetype applied to curriculum reform: Faced with inconsistencies from classroom to classroom and poor performance by some students (the problem symptoms), a principal (or a state governing body) institutes a top-down curriculum reform program. At first, there is an immediate improvement—teachers follow the guidelines and poorer classes improve. But over time, there are unintended consequences: Teachers lose interest in innovating, if only because they feel they have no time. After the initial burst of improvement, classes return to their previous levels of quality. As the feeling of accomplishment fades, overall performance subsides even more.

Stock-and-Flow Diagrams

Since nonlinear equations are needed to describe accumulations and exponential growth, and since these equations are generally too complex for people to manipulate beyond a rudimentary level, system dynamics often involves computer modeling and simulation—especially in the classroom and the school.

Causal loop diagrams, while they capture the universal structures embedded in, say, a reinforcing process, do not spell out the unique qualities of a particular situation. For instance, a causal loop that shows student population growth might show that investment in school activities leads to more students moving in. But how much investment is necessary before the school system crosses a threshold of attractiveness? How quickly will new students enter the district, and what does that speed depend on? To predict (or anticipate) a system's behavior in the future, you must look at the situation with more precision.

That's the value of the stock-and-flow diagram. It helps the student of systems specify the interrelationships in an explicit, mathematical way. Every arrow in the diagram can be linked to a formula, which allows one to comment not just on the assumptions underlying the relationship but on the exact way that one element influences another. Stock-and-flow diagrams are also a necessary next step for simulating the reinforcing process on computers.

A stock-and-flow diagram translates any sort of situation—even the most "qualitative," immeasurable situation—into five different kinds of mathematical entities:

1. "Stock" (shown in the diagram on the next page by the rectangle), representing the accumulation of some kind of quantity, either measurable or not. In this diagram, it is the number of students in the district this year, but it could also be the level of morale or the satisfaction parents feel with the school.
2. "Flow," representing the rates at which quantities flow into or out of the stock. Flows are like spigots on a faucet, controlling the amount of water moving, per minute or day, into a bathtub (a stock). Flows can also vary—rainfall per month is a flow that regulates the amount of water in a reservoir, adding copiously to it in the spring and sparingly in the summer. Understanding the pattern of flow is crucial, because it determines the delays in the system.
3. "Converter," representing factors that influence the rate of flow from one stock to another. For instance, the "attractiveness of new families per year in the district" is governed, in part, by the "school investment in capacity," along with other factors. In turn, it affects the rates of students entering and leaving the system.
4. "Connector," embodying the interrelationships among the other three types of elements, shown here by arrows. Each connector has a mathematical formula associated with it, explicitly defining the way that (for example) school investment will rise or fall as the number of students in the district changes.
5. "Cloud," represents areas that exist outside the system at hand, from which flows might originate (or to which they might discharge). In this diagram, clouds represent the population of students elsewhere in the nation.

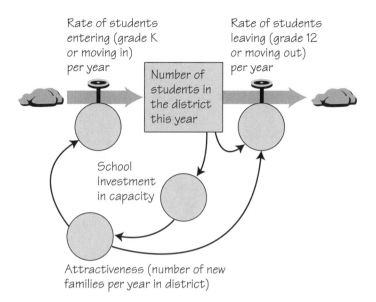

Rate of students entering (grade K or moving in) per year

Rate of students leaving (grade 12 or moving out) per year

Number of students in the district this year

School Investment in capacity

Attractiveness (number of new families per year in district)

Here is the same reinforcing process from page 136 presented in stock-and-flow form. The most significant "stock" or accumulated quantity—the number of students in the district each year—is influenced by two "flows"—the students entering the schools and the students leaving. These flows, in turn, are regulated in part by the attractiveness (the number of new families per year in the district) and, in turn, by the district's investment in new capacity. As the number of students goes up, the investment in capacity goes up, which contributes to higher rates for students entering that district.

A stock-and-flow diagram creates a model of the situation at hand—a model that can be programmed on a computer and tested against experience until you feel it is robust. The diagrams themselves are so versatile and variable, and yet so concrete, that they are particularly valuable for young people. Thinking in terms of inflows and outflows can lead to a fundamental shift in thinking for students and adults alike.

One group of teachers learning about stocks and flows was working to understand why the population at a psychiatric hospital kept rising. Finally, the system dynamicist teaching the course said, "Well, where do the patients go? How do they leave the hospital?" For a moment, there was silence. There was, in fact, no place in the community for patients to go, no outpatient clinics or group homes; thus, no outflow.

To help students learn to see the inflows and outflows, teachers can ask questions about how those stocks build and change. What is accumulating? What is causing that increase? What causes a decrease? In the American Revolution, the colonists' anger didn't just continually increase. Certain actions by the British actually served to lower the stock of "anger." What were those? Kids who work through the story see that anger doesn't just keep building: There must be release valves somewhere.

Stocks and flows can be diagrammed or drawn using only paper and pencil or a chalkboard. As questions and conversations develop, teachers can keep track, using lists at the side, of possible factors that might influence flows through the system. And if you draw a well-defined stock-and-flow diagram, you are halfway to building a computer model.

A STOCK-AND-FLOW UNDERSTANDING OF A REAL-WORLD CRISIS

One place where stock-and-flow analyses have made a difference is in our understanding of climate change. Levels of human-caused carbon dioxide (CO_2) emissions—the primary component of greenhouse gases—have grown exponentially throughout the industrial age. Today the level of CO_2 in the atmosphere is 35 percent higher than at any time in the past half million years, leading to a consensus among scientists that human actions are the primary causal factor of a very dangerous trajectory in the global climate.

The critical distinction is between the "stock" of CO_2 (the amount present in the atmosphere) and the "flow" of new emissions each year. This simple distinction has confused many people, including many in leadership positions who believe that stabilizing the flow of emissions, as mandated by the Kyoto Protocol in 1997, would be enough to solve the problem. The current flow of global CO_2 emissions is about 8 billion tons of carbon per year worldwide (the scientific convention is to measure emissions in tons of equivalent carbon). This is more than 2.5 times the amount—about 3 billion tons—that is removed per year from the atmosphere, either absorbed by natural biomass like trees, plants, and plankton, or dissolved in oceans.

The difference between "inflows" and "outflows" of CO_2 in the atmosphere works like water in a bathtub: As long as the inflow exceeds the outflow, the bathtub continues to fill. At some point, the tub will overflow. In other words, CO_2 levels will cross a threshold at which the effects of climate change are irreversible and are devastating to humans and other species. No one knows exactly when the bathtub will overflow, but the pace of climate change (such as melting glaciers and ice caps and increased weather instability) is leading to a consensus among scientists and some business leaders that catastrophic overflow can be avoided only by rapidly reducing emissions to equal or below the rate at which CO_2 is removed from the atmosphere in the next two to three decades. To achieve this will require a 60- to 80-percent reduction of worldwide emissions in 20 years. This is the "80/20 challenge" facing industrial society.

The source: Linda Booth Sweeney and John Sterman, "Understanding Public Complacency about Climate Change," *Climatic Change* (February 2007). Also see Peter Senge, Bryan Smith, Nina Kruschwitz, Joe Laur, and Sara Schley, *The Necessary Revolution: How Individuals and Organizations are Working Together to Create a Sustainable World* (Doubleday, 2008), and Peter Senge, Bryan Smith, and Nina Kruschwitz, "The Next Industrial Imperative," *strategy+business*, Summer 2008, www.strategy-business.com/article/08205.

Also see the dynamic video of this model, http://climateinteractive.org/simulations/bathtub.

Simulations and Computer Models

Computer simulations start as stock-and-flow diagrams with equations defining each of the interrelationships. The variables within the model can be manipulated by students to learn quickly how the elements in a system interact. Building a model can be as simple as experiment-

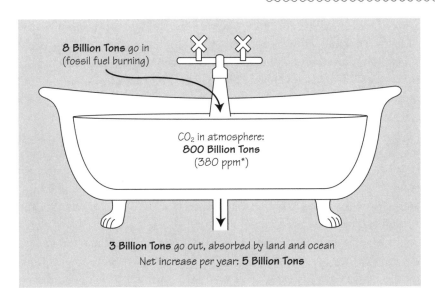

8 Billion Tons go in
(fossil fuel burning)

CO_2 in atmosphere:
800 Billion Tons
(380 ppm*)

3 Billion Tons go out, absorbed by land and ocean
Net increase per year: 5 Billion Tons

This bathtub represents the atmosphere, with annual inputs and outputs of carbon dioxide (CO_2). No one knows precisely when the tub will "overflow"—when climate change will accelerate dramatically and irreversibly. (1 part per million of CO_2 equals 2.1 billion tons of carbon equivalent.)

ing with one variable to see how changes in it affect an output graph. But models can be complex programs in their own right, with "pop-up" windows that ask questions or provide information as a student moves through the program.

For more on simulations and computer models in the classroom, see pages 275–292.

There is a great deal of value in working with existing simulations, to learn about the dynamics of a particular system. The simulation lets students play "What if…?" trying out different possible scenarios, comparing the results, and developing a much stronger understanding of the system as a whole. This requires lots of classroom discussion. Before each "run" of the simulation, it's important to ask students to predict how the graph will change as they change the probability numbers. Otherwise, they are simply playing a computer game. Comparing the actual results, in graph form, to their expectations leads to questions about why the system might have operated differently from what they predicted— and to larger questions.

Not every teacher will move to building models as part of the curriculum. It takes time to become comfortable with the software, and computer resources are still limited in some districts. But for those who do, the excitement and satisfaction of seeing what kids can do can more than make up for their own learning curve.

Using software presents a new, sometimes unexpected difficulty: debugging. Diana Fisher, a writer and educator who has pioneered using systems thinking in mathematics classes, once spent a week and a half with a student trying to figure out why the student's computer model didn't work. Finally they realized that the student was using inconsistent units of measurement—kilometers in one part of the model and meters in another. This was a valuable lesson—and one which, as she pointed out to the class, they had seen illustrated in the news several times with the Hubble space telescope and other hugely expensive projects.

A group of students from Bromfield High School in the town of Harvard, Massachusetts—with very little STELLA (a computer modeling program) experience—wanted to model something about their own community. The principal suggested looking at the school's yearly budgeting process. Larry Weathers, a science teacher who worked with the students, found a generic model for "trust and control" that the students could modify and build from. Once they played with and understood the model, they decided they needed to hear the perspectives of various parties involved in the budgeting process. They interviewed administrators and school committee members about the hurdles in the budgeting process. The students found that too much trust was just as destructive to a successful process as too much mistrust. Too much trust implied the possibility of collusion, which led to mistrust; too little indicated an inability to work together and reach compromises. A balanced amount of trust and scrutiny allowed both parties to reach consensus.

After developing the model, they showed it to the people they had interviewed and explained how it worked. The adults agreed it was a valid model and thanked the kids. That year, the budget was developed and passed almost painlessly—and though no one credits the model, the students like to think that the opportunity they gave the adults to think about the process had something to do with it.

Pegasus Communications

Daniel Kim and Colleen Lannon, *Applying Systems Archetypes* (1997); Daniel Kim and Virginia Anderson, *System Archetype Basics* (1998); Daniel Kim, *Systems Thinking Tools: A User's Reference Guide* (1994); Virginia Anderson and Lauren Johnson, *Systems Thinking Basics* (1997); *The Systems Thinker*; and more from www.pegasuscom.com.

Over the past 22 years, a body of training material has emerged to help business people make sense of systems through causal loops and archetypes. It is updated and collected by Pegasus Communications, a conference and publishing enterprise that was founded around the time *The Fifth Discipline* was published. The "Systems Archetype Basics" series, in particular, is a comprehensive, well-written, well-packaged users' guide to the archetypes. Though it's aimed at business readers, we would recommend it wholeheartedly for school administrators and educators trying to understand the systemic structures at play in their schools and communities. We also recommend their ongoing newsletter, *The Systems Thinker*. All are available from www.pegasuscom.com.

7. Are You Smarter Than a Thermostat?
Why Reflection Matters in Learning to Learn

Nelda Cambron-McCabe, Janis Dutton

People learn in cycles, moving naturally between action and reflection, between activity and rest. These cycles enable us to improve what we do. Most of us are somewhat proficient at this cycle (sometimes called single-loop learning): observing our previous action, reflecting on what we have done, using that observation to decide how to change our next action, and applying that decision to another action—all for the sake of improving our behavior or the norms of our organization. One of the most effective ways for people and organizations to increase their capabilities is to tap into this rhythm consciously and deliberately—to create not only time to think but time for different types of thought and collective discussion in classrooms, schools and communities.

These cycles of learning are effective in simple systems, but they are insufficient in complex systems. Suppose, for example, the behaviors and norms you are improving are ineffective or inappropriate for dealing with the changes you face. Suppose the problem is not how well you do what you do but what you choose to do in the first place? Suppose the answers you've found came from the wrong questions?

For example, a southwestern school district recognized that its system of tracking students according to ability was fraught with problems. The "smart" kids got all the "good" teachers, and the average or below-average students got all the other teachers. District leaders believed their overall goal of a quality education for all students was being compromised. But tracking was the way they had always operated, and it was

We adapted this in part from "The Wheel of Learning," by Art Kleiner, Rick Ross, Bryan Smith, and Charlotte Roberts, in *The Fifth Discipline Fieldbook*, p. 59. We've changed the practice on the wheel somewhat to provide a version that, in our opinion, is more useful in schools. In addition, this change allowed us to expand on the "reflection" stage. This article also draws on the works of Chris Argyris and Donald Schön, particularly Schön's *The Design Studio* (International Specialized Book Service, 1985), and his study of the implications in understanding the pedagogy of the architectural design studios in higher education as a means to reform and revitalize higher education across the disciplines. His discussion of working with ambiguity and uncertainty and the creative aspects of reflection-in-action apply to learners of all ages. Our focus on reflection-about-action is influenced by John Dewey, Paulo Freire, Myles Horton, and John Goodlad.

a school board policy. So they studied their tracking program, planned a new one, and put it in place.

The district leaders were very proud, at first, of their new program. They had expanded the number of tracks from three to five, with teachers working across ability levels. Indeed, they believed they had the best tracking system in the state. But they still never reached their goal of a quality education for all students. Devastating messages—about which children had value and which did not—were still loudly communicated to the children, parents, and larger community. The district also never questioned if the tracking itself, in trying to address the needs of "good, smart, average, and below-average" students, may have played a significant role in contributing to students' abilities. The district improved their practices to the highest possible degree, but they never reached their goals because they never went to a deeper level of reflection: questioning their norms or the overall sense of what was appropriate to do.

Gareth Morgan uses the example of a household thermostat to illustrate the limits of a simple system. The thermostat moves through the single-loop cycle of monitoring the environment for deviation from the set temperature (or norm) and correcting it. A thermostat, though, using this single loop, cannot determine if the preset temperature is appropriate for the people in the room. And since the thermostat cannot question the established governing variables—goals, rules, and values—or consequences underlying the set temperature, it cannot change its behavior and learn to do its job more effectively or responsibly.

A truly effective contribution to a system—akin to the thermostat changing the temperature according to the needs of the room's inhabitants—would require engaging in a second learning cycle. In this second cycle, connected to the first, the organization's norms would be subjected to critical scrutiny. Morgan calls this two-cycle approach "double-loop learning"; we also call it "learning to learn."

By stretching out time for reflection to incorporate double-loop learning (or thinking about the way they think) and deliberately challenging their own norms, attitudes, and assumptions, people can begin to understand the ways that their own choices (both conscious and unconscious) may contribute to the frustration they feel or the effectiveness of their organization.

Because the double-loop cycle questions norms people take for granted and often leads to new choices that feel uncomfortable at first, it is easily dismissed. According to Morgan and others in organizational research, organizations rarely engage in double-loop learning. In fact, the bureaucracies of many organizations actually impede this learning process. Yet it is this reflective, self-questioning ability that enables organizations to learn to learn.

To be smarter than a thermostat in any project or undertaking, develop a process like the one shown on this page. Give each stage below deliberate attention before you move to the next one and be prepared to go back and repeat if necessary.

OBSERVING

Focusing attention on an action you have taken. You might start with a just-completed project to learn from your experiences.

This type of observing is known as reflection-*on*-action, looking back on the past. How well did it go? What were you thinking originally? What assumptions or attitudes (what mental models) led you there?

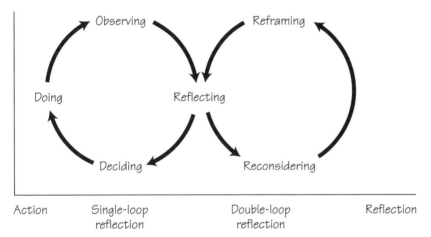

| Action | Single-loop reflection | Double-loop reflection | Reflection |

Reflection-*in*-action happens in the present, such as when something unexpected occurs and you need to shift course while you can still affect the outcome of the unfolding situation or project. What is going on here? What else looks odd? Why is this unexpected? How have you been thinking about this? What might you consider now?

Reflection-*about*-action encompasses the past, present, and future. Why are we proposing *this* action? What were/are/might be the broader and longer-term consequences of this decision?

REFLECTING (DOUBLE-LOOP)

Considering the implications of our observations and drawing conclusions from them. This stage in the cycle opens the door for new ideas and possibilities for action by questioning whether operating norms and assumptions are appropriate. Double-loop reflection contains at least two

For more about the concept of "double-loop learning," see Gareth Morgan, *Images of Organization*, (Sage Publications, Inc, 1996) pp. 86–88. Morgan bases his concepts on the work of Chris Argyris and Donald Schön: See their collaborative works *Theory in Practice* (Jossey-Bass, 1974) and *Organizational Learning: A Theory of Action Perspective* (Addison-Wesley, 1978). Donald Schön referred to the second loop as "reframing" in his book *The Reflective Practitioner* (Basic Books, 1983).

distinct components that together make up the inquiry about appropriateness. Each has its own set of questions to ask:

■ **Reconsider:** Start by reconsidering your basic assumptions and conclusions and the reasoning that led you to them. This is a form of self-questioning. "Is this project appropriate? Who wins and who loses? Is this the right way to do this project? What are the collective views of reality (the mental models) that underlie our choices? What will be the consequences of a new approach? What values are we communicating? Are the theories (and values) we are espousing the theories-in-use?"

⦃⦄ Tools of systems thinking can help here, particularly "The Iceberg," page 126.

■ **Reframe:** Articulate new possible guiding ideas and reflect on whether they will expand your capabilities. "How else might we approach our project? Is it the right project, the right goals, and the right objectives? Who decides? Who decides who decides? What are the conditions here that prevent us from taking risks? What images might we adopt of our preferred future and the most appropriate values and actions for us? Why are we doing this? To what end? What do we have to do to enact these images, values, and actions?"

For some people, this type of shared reflection will be a new experience. Even if they are accustomed to "reflecting" alone or with close friends, they probably haven't done it publicly, around a common table, on issues with this level of depth and uncertainty. That's why the skills of productive conversation—balancing inquiry with advocacy and the ladder of inference—are valuable here. Those tools help people talk safely about dangerous issues that come up.

⦃⦄ See the Ladder of Inference, page 101; and Balancing Advocacy and Inquiry, page 104.

DECIDING

Making a decision. W. Edwards Deming uses the word "planning" for this stage. But we use "deciding" because it incorporates an element of choice: "Here is the alternative we choose to take, and here are the reasons why." This stage assumes that group members have some influence on the overall process, whether it's a course or a school or a community team—not for the sake of showing they have "input," but because their participation in the decision is necessary and valued. Based on the reframing, the group thinks together about the nature of the steps it's going to take next. "What are we going to do? Who must be invited into the process? Based on past experience, what kinds of things are likely to come up? How will we design to anticipate them? What will our next step look like?"

DOING

Performing a task, with as much of an experimental frame of mind as possible. Now you, create, write, and produce. This can be carried out by team members individually—but it is coordinated. All the time spent observing, building shared meaning through reflection, and jointly deciding turns the action into a meaningful initiative.

PUTTING THE CYCLE INTO PRACTICE

When you reach the end of the cycle, you move immediately back to the observing stage, perhaps with a formal postmortem. How well did it work out?

A tight project deadline or a high-pressure curriculum (such as those aimed at performance on a standardized test) might influence people to shortcut the cycle. Who has time for "observing" or "reflecting" when you're trying to drill your way through the material?

But the first two stages (observing and reflecting) are the most crucial parts of the cycle. If you spend enough time building shared meaning, then people have a much clearer sense of why an activity is important—and why they are doing it. This understanding can make all the difference, for instance, in whether a drill is painful and fruitless or whether it leads to better results. The "double-loop" part of the practice will not just save time, it will allow you to revisit your practices regularly.

Double-Loop Reflection on Your Current Policies

The questions below were developed for double-loop reflection about student assessment. You may find it helpful to modify them to reflect on any issue in your school or organization.

■ What are you doing now to accomplish your goals (for example, to measure student progress)? Why are you using this approach? What assumptions drive your approach?

■ Do your current actions make sense educationally?

■ Are you measuring what you think you are measuring?

■ Who benefits from the current approach? Who does not benefit?

These questions were adapted from "Tool: Single-Loop or Double-Loop Learning," by Nelda Cambron-McCabe, in *The Superintendent's Fieldbook: A Guide for Leaders of Learning* (reviewed on page 427).

- What beliefs, attitudes, and values prevent you from creating other alternatives?
- What are your aspirations for student learning?
- What aspect of your thinking must change to promote transformation of present practices?

Incorporating the Five Disciplines into Your Life

Working with all these tools and practices in a classroom is only a first step. A systems understanding becomes a lifelong source of perspective and capability. Becoming proficient with mental models and team learning gives you a stronger, deeper connection with others that builds throughout your life. Clarifying your aspirations, through personal mastery and shared vision work, will establish a creative orientation: a focus on generating your destiny, rather than either reacting to it or trying to control it.

In the rest of this book, we will draw upon all of the five disciplines in a wide variety of contexts. By incorporating these practices into your work life (and the rest of your life), you can build your own capacity. This in turn will contribute to increasing capacity and competence in the three systems of education: the classroom, the school, and the community.

Classroom

~~~~~~~~~~~~~~

III. Opening the Classroom Door

1. Creating Classrooms That Learn

It's the first day of the new school year. You're preparing, as a teacher, for the arrival of your students, and it seems as if the room itself holds its breath in quiet anticipation. The whiteboard has no marks on it yet (except for one stray comment, left from last year, where someone mistakenly used an indelible Sharpie.) You leaf through your agenda planner; over the next few months, those blank pages will fill with circles and cross-outs. The students will become so familiar that it will be hard to remember a time when you didn't know them. You check off a mental laundry list of questions: Do I have all the materials I need? What kinds of students will I have this year? Am I prepared to make a difference to them? What will the leaders be like? The committed learners? The challenges and challengers? You can feel the impending presence of the students, like the tingling in the air just before lightning strikes.

There is also a sense of lightning striking from outside. Six parents have already left messages for you to return their calls. The local newspaper just reported test scores for every school in the region. The assistant superintendent has returned from a curriculum conference bursting with ideas. You would be happy to work on the new curriculum committee if there was time in the day, but your planning periods have been cut. The school board has chosen new textbooks and rearranged the bus and cafeteria schedules; they're adding five or six extra students to each class to save money.

If you are on the faculty of a college or university, you face a different array of pressures: teaching overloads, administrative duties, student counseling, recruitment, lack of time and support for innovation, and the expectation that you will "publish or perish." Or perhaps you're one of the increasing numbers of adjunct faculty members, hired to teach courses for almost no compensation, with security and status to match. No matter where you teach, there are social pressures and unprepared students, plus an array of institutional regulations and constraints. There is so much to complain about that the suffering of teachers is a latter-day cultural cliché.

Despite all this, veteran teachers return each year with renewed energy and enthusiasm; new people continually join the profession. There is always a deeper reason to teach: Teaching is an innately wonderful thing to do, and it is exhilarating to see students succeed because of the quality of your teaching. A classroom is one of the few workplace environments where people can experience their own commitment and creativity leading directly, and fairly quickly, to the development of others.

But the inner resources that teachers bring to the classroom—their creativity, training, capability, and love for teaching—will not sustain them indefinitely. What, then, do we know about designing classrooms that continually energize and engage the passion for learning of everyone within them? These questions lie at the heart of the "classroom" part of this book.

TEACHERS AS DESIGNERS OF THE LEARNING ENVIRONMENT

All teachers have moments when they step back and say to themselves: "Wow, this is what teaching is all about. Something went right today. I just wish I knew what it was!" If it was an interesting curriculum topic or an activity that generated discussion, they may be able to replicate the experience. Often though, they feel as if it will never be recaptured.

However, classrooms can be designed to lead people regularly to a state of "natural flow." That is the value of exercises that teach reflection and inquiry, of tools that foster systems understanding, and of taking the time for explicitly focusing on aspiration and collaboration. If what happens in the classroom is primarily a product of the ways people think and interact, then methods that improve the quality of thinking and interacting can make everything else that goes on in the classroom more powerful.

In a fourth-grade class in P.S. 116 in New York City, for instance, a group of so-called struggling readers is talking in a circle. They're not just parroting back to the teacher what they think she wants to hear; nor are they running around the room, unable to sit still. They're discussing the meaning of a book. "Usually I agree with you a little," says one boy to another. "But today I don't." A girl asks another, "When you said that it's a new stage, what would you call that stage?" In another room in the same school, a five-year-old kindergartner says she wants to "piggyback" a remark on another child's comment. This kind of conversational (and literary) sophistication doesn't happen naturally. It's the result of intensive design and implementation of new conversational practices in the classroom. In formal staff development and informal after-school meetings, teachers meet regularly to plan the ways they will introduce and set up conversation. They teach each other first, and then the children, to listen to each other closely, pull out "big ideas" from their reading, and build on each other's thoughts. "From September to October," says Nancy Bezzone, the teacher of that fourth-grade class, "it was strictly community-based work. And then the children were able to start opening up and taking some more risks and looking at each other as resources."

Classroom design can take many other forms as well. A second-grade teacher lets students correct their own homework. A principal plans recess so third graders can organize their own games instead of having them organized by adults. A sixth-grade student leads her parent-teacher conference, presenting a portfolio of work and diagramming her goals for middle school on the board. A middle school math teacher invites his students to challenge him; if they come up with a logical series of numbers, he'll guess the next one. Every day, they run out to the parking lot after him, trying to stump him. A university instructor asks that all students post their papers on the class blog to read, edit, and apply in their own projects. Another instructor sets aside a day at the beginning of the course for all students to establish their conversational ground rules.

The stories and techniques in this part of the book represent ways to develop better capabilities by redesigning the way teachers, students, and parents think and interact in class. They represent every kind of classroom subject and kind of school. In putting them together, we have relied on the experiences and precepts of dozens of educators. We have tried to be specific and helpful, without being prescriptive. We hope that you will find the next round of pages a valuable collection of tools and methods for creating classrooms that can learn.

ALL CHILDREN CAN LEARN

The concept that "all children can learn" is an established principle for many educational professionals. It is supported by research on cognitive and social capabilities that suggests that every child, every teenager, and every adult has the potential to achieve something significant—if conditions support learning and if each individual's capabilities are valued.

But as it's applied in many contexts, the principle is incomplete. It tends to be taken to mean that "all children are valuable in their own

The quotes from P.S. 116 came from *Building a Learning Community—A Portrait of a Public School District*, a videotape by High Performance Learning Communities Project (Learning Research and Development Center, University of Pittsburgh, 1998). For more about the LRDC, see p. 206.

way." Even in schools where this guiding idea is proclaimed, educators and parents often hold an implicit mental model about human potential: that once set, it is locked in and unchangeable.

This mental model leads to a culture of winners and losers, where some kids are labeled "advanced" and feel valued while others are written off as "uneducable," "disadvantaged," or simply "dumb." In such a culture, adults don't always invest the time and attention that would make a difference to the children in the latter group. This culture also encourages students and educators to focus on measurable, short-term assessments and goals, instead of on the more significant purpose of classrooms and schools: learning and enhancing the capacity to learn.

By contrast, a growing body of evidence suggests that human potential is not locked in at any point. Research into "neuroplasticity," a relatively new branch of neuroscience, suggests that the human brain is plastic, capable of forging new neural pathways all through life. Neuroplasticity appears to be triggered by conscious attention to new habits of thought and action. When students in a classroom practice a particular type of learning, day after day, this could affect the brain structure and function of everyone involved, including the teacher.

For more about neuroplasticity, see Jeffrey Schwartz and Sharon Begley, *The Mind and the Brain: Neuroplasticity and the Power of Mental Force* (HarperCollins, 2002).

See "The Cognitive Studies Group," page 404.

A learning classroom embodies not just the understanding that all children can learn, but that students learn in multiple ways, that their abilities are not fixed at birth, and that people can gain skills and capabilities to a remarkable extent at any age, no matter what their background or past experience. In such a class, students recognize that part of their purpose is making sure that everyone succeeds.

This is one reason why "instruction" in a learning classroom cannot simply mean "transmission"—the dissemination of information. If all students learn in different ways, the teacher must design and create an experience that enables everyone in the classroom to develop the knowledge, skills, capabilities, and awareness they need to participate in their world. In a learning classroom, it is relatively easy for the teacher to see what the learners need and want. The learners develop ways, both rapidly and slowly, to articulate their needs and wants. Both come together, over time, in a co-created experience of closing the gap between them. The classroom itself can take many different forms (as you'll see through this part of the book), but mutual respect, relevance to the learner's goals and needs, and spirit of discovery are common to all.

The full expression on the idea that all children can learn involves a deeper recognition of human potential. Embracing this idea does not mean turning a blind eye to the fallibilities of human nature. Children—indeed, people of any age—can be destructive or very difficult to reach. They may not fully understand their own potential or fully embrace the patience and dedication that they need to develop. Dealing with difficult people and situations is a critical challenge for any classroom and any teacher, from kindergarten onward, and for every community member as well. Used without reflection, the "learning organization" tools, (or, for that matter, any techniques) aren't enough to help with this challenge. It takes every ounce of our inner resources, throughout our lifetimes.

Nonetheless, the concepts that all children can learn and that everyone holds the potential to create a new future still holds true in every kind of human milieu and can be a source of strength for all. Taking this on as a guiding idea is perhaps the first step to creating a learning classroom. Hope draws many people to teach in the first place—remembering that all children can learn helps keep that hope alive.

CLASSROOM

LEXICON

The word "class" is derived from the Roman word *classis*, meaning a summons. It apparently evolved from the Indo-European base *qel* ("call") used in the sense of "a call to arms." In the sixteenth century, English speakers began using it to refer to groups of students, probably called to study together in the new ecclesiastic universities of that time. The Old English word for "chamber" was *cofa* (ancestor of modern English "cove" for "sheltered bay"). At that time, "room" meant simply "open space" (as its German relative *raum* still does). There is still a connotation of openness about the word. Classrooms are thus environments of continual openness, where people are called together to study the world around them.

2. Designing a Learning Classroom

Nelda Cambron-McCabe

PM
SV

Purpose:

For teachers to inquire deliberately into the assumptions that guide them as designers of the classroom.

Overview:

Instead of starting with the conventional aspects of design—such as the curriculum or arrangement of time— start with the image in your mind of a classroom that learns.

Participants:

Solo teachers or groups of teachers working together. This exercise can be a very effective starting point for getting involved, as a teacher, with creating a learning classroom.

When we turn our attention to classrooms, typically, our first thought is about teaching: What's going to be taught? How will it be taught? Who is going to be taught? And who is teaching? Our second thought has to do with success and achievement: How will performance typically be assessed? What will it take for the students to pass this grade level or course?

It's understandable that people focus on these two issues, but they are relatively low-leverage ways to increase the amount of learning in a classroom—at least if you are a teacher. The most leverage you have is in the design of the classroom as a learning environment. This exercise can help you create an environment that makes your presence, your relationships, and everyone's learning process more effective; in other words, it can help you begin to create a learning classroom.

STEP 1: "IF I HAD A LEARNING CLASSROOM…"

Imagine that you are teaching in the learning classroom you would design if you had complete freedom and control—including control over the curriculum and the forms of assessment used throughout the year. Think through, in your mind, the experience of being in that classroom. Ask yourself:

- What are students doing on a typical day?
- What structures, practices, or behaviors (on my part and the school's part) help these students thrive and succeed?
- How are the instructional activities—the lessons, assignments, and conversations—organized? Who organizes them? Who decides when they stop and start?
- Who makes the necessary decisions about students' learning goals and performance expectations—and what kinds of decisions are they typically making?
- How is the room set up? What types of equipment and supplies are present? What does it look like? How much time do students spend inside and outside the classroom?
- How do students interact with one another inside this classroom? (Do they engage one another in solving problems and working to-

gether? How do they help one another learn?)
- How do they interact with me, the teacher?
- What kinds of information do I, as the teacher, convey directly to students?
- What kinds of information do they get from books, magazines and newspapers, video, the Internet, games, and other resources? How do they find this information? What guidance, if any, do they receive in locating and working with it?
- What kinds of information do they get from learning experiences (and what kinds of experiences do they have)?

Write, draw, or dictate (using an audio or video recording device) your answers to these questions so that you will be able to retrieve them for later steps. To visualize the scene more vividly, write in the present tense. (Write: "Students work together to solve problems," not, "Students will work together to solve problems.") Be specific. Express, in as much detail as you can, the images, possibilities, and innovations that cross your mind. Don't worry about getting it "right" or "wrong," or whether it's "feasible," "realistic," or "politically awkward." You are designing your own learning classroom, and there will be plenty of chances to refine it later in this exercise.

STEP 2: ENHANCING THE DEFINITION

Now broaden your ideas by considering statements that other educators and writers on education have made envisioning the learning classroom. Take any statements from this list that fit your image and add them (perhaps changing them in the process) to further develop your ideal classroom image. If you are working through this exercise with a group of teachers, then you might include all of your individual responses from step 1 in this list, so you can further extend your definitions by building on each other's thinking.

In a learning classroom...

- "A variety of kinds of intelligence are cultivated, going far beyond the three Rs... Children develop a full range of the abilities that they will actually draw on to succeed." —Daniel Goleman
- "Students pursue problems that challenge and fascinate them and seek the knowledge and skills they need to follow through." —Seymour Sarason
- "Learners have substantial control over the purposes, the content, the form, and the pace of learning, and furthermore, the learner

This exercise is based in part on "Designing a Learning Organization: First Steps," by Rick Ross, Charlotte Roberts, and Bryan Smith, in *The Fifth Discipline Fieldbook*, p. 53.

If you have favorite quotes that might help others design a learning classroom, please use those in addition to or in place of these.

Sources for the quotes:

Daniel Goleman, *Emotional Intelligence: Why It Can Matter More than IQ*, 10th Anniversary Edition (Bantam, 2005), p. 37, reviewed on p. 207.

Seymour Sarason, *Letters to a Serious Education President* (Corwin Press, 2005), p. 97.

Peter Vaill, *Learning as a Way of Being: Strategies for Survival in a World of Permanent White Water* (Jossey-Bass, 1996), p. 58.

Nel Noddings, *The Challenge to Care in Schools: An Alternative Approach to Education*, 2nd Edition, (Teachers College Press, 2005), p. 63.

Mary Catherine Bateson, *Composing a Life* (Atlantic Monthly Press, 1989), p. 62.

Ellen Langer, *The Power of Mindful Learning* (Perseus, 1997), p. 135.

Robert J. Starratt, *The Drama of Schooling: The Schooling of Drama* (Taylor & Francis, 1989), p. 83.

Thomas Sergiovanni, *The Principalship: A Reflective Practice Perspective*, 6th Edition (Allyn & Bacon, 2009), p. 263.

Roland Barth, *Improving Schools from Within: Teachers, Parents and Principals Can Make the Difference* (Jossey-Bass, 1991), p. 44.

is the primary judge of when sufficient learning has occurred…" —Peter Vaill

■ "Students concentrate on problems instead of artificially and rigidly compartmentalized subjects." —Nel Noddings

■ "Students follow no single vision of excellence as a model for patterning their life; the real challenge lies in assembling something new from all the resources available for their creative imagination." — Mary Catherine Bateson

■ "We recognize that every inadequate answer is adequate in another context…Out of the questions of students come some of the most creative ideas and discoveries." —Ellen Langer

■ "There is a reflective mindset among students and teachers. They spend time thinking about the results of their actions, they puzzle out why some efforts work and others do not. Not only do they reflect after the fact, but they can bring this reflective frame of mind to the problem at hand." —Robert J. Starratt (discussing the theories of Donald Schön)

■ "Students collaborate by acting as a learning community that constructs shared understandings through sustained dialogue." —Thomas Sergiovanni

■ "Many conditions appear to foster profound learning: acknowledging one's inadequacies, posing one's own problems, risk taking, humor, collaboration with other learners, compassion, the importance of modeling, and the presence of a moral purpose." —Roland Barth

■ "All students are treated as gifted and talented students, because the gifts and talents of each child are sought out and recognized." —Henry Levin

■ "We must listen to each other's stories and we are each the authors of our own lives." —Daniel Pink

STEP 3: "WHAT WOULD IT BRING ME?"

One by one, consider each of the statements that you have written or chosen. Notice which elements intrigue you most as you think about these questions:

■ What sorts of benefits would happen as a result?
■ What would it bring to the students?
■ What would it bring to me personally?
■ How would it be different from the classroom where I teach now?

STEP 4: SELECTING AND REFINING THE TOP FIVE

Based on your deliberations in step 3, choose the five characteristics of a learning classroom that are most compelling to you. Don't worry about which ones seem plausible, easy to achieve, or most likely to win praise from the rest of the school. (You'll take up these concerns in step 5.) Try to include at least one or two characteristics that prompt you to think "It feels right, but I could never do that here."

Why five? The number is large enough to allow for a fully realized image but small enough that you can keep all the characteristics in mind.

This is a good place to make some of the abstract conditions specific. For example, you might have written "Classroom conditions are responsive to student learning needs." What kinds of classroom conditions do you have in mind? What would be an example? How might it address one particular student learning need? How might that be typical? You might end up writing a paragraph about a student who can't comprehend written material just by reading silently; he or she needs to read, reflect, and then talk through ideas to understand them fully. You might set up more frequent opportunities for small- and large-group discussions.

STEP 5: "HOW WOULD WE GET THERE?"

As a designer, what would you have to do to achieve each component of your vision? What practices would you follow? What capabilities would you build—in yourself and in your students? What policies would be put in place: at the classroom, school, community, and even state levels?

For example, your design might call for observing another teacher in your school system (or elsewhere) who has significant expertise in teaching something you want to teach more effectively. Maybe it would include coaching from other teachers. The school might provide substitute coverage for one or two weeks, so that teachers could work and learn by co-teaching alongside more experienced practitioners.

STEP 6: "WHAT STANDS IN THE WAY?"

What kinds of barriers and obstacles might exist for each idea raised in step 5? Consider the opposing forces you might face from the students themselves, from their parents, from other teachers, from the school establishment, from the community, and from the state.

Then consider the innate challenges that would arise simply as a natural consequence of your making the change. These challenges might include, for example, not having enough time to realize your aspirations; not having the kinds of help you need; an incomplete sense of how these

Henry Levin, "Accelerated Schools: The Background," in Christine Finnan, et al., (editors), *Accelerated Schools in Action: Lessons from the Field* (Corwin Press, 1996), p. 17.

Daniel Pink, *A Whole New Mind: Moving from the Information Age to the Conceptual Age* (Riverhead, 2005), p. 115.

The concept of opposing forces and how to manage them is the central theme in Peter Senge, Art Kleiner, Charlotte Roberts, Richard Ross, George Roth and Bryan Smith, *The Dance of Change: The Challenges to Sustaining Momentum in a Learning Organization* (Doubleday, 1999).

changes are relevant to your students; or opposition from others within the larger school system. Opposing forces of various sorts are a natural consequence when an established practice or value is threatened. Where would these opposing forces come from? How might you accomplish your goals without provoking that opposition?

STEP 7: "I'LL KNOW I'M MAKING PROGRESS IF…"

The rest of this book contains many strategies and methods that may help reach the goals you set in this exercise. Before you can proceed even partway, however, another step is needed in defining your vision. How will you recognize the progress you make?

Consider each of the five primary characteristics you chose in step 4 and the obstacles you described in step 6. Name one or more "indicators" for each set. An indicator is a piece of evidence that would signal that you have made some progress. Some indicators might be as simple as more students reading at grade level—but others might be less conventional, harder to measure, and yet more revealing of real change. Establishing an indicator that "Classroom conditions are more responsive to student needs" might be as simple as noticing that students regularly, and without your direction, bring in their own resources to share—a story, a family picture, or a special collection of objects that connect with the specific classroom learning experiences.

STEP 8: FIRST EXPERIMENTS

In nearly all schools, teachers have latitude to experiment with the design of learning in their classrooms. Hence the final step in this exercise: Design an experiment for yourself that might be effective in creating a learning classroom.

If you are interested in promoting more productive conversation, you could announce: "Let's talk about finding ways to engage together as a class. For example, what if we agree to say, 'Yes, and' rather than 'Yes, but' when we respond to someone else's comment? A lot of times, when you say 'yes, but,' you are appearing to agree, but you're really negating the speaker's position. Let's avoid doing that. If we become conscious of how we interact, hopefully it will make it easier to really listen to each other, instead of just listening for ways to get our own point across."

Then arrange, in two weeks or so, to conduct a postmortem. "Are we practicing 'inquiry'? What difference has the 'yes, and' rule made to us? Has it changed our conversation?" Based on that experience, you could add another guideline to further design the framework of class discussions.

A Teaching or a Learning System?

Nelda Cambron-McCabe

Reflective practice should be an integral part of an educator's training. In my classes, students often write personal reflections, and I also engage them in dialogue and reflection around particular issues or concerns. In recent years, I've found it valuable to pose the following questions to groups of teachers and administrators:

- How do you differentiate between a teaching system and a learning system?
- What does a teaching system look like in a classroom?
- What does a learning system look like in a classroom?
- Is there a difference in expected outcomes?
- What is the student's role/responsibility in a teaching system? In a learning system?
- How does change occur in a teaching system? In a learning system?
- What constitutes success in a teaching system? In a learning system?
- Is your school a teaching system or a learning system?

Purpose:

This reflection, conducted by a group, yields significant insight into teaching and learning and the implications for students' learning.

This exercise was adapted from "Reflection Exercise: A Teaching or a Learning System?" by Nelda Cambron-McCabe, in Cambron-McCabe, Luvern Cunningham, James Harvey, and Robert Koff, *The Superintendent's Fieldbook: A Guidebook for Leaders of Learning* (Corwin, 2005).

3. "Legal, Safe, and Something You Want to Learn"

Creating a Passionate Classroom

Carol Ann Kenerson

Teachers may rightfully wonder: "What am I getting myself into when I start using this 'five disciplines stuff' in the classroom?" Carol Ann Kenerson, a teacher who used the disciplines extensively in the classroom, provided us with this introductory guide for the first edition. Its precepts have stood the test of time.

As a classroom teacher, I used the five learning disciplines to create an environment that nurtured and energized my students and myself. The disciplines gave me an intentional, explicit framework that expanded many of my existing teaching practices and made the classroom into more of a space of learning, respect, and creativity. I have discovered that these disciplines are effective in any and all classrooms. As they become ingrained, students begin to "perform" at higher and more authentic levels and are present in a whole new way. The five learning disciplines, when tailored to the classroom, are invaluable for the thing I care most about: imbuing a passion for learning.

My first experiences were as an English teacher in a public high school. From there, I moved into a residential school where I taught writing. Most of the students had severe learning disabilities and emotional needs; they had suffered from various forms of abuse and neglect. These were children of both genders, aged thirteen to eighteen, with very low reading scores. Many were functionally illiterate.

I found that these students can thrive in an environment rooted in the learning disciplines. The dialogue circle reminded some of them of a twelve-step meeting or therapy group and was therefore a comfortable, natural setting. Conversely, many "advanced placement" students are focused more on grades than on the process of learning. This tends to cloud their sense of adventure. Although their work is usually thorough and creative, it saddens me when they ask, sometimes in agitation, "Please, will you give me four more points so that I won't ruin my 'A' average?" It is so much more enjoyable and inspiring, for all involved, when students say: "This is so interesting" or "I really learned a lot trying that."

PERSONAL MASTERY

The epitome of personal mastery in the classroom is helping children to decipher their passions, to explore whether they believe these are possible, and to nurture their courage to delve into it, without judging them right or wrong. A classroom is saturated with interests, desires, and talents; one of my goals as a teacher was to tap into these sources of energy. Thus, I regularly built lessons around students' personal visions. In the context of a specific piece of literature or topic of study, I would ask them to: "Write down two things that you could teach someone else as well as two things you would like to know how to do but have never tried." From their answers I would create a single working list that we would share and explore. Eventually, the students would choose partners and create projects that would incorporate each student's desires for teaching and learning.

"I am really good at writing and journalism," one student said, "but I really want to learn how to take and develop my own photographs." She connected with someone who had a camera and who wanted to strengthen research skills. The two developed a short newspaper that was directly related to the events, characters, and social context of the novel that we were studying. Other teams taped videos of character interviews relevant to a revolutionary essay, wrote rap songs based on the themes of an epic poem, or created an art display to illustrate the development of a storyline. My only guidelines were that the projects had to be legal, safe, and based on something they wanted to learn.

To allow the students this freedom takes trust on the part of the teacher. However, I know of no better way for students to become aware of their personal strengths and of the things that spark their curiosity. I always enjoyed the presentation of projects and assumed the role of learner among learners.

Sometimes the speeches, stories, or pieces of artwork seemed a bit inappropriate for school; they were rooted in themes of murder, drugs, disease, and high school pregnancies. Yet these were all facets of the students' lives and fears. When students can speak and create with their own voices, the insights and learning are huge. On more than one occasion I returned to my office and sobbed. "What's wrong?" others would ask. "You can't believe what just happened in there! They have created projects and papers that are so beyond what I could have assigned, it is really amazing!"

Over time I began to recognize the importance of meditative relaxation, not only in my own life but in the lives of my students. To spend time quietly reflecting and sitting still is an effective way to bring personal mastery into the classroom. Although most students took part in this exercise, it was not a requirement. However, they all needed to honor the silence in the room, even if they wanted to do other work, doodle, or read. We would turn the lights down, they'd close their eyes and I would talk them through a brief visualization.

After we had done this a few times, the students began to ask me to let them relax and meditate for five minutes at the start of class. "We have so much going on; we can't concentrate." They would promise effusively to work afterward. I trusted that they knew what they needed and often honored the requests. I never regretted it. Each class that followed such a meditative beginning was rich with creativity and fertile with learning.

Meditation is more difficult in some settings than others. In the residential school, for instance, some students (who had experienced various forms of abuse) were afraid to close their eyes in a vulnerable place. Instead, we would just sit quietly, with soft music playing in the background. In all situations, I tailored this practice to the needs of the students; when they had two exams in a single morning, I understood their need to have a space where they could recenter themselves.

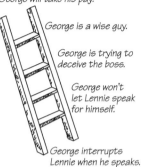

If Lennie doesn't watch out, George will take his pay.

George is a wise guy.

George is trying to deceive the boss.

George won't let Lennie speak for himself.

George interrupts Lennie when he speaks.

— A "ladder of inference" derived from John Steinbeck, Of Mice and Men, chapter 1.

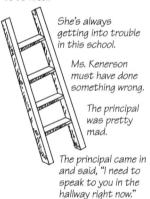

Ms. Kenerson is going to be fired.

She's always getting into trouble in this school.

Ms. Kenerson must have done something wrong.

The principal was pretty mad.

The principal came in and said, "I need to speak to you in the hallway right now."

WORKING WITH MENTAL MODELS

The ladder of inference (page 101) is another very powerful classroom tool. It can be referred to during any conversation or lesson about literature, history, or even science and math. For an episode about John Steinbeck's *Of Mice and Men,* I would ask the class: "What might some of Lenny's leaps up the ladder be?" Or, "What assumptions is George making?" You can also ask about the mental models held by the writer and their discrepancies from the reality that the children, as readers, understand. The ladder sounds abstract, but it is actually quite easy to teach. Children know that these "leaps of abstraction" exist, but no one has ever offered them a way to articulate the various levels of thought. If someone made an assertion during class, another student would ask, "Is that really what happened? Or is it what you heard happened?"

I found a multitude of ways to introduce and practice this material. I might ask the principal to step into my room and say to me, "I need to speak to you in the hallway right now." I would purposely return from the corridor a minute later, visibly flustered. Then I would ask the students what they thought had occurred. Everybody had his or her own theory. I'd guide them through the structure of the ladder of inference and ask them to think about the incident and consider, "Why do we have such different stories about why the principal wanted to speak to me? What was the data?"

To create this type of environment, a teacher must be fully engaged. Full engagement can be very exhausting in some ways, but it is also more joyful and inspiring in the long run, because you are never stuck sitting at your desk in the front of the classroom. Over time, discipline problems decline, creativity levels soar, and a collective respect permeates the classroom.

TEAM LEARNING

One of my goals was to create a dialogue-like environment in class. I never required students to raise their hands to speak. Instead, we sat in a circle or in a way that allowed us each to feel comfortable and let the conversation flow through us. Over time and with consistent practice, students learn that it is okay to wait for someone to finish speaking a thought before they jump in. To introduce dialogue, it may be effective to use an object, such as a globe, as a "talking stick," until dialogue becomes a pattern in the classroom.

The "discount revenge cycle," developed by George Prince of Synectics, Inc., is a powerful concept for classroom dialogues. I would point out the many ways that people discount each other—subtly or not, with body language or verbally. For instance, some students whisper while others talk, murmur "Oh, God, do you believe it?" or simply roll their eyes and yawn.

As Prince notes, any time someone feels discounted, a revenge will follow. It might not be today, or tomorrow, but the cycle will continue and revenge will be acted out, only to be followed by another discount. In dialogues, I strove to bring this destructive pattern out in the open in a way that was respectful and clear, drawing attention to it as it happened and helping the students to become aware of the costs. This is an important reason for teachers to be involved in dialogue as well, not only with the children, but with one another, as one of the most powerful ways to teach is to embody and to model the practices that we present. Teachers listen differently to different students; we allow some a chance to think as they speak, and we interrupt others. Practicing dialogue helps to build and nurture our capacity to listen to everyone on a deep and authentic level.

Also see "Check-ins," page 258.

THE CHALLENGES OF A LEARNING CLASSROOM

There certainly may be moments when practicing and modeling these disciplines feels like struggle, and one tendency is to revert to old ways and habits; however, I firmly believe that continuing to forge ahead will bring innumerable rewards and gifts.

You may feel sad when you say goodbye to your students in June. They will have other teachers, who may not teach in the same style or be aware of the disciplines and tools in which you've become proficient together. Some students may also find that the disciplines make their home lives tougher. One of my students, after learning the difference between "good" and "well" in my English class, went home and corrected his dad one evening. He was hit as punishment for thinking that he was better than his father. I felt tremendous guilt after hearing about this boy's experience; no matter how much a school may thrive and instill systems thinking and good communication, how does one manage the discrepancy that may appear for the children? How to integrate what they are learning with us, their teachers, with the rest of their lives?

When I first began teaching, one of my students asked me a great question. "I'm not sure," I said. "I'll go home tonight and do some research. Why don't you go home and look too. Tomorrow we'll compare notes and see if we can find the answer." My more experienced co-teacher was horrified; she said I should have either looked up the answer surreptitiously or made something up in the moment. I was never, ever to admit that I didn't

For more about Prince's work see W. Timothy Weaver and George M. Prince, "Synectics: Its Potential for Education," *Phi Delta Kappan* (January 1990), pp. 378–388; and W. Timothy Weaver, "When Discounting Gets in the Way," Training and Development, 48, 7, (July 1993a), pp. 55–62.

Also see Robert Fuller, *Somebodies and Nobodies: Overcoming the Abuse of Rank* (New Society Publishers, 2004).

have the answer. This was one of my first moments of struggle as a teacher—I had to fight for the right to admit that I don't know everything. Not having the answers is one of the greatest ways to arrive at a true solution.

One thing that I know to be true is that I must continue to model and to live that which I teach. There is no line of demarcation between what I present as a lesson and what I practice in my everyday life. I believe that these disciplines add to my collection of tools, methods, and processes not as additional requirements that I must fit into my already overly filled class schedule, but rather as a way of being—in the classroom, and in my life.

THE COURAGE TO TEACH

Exploring the Inner Landscape of a Teacher's Life, by Parker J. Palmer (Jossey-Bass, 1998)

"We teach who we are." In that simple statement Parker Palmer challenges those of us in education to turn our thoughts inward to explore our life's work of teaching and to reconnect with what, for many of us, is an avocation not just a vocation. The book provides a powerful tool for individual readers or study groups to reflect on Palmer's premise that teaching and learning lie at the dangerous intersection of personal and public life and that good teaching comes from the integrity and identity of the teacher, not methods and techniques.

You could read this book as an exercise in personal mastery. *The Courage to Teach* helps you focus on how you can commit your whole self, undivided, to lifelong learning in order to be more fully available both to your subject and to your students. By understanding who you are, you can engage yourself more fully in the world, with all your talents, in more meaningful relationships. —Paul Mack

EDUCATING ESMÉ

Diary of a Teacher's First Year, Expanded Edition, by Esmé Raji Codell (Algonquin Books, 1999, 2009)

When she first wrote this book, the author—now a librarian and children's literature specialist—was an enthusiastic twenty-four-year-old who took a job teaching fifth grade in an inner-city Chicago elementary school. Educating Esmé is essentially the no-holds-barred diary of that first year. She rebukes her principal when he imposes his authority, renames math as "puzzling" so kids won't feel they have a history of failure with it, collects their anxieties in a "trouble basket" (a nice form of check-in, page 258), sets up a storytellers' workshop for children after school, lets one of her toughest students teach her class for a day—and describes her experiences on National Public Radio. The point is not to hold up Esmé as a model for teachers; many have done this kind of thing. But *Educating Esmé* can be read as an avatar of brash candor, a vial of direct empathy, a vehicle for bringing out your own inner Esmé when you need it. (Bel Kaufman, who provided the same gift two generations earlier with *Up The Down Staircase*, contributed a blurb.) —Art Kleiner

IV. Seeing the Learner

The "Newer Views of Learning" website, developed by University of Wisconsin-Stevens Point professor Leslie Owens Wilson, provides a comprehensive overview of emerging views of intelligence, along with links to many of the leaders of the field. There is also guidance on creating teaching environments that support and nurture learning for all the students you are likely to encounter. See www.uwsp.edu/education/lwilson/learning/index.htm.

Since the mid-1970s there have been remarkable advancements in research on the ways people learn. One result has been the growing awareness of multiple intelligences and ways of learning and the realization that intelligence is neither fixed nor simple to measure. Students and schools may still be ranked and rated according to standardized test scores, but no one can claim (with validity) that these scores reflect any more than a fragment of actual capabilities or potentials.

This chapter includes a variety of efforts to incorporate awareness of multiple ways of learning into classroom practice. But it does not stop there. The current understanding of how people learn is still emerging, and it raises fascinating, significant questions. If IQ tests don't measure learning capabilities, what kind of assessment would? Which forms of intelligence and learning styles are worth investment in developing in children? And in adults? What effect does the teacher's learning style have on breakdowns in class communication? Which forms of intelligence represent prerequisites for the practice of the learning disciplines? (For example, does shared vision require an innate capability for spatial visualization?) Do teams and groups vary in their kinds of intelligence, the way that individuals do? And what difference does this body of knowledge make to the design of a curriculum, a school, or a community?

We make no effort to be comprehensive—only to provide starting points that we find valuable or intriguing. Our guiding principle is the importance of valuing all learners and treating them with dignity. What are your mental models about learning, and how do they differ from those around you? What are your gifts—as *a teacher, as a learner? What are your less proficient learning capabilities? What are the gifts of others around you? What can you learn from one another? This inquiry is the purpose of the articles, exercises, and resources in this chapter.*

Also see "The Cognitive Studies Group," page 404.

1. The Dignity of the Child

Tim Lucas

Anna is in the third grade. Like many eight-year-olds, she bubbles with energy. This morning she skipped to the bus stop and laughed with her best friend on the ride to school, but as soon as she arrived things went wrong. First, the math homework she had completed the night before wasn't in her book bag. When she told her teacher she couldn't find it, the teacher, with hands on hips, said, "You forgot your homework again? You are so disorganized!"

Later that morning, the class attended an assembly in the auditorium. On the way back to class, two girls shoved Anna into the wall, causing her to trip and fall. "You're so disorganized," they jeered, echoing the teacher. Two boys pointed and laughed; when the teacher told them to quiet down, they looked at Anna as if it were her fault that they were reprimanded. Back in class Anna looked down at her hands while the rest of the class went over the math homework. The girl sitting next to her said, loud enough for everyone to hear, "No wonder you're so dumb." The teacher decided to ignore it and continue on with the lesson. At lunch Anna couldn't eat much because her stomach hurt. And so on it went, through the day; on the bus ride home, she sat, silently, glumly, unaware of anything around her.

I sometimes tell Anna's story at school assemblies. First I hold up a large sheet of paper with the words "I am a person with dignity." I ask the students and teachers to think of the paper as Anna's dignity—the way she sees herself. At each incident in the story I rip off a piece of paper, making the visible surface smaller each time, until only a small fragment is left. "Every time you take away a piece of Anna's dignity," I say, "she believes she is less than she really is. How can you fix the damage? Once the words have been said, can you really take them back?"

We have all heard stories similar to Anna's. Most of us have been Anna sometime during our education. If we made it through elementary school with our dignity relatively unscathed, the assaults of adolescence, high school, and college awaited us. A girl tired of jokes about her breasts was told by adults to ignore it and sit somewhere else. A university design student was told by a professor, "Next time you draw a picture, try using your hands." An administrator transferred a group of sixth graders away from the subject they wanted because, he said, they would never be capable of handling it. A teacher said, in a thoughtless moment, "Nobody can do anything with you." In all of these and in countless more cases, we are told that we are not worth very much. We may spend the rest of our lives fulfilling that prophecy. We may remember these attacks on our dignity in great detail for most of our lives. Ask children to write about a time they were teased or bullied, and you'll get a piece with vivid detail.

Bullying has long been a national concern in our schools, and one that has come into even sharper focus in recent years with the prevalence of, and media attention to, cyberbullying. However, we all too rarely hear educators—or other people—reflect openly about the dignity of the children they teach. They talk about curriculum content, teaching methods, and, occasionally, new research in developmental stages or multiple ways of learning. But how often do they say that each child has value and deserves respect and that learning is tied to student perceptions of the respect they receive and their own sense of worth? How often do they look at children through the lens of dignity?

As people concerned with school, we need to step back and reflect on the meaning of the dignity of the child. Many educators and parents seem to believe that the principle is self-evident, especially with the notion of raising self-esteem prominent in many schools. Unfortunately, that isn't true. If the primacy of children's dignity was obvious to everyone, then we would look more often at children through the lenses of their own perceptions of themselves. There would be far fewer labels—such as "at-risk," "tough," "special," and "disturbed"—applied to children.

ENGAGING CHILDREN THROUGH THEIR DIGNITY

I first became aware of this concept in my second year as a science teacher. I knew I was reaching kids, but I couldn't understand why I couldn't reach more of them. I was lucky. I taught in the same building as a woman named Trudy Creede. Trudy was a remarkable teacher and mentor. A frail, elderly woman, she taught reading, using photography, to a group of twelve- to fourteen-year-old kids whom most of the teachers would have labeled "at risk" or "problem students." This took place during the mid-1970s—a turbulent time for American education in general. Our junior high school held 1,200 kids in a building designed to

The literature on bullying has now become extensive and multifaceted. The work we appreciate includes Paulo Freire, *Pedagogy of Freedom* (Rowman and Littlefield, 1998), pp. 62–64; Jonathan Kozol, *Savage Inequalities* (HarperCollins; 1991); Ira Shor, *Empowering Education: Critical Teaching for Social Change* (University of Chicago Press, 1992); Barbara Coloroso, *The Bully, The Bullied, and the Bystander* (HarperCollins, 2003); and Rosalind Wiseman, *Queen Bees and Wannabes: Helping Your Daughter Survive Cliques, Gossip, Boyfriends, and Other Realities of Adolescence* (Crown, 2002 and 2009).

hold 600, and we shared classrooms with a high school that was similarly "overcrowded." Use of marijuana was prevalent, and the local police often had to visit the school. No one knew yet how to deal with cigarette smoking in school lavatories, let alone with drugs in schools.

I was part of a group of eight or nine young teachers who were a little beyond the norm. We were unmarried and often seemed only a little less wild than the kids we taught. We had long hair, rode motorcycles or bicycles to work, and often used unorthodox teaching methods to reach our students. Other teachers sometimes lodged complaints against us. (Once I took my science class outside to collect soil samples. Another science teacher complained, "You can't take your class outside. When my kids look out the window and see yours, they think your class is more fun than mine. That's not fair!")

Trudy invited us all, once a month, to have dinner with her and her husband. We would have long discussions about her success with "incorrigible" children. Trudy engaged her students in taking pictures, developing them in a darkroom, writing about them, and reading one another's stories. The graduates of her class often succeeded in the long run. "How do you do it?" I would ask her.

"It is just about their dignity, Tim," she told me. She always knew that her students were at that challenging developmental stage when they could easily drop back into preadolescent ways of thinking. But in each case, she would say to herself, "This child has dignity built right in. It's there already; we don't have to put it there. Our job is to acknowledge it and work with it."

To Trudy, these children weren't "cases." They were unbelievably complicated organisms, with a great deal going for them. She had the gift of stepping back and seeing her children as people—seeing the ways they worked, moved, thought, talked, and processed information. And she never lost her awe of them and her respect for them. As she explained it to us, she didn't have a choice; as much as she might want to take a kid for granted, "I can't. Because there they are. There is that person."

Recognizing the dignity of a child is easy when you see, say, a group of eight kindergartners walking down the street or on a field trip, holding hands. But those same eight children, nine years later, may well look like a gang to you, especially if they come from a "bad" background. Every child, at age fifteen, seems challenging and disruptive at times; that's natural for their developmental stage. Trudy taught me that there are no good kids or bad kids. There are just kids. This frail woman held her classes together because she understood dignity and gave it back to her students. You can't teach people how to do that by lecturing them. You have to model it for them.

EDUCATING FROM A SENSE OF DIGNITY

I still talk with some teachers I knew during those years, and we speak often of the idea that every child has dignity and the ways in which Trudy modeled that belief and talked about it. I took those lessons with me as I moved into the roles of principal, superintendent, and university educator. It is part of my vision. If I believe that children are lovable and capable, then it is my responsibility to honor their dignity by meeting them where they are.

When I was the superintendent of schools in Ho-Ho-Kus, New Jersey, our learning consultant screened all of our incoming kindergartners in one-on-one interviews with each child and his or her parents. When the school board questioned that expense, I told them about an incident at the school's opening day. While I was blowing up some balloons for the kindergartners to take home, our learning development specialist said, "I screened one child this summer who is deathly afraid of balloons. If you walk into that kindergarten room with twenty balloons, this girl will freak out."

We would have never known that if we didn't screen. We would have embarrassed her, threatened her, and damaged all the children's impressions of school on their first day. Instead, the counselor took the girl aside before the day started. She told her that I was going to give out balloons, that she didn't have to take one home, and that they could leave the room together and walk around the school during that time if she wished.

"That's okay," said the girl. "As long as I don't have to take one." For the rest of her time at school, she knew (and the other kids knew) that we respected her.

In daily practice, it's as simple as treating other people as you would want to be treated. As a teacher and administrator, I greeted children in the hallway by name, because I believe if you walk by someone (child or adult) and don't acknowledge them, you rob them of a piece of their dignity. The best educators I know focus a great deal of attention on getting to know kids. Teachers deliberately set up activities in class where kids can talk about their hobbies and family backgrounds, in a way that they won't be judged or picked on. Once you have that knowledge about the children—once you really see what they care about—then you can do a great deal more for them.

You can improve your activities and practices by asking "Does this add to, or take away from, the dignity of the child?" Talking about the dignity of the child as a primary value provides a powerful starting point for building a shared vision and focusing staff development programs aligned with that vision. It affects the ways that educators talk to each other—in the classroom, in meetings, and in the lunchroom. You can build a practice of seeing students for who they are by deliberately incorporating the research on multiple intelligences and learning styles into your lessons, creating fruitful obstacles for all the different learning styles in the room, challenging them to reach beyond their natural limits, and showing them that we recognize their strengths and limits. The end result is a system that continually communicates to children "We're going to add value to your life today, and your teacher next year will add more value to you—because we know you're worth it."

《《 Also see "What Signals Are You Sending," page 204.

I consider myself fortunate to have been exposed to the idea of the dignity of the child so early in my career. It has motivated me to keep learning from new research on different types of learners and their varied strengths, to celebrate those differences, and to promote diverse ways of thinking and interacting. Only students with a strong sense of their own dignity can grow up to be adults who can take risks, handle minor failures, and act to protect other people's dignity.

In some schools, teachers and administrators talk openly about this. Any time someone wants to make a decision about any group of kids, they ask: Have we stepped back to see the ways in which these are great kids? Do we see the potential in these kids? Or have we written them off? In the end, recognizing the dignity of the child means reconnecting with the sense of primal wonder that every child's learning can spark sometimes— for instance, when they first read a street sign or put together a complete sentence. You have to learn not to take such episodes for granted and to view every child through the lens of respect. Then the theory of "the dignity of the child" is no longer a theory. It is simply the way you see.

HOWARD GARDNER AND MULTIPLE INTELLIGENCES

The Disciplined Mind: Beyond Facts and Standardized Tests, the K-12 Education That Every Child Deserves (Penguin, 2000); *Five Minds for the Future* (Harvard Business Press, 2009); *Multiple Intelligences: New Horizons in Theory and Practice* (Basic Books, 2006); *Truth, Beauty, and Goodness Reframed: Educating for the Virtues in the Twenty-First Century* (Basic Books, 2011); all by Howard Gardner.

In his research and writing on multiple intelligences, creativity, and leadership, Harvard psychologist Gardner has raised a series of powerful questions about the appropriate ways to foster teaching and learning. While he has never been directly involved in working with the five disciplines of organizational learning, the theory of multiple intelligences resonates powerfully with the five learning disciplines. At its core is an evolving taxonomy of diverse cognitive and emotional strengths: verbal-linguistic, logical-mathematical, spatial (artistic), physical-kinesthetic, musical, natural (awareness and sensitivity to the environment), interpersonal, and intrapersonal (reflective). In facing the challenges of life, Gardner says, people must bring each of these forms of intelligence to bear: to bear throughout their lives, from childhood onward. Since everyone has a different mix of intelligence, people must complement each other's skills and strengths in every social milieu.

Gardner's work reframes one of the subtlest, most pervasive, and most destructive mental models about school: the linking of achievement to the most intellectual forms of intelligence (verbal-linguistic and logical-mathematical) and the devaluation of all other forms. This view of intelligence (and thus of human value) has devastating effects on the vast number of children whose gifts are overlooked or ignored in school. In adult society, it leads to the promotion of leaders who may be "book smart" but who lack the physical, social, ecological, reflective, and interpersonal skills that they (and the rest of us) need them to have.

Each of Gardner's books expands this body of work, often taking it into new domains. For educators, *The Disciplined Mind* is probably the best starting point. Published in 2000, it was deeply informed by Gardner's work with school reform in the 1990s. While he deliberately avoids fostering a particular program (there are no "Gardner schools"), he writes explicitly and eloquently about designing curricula and classrooms for a wide variety of ways of learning and being. He also puts forth his view of the purpose of school: That is to teach students what it means to operate within a discipline—to think scientifically, historically, artistically, ethically, mathematically, and musically, even when those ways of thinking seem counterintuitive or difficult at first. As demonstrators, he uses three ideas: the theory of evolution (science), the history of the Holocaust (history and morality), and the music of Mozart (the arts). Then he shows how different intelligences, brought to bear on these (and other) topics, lead to a richer, more pragmatic body of knowledge.

Multiple Intelligences, updated in 2006, lays out the theory underlying Gardner's taxonomy and provides a useful overall introduction. *Five Minds for the Future*, which Gardner published in 2007, synthesizes the intelligences into more general forms of mastery that people can (and he says should) apply to the challenges of the next fifty years. These are, in effect, his own version of learning disciplines. They include working steadily over time to improve skill and understanding (the disciplined mind); putting information from diverse sources together (the synthesizing mind); breaking new ground (the creating mind); understanding others (the respectful mind); and coming to a better understanding of purpose and value (the ethical mind). *Truth, Beauty, and Goodness Reframed*, published in 2011, focuses on the three great Platonic virtues and how they can be cultivated in modern times. —Art Kleiner

ROBERT STERNBERG

Robert Sternberg, *Successful Intelligence: How Practical and Creative Intelligence Determine Life* (Simon & Schuster, 1996), and Robert Sternberg with Elena L. Grigorenko, *Our Labeled Children: What Every Parent and Teacher Needs to Know About Learning Disabilities* (Perseus Books, 1999).

Oklahoma State professor of psychology and education (and provost) Robert J. Sternberg is an important voice in the field of modern learning theory. He challenges not just disability labels but the rigid school practices that focus narrowly on "componential intelligence" (linguistic and logical mathematical abilities). Two other kinds of intelligence, creative and practical, are not only important for society, but have a determining factor in people's success. These abilities are given little opportunity to develop in most schools. His multiple intelligence identifications, though different, are not contrary to Howard Gardner's. Sternberg is widely published in a range of books on cognitive psychology, creativity, and teaching. These books are two good places to start. —Janis Dutton

2. Revealing the Learner

Tim Lucas

Ask a group of schoolchildren on the playground to choose a team for a game. The most talented athlete is always picked first; everyone knows who that person is. If the same students must choose a team to work on a science poster, the most talented artist will always be picked

Purpose:

*To help students—
working either with
parents or teachers—
realize their individual
strengths, identify
the areas they need
to develop further,
and begin to value the
different strengths and
skills that others bring to
the classroom.*

Overview:

*In small groups, students
develop images of the
intelligences, the different
kinds of "smartnesses"
they engender, and their
own smartness.*

Participant:

*Class of students divided
into groups of three.*

Materials:

*A description of the
multiple intelligences and
circular chart for each
participant.*

Environment:

*Space for both group
discussion and small
group activity.*

first. If a geography or spelling bee is on the agenda, someone else will always be the consistent "first pick."

It's a great system—for those who are chosen first. Most of us are familiar with the typical feeling of anticipation that ensues, wondering how soon we will be picked, relieved and yet disappointed to be picked somewhere in the middle. We also know the embarrassment of being chosen as the last resort, labeled in effect as "worthless" because our particular talents don't fit today's activity.

The first-pick mindset is so deeply ingrained in us that it seems impossible to break. But this exercise can help. I have used it with children as young as eight or nine, yet I find it particularly effective in middle school, where kids are acutely aware of their similarities and differences and where they need to learn how to deal with disappointment while keeping their own innate sense of dignity.

STEP 1: REFLECTING ON SKILLS AND CAPABILITIES

Ask your students to reflect on what happens in group contests and projects: "How do you decide whom you want to work with or pick first? How do you know that they're good at this thing?" Discuss the different skills that might be helpful in these activities and how most people are better at some activities than others.

Move into a conversation about the reasons why different people have different mixes of talents: "How do people develop certain skills? Are they born that way, or do they have more opportunities and experiences?" (For example, is a person good at geography born that way, or has he or she traveled a lot? Do musicians have to practice and study with a music teacher?)

STEP 2: INTRODUCING NINE INTELLIGENCES

I generally move to a short lecture on multiple intelligences: "As a group we have a full range of skills, but some of us are better in some areas than others. The question is not if you are smart, but how you are smart." Then we look at nine established types of human intelligence, with language that makes it easier for elementary and middle school students to distinguish them:

- If you are *word smart* (high verbal-linguistic intelligence), then you are good at language, writing, creating poetry, and storytelling.
- If you are *logic smart* (high logical-mathematical intelligence), you have strong skills for problem solving, inductive and deductive thinking, working with symbols, and recognizing patterns.

- If you are *picture smart* (high spatial intelligence), you have visual talent (drawing, painting, and sculpture) and assembly talent (you grasp how things work, come apart, and are put together).
- If you are *body smart* (high physical-kinesthetic intelligence), you can eloquently use your body coordination to play sports, games, dance, act, and move.
- If you are *music smart* (high musical intelligence), then you are gifted in recognition of tones and rhythm and sensitive to vocal, instrumental, and environmental sounds.
- If you are *nature smart* (high natural intelligence), then you have well-developed awareness and sensitivity to the environment around you, and you can operate effectively among plants, animals, and natural habitat.
- If you are *people smart* (high interpersonal intelligence), then you know how to work well with others, interpret their moods and meanings, and predict what they will do next.
- If you are *self smart* (high intrapersonal intelligence), then you are capable of deep self-knowledge, metacognition, and internal reflection.
- If you are *philosopher smart* (high existential intelligence), then you engage readily with abstraction and are capable of deep reflection about the meaning of human existence and other complex issues.

This exercise is based on a common set of paraphrases of multiple intelligences in Howard Gardner, *Multiple Intelligences: New Horizons in Theory and Practice* (Basic Books, 2006).

STEP 3. IMAGINING THE INTELLIGENT

In groups of two or three people, write out descriptions of people high in each intelligence type. What would their favorite hobby be? Their best subject in school? The job they're likely to get? A good vacation spot for them? What person in history displayed this trait? What TV or movie character embodies it? What song lyric evokes it?

STEP 4: INDIVIDUAL REFLECTION

Having gone through the previous discussion, the class is now prepared to reflect on (and write answers to) the following questions:

- What three intelligences are your strongest? Give an example in your everyday life that illustrates why you chose those three.
- If there were two intelligences you would like to get better at, what would they be and why?
- What intelligences are members of your family strong in? (Think about their jobs, hobbies, and daily work.) Please give examples to back up your thoughts.
- Why couldn't a person be great at all nine intelligences at once?

- How can school (and this classroom) get better at helping you improve in all nine intelligences?
- Sometimes, if a young child is really strong in one area such as "musical," the parents will send him or her to a special school with an intensive focus on music. Such children become gifted performers by their early teens. Olympic gymnasts go to special elementary schools. Child actors use tutors. What is your opinion of this?

USING THIS EXERCISE AS A FOUNDATION FOR OTHER WORK

A class that has been through "Revealing the Learner" has a language for talking about differences among people, without putting anyone down. You can talk in more dispassionate ways, for instance, about people who seem different from everyone else. They may seem to have obvious weaknesses, or even disabilities; but what are their strengths? Rather than simply saying "Everyone is good at something," you can begin to talk about the things that different people in the room are good at.

If you are a teacher, the exercise will help you learn along with the students, making you more aware of their individual ways of learning and processing information. That, in turn, helps you tailor a range of experiences for them—some to exercise their "stronger" intelligences and others to improve their "weaker" skills.

⟩⟩ Also see the 4MAT review on page 188.

The exercise can also make a difference for teams of adults, such as a staff group trying to design or implement a school change initiative. Two teachers, for example, may unconsciously adopt different views of the same child based on the "intelligences" they are comfortable with, without ever realizing the source of their different opinions. The first teacher, strong in interpersonal intelligence, may convene a team of people to help the child. The second teacher, with highly developed linguistic intelligence, may approach the child through reading or writing. Whose approach is "right"? Not necessarily the teacher with the most experience or even the teacher who knows that child best. It may be the teacher most unconsciously attuned to the child's innate strengths.

Similar differences can occur among parents, people in the community looking at school issues, and any two organizational employees. We have seen adaptations of this exercise make a difference in staff development workshops, in school and community meetings, and even in families. (Children bring it home and try it with their parents and siblings.) It always opens minds to the recognition: We are not all gifted the same way. And we don't see the differences until we look for them.

HOW YOUR CHILD IS SMART
by Dawna Markova (Conari Press, 1992)

Dawna Markova bases her work on clinical research about the diverse states of brain activity. Some of us are consciously oriented to visual primacy (paying most attention to what we see), others to auditory learning (focusing on what we hear), and others to kinesthetic knowledge (learning through the body and movement).

One of my daughters, for example, is predominantly kines thetic in her conscious mind. When she was in school, obeying demands to "sit still and pay attention" took all her energy, will-power, and attention. She had none left for listening. I talked to her teachers about this and got their permission to give her little rubber balls to squeeze in her hand when she was listening. (She understood why she couldn't interrupt the rest of the class with them.) It was amazing how much they helped her sit still and lis-ten better, and she remembered every bit of content much better when allowed to fidget in this way.

How Your Child Is Smart is written directly for parents—the people with the greatest incentive for considering their child's learning styles. It describes how to stimulate children's conscious, subconscious, and unconscious minds to help them learn better. It also tells some of Markova's own story as a classroom teacher who had to hit bottom in her own career before she understood how to listen to children in the way this book describes. —George Roth

See also Dawna Markova's other Books on learning styles: *Learning Unlimited* (1998), centered on helping children with their homework; *The Open Mind* (1996) for adult learners; and *An Unused Intelligence* (coauthored with Andy Bryner, 1996), a workbook for the kinesthetic learner, all from Conari Press.

HUMAN DYNAMICS
A New Framework for Understanding People and Realizing the Potential in Our Organizations, by Sandra Seagal and David Horne (Pegasus Communications, 1997).

Seagal and Horne have identified five predominant personality dy-namics, each with its own cues and capabilities: Mentally centered, physical-mental, physical-emotional, emotional-objective, emotional-subjective. Members of each group differ remarkably from members of others in the way they interact and perform tasks. A personality dynamic is not a label someone applies to you. You determine which group you belong to—but it is not a choice—you discover it through reflection. —Janis Dutton

THE 4MAT SYSTEM

Educator Bernice McCarthy and a host of her colleagues and teachers have developed an ingenious approach to learning styles in schools. The 4MAT software, which is very inexpensive, is available at their website: www.aboutlearning.com. They have more than 300 sample lessons for all PK–12 grade levels and modules for teacher training and individualized instruction. There are also diagnostic tests for students, teachers, and parents. McCarthy suggests that there are four main learning styles, each of which has a left- and right-brain component, leading to eight different types of lessons, each attuned in different ways to different students' strengths. —Tim Lucas

Techniques that get children engaged and motivated in the classroom also seem to work well for adults. I used Bernice McCarthy's leadership survey as an administrator to help school teams assess themselves. Since we planned the curriculum and tea ching practice together in grade-level teams, we sought to understand the diverse strengths and skills we brought. McCarthy's book on the 4MAT approach to instruction also includes a section on components for leading a successful staff meeting. —Victoria Kniewel, superintendent, West Windsor-Plainsboro Regional High School District, New Jersey

3. Overcoming Absurdity

A "whole-systems" approach for helping students overcome the hurdles of disability...and of everyday life

Terry O'Connor, Deirdre Bangham

At the time of this book's first edition, Terry (who passed away in 2008) was the director of the Center for Teaching and Learning at Indiana State University in Terre Haute, Indiana. Deirdre was the director of Festina Lente, formerly the National Specialised Equestrian Training Centre in Bray, Ireland (http://www.festinalente.ie), where much of this story took place. This article, ostensibly about the educational challenge made explicit by students with disabilities, is really about staff development for all teachers, and about creating better learning environments for all students. We're not suggesting every student needs a horse. But maybe every teacher would benefit from some work with students with disabilities—and certainly from the exercises that follow.

There was an outbreak of serious crimes in a neighborhood where people saw Niall change buses every day. Niall is easy to pick out in a crowd—not so much by appearance, but by his mannerisms. He is generous and kind of spirit, displaying anxiety if he perceives he is under pressure. His social sense is tuned to its own wavelength. If he does not know you, he is wary. If he thinks he knows you, you are his best friend almost immediately. He has a large vocabulary but does not speak in the most coherent way—topics switch without clear reasons or clues. It didn't take long for someone to bring this "suspicious" person to the attention of the police.

The police picked him up and questioned him for two hours. Niall warily bantered with them. He would not respond directly, and the police thought he was evading their questions. So they increased the intensity of the interrogation, hoping to break through his attitude. Then Niall mentioned the Specialised Equestrian Training Centre (SETC) he had attended, and suddenly one of the officers understood. Students at SETC have a range of disabilities, but they have learned there to live and work in local communities. Fortunately for Niall, this understanding police officer was able to redirect the interrogation; otherwise, the incident threatened to dehumanize a young man who had only recently mastered the basic skills for living responsibly in public.

When we think of people like Niall, we are often reminded of the theater of the absurd—the dramatic movement that explored mid-twentieth century people's feelings of bewilderment, alienation, and despair. One of the best-known playwrights from this tradition, Eugene Ionesco, placed his characters in dialogues that trapped them in the inhumane cages forged by their unexamined habits. His plays portray a truth that most of us can relate to. We all sometimes find ourselves in situations that are alienating and without meaning. We may work in places where rules and regulations don't make sense because they were created decades ago and nobody has bothered to change them, where people don't relate in authentic ways, and where there's seemingly no way out.

The lives of people with disabilities can be one long performance of the theater of the absurd. The institutions that house them often magnify the absurdity, by putting them into routines that make no sense, such as stuffing mattresses, and by isolating them from other people and from an understanding of the whole systems around them. But it is also possible to design a school for the disabled that helps students learn to escape the absurd. By rescripting our blind educational habits for these deserving and responsive students, we can also discover essential ways to restore the delight and power of learning for all students.

INSIDE THE EQUESTRIAN CENTRE

Until recently, most training programs for the disabled in Ireland expected that the students would remain in constant care facilities for the rest of their lives. The graduates of chef's schools, for example, would cook and live in institutions for people with disabilities. Their education was narrowed to drill them in accomplishing simple manual tasks. Their schools were oblivious to poetic, social, athletic, and other potential talents that would reach beyond the absurd.

The SETC has a different goal—to teach students the social, work, and academic skills that would allow them to leave constant care and to function in the real world. The two dozen students at the college are eighteen to twenty years old and have a range of disabilities. At least that is the label that admits them into the official system. The school does not allow these labels to follow them into the school. They are viewed instead as people who have experienced a variety of constraints that interfered with their learning. Their disabilities have made them vulnerable to judgment, critique, and abuse. They have suffered and struggled with debilitating scripts written by their families, schools, or neighborhoods.

The learning approach at the school looks at the whole person. It builds on students' successes and potential rather than focusing on their deficiencies. The students are promised respect and dignity, which for most is a new experience, and they are challenged to succeed. Perhaps for the first time in their lives, if they fail at something they will not be made to feel stupid, second rate, or have it held against them. They will be expected to work with the teachers again and again until they succeed. After experiencing years of alienation, they start to connect to a sense of purpose, the joy of learning, and the pride of success.

That's where the horses come in. The students are trained to work in the horse industry, caring for the horses, riding, and managing the stables and the riding arenas. The teachers help the students develop trust and empathy first with the animals and then with one another. Lessons in math or reading or other traditional "subjects" are tied to the skills they need to do their work.

Helen swore she could never learn to read, but to care for the horses she needed to be able the read the word "oats" on a bag of feed and to distinguish the different horses' nameplates on their stalls. At night a teacher, busy washing dishes, might ask Helen to look up something in a horse magazine. "My hands are too wet," the teacher would say. "Just turn to page 10 and tell me what it says about grooming your horse." Helen never considered it reading; she was just helping. Soon enough, with little fanfare, she was comfortably reading.

On my visits to the school, I am touched by the ability of these students to learn and succeed, in a way that supersedes their disabilities. Maggie was considered too autistic for regular employment. When I first met her, she wouldn't address people. If someone entered the stables, Maggie would look at her shoes and refuse to answer questions. Three years later, when a new instructor arrived at the school, Maggie stepped forward and reached out her hand to greet him. It was no small act.

THE AESTHETICS OF LEARNING

Almost every educator would agree that there are many factors that interfere with learning, though they are not always easy to identify. Teachers at SETC have created a learning environment that responds to the complex range of needs that undergird the success of any learner. They balance four dimensions of learning: intellectual, emotional, physical, and spiritual.

Colm knew that he had only two options, the equestrian school or a sheltered workshop—a fate he desperately wanted to avoid. Unfortunately, he had no interest in horses or their care, so he faked it. He fooled everyone and was admitted. Faking, we found out later, was one of his coping strategies, and he was quite skilled at it—up to a point. But he couldn't keep it up forever. When it became obvious that Colm didn't fit in, the school was faced with a dilemma. Recommending another career direction to Colm would likely condemn him to the assembly-line work he wanted desperately to avoid. Yet encouraging him to continue would use up his training funds, preparing him for a career he would not choose. A staff member observed that Colm had an interest in an old tractor. When they reorganized his program around tractors, cars, and other mechanical items instead of the horses, they discovered it was the horse part that didn't fit, not Colm. Soon he was happily learning new skills and was able to graduate and get a job using them.

Students without a purpose for their studies are lifeless learners. For any educator, the challenge is to identify the personal vision that motivates and guides the learners and to help create connections between that vision and the learning that needs to occur. One way to do this is to recognize when those fundamental moments of learning—the "ahas"—light up a student's face. Donald Arnstine calls this the "aesthetics" of learning. At SETC, these aesthetics represent the key to SETC's success: they make connections between purposes and practices that are seemingly unrelated.

The aesthetics of learning may be the only way people have to counteract the "theater of the absurd" nature of schools that continue to isolate, alienate, and disconnect students and teachers from the joy of learning. Schools don't have to provide every student with a horse; but they do need to provide an environment that gives students a belief in their own inherent value. How quickly the little slights, labels, and expectations that they should reach beyond their developmental ability can undermine that belief and lead to failure. Many teachers (and other people) unconsciously compound these slights and labels, even as they agree to the abstract goal that every student is valued.

This problem is not limited to students with disabilities. We can all remember absurd times in school that taught us to turn off to our talents. When I (Terry) was in third grade, the teacher gave us blunt evaluations of our singing ability. I learned to give up singing, a joy that I abandoned until thirty years later, when I decided to sing out despite her advice. The results of "education of the absurd" are evident in the resistance that builds up inside kids and bubbles to the surface, usually around high school. Students recognize the absurdity of their situation but don't know how to respond to it. Unable to find the connections they seek in school, they look outside for it, in ways that may not be appropriate, safe, or in their long-term best interests.

In the end, the most crucial disability anyone may have is the inability to continue to learn. When schools cast learning in absurd ways, even the most willing student may wisely choose to withdraw from meaningful engagement. The only way to avoid this is to remain in touch with the joy—the aesthetic—of learning.

Reconnecting to the Aesthetics of Learning

Terry O'Connor

1. DESCRIBE THREE TO FIVE AESTHETIC LEARNING MOMENTS.

These are moments when something at school, or in your learning outside of school, clicked with your own aspirations and you felt a charge of connection.

What are some of the ways you felt? Describe them, using adjectives or metaphors. If you felt valued or valuable, describe that feeling or experience as you remember it.

Share your insights with others and begin to draw up a list of qualities found in aesthetic learning moments. Make this into a list of guidelines for your class.

2. DESCRIBE THREE TO FIVE ABSURD LEARNING MOMENTS.

In these moments, you felt pushed into a situation of bewilderment, alienation, or despair. Again, what are some of the ways you felt? If you felt belittled, frustrated, or angry, describe that experience as you remember it.

Share these insights with others and begin to draw up a list of qualities found in absurd learning moments. Make this into a list of warning signs for your class.

3. HOW DO YOUR STUDENTS APPROACH THEIR LESSONS WITH YOU?

Use your lists of guidelines and warnings to see how your students are feeling. Are their lessons full of aesthetic moments? Absurd moments? Are they interested and intrigued, challenged and alert? Are they dull and lifeless, bored or anxious?

Reflect on what rules, relationships, assumptions, or learning patterns have helped to produce your success or your absurdities.

4. WHAT ARE THE SIGNS OF STUDENTS WHO HAVE LOST THEIR CONNECTION TO LEARNING?

When you see students who have been caught in the realm of absurdity for too long, what behavior do you see? How do these students talk or act? What else do you notice?

5. HOW CAN YOU HELP THEM RECONNECT TO REAL LEARNING?

How would you find out more about them? What are their passions? How can lessons be adapted to connect their learning practice to these important purposes?

Purpose:

Sensitizing oneself to the emotional tone of students so that you, as a teacher, can better respect their dignity, build confidence, and help them address learning challenges.

Overview:

A series of reflective questions that connect your own learning moments to those of your students.

LEARNING DISABLED

The term "learning disabled" has been defined as a deficit in "school skills"—speech, language, reading, spelling, writing, or arithmetic—that stems from some innate factor about the child, not from the environment at home or school. Being branded "learning disabled" (or an equivalent phrase) is often a prerequisite for special services or counseling. Even when the services are valuable, the individual is often pulled visibly out of class or normal study hall to receive them, and the implication remains—that the person has something wrong with him or her, and the task at hand is diagnosis and cure.

In all too many cases, labels like "learning disabled," "attention-deficit disorder," "dyslexic," and "LDNOS" (learning disorder not otherwise specified) represent a quick fix to the challenge of multiple intelligences and learning styles—a way of fitting children into the industrial model of schools. Many children struggle in schools not because they are "disabled," "disordered," or "deficient," but because the way they are being taught is incompatible with the way they learn; they don't fit conveniently into the processes of the school. The label is the school's way, or society's way, of equating this lack of fit with a deficiency in the student. The deficit actually lies in the system.

Worse still, the "learning-disabled" label makes it harder to distinguish students who have a genuine brain injury or disability from those who are simply "differently abled." Then the label leads to prescriptions—medical or social—that treat the student, not the situation, with terrible potential for cost, waste, and risk. One consequence is the inaccurate and disproportionately prevalent labeling of certain economic classes and ethnicities.

Some educators are becoming more sophisticated: more capable and aware of managing learning for a wide variety of students. They sometimes go out of their way, in their speech and their actions, to show that the label "learning disabled" is not a judgment, but rather an institutional convenience: a way to qualify students for funding or services without having to label them as mentally retarded, autistic, or otherwise impaired. But the prevalence of this subterfuge, and the stigma still attached to the label by many people (including the students themselves), shows how far there is to go before we have schools that recognize the value and learning path for every child, whatever their learning styles, predispositions, and backgrounds may be. —Janis Dutton and Art Kleiner

Researchers in this field are keenly aware of this issue. In Renee Bradley, Louis C. Danielson, and Daniel P. Hallahan, *Identification of Learning Disabilities: Research to Practice* (Psychology Press, 2002), a report on a learning disabilities summit conference convened by the U.S. Office of Special Education Programs, there is an extensive history of the ongoing debates over this definition, and the real-world consequences for many children. The report settled on this definitional statement: "The central concept of SLD [specific learning disabilities] involves disorders of learning and cognition that are intrinsic to the individual. SLD are specific in the sense that these disorders each significantly affect a relatively narrow range of academic and performance outcomes."

4. We Dance Together

Candee Basford

PM   MM

People are quick to label those who learn differently, drawing conclusions from the labels rather than from any direct contact or relationship. In this article, Candee Basford—an artist, consultant, and adult educator—describes her experience of advocating for her daughter Katie, who has Down syndrome. For most of her daughter's life, Candee (and ultimately Katie herself) refused to accept prejudiced views of Katie's abilities and potential. This led them both to continually challenge traditional ways of thinking and interacting. The experience transformed Candee into a community activist involved in broader issues—posing the question, "Whose disability is it, the person's or the systems'?"

Boarding a school bus with a group of fifth graders embarking on a field trip to the zoo was like being inside a popcorn machine. The students hollered and cheered as they randomly scattered throughout the bus and bounced into their seats. I took photos of my daughter Katie arm in arm with her friends getting ready to leave, and I knew how excited they all were. We live a good distance from the zoo, so it was a rare opportunity for many of the children. I sat with Katie and another child. Everyone cheered when the bus started to move.

But then the bus stopped at the front of the high school, and a special education class of children with mild developmental disabilities emerged with their teacher. The cheers were replaced with groans "Oh no, not them!" Even the other chaperone groaned. All of the children on the bus got up and moved to the back so they wouldn't have to sit with *those* kids. And Katie moved back there too, even though, as a child with Down syndrome, she had far more significant disabilities than the others who were about to board the bus.

Katie's classmates probably didn't know much about the other children except that they were in a special education class and they came out of another building. Neither did the other chaperone. At that moment I realized that it's not the differences that separate people, or even the degrees of difference (as in the level of disability). It's the way that people, often those in positions of power, assign status based on the label they have carved in their minds. This positioning results in a lack of opportunities to interact with others in positive ways. Spending time with people—being in close proximity with those who are different—

can break down the labels and the assumptions and give relationships a chance to develop.

Katie's classmates knew her because they interacted with her daily. She was their friend and accepted as a member of their community. They knew she was different, but they saw her as a member of the class, and she saw herself the same way. In that classroom the children were learning much more than curriculum. They were learning with, from, and about each other.

FROM DEFICITS TO GIFTS

Before Katie was diagnosed with Down syndrome, her future seemed full of possibilities. After the diagnosis, her future appeared dark and unknown. I didn't know what to expect or what to do. I didn't think I could possibly parent this child.

When Katie was two, and the umpteen-hundredth professional asked me how old she had been when she first walked, I said, "She could take ten steps nine out of ten times when she was eighteen months old, and…" Suddenly, I stopped. I realized I was answering questions as an objective caregiver, and even as a distant one, not as a mother. The awareness took my breath away.

I started examining my own prejudices. I realized I had been socialized to value certain characteristics in human beings: intelligence, achievement, success, and money. I tied all those characteristics to some word we call "normal." I had been socialized to believe that my own child was defective, less than normal, not worthy. I loved her too much to believe it any longer.

Against the advice of professionals, we did not enroll Katie in a school designated for children with disabilities. Instead, we chose a preschool in the community. That was when I first had a chance to see Katie's learning in relationship with other students—and to see, lo and behold, that they also learned from her. I began to recognize that she was not an individual learner, but that she learned more when she was with others learning together. I became convinced that her potential was—and is— bound up in relationships.

More on John McKnight's work with others on focusing on gifts rather than deficits can be found on the website of The Asset-Based Community Development Institute at Northwestern University at http://www.abcdinstitute.org/.

John McKnight says that when you look at deficits and needs, you create services, and the people you serve become clients of the system. But if you shift your focus from looking at what's wrong with people to looking at their gifts and capacities and what they have to contribute, you create citizens. Coming to understand this was a powerful, powerful shift for me.

Katie went into kindergarten against the school's wishes. They did not want her there. I wish more school leaders would see the relationship between what they do and the level of community they create. Schools have a choice: They can create citizens or clients. The schools that create citizens are those where building community is critical; where school is about building relationships and learning how to be a friend.

The Chilean biologist Humberto Maturana says that love expands intelligence and enables creativity, and "when the emotion of love is there, vision expands." I certainly subscribe to this idea; I think it was through focusing on my love for Katie that I began to have visions for her life that were much higher than the goals put forth by the systems designed to help people like her.

Learning to make her bed, to tell time on an analog clock, and to count change were among the goals that the professionals deemed essential. They were preparing her to function in an institution or sheltered workshop, and they set low expectations. The scary thing was that so many people thought Katie needed modest goals because her life would be different from everyone else's. They assumed she would not work, or that she would not do all the things the rest of us think we want to do. Learning about the world and learning math and science weren't deemed important for her. Being with her friends wasn't seen as relevant because nobody thought about her that way.

Learning about the world was very important to Katie, even if others didn't think it mattered. It was important to me that Katie have the opportunity. One day I visited her first-grade classroom and observed the children away from their desks sitting in reading circles, except Katie. She was at her desk with a pencil and paper. I asked the teacher why Katie wasn't in a reading group. She told me she had a rule that the children had to be able to recite their ABCs from A through Z, without missing a letter, before they could join a reading group. Until then they sat at their desks.

I knew I was no expert in teaching reading, but I thought Katie would benefit from being in a reading group, whether she ever learned to read or not. I knew that she would learn something from hearing the stories and being with the other kids. I asked the principal for help, and Katie was let into a reading group.

THE LEARNER AS TEACHER

Eventually, Katie learned to read quite well, and she graduated from high school, though she still hesitates when reciting the alphabet. Some days it scares me to death to think that we would still be working on the alphabet. We could have spent ten years of school on just that before she learned to read and was able to discover more about the world.

When Katie first told me she wanted to go on to college, I was reluctant to agree. Frankly, I was tired from the years of advocating for her

For example see Humberto Maturana and Pille Bunnell, The Biology of Business: Love Expands Intelligence. *Reflections, 1(2)* (1999). Society for Organizational Learning and the Massachusetts Institute of Technology, 1999.

presence and participation in public school. I also thought she would only be able to audit the classes. I really didn't think about the success she had already achieved in the face of tremendous adversity, or about giving her more chances to be successful. But Katie had a vision and, again, she taught me a lesson. Despite the weight of her disability, she has completed courses in subjects such as anatomy and physiology, microbiology, and art at our local community college. She has a 3.0 grade point average. Her friends from elementary through high school still drop by to visit.

Katie has her own dreams and her own visions for her future. Her visions have helped expand my vision for her, partly by allowing her to try things I didn't think were possible. She wants to finish her associate degree, work as a lab assistant, get married, join a rock band, and write a book.

Katie has shifted my thinking in innumerable ways. I still read a wide range of books and network with people all over the country who are having conversations about learning and being together in community. I facilitate meetings with parents to create stories and portfolios about the gifts their children have to offer and to explore what it means to learn in community with others. I have learned that when people are different, a lot of time is spent determining what's wrong with them, and very little time is spent understanding their gifts and potential contributions. In fact, I think too little time is spent looking at the gifts and capacities of people who are labeled "normal" or even "above normal."

I guess I never expected that Katie would become one of my most powerful teachers. Knowing her has taught me what it means to be uncertain and to not be sure about anything that I'd always been certain about before. She taught me the importance of ambiguity: the importance of not knowing how the world should be structured and then relearning or maybe rethinking the possibilities.

My learning with Katie is an upward spiral and each cycle leads to a deeper understanding of the perceptions and gifts she has to offer.

Recently I asked Katie what people could do to help her reach her dreams, and she answered, "You can dance."

"If I dance, how can that help you reach your dreams?" I asked.

"That tells me that I can dance, too. I can follow the moves and the steps. If you're dancing, I can feel the motions," she replied.

"Okay," I said, "I get you. If I dance and we all dance, then…"

Katie said, "We dance together."

WE DANCE TOGETHER

A Painted Essay About My Education with Katie,
by Candee Basford (Candee Basford, 2005), http://www.wedancetogether.com

Candee Basford's life changed drastically when her daughter Katie was born with Down syndrome. She never expected that Katie would become one of her most inspirational teachers in a twenty-six-year (and counting) journey of discovery and transformation. In this collection of her paintings accompanied by short essays, the author reflects on her experiences. When I share this book with others, their eyes often water with tears, but they stem from inspiration and promise rather than sadness. It is a useful tool for generating conversations among educators, parents, and community members by raising questions that have no easier answers. What does it mean to work and learn in community with others? What prejudices do we hold toward people with disabilities? Or toward people who are just different? In what ways do prejudices prevent people from seeing the gifts that people of all abilities have? What can we learn from Katie? —Janis Dutton

I love how my mother created this book with watercolor paintings and words. She is very creative. She brightens my eyes with rainbows. My mother Candee is a spirit with nature. She always loves her kids. She loves me. We go to conferences together, we pass notes back and forth. Some of the notes became paintings in this book. I do love my mother. She has been supportive, caring, sweet, and loving. This book makes me happy. I want to learn and be creative like my mother. I want to write my own book. The title of my book will be called "Facing the Future." Look for my book next. —Katie Basford

Creating a Book About Your Child's Gifts

Candee Basford

Ask a roomful of parents of children with disabilities to describe their sons or daughters, and you often get a laundry list of deficits, including visual, hearing, behavioral, and cognitive problems. So much time is spent labeling deficits and delays that eventually the labels take over. Seeing children only in this way leads people to overlook their children's gifts and potential. A portfolio can be a way to shift that perspective, a chance to remember a child's gifts and capacities, and an opportunity to reveal and then share with others his or her contribution to community.

This exercise grew out of a series of workshops I began for parents of children with disabilities to explore the question "Who is your child, really?" Over time, parents of children who aren't branded with the "disability" label started attending, often outnumbering the other parents, and shedding as many tears. Sadly, there is so much emphasis on performance on achievement tests, grades, and in sports it seems too many parents don't have the opportunity to stop and think about who their children really are.

Creating activities around gifts and contributions opens up possibilities for making connections and building community—whether the focus is on children or the adults in the room.

The First Session: Beginning the Book

STEP 1: IMAGINE

Start with a conversation about community. Imagine that an alien from outer space landed in your backyard and asked you to take him to your best example of community. Where would you take him and why?

Then ask: What are the common themes about the places that everyone chose?

You will undoubtedly discover that each story is really about one person or a group of people giving something to the newcomer. Discuss the concept of gifts. Some people have the gift of making people happy or welcome. Consider your own gifts and how you are currently giving your gifts and strengthening community.

STEP 2: REMEMBER

Think about your child's gifts and contributions. What does she or he bring to the world? This conversation can first take place in groups of two before sharing with the larger group. Partners interview each other; one person tells some stories about his or her child, while the other person listens, offers encouragement, and records the child's gifts and strengths found in the story.

Some examples of questions that might be asked: Is your daughter's smile a gift? Does your son make people happy? Does she know a lot about dinosaurs or some other topic? Does he sing songs?

For parents of children with disabilities, this is not always easy. One mother whose child is autistic cried through most of the workshop. Her son's recent difficult behaviors had left her empty of ideas about his gifts. But another member of the group started telling a story about this little boy—something good that happened on the playground. That started a shift, and she remembered his gifts and strengths. Looking back on that session later, she said the shift in thinking about her son changed her life and his in profound ways.

STEP 3: DREAM

Now discuss your dreams with the same partner. What five things do you most want for your child's future?

Then share your ideas with people in the room.

Have someone record the list of visions and dreams.

Ask what surprised people and how those surprises expanded or confirmed their own thinking.

Think about how you can illustrate all this in the portfolio you will be creating.

The questions in this exercise were posed by John McKnight at a workshop on building community. For more on McKnight's work and the Asset-Based Community Development Institute go to: http://www.abcdinstitute.org/.

STEP 4: CREATE

Begin to make pages for a portfolio of your child's gifts. Try to complete at least one page that you may use or redraft later for the final book. Use images, words, or both. You can choose to draw your own pictures or use family photos or images out of a publication. You can describe your child's gifts and dreams using prose, poetry, or individual words. Be sure to include your dreams and visions for your child.

Some parents create a table of contents for their book. Here is one example:

A Little History

Meet the Family

Jessica's Hobbies

Mom's Recommendations

My Vision for Jessica

Session Two: Reflection

STEP 5: SHARE

Work on the book between the two sessions. Then bring what you have created to share with the group. It doesn't have to be complete. Like the children, it is a work in progress.

Designate someone to record the group conversation on flip charts.

What was it like to make this portfolio? What was it like to remember these stories? What were the difficulties or challenges? What insights or surprises did you discover about your child or yourself? Who else became involved in creating the portfolio? What happened when you shared it with others? Who might you share this portfolio with?

What have we learned about each other?

What have we learned about community?

Jessica's mom wrote a note to the teacher on the table of contents page.

"Thank you for taking time to learn a little more about my daughter. Your job is so very important. You have the opportunity to see my daughter interact with her peers, struggle with new concepts, and see the success of her hard work. You are her role model, teacher, and future friend. I look forward to getting to know you as we work together to help this child excel."

STEP 6: TAKING IT BACK HOME

After the session, share your child's portfolio with your family and neighbors. Don't forget your child's current and future teachers.

Variation: Focus on one story

Find a photograph of your child that tells a story. Think of that story, of that time, and talk (or write) about the gifts revealed within the story.

Variation: A frame for a longer story

This is for groups who meet over a longer period of time. At each meeting, participants discuss the gifts associated with their children, and their own gifts, and draw pictures of them. These drawings are then taped one at a time around the edges of a large wall chart, illustrating the idea that real community is framed by the gifts of its citizens. The center of the chart, now framed by gifts, is later filled in by the stories the group will share as they continue to meet.

50 YEARS WITH AUTISM

A Mother and Advocate Looks Back on the Personal and Social Challenges of an Autistic Disability, by Irene Slovak Kleiner with Edward Kleiner (Spyral Publisher, 2011), www.50yearswithautism.com.

As it becomes easier and less expensive to self-publish books, a growing number of people are putting out memoirs of their experiences raising or teaching children with special needs. This story is one I know personally.

A boy with autism grows up in the early 1960s; his parents struggle with a lack of diagnosis, support, and help. They are determined that their child will have a chance for a normal life. Their son Edward is determined to make his own way and not accept the limits of others' labels. He goes to the public schools, at first with powerfully encouraging results, and then—as the politics of the school district shift against him—with heartbreak. Being put into regular classrooms is not a panacea, because he is bullied mercilessly, and there is no room for him.

Later, in the 1970s, he attends a series of private schools. Some are criminally negligent, getting away with it because the parents know they have few other options. Others are genuine learning organizations, in which the entire community seems to be developing an understanding of what this very special kind of education requires.

For Edward, the biggest challenge of all comes from within. In the late 1970s, at age thirty and facing expulsion from a group home, he has to decide whether to take responsibility for his own life or to remain dependent on his parents. Going on his own, though he desperately wants to do it, is extremely difficult, and he almost doesn't make it. But since he will almost certainly outlive his parents, dependency is not an option.

That's the moral of this memoir. It is always tempting to set "difficult" children aside when they are young. But for each, there is a similar moment of truth, when they can choose to be a citizen or a client, a contributor or a burden. The challenge is to give them enough skills and support, over the years, so they can make that choice when the time comes. For they will not always be children. Today there are many more opportunities for autistic children, but they still face many of the same challenges that my brother did so many years ago. —Art Kleiner

EDUCATING ALL STUDENTS TOGETHER

Educating All Students Together: How School Leaders Create Unified Systems, by Leonard C. Burrello, Carl A. Lashley, and Edith E. Beatty (Corwin Press, 2000)

I'm often struck by the struggle involved in meeting the educational needs of the growing number of students at the margins of our educational systems. These are the students with racial, ethnic, or ability differences, students living in poverty, and students with language differences. Too often these students are placed in "special" or "alternative" programs—in effect, a parallel system. Even when included in the "regular" program, the students generally do not experience learning environments that respect diversity and build on what they bring to the classroom.

Burrello, Lashley, and Beatty develop a conceptual framework and process for moving toward a "unified" system that is learner centered. Using a systems approach, they argue that the process must begin with confronting the discrepancy between a community's vision for its schools and its current reality. Doing this can form the basis for dialogue and inquiry about the purpose of schools and the kind of education the community wants for its children. For educators attempting to create a unified system, the authors provide guidance in organizational structure, curriculum, instructional delivery, and program evaluation. —Nelda Cambron-McCabe

5. What Signals Are You Sending?

Unearthing the Messages in the Language We Use with Children

Janis Dutton, Nelda Cambron-McCabe, Tim Lucas, Art Kleiner

Adam is an intelligent and sensitive seventh grader. One day his teacher pulled him aside and said, "Adam, your last assignment is fabulous. I think it is the best one in the class." That afternoon he surprised his parents by starting his homework as soon as he got home from school and finishing it early. "I loved school today," he told his parents. "I learned so much in every class, and I did all my work without being reminded. Mrs. Jones really liked my paper. I never knew school could be so much fun."

Unfortunately for Adam, school is rarely fun. He thinks he is stupid because over seven years, more than one teacher has communicated this perception through their interactions with him. When Adam's mother told his writing teacher about the effect of her compliment, the teacher said, "Thank you so much for telling me. I know my personality is rather abrupt, and sometimes I am so busy I don't often think about the things I say. I have been looking for a way to reach Adam. I'm so proud of the paper he did. I will look for more opportunities to encourage him."

Often when people are in a position of power over others, their use of invalidating language—language that communicates that the other person is flawed or incomplete—can have a much longer-term impact than they realize. Many kids can't read social situations well, but negative messages from teachers come through loud and clear and linger for years, much more vividly than the lesson being taught. "Don't try to sing, dear…just mouth the words," says a teacher during rehearsal for a class play, and that person is silent thereafter whenever people gather to sing. Or "You're always picked last, aren't you?" says a coach on the playing field, and the kid turns off from sports forever. The teacher doesn't intend to hurt the child; the teacher is probably unaware of the signal he or she has sent, the way that he or she has invalidated the child. But those experiences take a toll.

Teachers also send signals nonverbally—for instance, in the way they grade homework. Marking an assignment with a big red "X" sends a signal of judgment and blame. Handing back the papers in the order of highest grade to lowest, or asking students to grade each other's papers, is a devastating signal. It says that poor performance is public knowledge. When a principal we know told a teacher that she was embarrassing her students this way, she said, "Well, I don't have time to grade all these papers." The efficiency of her classroom had overtaken her respect for the students in her class

Positive messages linger too. One of the authors of this book was once told by a middle school assistant principal, "You can be anything you want to be." That message is continually remembered and leaned on in difficult times. A similar story appeared in Bob Greene's syndicated column several years ago. A young boy, who wasn't a particularly good student, received an English paper back marked "This is good writing." That statement changed his life. He had always liked writing, but never thought he was good enough. The statement was important, not because it built his self-esteem, but because he suddenly saw that it was true—he had produced good writing. Today, he is a professional writer.

Busy people in positions of authority—teachers, parents, principals, bosses, colleagues—are often unaware of how the language they use affects the way they think and the way others interpret their messages. Teachers who use the phrase "at-risk students," for example, are unconsciously reinforcing the belief that the students' own flaws—of personality, character, or background—have put them in jeopardy. Since those flaws aren't going away, it can be inferred that the student will always be in jeopardy. By contrast, teachers who talk about students in an "at-risk situation," are reminding others and themselves that circumstances can change (or be changed). This helps them move away from blaming the student and leads them, instead, to seek more fundamental solutions to the student's problems.

How, then, can we use language to support a child's learning instead of interfering with it? Anyone in a position of power or leadership might

I remember spilling paint in second grade while working on a pioneer bonnet for a playground celebration. The teacher yanked my arm, said, "You never listen to directions!" and sent me back to sit at my desk. The next day I was "permitted" to paint my bonnet in the back of the room while everyone else worked at their desks and snickered at me. I was probably the only person at that celebration who still remembers it; the misery I felt then returned, years later, when I attended my children's class events on pioneers. Everyone I know, just about, has some similar memory. —Janis Dutton

The writer's name is Malcolm Dalkoff; the story appeared in Bob Greene, "Good or Bad, Words Echo Forever," *Middletown Ohio Journal*, December 5, 1997.

Some of these examples were adapted with permission from the "EQ in Education page" (www.eqi.org/educ.htm), from EQI, a website on emotional intelligence developed by Steve Hein.

When you say . . .	They might hear it as . . .	But you could turn it into an opportunity for learning by saying something like this:
"You're not getting it."	"You're not capable of getting it."	"Have you tried looking at it this way?"
"So you forgot your homework again."	"You are irresponsible."	"What strategy can we work out to help you turn in your homework on time?"
"You are so slow!"	"You are dumb."	"Would you like some help with this part of the assignment?"
"No, you're wrong."	"You are dumb."	"What is it that led you to that answer? How do you know it's a good answer? How else might you look at it?" Or, "That's a great answer, but it's not quite the question we're asking right here."
"You're trying hard, but it still won't get you an "A.""	"You'll always be dumb, no matter how hard you try."	"I have noticed that you're really making progress. I'm happy to see how much you've practiced."

"As a teacher I possess tremendous power to make a child's life miserable or joyous. I can be a tool of torture or an instrument of inspiration. I can humiliate or humor, hurt or heal. In all situations, it is my response that decides whether a crisis will be escalated or deescalated, and a child humanized or dehumanized." — Haim Ginott. See Haim Ginott, *Teacher and Child* (Collier Books, 1972).

do well by drawing on the cardinal rule of medical practice: First, do no harm. Haim Ginott's guideline for effective communication—between parent and child or teacher and student—is to talk to the situation, not to the character or personality. In the table that follows are examples of thoughtless statements that send a signal that "something is wrong with you"—and alternatives that open the door to more fruitful learning. The underlying principle for each alternative: Instead of describing something about the student, describe an observation about the student; let the student become your partner in figuring out what to do next.

Also see "Balancing Advocacy and Inquiry," page 104.

LEARNING RESEARCH AND DEVELOPMENT CENTER

For those who seek insight on the nature of learning and on ways to improve it, this center is particularly valuable. Based at the University of Pittsburgh, it maintains ongoing intensive research in subjects ranging from educational technology to learning in the workplace to children's museums. Its materials are accessible to educators, parents, and community members through comprehensive websites, publications, and other media. They are broad and flexible but relevant to everyday school activity. And they pay attention to the whole system of influences that affect a child's learning, including the parents' lives and work environment and the social networks of the school.

One component of LRDC, the Institute for Learning, sets up partnerships with educators and schools; it focuses on professional development based on cognitive learning principles and the development of effort-oriented educational programs. Director Lauren Resnick is best known for research challenging the validity of norm-referenced test results ("bell-curve" style results that compare one student against another); LRDC's New Standards project (a joint project with the National Center on Education and the Economy) has led the nation in standards-based reform efforts. A good starting point is the nine broad principles of learning that Resnick and her colleagues have identified that must be evident if students are to learn at high levels. These are: being organized for effort, clear expectations, recognition of accomplishment, fair and credible evaluations, rigor in a thinking curriculum, accountable talk, socializing intelligence, self-management of learning, and learning as apprenticeship. —Nelda Cambron-McCabe

The best starting points online are the LRDC website (www.lrdc.pitt.edu) and the Institute for Learning website (www.instituteforlearning.org.)

EMOTIONAL INTELLIGENCE

Why It Can Matter More Than IQ, by Daniel Goleman (Bantam, 1995)

As Goleman puts it, "There is a role that emotional competence plays over and above family and economic forces—it may be decisive in determining the extent to which any given child or teenager is undone by hardships (like poverty or child abuse) or finds a core of resilience to survive them." Unlike most popular psychology books, this one has substance (building on the work of cognitive scientists and educational researchers), and in its last chapter, it suggests ways that schools can foster emotional intelligence in their students.

Mary Leiker, during her tenure as superintendent of the Kentwood, Michigan, school district, read and discussed this book with thirty-seven administrators and the seven school board members in her district. They met monthly and, chapter by chapter, discussed the implications of emotional intelligence. According to Leiker: "For example, when students came back from being suspended, we began to 'go that extra step' and discuss with them the reason for their emotional state—to make the suspension a learning opportunity. I also use emotional intelligence as an opening point in our programs on parenting skills." —Nelda Cambron-McCabe

Also see "No Throw-Away Children," by Mary Leiker, page 434.

Some of Goleman's follow-up books add other dimensions to our understanding of human competence. *Social Intelligence: The New Science of Human Relationships* (Bantam, 2006) describes the ways in which other people affect people's mental and physical functions—and how social environments, including schools, can be designed to improve the quality of life for everyone within. *Ecological Intelligence: How Knowing the Hidden Impacts of What we Buy Can Change Everything* (Broadway Books, 2009) describes the cognitive link between human awareness and ecological sustainability.

I have used *Emotional Intelligence* very effectively with adults. One insight in particular, the amygdala hijack, is very useful; it points to the way we are hardwired to fly off the handle, through reflexive parts of our brain, at certain emotional stimuli. Everyone has that tendency, and making people aware of it lends humanity and compassion to a common and debilitating predicament. Just as you learn to watch yourself go up the ladder of inference, you can learn to watch yourself get "hijacked," feel the voltage of anger or anxiety hit, and then simply react differently. I've used this to help a group of bankers; if they can learn to lighten up, anyone can. —Bryan Smith

See "The Cognitive Studies Group," page 404.

V. Practices

1. Teaching Structural Tension

PM

Robert Fritz

*The practice of personal mastery focuses on some of the most signifi-
cant questions an adult can reflect upon: What are you really trying
to create in your life? What is the nature of reality right now for you?
And what do you choose? The practice works in a transcendent and yet
matter-of-fact way, a way that every creative person recognizes and
that is difficult to put into practice and into words.*

*It works for adults, but how well would it work for children? We
asked the man who had formulated the concept of personal mastery.
Robert Fritz, a composer and filmmaker, formalized his theories about
the creative process in the 1970s and 1980s, when he codesigned (with
Peter Senge and Charles Kiefer) the original Leadership and Mastery
course on which The Fifth Discipline is partly based. He developed the
concept of "creative tension," which he originally called (and still calls)
"structural tension."*

Also see Personal Mastery, page 76.

What is the point of education? Is it to socialize young people so
they can fit into the fabric of society? Is it to train a workforce? Is
it to introduce young people to the greater possibilities that life has to
offer? These are all legitimate and, therefore, correct answers. But they
leave out the most profound purpose that education might have: helping young people learn how to create the lives they truly want to create.

There are a few interesting reasons why adults don't teach—and
young people don't learn—how to create what they truly want to create.

First of all, most teachers have not been trained in the skills of the cre-

For more depth about structural
tension, see Robert Fritz, *The
Path of Least Resistance* (Fawcett-
Columbine, 1989) and Robert Fritz, *The
Path of Least Resistance for Managers*
(Publishers' Group West, 1999).

ative process. The topic can seem as if it belongs more to after-school extra-curricular activities such as band or theater. It doesn't sound like a center-piece of mainstream education like math, science, or language skills. And yet the creative process is the most successful process for accomplishment in the history of civilization. It has created all of the arts, most of science and technology, pop culture, literature, and poetry, and it has fueled invention and innovation in business and organizations. Can it be understood by most teachers, parents, and students? Can it be taught? The happy answer to both questions is yes. But before we can begin to do it, we need to think differently about our goals, our understanding of reality, our ability to generate original processes to enable us to accomplish our goals, our relationship to success or failure, and the nature of discipline and momentum.

STRUCTURAL TENSION: THE KEY

The key to the creative process is structural tension. Whenever we establish a tension, it strives for resolution. Structural tension is established through contrast: between our desired state (our goals, aspirations, desires) and our current reality in relationship to those goals. We can move toward resolving the tension by taking actions that bring our goals and reality closer together. The ultimate resolution happens when we accomplish our goals. Moving toward our goals sounds simple but requires the development of many skills.

DISCIPLINE

All disciplines are unnatural. That's why they are disciplines. When we have an itch, it is natural to scratch. It takes discipline not to scratch. When learning to ski, the student stands on top of a mountain looking down to a distant valley below. Any novice's natural instinct would be to lean back. But the instructor says, "Lean down the mountain!" As it turns out, the way skis are designed, leaning down is like putting the brakes on the skis, while leaning back is like putting the pedal on the floor. It takes discipline to go against our instinct and lean down, but that's what the skier must learn to do.

See *The Path of Least Resistance*, p. 197.

In establishing structural tension, it takes discipline to define the actual end result we want to create and to define reality objectively outside the distortions of our assumptions, theories, and concepts. It takes discipline to confront moments that are filled with frustration, disappointment, and setbacks. It takes discipline to learn from mistakes and successes—ours and other people's.

Many of the most demanding careers, such as in music, filmmaking, medicine, and sports, place extreme physical and mental pressures on people and pit them against tremendous competition. Without a discipline for establishing and maintaining structural tension, it's very difficult to accomplish any great mastery. Every time the situation becomes uncomfortable—for example, when you face rejection—you will be prone to give up. By contrast, if you operate with a discipline based on what you genuinely want, you may still feel disappointment, but you won't give up. If anything, the disappointment tempers you and helps you keep moving forward.

THINKING ABOUT WHAT WE WANT

Many well-meaning people think that they have asked their children or students what they want to create, but they haven't really. They have asked a subtle variation: "Of the things we've made available to you, what do you want?"

Notice the difference. "What do you want to create?" asks the young person to consider his or her overall life goals, values, aspirations, and dreams. The more controlling version begins by providing a menu of acceptable possibilities, and then says "From what is available to you, pick something." What if the goals and dreams they truly want aren't on the menu? Then the children or students are out of luck. The message is delivered to them that the circumstances of life are the dominant force, and "You'd better learn to comply." This idea eventually becomes an orientation, which in my first book, *The Path of Least Resistance*, I called "the reactive-responsive orientation." I was describing the way people get trapped in a life-stance that seems to say "Limit your aspirations to something reasonable." There is another orientation available: the "creative" (or self-generative) orientation, in which the individual's choices are the organizing principle in his or her life.

When my colleagues and I first started teaching adults the creative process back in the 1970s, many people had a lot of trouble answering this simple question: What do you want? Instead of considering what they actually wanted, they would attempt to describe what they thought they should want, or they would name the elimination of problems as what they said they wanted, or they would use vague slogans, or they would think about processes rather than what the processes were supposed to produce.

The situation was all rather puzzling at first, until the obvious became obvious: A lot of people don't know how to think about what they want. They have had the subject so drummed out of their brains that it's as if they can't think about certain ideas because they don't know the right questions to ask. Too many young people are taught to give up their dreams before they have had any experience attempting to pursue meaningful goals. These young people are thought to be unable to fulfill their ambitions. This happens, paradoxically, because we love our kids, and we don't want to see them suffer. Our tendency is to protect them and control them so they will be saved from the emotional upheaval that disappointment can bring. To protect them from disappointment, adults inadvertently censor young people not only from trying to create what might matter to them but from even thinking about trying.

Because we protect young people from these experiences, they don't have the chance to toughen up and build important life muscles. They never develop the discipline for going the extra mile when it's called for. They never learn the lessons of consummate professionalism so important when developing character or the ongoing learning skills needed to accomplish anything difficult.

IT BEGINS WITH A QUESTION

The creative process begins with this deceivingly simple question: What do you want to create? Can we ask our young people that question? At first they will not know how to answer. They will tend to say what they think adults want to hear. But if we persist, eventually they will realize we really want them to give us their answer, not the answer we might have wanted them to tell us in the past.

When we get into the habit of defining our goals, visions, and aspirations, we are developing a true skill—a skill that young people need to learn if they are to master their life-building process. When young people don't know what they want to create in life, their education can seem arbitrary to them. When they do know what they want, their education takes on a focus and purpose—at least to the degree that it supports their long-term goals.

Defining goals is a good beginning to have in place, but only a beginning. The next step is even harder for both young people and adults, and that is to describe current reality accurately and objectively.

JUST THE FACTS

Most people learn to distort reality. They do so because reality often includes things they don't like. Kids learn to lie for many reasons. They lie to avoid criticism and punishment. They lie because they see that it is socially acceptable. They lie because sometimes it is hard to see reality without the distorting lens of assumptions, concepts, theories, worldviews, and speculation.

Rosalind and I were always honest with our kids, but many other people in our life were not. When our daughter Eve was four, our nanny would often lie to her by saying things like "There's no more candy," when there was. We would tell Eve, "There is more candy, but you can't have any right now." The nanny would ask Eve, "Would you like to go to school today?" pretending she had a choice. Eve had no choice; she had to go. So we had to train Eve's nanny in something that sounds simple but actually was hard for her at first: Tell Eve the truth.

If we lie to our young people, they will learn to distort reality. They will begin to misrepresent reality not only to others but, even worse, to themselves. Without a fix on reality, they will not be able to know where they are in relation to their goals.

Learning requires the ability to evaluate our actions: Did they work? Did they not work? We need to consider two essential data points: the current state and our desired outcomes. The skill of evaluating the actual situation must be developed deliberately, because it is easy to distort reality when we don't like what there is to see. To develop this skill, young people must be able to tolerate disappointment and frustration but not let those experiences stop them. Rather than overcome these feelings, they must learn to take them in stride, because when they learn something new, they are often incapable of success at first, and that can be hurtful and misinterpreted as a matter of self-worth. They must be able to separate who they are from what they do.

THE SELF-ESTEEM TRAP

One of the concepts that has become popular over the past twenty years is the idea that in order to be successful in life, one must have high self-esteem. This is simply not the case. If we read the biographies of some of the most successful people in history, we find that a majority of them had grave doubts about themselves but still were able to achieve their aspirations and influence the world. The question of self-esteem is independent from your ability to create what most matters to you in your life. And here are two reasons why:

- Where is the focus? When we are creating something, we have one of two places we can place our focus: on ourselves or on the object of our creation. These different points of focus lead to very different possibilities. If the focus is on us, then our performance becomes a reflection of our identity, and our worth becomes tied to how well we did. The purpose of any action becomes "what it says about me" rather than "how well it supports my accomplishment of my goals." But in the real world, learning often includes being pretty bad at something before it is possible to be competent. How can young people tolerate being inept on the way to mastering new skills and abilities if their focus is on themselves? How can they be objective and honest about reality if they are trying to manage their self-esteem at the same time? Most successful people learn that self-esteem and self-opinion are totally irrelevant when it comes to creating what matters to them in their lives. "Take what you do, but not yourself, seriously," is the oft-quoted phrase.

Some would argue that the point of accomplishing anything is the satisfaction that one receives for having done it. Certainly this is true of hobbies and entertainment. But there are many other types of human endeavors in which the point is something more significant than satisfaction. If we are parents, we may take our children to dance, skating, soccer, or music lessons, not because we are after glory for ourselves or to be seen as good parents by the community or even in the hope that our kids will thank us. We do it for a much better reason: We do it because we love them. The point is to support their growth and well-being, and not our own. And this is the most common orientation within the creative process. The reason to act is in support of the outcomes we care about.

■ Generative love: Most people think of love as responsive: "They met, they fell in love." The situation first, the love second. But in the creative process, it is the other way around. Creators love creations before they exist. The filmmaker loves the film before it begins to shoot. The painter loves the painting before it begins to appear on the canvas. The architect loves the building before the ground is broken.

Today, a common complaint about young people is that they are indifferent and uninvolved. To the degree that it is true, it is true because these young people don't have something they love enough to do what it takes, learn what they need to learn, and change what they need to change to accomplish their goals.

But education can take on a new meaning if we think of our job as teaching generative love. What can the individual love enough to bring into being, even though that will usually mean going well beyond his or her current abilities? When that question is answered, uninvolvement, indifference, and rebellion become commitment, caring, and collaboration. Generative love leads to true discipline in the highest sense. It can help us learn what at first might be hard and frustrating. It is the best reason to act in favor of our aspirations.

THE LESSON OF ACTION

Once we have established the desired outcomes we want and the current reality we have, the next natural step is to act. There is a feedback system that kicks in when we act within the context of structural tension: Action produces results that are evaluated ("How well did the actions move us toward our goal?"), which leads to adjustments of future actions. This feedback system continues until the goal is accomplished. Some of the best life learning takes place within this context, because the lesson is both specific to the actual goal that is being pursued and the general understanding that the person can learn what is needed to learn.

Actions are choices. There are three major types of choices: the fundamental choice, the primary choice, and the secondary choice. The fundamental choice is a choice about our basic values and resolve in life. If you've never made the fundamental choice to be a nonsmoker, for example, any process you choose to quit smoking probably will not work. If you have made the fundamental choice, then almost any method you choose will work. One of the most basic fundamental choices young people can make is to be the predominant creative force in their lives. Having made this choice doesn't mean that suddenly they can create everything they want and the world will revolve around them, but it does mean that they are ready to take responsibility for their own lives.

Another type of choice young people can make is the primary choice. The primary choice is about major results in their lives. These include choices of goals, aspirations, and ambitions. These are often the goals found in the formation of structural tension.

Once a primary choice is established, then other choices have to be made to support the primary choice. Often these secondary choices are things that we don't like doing but need to do to support our primary choice. By making secondary choices to support primary choices, young people learn to act in their own best long-term interests by managing their short-term activities. They might not like doing hours of homework, but they do it if they have made a primary choice, for example, to become a biophysicist (or anything that requires graduating high school and going to college).

Developing the capability of making choices takes practice. The more choices a young person can make, the more chance he or she has of seeing the consequences of the choice. But too often adults are afraid to let young people choose their own path.

In our family, we have handled the situation with a practice we call "the deal." The deal was this: It was our job to take care of our children while it was their job to learn how to take care of themselves. As they got older, they could make more and more choices on their own. We all knew that we would transfer choices to them when they demonstrated that they could make those choices in their own best interests. Soon our kids were making choices about their clothes, their bedtime, their music, the way they spent their time, and many other aspects of their lives. While we were the judges about what was in their own best interests, our criteria were pretty obvious. Someone who continually stays up so late that he chronically jeopar-

Robert Fritz and his wife, Rosalind Fritz, are cofounders of Robert Fritz, Inc. in Williamsville, VT. For more information, see their website at www.robertfritz.com.

dizes his health and ability to function is clearly not ready to decide what time to go to bed. The final part of the deal was this: In any area where they were not ready to make choices on their own, it was our job to teach them how to make good choices so they could make them on their own as soon as possible. The deal worked well in our family because it was a fair deal.

The basic insight of "the deal" is to understand the role of adults and children. A child starts off life being taken care of by adults. The young person's job is to learn over time how to take care of him- or herself. Who has the best chance of making good choices in life: the adolescent who has made thousands upon thousands of choices or the one who hardly has any experience of making choices? When it comes to making choices about sex, drugs, and safety, we are better off helping young people make lots of various types of choices so they can get hands-on experience of the consequences of their choice-making.

2. A Shared Vision Process for the Classroom

Tim Lucas

On the first day of school, the teacher opens the discussion by asking: "What would you like this classroom to be like? How would you like to be treated here—by me and by one another? What would make you look back and say 'This was a great class?'"

The teacher, by doing this, is drawing the kids to actively say what they want from this class and from school in general. They might never have been asked before. But if they got drawn into this kind of process year after year, over time they would learn to think for themselves about what they want school to do for them. They would stop shifting the burden of deciding what school should be onto the adults around them: the teachers, administrators, counselors, and parents.

What would kids say during this first class discussion? Some might talk about the irritations of the past that they never had a chance to voice before. "When we do work, I don't want anyone else coming over and taking stuff off my desk." Or, "I want the teacher to be polite to me; I don't want to be teased by teachers." Or, "If I get answers wrong, I don't want that announced to the class. I don't want everyone knowing the scores I get." Or, simply, "I don't mind sitting near other people, but I don't want to be stuck next to the same kid all year long."

In personal mastery terms, these are largely negative visions—they are images of something we want to avoid. So it might be up to the teacher to draw some of the students out further, to bring to light the positive visions that underlie their attitudes. The teacher might ask: "When you say you hate being teased, that suggests what you don't want. But can you think of anything you *do* want? In the classes you liked best, or in the best classes you can imagine, what kinds of things happened?" If more prompting is needed, the teacher can say: "Do you think you should have to raise your hand to talk? What about when we're doing math? How do you like to be treated then?"

Different students will say different things, and some kids won't know what to say at all. But at least one message will probably come through: "When I talk, I want to be heard." Out of that comes a vision for classroom etiquette and procedure for how they all want to be treated and how they feel a class should run.

This vision can be kept alive for the rest of the year by continually referring back to the ground rules that they co-created. From here on out, discipline is no longer just in the hands of the teacher. When there's a transgression, everyone knows whether it's serious or not—and how to respond to it. When there's a report from a substitute teacher that the kids were rowdy, the teacher can use the vision as a comparison point: "OK, all of you contributed to this vision. What happened here yesterday? What should have occurred? How would you want to deal with it next time?" Self-discipline begins to click.

3. Homework: The Beast

Betty Quantz

Betty Quantz played a number of roles in the evolution of this book, including correspondent, designated "critical friend" at some of our meetings, and project partner to one of the authors. Throughout the process, she also participated in a number of conversations about the many ways the five disciplines, particularly shared vision, affected interactions among students, parents, and teachers. Her reflection on homework from both a parent and teacher perspective—written originally in 1999 and updated for this edition—raises questions about whether commitment versus compliance is an issue for everyone, not just students. One of her daughters shared this article with her friends. Their response: "We didn't know anyone noticed—or cared!"

Homework is such a pain! I think that statement could have been made by a teacher, a student, or a parent. Considering how much a part of schooling homework is, it's fascinating how much everybody hates it. Except for the occasional project, my kids have generally thought of homework as boring and a waste of their time. Their teachers continuously complained about the amount of time they spent checking and grading homework. And as the parent supervising homework, I alternated between fury and tears.

If students can't stand it, teachers don't like the bookkeeping it requires, and parents don't like standing over their children, why are we still fighting this beast?

Conferring with a teacher one year, I asked, "Why do you grade the homework?"

"That's the only way to get them to do it."

A picture began to emerge. At school, teachers punish children to get them to get the work done: low grades, after-school sessions, no recess. With homework, the student gets a double whammy: the grade-book threat at school and no-privileges threat at home.

"So the kids who still haven't 'got it' are still getting bad grades on their homework?"

"Yes," she said, "but they get more worksheets and additional homework to help them."

From the teacher's view, more work meant getting these kids closer to mastery. But I could not even begin to imagine all the pain and frustration the children and their parents had to endure at homework time. Kids learn at different rates, so those who take a little longer to master new ideas are penalized when homework is graded. In fact, the practice and repetition reinforces his or her misunderstandings and causes further frustration. As for those who already know the material, the practice has some reinforcement value at first—but then boredom sets in.

Unfortunately, some people believe that if a student does not have homework every night—and lots of it—the student is not learning, and the teacher is not doing a good job. Moreover, the focus on standardized testing as a way to rate schools has turned homework into a vehicle to push sample questions, priming students for the upcoming tests.

As an English teacher, I have confronted the homework beast, too.

Grading repetitive homework was a nightmare for me. If I got bored grading it, I knew the students were on autopilot (read: not thinking) while doing it. Many graduates returning to visit from college told me that they had much more homework assigned in high school than they ever had their first year in college.

As a teacher, I like the idea that less is more. I think that by decreasing the amount of homework and increasing quality, we might find critical advantages for students and their success in schools. Quality homework has some of the following characteristics: evaluation, synthesis, and analysis of ideas and material (in other words, the higher levels in Bloom's Taxonomy). The level of thinking needed to complete the assignment determines the quality of the homework. Homework can move the student to higher-level thinking skills, instead of shutting down thinking and turning on zombie pilot.

The urban public school where I now teach has about 65 percent of our students receiving free lunch; about one-third get Social Security Disability. The kids in my lower track classes will straight-out confess that one of the major reasons for their placement was their failure to do homework.

I give my students a choice of homework assignments within a two- or three-week period. The assignments are divided into categories; one category is always oral presentation and another is always writing. Each category has two or three options, solo or collaborative, appealing to a variety of learning styles and ability levels. Creativity is encouraged and rewarded. For instance, my seniors read John Steinbeck's *The Grapes of Wrath* as part of a National Endowment for the Arts program called "The Big Read." How could I get my urban high school students to identify with the "Okies" in Steinbeck's 1939 novel? I constructed the homework choices (see margin note) to appeal to multiple areas of interest and abilities, to extend the ideas disucssed in class, and to be heavily weighted toward internet use. Luckily, our library is open after school (staffed by volunteer teachers because decreased library funding had eliminated extended hours). So students who do not have Internet at home or do not own a computer (about 70 percent of our students) had access to both in our library after school. They were also reading the book and preparing for class discussions as homework during this period.

Sometimes during our discussions students will find something that interests them and propose a homework assignment designed just for them. I consider those assignments real victories in the battle with the Beast. Now the kids are looking for ways to grow their knowledge and interest— and boy! Do those assignments improve our class discussions and learning!

Bloom's Taxonomy is an established American classification of learning goals dating back to 1956, when it was first proposed by a committee of educators chaired by educational psychiatrist Benjamin Bloom.

The Grapes of Wrath Assignment

WRITING CATEGORY: 1. Watch and respond to the PBS series called *Surviving the Dust Bowl*. 2. Go to the local news sources online and find articles about foreclosures in our area and document the stories of the families involved. 3. Examine the role of women in the 1930s.

ORAL PRESENTATION CATEGORY: 1. Follow Route 66, the primary road to California for migrants. 2. Imagine you are an investigative reporter sent to find out about the migrant camps. Tell us about them.

ART CATEGORY: 1. Examine the work of particular artists like Woody Guthrie and explain their influences on music now. 2. Choose three photographs taken by Dorothea Lange or others of the period and present your findings about the people or places in the pictures.

SOURCES FOR BETTER HOMEWORK
thinkfinity.org and webenglishteacher.com

I often cruise online lesson plans for ideas of homework choices, and these two are indispensible. *Webenglishteacher.org* has a
wealth of lesson ideas. If you have not been to the classroom portal
called *thinkfinity.org,* then you are missing the best brainstorming
source in the world. I look not only at the high-school-level material but also the elementary and middle school levels. Since I have
a wide range of abilities in my classroom, I often find inspiration
in the plans of elementary teachers and change the ideas to fit my
high school students' needs. —Betty Quantz

Making Homework Meaningful Betty Quantz

Pull out one of your homework assignments. Answer the following questions with *Yes* or *No*. Be honest!

Purpose:

*To analyze the mental
models that drive your
homework assignments
and to assess where you
can intervene to increase
student learning.*

1. Is a purpose for the assignment clearly stated on the paper that goes
   home with the student? Communicate the purpose behind your assignments on the assignment sheet itself. If every teacher did this,
   parents would no longer have to wonder, while helping their children, "What was this teacher thinking?"
2. Are student-centered objectives clearly stated on the paper that goes
   home with the student? What skills do you hope to reinforce?
3. Does the assignment expand on class work or merely repeat work
   done in class?
4. Are multiple learning styles and interests represented in the assignment?
5. Will you have to think when you grade this work or will you "skim" or
   follow a key? Are you interested in the students' responses or are you
   bored?
6. Are you covering only one standard or is the assignment doing double (or more) duty? For instance, I cover knowledge-based objectives, oral presentation objectives, as well as writing standards in the
   Grapes of Wrath assignments.
7. Why is the assignment relevant? What connections does the assignment make between the students, their past experiences, and their

lives now?

8. Think about the quality of each assignment and begin to open a dialogue about the purpose of learning with students and parents. Are you listening to what your students (and their parents) say about the assignments? Are they saying, "I've done (or not done) this a million times?" or are they saying, "While I was doing this homework, I remembered—" or, "I thought about—," or, "I had a question about—"? The assignments should, and could, generate more questions than they answer.

THE HOMEWORK MYTH

Why Our Kids Get Too Much of a Bad Thing, by Alfie Kohn (Da Capo Press, 2007).

Malcolm Gladwell famously argued that proficiency requires 10,000 hours of practice. Alfie Kohn might reply that deadening the spirit of learning takes only a few hours of being forced to practice. This book marshals the arguments, including a fairly robust body of research, to show that homework does not help students learn—it fosters rebellion, argument, grudging compliance, and extrinsic motivation. The alternative: practice during class, aided by peers, in a fully engaged environment. —Art Kleiner

4. Assessment as Learning
Are We Assessing What We Need to Know?

Bena Kallick

There's nothing intrinsically wrong with assessment in the classroom. Designed well, it can be a vehicle for learning and awareness; indeed, learning and awareness are far more difficult without it. Bena Kallick, based in Connecticut, has been a faculty member at Yale and Fairfield universities, a community activist, a cofounder of a children's museum, a cocreator of a teacher center, and a consultant to the innovative Tri-State Consortium (fostering educational improvement in Connecticut, New Jersey, and lower New York State). She has been involved in a number of startups, including Technology Pathways and Performance Plus, companies dedicated to creating and managing teacher knowledge about student learning; and currently Eduplanet, a company that is designing online learning that blends author experts with the social learning among teachers. Throughout all of these endeavors, she repeatedly has found herself dealing with the question of assessing learning: How do we know that the capabilities of a student (or a school, or an innovative group within a school) have genuinely been bolstered? We asked her to tackle the question of assessment for those who recognize its value, as long as it can be done in a way that fosters, instead of kills, learning.

Imagine that you have a teenage son who is old enough to get a driver's license—and you are a little nervous about it. You drive him to the licensing agency to take the multiple-choice written test on state driving laws. When he returns with a big grin to tell you that he scored well, you are pleased and relieved. At least he knows the shape of a stop sign, the speed limit in a school zone, and the need to yield to pedestrians. He has proven his mastery of formal knowledge: He knows (or knows where to find) the academic, explicit, codified facts that any expert would need at his or her fingertips.

But are you ready to turn him loose with an automobile? Probably not. Passing the written test alone is inadequate until you know how he applies his knowledge of driving. Can he parallel park? Does he look both ways before moving into an intersection? Does he use the rear-view mirror? Does he exercise caution? Eventually, after further hours of instruction behind the wheel, he passes the full-performance driving test. He proudly brings home his provisional driver's license. He's demonstrated applicable knowledge: the ability to transfer knowledge into action, even in situations that are less than routine. Under a variety of conditions, he has the proficiency he needs to produce results.

You congratulate him, and he immediately asks for the keys to the car. What do you do now? The tests—both the written and the performance test—are inadequate in themselves. All they show is that he knows how to pass the tests. Before you hand over the keys, inevitably you will think about your history with that child. Is he responsible? How does he exercise self-control? Do you need to set limits on night driving, the number of other teenagers in the car, or the distances from home or school? In the end, do you know him well enough to know how capable he is? For example, do you know how well he can handle unexpected situations— the kinds of events that can't be anticipated by any test?

Formal tests, even good ones, are not enough to assess learning authentically. Before your son can drive your car (or at least mine) alone, he must also show signs of longitudinal knowledge: the basic capability for acting effectively over time in a way that leads to ongoing improvement, effectiveness, and innovation. Can a student of any subject evolve from merely being a student to being a reliable, careful, competent, good practitioner of this skill? If so, then you probably will trust him or her—after you have made that assessment. And if you make the wrong, assessment, crediting someone with longitudinal knowledge when he or she actually doesn't have it, then you will face potentially dire consequences: botched assignments, missing work, incompetent results, damaged relationships—and conceivably a crashed car.

ASSESSMENT AS LEARNING FOR STUDENTS

In many schools and departments of education today, we have come to rely on a single measure for evaluating student progress—conventional, standardized paper-and-pencil test assessments. These tests, including most state-level tests, are like the written driver's test; they only measure formal knowledge. Worse still, the results arrive after months of delay, often after students have moved on to another grade level. This is far too late to be meaningful as guides to further learning. The test results display only one or two highly aggregated scores, giving students extremely limited information about their performance. By showing only the percentage of items that each student got wrong, they subtly lead students to feel that their skills are inadequate, which, in effect, goes against the grain of what we know about learning. (You start with the strengths of a person's work and then move to where the person needs improvement.)

The current trends in assessment, as of 2011, have brought us closer to making decisions on the basis of cost-effective and efficient tests that measure how well the student can reproduce what has been learned. But most tests still do not provide sufficient information to let us know whether a student can actually apply what he or she has learned in a more authentic context. Thus, when educators focus on helping students learn how to do well on tests, we may fail to help them learn how to meet the tests of life. We talk to students about college and career readiness without truly understanding what is required to be successfully both in higher education and in careers.

The Common Core Standards Initiative, launched in 2010 by state governments in the U.S., is encouraging in this regard. The standards make explicit the need for students to work at higher levels of engagement, become more self-directed, and learn how to integrate work from different disciplines as they become more effective problem solvers. The challenge for the states that have adopted the Common Core Standards is to develop assessments that offer students an opportunity to show evidence of those higher levels. There are consortia that are working on this question to see whether there might be a common assessment set for all states using common core standards.

However, educators need not wait for these assessments to appear. Similar assessments can be designed locally. They should take into account students' progress-providing data from three perspectives: assessment *of* learning, assessment *for* learning, and assessment *as* learning.

The Common Core Standards initiative website is www.corestandards.org. The consortia working on assessment issues include the Partnership for Assessment of Readiness for College and Careers (www.parcconline.org) and the Smarter Balanced Assessment Consortium (www.k12.wa.us/smarter).

- **Assessment *of* learning** is summative. It provides data regarding how well a student is performing at a specific point in time. Examinations at the end of a course, mid-term exams, and standardized state tests are examples of summative assessments.

- **Assessment *for* learning** is formative. It provides information for teachers, parents, and students, along the way, about how a student is performing, with the intention of better guidance. In most instances, formative assessments are not graded. Rather, they are scored. This is a critical distinction. When you grade papers or assignments, you give students feedback about how they are doing at that point in time. However, when you score student work, you provide feedback, coaching tips, and an opportunity for the students to continue to demonstrate learning as they progress toward a summative assessment.

For the distinction between assessment *of* learning and assessment *for* learning, see Rick Stiggins, "From Formative Assessment to Assessment for Learning," *Phi Delta Kappan* (December 2005); and the Assessment Training Institute, founded by Stiggins, www.assessmentinst.com.

- **Assessment *as* learning** is designed so that the assessment itself is instructional. As the teacher provides feedback, students are engaged in learning about how to improve. For example, when a teacher uses a scoring rubric to show the distinction between a low-quality paper and a high-quality paper, the students who did not perform at the highest quality are given the opportunity to re-do the assignment, taking into consideration what they have learned, and varying the details enough that it does not seem tedious.

In a system where assessment is seen as a learning event, students have access to their own data. They are well aware of how they are doing and what needs to be improved, and they can take more responsibility for their learning. They set goals based on the data and monitor their own improvement. In this system, they learn to become self-directed and begin to internalize the ability to become more self-evaluative.

Qualities of Assessment for Learning

We need assessments that are designed for learning, not assessments that are used for blaming, ranking, and certifying. That, in turn, requires deep shifts of attitude about testing and learning for parents, educators, and students themselves. There are places where that shift in attitude has taken place—and where we have seen remarkable turnarounds and the growth of new capabilities. Here are some of the principles and practices that make this shift possible.

Before going any further, think of a time in your life when assessment (grading, feedback, or evaluation) actually served you for learning. What were the common characteristics in those experiences?

I've asked this question many times in workshops (in fact, it's a very good question for a group of teachers and administrators to talk through). Chances are the best assessments did not happen in school. My personal favorite occurred in a repertory theater. A great director made a point of coaching me and other actors with in-depth, constant feedback about the nuances of our performance. Other people often remember a sports coach who did something similar.

We find in these workshops that the same characteristics come up again and again, as features of assessments that people remember.

Purpose:

To help educators rethink their grading, feedback, and evaluation approaches in light of assessment for learning.

TIMELINESS

The importance of timeliness is especially significant in this age of immediate gratification. If students get feedback about their work many weeks after the test is taken, they probably are on to new work and no longer focused on the work that was done. Whether the assessment is a standardized test or a classroom-based performance, the closer students are to the feedback, the more meaningful it is. When teachers are required to teach as many as 120 students in a given high school course of study, timeliness is very difficult. School schedules need to be designed so that teachers have regular conference times with students in which they review and give feedback regarding their work.

HONESTY

Evaluations challenge learners to make changes on the basis of the data they provide. Sometimes it is difficult to face this data; after all, if people don't take it seriously, they won't need to change. However, an honest assessment will tend to create a sense of cognitive dissonance or disequilibrium—that makes people face the need for change.

I know one California school system that got caught up in the drive for "higher scholastic standards." They raised the bar on academic achievement and pushed kids to meet the challenge. Test scores went up overall, but they also showed one group of students routinely falling through the cracks. To "fix" this last remaining problem, a group of teachers applied for an instructional improvement grant. The funding agency asked why they needed the money. "Aren't most of your students doing well? Which students are doing poorly?"

The teachers couldn't answer at first. The answer made them so uncomfortable that they had never talked about it; they did not want to draw attention to it even now. The assessments had singled out African American males as the poorest performers in the school. Forced to confront the data, teachers decided to do something they had never considered before: interview students themselves ask them for suggestions.

It turned out, to the teachers' surprise, that the students were also very frustrated. They knew the school expected higher standards, and they ardently wanted to meet those standards, but they didn't know how to do it. The school had been working under the assumption of "teaching by assignment": If you just assign a challenge, students will naturally rise to meet it. The kids knew what they needed. They wanted easier material to start reading with. They wanted to read with an adult, and they ardently wanted their own "book talk" sessions where they could discuss what they were reading, without more advanced kids overwhelming them. They felt that their parents weren't understanding the school's new imperative, and they wanted their parents to come in and work with the teachers more closely. And they wanted more adult role models who could show them how to make their way through the demanding workload. Essentially, they wanted someone to reveal the strategies for learning that other students already seemed to know.

The students and teachers sat down and rethought their approach together. They started by writing the proposal for that grant; but now they proposed changes in the long-term educational practices, changes that they would never have considered if they had not been led by that "offensive" data to learn from one another.

REFLECTION

Educators often think of the "feedback" of assessment as a loop, as shown at left.

But it is more accurate to draw it as a spiral, which does not continually return the learner to the same place.

When I showed this spiral diagram in a workshop, a teacher said, "We love this because it supports something we believe: 'Anything worth

Further resources on assessment include: Linda Darling-Hammond, Ray Pecheone, et al. (Stanford University), *Developing an Internationally Comparable Balanced Assessment System that Supports High-Quality Learning* (2010); Marc Tucker (National Center on Education and the Economy), *An Assessment System for the United States: Why not Build on the Best?* (2010); Stephen Lazer (Educational Testing Service), *High-Level Model for an Assessment of Common Standards* (2010); and Larry Berger (Wireless Generation) and Lynn Resnick (University of Pittsburgh), *An American Examination System* (2010), all available online from the Educational Testing Service's Center for K–12 Assessment & Performance Management, www.k12center.org.

doing is worth doing poorly the first time.'"

I said, "That's nice—but when do you take the time to learn from what you do poorly?" Very few teachers have built in time for their students (or themselves) to reflect on their evaluations. This means that they are missing the metacognitive work of standing back and saying, together: "OK, what did we just get from the last two weeks of class?"

Every teacher can set up a system where students assess themselves—and still meet society's criteria for advancing through the education system. But each class requires a different design. Teachers can start by considering three main questions:

- Self-management: How can students plan and organize their own learning? How can they set their goals and name the milestones they expect to reach along the way?

〉〉 See "A Shared Vision Process for the Classroom," page 216.

- Self-evaluation: How can students evaluate and critique their own work? How can they critique the work of their peers and reflect on the differences in perception?
- Self-adaptation: How can students modify their working methods based on the feedback they receive? How can they be best prepared to learn?

Much of this reflection will take place in conferences that teachers set up—individually, with teams of students, and with parents. Setting up time is the easy part; the hard part is scrupulously paying attention to what the students have to say and letting it inform the way teachers design their instruction.

Heretofore, grades have been a form of judgment subject to the authority of the teacher. Students have learned to get good grades by pleasing the teacher. The teacher, in effect, has told them whether they were learning or not.

But when students assess themselves, grades become an evaluative process. Students manage their own judgment about their progress. In the end, this situation puts much less stress on the teachers, but it takes a great deal of getting used to.

By the time a kid is seventeen years old, he or she should be responsible for, and skillful at, presenting evaluations to parents: the report card, the work, and the goals. That communicates to everyone—teacher, parent, and student—that the school believes assessment is a process for learning, not just for accountability.

Students who develop this skill need not be held back by a teacher who doesn't assess them openly. Suppose, for example, that you're a sixteen-year-old high school junior writing an essay on Romantic poetry, sticking your neck out to express some original ideas. You get only two comments back: a "B-plus" grade and a margin notation: "minus twelve points," with no further explanation. Having evaluated yourself for years, you can go to your teacher and ask: "Can you show me where the twelve points were dropped?" If the teacher can't articulate it, then you still have the skills to look at the paper yourself, as if you were your teacher, to find the reason for the minus twelve. Meanwhile, your teacher is likely to recognize that you're not hustling for an A—you genuinely want to know.

A similar process can help teachers reflect on their own teaching. When working with teachers I spend a great deal of time on three questions, each of which is designed to draw forth the teachers' grasp of different types of knowledge of their field and of teaching itself. This reflective process can also be thought of as a spiral. First teachers plan their teaching practice, including a way of assessing students' performance. Then, after the actual teaching, teachers study and reflect on the assessment. For example, teachers might use a scoring rubric (or another multidimensional methodology) to analyze a student's particular problems. In one case, it might be discovered that a student gets inaccurate answers in math because of a problem in reasoning. That case will lead to a new plan for teaching practice: perhaps, for example, teaching some students how to "create a simpler problem" to help them deal with their reasoning difficulties. The better teachers can analyze exactly what the students are missing individually, the more effective a teaching intervention they will make next time. That's why, on some trips around the spiral, it's important not just to assess teaching but also to assess the assessment—to reconsider the rubrics and other scoring methods being used and whether they are revealing the things teachers need to know.

CONSTRUCTIVE GUIDANCE

I sometimes bring together teachers from all grade levels, kindergarten through twelfth grade, to look at a pile of elementary students' writings—replete with scribbled handwriting, misspellings, and lack of capital letters and punctuation. Many of the high school teachers immediately say, "I can't read this." I ask them not to notice what's missing (say, commas or spaces) and only to read what's there. It typically takes three or four rounds before they can retrain themselves to read what the kids wrote. Suddenly they see (or hear) the voices of the children coming out in the papers. They notice the authorship.

This is a valuable exercise for any teacher; it shows how to shift the frame of mind from looking for deficits to looking for strengths. Teachers who understand this tend to grade papers very differently. They no longer mark up "things you didn't do right," with red circles around each one. Instead, they articulate "what you did," and focus their remarks on "what will stretch you for the next step." The kids get the point, because they are continually looking for the answer to one question: "What am I supposed to do next?"

In addition, students who are graded this way learn how to refer to what they *can* do rather than what they *cannot* do. With the help of their teachers, they develop a series of "I can" statements such as:

"I can read aloud easily."

"I can respond and give details when answering questions about a story I am reading."

Notice that each "I can" statement references a standard. So, not only are students keeping track of their capabilities, they are also learning how they meet the required standards for their class.

FOCUS

In a Maryland high school a few years ago, the administrators proposed making all the students wear uniforms. The teachers rallied for the idea: "We're sick of the caps and the pants that fall below the waist." Then they delivered the clinching argument: "There's lots of evidence that uniforms make a difference to morale and test scores."

Challenged to substantiate that claim, they found assessments from other schools. Unquestionably, when school uniforms were instituted, behavior scores (such as truancy rates) improved. Unfortunately, there was no qualitative information here, so it wasn't clear whether the improvements came from uniforms per se or from another factor, of which the uniforms were just one symptom: greater consistency and uniformity.

To test this, we asked them to consider equivalent assessments from a second set of schools: schools that followed the work that Art Costa and I have done on habits of mind. In these schools, the attributes were posted and discussed by teachers, children, and even parents in groups; and the schools as a whole did their best to live up to them. This case produced an even greater leap in behavior scores, plus the highest scholastic test scores in the state.

〉〉 See "Intelligent Behaviors," page 240.

The schools with uniforms had focused on getting better discipline. The sixteen-attribute schools had focused on improving learning. They each got what they measured for. Choose the focus of your assessments carefully: Whatever you make relevant, you'll get.

THE ROLE OF PARENTS

Ironically, parents are often the most resistant to changes in the ways their children's work is assessed. I believe most parents know that grades and test scores don't reflect their children's learning. But parents are so used to the grading systems from their own school experiences that they still give them a primary focus. They worry about how their child compares with the neighbor's child, what to tell Grandma, and whether their son or daughter can get into a competitive college. They also worry about their child's feelings and often try to intervene around the question of grades.

Such intervention can be counterproductive. If parents intervene, the teacher assumes they are interested only in improving the assessment. The teacher groans inwardly ("Here comes Ms. Walker again. I don't have time for this"), placates the parents ("Yes, I understand what you are saying"), and concentrates on fending off "problem" parents. The teacher learns nothing about the student. The student's work (and assessment) remains stable. And the parent leaves thinking, "Once again, nothing's going to happen here."

Teachers can make a difference here by simply letting parents speak first and at length—and by truly listening—before they present their case. But the most effective approach is to let students lead the conference. Students should not just attend but should moderate the conversation and raise the critical questions. When a student asks a teacher directly to explain why points were taken off in an essay or how to improve work on the next assignment, it shows everyone that the student is actually interested in learning.

In the end, the most powerful tool that parents have, as advocates for their children, is to educate the children to ask teachers the necessary questions. Teachers listen more carefully, and students learn one of the most valuable life skills they will ever have as an adult: to manage their own learning. Kids already know that the adult world doesn't know as much as they do about their own learning. By giving them self-managing processes where they learn how to be more critical of their work, modify on the basis of feedback, and take responsibility for what they're doing, conditions in which they care about the quality of their efforts are created.

ASSESSMENT FOR SCHOOLS

At the schoolwide level, a truly useful assessment system would be comprehensive and complete enough to enable school leaders to talk honestly to parents, teachers, and community members: "This is our how our school is doing based on data from a variety of assessments, this is what it means, and this is how our programs are working." The Board of Education would become sophisticated enough to encourage the schools to be certain that they are assessing what is truly valuable.

Very few assessments are in place right now with those qualities. In most school systems, at the district level, the test results are insufficiently analytic to give school leaders the information they need for improvement.

Furthermore, test scores are published in newspapers. This gives parents, real estate agents, and politicians an impression—accurate or not—of how effective the schools are and how they compare to others nearby. Naturally, people assume schools are doing a bad job if the scores are low or a great job if the scores are high. They blame or praise the schools accordingly. Educators try to defend themselves by asking for a less "judgmental" form of evaluation or discrediting the idea of evaluation itself. But judgment is, by definition, the purpose of evaluation—the word "evaluation" means "to assign a value to results." We don't need less judgment, we need more informed judgments. We need them delivered in a more timely manner, in a way that leads to more effective change, without turning people off to their own capabilities.

ASSESSMENT IN THE LEARNING ORGANIZATION

Shifting the Paradigm, edited by Arthur L. Costa and Bena Kallick
(Association for Supervision and Curriculum Development, 1995)

Educators willing to take up the challenge of improving assessment—of their students, teaching practices, and school change initiatives—probably won't leave this book on a bookshelf collecting dust. Teachers from a variety of disciplines and grade levels provide examples of their personal experiences and strategies for rethinking traditional forms of assessment. Administrators share the insights they've gained and practical examples of techniques. Fieldbook-style chapters cover tangible techniques and tools: portfolios, feedback spirals, student self-evaluation, new kinds of report cards, shared vision exercises, and more. Interwoven throughout are clear discussions on how the theories and practices advocated by Deming and Senge apply in the arena of schools and assessment. While the book wasn't written with parents in mind, the editors' well-written and compelling introductions to each of the sections based on the five learning disciplines are worth reading by anyone interested in schools as learning organizations. —Janis Dutton

PUNISHED BY REWARDS

The Trouble with Gold Stars, Incentive Plans, A's, Praise, and Other Bribes, by Alfie Kohn
(Houghton-Mifflin, 1993)

This book patiently unravels every commonplace assumption we, as parents and educators, carry about the roles of motivation and grading in learning. There is no mistaking Kohn's point: Grades are not only poor substitutes for true motivation, they are counterproductive to real learning. The fact that this seems so counterintuitive only proves the depth to which we have to reconstruct our thinking. In my own institution, groups of us are questioning whether the problem is grade inflation or grades. Kohn clearly distinguishes between grading and assessment, noting that all learners need feedback in order to grow, while grading is actually destructive. It is written in such an accessible nonacademic style, I was astonished to see the amount of research that Kohn leverages to support his points. —Thomas A. Dutton

5. Assessment and Accountability

A Superintendent's Perspective

Steve Price

Increased pressure for accountability in American public schools is evident from the intense focus on measuring students' performance. Low-performing schools face punitive solutions and public recrimination. For all the uproar and attention, we've seen few or no results to indicate that schools are closing the achievement gaps among student subgroups or that learning has increased overall for students. Dr. Price, Superintendent of the Hazelwood School District in Missouri and former Superintendent of Middletown City Schools in Ohio, questions the unintended consequences of current accountability measures that rely on punitive testing and shares his work on assessment for learning in Middletown and Hazelwood.

On a cold January morning in 2007, a man with a violin played six Bach pieces for about forty-five minutes in the Washington, D.C., metro station. During that time, approximately two thousand people went through the station, most of them on their way to work. Only six adults stopped to listen and only for a very short time, quickly realizing they needed to move on. Several children slowed to listen, but without exception their parent forced them to quickly move on. At the end of this short concert, the man had collected $32 from about twenty people who left donations in a hat lying in front of him. No one noticed when the playing stopped and the music was replaced with the dull hum of a busy train station. No one applauded, and there was no recognition.

Unknown to the busy commuters in the station that day, the *Washington Post* was conducting a social experiment. The violinist was Joshua Bell, one of the greatest musicians in the world. He played, on a violin worth $3.5 million, some of the most intricate pieces of music ever written. Two days before, Joshua Bell had played to a sold-out theater in Boston where the price of seats averaged $100.

The Post raised several questions about the spectators: In the daily commonplace environment of classrooms at an inappropriate hour, do we perceive beauty—that is, the special talents and gifts of students? Do

Gene Weingarten, "Pearls Before Breakfast: Can one of the nation's great musicians cut through the fog of a D.C. rush hour? Let's find out." *Washington Post*, April 8, 2007; http://www.washingtonpost.com/wp-dyn/content/article/2007/04/04/AR2007040401721.html.

we recognize talent in an unexpected context? These questions can very well be asked when we assess the effectiveness of schools. The current overreliance on a narrowly defined standards-based curriculum and the accompanying assessment has become the expected context, making it difficult for educators to recognize talent beyond that context. This is especially true in our lowest performing schools across the country.

In short, when we look for specific performance on narrow assessments, the classroom—the very place we would expect to nurture and discover the talents of our students—becomes an "unexpected context" or an "inappropriate hour" for this to occur.

A NARROW DEFINITION OF SUCCESS

Consider the context from which many teachers in our lowest performing schools, located mostly in urban and low socioeconomic communities, view the classroom world. They face tremendous pressure for their students to perform well on standardized accountability tests. The curriculum includes primarily the standards that will be tested (content from the core subjects, immediately diminishing the importance of all the other rich opportunities students might experience in their school lives). To ensure coverage of content, lessons are often scripted and leave little room for improvisation or inspiration. And if that's not enough, students bring issues related to race, class, and language to the classrooms that often frustrate the teachers. As such, the teachers see the students as problems to be "fixed" and "remediated" rather than unique individuals who bring gifts and talents to the classroom. Under these circumstances, students are blamed for not learning at acceptable levels, and the system takes on a "blame the victim" mentality.

If gifts and talents are not evident and developed in our "expected contexts," we will be doomed to the continued use of a deficit model directed at remediating and fixing students. We will miss the richness of opportunities and possibilities within the very student communities we espouse to help. The current model of schooling encourages teachers and administrators to define problems, look for quick solutions, and assign blame. I fear the "expected contexts" of many classrooms have rendered invisible many of the gifts and talents that lowest performing students need to have discovered.

If you believe the function of schooling is for students to get high test scores and do better in school, then most high-performing schools in the country are designed perfectly to get those results and will be considered successful under the current accountability system. Unfortunately, the system is not working for a growing number of students. As in the

After reading about the *Washington Post* experiment, Tom Dutton, a professor of architecture at Miami University, commented:

"Contexts frame perceptions, many times in unfair ways that eclipse people. It's like we use context as stereotypical shorthand for understanding people. The congruence is disturbing: 'good' contexts produce 'good' people, and conversely, 'bad' contexts produce 'bad' people. End of story."

"Success to the Successful" archetype, the schools that show success on mandated tests will be rewarded with resources, while the unsuccessful schools will continue to struggle with less and less.

⟩⟩ See "Success to the Successful," page 372.

As school superintendent for seven years of Middletown City Schools, a small urban school district, I was challenged by Ohio's high-stakes assessment system—a system used to judge the success or failure of our students and our schools. I fully understood and supported the need for our schools to be accountable to the community. But, at the same time, I also watched the intense pressure administrators and teachers experienced, fearing that their schools would be labeled as failures. Inevitably, this pressure led to a narrow curriculum focus to emphasize and teach what was on the test. Classroom assessments became more summative in nature and much less formative. I thought this focus actually moved our staff further away from assessing the real learning needs of students.

Each year, the staff and I disaggregated state testing data by content strands to identify those areas of our curriculum that were working and those areas that needed further attention. Often quick and expeditious solutions were designed in the form of new math and reading programs, short-cycle assessments, or some other assessments that promised to turn around failing schools. Those quick and simple solutions, however, deterred us from an in-depth examination of our organization—an investigation that might have revealed the very thinking that underpinned our poor results. Instead, when the test results remained disappointing, it allowed blame to be placed on the new programs and the personnel responsible for implementing those program changes.

Also, by disaggregating data by student subgroups (race, gender, socioeconomic) to identify students in need of remedial support, the focus shifted away from the system as the problem and placed it squarely on the shoulders of specific groups of students in our school system. This shifting of the blame was further reinforced by the use of summative classroom assessments that were mini versions of the state test. Teachers and students seldom experienced assessment "for" learning as advocated by Rick Stiggins—assessments that are non-evaluative and used to provide timely information that creates valuable scaffolding for student learning.

⟩⟩ This is an example of "Shifting the Burden;" see page 375.

Defining student success in narrow terms has sucked the life out of classrooms in many communities. Educators, communities, parents, and students have been led to believe that the most important thing is passing a high-stakes standardized test that measures a limited number of core content standards. Our students have been pigeonholed by the need to perform well on an annual test, making it virtually impossible for them to share and discover their true gifts and talents. Our classroom assessment system reflects the need to do well on state exams and fails to utilize the full array and richness of all assessments available to our teachers.

In short, our current accountability practices, relying primarily on tests, unwittingly reinforce a system that narrows learning for all students. I am not arguing for the elimination of standardized tests, but rather to balance the scales with a much greater emphasis and investment in quality classroom assessments that enhance teaching and learning. As Elliot Eisner stated, "The function of schooling is to enable students to do better in life. What students learn in school ought to exceed in relevance the limits of the schools program."

ASSESSMENT FOR LEARNING

Significant resources must be invested to balance the current system of high-stakes testing with effective classroom assessments. Helping educators become assessment literate is the first step. We need to provide the means to teach and assess a much broader range of learning targets beyond the narrow scope of those measured on high-stakes state accountability tests. It is important to implement a system where teaching, learning, and assessment are seamlessly integrated in the classroom.

In the Middletown school system, we used Rick Stiggins's concept of *assessment for learning* to guide our work. Rick helped us understand that:

> Assessment for learning turns the classroom assessment process and its results into an instructional intervention designed to increase, not merely monitor, student learning. It acknowledges the critical importance of the instructional decisions made by students and their teachers working as a team. Assessment for learning motivates by helping students watch themselves succeeding—by helping them believe that success is within reach if they keep trying.

Stiggins describes our current assessment system as one based on rewards and punishment. Students are told throughout their school lives that they need to study hard to do well on tests. If you do well on your tests, then you will get good grades. If you get good grades, you will get into a good college and good things will happen when you try to find a job. The reverse is also true. If you don't study hard, you will do poorly

lliott Eisner, "What Does it Mean to Say that a School is Doing Well?," *Phi Delta Kappan* (April 2000).

ee Rick Stiggins, Judith Arter, Jan Chappuis, and Steve Chappuis, *Classroom Assessment for Student Learning: Doing It Right—Using It Well* (Pearson Books, 2006).

ee Rick Stiggins and Jan Chappuis, *An Introduction to Student-Involved Assessment for Learning,* (6th Edition, Addison Wesley, 2011). Stiggins founded the Assessment Training Institute, whose website is ati.pearson.com.

on tests and get bad grades. You won't get into a good college and bad things will happen. When most of us close our eyes and think back on our school days and the feelings we had just before a big test, it doesn't conjure up warm and confident feelings. We usually remember the fear in the pit of our stomach and the negative consequences that awaited us for a poor performance. This system of reward, punishment, and fear works for some students, but more and more of them begin to feel helpless and give up trying. They don't believe success is within their reach.

Assessment *for* learning begins first with the end in mind: a clear vision of what we want our students to look like when they finish a course, a grade level, and eventually graduate must be created before teaching ever begins. This preferred picture of students should include skills and knowledge measured by our state standards but should also consider the many other rich targets we hold valuable to becoming a well-rounded and fully functioning citizen in our society. A collaborative process that involves the community, parents, staff, and students should be undertaken to identify the knowledge, skills, dispositions, and performance targets we want our students to attain.

It is especially important to make students partners in this process. When learning targets are transformed into curriculum maps written in both adult language and student-friendly language, students are able to clearly understand the learning for which they are responsible and what comes next in the sequence. Too often our students are taught with little understanding and clarity of what it is they are to learn and with little relevance in their lives.

Is it possible to use assessments that motivate students—assessments on which our students feel confident of doing well and can't wait to take? Is it possible to use assessments to help provide relevance and clarity for student learning? The answer is "yes," but it takes dedicated work and time to shift the thinking and practices underpinning the current system of assessment.

Assessment-literate professionals first recognize the purpose of the assessment they are administering. The users as well as the use of the assessment results define the purpose. In the Middletown school district, we had three levels of definition: the instructional level, the instructional leadership and support level, and the policy level.

At the instructional level, users included students, teachers, and parents. Assessments for learning are associated closely with this level of users. The information from assessments given at this level is needed on a continuous basis and measures individual mastery of required material. These assessments try to answer questions about next steps in learning and where help may be needed. They are used to track individual success and individual needs, evaluate instruction, and assign grades.

It is critical for these assessments to provide scaffolding for student learning—a map of next steps in the learning process. A teacher might have her students analyze samples of poor, fair, and excellent writing to help them create a shared vision of what quality writing looks like. The teacher uses this exercise to help guide the growth of students and provide non-evaluative (not graded) feedback to their ever-improving writing samples. As the students learn what makes a piece of writing poor versus excellent, they begin to internalize their understanding of quality writing. They apply this understanding to their own work and no longer need someone else to tell them when their writing is of high quality. We found that students quickly became partners in the learning and assessment process.

At the instructional leadership and support level, our users included building administrators, psychologists, and curriculum directors. The information was used to evaluate programs, evaluate teachers, identify students with special needs, and allocate resources. The data allowed us to answer questions about quality of instruction and desired results, possible professional development and who might need remedial support. We gained this information through periodic assessment of group achievement.

Policy-level users included the superintendent of schools, school board, Department of Education, legislators, and the citizenry. The information needed required periodic assessment of group achievement on building, district, and state curriculum. It provided public accountability and sought to answer questions about program and curriculum effectiveness.

We worked to develop assessment-literate professionals, who clearly understood the targets they were trying to measure. They needed to understand the different types of knowledge, reasoning, skill, product, and dispositional targets students are expected to master. It is only then that professionals will know which assessment option is best to measure the desired target. Professionals understand the target being measured determines whether to use a selected response, essay, performance assessment, or personal communication assessment option. They know how to select an appropriate sample size for the assessment option chosen and how to minimize possible bias that may exist in a particular assessment option.

As I moved from the Middletown City Schools to the Hazelwood School District in Missouri, my own work on assessment literacy has continued. Lessons learned in Middletown about organizational change have helped move this work forward in Hazelwood. Using systems tools, like the iceberg and the ladder of inference, has helped the staff identify and better understand the beliefs and mental models underpinning our current assessment practices.

Last year an assessment literacy steering committee convened several meetings throughout the school district to share a different vision of student assessment. The vision challenged current mental models of assessment (blame the victim, deficit thinking, and a narrow definition of what constitutes learning) present in our school district. An invitation was extended to all who wanted to learn more about assessing students to promote learning. More than 250 teachers elected to participate in professional development activities about assessment literacy. That number promises to expand, as the first waves of volunteers have become disseminators and supporters of the work back in their own buildings. With the broadening of assessment practices, our classrooms will reflect more than the current narrow definition of success and once again become places that discover the countless gifts and talents students bring through the classroom door each day.

All of this may initially sound overwhelming, but educators around the world are undergoing this transformation every day. It offers our students hope for a rich educational experience that holds relevance in their lives. The journey is rewarding for professionals and often restores the excitement and enthusiasm for teaching that has been dulled by a narrowly defined curriculum and the pressure of mandated testing. We owe this effort to our students and our profession.

Assessing Assessment's Purpose

- List the different types of assessments used in your building and in your classroom. Label the purpose for each assessment.
- Identify the primary uses and users of the data generated from the assessments you have listed.
- How do the assessment structures frame expectations of both adults and students?
- Which assessments are used as assessments for learning—assessments that provide effective scaffolding for student learning in the classroom?
- What are your aspirations for student learning? What are students' aspirations for their own learning?

Purpose:

These reflection questions can help you as an individual teacher or a group of educators examine your own classroom and school assessment practices.

- How do your existing assessments help students fulfill those aspirations? How do they get in the way?
- What additional assessments do you need in the classroom to address your aspirations for student learning? What is required to integrate these into your teaching?
- What aspect of your thinking must change to promote transformation of the current practices?

6. Intelligent Behaviors

Art Costa

For more depth and detail on intelligent behaviors, see Art Costa and Bena Kallick, *Learning and Leading with Habits of Mind*, (Association for Supervision and Curriculum Development, 2009), and Art Costa, "The Search for Intelligent Life" in *Developing Minds: A Resource Book for Teaching Thinking*, edited by Art Costa (Association for Supervision and Curriculum Development, 1991).

In his well-known work on intelligent behaviors and habits of mind, Art Costa enfolds many of this book's guiding ideas—multiple intelligences, the value of systems understanding, the importance of a learning community—within a hands-on practice for teachers and parents. These "sixteen behaviors" offer a straightforward, effective, and profound alternative to conventional assessment. They are distinct from learning styles because of the way they are used: as criteria for judging the intellectual development of our students, our children, and ourselves. When systems thinking, team learning, and shared vision are practiced, these behaviors come into play. Costa, a professor emeritus of education at California State University in Sacramento, codirects the Institute for Habits of Mind in Westport, Connecticut.

When we teach people to think, we are interested not only in the answers they know. We want to closely observe them when they don't know the answer. To solve an unknown, challenging problem demands all of the capabilities we think of as intelligence: strategic reasoning, insightfulness, intellectual perseverance, creativity, and craftsmanship.

Also see Barry Richmond's critical skills for systems thinking, page 296.

Thus, the best way to gather evidence of student growth is to engage in kid-watching. As students interact with real-life, day-to-day problems—in school, at home, on the playground, alone, and with friends—they demonstrate the development of their intelligence. If you really want to know about a child, don't rely on standardized tests; keep records of the child's spontaneous acts, collecting anecdotes and examples of his or her written and visual expression.

But what should you watch for? Based on the work of a half-dozen key researchers on creativity and intelligence, there seem to be at least sixteen key characteristics of intellectual growth that teachers and parents can observe and record. The characteristics on this list seem to recur, again and again, among people who have developed their thinking abilities: successful mechanics, teachers, entrepreneurs, salespeople, parents, and people in all walks of life.

1. PERSISTING

Students often give up in despair when the answer to a problem is not immediately apparent. They crumple their papers and throw them away: "I can't do this," they say. "It's too hard." Or they write down any answer, just to finish the task as quickly as possible. They lack the ability to analyze a problem, to develop a strategy for attacking it.

When students gain persistence, they begin to use alternative strategies for problem-solving. If they find that one strategy doesn't work, they know how to back up and try another, starting over if necessary. Over time, they develop systematic methods for analyzing problems. They know how to begin, what steps must be performed, what data need to be generated or collected—and how to keep going, without losing heart, until they have learned more about the problem.

2. MANAGING IMPULSIVITY

Often, students blurt out the first answer that comes to mind. Sometimes they shout it out or start to work without fully understanding the directions. They may take the first suggestion given to them or operate on the first idea that pops into their head. But as they gain intelligence, they learn to consider the alternatives and consequences of several possible decisions. That's when we see them making fewer erasures on their papers; gathering much information before they begin a task; reflecting on their answers before talking; making sure they understand directions before beginning a task; planning a strategy for solving a problem; and listening to alternative points of view.

3. LISTENING WITH UNDERSTANDING AND EMPATHY

Some psychologists believe that the ability to listen to another person, to empathize with and to understand another's point of view, is one of the highest forms of intelligent behavior. Indications of listening behaviors include: being able to paraphrase another person's ideas, to empathize

I've used the sixteen behaviors as a lead-in to three critical questions during our university department's review of its grading practices: "Do these behaviors represent the capabilities we want our students to develop? Are we accomplishing this in our school? Is our grading system helping or hindering us? —Thomas A. Dutton, professor, Miami University School of Architecture, OH.

She felt sure that if she thought long enough about Wilbur's problem, an idea would come to her mind. —E.B. White, *Charlotte's Web* (Harper and Row, 1952).

After a while her silence beat my talking like paper covers rock, so I kept my mouth shut even though the list of questions kept sprouting in my brain. —Jack Gantos, *Joey Pigza Loses Control* (Farrar, Straus and Giroux, 2000).

Whee! Grandpa!" exclaimed Paul. "I like the way you talk about history." —Marguerite Henry, *Misty of Chincoteague* (1947).

(to detect cues of their feeling or emotional state in their oral and body language), and to accurately express another person's concepts, emotions, and problems. Jean Piaget called this capability "overcoming egocentrism."

Children, without this form of intelligence being well developed, will ridicule, laugh at, or put down other students' ideas. We know their listening skills are improving when they can demonstrate an understanding of someone else's ideas or feelings by paraphrasing them accurately. We should look for students to say "Let's try Shelley's idea and see if it works," or "Let me show you how Gina solved the problem, and then I'll show you how I solved it."

4. THINKING FLEXIBILY

Some students have difficulty considering alternative points of view. Their way to solve a problem seems to be the only way. Their answer is the only correct answer. Instead of being challenged by the process of finding the answer, they are more interested in knowing whether their answer is correct. Unable to sustain a process of problem solving over time, they avoid ambiguous situations. A need for certainty outweighs an inclination to doubt. Their minds are made up, and they resist being influenced by any data or reasoning that might contradict their beliefs.

As students become more flexible in their thinking, they can be heard considering, expressing, or paraphrasing other people's points of view or rationales. They can propose several ways to solve problems and evaluate their merits and consequences. They use words and phrases such as "however," "on the other hand," and "if you look at it another way." While they progressively develop a set of moral principles to govern their own behavior, they can also change their minds in light of convincing data, arguments, or rationales. This ability makes it easier for them to resolve conflicts through compromise, to express openness about others' ideas, and to strive for consensus.

Now look, Calvin, don't you see how much easier it would be if you did [the math assignment] this way?" —Madeleine L'Engle, *A Wrinkle in Time* (1962).

5. METACOGNITION (THINKING ABOUT OUR OWN THINKING)

Some people are unaware of their own thinking processes. When asked, "How are you solving that problem?" they may reply, "I don't know. I'm just doing it." They cannot describe the mental steps that led them up to the act of problem solving or where they expect to proceed next. They cannot transform into words the visual images held in their minds. It is hard for them to plan for, reflect on, and evaluate the quality of their own thinking skills and strategies.

When students become more aware of their own thinking, they can

But while I walked, I got to think a little bit, which is something I don't usually like to do because it makes me feel nervous, and I wondered if my dad would mind if I stopped hating... —Chris Crutcher, *Athletic Shorts* (Greenwillow Books, 2002).

describe what goes on in their heads, what they already know versus what they need to know, what data is lacking and their plans for producing that data. Before they begin to solve a problem, they can describe their plan of action, list the steps, and tell where they are in the sequence. In retrospect, they can trace the pathways and blind alleys they took on the road to a problem solution.

We hear them using such terms and phrases as "I have a hypothesis…" or "My theory is…" or "When I compare these points of view…" or "By way of summary…" or "The assumptions under which I am working are…"

6. STRIVING FOR ACCURACY AND PRECISION

Students are often careless when turning in their completed work. When asked if they have checked over their papers, they may say, "No, I'm done." They seem to feel little inclination to reflect upon the accuracy of their work, to contemplate their precision, or to take pride in their accomplishments. The desire to finish overrides their interest in craftsmanship. When they grow in their desire for accuracy, they take more time to check over their tests and papers. They grow more conscientious about precision and clarity. To confirm the quality of what they have done, they will return to the original rules that they were to follow and the criteria they were to employ: Have they fulfilled the spirit as well as the letter of the problem?

7. QUESTIONING AND PROBLEM POSING

One of the characteristics that distinguishes humans from other life-forms is our inclination and ability to find problems to solve. Yet often students depend on others to ask questions for them. Sometimes they refrain from asking questions for fear of displaying ignorance. Over time, as students develop intelligence, there should be an observable shift from teacher- to student-originated questions and problems. Furthermore, the types of questions that students ask should change and become more specific and profound. For example, there will be requests for data to support others' conclusions and assumptions: "What evidence do you have?" or "How do you know that's true?" More hypothetical problems will be posed: "What do you think would happen if…" or "If that is true, then…?"

We want students to recognize discrepancies and phenomena in their environment and to inquire into the causes. "Why do cats purr?" "How high can birds fly?" "Why does the hair on my head grow so fast, but the hair on my arms and legs grows so slowly?" "What would happen if we put the saltwater fish in a freshwater aquarium?" "What are some alternative solutions, besides war, to international conflicts?"

But wherever Thorin's smoke-ring went it was not quick enough to escape Gandalf. Pop! He sent a smaller smoke-ring from his short clay-pipe straight through each one of Thorin's. —J.R.R. Tolkien, *The Hobbit* (1937)

How to get down to that glittering palace? As soon as she posed the question, she had the answer. She laid the box down and climbed aboard. —William Steig, *Brave Irene* (Farrar, Straus and Giroux, 1988).

8. DRAWING ON PAST KNOWLEDGE AND EXPERIENCES

Too often, students begin each new task as if for the very first time. Many times teachers are dismayed when they invite students to recall how they solved a similar problem in the past, and the students don't remember; it's as if they never heard of the problem before. Thinking students, by contrast, learn from experience. They can abstract the meaning from one experience, keep it in mind, and apply it to the next experience. Students can be observed growing in this ability when they say, "This reminds me of…" or "This is just like the time when I…" Analogies and references to previous experiences are part of their explanations.

Probably the ultimate goal of teaching is for students to apply school-learned knowledge to real-life situations and to other content areas. Yet we find that while students can pass mastery tests in mathematics, for example, they often have difficulty deciding whether to buy six items for $2.39 or seven for $2.86 at the supermarket.

When parents and teachers report that they see students using their school knowledge at home or in other classes, we know that students are transferring. For example, a parent reported that during a slumber party his daughter invited her friends to "brainstorm" the activities and games they preferred. (This came after she learned brainstorming techniques in school.) Similarly, a wood shop teacher described how a student volunteered a plan to measure accurately before cutting a piece of wood: "Measure twice and cut once"—an axiom learned in math class.

9. CREATING, INNOVATING, ORIGINATING

All human beings have the capacity to generate novel, original, clever, or ingenious products, solutions, and techniques—if that capacity is developed. Creative human beings try to conceive problem solutions differently, examining alternative possibilities from many angles. They tend to project themselves into different roles using analogies, starting with a vision and working backward, imagining they are the object being considered. Creative people take risks and frequently push the boundaries of their perceived limits. They are intrinsically rather than extrinsically motivated, working on the task because of the aesthetic challenge rather than the material rewards. Creative people are open to criticism. They hold up their products for others to judge and seek feedback in an effort to refine their technique. They are uneasy with the status quo. They constantly strive for greater fluency, elaboration, novelty, parsimony, simplicity, craftsmanship, perfection, beauty, harmony, and balance.

I really did have to live near water for cooking and drinking and comfort. I looked sadly at the magnificent hemlock and was about to desert it when I said something to myself. It must have come out of some book [I had read]: "Hemlocks usually grow around mountain streams and springs." —Jean Craighead George, *My Side of the Mountain* (Puffin, 2000).

We even make up his history—where he was born and how he ended up as a sideshow owner. —Kimberly Willis Holt, *When Zachary Beaver Came to Town* (Henry Holt ,1999).

10. THINKING AND COMMUNICATING WITH CLARITY AND PRECISION

Some students' language is confused, vague, or imprecise. They refer to objects or events as "weird," "nice," or "okay"; they name them as "stuff," "junk," and "things." They offer vague nouns and pronouns ("They told me to"; "Everybody has one") and unqualified comparisons ("This soda is better," "I like it more.")

As students' language becomes more precise, we hear them using more descriptive words to distinguish attributes. They refer to objects or events with analogies: "crescent-shaped"; "like a bow tie." They offer criteria for their value judgments, explicitly saying why they think one product is better than another. They speak in complete sentences; they volunteer evidence that supports their ideas; they elaborate and operationally define the terms they use. Their oral and written expressions become concise, descriptive, and coherent.

His dollop of a nose reminds me of a lamb's snout. —Carolyn Mackler, *The Earth, My Butt, and Other Big Round Things* (Candlewick, 2003).

11. GATHERING DATA THROUGH ALL THE SENSES

Information enters the brain through our sensory pathways. To know a wine it must be drunk; to know a role it must be acted; to know a game it must be played; to know a dance it must be executed; to know a goal it must be envisioned. Those whose sensory pathways are open, alert, and acute absorb more information from the environment than those whose pathways are withered, immune, and oblivious.

We see young children using all the senses when they touch, feel, and rub the objects in their environment. They put things in their mouths. "Read me a story," they say, again and again. With the same enthusiasm, they act out roles, to "be" the thing they play: a fish or a flatbed or a father. "Let me see," they plead. "I want to feel it. Let me try it. Let me hold it."

As they mature, their intelligence is revealed in the way they solve problems by using the senses. They make observations, gather data, experiment, manipulate, scrutinize, interview, visualize, role-play, illustrate, and build models. They use a range of sensory words: "I feel like…" "That touches me…" "I hear your idea…" "It leaves a bad taste in my mouth…" "Do you get the picture?"

The sharp-seeming glass blades, waist high, were tender to the touch and sprang back lightly behind her as she passed…The bank was warm, almost too warm here within the shelter of the tall grass, and the sandy earth smelled dry. —Mary Norton, *The Borrowers* (Sandpiper, 1952).

12. DISPLAYING A SENSE OF HUMOR

Smiles and laughter are exceptional human responses. Physiologically, they cause a drop in pulse rate, the secretion of endorphins, and increased oxygen levels in the blood. They have been found to provoke higher-level thinking and to liberate creativity. Some students do not have fully developed senses of humor. They may be able to laugh at

I don't know how to break this to you," said Ron, "But I think they *might* have noticed we broke into Gringotts." All three of them started to laugh, and once started, it was difficult to stop. —J.K. Rowling, *Harry Potter and the Deathly Hallows* (Arthur A. Levine Books, 2007).

"slapstick style" visual humor or at the expense of others. But they can't appreciate the humor in a story or remark about the human condition.

People who behave intelligently have the ability to perceive situations from an original, and often humorous, vantage point. They place greater value on having a sense of humor; they appreciate others' humor more; and they see the humor in situations. They thrive on finding incongruity and have that whimsical frame of mind characteristic of creative problem solvers.

13. RESPONDING WITH WONDERMENT AND AWE

Some children and adults avoid problems. "I was never good at puzzles," they say. They don't enroll in math class or "hard" academic subjects after completing their required courses. They perceive thinking as hard work and recoil from situations they deem "too demanding."

Students who behave intelligently grow not just in their ability to use thinking skills but in their enjoyment of problem solving. They seek problems to solve. They make up problems, request them from others, and solve them with increasing independence, without an adult's help or intervention. Such statements as "Don't tell me the answer; I can figure it out by myself" indicate growing autonomy. These students will be lifelong learners.

The critical behavior here is approaching the world with a sense of wonder and openness. Do we notice children reflecting on the changing formations of a cloud? Being charmed by the opening of a bud? Sensing the logical simplicity of mathematical order? Finding intrigue in the geometrics of a spider's web or exhilaration in the iridescence of a hummingbird's wings? Recognizing the orderliness and adroitness of a chemical change or the serenity of a distant constellation?

As they advance to higher grade levels, children who exhibit this kind of intellectual behavior derive more pleasure from thinking. As the problems they encounter become more complex and their senses capture more of the rhythm, patterns, shapes, colors, and harmonies of the universe, their curiosity becomes stronger. They show greater respect for the roles and values of other human beings; they display more compassionate behavior toward other life-forms; they perceive the delicate worth and uniqueness of everything and everyone they encounter. Wonderment, a sense of awe, passion—these are the prerequisites for higher-level thinking.

14. THINKING INTERDEPENDENTLY

We are social beings. We congregate in groups, find being listened to therapeutic, draw energy from each other, and seek reciprocity. Prob-

The Spring sunlight lit up the house so beautifully that nobody remembered it needed a coat of paint and new wallpapers. On the contrary, they all found themselves thinking that it was the best house in Cherry-Tree Lane. —P.L. Travers, *Mary Poppins* (Harcourt Brace, 1934).

ably the foremost intellectual behavior for the citizens of the twenty-first century and beyond will be a heightened ability to think in concert with others. Problem-solving has become so complex that no one person can do it alone. No one has access to all the data needed to make critical decisions; no one person can consider as many alternatives as several people could. Working in groups requires the ability to justify ideas and test the feasibility of solution strategies on others.

Students do not necessarily come to school knowing how to work effectively in groups. They may exhibit competitiveness, narrowness of viewpoint, egocentrism, ethnocentrism, and criticism of others' values, emotions, and beliefs. Cooperative skills need to be taught directly and practiced repeatedly. Listening, consensus seeking, giving up an idea to work on someone else's idea, empathy, compassion, leadership, knowing how to support group efforts, altruism—all are behaviors indicative of intelligent human beings.

15. TAKING RESPONSIBLE RISKS

Intelligent people seem to have an almost uncontrollable urge to go beyond established limits. They are uneasy about comfort; they "live on the edge of their competence." They seem compelled to place themselves in situations where they do not know what the outcome will be. They accept confusion, uncertainty, and the higher risks of failure as part of the normal process of life, and they learn to view setbacks as interesting, challenging, and growth producing.

However, they do not behave impulsively. Their risks are educated. They draw on past knowledge, are thoughtful about consequences, and have a well-trained sense of what is appropriate. They know that all risks are not worth taking. They develop a capacity for intelligent risk-taking—a cross between intuition, past knowledge, and a sense of meeting new challenges.

There are two types of risks: ventures and adventures. Most venture capitalists, when approached to take the risk of investing in a new business, proceed with care. They look at the markets, see how well organized the ideas are, and study the economic projections. If they finally decide to take a risk, it is a well considered one. That is the venture way.

The adventure way involves spontaneity and a willingness to take a chance in the moment. Adventurers will only take this chance if they know—from past history or their current group support—that this activity is not going to be life threatening or they will be protected enough from harm. People who take high-risk experiences in this way develop the ability to take more actions, often more than they previously believed they could.

Just write it all down like you're talking. Put in all the fun we had, the cool things we did. Our adventures."

"But you know I can't write, Kevin."

"It's all in your head, Max, everything you can remember. Just tell the story of Freak the Mighty, no big deal."

– Rodman Philbrick, *Freak the Mighty* (Scholastic, 1993).

If the bear had wanted you," his brain said, "he would have taken you." It is something to understand, he thought, not something to run away from. The bear was eating berries.

Not people.

And the bear had almost indicated that it didn't mind sharing—had just walked away from him.

And the berries were so good.

He walked slowly back to the raspberry patch and continued picking for the entire morning, although with great caution. —Gary Paulsen, *Hatchet* (Bradbury Press, 1987).

Some students seem reluctant to take any risks. They hold back in games, new learning, and new friendships because their fear of failure is far greater than their experience of venture or adventure. A mental voice within them says, "If you try it and you are wrong, you will look stupid." The other voice that might say "If you don't try it, you will never know" is trapped in fear and mistrust.

When someone holds back from taking risks, they are confronted constantly with missed opportunities. But as students become more venturesome, they become capable of being different, going against the grain of the common, thinking of new ideas and testing them with peers as well as teachers. They are more likely to be successful in an era of innovation and uncertainty because they learn to take risks effectively through repeated experiences.

16. LEARNING CONTINUOUSLY

Intelligent people are in a continuous learning mode. Their confidence, in combination with their inquisitiveness, allows them to constantly search for new and better ways. They are always striving for perfection, always growing, always learning, always modifying and improving themselves. They seize problems, situations, tensions, conflicts, and circumstances as valuable opportunities to learn.

A great mystery about humans is that we often confront learning opportunities with fear rather than mystery and wonder. We seem to feel better when we know rather than when we learn. We defend our biases, beliefs, and storehouses of knowledge rather than inviting the unknown, the creative, and the inspirational. Being certain and closed gives us comfort while being doubtful and open gives us fear.

Perhaps this is a consequence of traditional education—both at home and at school. From an early age, employing a curriculum of fragmentation, competition, and reactiveness, students are trained to believe that deep learning means figuring out the truth rather than developing capabilities for effective and thoughtful action. They have been taught to value right answers rather than to inquire, to know which choice is correct rather than to explore alternatives.

Our wish is for creative students and people who are eager to learn. That includes the humility of knowing that we don't know, which is the highest form of thinking we will ever learn. Paradoxically, unless you start off with humility, you will never get anywhere; so as the first step, you must already have what will eventually be the crowning glory of all learning: the humility to know—and admit—that you don't know and then not be afraid to find out.

But I figure if the world were really right, humans would live life backward and do the first part last. They'd be all-knowing in the beginning and innocent in the end. —Angela Johnson, *First Part Last* (Simon & Schuster, 2003).

The quotes next to each "intellectual behavior" were selected by children's librarian Jennie Dutton, children's literature aficionado Martha Piper, and *Schools That Learn* coauthor Art Kleiner. Some are included on a list of recommended children's books, tagged to each intellectual behavior, published by the Institute for Habits of Mind. To see the list, visit instituteforhabitsofmind.com, click on "Resources" and then "Bibliography of Student Books."

REUVEN FEUERSTEIN AND INSTRUMENTAL ENRICHMENT

Books and videos available through http://www.icelp.org

Cognitive psychologist Dr. Reuven Feuerstein began his career teaching disturbed children in Bucharest at the beginning of World War II. He later escaped and fled to Palestine, where he worked with thousands of child survivors of the Holocaust. These children's cognitive processes had been severely stunted by their trauma. Feuerstein developed materials and techniques for assessing and mediating the learning process, helping to reveal children's strengths and build the skills they lacked.

Feuerstein's Instrumental Enrichment (IE) program focuses on metacognition—thinking about your thinking—and developing strategies for organizing and processing knowledge.

One cornerstone is the need to reduce impulsivity. Feuerstein's slogan is: "Just a minute, let me think." Just a minute—stop and reflect, whether you're a teacher, a kid with ADD, or someone who has been diagnosed as learning disabled. The mediated learning of IE raises people's awareness of their own cognitive patterns and styles by teaching thirty-three different ways to describe flavors of human thinking. A personal favorite is: "I'm having an episodic grasp of reality."

His award-winning documentary video *The Mind of a Child* tells a poignant story about children affected by poverty, racism, and war, and the adults who work with them using Feuerstein's methods. Feuerstein founded the International Center for the Enhancement of Learning Potential and the Hadassah-WIZO-Canada Research Institute in Israel. —Tim Lucas and Janis Dutton

Ferris Bueller's Day Off, directed by John Hughes (Paramount, 1986). The economics teacher was played by Ben Stein.

7. Knowledge and Power
Education for Social Justice

Nelda Cambron-McCabe, Janis Dutton

A high school economics teacher stands in front of a chalkboard. In a monotone, deadpan delivery, devoid of a shred of enthusiasm, he addresses the students with a fill-in-the blank lecture. "In the 1930s," he intones, "the Republican-controlled House of Representatives, in an effort to alleviate the effects of the—" He pauses for a second. "Anyone? Anyone?" Having received no answer, he fills in the blank "—Great Depression—" and continues with the sentence: "passed the—Anyone? Anyone? The Tariff Bill." Students sitting at their desks, eyes glazed over, bored, disinterested, comatose, or asleep. This classroom parody from the movie *Ferris Bueller's Day Off*, though cartoonlike in its exaggeration, taps into people's shared experiences or beliefs. We have yet to see a group of teenagers watch this movie without a hilarious response and comments like "That is so true!"

Sadly, many of us can relate to this transmission model of teaching—whether in high school or college, workplace training sessions, community lectures, or conference keynotes where experts "tell" us what they think we need to know. As in Ferris Bueller's classroom, both the lecturer and the recipients seem anesthetized against the painful experience, as if teaching and learning are as much fun as getting your teeth drilled. Whether you are in the dentist's chair or lecture hall, both experiences place you in a passive role of having something "done to you," with no power and no agency. The humor in the film scene above lies not just in a recognition of common experience, but also in the irony that a class about democracy is so disempowering.

⟫ See "The Industrial Age System of Education," page 32.

Many teaching and learning practices—in classrooms and in professional development in workplaces—have been moving away from this approach, by coaching learners through a process of inquiry, exploration, and discovery of the subject. Encompassing theories and methods from constructivism, collaborative learning, cooperative learning, engaged learning, and others, these practices are based on the belief that students will create a deeper understanding of the content and retain more by building on their own experiences and by interacting with the subject matter and with other people, including peers, teacher/facilitator, or members of the community.

But what do you do with that knowledge once you have it? To what end are people being educated? Why this particular content? How does it relate to the larger context? How are the content and distribution related to issues of power? Is the knowledge useful to help question the very processes by which certain knowledge is legitimated in the first place?

That is why we are drawn to the theories and practices of popular education and critical pedagogy and inspired by the power they bring to our practice with the five disciplines. We believe they can help people create significant and enduring change in their organizations—especially schools—by developing fundamental shifts of attitudes and beliefs about the nature of schooling, the social construction of learning, and how knowledge always forms the basis for social action—in any organization.

POWER

The word "power" can have both positive and negative connotations. You can power up a generator, be powered by an engine, have powers of concentration, have the power to accomplish, or have power over others. Some forms of power can be measured and controlled accurately, such as power of magnification, horsepower, watts, and ergs. The innate powers driving human behavior may not be so easily measurable, but the effects of their absence or presence are quite noticeable.

The word "power" stems from the Latin *posse*, "to be able." It passed into French as *pouvoir* and became a noun meaning "ability to do things." This root also gave us the words "possible" and "potent." Power is not only about control or authority; we draw on our own powers to increase our capabilities.

But in many cases, power (and its variants, like "empower") have developed connotations of one-directional action. Most people who say, for instance, "We have to empower people" are subtly implying that the receivers have no power other than the power given to them and that the internal powers that human beings have are valid only when granted legitimacy by external agents who possess knowledge, authority, or control. In this book, when we describe power, we try to maintain awareness that power from outside (an individual, group, or organization), especially when unseen and unacknowledged, often disconnects people from their potential power from within. —Janis Dutton

When the military took over the Brazilian government in 1964, Freire was forced into exile; in the eyes of the totalitarian regime that followed, an empowered or even literate citizenry was subversive. Only after an amnesty was declared in 1979 did Freire return to Brazil; and in 1989, he was chosen as minister of education for the city of Sao Paolo. In 1993 he was nominated for a Nobel Peace Prize for his work. See Maria del Pilar O'Cadiz, Pia Lindquist Wong, and Carlos Alberto Torres, *Education and Democracy: Paulo Freire, Social Movements, and Education Reform in Sao Paulo* (Westview Press, 1998).

The term "popular education" emerged from the Latin American movement *educacion popular* in the 1960s–1970s. It moved into North America through the work of its internationally known proponent, the late Brazilian educator Paulo Freire, who is considered one of the most influential thinkers on education in the late twentieth century in much of the world but receives little notice in North America. The term means "education of the people"—not, as some may think, an education that is well liked or commonly accepted. Popular education, known as informal education in Great Britain and other parts of the world, has the express purpose of creating environments and opportunities for oppressed or repressed groups of people to raise political self-awareness, build community, and take action to change their social conditions. It is guided by the principles of working for the well being of all; respecting the unique value and dignity of each human being; dialogue; equality and justice; and democracy and the active involvement of people in the issues that affect their lives.

The practice of popular education situates itself outside of and provides a stark contrast to formal institutionalized schooling and training, which too often reinforces powerlessness through assimilation or adjustment to the status quo. The late popular educator Myles Horton, cofounder of what is now known as the Highlander Education and Research Center, said, "What ought to be rather than what is—that is Highlander's mission. From two words, *ought* and *is*, arises the tension out of which people will learn and act." In many ways it is like people engaging the five disciplines to analyze current reality and engage in productive conversations to create a desired future—but with a key distinction. In popular education, the education and the educator are understood as inherently political. According to Horton, "There can be no such thing as neutrality. It's a code word for the existing system."

Quotes from: Frank Adams with Myles Horton, *Unearthing the Seeds of Fire: The Idea of Highlander* (John F. Blair, 1975), p. 214, and Paulo Freire and Myles Horton, *We Make the Road by Walking: Conversations on*

PEDAGOGY, CRITICAL PEDAGOGY

The word "pedagogy" stems from the Greek word *paideutike*, meaning "the art of teaching the young." (The English word "ethics" derives from the same Greek base, which stemmed, in turn, from an older Greek word *paido* meaning "child.") Today, the word "pedagogy" typically invokes a more narrow meaning of "what teachers do" or even "teaching techniques." Yet education is a lifelong experience, and teachers show up not just in learning institutions but everywhere, in a multitude of guises. Many adults have pedagogical roles even if they aren't called "teacher." Within this view, pedagogy is defined to include all of the practices and processes that shape what people know and how they come to know it. These processes and practices are inherent in any organization or social interaction, not just in schools.

~~~~~

The practices and theories of critical pedagogy bring forth the hidden motivations, a hidden curriculum behind the social construction of knowledge. Knowledge is always produced and distributed for particular ends, by voices within relations of power in an organization, community, or school. Schools, in particular, are never neutral sites or free spaces; they may pretend to exist outside the conflicts of internal and external politics, but they are always shaped by the political structures around them. Like any organization, schools are places of ongoing struggle over meaning, values, assumptions, the construction and dissemination of knowledge ("Who decides what is taught?"), classroom practices ("Who decides how it is taught?"), and interpersonal relations among staff members, students, and people from the outside community ("Who decides who decides?"). The lens of critical pedagogy helps bring into focus why some students and schools succeed and why others must strain to succeed against overwhelming odds.

The field of critical pedagogy, sometimes called transformative pedagogy, also grew out of the work Paulo Freire and focused the principles of popular education back into classrooms and schools. Freire critiqued transmission pedagogy, what he called the banking concept, in formal schooling where experts deposit knowledge into passive students who are taught to accept the world as it is with little hope of being able to change it. Freire believed that literacy was critical to democracy and felt that both child and adult learners' ability to "read the word" was intimately tied to being able to "read the world."

In his early work, Freire and his team members met with impoverished and illiterate villagers and engaged in culture circles about their lives and their hopes. Through this dialogue common words emerged as a primer for learning to read, but more importantly the villagers began to understand that their lives and conditions were socially constructed rather than absolute and that their silence contributed to their own powerless position in society. It took only thirty hours for villagers to achieve functional literacy once they realized they had the power to transform their world.

Freire's success in the national adult literacy campaign in Brazil in the 1960s influenced literacy campaigns around the world. Unfortunately, too often, especially in North America, people imported Freire's meth-

Education and Social Change (Temple University Press, 1990) p. 102.

For more on Highlander and Popular Education see Myles Horton with Judith Kohl and Herbert Kohl, *The Long Haul: An Autobiography* (Teachers College Press, 1997), the resources reviewed below, and visit www.highlandercenter. org. See also The Encyclopedia of Informal Education at www.infed.org.

The term "critical pedagogy" developed out of the work of a network of educators influenced by the writing and teaching of Paulo Freire. Significant voices in the field include Peter McLaren, Henry Giroux, Richard Quantz, Jeanne Brady, Dennis Carlson, Ira Shor, Donaldo Macedo, Thomas Dutton, bell hooks, and Michael Apple. For more information on the work in critical pedagogy and cultural studies see: Ira Shor, *Freire for the Classroom*, (Boynton/Cook, 1987); Henry Giroux, Teachers as Intellectuals, (Bergin & Garvey, 1988); Michael Apple, *Cultural Politics and Education*, (Teachers College Press, 1996); bell hooks, *Teaching to Transgress*, (Routledge, 1994); and http://www.paulofreire.org (Portuguese and English). See also the resource reviews following this article.

ods, depoliticized them, reduced them to mere "techniques," and left his theories and principles behind. Not surprisingly, their efforts fell short.

LITERACY

The word "literacy" stems from the Latin *littera*, meaning "letter." From that root was derived *literatus*—having knowledge of letters, and hence our current meaning of "educated, learned." Today, however, the word "literacy" is used to describe sets of skills beyond the ability to read and write. Reading and writing are unquestionably important but so are other literacies.

Just as Howard Gardner has described multiple intelligences, there is more and more talk of multiple literacies. It is valid to talk about emotional, computer, cultural, environmental, visual, financial, functional, musical, community, and systems literacy. Each represents a form of power: the power to name or identify things and ideas and to communicate effectively with or about them. In our view, each type of literacy includes the ability to reflect on the meanings of symbols, on our feelings and actions about them, and about the effect they have on others. Literacy is a kind of leverage.

According to Robert Moses, an organizer of the Civil Rights Movement with ties to Highlander and founder of The Algebra Project, math literacy is just as critical to agency as reading. For more see Robert Moses and Charles E. Cobb, Jr., *Radical Equations: Civil Rights from Mississippi to the Algebra Project* (Beacon Press, 2002) and www.algebra.org.

Literacy is best understood as a myriad of [communication] forms and cultural competencies that construct and make available the various relations and experiences that exist between learners and the world."
—From Paulo Freire and Donaldo P. Macedo, *Literacy: Reading the Word and the World* (Bergin and Garvey, 1987), p.10.

POSSIBILITIES FOR THE FIVE DISCIPLINES

What value, then, do popular education and critical pedagogy offer practitioners of the learning disciplines? At the very least, they offer the understanding that schools are unavoidably political sites—that no content or process of teaching and learning, or determining policy, is politically neutral. But more importantly, they offer an understanding that the five disciplines are not neutral either.

People in schools and other organizations often create teams that hold deep conversations about their purpose, the nature of their organizations, their shared values, and their goals. Yet they appear to be unaware of the political and social forces that have shaped the system around them and that their silence on many issues contributes to the conditions with which they struggle. This makes it more difficult to see the interconnections in their actions or inaction, where to apply leverage, or even that they are part of creating the system.

According to Horton, there are two types of education. One enslaves people in service to the existing system; the other liberates people and allows them the power to make decisions about their lives, so that they can acquire knowledge as tools to change society. So when some teams regularly use the language of systems thinking and visioning but omit serious attempts to identify and critically question mental models about the political and social forces that shape their system—their own mental models and those of people in positions of authority—they can end up in reinforcing loops of ignorance.

Proponents of popular education and critical pedagogy continually ask questions that provoke people to focus on power and the purpose of learning, in classrooms, in schools, in communities, in democracies. While these kinds of questions and discussions may be uncomfortable, true learning often is.

See "Are You Smarter Than a Thermostat?," page 151.

Paulo Freire and Myles Horton were often labeled revolutionary (as were Thomas Jefferson and Benjamin Franklin in their time). To them, education was not an end in itself or merely a means to employment. They saw schools as political sites that either engaged people in informed political participation for a stronger democracy and a better future or prevented them from becoming engaged. Both Freire and Horton believed in democracy and equality and didn't shy away from explaining how these were enabled or disabled by power and politics.

Freire said: "A humanizing education is the path through which men and women can become conscious about their presence in the world. The way they act and think when they develop all of their capacities, taking into consideration their needs but also the needs and aspirations of others." From our perspective, in order to create a better and sustainable future for our children, schools, and communities, the first step is to bring mental models about knowledge and learning to the surface in the interest of democracy, equity, and social justice. If that is considered unsettling or even revolutionary, then so be it.

PAULO FREIRE AND MYLES HORTON

The Paulo Freire Reader, edited by Ana Maria Araújo Freire and Donaldo P. Macedo (The Continuum Publishing Company, 1998); *The Myles Horton Reader: Education for Social Change*, edited by Dale Jacobs (The University of Tennessee Press, 2003); *We Make the Road by Walking: Conversations on Education and Social Change*, by Paulo Freire and Myles Horton (Temple University Press, 1990).

Whenever anyone asks "Which Paulo Freire or Myles Horton book should I read to get started?" I say: Start with the two Readers and then read the conversation between them. Freire, for example, wrote prolifically so that he could engage in reflection-action cycles of his own learning and communication, and this Reader provides a glimpse of his transformation. A collection of Freire's most incisive writings, it includes his "Banking Concept of Education" (in which he discusses the prevalence and authoritarian influence of the transmission model), the dialogues with the villagers of Recife, the challenges of urban education, and his explorations on "reading the world." If the notes I've made on the pages are any indication, I do have a favorite: "The Pedagogy of Hope."

The Horton Reader is a collection of his writings, speeches, and interviews on the ideas and people who influenced him to start the Highlander Folk School, the successes and challenges Highlander faced through the labor and civil rights movements, and an engaging section on Horton's educational philosophies. I am particularly drawn to the parallels with the five disciplines in a 1972 speech on "Why Don't Reforms Reform?" and how real reform requires reexamining the idea that "by being good people, people of goodwill, people who are trying to change here and there, that we will make progress."

Though Freire and Horton knew of each other for years and met briefly on different occasions, in 1987 they had the opportunity to come together for a week to "speak a book" and then reunited two years later to reflect on their dialogue. *We Make the Road by Walking* captures this remarkable conversation and guides the reader through the similarities and differences of their philosophies, histories, and contexts in Latin America and the southern U.S. Freire chose to work within institutions and Horton from the outside, and I believe this book reveals how both are necessary. The margins of my copy of the book, where they discuss the difference between education and organizing, are heavily marked in different colors of ink, as each time I read it, it raises more questions. —Janis Dutton

CRITICAL PEDAGOGY

Notes from the Real World, by Joan Wink (Longman, 1997)

This book is a breath of fresh air and an inspiration. Wink provides access to the theories and practices of critical pedagogy through a reflection on her own experiences and explorations as a teacher of children labeled "at risk," "minority," "limited English proficiency," or "problems." She quickly learned to hate those labels because they hid the child and families behind them and limited their possibilities.

Some books on critical pedagogy can get pretty dense. Wink writes about her struggles with the language of critical pedagogy while introducing the reader to that language by communicating its importance in understanding and describing her work as a teacher. She tells stories, provides exercises and tools, teaches theory, and uncovers the history of that theory in a writing style that makes everything accessible—and even fun. —Janis Dutton

VI. Productive Conversation

TL

1. Check-In

Carol Kenerson, Micah Fierstein, Janis Dutton

Purpose:

Taking a few moments at the beginning of class to give students a chance to be present together.

Participants:

Any group of two or more people. In addition to staff meetings and classrooms, some people use it around the dinner table at home.

Time:

A few minutes (or less) per

There are many variations and very few rules. Some students will be silent for a minute, focusing inward, and then simply say, "I'm here." Others will talk about their current problems or triumphs, while others will offer a simple statement about their perspective. It need not be done every day, but to conduct check-ins on Monday and Friday offers a stable frame to the week. Each person has an opportunity to speak. People speak to the whole group. Students who are shy or just don't feel like talking can say "Pass," instead of being forced to speak, but they need to acknowledge their passing out loud, so their voices are heard.

Listeners who can focus on what is said without having to worry about making a response develop a deeper appreciation of each person. If class time is tight, a one-word check-in takes a couple of minutes. Go around the circle and let each individual offer a single word: "Purple." "Running." "Basketball." Some students prefer going around in a circle and knowing when their turn will come. Others prefer check-ins where each person speaks when the feeling moves him or her, until everyone has spoken. Either process causes stress for someone in the room; this is a great marker for the different needs and styles of individual learners.

As a teacher, you can open by checking-in yourself, talking about a book you have read or something on your mind, to model what it takes to be present. Make check-in absolutely safe. Classroom students should know they can admit, for instance, that, "I woke up late today, and I was rushing and I'm kind of frazzled, so the first five minutes

258 ■ ~~~~~~~~~~~~~~~~~~~~~~~~~~~~~

may be a little out of sync," and it will be heard in the spirit in which they mean it.

Check-ins transform a group. One high school teacher, who normally began each class with check-in, had a compressed schedule one week and said, "No check-in today." The students protested vehemently. "I have been waiting all day," said one, "to say what I was thinking."

CHECK-OUTS

If "check-ins" help students feel present, a similar technique—called "check-outs"—can provide a sense of closure. At the end of a unit, allow every individual a chance to speak (if the student wants it):

- What did you find particularly interesting?
- What would you like to know more about?
- If there was something that confused you that you finally figured out, how would you explain it to someone else?
- What do you still feel confused about?

person. In fifty-minute classroom periods, check-ins can be useful at the start and end of each week.

2. Opening Day

Nelda Cambron-McCabe

See Parker J. Palmer, *The Courage to Teach: Exploring the Inner Landscape of a Teacher's Life*, 2nd edition (Jossey-Bass, 2007), pp. 76; reviewed on p. 174 of *Schools That Learn*.

Introducing mental models in the first session of a course can open up an atmosphere of trust and inquiry throughout the entire course. I've seen this firsthand in the university seminars I teach; my students have taken it back to their high school and grade school classrooms and report the same effect. I start during the first class of a semester. First I encourage students to explore the concept of mental models, the ladder of inference (page 101), the systems thinking iceberg (page 126), and the need to balance inquiry and advocacy (page 104). I explain that the course structure and readings are set up to provide the boundaries for our conversation together during the semester. I quote Parker Palmer: "The [classroom] space should be [both] bounded and open."

I emphasize that if we are to learn together, this class must be a safe place to raise issues that are hard to talk about elsewhere. In my university, as in most educational institutions, there are often many concerns about culture, race, class, and gender below the surface. In this course, these issues may be laid on the table. I say that the students' role is not to talk to the professor, as they often do, but with one another. My role is not to give them information but to set up a structure in which we can all learn together. All voices have value in the classroom, and I expect to learn from them as well.

This classroom environment requires a very different orientation for students. Even at the graduate school level, they still expect teachers to present the knowledge and information. If they don't learn at the end, they assume it's because the teacher didn't do a very good job of imparting knowledge to them. So we talk about this during the first session. Then I say something like this:

> We're going to establish some structure for our conversations. I intend to hold myself to them as well as you. Each of us must be accountable to the whole class for promoting and supporting a deeper conversational level.
>
> First, we listen intently as others talk. We don't just hold our own thought, waiting for our turn. Instead, we listen for the meaning others are attempting to share. We may build on another's comment or ask questions about what thinking lies behind the comment.
>
> Second, we recognize the importance of silence. Space is needed to reflect on what is being said.
>
> Third, no one interrupts. We let each other finish.
>
> Fourth, we don't criticize others' comments as "right," "wrong," "smart," or "stupid."
>
> Fifth, we forbid the phrase "Yes, but"—a phrase that automatically labels the previous comment as invalid. Instead, we urge the use of "Yes, and," which validates and extends the contribution.

Before beginning this kind of redesign, it's helpful for teachers to have gone through the Designing a Learning Classroom exercise (see p. 164). Having envisioned the kind of interactive, divergent classroom they want to create, they are more aware of the information about students that will be helpful. Parents will also find this exercise useful for thinking about the kind of classroom that will draw on their child's strengths.

The first time I opened a course this way, I didn't realize how much of an impact it had made until the final paper, when students were asked to critique their learning in the course. One student wrote, "This was the first time a professor ever laid out a structure for conversation like this. And you didn't just talk about it; you modeled it." She added, "I often marveled how you not only allowed us to get off task but actually encouraged conversations seemingly irrelevant to that day's topic. However, over time I came to recognize the importance of this strategy, because it was through these conversations that the material became rich and relevant to each of us." She concluded: "I would never have allowed that in my own teaching because I wouldn't have trusted the learning process. But nothing was irrelevant, and the course was much more powerful this way."

Students often comment about the "yes, and" technique in particular: People critique each others' ideas just as much, but their responses show that they have truly listened and considered another's view before commenting."

⟩⟩ See other tools for productive conversation in the Mental Models primer on page 97.

3. Reframing the Parent-Teacher Conference

Nelda Cambron-McCabe, Janis Dutton, Tim Lucas, Betty Quantz, Art Kleiner

PM   MM
   SV   TL
       ST

If the classroom is a system (page 16) involving the teacher, student, and parent, then the link between the teacher and parent is the weak link in the system. All day long, communication occurs between teacher and student. Evenings and weekends, it occurs continually between student and parent. But between teacher and parent, there is just one quarterly communication: a group of letters and numbers on a report card, perhaps with a comment or two scrawled in the margin. The important knowledge within this system is not being shared effectively.

The parent-teacher conference was created to improve this link—but it, too, is rarely a learning experience. The teacher has a folder of notes about the child's strengths and weaknesses. The parent listens as the teacher runs down the notes for the scheduled fifteen minutes. Sometimes the teacher listens while the parent vents frustration. Both sides leave with their mental models of the conference intact—a ritual that ought to be fascinating for both sides but seems to end up being lackluster and frustrating. After a year or two, many parents stop going, and some teachers wish they could as well.

This article is not an exercise, because no single exercise will do. Every student situation, and every teacher, is different. Some teachers have a half hour or longer per semester to devote to each child. Others have a few minutes (and have to design accordingly). This menu of possibilities is based on the five disciplines:

1. Personal mastery—being honest about the strengths and weaknesses of current reality and nurturing to a child's own aspirations;
2. Mental models—surfacing assumptions about what is happening in class, the child's developmental stages, and the home environment;

3. Shared vision—talking about goals for the teacher, parent, and student;

4. Systems thinking—understanding academic performance in light of the full complexity of a student's life;

5. Team learning—Teachers, parents, and students all have the same purpose: to achieve the best possible learning experience for each student for that year. Each member of the team possesses unique knowledge and understanding that the others lack. Each has the ability to act within his or her milieu: the teacher in class, the parent at home, the student everywhere else. And none of them has control over the whole situation.

The conference should be influenced by each person, and each participant's views, including the student's, should be seen as equally valid. Team learning, after all, is a process of seeing what each member of the team knows, so the team as a whole can act more effectively than the mere sum of its individual member's actions.

QUESTIONS FOR PARENTS AND EDUCATORS

Even when there's very little time, parents or educators can effectively reframe a parent-teacher (or parent-administrator) conference by asking questions to build a common understanding of current reality. Educators can ask:

■ What strengths do you see in your child?

■ What does your child say about school?

■ What kinds of activities, at school or elsewhere, seem to frustrate your child most?

■ What kinds of activities excite your child? What does he/she play?

■ Tell me about your child's peers and social relations? Whom does he or she socialize with outside of school?

■ What kinds of responsibilities does your child have at home?

■ What goals do you have for your child?

■ What goals does your child have?

■ What is your child's favorite subject or activity?

■ What would you like me to know about your child?

Parents can ask questions like these:

■ How does my child interact with you and other adults?

■ How does my child interact with classmates?

■ What activities engage or frustrate my child in class?

- What does my child do with unstructured time?
- What activities hold my child's interest the longest?
- How does my child work in teams?
- Whom do you team my child with and why?
- Based on your experiences with my child, what kind of classroom structure or instructional style would you recommend next year?
- What are my child's strengths?
- What areas need improvement?

MAPPING THE CHILD'S CURRENT REALITY

If time permits, mapping is a remarkably powerful tool for educators, students, and parents—any of whom can initiate the process—to set goals and monitor them and to document ongoing team learning. Families keep a copy and the school keeps a copy. Mapping also can help groups of teachers, or teachers and administrators, consider the whole-life situation of a child in difficulty. If issues arise, or if you are seeking expanded opportunities for the student, you can go back and ask, "What do we know about this child?" And if you can create the time, mapping can help turn parent-teacher conferences into beginning a shared vision.

On a sheet of paper, write the student's name. Then, in ever-widening circles out from the center, write in everything you can think of that represents an aspect of the child's life. You can use the "parents" and "educators" questions from this article to help generate elements for the map. Since everybody's thoughts go on the same map, they can reach insights together that neither would make on their own. The parent may say, "We've moved four times in the last five years, and my child doesn't make friends easily." The educator might then respond: "You know, I've seen your child sitting back and watching the activity nearby without jumping in. Now I understand better what to look for, and I think I have some ways to work on this."

If parents jump up the "ladder of inference"—making a broad generalization about the child or the school—the educator can say: "Let's talk more about that; tell me what you've seen, because I want to record this accurately on the map." The parent can do the same. If the educator says, "She's a great kid," the parent can say, "Well, in what way? What else on the map is the 'great kid' connected to?"

One map showed that a fourth grader had tremendous rapport with younger children; the teacher arranged for her to visit a first-grade class and tutor students there occasionally, learning a great deal about herself and her skills in the process.

If the map is drawn in September or October, then both the parent and educator can keep a copy. As issues arise during the year, they can look back at the map, reconsider what they know about the child, and add to it. It's always fascinating to watch the maps grow or change as the child moves through the grade levels.

}} For a sample concept map (in the primer), see page 121.

4. "Don't eat the pizza..."
Exercises for Taking Stock of the Classroom Experience

Bryan Smith, Nelda Cambron-McCabe, Tim Lucas, Art Kleiner, Janis Dutton

Purpose:

A variety of ways for children and students to take stock of their own classroom experiences and make reflective statements for others.

Sometimes schools invite their alumni back from the next school level as guest speakers. "Let us tell you about what it's like in high school," say ninth graders to the eighth graders who will follow them from middle school. "I wish I'd had more complete lessons in geometry, because you really need it up here." One of us asked Patrick, a third grader, coming back from meeting with fourth and fifth graders, what he had learned. "They told us whatever we did, don't eat the pizza in the cafeteria," he said. "It has bugs in it."

Taking stock of school experience can be one of the most valuable ways for students to reflect—and to pass on their reflections to others. This can start at a very young age. One of the great milestones from kindergarten to first grade in many schools is staying a full day—including lunch. First graders have a lot to tell their successors: "You have to label your lunch bag with your name and don't forget to wear gloves when it's cold, because they send you outside."

THE TIME CAPSULE

At the end of every year or every semester, students design a "time capsule" of advice and perspective for the students who will come after them. This time capsule could take the form of a letter written to the next class or a videotape or audiotape where they interview each other. Websites are a natural medium for this. A good rhythm would be: Make a tape just before winter holidays, look at it and add to it in the spring, and then offer it to the students coming in next fall.

The students making this time capsule, no matter how young, are taking a stand—on behalf of their compatriots who will move, grade by grade, behind them in the system. For that reason, if you're a teacher, your participation should be minimal. Discourage and edit out personal remarks (including those about yourself). Offer constructive critique but resist making changes in content. This is an exercise by kids, for kids.

Questions to ask:

- What did you expect when you started?
- What surprised you?
- What do you wish someone would have told you before you started?
- What are you glad you studied, and why?
- What do you wish you'd studied less of, and why?
- How do you think about things differently than you did a year ago?
- What gave you a tough time, that you wish you'd gotten more help with?
- What do you want to do next year?

RETROSPECTIVE REFLECTION

These questions, at the end of a session or a week of classes, can help a group of people reflect on their own team learning capabilities.

- Have we been open to other people's ideas?
- Have we been able to express the kinds of thoughts that normally remain unspoken but that would have made a difference for the better here?
- Did everyone get a chance to speak?
- Did we move toward our common goals?
- Were we open to different learning styles, personality styles, and levels of verbal ability? Did we draw forth the generally silent people?
- Did we model the kind of behavior we would like to produce?
- Were we in "flow"? Did we feel the conversation move forward with its own creative momentum?
- Did we feel aligned? Did we understand each other's attitudes, why the other people held them, and how that might affect the next step? Can we work together even if we know we don't agree?
- Did my behavior help or hinder the group?
- Do I treat others with respect for their dignity?
- Did we model reflective learning?

The Classroom Reflective Journal

Nelda Cambron-McCabe

Any form of regular taking stock is valuable, in a classroom, for helping teachers understand their own learning. In my seminars at Miami University's graduate school of education, I require students to keep an ongoing reflective journal. They turn in about 1,000 words per week, thinking in depth about the class discussion, the papers they are writing, or any reactions they have had to the course. It represents a lot of reading for me, but I continue to require it, because it significantly improves the quality of their learning as well as my own.

At first, everyone hates these assignments—on top of all the other course work, they have to write three to five pages a week to me!—but at the end, they all say they could never have learned as much without it. By the third or fourth week, most of them have gotten into the habit of making time for the journals just after class, when their thoughts are fresh; then they revise their writing a few days later, when their thoughts have had time to settle in. The journal represents a commitment to the course—a way for them to take the complex ideas of a seminar and connect them back to their own lives.

In return, I promise them not to critique or assess their journals but only to add my thoughts back to them—and to keep the journals absolutely confidential. Students feel free to write some very personal, painful things, because they know that I will be the only person who reads them. One young African American doctoral student wrote that the course in organizational learning was very painful for him. "I want to know," he wrote, "why I never took courses in high school or college that encouraged me to raise questions about power and inequities in school. Why isn't all learning like this?"

For students who are going to go on to become teachers, the reflective journal provides a missing piece. Experiencing some kind of metareflection about your own learning makes you a much more caring and committed teacher of others, not just in intention but in practice. When the term ends, the doctoral students sometimes tell me that they've now made a lifelong commitment to keeping a reflective journal on a regular basis, because they find it so useful in understanding their own growth in learning.

For more about teacher education, see page 409.

BROOKFIELD'S SERIES ON CRITICAL REFLECTION

Becoming a Critically Reflective Teacher (Jossey-Bass, 1995); The Power of Critical Theory: Liberating Adult Learning and Teaching (Jossey-Bass, 2004); The Skillful Teacher: On Technique, Trust, and Responsiveness in the Classroom (Jossey-Bass, 2006); Teaching for Critical Thinking: Tools and Techniques to Help Students Question Their Assumptions (Jossey-Bass, 2011), all by Stephen D. Brookfield.

When I was department chair, I ended up purchasing fifteen copies of *Becoming a Critically Reflective Teacher* for faculty after more than one colleague tried to talk me out of my only copy. Brookfield writes from his experiences in a university combined with his expertise in the field of adult learning. Filled with humorous stories, this book is not written in an academic language; teacher/learners at any school level and across disciplines can learn to improve their teaching through the practices of reflection he describes. Brookfield suggests that teachers view their practice through four different lenses: their own, their students' eyes, their colleagues' perceptions, and theoretical literature. Those without much experience in social science may be surprised at how valuable educational theories are in helping them improve their own teaching. Educational institutions across all levels are notoriously unsupportive of critically reflective teaching, and Brookfield offers some suggestions for creating a more supportive culture. *The Power of Critical Theory* applies the same principles to adult education; *The Skillful Teacher* is particularly valuable for college educators; and *Teaching for Critical Thinking* focuses on inquiry skills in the classroom. —Nelda Cambron-McCabe

VII. Systems Think-
ing in the Classroom

This book would never have been initiated if not for a dedicated group of educators who have sought, for the past decade, to instill systems thinking skills into elementary and secondary education. Over the years, the systems-thinking-in-the-classroom community has developed an impressive body of theory and method for making complexities clear, along with a series of powerful tools. The systems work is powerful precisely because it doesn't stand alone: It reinforces, and is reinforced by, the other insights about learning and teaching that occur throughout this part of the book.

Some people may find the tools of systems thinking daunting at first, but we have tried to present them here in a way that can help any teacher (or parent, or student) to experiment fruitfully. We have also avoided any sort of "party line"—you will find some writers arguing that computer modeling is vital for systemic awareness and others asking, as Janis Dutton does, "Where did the Native Americans plug in their laptops?"

"Systems thinking has been around forever," says Mary Scheetz, the former principal of Orange Grove Middle School in Arizona and an eminent pioneer in the field. "The world, after all, is made up of dynamic systems. There are a lot of different ways to build the capacity to think systemically and to ask the kinds of questions that lead to greater understanding. System dynamic computer models are one way we've found to do that, and they have proven to be a particularly powerful way, but I don't think they are the only way." In this part of the book, we hope to make the range of tools accessible and inviting enough that you can go as far as you want, without feeling over your head.

1. Systems Study for the Long Term

Jay W. Forrester

ST

Professor Emeritus at MIT's Sloan School of Management, Jay W. Forrester is the founder of the field of system dynamics and the developer of much of its conceptual theory, its mapping and modeling methods, and its software-based tools for simulation. In the mid-1950s, after inventing the magnetic core memory technology that nearly all computers still use today, he left computer design to work on the more interesting problem of trying to understand the behavior of complex systems. Since then, he has been an advisor and mentor to several generations of researchers in the field (including Peter Senge). His critical work on industrial dynamics, urban dynamics, and world dynamics led to dramatic shifts in the prevailing dialogue about, respectively, corporate strategy, urban renewal, and the global interdependence of population, resources, and the environment. In the 1980s, Jay began to focus his attention on bringing systems study to education. He is the director of the MIT System Dynamics in Education Project, a group of students working to foster learner-centered learning using the tools and concepts of system dynamics.

For more about the System Dynamics in Education project, see their website at: http://web.mit.edu/sysdyn/sdep.html. We would like to thank Nan Lux, SDEP Administrative Officer, for her help in developing this article. Much of the SDEP work is available through the Creative Learning Exchange, p. 290.

It is commonplace to assert that people take only a short-run view of life, but that is only partially true. In fact, most people hold long-term personal goals—they hope for the future well-being of their children and grandchildren. But they don't fully understand the systems they operate within, and therefore they make short-term decisions that jeopardize these long-term goals. For example, they put both the economic and environmental welfare of future generations at risk.

Over the last several decades, I have come to believe that people can learn to break this pattern. But for most people, doing so requires being introduced to the study of systems at an early age. And it requires more than talking about systems conceptually. People need time with hands-on tools—computer-based simulations that they take part in designing themselves and that allow them to experiment and create their own models of real-life complex systems.

There are several hundred PK–12 schools throughout the world where students are studying systems using computer-based models. At least a dozen of these are doing pioneering, excellent work. They have applied system dynamics modeling to mathematics, physics, social studies, history, economics, biology, and literature. In the more successful schools, system dynamics is combined with a project-oriented approach: learner-centered learning, where teachers are no longer necessarily seen as lecturers in command of the flow of wisdom or even as authority figures. Teachers become advisors and coaches to students who are creating projects that may lie beyond a teacher's experience. In this way, a junior high classroom can become much like a university research laboratory. Students address projects with real-world significance, facing the challenge of learning what they need to know to accomplish the project.

We do not expect most students to spend their lives in front of a computer, building system dynamics models. What, then, should be the outcome of a systems education? The objectives of a system dynamics education might be grouped under three headings.

1. UNDERSTANDING THE NATURE OF SYSTEMS

System dynamics gives students a more effective way of interpreting the complexities of the world around them. It helps us unlearn our intuitively "obvious" mental models about the world, the mental models that prevent most people from acting effectively. These mental models have been acquired since childhood, often from our most easy-to-understand experiences. A child touches a hot stove, and the hand is burned here and now. After several such mishaps, the child learns to assume that cause and effect are closely related in time and space, and that the cause of a problem must lie nearby and must have occurred shortly before the symptom appeared. However, when the child grows up to confront the complex systems of adult life, those lessons of the past will be aggressively misleading. In most systems, the causes of an observed symptom may come from an entirely different part of the system and lie far back in time. Remedies that seem "obvious" because they are close at hand may in fact be irrelevant to the real problem, or may make matters worse.

See Jay W. Forrester, *Urban Dynamics* (Pegasus Communications, 1969) and Lawrence M. Fisher, "The Prophet of Unintended Consequences," *strategy+business*, Fall 2005, http://www.strategy-business.com/article/05308.

I saw this situation firsthand when I conducted a systems simulation of urban development in the late 1960s. The model showed that the most "obvious" (and popular) city government policies were either neutral or highly detrimental—both for the city as a whole and for its unemployed low-income residents. Building low-income housing seemed, to many city officials, like a natural solution to housing problems; it would make it easier for poor people to find comfortable places to live. However, low-income housing projects accelerated urban decay. They occupied land that could be used for job-creating business structures. They attracted relatively unskilled people who competed for low-paying jobs, in an area where such jobs were hard to find. The apparently humanitarian policy of building more housing actually created poverty by pulling people into areas of declining economic opportunity.

Assertions such as this one, about cause and effect in a complex system, carry little weight when you read them in an article. After all, anyone can assert that a causal relationship exists. But when a student has worked repeatedly with models that demonstrate such behavior, has tested that model by incorporating a variety of real-world observations into its design, and has had time to observe the same kinds of behavior in other real-life systems, then the idea is internalized and becomes part of normal thinking. The student becomes unusually skilled at dealing with complex problems and situations.

The models themselves often reveal surprising new insights about real life. One weekend I added a job-training program to the urban dynamics model. It was a "perfect" job-training program—it transferred people from the "unskilled" category into "skilled labor," and no charge was assigned, so it cost nothing. Yet this perfect program caused unemployment to go up. This fact surprised me until I spent a day discovering what the model had done: decreasing the amount of other job-training efforts (because they were no longer needed), increasing the number of skilled workers (thus increasing unemployment among the skilled), and attracting unskilled, unemployed workers from other cities. I took the computer runs back to a group of Boston politicians and business executives. They looked at the rising unemployment in silence for several minutes until one said, "Oh! Detroit has the best job-training program in the country and the most rapidly rising unemployment rate." Still unsure of the model, I asked some job training professionals if they knew of any situation where their work could increase unemployment. I expected them to pooh-pooh the idea. Instead, they replied: "When that happens, we go to another city."

New knowledge can be created at university and PK–12 levels, often by people working outside their fields. One student at MIT modeled the behavior of insulin and glucose in various aspects of diabetes. He got a result from his computer "patient" that had never been reported in the medical literature. Was there something wrong with the model? He showed the results to doctors doing diabetes research. Their response was: "We had a patient like that once but always thought there was a mistake in the measurements." By this process, a new medical syndrome was identified.

2. DEVELOPING PERSONAL SKILLS

Systems modeling imposes a discipline for clarity and consistency that ordinary language, either spoken or written, does not require. In ordinary conversation, people often hide behind ambiguous, incomplete, and even illogical statements, such as: "The way people respond depends on the situation." A systems modeler who wanted to describe that phenomenon would have to specify: which people, what kinds of responses, and exactly how different conditions would lead to particular actions. Otherwise, it could not be translated into explicit statements in a simulation model.

Equally as important is the ability to make the reverse translation: to write or speak clear statements that express the precise understandings that came from building and using the model. It takes courage and skill to be unambiguous and clear. But by developing this capability, students learn to put their own assumptions up for critique and learn to improve them. They develop the judgment to think more deeply, to look beyond the immediate situation, and to stand against majority opinion that is ill-founded and shortsighted. In solving problems, they search for a wider range of alternatives than the first "intuitively obvious" answer. And they are sensitized to the importance of the interconnections that give meaning to events that would otherwise seem isolated and capricious.

Not long ago, I asked a recent university graduate what system dynamics study had done for him. His answer: "It gives me an entirely different way of reading the newspapers." He meant that he sees the relationships between different events, he understands the relationships between today's news and what happened last week or last year, and he reads between the lines to know what must have been part of the story but was not reported.

3. SHAPING AN OUTLOOK TO FIT THE TWENTY-FIRST CENTURY

A systems education should give students confidence that they can shape their own futures. A PK–12 system dynamics thread, in particular, should leave individuals optimistic about understanding those problems of society that earlier generations have found so baffling. Inflation, wars, unfavorable balance of trade, and destruction of the environment have persisted for hundreds of years without public understanding of the causes. Such problems are too serious to be left to the self-appointed experts; the public must acquire the insights that permit participation in debates of such importance.

Even if individual students do not construct models in later life, they should expect that system dynamics models will be constructed by those who propose changes in economic and social policies—and that those models will be made available for public inspection. In order to participate, the public will need to know the nature of such models, to evaluate the assumptions embedded in them, and to feel comfortable in pushing their proponents to reveal their assumptions and to justify their conclusions.

Such understanding comes in incremental steps. A television producer working on a program on systems education once turned to a junior high school boy and asked, "What have these systems studies meant to you?" His immediate answer: "I am much better able to deal with my mother." By the time systems students enter their first jobs, however, they can acquire remarkable prescience. One of our MIT graduates, working for the Department of Energy, used a very simple two-level simulation to demonstrate a point. He was amazed by the amount of influence this model gave him on the thinking of those around him. Even such a simple system often goes far beyond the existing thinking of people in important policy positions.

Finally, a systems education should influence students' personalities: enhancing their innovative tendencies and counteracting the forces in society that convert innovative personalities into authoritarian ones. The purely authoritarian personality, the person who feels his or her lot "is not to reason why, but to do or die," expects no reasons for why things happen and has no will to search for reasons. By contrast, the innovative personality assumes that reasons exist, even if they are unknown. Furthermore, it is worth looking for the reasons because, if one understands, then one probably can change and improve what is happening.

I believe that babies are born as innovative personalities. They want to explore, to understand, and to see how things work and how to master their environments. But our social processes work to stamp out exploration and questioning. Children are continually confronted with "Do as you are told," or "Stop asking questions and just mind me," or "Study this because it is good for you." Repeated restraint of innovative inclinations gradually forces personalities into the authoritarian mold.

A system dynamics modeling curriculum, by letting students formulate the structure and policies causing behavior under study, will help preserve and rebuild the innovative outlook. To be innovative, one must be willing to make mistakes while searching for reasons and improvement. Computer simulation modeling is a repeating process of trial and error. One learns that progress is made through exploration and by learning from mistakes. An authoritarian personality fears mistakes and does not try the unknown. An innovative personality knows that mistakes are stepping-stones to better understanding.

I am using authoritarian and innovative personalities in the sense described by Everett Hagen in his book, *On The Theory of Social Change: How Economic Growth Begins* (Dorsey Press, 1962). The quote comes from Alfred Lord Tennyson, "The Charge of the Light Brigade," stanza 2.

ACHIEVING THE BENEFITS OF A SYSTEMS EDUCATION

A systems thinking and systems modeling curriculum will not automatically yield the deeper lessons that should be absorbed. Even a reliable and well-crafted model cannot test the assumptions that were built into it. These assumptions can be judged only by their comparative usefulness—the ultimate value of the actions recommended by the model. If there are discrepancies between the model's assumptions and its real-world effects, then students should examine those discrepancies and use them to improve both the mental and the computer models that underlie the simulation. They should relate what they are learning to systems they already know in families, community, and school. And as early as possible, schools should move away from canned models that have been previously prepared for student use. Instead, students should create their own models, examine their shortcomings, and learn from improving them.

Other "systems thinking" methods—talking about the characteristics of systems, discussing insights from system archetypes, and relating the experiences people have with systems—are all valuable as door openers and incentives to go deeper. But these forms of "systems thinking" represent no more than 5 percent of a useful systems education. They will change very few of the mental models that students will use in their future decisionmaking. Only immersion in active system dynamics simulation modeling can change mental models.

Ultimately, the great challenge for the next several decades will be to advance understanding of social systems in the same way that understanding of the physical world advanced over the twentieth century. This would mean learning to accept the fact that the interrelationships of a social system have a strong influence over individual human behavior. To put the matter even more bluntly, if human systems are indeed systems, then people are at least partly cogs in a social and economic machine; they respond in a significantly predictable way to forces brought to bear on them by other parts of the system. Even though this view is contrary to our cherished illusion that people freely make their individual decisions, I suggest that the constraints implied by the existence of systems are true in real life. "Redesigning" social and political systems may seem mechanistic or authoritarian. But all governmental laws and regulations, corporate policies, and other social systems have already been designed—often by default—without questioning the assumptions underlying their designs. These designs are tested "experimentally" on real people and real communities, without first modeling the long-term effects or running small-scale pilot experiments. In the twenty-first century, it is my hope that better systems education will lead to better systems design everywhere.

2. A Guide to Practice for Systems Thinking in the Classroom

Assembled and edited by Lees Stuntz and Nina Kruschwitz

ST

This guide was updated from the last edition of this book and represents the collective wisdom of a group of practitioners in the field. Lees Stuntz is the director of the Creative Learning Exchange (page 290), one of the primary sources of research and development in the field. Nina Kruschwitz is the managing editor of the Fifth Discipline Fieldbook Project and the MIT Sloan Management Review. She learned the tools and skills of systems thinking in her previous work at MIT's Organizational Learning Center.

We wish to thank Deb Lyneis, Sheri Marlin, Tracy Benson, and Anne LaVigne for their guidance and help.

The use of systems thinking and system dynamics in PK–12 classrooms has been going on since the 1980s. If you are a teacher, you may be intrigued; but where do you begin? How much do you need to know about the field before introducing systems thinking in your own classroom? Where can you turn for help? What should you expect for—and from—your students?

There is no single right way to proceed. People enter this territory from every discipline and with a wide range of experience. You and your students may be satisfied simply to use systems thinking to gain new perspectives on existing curricula, or you may want to learn enough to develop your own computer models. But no matter where you start or how far you go, there are some things you can expect to encounter, activities we encourage you to try, detours we hope you can avoid, and resources we think you may value.

WHY SYSTEMS THINKING IN THE CLASSROOM?
Systems thinking is the ability to understand (and sometimes to predict) interactions and relationships in complex, dynamic systems—the kinds of systems we are surrounded by and embedded in. Some of the systems already under study in classrooms (population growth; land use, climate, and agricultural production; the causes of revolution; and traffic patterns) readily lend themselves to the use of systems thinking and its tools.

The ability to think systemically is neither new nor mysterious. One teacher, after an introductory course, gave voice to many people's reactions when she exclaimed: "This is just common sense!" In many ways that is true. Systems thinking enables you to see the big picture, the minute details that make it up, and the way parts interact over time, making explicit the patterns of behavior that people see all the time but that are rarely explained.

The tools of system dynamics—behavior-over-time graphs, stock-and-flow diagrams, causal loops, computer models, simulations, and archetypes—are all ways to help us more effectively understand those patterns and the systemic dynamics that drive them.

For a more general introduction, see the Systems Thinking primer on page 123.

With these tools available to enhance existing curricula, students can learn how to specify and quantify the precise kinds of influences that cause systems to grow and stabilize and then to simulate those influences to observe the behavior of the system over time under varying assumptions. With practice, students can learn to identify the parts of a defined system, to analyze and understand the interdependencies among parts of a system, the conditions that create those interdependencies, and their effects over time and space. Different tools are suited to different tasks, and, as with anything, both teachers and students will be predisposed to use particular tools. However, as we have gained more experience in using these tools in the classroom, we have learned that using them together significantly enhances learning and comprehension.

A group of educators from Singapore visited a seventh-grade class at the Tubman Middle School in Portland, Oregon. One student, explaining the fine points of a model she had made, casually remarked "I use these tools anywhere—like I use behavior-over-time graphs in any of my classes—but, you know, my own personal favorite is the causal loop." To the teacher standing nearby, this girl's words represented a kind of victory. This easy sense of familiarity, confidence, and ownership is rare with intellectual tools. Ideally, students should feel that way about all the skills they gain in school—even algebra and sentence diagramming. Too often, this sense of ownership has been taken away from students by the standard way of teaching things. With systems thinking, teachers have an opportunity to provide students a set of tools that will give them an edge for the rest of their lives—in school and out of school.

When math teacher Diana Fisher discovered systems thinking and computer modeling, she felt she had found a tool she'd been looking for all her life. She saw a way for students to understand how "things in the real world" actually worked. "Equations don't speak to most people," she says. "Even with my training and math teaching experience, when I look at an unfamiliar equation I say to myself, 'Oh my gosh, I'm going to have to sit and analyze each of the pieces of this.' But a diagram is a natural way to show a story, because of its visual nature. There are students who have outstanding analytical abilities that we don't even begin to tap. If we show them a tool like STELLA (the system modeling software described on page 292), we can let them fly. We can reach student populations we have never reached before."

Systems Thinking in the Elementary Grades

by Sheri Marlin, lessons by Barbara Casanova, Borton Primary Magnet School

STONE SOUP, STOCKPOTS, AND STOCK/FLOW DIAGRAMS

A stockpot is typically used for making soup, but it can also be a very concrete tool to teach kindergarten children about what causes change in a system and how that change can be measured in the slope of a line. After several years of using behavior-over-time graphs with young children and observing how the visual nature of these tools supports children in being able to articulate their thinking, teachers became excited about the possibility of using stock/flow diagrams as well.

Kindergarten teacher Barbara Casanova took a familiar fall lesson and created a learning opportunity that clearly illustrates for her students how a stock/flow model works. The children's story *Stone Soup* recounts the folktale of a clever young man who tricks an old lady into making him soup by convincing her that he can make soup from a stone. He does indeed make soup from the stone, but only after she adds the onions, carrots, beef bones, salt, pepper, barley, and butter. In Barbara's classroom, students make their own "stone soup"—they shop for tasty vegetables at a nearby market, return to school, wash and chop the vegetables, and then are ready to begin preparing the soup. This is when the systems thinking begins.

Based upon their personal preferences, students are asked to decide whether to add one-quarter, one-third, or one-half a cup of vegetables to the stockpot. Simultaneously, students graph the rate at which the pot is filling up with vegetables. Students also create a paper stockpot with various paper representations of the vegetables being added to the soup. This paper version of the stockpot serves as an ongoing reminder to students creating stock and flow maps throughout the year that the rectangle in the middle of that diagram represents an accumulation.

Ann McGovern, *Stone Soup,* illustrated by Winslow Pinney Pels (Scholastic Books, 1968).

Once the pot is full, the cooking begins. In one classroom, as the full pot of soup cooked, one student astutely observed that there was steam coming out of the pot and that steam needed to be recorded as a change in the level of the stock.

Finally, it is time to eat the soup. Generously, students have invited friends and family to share in the eating of their soup. As the soup is eaten, children record the number of cups and bowls that are taken from the pot. They note that the larger bowls require a steeper drop in the outflow of soup from the stock. Familiar with behavior-over-time graphs, students predict the slope of the line as they draw it on the graph. They generate conclusions about what happened during the process of preparing, cooking, serving, and eating the soup.

Soup in and of itself is not a highly complex system. But the ability of five-year-old children to explain an accumulation, to use the terms rate and slope, and to transfer this information to other systems that accumulate is significant. Even more powerful is the ability of these kindergarten students to return to the model weeks after the lesson and still explain these concepts with accuracy and clarity. Young children can and do think deeply and even abstractly. Providing them visual tools ensures that misconceptions can be clarified, so that they are also thinking accurately. The stockpot is a concrete example that creates a clear analogy to help students produce their best thinking.

VISITING THE ZOO TO CLARIFY THE CONCEPT OF ACCUMULATION

Young children have the ability for abstract thinking when it is carefully scaffolded by a concrete example. Hence, kindergarten teacher, Barbara Casanova, has increased her students' success by using the example of going to the zoo to teach her students how a stock/flow model works.

Going to the zoo is a fairly common spring field trip for kindergarten children. In Barbara's class, students learn not only about the animals but also how the rate of traffic going in and out of the zoo affects the zoo-going experience for patrons. They examine the factors that affect people going in and coming out of the zoo. For example, people might leave the zoo if they are hungry, finished seeing the animals, or tired—for example, "the baby needs a nap." Students also recognize that special events, such as the birth of a new baby animal, will affect the number of people entering the zoo.

To represent this accumulation of people in the zoo, Barbara tapes off a large rectangle in her classroom. Students create a large story book. Each page represents an hour of the day and each student chooses a time to enter and exit the zoo. Using a large clock, Barbara ticks off the zoo

---

The use of books, as in the *Stone Soup* example, or the use of games, in several of the curricula that follow, sets the context for learning about complex systems. If students have a mutual experience or reference point, they are able to delve into the complexity and interrelationships of the system as it is experienced.

hours. At 9 a.m., four people enter the zoo. Six more enter at 10 a.m. At 11 a.m., five people enter, but three people leave. The recording continues on the stock and flow diagram until 4 p.m., when the zoo no longer has any visitors.

This lesson establishes the idea that a stock is an accumulation—in this case, of visitors to the zoo. By physically moving in and out of the large rectangle, students are simulating the rate of change and the accumulation within the stock. Following this kinesthetic experience, students are able to analyze the factors that affect traffic at the zoo.

The physical representation of the stock used in the zoo game closely mirrors a math game that is part of the kindergarten curriculum. The game requires students to roll a specially designed cube with sides that read +1, +2, +3, -1, -2, -3. Starting with three counters, students move counters in and out of a box based on the roll of the numbered cube. The purpose of the game is to help with rote counting and build the foundation for addition and subtraction. Using people instead of counters, Barbara asks her students to simulate the zoo story while writing out the corresponding equations. She thus reinforces the mathematics connected to a very simple stock/flow diagram.

When this math activity is paired with the kinesthetic zoo stock/flow game, students have greater opportunities to make connections and thus create more meaning from both activities. The zoo stock/flow game is a great example of using a systems thinking tool to enhance the teaching of an existing academic standard by increasing student thinking required to complete the activity.

THE MAMMOTH GAME

Third-grade students in Carlisle, Massachusetts, are introduced to the Mammoth Game as part of their curriculum about the ice ages in social studies. They create behavior-over-time graphs by rolling dice to represent births and deaths of mammoths; with each round of the game the group's herd declines. As the numbers of the total herd are plotted year by year, a picture emerges. Helping students to see the pattern in their graph is key, and questions such as "What is changing? How is it changing? Why is it changing?" help guide the conversation. A steep curve means a sharply decreasing population, while a flatter line indicates a slower rate of decline.

The students and teachers then use two different systems thinking tools to explore the relationship between population and births and deaths. With the first, the causal loop diagram, they talk as a class about the characteristics of feedback loops. In Carlisle, Massachusetts, where

The Mammoth Game and ten other student-friendly games can be found in Rob Quaden, Alan Ticotsky, and Debra Lyneis (Nathan Walker, Illustrator), *The Shape of Change, Including The Shape of Change: Stocks and Flows* (Creative Learning Exchange, 2009) http://www.clexchange.org/cleproducts/shapeofchange.asp.

the mammoth lesson was developed and written up, teachers were astounded by the eight- and nine-year-old students' understanding of exponential decay. The class was talking about extinction—the mammoth population always died out when deaths were greater than births—and one student asked whether anything would be different if, instead of starting with one hundred mammoths, they started with 1,000. No one was quite sure, including the teacher. Some thought if they started with ten times more mammoths, the mammoths would last ten times longer. Then another student said no: If one out of three mammoths died every year, the herd would still be cut in half at the same rate and become extinct at the same time. The class ran a simple STELLA model of the game, and he was right. By the end of the session, with additional discussion, most of the class understood the concepts of exponential decay and half-life—though without using those terms. When the teacher introduced those terms, the students immediately understood them.

Causal loops like these give teachers and students a schematic way to show how different elements in a system influence one another. More important, they identify circular feedback: As different parts of a system affect each other, causes become effects which in turn become causes. While behavior-over-time graphs describe "what" happens in a system, causal loops tell "why." Many teachers are drawn to causal loops and develop an intuitive feel for mapping out cause and effect. The diagrams can be useful in providing a quick visual of a complex pattern of influence. However, while causal loops can be drawn with many intertwined loops, depicting fairly sophisticated and complex systems it's usually best to keep them simple.

As a next step, the Carlisle teachers use a stock-and-flow diagram of the Mammoth Game with the class. Stock-and-flow diagrams are much more versatile than causal loops, and yet they are so concrete that they are particularly valuable for young people. When students (and adults, for that matter) start to think in terms of inflows and outflows, this can generate a fundamental shift in their thinking. The students can discuss the actual numbers they talked about in the game and relate them to concepts of accumulations and flows over time.

Stocks and flows can be diagrammed using only paper and pencil or a chalkboard. As questions and conversations develop, teachers can keep track of possible inputs, outputs, and influences on rates of flow in lists on the side. These can be useful to bring back in as the diagram develops and becomes more complex.

Stock-and-flow diagrams are not always created in isolation, however. Often they are drawn as part of a progression toward simulation or building a model. Indeed, if you draw a well-defined stock-and-flow diagram, you are halfway to building a computer model. A final step taken in many classrooms is to program a simple computer model and run it to see the patterns of the graphs, as was done with the Mammoth Game in this example.

—Rob Quaden, Alan Ticotsky, and Debra Lyneis

Systems Thinking in Middle School Classrooms

One of the important uses of systems thinking in the classroom is the development of an understanding of the important issues of our era and how they might be addressed. Two of those issues are the sustainability of our planet and the real possibility of widespread devastating infection. The following two middle school units address these issues clearly.

THE BEAN GAME

Most social studies, science, and environmental education curricula have common standard elements that address limiting factors, effects of interactions between humans and natural systems, carrying capacities, the relationship between scarcity and choice, and the distribution of natural resources. Cheryl Dow and Tracy Benson from the Waters Foundation's Systems Thinking in Schools project created a role-play simulation that helps students experience many of these essential concepts. "The Bean Game" traces the effects of multi-generational families over time as each generation (great-great-grandparents, great-grandparents, grandparents, parents, and children) decides what resources they will need to live healthy, prosperous lives.

The game is structured so that each family has access to a different kind of consumption utensil (a spoon, small cup, or tweezers) that they use to access and consume resources (represented as pinto beans) from a large tub that holds the world's resources. Knowing that the game does not incorporate renewable resources, students quickly see a rapid depletion over time and the effects that mental models, greed, and the type of utensil can have on the rapid depletion of world resources. Typically, at first family members get competitive and try to take as many beans (resources) as they can. A fun-loving animosity develops between families who have utensils that enable them to collect many beans (small cups) versus those who have clear limitations (tweezers). Towards the end of the simulation, the youngest generation is faced with an alarming deple-

For more about The Bean Game, see http://www.watersfoundation.org and search for "beam game."

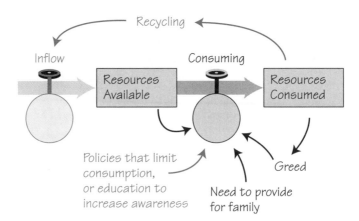

tion of available resources, therefore generating an emotional reaction that fuels a lively debriefing.

A stock-and-flow map is a helpful tool when debriefing this simulation. Students first map the system they experience, a system void of renewable resources (shown in black in the diagram), and then add leverage actions to the map that would help sustain the system (shown in blue). Students leave with a sense of empowerment knowing that they have an effect on both the outflow (consumption of resources) and the inflow (renewable resources). The experience of this game and debriefing tends to increase their awareness and will hopefully have an effect on their future behaviors.

—Tracy Benson, Waters Foundation

HELPING MIDDLE SCHOOL STUDENTS EXPLORE HOW INFECTIONS SPREAD

At times, middle school students may seem more interested in the latest social news among their peers than in the latest science lesson on the spread of a disease. But these two systems are actually more similar than many students realize.

Students are very familiar with how quickly a rumor can spread; everyone seems to hear the gossip within a very short span of time. Connecting with this real-life experience, Shea Van Rhoads and I worked with her eighth grade science students to help them see how diseases, such as human immunodeficiency virus (HIV), can spread in a very similar way. (The game has also been used in health classes.) Students played a kinesthetic game, in which they shook hands with other students in the class over a series of rounds. Sometimes the interaction would transmit an imaginary "infection," and sometimes it would not. After each round, the students recorded their infection status: healthy or infected. Initially,

A detailed description how to set up and use the Infection Game as a classroom activity can be found in *The Shape of Change* (see "The Mammoth Game," p. 279).

The Infection Game is based on work by Holly Cluff, Sam DeVore, Will Glass-Husain, Anne LaVigne, John Sterman, Shea Van Rhoads, and many other PK–12 educators and practitioners.

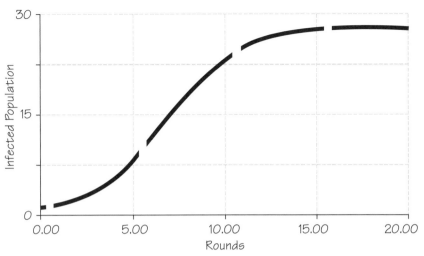

For more about the Epidemics Game, see Will Glass-Husain, *Teaching System Dynamics: Looking at Epidemics* (Creative Learning Exchange, 1991) http://clexchange.org/ftp/documents/Roadmaps/RM5/D-4243-3.pdf. The model is based on the two-stock infection model created by John Sterman.

only one student had the imaginary disease, but over the course of a dozen or so rounds, all students became infected. Students then collated their data to graph the total infections over time. The general S-shaped growth pattern showed how the infection spread slowly at first, then accelerated as more and more students had the disease. Eventually, everyone was infected, and the graph leveled off.

Using the graph, the class talked about the underlying structure that created this pattern of growth. They then set up a computer software model including other components of the system (for example, the number of infected individuals, the number of healthy individuals, and the rate of contact between them). Running the very simple model generated an S-shaped pattern similar to the one experienced in the game. Students then used the model to test different theories about what caused the spread of the infection and what might have prevented it.

After achieving a general understanding of how infections can spread, students explored a specific disease: human immunodeficiency virus (HIV), which was part of their science curricular materials. Students ran a simulation to explore the dynamics of HIV, using statistical data about how the spread has affected a sampling of countries, such as Zambia, the United States, and Botswana. Each country had very different infection patterns, relating to elements such as the percent of the infected population at the beginning of the simulation, the availability of medical treatments, and the percent of people exposed to the virus. Because the original, imaginary infection game had not included the possibility of either recovery or death, the patterns of HIV spread were somewhat different from the handshake game; it was possible for the disease to decline over time.

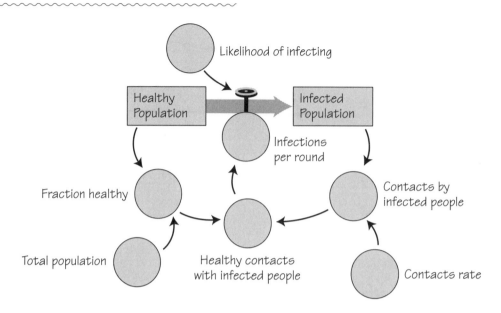

Based on the simulated conditions in different countries, students made predictions about what would happen to their populations over time. After running the simulation, students talked about the economic, political, and cultural implications. They also began to ask and explore some difficult questions about possible leverage for desirable change and potential long-term effects of policy decisions. For example, "What would happen if all new infections could be eliminated with prevention methods?" and "What effects might medication have on prolonging the life of those who are infected and on the rate of disease spread if no preventative measures were taken simultaneously?"

In a similar way to seeing the connection between the spread of rumors and the spread of HIV, classes have explored this pattern of growth in a variety of contexts. These included the Black Plague, the spread of new ideas or innovations, and the evolution of fashion and product fads. Students have built their own models, experienced kinesthetic simulations, built stock/flow representations, and explored simulated environments. Through these varied experiences, students can understand this generic pattern of growth and recognize it in a variety of real-world contexts; they are also aware of some of the effects on real people who face (or have faced) these issues around the world and throughout history.

—Anne LaVigne, Waters Foundation

Systems Thinking at the High School Level

The use of systems thinking tools is not limited to math or science. In a tenth-grade English class, students reading *Lord of the Flies* worked in groups to graph how the characters' level of power changed as the events of each chapter unfolded. Comparing results, the students got into a set of deeply engaging questions and discussions. Since each group's graph was different, each group must have started with a different set of premises about the nature of "reality."

William Golding, *Lord of the Flies*, (Faber & Faber, 1954).

}} See the description of the Lord of the Flies simulation in The Primer, page 140.

"I'd done a bit of reading about behavior-over-time graphs," said Tim Joy, their teacher, "but had no idea if I could pull this off. Their task was to trace the thread of the characters over the course of the book. They finished at home, and when they came in the next day, I could barely get through attendance. They were showing each other their graphs, and their arguments were already unfolding. Even in the best of circumstances in honors classes, we'd never had such animated discussions. I had them get together and do graphs representing their consensus viewpoint. That was a stroke of dumb luck, because it led to homework where they chose a graph they disagreed with and stated their cases in a brief paper. Once I saw the students' responses—the degree of participation, the level of thinking and conversation—I knew this was a tool I wanted to keep using."

As Tim continued with his class, he segued into stock-and-flow diagrams and finally into a computer-based simulation model that he had constructed, with equations defining each of the interrelationships. The variables within the model were manipulated by students to learn quickly how the elements in a system interact.

There is a great deal of value in working with existing simulations to learn about the dynamics of a particular system. The simulation lets students play "What if…?" trying out different possible scenarios, comparing the results, and developing a much stronger understanding of the system as a whole. Many simulations are accessible even for elementary school students. The Mammoth Game shows what happens when birth and death rates change or when hunters are introduced into the scene. The "board game" version, using throws of dice, can take days to generate the same "runs" that a computer can demonstrate in minutes.

Using simulations in the classroom requires lots of classroom discussion. Before each "run" of the simulation, it's important to ask students to predict how the graph will change as they change their input variables.

Otherwise, they are simply playing a computer game without the synthesis or understanding. Comparing the actual results, in graph form, to their expectations leads to questions about why the system might have operated differently from what they predicted—and to larger questions. Every graph has a story to tell. Why didn't the mammoths stay alive? Wasn't there enough food? Did the number of hunters grow too fast?

Adults may be surprised by how quickly young people take to working on computer simulations. Because teachers may be unused to working with computers in the classroom, they may err on the side of too much explanation. A brief explanation followed by fifteen or twenty minutes to let students experiment on their own is usually sufficient. Accustomed to video and computer games, kids probably will want to immediately test the limits of the model—to "win" or beat the computer. Few are intimidated by working with or manipulating simulations and many may want to go directly from simulations to building their own models.

Once they understood how the model was structured, the high school students who worked through Tim Joy's simulation for *Lord of the Flies* began to question it. It didn't allow them to include some of the relationships they saw in the novel, and some of them took the model home to amend it.

Tim told us: "They added some stocks and had some trouble with the inflows, but that's when I discovered that even a bad model is better than some traditional teaching tools. It forced them to be explicit about their thought processes and the questions they were asking."

Not every teacher will move to building models as part of the curriculum. It takes time to become comfortable with the software, and computer resources are still limited in many districts. But for those who do, the excitement and satisfaction of seeing what kids can do can more than make up for their own learning curve.

There's reason to think that the effort to learn modeling and teach it to kids will consistently pay itself back in unexpected ways. Martha Lynes, a former physics teacher in Northampton, Massachusetts, developed a curriculum a number of years ago in which her high school students built rockets out of soda bottles. The students were first introduced to behavior-over-time graphs and stock-and-flow diagrams and then to some preliminary modeling. The greatest thrill, of course, came from constructing the rockets and setting them off in a field near the school. They took videos of the rockets' flights and later covered the video screen with plastic to chart the courses of the rockets. Working in teams, they developed models to explain those flight paths, which they presented to the class.

After he graduated, one of the students from her first class wrote to Martha from Stanford University. He was in a physics course there, he said, with many students from privileged schools who had taken years of calculus-based physics. But he found that, unlike him, they lacked enough real understanding of the concepts to do as well on the exams as he did.

A few years later, he wrote her again, this time from an internship program at an automotive research institute. He was working to develop a realistic computer model of an airbag. It reminded him, he said, of the models of water rockets. He thanked her again for her class, which was "years ahead of other high school classes." It was clear from his letter that if enough students went through similar practices, we could expect technological development to become not just increasingly advanced—but increasingly rich with diverse and human perspective.

At an exposition of student work in Portland, Oregon, one team of seniors who had taken some forensic science grew interested in the process by which a coroner figures out how long a body has been dead. They found a coroner to interview; he also lent them some of his original journal articles. The students chose three variables that gave a clue to the time of death: ambient temperature, body weight, and condition of the clothing—whether it was wet, dry, or missing. They figured out how to model the first two without too much trouble, but the issue of clothing posed a problem. How could they represent all the variables in a single formula? The students filled three milk containers with ninety-eight-degree water and put a wet towel around one, no towel around another, and a dry towel around the third. Over a couple of hours, they took temperatures of the water every fifteen minutes to understand the curve.

LEARNER-CENTERED LEARNING

One benefit of systems thinking tools at all levels is that teachers tend to have students work in pairs and groups. Students who pair up to work on building a STELLA model, for instance, have a peer to ask questions of and test their thinking with. An eighth-grade math class, using STELLA to graph simple equations nearly a year after their last encounter with the software, resounded with questions like: "What will happen if we change that variable to 5?" "Do you remember how to set the scale for consistent units?" "Does this seem like the same kind of problem we did in social studies?" "What made you write the equation that way—can't we do it this way too?"

Students working together in this kind of environment are far more likely to ask new questions about a problem than become obsessed with getting the right answer. Although they may need some guidance to stay on track, questioning can lead them further than they—or their teacher—expected. Dorothy Johnson's students finished their Romeo and

Juliet curriculum by writing short essays. One optional question asked students to work in teams to develop a stock-and-flow model, and then a STELLA model, of a story of their choice. She suggested they keep it simple. Confident that no one would choose that option, she was surprised when every pair chose to model stories ranging from simple fairy tales to *Of Mice and Men*—and many came in after school to do so.

Will Costello, a teacher in Vermont, co-taught a modeling class for high school seniors. Two students from his science classes became interested in the question of whether the Civil War was inevitable. They decided they needed to conduct some research on cotton production to understand plantation growth and the demands for land over time. Unable to find the information they needed in the library, they traipsed over to the agricultural school of a nearby university. There, serendipitously, they found a professor who had done twelve years of research on cotton in the South, who helped them understand the variables they needed to build their model.

"You can imagine how empowering it was," says Costello, "for high school kids—who were not history buffs—to come up with the kind of insights they were coming up with that they almost shouldn't have been able to come up with. They saw the connection between soil exhaustion—cotton exhausts the soil in two years—with the limited supply of arable land that southern plantation owners had available. The students discovered through their own research that there were economic reasons for the South to go to war. I think students can learn and perform at levels we can't even imagine if they're given the tools, and encouragement, to do so."

BRIDGING SUBJECT BOUNDARIES

Once students understand a concept in systems terms and experience the excitement of being engaged and curious, they naturally seek to apply systems thinking in other settings. Students reading *Lord of the Flies* in a Catholic high school English class brought their discussions of innocence lost into their religious studies course. Impressed with the intense discussion of good and evil, and unfamiliar with the diagrams and language the students were using, the religion teacher went to the English teacher to find out what was going on. After seeing the graphs the kids had created, he guided the students in a continuing discussion about William Golding. "The author's belief that man has an innately evil core is at odds with the teachings of the Catholic church," said the religion teacher. That statement, in itself, provided a springboard for an in-depth conversation about the possible meanings of original sin and redemption.

Although the religion teacher had previously heard about systems thinking and system dynamics tools in meetings, he had avoided them as too technical, geared toward math and science. A semester later, teachers in the religious studies department had picked up on the tools. Now, several years later, juniors in religious studies are using many system tools and building computer models of the effects of building dams on salmon populations in response to a bishop's directive to name a nearby river "sacred waters."

MODELING SYSTEMS WITH INTANGIBLES

Sometimes teachers think it will be too difficult to assign mathematical values to "soft" variables such as innocence or happiness or self-confidence. Since they can't be measured, how can they be modeled? Yet it's possible to model everything from a school administrator's mistrust to Romeo's intense emotions.

You do this by assigning numbers that represent comparative quantities (of, for example, enthusiasm). As Barry Richmond, the creator of the STELLA modeling software, noted, many qualities that cannot be measured still can be quantified. To quantify simply means to assign a number assessing something. If quantifying a "soft" variable, such as an emotion or group's attitude, seems difficult, that may be because many of these quantifications are easy to mistrust, unless they are transparent: unless the assumptions underlying the quantity are made explicit. You may set up a formula, for example, in which Macbeth's capacity for murder doubles every time he (or his wife) perceives an insult. But can you defend that relationship? Why does it double? Which raises the capacity for murder more—insult or ambition? Deciding how to quantify "soft" variables can take a fair amount of discussion and rigorous thinking about the relationships between the "soft" variables and others in the system. Some people prefer to call these "rhetorical" values. When you choose a number you are, indeed, staking a position that you must be able to defend by telling a story that demands respect for that number.

CAN YOU CHANGE THE WORLD?

Addressing the issues and challenges of our ever-increasing, complex world demands tools that help us, and especially our students, understand and cope with that complexity. Systems thinking tools are uniquely adapted for that purpose. Issues of sustainability, our social systems, and international systems all cry out for the use of these sense-making tools.

The activity in Diana Fisher's system dynamics modeling class at Wilson High School in Portland, Oregon, shows the huge variety of topics that these tools can address. At a recent International System Dynamics Conference, four of her students presented projects on such varied subjects as: "Can Automakers Cope with the Increasing Demand for Hybrid Gasoline-Electric Vehicles?," "What Happens When an Invasive Species is Introduced into a Stable Ecosystem?," "How Are We Contributing to Global Warming by Transportation of Milk from Producers to Consumers?," and "Global Warming, How Much Time Do We Have?"

With students able to generate productive, insightful answers to questions like these, grounded in their own understanding of the interrelationships that shape reality, change in the world is a real possibility.

See Peter Senge's essay, "The Systems Citizen," page 558.

THE CREATIVE LEARNING EXCHANGE

Curricula are available directly on the web at http://www.clexchange.org or by CD-ROM. Contact Lees Stuntz, Executive Director, 27 Central Street, Acton, MA, 01720; stuntzln@clexchange.org.

The Creative Learning Exchange (CLE) helps teachers (and citizens) get started using system dynamics, systems thinking, and learner-centered learning in PK–12 schools. Papers exist on everything from how to explain systems thinking to rubrics to curricula; a newsletter comes out four or five times a year with stories and encouragement; and a national conference occurs every other year with speakers ranging from teachers with hands-on experience to some of the world's foremost authorities in the field of system dynamics. Most important of all, the CLE network offers educators the kind of community contact they need when coming to terms with a new technology, including telephone and email support.

One of the CLE's most valuable offerings is teacher-created systems thinking curricula that can be downloaded and used for free for educational purposes. There's an "open software" feel to the CLE material; teachers and students build on, and refine, each other's efforts, so that the body of curricula is continually evolving. Lessons include the "Friendship Game" (depicting the reinforcing process between your friendship skills and the number of friends you have); "Banzai Barbie" for middle school students who learn graphing and modeling techniques by taking their dolls on bungee jumps; "Understanding the Tragedy of the Sahel," a simulation of humanitarian aid in Africa's Sahel regions, showing how aid can backfire, destroying culture; and "Simulating the End of

The Creative Learning Exchange also cosponsors (with the Waters Foundation and the Society for Organizational Learning) Camp Snowball, an annual immersive learning event on systems thinking tools for educators and individuals (including students). Information is available at http://www.campsnowball.org/.

Innocence," the simulation based on the descent into savagery in *Lord of the Flies*. —Nina Kruschwitz and Tim Lucas

DIANA FISHER'S MATH AND MODELING GUIDES

Modeling Dynamic Systems: Lessons for a First Course (2005) and
Lessons in Mathematics: A Dynamic Approach (2001), by Diana Fisher (iSee Systems).
Both are spiral bound and bundled with a disk of STELLA materials.

Diana Fisher wrote the first edition of *Modeling Dynamic Systems* after five years of experience teaching system dynamics modeling in the Portland Public Schools. It offers practical hands-on advice and detailed lesson plans for teaching students in high school how to model, step-by-step. Motivated adults or students could use it as a self-paced course. It can help a teacher who has experience with system dynamics modeling to set up a course for students, either in the regular curriculum or in a club setting after school hours.

Lessons in Mathematics illustrates how to integrate system dynamics into an existing curriculum. Diana often maintains she now couldn't teach mathematics without system dynamics because it helps elucidate concepts that cannot be taught in the standard math curriculum. —Lees Stuntz

Diana Fisher also has a website with resources and powerful videos of student learning http://www.ccmodelingsystems.com.

INSPIRATION

Published by Inspiration Software: www.inspiration.com

This conceptual mapping software allows you to brainstorm freely and easily and put all of the points and links you conceive of into a workspace on your computer screen. The ability to project the computer on a large screen enhances class discussions. Each student, in turn, describes concepts of a problem or topic, and bit by bit a visual definition of all the relevant facets is built.

 For examples of maps created in Inspiration, see pages 121–122.

Any teacher can get up to speed with Inspiration after a half-hour's tutoring or a couple of hours of experimentation, and kids can hook into it from second grade onward. The software continues to be updated; recent versions make it easier to add your own symbols and export diagrams to the Web. —Richard Langheim, Associate Professor of Education, Ramapo College of New Jersey

STELLA

Published by iSee Systems (formerly High Performance Systems): www.iseesystems.com

STELLA is a very elegant adaptation, designed for educators, of the original system dynamics computer languages developed by Jay Forrester. (A similar program, iThink, is oriented to business decisionmakers.) To create a STELLA model, you must specify stocks and flows (see page 145) and the interrelationships between them. Keeping all this clear is a struggle; for example, you can't have an inflow to a stock be water and the outflow be energy. But working through that struggle causes a student to come to a much deeper understanding of the material. Finally, STELLA allows you to design an interface so other people can test your model more easily, without being confronted by the underlying structure (though they can still find it if they want to).

Elementary school students can work with STELLA models and can understand stocks and flows. But building models would start in the middle school grades. Teachers need a couple of days of training to learn STELLA well enough to introduce it into a class. In my experience, students are capable of the math they need to create models using STELLA formulas by middle school or earlier. Using STELLA teaches them to translate from verbal descriptions to diagrams to mathematical formulas, and it teaches them to translate between the principles of systems in history, biology, literature, and every other field.

To get involved with these three programs, you need to feel comfortable with the mental exercise of looking below the surface at the underlying structure of a situation. These maps and simulations are tools for asking: "How does this work? And what does it mean?" You can solve two plus two equals four from a table of answers. A map or simulation asks why addition (or any subject) is appropriate, how it works, and why it is important.
—Richard Langheim

3. Context and Engagement

Peter Senge

ST

I n 1988, the first systems thinking classes were started at Orange Grove Middle School in Tucson, Arizona, instigated by Frank Draper, a science teacher, and encouraged by Mary Scheetz, then Orange Grove's principal. When my wife, Diane, and I first visited Frank's eighth grade science class in 1991, it was hard not to notice that something was different. First, Frank was nowhere to be seen. In fact, there was no teacher in the room. A couple of students had some questions about their library research, and Frank had gone to the library with them (back in the pre-Internet walk-to-the-library days). But, to our amazement, the classroom had not descended into chaos. Instead, the thirty or so students were glued to their new Macintosh computers, two to a machine, deeply engrossed in their conversations with one another.

We learned that Frank and his colleague Mark Swanson had built their semester science curriculum around a real project: the design of a new state park to be developed north of Tucson. After studying the sorts of conflicts that inevitably arise in park and wilderness area management, they were working with a STELLA-based simulation model that showed the impacts of different decisions. They had an overall budget and a prescribed mission based on environmental quality, economics, and recreation and education targets they had set out for the park. At the time, the students were working on designing the park's trail system. Once they laid out a proposed trail, the simulation model calculated the environmental and economic consequences, prompting energetic debates over tradeoffs among different options.

We had only been standing in the back of the room for a few minutes when a couple of young boys came over and grabbed us. "We need your opinion," Joe said. "Billy and I have different trails. He thinks his is great because it makes a lot of money (routing hikers past the best views), but it also does a lot of environmental damage. Mine does less environmental damage, but he thinks it's too close to the Indian burial grounds and will stir up protests."

We listened for a while as the two boys explained their different trails and showed us some of the simulated consequences. There were no black and white answers, and it was clear that they understood this. This was about design and making choices. The bell rang, signaling the end of the period, and they said goodbye, agreeing as they left to come back after school to see if they could agree on a proposal to share with the rest of the

T his essay was adapted from part of "Education for an Interdependent World" in Joy Richmond, Lees Stuntz, Kathy Richmond, and Joanne Egner (editors), *Tracing Connections: Voices of Systems Thinkers,* (iSee Systems and Creative Learning Exchange, 2010). *Tracing Connections* was a commemorative volume in honor of Barry Richmond, a pioneer in systems thinking, managing director and founder of High Performance Systems, and designer/developer of the STELLA modeling software, who passed away suddenly in 2002.

class at the end of the week. (The students' proposals and analyses were presented to the actual park planning commission at the end of the term.)

The students also learned a variety of conceptual tools for mapping systems and for expressing and communicating with others about their understanding of the interdependence in developing a park plan. Today, tools like behavior-over-time graphs, connection circles, causal loop diagrams, stock-and-flow mapping, and system archetypes are introduced in this school system as early as kindergarten. These young children are invited to look at daily experiences like how trust builds or deteriorates in a friendship, or what happens during the process of breaking a bad habit. As students get older, they can naturally extend these tools to more complex subjects, and start to develop their own simulation models (see pages 148–150 and 275–292). This process develops not only deep content knowledge but thinking skills to see how common system dynamics can underlie very different situations.

"Our approach was to invite kids to consider a world view of complex interdependent systems. Instead of abstract learning, we use simulations to begin to confront and to penetrate this world of interdependence as it is embodied in particular real-life situations and how these systems relate to other systems," says Frank Draper.

ROOTS OF ENGAGEMENT

What was evident from the outset in the state park exercise at Orange Grove was the engagement of the students. What made them so involved?

First, the students were wrestling with real-world problems rather than artificial schoolroom exercises. They could identify not only with the challenges of developing a new state park but also with the benefits of designing the park well.

Second, the students were thinking for themselves. They knew there was no single right answer to the challenges they were facing. Ultimately, they had to understand more clearly what would happen if different decisions were made, and they had to frame the resulting trade-offs appropriately. No single formula was presented by the instructor to point to the right answer. Rather, the students had to sort out their own thinking about a real issue and explore different proposals, ultimately coming to their own conclusions.

Third, the teachers operated as mentors, not instructors. The teachers' role was not to give a prescribed method or guide the students to a predetermined right answer. Indeed, the teachers did not know the best outcome and were co-learners with the students. But the teachers' roles were no less crucial: they had to help the students make sense of the outcomes of different scenarios. Having been involved in building the computer simulation gave the teachers important knowledge for this task, but no simple answers. A complex dynamic simulation model will often respond to changes in ways that its developers do not anticipate, as different feedback interactions play out over time.

The entire process engaged both teachers and students in mutual learning around a complex domain. They had to recognize that they were working with a model and thus, by definition, their view was incomplete. One of the teachers' roles was to help the students describe the assumptions upon which the model was based and to invite the students to critique those assumptions and consider the implications of alternative assumptions, a critical aspect of scientific thinking.

》》 For examples, see Diana Fisher's Math and Modeling Guides, page 291.

Fourth, working with partners drew the students into a joint inquiry. This not only enabled them to get to know one another but forced them to continually confront alternative views and assumptions. This drew students into a natural process of seeing how each reasoned, employing past experiences and assumptions to draw conclusions that guided actions. Appreciating this in the other made them more open to testing their own reasoning.

Of course, human beings follow such processes of inferential reasoning all the time, but it is often easier to see how this works in another person, since our own reasoning is often "transparent" or invisible to us. Educators understand the importance of reflection (i.e., learning how to examine our own assumptions and reasoning) in developing higher-order skills, but it remains an elusive educational goal, all but completely ignored by traditional schooling. Didactic instruction bypasses it entirely. Teachers' efforts to try to get students to reflect are easily undermined by teachers' authority and formal power, which intimidates students programmed to seek correct answers. As Scheetz said, reflection requires safety, which benefits from an environment of mutual inquiry. In this sense, students helping one another reflect is a powerful approach that goes well beyond teacher-centered strategies.

For example, consider the following (slightly stylized) interaction between Joe and Billy, working on their park trail system.

Billy: "Your trails are a bad idea because they are too close to the Indian burial grounds. You shouldn't do that."

Joe: "Who says? There are no rules that say we can't do that. They do a lot less environmental damage than yours."

Billy: "Yeah, mine are a problem. But which is worse?"

Joe: "I didn't really think about the burial grounds. Maybe there is a way to avoid the burial grounds and also do less environmental damage?"

Barry Richmond was an educator and lifelong student of systems thinking who designed and developed the modeling software STELLA. From his work with educators, Barry identified eight component skills of systems thinking. They were:

1. High-altitude thinking: to gain a view of the interdisciplinary big picture rather than the minutiae of any particular field of study

2. System-as-cause (endogenous) thinking: to distinguish the factors most relevant to an issue or behavior of interest and how they interact to generate observed behavior

3. Dynamic thinking: to visualize behavior patterns over time and see incidents as parts of patterns of behavior rather than isolated events

4. Operational thinking: to understand how the parts of a system interact to generate these patterns of behavior

5. Closed-loop thinking: to identify the web of interacting feedback loops (causal relationships) that link together all the interacting parts

6. Scientific thinking: to use mathematic models and simulation experiments as hypotheses, explaining the links between feedback and behavior

7. Empathic thinking: to inquire about working hypotheses and communicate

them effectively for individual and organizational learning

8. Generic thinking: to understand how certain feedback structures generate the same behavior in a variety of settings and contexts.

Also see Barry Richmond, "The Thinking in Systems Thinking: Eight Critical Skills," in *Tracing Connections: Voices of Systems Thinkers*, (iSee Systems and Creative Learning Exchange, 2010), page 3ff.

Billy: "Yeah, maybe, but I wonder how much less money we'll make; the park has to generate enough money to stay open. Let's try some other routes."

Today, many educators advocate for a "systems view" in education, but this simple interaction shows a critical but often missing element. The two boys are debating about the way specific features of a system interact over time in response to alternative actions—for example, how trail location affects the hiking patterns of visitors, the environmental effects, and park revenues. They step back to see how specific choices can have many different effects. They see different parts of the system interacting as a result of the choices they have made, and they adjust their choices accordingly. This is what the late pioneering educator Barry Richmond called "operational thinking." It was one of eight interdependent systems thinking skills that he saw as critically important. Other skills were also evident: The students were learning to see change—the consequences of how the park's trail system was laid out—as differing patterns of behavior over time, exhibiting dynamic thinking. And they learned how to formulate a hypothesis—what consequences they expected from different changes—and to test their expectations against a formal model of the system. They thus engaged in scientific thinking.

Operational thinking really comes alive when students can use interactive models to simulate and analyze the effects of different actions on overall system behavior. In concert with scientific thinking—where the model's assumptions are made explicit and challenged—even young learners can engage in sophisticated processes of building rigor and relevance.

The exchange also illustrates the dance of collaborative inquiry—thinking together about a complex matter. The boys are probing each other's ways of thinking through the design problem they face and making their own thinking more explicit in the process. In this way, collaboration and reflection become inseparable elements of mutual learning. They are helping one another; neither is right nor wrong; both are learning. Joe hadn't really thought about the Indian burial grounds as a constraint; this was outside the assumptions upon which he was operating. Likewise, Billy had not paid a lot of attention to the environmental damage of his trails because he was focused on maximizing hiker traffic and park revenues. Both conclude that there may be still better overall designs if they expand their assumption sets. In short, the boys are becoming more aware of their own taken-for-granted assumptions as they think through ideas together.

Of course, such interactions both build and depend upon mutual respect. It is easy to imagine two young boys simply arguing about who is right and never challenging their own reasoning. This is why educators like Scheetz understand that realizing the benefit of systems thinking tools is inseparable from deep and broad engagement of students, and that how, in turn, this depends on the overall school environment. As Scheetz says, "an environment where learning is likely to occur is one that is safe and secure and where taking risks is okay."

THE GLOBAL ACHIEVEMENT GAP

Why Even Our Best Schools Don't Teach the New Survival Skills Our Children Need—
And What We Can Do About It, by Tony Wagner (Basic Books, 2008).

This book describes seven skills that people need to thrive in the world at large: critical thinking and problem solving, collaboration across networks and leading by influence, agility and adaptability, initiative and entrepreneurialism, effective oral and written communications, accessing and analyzing information, and curiosity and imagination. Wagner then describes how schools might evolve to foster these skills. Tracy Benson, praising this book, noted that many schools are using it as they develop curriculum and classroom approaches to prepare students for the twenty-first century. —Art Kleiner

4. Pitfalls and Skills

Precepts for Building a Robust, Compassionate Systems Thinking Practice

Michael Goodman

Michael Goodman, director of the systems thinking practice at Arthur D. Little/Innovation Associates, has been one of the most valued ongoing contributors to the Fieldbook project. He oversaw The Fifth Discipline Fieldbook's *section on systems thinking, which is still one of the most authoritative guides extant to the practice of systems thinking in organizations. He is familiar, in depth, with most of the variations of the craft, from mapping as a communications tool through the de-*

sign and use of complex simulations. He has taught system dynamics and systems thinking tools to classroom teachers (at Boston's Lesley College). And he is keenly aware that systems thinking practice has potential pitfalls. This set of guidelines is designed for teachers, as they develop models or maps, to help avoid those pitfalls and reach the students (or colleagues) they want to reach.

RECOGNIZE DIFFERENT KINDS OF LEARNERS

Different people learn systems, like everything else, in different ways. Some people grasp maps more easily than models and simulations; others have an intuitive feel for stocks and flows but don't follow causal loops. Others prefer telling systemic stories verbally.

All too often, however, a "systems thinking" class requires everyone to approach the subject the same way, often by using a system dynamics model. But doing that requires a basic level of confidence in math. If students are forced beyond their level of confidence, then they will be frustrated and think that they are inadequate for not "getting it."

The same, incidentally, is true of teachers. When educator Nancy Roberts first introduced system dynamics modeling to classroom teachers in the mid-1980s, they had to use a programming language called DYNAMO, much like Fortran. I remember feeling (naïvely) shocked and dismayed to discover how difficult this approach was for teachers. Today, STELLA is much easier to learn, but it is still a programming and simulation tool, and it is still unreasonable, in my opinion, to impose it on classroom educators.

Causal loop diagrams are much less complex than the models; that's why we developed them. But they also have limitations. Some readers have complained, for instance, that there was "too much" systems thinking in *The Fifth Discipline Fieldbook* and *The Dance of Change*; they skipped those sections. I've found that nonvisual learners, for example, have a hard time relating personally to the diagrams, and they feel excluded. Sadly, they lose interest in this very powerful set of concepts and tools.

Have you designed your models—and the conversations around them—to reach people with a variety of learning styles? Do you allow students to enter the conversation through work with the model, through mapping and considering loops, or through telling stories? If not, you run the risk of alienating a significant part of your audience, who may never tell you they are alienated for fear of looking stupid.

}} See the material on learning styles on pages 181–188.

USE THE RIGHT TOOL FOR THE RIGHT PURPOSE

Sometimes teachers are told, in effect, "You're inadequate as systems thinkers unless you build a computer simulation model," and the imposed learning curve leads to resentment and fear. In my view, all forms of systems thinking are appropriate for some purposes, and all are credible parts of the field. Some of the best systems thinkers never drew a loop or turned on a computer in their life.

If you've got a tough problem, with solutions that aren't obvious, then something as rigorous and analytical as a computer model is called for. As MIT professor John Sterman puts it, causal loops are like "training wheels" in comparison, and they can lead to as many misunderstandings as they lead to understandings. Elementary and middle school educators also often prefer stock-and-flow models because they engage children in thinking about critical distinctions that causal diagrams ignore.

If more people were willing to take the time out to rigorously learn computer simulation, then we would have a world of much better decisions. But that is not very likely. Thus, causal loops also have value and often reach a larger audience. Consultants and trainers, as well as those involved in school change initiatives, often use them to make a point that can't be made any other way, to an audience who will have little patience for the learning curve involved with stocks and flows. If your purpose is to make mental models explicit, to notice conflicts, and resolve apparent differences, then causal loops are highly effective.

In the end, as Jay Forrester has noted, system maps and models should be judged not on their validity but on their usability, insight, and relevance. In fifteen minutes, I can draw a loop of a vicious cycle with a team of kids or executives and say, "This is a trap. Someone is stuck in this. What can they do?" The resulting discussion can be just as valuable as the discussion that results from demonstrating a model that I spent five days programming. Your choice of approach should depend on the constraints involved, your skills, the complexity and riskiness of the issue, the degree to which you need to come up with a rigorous solution, and the needs and expectations of your audience.

WATCH OUT FOR THE "NINTENDO EFFECT"

Simulations are seductive and exciting. Plug in numbers, and you create a coherent-looking graph of the system's behavior over time. Unfortunately, the graph doesn't tell you if the assumptions of the model are correct, and you can end up with a model-generated "solution" that is irrelevant or even misleading. When the results don't seem accurate, there's an irresistible temptation to "play" the simulation again, plugging in other numbers until the behavior-over-time graph comes out right and you "win" without ever trying to understand or question the assumptions that were written into the model. In an atmosphere full of this type of model-building and model-using, people start gaming the system rather than using it for learning.

That's why it's so important to build in sessions where students talk about their expectations ahead of time and work out a description of the system on pencil and paper (or, together, with a chalkboard), before they ever put fingers to the keyboard. The most important thing you create is not a model, but a thinking process—especially in a group where you can challenge one another's thinking and assumptions.

USE YOUR SYSTEMS WORK AS THE FIRST WORD, NOT THE FINAL WORD

System models, whether created by computer or on paper, often are granted the weight of truth and authority by the people who use or build them. But a model merely represents the assumptions and beliefs of one person (or group of people), codified at one moment in time. If the designers change their minds, or if new data comes in, the model may become out-of-date. The best modelers realize this; they know their models will never be finished, because there will always be new information, new perspectives, and new opportunities to learn. That is why the use of systems thinking in the classroom needs to be open to inquiry and challenge from others. Most systems modelers will tell you that their models are just the first step of inquiry—they welcome critique of their structure and formulas. Yet in practice, it's all too easy for a model-builder to fall into the traps of arrogance and attachment. They get carried away with the "truth" of their model, simply because they have gone through the process of creating it. To prevent this, models should be designed as open (and unprotected by passwords), so students are encouraged to look "under the hood," see how the model is structured, and ask why it has been set up in this particular way.

USE THE MODEL AS A STARTING POINT FOR TESTING AND EXPERIMENTATION

By definition, all models (mental or computer models) are flawed simplifications of the only "perfect" model—the real world. Thus, when a model suggests a course of action, either in an organization or in a classroom, it needs to be tested. That is the value of the scientific method. The model is a working hypothesis that has its limitations. What flaws can you uncover in it? What do your tests tell you about modifying the hypothesis, your future tests, or the model itself?

There is concern that increasingly sophisticated models can be (and may be) used to justify manipulation and control. The antidote is to keep a focus on open learning and experimentation. Students who build models will be challenged, in ways that may not be obvious even to them. They need time to come to terms with those challenges, a safe place to talk about them, and skills to invite inquiry and productive conversation.

5. Learning to Connect the Dots

Nurturing and Developing on the Natural Systems Literacy of Children

Linda Booth Sweeney

How can parents, through everyday conversations and activities, nurture their children's capacity to think in systems terms? How can educators build an environment that leads children to see the patterns that make a difference? In this article, educator and writer Linda Booth Sweeney points out that thinking about systems means paying attention to the interrelationships, patterns, and dynamics that surrounds us—and that children are naturally attuned to this. In cultivating systems literacy, you build upon this natural understanding to help promote this integrated way of thinking with the children in your life.

The road construction project around the local rotary had been going on for over a year. As a result, the whole town was cranky. One afternoon, my son and I drove through the rotary just before 5 o'clock, along with throngs of irritable commuters anxious to get home. Tempers were short and the sound of car horns pierced the air. Pointing to the tangle of traffic in front of us, my then four-year-old asked: "Mommy, what happens when everyone says, 'Me first!'?"

I was used to his asking questions. Typically Jack asked about categories ("Animals aren't people, are they?") or how things work ("Why do bees kiss the flowers?") or facts ("How hot is the center of the earth?"). But this question was different; this one had to do with causes and consequences. I considered talking to him about the cost of maximizing individual gain but held back and asked instead: "What do you think would happen if everyone said, 'Me first!'?"

He pressed his nose against the window, paused and said, "Well, there might be a lot of accidents. Or maybe even a huge crash!"

"Can you think of other times when everyone says 'me first'?" I was thinking about gas guzzlers, Napster, and our overcrowded community pool.

Jack responded, "You know how you said it's not good to let the water run when we brush our teeth, 'cause if everyone did that the reservoir would go down? Well, it's kind of like that."

At the age of four, he had made an important observation: the rotary and the reservoir were common resources. Like water, air, and playgrounds, these are resources that many people use and for which no individual is solely responsible. Moreover, in asking the question, "What happens when everyone says me first!" my son was curious about the impact of individual decisions on the larger whole. Without knowing it, he stepped right into the middle of the greatest dilemma in commons-related issues: each individual action is defensible on its own, but they can combine to have devastating impact on the larger whole.

Many children intuitively grasp the nature of systems as Jack did. They can see, for instance, how a common but limited resource, such as water, air, land, highways, fisheries, energy, or minerals becomes overloaded or over-used, and how everyone experiences diminishing benefits. But they don't always have many opportunities to develop those insights into a systems awareness that will serve them all their lives. Parents, educators, and other adults can help them learn to "connect the dots": to see beyond the surface, to recognize interconnections and dynamics among people, places, events, and nature, and to begin thinking about how to use those interconnections to improve their world.

Where do our children learn to think this way? How do you nurture a child's natural intelligence about systems and help him or her to become systems literate? How can you confirm for your children what they already know: that their world is interconnected and dynamic, a tightly woven web of related, interacting elements and processes and, as such, is indeed meaningful? How can this insight become an underlying learning aesthetic with which they can build their lives?

WHY SYSTEMS LITERACY MATTERS

Children today are growing up in a world in which oil spills, global warming, economic breakdowns, food insecurity, institutional malfeasance, biodiversity loss, and escalating conflict are all too commonly at

One of the essential components of higher-order thinking is the ability to think about a whole in terms of its parts and, alternatively, about parts in terms of how they relate to one another and to the whole."
—Chapter 11 ("Common Themes") in *Benchmarks for Scientific Literacy: A Tool for Curriculum Reform*, Project 2061, American Association for the Advancement of Science (Oxford University Press, 1993) http://www.project2061.org/about/default.htm.

the top of the news. For children to make sense of these catastrophes, they must become aware of the causes and consequences in a slew of interconnected systems, including families, local economies, the environment, and more. Ideally, we want our children to take what author Edith Cobb calls "a reticulate approach" (resembling a net or network) to knowledge and sense making.

To be literate means to have a well-educated understanding of a particular subject, like a foreign language or mathematics. In many fields, the knowledge must be comprehensive and capable enough that you can put it to use. Systems literacy represents that level of knowledge about complex interrelationships. It combines *conceptual knowledge* (knowledge of system principles and behaviors) and *reasoning skills* (for example, the ability to place situations in wider contexts, see multiple levels of perspective within a system, trace complex interrelationships, look for endogenous or "within-system" influences, be aware of changing behavior over time, and recognize recurring patterns that exist within a wide variety of systems).

When people aren't literate about systems, too many human activities are like those cars jammed into the roundabout: unaware of the pattern that connects them and thus prone to exploitive and destructive results. Systems literacy is a prerequisite for realizing the kinds of aspirations that people increasingly have in an interconnected world but that seem impossible to achieve from a fragmented point of view. As the poet, novelist, and essayist Wendell Berry puts it, "We seem to have been living for a long time on the assumption that we can safely deal with parts, leaving the whole to take care of itself. But now the news from everywhere is that we have to begin gathering up the scattered pieces, figuring out where they belong, and putting them back together. For the parts can be reconciled to one another only within the pattern of the whole thing to which they belong."

When children learn about systems and become more explicitly systems literate, their worldview shifts. In The Power to Transform, Stephanie Pace Marshall explains that the value of nurturing systems literacy comes from "the power of an alternative worldview." She continues, "When we perceive and experience wholeness, we are transformed. We no longer see nature, people, events, problems, or ourselves as separate and unconnected."

One natural consequence is greater compassion for others. This is a part of people's makeup that can get suppressed by the prevailing culture in many places but that can be uncovered and drawn out by experience and learning. When children look for the connection between

Edith Cobb, *The Ecology of Imagination in Childhood*. (Columbia University Press, 1977).

Research on children's and adults' intuitive understandings of complex systems shows that deep misconceptions about the dynamics of complex systems persist, even among highly educated adults. Research in dynamic decisionmaking shows that when adults are faced with dynamically complex systems—containing multiple feedback processes, time delays, nonlinearities and accumulations—performance is biased and suboptimal. See, for example:

Tina Grotzer, "Learning to Understand Forms of Causality in Scientifically Accepted Explanations," *Studies in Science Education*, 39 (2003): 1–74.

John D. Sterman, "Misperceptions of Feedback in Dynamic Decision Making," *Organizational Behavior and Human Decision Processes*, 43(3) (1989): 301–335.

John D. Sterman and Linda Booth Sweeney, "Understanding Public Complacency About Climate Change: Adults' Mental Models of Climate Change Violate Conservation of Matter," *Climatic Change* 80(3-4) (2007): 213–238.

themselves and other people, places, events, and species, they no longer feel like outsiders looking in at others' worlds. They are now insiders, experiencing the connection to "other" as the farmer is connected to the soil and the salmon is connected to the river.

Another consequence is that children start to see themselves as part of, rather than outside of, nature. Imagine that a twelve-year-old, living in a suburban village, is presented with two pictures of a lawn. The first is filled with wildflowers and looks somewhat messy and random. The second is lush, green, neat, orderly, well-groomed, and obviously well-fertilized. Which is more beautiful? The second image, of course, represents the way that a beautiful lawn is conventionally expected to look in many communities, and many twelve-year-olds would pick it. But a student with a high level of systems literacy might well prefer the disorderly lawn. He or she would know that that the lawn worked with the landscape's natural processes, encouraging a diverse group of plants and animals to grow, maintaining its own ecological balance and adding little or no waste to the ecosystems around it.

On the other hand, the orderly, straight, groomed lawn could only survive by contradicting natural processes. It would require ongoing management, and its continued success would lead to a variety of unintended negative consequences: greenhouse gas emissions from the lawn mower, use of fossil fuels to make chemical fertilizers and treatments, the death of beneficial insects from pesticides, the added economic costs of lawn supplies and maintenance and the stress this puts on the family's budget, the removal of some plants allowing others to overrun the ecosystem (potentially causing the need for more pesticides), and the run-off of chemicals into local water sources with unknown effects.

As they grow up and learn about the economy, climate, education, energy, poverty, waste, disease, war, peace, demographics, and sustainability, children who are systems literate will tend to look at all these issues as interrelated. From the systems perspective, nothing stands alone: my climate is your climate, your infectious disease is my infectious disease, your food shortage is my food shortage. Systems literacy makes people less likely to blame a single cause for challenges and problems. Instead, it becomes a habit to look for recurring patterns that exist among a wide variety of systems, to seek out indicators of interrelated causes (knowing that very complex causes can leave deceptively simple tracks), and to conduct thought experiments to anticipate how the functioning of a living system will change if a part or a process is changed. Systems thinkers recognize that big actions can have small consequences—and vice versa.

Wendell Berry, *The Way of Ignorance and Other Essays* (Shoemaker & Hoard, 2005), p. 77.

They seek diversity, knowing that living systems depend on the variety, complexity, and abundance of species to be healthy and resilient. They look for closed loops of production and consumption, where waste from one source can be "food" for another. They question the assumption that bigger is always better.

Paying attention to living systems also raises awareness of Earth's (or biosphere's) pace of change, often in stark contrast to the hurried, mechanistic pace of the technosphere. Systems literacy makes it easier to see the commons: the shared gifts of nature such as water, air, land, fish, and also the shared efforts of our communities, upon which we depend and for which we are all responsible.

Learning about systems, and about living systems in particular, can help children come to a deeper, more compassionate, more accurate, and more sustainable sensibility about what is beautiful, what is peaceful, and what is essential.

Stephanie Pace Marshall, *The Power to Transform: Leadership That Brings Learning and Schooling to Life* (Jossey-Bass, 2006).

CHANGING THE LEARNING AESTHETIC

When we ask students to move beyond simple, linear explanations of causes, we are asking them to be literate about systems. Yet most adults in the U.S., including most industry and government leaders, were not explicitly taught skills related to seeing systems of multiple causes, effects and unintended impacts. Rather, people were taught that the best way to understand a subject was to analyze it or break it up into parts.

Herein lies an intriguing opportunity. When it comes to developing greater literacy about systems, most adults are learning along with their children. Rather than an obstacle to children's learning, this could be a major asset. For most students, co-learning (with parents, teachers, or peers) offers a chance to take an active role and develop higher-order skills such as critical and divergent thinking, analysis, synthesis, and problem solving.

While the world is becoming increasingly more complex, many classrooms continue to fragment knowledge and real-world problems through compartmentalized curricula; science is taught in one class, math in another, English in another. Courses in natural science focus on the material world while courses in the social sciences focus on the social world, and neither class acknowledges the intensive, ongoing ways in which these two worlds influence each other. When we talk to children about issues such as climate change, terrorism, and water use, we can raise their awareness of the material and social worlds, bringing together insights from history, biology, and literature, as well as the daily newspaper. Most importantly, we can come to richer understandings by tapping into the experience and insight that children already have.

Conversations with Fritjof Capra helped me clarify this division between the natural and social sciences. According to Capra, "This division will no longer be possible, because the key challenge of this new century—for social scientists, natural scientists, and everyone else—will be to build ecologically sustainable communities, designed in such a way that their technologies and social institutions—their material and social structures—do not interfere with nature's inherent ability to sustain life." (See Capra's book *The Hidden Connections: A Science for Sustainable Living* [Doubleday, 2005] p. xix.)

Seymour Papert, "Papert on Piaget," in *Time* magazine's special issue on "The Century's Greatest Minds," March 29, 1999, p. 105.

In one of his most famous experiments, Jean Piaget, the Swiss psychologist, conducted this dialogue with a five-year-old girl named Julia:

Piaget: What makes the wind?
Julia: The trees.
Piaget: How do you know?
Julia: I saw them waving their arms.
Piaget: How does that make the wind?
Julia: Like this (waving her hand in front of Piaget's face). Only they are bigger. And there are lots of trees.
Piaget: What makes the wind on the ocean?
Julia: It blows there from the land. No, it's the waves.

Piaget was interested in the child's own theories of how the world works. Most educated adults would not consider Julia's answers "correct." We would point to air pressure, ocean temperatures, and the heating effect of the sun. All these things cause the wind. Yet it is not correct to say that trees do not make the wind. Trees play a role in ecological temperature regulation—they are part of the system that creates the wind. So are the waves. That is one reason why the wind is different over the forest, the ocean, and the desert. As an adult, you probably wouldn't want to simply agree with the child that the trees create the wind; nor would you want to shut down the conversation by saying that trees don't have any role. Either approach might unintentionally discourage a child's natural inclination to take an integrated, systemic view of his or her environment. Instead, you would talk about the many factors involved and the ways in which they interrelate, perhaps going to look up the answer so you and the child can figure it out together.

Opportunities to develop systems literacy are low-hanging fruit, ready for picking. A growing number of educators are making serious inroads into their schools and communities, integrating systems thinking or its cousins—ecoliteracy, decentralized thinking, eco-logic, and integral thinking. But it isn't necessary to wait for educational reform to foster systems literacy with children, starting right where they are.

EVERYDAY WAYS TO FOSTER SYSTEMS LITERACY

The argument has sometimes been made that because systems operate in nonlinear ways that can be difficult to assimilate, systems thinking requires access to advanced training in complex systems theory, system dynamics, and agent-based modeling. Certainly, these fields of study can help people move beyond natural, intuitive understanding of systems to more expert levels of systems literacy. At the same time, there is a growing body of research (including my own research with ten- and eleven-year-olds) that shows that many students intuitively "think about systems," both natural and social systems, without any formal training and long before they're ready for graduate school. Children as young as four and five show capacity for understanding systems behaviors, which suggests that systems thinking may be part of a child's innate intelligence that is "corrected" by adults, who have themselves been taught to compartmentalize phenomena.

See, for example, Linda Booth Sweeney and John D. Sterman, "Thinking About Systems: Student and Teacher Conceptions of Natural and Social Systems," 50th Anniversary issue of *The System Dynamics Review*, 2007.

Robert W. Kates and Cindi Katz (1977) studied three- to five-year-olds and their understanding of the hydrologic water cycle. These researchers found that "some sense of cycles" (for example, the domestic water cycle and the cloud-rain cycle) existed among the four-year-old children, while the five-year-old group described "a more complex and extensive hydrology."

Robert W. Kates and Cindi Katz, "The Hydrologic Cycle and the Wisdom of the Child," *Geographical Review*, 67 (1977); 51–62. Available online at: http://rwkates.org/pdfs/ a1977.01.pdf.

Piaget, who was familiar with Austrian-born biologist Ludwig von Bertalanffy's notion of "open systems," recognized this natural systems intelligence when he observed: "There is in the child…a spontaneous belief that everything is connected with everything else and that everything can be explained by everything else."

Jean Piaget, *The Language and Thought of the Child*. (Humanities Press, 1959), p. 91. Also see Ludwig von Bertalanffy, *General System Theory: Foundations, Development, Applications* (Braziller, 1968).

We see this natural intelligence in young people playing role-playing games such as Dungeons and Dragons and computer games like Zoo Tycoon and SimCity. In the thick of this "play," children track numerous interdependencies, manage large amounts of data, and anticipate unintended consequences. In play, they flex their systems thinking muscles.

Opportunities for nurturing systems literacy in children are all around us, from the classroom and the playground to the car, the library, the dinner table, the bath, and the grocery store. With a thoughtful guide, for instance, the great outdoors offers a fertile classroom for understanding the interrelationships and dynamics of ecology. Why not encourage the seven-year-old child, enthralled with the life cycle of a butterfly, to explore other "life cycles?" Why not wonder, with the ten-year-old fish-

The word "ecology" comes from the word *okologie*, from the Greek *oikos* "house, dwelling place, habitation" and *logia* "study of", a word coined by German zoologist Ernst Haeckel (1834–1919) in 1873.

ing enthusiast, how a worm in the garden might not only be useful for his next fishing trip but also function as a soil tiller and a potential food source for a hungry robin?

In these ways, we can give children direct experiences with unadulterated nature, so that they, as Masanobu Fukuoka, farmer and author of *The One-Straw Revolution*, urges, "…can instinctively understand what needs to be done and what must not be done—to work in harmony with (nature's) processes."

Here are some other examples of conversations and activities that can help young people become more systems literate:

- **Set an example by talking not just about objects, but the relationships among them.** Instead of simply saying, "That's a brown chicken," point out that the chicken lays eggs and eats the insects in the farmer's garden. Recognize and encourage the child's natural tendency to see a network of possible causes and consequences. Ask the child to draw the connections he or she sees among cars, air, plants, and people.

- **Use systems diagrams to reveal the structural patterns underlying chronic problems.** For instance, think of any ongoing household battle. Perhaps your son hates to clean his room. You hate to ask him to clean his room. Throughout the week, you remind him about the chore. Your son resists. By the end of the week, your frustration is boiling over. Finally, you threaten a week of no TV. Your son relents. When he shows his clean room, you are happy. But the next day, with the pressure off, he slowly reverts to his old habits. Midway through the week, you feel your frustration build again, this time with more pressure.

  One way out of this dilemma is for you and your son to sit down together and each draw simple diagrams showing the situation as you see it. By connecting the dots, both you and your son can see that you're caught in a closed causal loop: a balancing feedback process. Your son only cleans when the pressure from you is on.

  Once you see this pattern, you can look for ways to break it. You may be aware, for example, that balancing feedback processes are goal seeking. One strategy is to revisit and reset the goal. Perhaps your standards as a parent are too high—you're looking for the pristine child's bedroom that one might see in *House and Garden*—while your child's are too low. Can you develop a "maintenance" goal that both parent and child agree upon? Since that may not be enough to overcome this ingrained systemic structure, can you also add in a link to the system—such as planned clean-up time twice a week—to achieve the maintenance goal?

Masanobu Fukuoka, *The One-Straw Revolution: An Introduction to Natural Farming*, translators Chris Pearce, Tsune Kurosawa, and Larry Korn. (Rodale Press, 1984)

Time in nature is not just healthy (as Richard Louv, author of *The Nature Principle: Human Restoration and the End of Nature-Deficit Disorder* reminds us), it is also important if we are to learn to live sustainably with our natural environment. Buckminster Fuller, the American engineer, systems theorist, author, designer, and creator of the geodesic dome, too pointed to the nature-as-teacher: "I am confident that humanity's survival depends on our willingness to comprehend feelingly the way nature works." See Amy Edmondson, *A Fuller Explanation: The Synergetic Geometry of R. Buckminster Fuller*, (Birkhäuser Boston, 1986), p. 5.

A great guide to this type of systems strategy is Draper Kauffman, *Systems 1: An Introduction to Systems Thinking* (Pegasus Communications, 1980). This short book has helped many understand why fundamental change to balancing

- **Help children to connect the dots:** to shift their attention from a single dot (or event) to the pattern of interrelationships that you see when you connect several events together. For example, a teenage daughter might say: "Mom, some teachers at school think that the more homework you have, the better you get. But when I get too much homework, I start to think I'll never get it done, and then I get frustrated."

  As you talk it through, encourage your daughter to think about "homework overload" as not only a singular event, but as part of a larger pattern. You can ask, for instance, "What happens next, after you feel frustrated?"

  She might say, "Well, then I feel overwhelmed, and I can't pay attention. Then I want to give up, and that makes my grades even worse." You can point out that frustration has an effect on her capabilities. Try to brainstorm. How can you modify the links between homework and frustration? What can you do about it?

  Here is one hopeful middle schooler's suggestion: "If teachers give us less homework, or no homework, on weekends, we won't get behind and start feeling bad about ourselves. We definitely would be able to pay attention in class and would do better all the way around." Can you, as a parent, speak to the teachers or the school? If that's not likely to yield results, are there other solutions? Can your daughter's schedule be designed differently? Can some of it be done in advance or in groups—or can some of it be linked to your daughter's interests and thus made less frustrating?

  See Homework: The Beast, page 217.

- **Talk about change over time.** Trace and anticipate temporal and spatial changes over days, months, and years. For example, a child may notice the slow decomposition and changing states of a fallen tree in a park or in the back yard, or the changes in a pasture when chickens are allowed to roam free.

  You can work with your child to draw simple line graphs to track behavior over weeks or months—anything from the levels of happiness at school to the money in your savings account to the number of beavers in the pond. Once you have a graph, and you can see some behavior rising, falling, or oscillating, ask: what set of interrelationships might be causing this?

  For a highly effective demonstration of change over time, encourage children to find a "sit spot" where they can focus on some outdoor phenomenon, returning on a regular basis to see how it changes. Examples might include a tree with leaves that turn color, a pond whose

and reinforcing forces makes the different between temporary and long-term change: "Essentially, any change—no matter how big—which does not change the important positive and negative feedback loops, will be only temporary. At the same time, any change—no matter how indirect or small it seems—which affects the relationship between the plus and minus loops is going to alter the long term behavior of the system." (p. 27).

This student attended the Sunnyside Environmental Middle School in Portland, Oregon.

The "Sit Spot" was originally developed by tracker and author Jon Young. See Jon Young, Evan McGown, and Ellen Haas, *Coyote's Guide to Connecting with Nature for Kids of all Ages and their Mentors* (OWLink Media Corporation, 2008).

water level rises or falls, or a place with a barometer and thermometer. Encourage them to leave a small notebook near their *sit spot* so they can keep track of the changes they observe over time.

■ **Recognize patterns that exist across systems.** When a child observes a drivers' behavior at the traffic rotary being similar to people letting the water run when they brush their teeth, or that the growing conflict between two kids at school is similar to the escalating conflict between two nations, compare those patterns together. Give your own nicknames to the patterns you see. For instance, you might call that escalating conflict "snowballing," and then when a fight between siblings begins to escalate at home, you can ask, "Are you snowballing now yourselves?"

■ **Look at the same "systems" from different perspectives.** When there's a case of bullying at school, try to talk about the perspectives of the aggressor, the target, the teachers, and the bystanders. Create a role play so the students can act out the situation or problem from different perspectives. What new ideas or insights come from changing some of the situational factors—such as how close they stand to each other when they tell the story?

■ **Talk about the difference between stocks and flows.** An accumulation of something—trees, fish, people, goods, good will, money—is a stock. The rate at which a stock changes is its *flow*. Consider the laundry pile. What influences the flow into the laundry pile? How fast does the laundry pile up? What affects the flow out of the laundry pile?

Confusion between stocks and flows can generate some of the most perplexing dynamics we encounter. For example, studies of the pesticide DDT (dichlorodiphenyltrichloroethane) have shown that while DDT evaporates from the surface of plants and buildings over six months, it remains in the tissue of fish for up to fifty years. The amount of DDT in fish tissue is a stock with very slow outflow. The same distinctions can be used to explain global climate change (the amount of carbon dioxide in the atmosphere is a stock), or the national debt (where the debt is a stock, and the deficit is a flow.)

For more on global climate change, see page 148.

■ **Look for the influence of actors within the system.** For example, in traffic congestion, ask: "How are we contributing to this?" Look for indirect influences as well: "Does our driving have an effect on a polar bear's life?" Eventually, this type of activity shifts one's focus to understanding the system's structure, not on blame.

For the systemic causes of traffic jams, see page 132.

■ **Look ahead to anticipate unintended consequences.** Ask children to adopt what sociologist Elise Boulding called "the extended present": a view of time that extends the present fifty to 200 years ahead and behind. For example, disposable diapers take between one hundred and 500 years to decompose. Talk about the fact that no one knows exactly how long it takes, because no one has lived long enough to see it happen. The extended sense of the present is particularly appropriate for living systems because many living systems, both natural and social, don't generate a full cycle of behavior over short time intervals. You won't understand the seasonal cycle of your garden, for instance, if you observe it for only a day or two.

■ **Talk about the integrity of the systems you see.** They have essential parts and processes, and the way the parts are arranged matters. You might see this understanding in the child who says: "When Mommy is sick, everything is out of whack" or "Don't get rid of the spiders! They eat the flies." Talk about what happens if one of the elements is removed. For instance, if you remove the heart from the body, neither the part (the heart) nor the system (the body) functions. Is the same true for a soccer team or a classroom? It matters, too, how the parts are arranged. Ask any four-year-old this question: if you cut a cow in half, do you get two cows? They will all say "no!" Why? They intuitively know that the cow needs both halves of its body to function.

■ **Introduce the idea of non-linear behavior** by showing children how consequences are not always proportionate to actions. For example, when a child teases another child, it seems very small. But after the thirtieth or fortieth time, the other child might strike back and someone gets hurt. On the other hand, someone can yell loudly and energetically and not have much impact. Look for other instances where small changes have had a big impact or big changes have had none. Traffic jams, weather patterns, and epidemics are all examples of nonlinearities.

Proverbs can be useful for thinking about non-linearity. Ask a young person to think of the proverbial camel and the straw that broke its back. The camel has 1,000 straws on it. Each of those straws has produced some effect on the camel. If the camel-as-system exhibited linear behavior, the last straw would have the same effect as the previous 999 straws.

FROM AWARENESS TO ACTION

With the help of adults, children's intelligence about systems can be developed further into models of problem solving. This enables them to analyze and act in informed ways; aware of recurring patterns, they

Boulding observes: "...the futures-creating individual must learn to live in an extended present. The present as defined by the year, the decade, or even the quarter century is too small of an adequate grasp of significant social processes." From *Education for Inventing the Future*, by Elise Boulding in *Alternatives to Growth I: A Search for Sustainable Futures* (Ballinger Publishing Co.,1977), p. 304.

Buckminster Fuller, the American engineer, systems theorist, author, designer, inventor, and creator of the geodesic dome, reminds us that, "The fact that 99% of humanity does not understand nature is the prime reason for humanity's failure to exercise its option to attain universally sustainable physical success on this planet." –Buckminster Fuller in collaboration with E.J. Applewhite, *Synergetics: Explorations in the Geometry of Thinking* (Estate of R. Buckminster Fuller, 1997), p. 28.

will be less likely to react viscerally and ineffectively and more likely to understand the patterns of behavior. They can use this understanding to correct their own actions, anticipate unintended consequences, and help others operate more effectively.

When children are systems literate, they help their parents learn as well. For example, they can talk about and make visible "commons dilemmas"—those conflicts that arise around shared resources for which everyone is mutually responsible.

My four-year-old at the rotary is now a strapping thirteen-year-old. Not long ago, he ended up in a not-so-playful snowball fight with his brother. I took each one aside to find out what was going on. They both told a similar story: a cutting comment from one led the other to comment back, which led the first boy to poke, the second boy to squash, and then both to out-and-out battle. This was an example of the common pattern called escalation. Feeling at my wit's end, I quickly sat them down and sketched a diagram that looked like this:

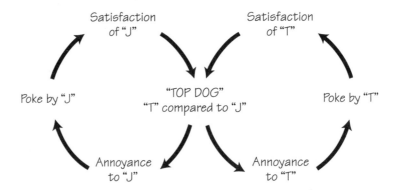

"Look," Jack said, "it's a figure eight lying on its side. That's infinity. This thing could go on forever".

"And just keep getting worse," his brother groaned.

As we talked about it, we realized together that the growing conflict was driven by each one trying to "out-cool" or "top-dog" the other. The more "cool" behavior one kid put on, the more the other wanted to squash it. Suddenly, they saw themselves as part of the "system," rather than separate from it. They "got" that blaming each other wasn't going to solve the problem. When they could see how their actions were actually fueling the actions of the other (with the help of a simple picture), they then could talk about how they might break the cycle. When I asked what they could do differently, the answer came easily. The poker would lighten up on the poking, and the squasher wouldn't squash so much.

The rotary, of course, has long since been fixed; traffic is back to normal. In our family, we try to do our part to solve the problem of the commons. Though I still rely on the car to drive to soccer practice, we walk to buy groceries, and we share eggs with neighbors from our own chickens. We try to talk in ways to make it easier to connect the dots in everyday situations. A common phrase in our house these days—*what if everyone did that?*—is our way of attempting to magnify the consequences of our individual actions so that we can imagine the broader impact.

Everyone is born with a natural intelligence about living systems. With just a little effort, you can encourage that natural intelligence in young people and remind them that their world is interconnected and dynamic, a tightly woven web of related, interacting elements and processes. As such, it is both purposeful and meaningful.

Hidden Connections

On any trip or in any new location, ask students to pick a target object and ask, "How many connections can we make to this?" Encourage them to keep notes, using a pencil and paper, or to make simple conceptual maps, using words or pictures to describe interconnections and causality. On a farm, the object might be a chicken, a tractor, or a pail of fresh milk. On a beach, it might be a fishing net, a crab in a tide pool, or a shell. In an urban environment, it could be a water pipe or a construction crane. Where possible, draw on local "informants"—people who work with this object in their everyday lives—to help the students build their story.

A conversation between a farmer and a group of students might go like this:

Student: "Well, you feed the chickens. And give them water." (Students draw a chicken, a farmer, food, and water.)
Farmer-educator: "Where does the food come from?"
Student: "You go to a store to buy it."
Farmer-educator: "What do I use to get to the store?"
Student: "That truck outside. And you need gas for the truck." (Student adds a truck and gas to his picture).
Another student: "Well, the chickens lay eggs and the farmer eats the eggs. You also sell the eggs to the farm stand down the road."
Another: "And then you have to buy feed for the chickens."
Another: "And do something with the manure."

For more about systems mapping techniques, see pages 134ff.

Purpose:
This simple activity can foster thinking about interdependence.

Linda Booth Sweeney and Drumlin Farm (an Audubon site near Boston) created a *Making Connections Playkit* (with playing cards and wikki stix) to help children think deliberately about living systems in a farm setting. The playkit is available through the Creative Learning Exchange: www.clexchange.org.

Systems Stories for Children

Linda Booth Sweeney

A growing number of children's books have great examples of balancing and reinforcing feedback, or they embody systems principles and archetypes in other ways. These are a few favorites.

Linda Booth Sweeney has published two collections of stories with systems themes: *Connected Wisdom: Living Stories About Living Systems* (SEED, 2008); and *When a Butterfly Sneezes: A Guide for Helping Kids Explore Interconnections in Our World Through Favorite Stories* (Pegasus Communications, 2001). See review of *Connected Wisdom* on page 316.

Other books by Numeroff that reinforce the notion of circular causality include: *If You Give a Moose a Muffin* (1991); *If You Give a Pig a Party* (2005); *If You Take a Mouse to the Movies* (2000); *If You Give a Cat a Cupcake* (2008) (all from HarperCollins), and *If You Give a Dog a Donut* (Balzer and Bray, 2011).

IF YOU GIVE A MOUSE A COOKIE

By Laura Joffe Numeroff, illustrated by Felicia Bond (HarperCollins, 1985)

This is the story of the unforeseen consequences of giving a hungry little mouse a cookie. Seems innocent enough? But the next thing you know, the energetic mouse will want a glass of milk. Then he'll want to look in a mirror to make sure he doesn't have a milk mustache. Then he'll ask for a pair of scissors to give himself a trim. The mouse mischief tumbles on like dominoes throughout this adorable book, ending where it started, with the mouse requesting yet another cookie.

This is a good story to help children practice the skill of tracing cause and effect relationships to see how an event (giving the mouse a cookie) feeds back on itself. What other types of chain-of-events situations can they think of that eventually feed back on themselves? And for older kids: What are the possible unintended consequences of some everyday actions? (For instance, suppose city planners add an extra traffic lane to a crowded highway. Would this produce less traffic or more traffic?)

"This is one of the best books I have found for introducing very young children to systems," says Tim Lucas. "From here, ask children 'Can you think of other sequences like that?' Have them draw a cartoon strip of their ideas, then tape the ends of the paper together so it forms a never-ending loop. Where's the beginning? Where's the end? I've watched teachers expand on this idea to talk about the ways in which events come together into patterns. Some patterns are cyclical. And you don't end up quite where you started, but you always go around again."

THE SNEETCHES AND OTHER STORIES

by Theodor Geisel (Dr. Seuss), (Random House, 1961)

In this gem from Dr. Seuss, we see how prejudice and the drive for exclusivity result in wasted energy and depleted resources. Star-

Belly Sneetches are fuzzy green animals with neon green stars in the middle of their stomachs. Plain-Belly Sneetches have no star. Just as bell-bottoms, miniskirts, Izod shirts, and Tommy Hilfiger have (at various times) made students feel superior, so the small green star allows some Sneetches to brag: "We're the best kind of Sneetch on the beaches." Eventually an enterprising imp cashes in; for a pretty penny, he adds stars to the Plain-Belly Sneetches with his peculiar machine. Suddenly green stars are everywhere. To remain distinctive, the Star-Belly Sneetches go through the imp's "Star-Off Machine." The cycle continues until they spend every last cent of their money. Finally outwitting the imp, the Sneetches learn to accept their differences and themselves.

The Sneetches, in short, are "shifting the burden" from a fundamental but difficult solution (learning to accept and embrace their differences) to an easier but devastatingly expensive "quick fix" (tattooing themselves with stars).

Questions to ask include: What other consequences or side effects might occur that would make it more difficult (or easier) for the Sneetches to see what's going on? If you visited the Sneetches, would you try to break the cycle? How would you do it?

}} For more on Shifting the Burden, see page 375.

Other systems-conscious books by Dr. Seuss include: *The Lorax* (Random House, 1971) and *The Butter Battle Book* (Random House, 1984).

ANNO'S MAGIC SEEDS

by Mitsumasa Anno (Philomel, 1992)

In this Japanese folk tale, a magic wizard gives a farmer named Jack two mysterious golden seeds. He instructs Jack to eat one, which will sustain him for a full year, and to plant the other. Jack obeys, and a plant grows bearing two seeds. The following year, Jack plants both seeds—and the plant bears four. He eats one seed and plants the other three—and reaps six the following year. As the years go by, he continues to plant all but one seed, and his crop of seeds doubles annually. He marries, raises a family, plants many crops, endures a flood, and saves enough seeds to feed his family and start planting again.

This is a story about exponential growth—where the doubling time is constant. But nothing grows forever, and the story also shows the process of boom and bust; inevitably, some kind of limit (such as a flood) will cut off growth and even cause a near collapse. What would have happened to Jack if he had followed the wiz-

In another book—*Three Strands in the Braid: A Guide for Enablers of Learning* (A Tribe of Two Press, 1994)—Underwood describes her grandfather's "rule of six": for every perceivable phenomenon, devise at least six plausible explanations. "There will probably be sixty," her grandfather said, "but if you devise six, this will prevent you from fixing on the first plausible explanation as 'the Truth.'"

ard's instructions and only planted one seed? What would have happened if the flood had never come? How long would it have been before the world was overrun with seeds? Where else do you see this type of explosive growth?

WHO SPEAKS FOR WOLF?

by Paula Underwood, Illustrations by Frank Howell (A Tribe of Two Press, 1991)

Who Speaks for Wolf is the story of an eight-year-old boy who asks his grandfather to tell how their family came to live with the wolves. We hear of the dilemmas and unintended consequences that occur when the tribe moves into the wolf community's "Center Place." What do you think the boy learned from this story of Wolf-Looks-at-Fire? Why do you think the community did not listen to Wolf's brother? How might the boy and his community have considered the wolf community in their decision?

CONNECTED WISDOM

Living Stories About Living Systems, by Linda Booth Sweeney.
(SEED [Schlumberger Excellence in Educational Development], 2008).

Linda Booth Sweeney has selected folktales from across cultures to demonstrate systems thinking principles. The fables are not only engaging, but beautifully illustrated by artist Guy Billout. Educators and parents will find this book an engaging way to learn and practice systems with children and other adults. At the end of each story, there are comments and questions to guide conversations about specific systems issues exemplified in the stories. One of my favorite stories is "Gecko's Complaint," a Balinese folktale of interdependence. We find Gecko complaining to the Village Chief about Firefly disturbing his sleep. In this tale of connection, we meet Firefly, Woodpecker, Frog, Black Beetle, Water Buffalo, and finally Rain. Each relates their connection to another character as the story moves along to finally discover that Gecko is dependent on Rain for mosquitoes. At that, the Chief calls in Gecko and orders him to stop complaining and live in peace with all his neighbors. This rich story, like the others in the book, can generate numerous questions and deepen your understanding.
—Nelda Cambron-McCabe

School

VIII. Entering School

1. Creating Schools That Learn

Joan has been teaching first grade for twenty-five years. She is known in her small district as a dedicated and effective educator. One day a neighbor pulls her aside to ask about the school. "I just don't think the high school teachers are very motivated," says the neighbor. "I've tried to meet with them to find ways to help my kids be more enthusiastic about school, but the meetings never seem to go anywhere. Some of them act like they're in foxholes, afraid to come out; some of them seem to think that our girls' problems are our fault, and they have no responsibility to help us. And I don't know what to do next."

Years before, Joan's own children had had similar problems in high school. "I don't think it's the teachers," she says. She tells her neighbor about a project she had initiated several years back with two other teachers to redesign the math curriculum. Merely by telling the story, Joan relives some of the excitement she had felt. Her eyes light up; her hands play a lively duet in the air as she talks. She tells her neighbor that the principal was very supportive and had a few ideas of his own. Then he said that they needed to get permission from the superintendent.

Joan's shoulders suddenly slump and her eyes grow opaque. "All the superintendent could talk about," she says, "were the reasons it could not be done. He said he'd been through it all before. First, the parents would protest. The school board wouldn't approve. And the state wouldn't allow it. Sure, he cared about the education of the children in the district. But all he could focus on were the 'why nots.' And without his support, our plan was dead." Neither Joan nor her partners have ever tried to innovate anything beyond their classroom doors since then.

Joan and the superintendent, of course, never talked directly about this. And the superintendent has long forgotten the conversation; he's had so many like it. He genuinely wants the district to improve, and he recognizes that it must change. But he sees himself as continually struggling with the worst tendencies of his partners. The state regulators can be inflexible; the school board tends to micromanage; some parents are intransigent; the teacher's union leaders are often suspicious; and the union itself has voted down innovative measures in the past. In his mind, his job represents a continual battle on many different fronts, with himself as the only person who sees the needs of the district as a whole. Sometimes he wishes he could get more support, but he never expects it and never asks for it, because there's no reason in his mind to think that anyone would give it to him.

The school board members, meanwhile, feel a great deal of pressure from the community; they perceive the people of the area as unwilling to spend any more in taxes. The union leaders, the principals, the staff, the local community members, the teachers at all levels, and the students themselves all have their own story to tell. Their perspectives couldn't be more different, but they all have two things in common. First, they all have the same goal: a school system that works more effectively and more compassionately, a system that doesn't let students like Joan's neighbor's daughters slip through the cracks this way. Second, they all feel utterly alone. Even when they compare notes, as Joan and her neighbor did, they do not imagine acting together.

But suppose there were ways for all of them to talk together—not once, but repeatedly, starting from the assumption that they all had the best interests of the school and its children in mind. Then the school system could begin to shift from a complex set of interlocked but separate constituencies to a body of people who were learning together, on behalf of their common purpose.

LEARNING SCHOOL

The word "school" comes from the Greek *skholé*, which originally meant leisure. It gradually evolved (via the Latin *skola*) to mean "leisure devoted to learning or intellectual argument." From this came the many meanings we have today for the word: a physical space for educational assembly (a "school building"), the process of being educated ("schooling"), the generic learning experience (the "school of hard knocks"), and a group that has learned a common way of looking at the world (a "school of thought"). One meaning, a group of fish traveling together, derives from a different root: the Germanic *skulo*, meaning "split" or "divide." This ambiguity is fitting. A school is a physical place; people speak of "going to school." Yet a school is not entirely bound by its building. We use the term in this book to mean the formal environments created to provide places and opportunities for education—everything from a one-room schoolhouse to an elementary school to an entire urban school district. The word also refers to institutions for adult learning, from alternative meeting places to community colleges to large universities. Increasingly, people also use the word "school" to refer to learning environments in the community. Thus the idea of school continues to evolve—and maybe it will mean "leisure" again one day.

As you will see in this part of the book, there are a growing number of places where this kind of profound change—a change not just in policies and practices, but in the ways of thinking and interacting in the school—is beginning to happen. It is never easy, but it is always rewarding. From the experience to date, there seem to be several key principles for success.

■ **Change starts small and grows organically.** We often hear of school districts trying to "roll out" a program quickly from one successful school to many other schools at once. But sustainable change in organizations is like the biological growth of any living population. In nature, all growth follows the same pattern: starting small, accelerating, then gradually slowing until "full" adult size is reached. This pattern recurs again and again because it reflects the interplay between the forces that reinforce growth and the constraints that limit it.

What if change in schools followed a similar growth pattern? Then those who wish to produce change would focus, first and foremost, on understanding the limiting processes around them. They would not hover over the school personnel, exhorting them to change, any more than a gardener would stand over a plant, imploring: "Grow! Try harder! You can do it!" Successful agents of change would learn instead to appreciate the statement by Chilean biologist Humberto Maturana: "Every movement is being inhibited as it occurs." They would develop a balance between urgency and patience, so they could start small, accelerate appropriately, and reflect on each new

For a more comprehensive analysis of the reasoning behind a learning-based school change initiative and the challenges of change, see *The Dance of Change*, pp. 5–64.

development before moving on to the next phase. They would let innovation occur not through exhortation or command, but through careful tending and sustained deliberation.

■ **Sustained learning requires personal commitment.** A person in authority—a superintendent, school board president, principal, chancellor, or legislator—can't dictate that people will become inspired or engaged in improving the school. Such dictates will, at best, make people comply with the changes without feeling any commitment to them. When the imperative to change fades, so will their interest in it. People will only sustain interest if they choose to make a commitment on their own and if this kind of learning orientation continues through the life of the initiative (and the school).

But if you can't force commitment, what can you do? You can do the same things that a teacher can do to foster genuine learning with students. You can nudge a little here, inspire a little there, provide a role model. Your primary influence is in the environment you create—an environment that encourages awareness and reflection, that gives people access to tools and training that they ask for, and that enables them to develop their own ability to make choices.

■ **Money is not the most important resource.** Having an adequate budget is, of course, important, but other factors matter more than financial resources. Many of the schools with the greatest track records in the learning disciplines are located in relatively low-income neighborhoods or in districts with very sparse budgets. The Waters Foundation, which has introduced systems thinking into many schools, has concentrated on schools with large subsidized lunch populations, just to demonstrate that success can take place in a variety of environments, including schools that have been written off as unworkable. Probably the most critical factor, as with any innovation, is knowing how to create an environment where people trust each other and can work together effectively.

■ **Organizational learning takes less time than the alternative.** Administrators and teachers, eager for new types of school reform, often say: "We just don't have time for this learning organization stuff." But, in fact, perhaps they don't have time for any other approach. As MIT professor Lotte Bailyn, who has studied time pressures for thirty years, puts it, "Often a perceived 'lack of time' problem is caused by the way the work is organized." An overly structured school day without flexibility or a highly politicized work environment can lead to much unnecessary work—time spent spinning wheels, recovering from unnecessary errors or dealing with problems created by people in other parts of the school system who did not realize they were undermining each other's efforts. Organizational learning initiatives may take more time at first, but they tend to resolve these types of problems, relieving much more of the pressure on time in the long run.

- **Pilot groups are the incubators for change.** Once it is understood that all great things have small beginnings, people think naturally in terms of "pilot groups." These groups may be as small as two teachers or as large as a districtwide initiative of several hundred people. They may be commissioned formally by the superintendent and school board or formed through a series of informal lunches with no hierarchical authority or mandate but an influence based on members' credibility and commitment. The one constant in successful pilot groups is a predisposition toward pragmatic curiosity. Members have seen success in a classroom or community group, and they are intrigued. They know they cannot pursue the ideas on their own, so they gravitate toward others who are similarly intrigued. The pilot group emerges out of that impulse. In many pilot groups, people are insulated from the overarching pressures; this helps them reconnect with their own purpose, their drive to learn, and their willingness to take risks on behalf of children.

- **Organizational learning takes place through multiple layers of leadership.** Like the myth of the "heroic CEO" in corporations, the myth of the "heroic school leader" (who operates, against the odds, to turn around a troubled learning environment) usually makes real change much harder. Instead of inspiring people, it makes them feel dependent on the few special people who have skill, ambition, vision, charisma, and hubris enough to overcome the blocks that stymie everyone else. When the hero's grand strategies fail to get implemented, people cling instead to habitual ways of doing things.

  Successful school change, by contrast, requires multiple layers of leadership roles. Formal and informal leaders, at the classroom, school, and community levels, each provide different resources to any organizational learning effort. There will need to be imaginative, committed local classroom leaders who are accountable for particular results and who can undertake their own initiatives and projects that affect a classroom, a grade level, or sometimes a school. When people throughout the system become stewards of the children, the system, and one another, they provide the context for change.

- **Challenges are a natural part of organizational learning,** just as the challenges faced in adolescence are a natural part of the growth of the child. As powerful as it is, and amid all of the success and satisfaction it

See "Integrating Work and Personal Life…in Practice," by Lotte Bailyn, in *The Dance of Change*, p. 95ff.

For more about the challenges of organizational change, see *The Dance of Change*, p. 60ff.

generates, this "learning organization" work can easily lead to failure, setbacks, and backlash. Some learning initiatives never seem to get off the ground. In other cases, innovators who expected to be rewarded and promoted lose their jobs instead. Or they just move on, searching for school systems that are more open to their ideas. Even after years of success, learning-oriented cultures can come under relentless attack.

But perseverance pays off, as long as it is buttressed by a genuine appreciation of the value of the students. One powerful success story is from a "turnaround school" in Tucson—a school that did so poorly on standardized tests that, by state law, a full staff turnover was mandated. All the adults in the school—including teachers, administrators, and staff members—were fired, and only about twenty-five percent were hired back. The new incoming principal (whose previous job had been at an Indian reservation school) was a tough-looking, plain-spoken woman. At the end of her first year, reflecting on the challenges they had faced, she said, "Everyone thinks you're starting from scratch. But you're not. There are ghosts in the building."

Asked to elaborate, she said, "They fired all the adults, but the kids are still there. This turnaround certified them as losers because all their teachers were fired. Think of what that's like for the kids. It's like the ultimate validation of what they knew all along—they are the bottom, the rock bottom. They have no chance."

Yet the students and the school persevered. The principal, at the time she made these remarks, had recently held a talent show. "I've been to middle school talent shows many, many times," she said. "They're brutal. Kids make mistakes, they get booed, they get hissed." But at this show, every time a kid made a mistake, the audience had cheered them on. "I felt we'd made it," she said. "I had one and only one goal the first year: the kids are not losers."

Challenges can be draining, but they should also give you confidence—they are signs that you are having an effect. No challenges would be a sign that you were making no progress.

MM

What Is the Purpose of School?

Any significant organizational learning initiative in an educational setting raises a fundamental question: What are we here for? Before too long, the members of the school community—parents, teachers, administrators, students, and staff—begin rethinking their values, their contribution to the community, and their identity. There is a lot to think about, because there is little consensus around the profound question of the purpose of school. Instead, there are many answers, each with its own strong advocates:

- School has an economic purpose, as a supplier of talent: to prepare the skilled workers that employers need. But which workplace are they being prepared for? The workplace of 2012, when this year's kindergarteners enter school? That of 2025, when they will probably graduate from high school? That of 2030 through 2040, when they will probably begin their employment? Or the workplace of the 2050s, 2060s, and 2070s, which some of today's kindergarteners will be leading and which might well be so different from the workplace of 2012 that any direct preparation would be meaningless?

- School is also tied to individual economic success—equipping students for a better life by giving them the skills they need to compete and hold a job. But whose view of competitive skills should guide their choices and the offerings the school provides? The students' view, which is limited by lack of experience? The faculty's view, which may be attuned to the skills needed in the past rather than those needed in the future? The view of the parents, who may be too close to their children, or too biased by their own experience, to see the value of different options clearly? Or that of outside experts, who may have a broader perspective but little or no insight into the individual students themselves?

- Or should the purpose of school be to instill skills and knowledge for their own sake? And if so, which skills and knowledge? Should they be relatively mainstream: literacy, science, math? Should they expand to skills that have not always been recognized but are crucially important in today's world: computer modeling, physical exercise and health awareness, financial literacy, or media awareness? Should schools exist to demystify this knowledge or to codify it and make sure that only a small group of qualified and credentialed people have license to practice it as professionals?

- Schools also (if only unconsciously, sometimes) follow a mandate about scaling knowledge, assuming that their purpose is to standardize capability—so people everywhere have a common base of knowledge and competence. Or should educational institutions seek to differentiate, to bring out the unique differences in everyone? Should schools cultivate a few people as elite and focus on providing great opportunities for them so that they can serve society? Or should they devote as much, in resources and attention, to developing the children of all social and economic groups as they do to developing the children of the privileged?

The John Goodlad quote comes from his essay "Education and Democracy: Advancing the Agenda," *Phi Delta Kappan* 82(1) (2000) 86–89.

Goodlad (who is the president of the Institute for Educational Inquiry) also argues that public schools are the most appropriate public forum for participation to preserve our democratic processes. See John Goodlad, Roger Soder, and Bonnie McDaniel (editors), *Education and the Making of a Democratic People,* (Paradigm Publishers, 2008). Also see the Institute's website, http://www. ieiseattle.org.

■ Or perhaps schools should be dedicated primarily to social and political goals: to develop, as John Goodlad puts it, "the essence of each individual self in the contest of justice, fairness, responsibility, and mutual caring to which the Declaration of Independence and the Constitution speak so eloquently." But what social and political goals are the right ones? Should schools produce the kinds of aware, conscientious citizens who can participate fully in democracies? Should they help to reduce differences in capability, status, and privilege and thus advance the goals of broadening opportunity and increasing social equity? Should they further the goal of sustainability or community, as Jaimie Cloud and Peter Block suggest? Are schools vehicles with which a community invests in its future: to enable children to live better than their parents did, not just economically but in terms of their ecology, humanity, and society as well?

See "Reclaiming Citizenship Through Conversations," by Peter Block, page 479; and "It Takes a Child to Raise a Village," by Jaimie Cloud, page 537.

■ Or do schools exist primarily for personal goals: to help each individual grow as a learner, to move closer to the core of their own aspirations, whatever those may be? Should they help students cultivate self-awareness, to become more like "bowlers" (as Stanford University professor Mary Budd Rowe calls them), continually trying to improve their game, as opposed to "crap-shooters," playing a game of chance and relying on luck for their success? Alternatively, should the purpose of school be to help people "grow up"—to acquire self-discipline, take difficult burdens in stride, and learn to control their impulses?

■ Or is the purpose of schools to simply be present for the children who attend them and, indeed, for all the people in them?

Finally, is there a way for schools to fulfill all of their objectives and priorities at once, or is education a zero-sum game, in which some will be chosen as winners while others by definition become losers? Can schools be designed so that success for some of their members reinforces success for all? And whichever goals are chosen for a school, are we (the school leaders and constituents) aware of why we want them?

Most school system leaders haven't raised these questions in a clear and meaningful way. And when there are no clear answers, people in authority often resort to the goals that are most expedient. In school systems, that means the purpose in practice becomes threefold: to keep the institution running, to provide as many "passing" scores on key indicators (like standardized tests) as possible, and to fulfill the perceived needs and priorities of the key stakeholders of the school system (the most influential teachers, parents, administrators, and political influencers).

The top-down hierarchies of most school systems (in which budgets, for example, are determined by a central office and not by local teachers and principals), reinforces this push to expediency. So does the politically shaped governance of most school districts, in which pressure groups can easily form to achieve narrow goals but broad change is inevitably resisted. If we are adults involved with schools—as parents, community leaders, or educators—our ability to think about this clearly is also complicated by the natural human tendency to carry forward our own memories of school and use them as a template in determining the shape of schools to come.

Or as *Fifth Discipline Fieldbook* coauthor Charlotte Roberts asked a group of educators recently, "Do we really want to re-create the schools we remember from our own childhoods? Do we want to stop the flow of change and create stagnant pools of schooling because that's what educators were molded to fit into?"

As the authors of this book, we want to propose a more fundamental aspiration: to work toward a system that allows children, their parents, educators, and the community at large to have everything they need from schools. We want it all. We want schools that educate all students affordably, that draw out the inner potential of every child, that are enjoyable to teach in and invigorating to learn in, that enable students to pass standardized tests with ease, that stretch everyone in the building, that help children and adults understand systems, and that graduate a generation of capable, committed people around the world who are ready for the challenges facing us. Finally, we want to achieve this consciously—thinking and acting together in a way that builds our own collective capacity and awareness.

This aspiration may seem impossible to achieve, and perhaps it is, especially when you remember that there are no quick fixes to most school problems. They are too complex and profound. But as you explore the techniques, concepts, and practices in this chapter, remember the importance of a strong vision. It is important not to let our goals erode, even as we seek a clear view of current reality.

⟩⟩ See Personal Mastery, page 76; and Teaching Structural Tension, page 209.

Finally, there is reason for hope. As we revise this book in 2011, we conclude that many of the schools we know are better than they were in the past and are growing better still—judged either by objective measures or (more importantly) by the enthusiasm and commitment of people within them. People know more about what makes a good school and how to turn an institution of learning into a learning organization. Efforts to make education better are evoking the passion that people feel—not just for children and learning, but also for schools as a place where people come together to learn. We take heart from this, and we believe many others involved with school—educators, parents, and students themselves—may do the same.

THE FINLAND PHENOMENON

Inside the World's Most Surprising School System, directed by Robert Compton, (Broken Pencil Productions, 2010) www.2mminutes.com.

Here is a film about a school system built around trust: administrators trust teachers, teachers trust students, and students trust the system. The narrator and researcher, Tony Wagner of the Harvard Technology and Entrepreneurship Center, known for his studies of education innovation around the world, describes the remarkable results achieved by schools throughout Finland. By many conventionally accepted measures, they fall short. Kids spend 20 to 30 percent less time in school than in other places. The school day is compressed. There are no standardized tests or homework assignments. And yet, in the end, the students of this country outperform most others, even where the workloads are a great deal heavier.

That doesn't happen by accident or because of Finland's social or cultural homogeneity. (The country's population, 5.3 million, is larger than that of Colorado; 15 percent are minorities, many of whom speak a different language than Finnish.) It happens because of a series of decisions made by Finnish leaders, starting with the way that teachers are hired and treated: as highly respected professionals, drawn from the top university students. They focus on kids' development and manage stress and effort in very mindful ways. Though the film is only sixty minutes long, it is not a montage of sound bites; it includes extensive interviews with educators and demonstrations of classroom teaching. Films like this can become the beginning of a global dialogue—schools *can* break out of the industrial age norm, once people look at the assumptions underlying them. —Peter Senge

THE DEATH AND LIFE OF THE
GREAT AMERICAN SCHOOL SYSTEM

How Testing and Choice are Undermining Education by Diana Ravitch (Basic Books, 2010).

Diane Ravitch, professor of education at New York University, long championed the conventional wisdom of more testing and charter schools. But as the evidence of the ineffectiveness of these approaches mounted, she became convinced that school improvement was not well served by the existing consensus. In this book, she argues that if the nation is falling behind in global competition, if the economy is a shambles, if poverty persists, if American kids are not as serious about their studies as their peers in other nations, too many people think the school must be to blame. It's not globalization, or deindustrialization, or poverty or our coarse popular culture, or predatory financial practices. It's the public schools, their teachers, and their unions. Ravitch counters that it is far too simplistic to blame schools and teachers. "Leadership," concludes Ravitch, "doesn't require beating up on your teachers." She recommends following the example of Finland, typically the Western nation with the highest international assessment results: invest in the preparation, support, and retention of excellent teachers; establish a demanding national curriculum; and greatly improve social welfare programs for children and families. —James Harvey

James Harvey is the director of the National Superintendents Roundtable, http://www. superintendentsforum.org.

~~~~~

2. Schooling as an Ethical Endeavor

Nelda Cambron-McCabe

A doctoral student approached me with frustration as he was completing our course work in educational leadership at Miami University. "This program," he said, "has been troubling for me, because I have worked hard to be a good teacher and a good school administrator. But I realize now after all this time that I'm part of the problem." He said that he recognized that many of the instructional practices and organizational structures in his school had created problems for some of the children. But he had seldom questioned those practices; he had accepted them as givens in the system. "My exasperation," he told me, "is that no one prepared me to raise these kinds of questions earlier in my professional life. Now I feel like I have conspired to maintain the present schools by not asking difficult questions of myself and others."

Every occupation needs some form of reflective "questioning," but it's particularly important for teaching because teaching is a moral undertaking. Teaching is not simply a set of technical skills for imparting knowledge to waiting students. It involves caring for children and being responsible for their development in a complex democratic society. In other words, teachers need to think not just about the "means" by which they teach but the "ends" they are teaching for. Doing that places a heavy obligation on those who teach—especially those who teach in public schools where state laws compel students to attend.

Yet the idea of moral responsibility typically is not raised in most educational preparation programs. Nor is it discussed when one enters the teaching field. Rather, when educators talk about responsibilities, they tend to focus on professional accountability—developing students' knowledge and understanding of subject matter, equipping students with high-level skills to succeed in the academy and workplace, designing rigorous curricula, and challenging students to meet high standards.

Focusing attention solely on these technical aspects of teaching (the "means") ignores the overarching moral principles that must guide the work of teachers and administrators. For example, a teacher may be a highly trained specialist in reading instruction. Few educational requirements are as critical to an individual in life as basic literacy—becoming a reader. Yet few academic challenges are as complex. Regardless of which approach one takes in the hotly contested and divisive debate surrounding reading and literacy approaches, reading specialists possess extensive technical skills (decoding processes, whole language, phonemic awareness, literature centered, encoding or spelling, vocabulary understanding). They can pull multiple techniques from their repertoire, without a lot of deliberation, to teach young children. And that's where the problem arises. If some children are not learning to read, a reading specialist may conclude that those children simply lack the capability to read. After all, the specialist has tested all of the tools and techniques.

An opportunity exists here for this specialist to question the assumptions underpinning those technical approaches or the way that he or she has framed the problem. By examining the poor reading performance from the children's perspective, the specialist can raise questions with ethical dimensions. Who are the children experiencing difficulties? Are they disproportionately from poor families or ethnic minority backgrounds? Is the focus of instruction on the "deficits" that they bring to the classroom? Are ethnic, cultural, or learning style-oriented differences seen as deficits? What important skills and knowledge do they have? How can instruction relate to the knowledge and skills they bring to the classroom? What is the purpose of teaching them reading in the first place, and what kind of reading materials does that suggest they should be introduced to? Through reflective questioning, the teacher can consciously engage the moral dimensions of schooling connected to his or her relationship with the students and their access to knowledge.

One value is not as good as any other value in schools. People in democratic societies have a right to expect their schools to be guided by moral principles such as justice, fairness of treatment, liberty, honesty, equity in the distribution of resources, and respect for differences. As educators, we make decisions every day with tremendous moral implications for the students in our care. How do we divide our time and attention among the students in our classroom? What impact do our instructional grouping practices have within the classroom and across the school? Whom do we recognize or ignore, encourage or discourage in classroom interactions? What knowledge do we choose to emphasize or to gloss over? Which classrooms or schools are assigned the recognized expert teachers?

Each of these questions is first and foremost an ethical question. Since most teachers answer not in words but in educational practices, it follows that our choice of teaching methods and school designs is also an ethical decision. Some educational practices are moral and others are immoral. Our actions in the classroom, whether in a public or private school, can enable or disenfranchise the students in our care. How we instruct validates some students and not others; how students are graded, grouped, and rewarded may place some students at serious risk.

Moreover, there is no guidebook or listing that can automatically sort these dilemmas for us, nor can there be—not in a world of ambiguous interpretations and incomplete awareness of our mental models. It is only through study, reflection, and inquiry that we, as educators, can come to understand the impact of our decisions. If we fail to undertake that kind of inquiry into the moral nature and consequences of our actions as educators, then our practices remain unquestioned. Even those practices that have devastating consequences for certain students will continue, unquestioned. We will believe them to be neutral and beyond our control—simply the way schools operate.

Without explicitly inquiring into the moral obligations inherent in our work, we insulate ourselves from personal responsibility for any negative consequences that students may suffer from our decisions. We are, thus, shielded from the burden to take action. When we are part of a school system that doesn't work for a growing number of its children, this insulation allows us to blame others—the administration, the parents, the state, policymakers, the community, the "no child left behind" law—instead of thinking about our own role. Embracing our own moral responsibility, however, pushes us to ask ourselves: "What about my thinking impedes kids' learning?" "What am I doing that keeps children where they are?" Without this difficult inquiry, the Fifth Discipline concepts in this book may bring only superficial changes to the work in schools. The use of learning disciplines also has an ethical dimension. Does the design of inquiry or dialogue favor some students over others? What assumptions are built into systems models? When talk of current reality gets too close to home, or too wrenching, is it allowed to continue, or is it cut off?

THE MORAL DIMENSIONS OF SCHOOLING

Where does one start to gain insight into the moral responsibilities connected with schooling? I have found John Goodlad's writings helpful in giving shape to the idea of schooling as a moral endeavor. "We created schools primarily out of concern for the welfare of our culture," says Goodlad, "particularly in regard to the preservation of our religious and political values. We broadened the purposes over time until they included the whole process of developing effective citizens, parents, workers, and individuals; these are now the educational goals of our school districts as well as our nation. Schools are major players in developing educated persons who acquire an understanding of truth, beauty, and justice against which to judge their own and our society's virtues and imperfections…This is a moral responsibility." The four dimensions include:

Goodlad's four moral dimensions of schooling have been powerful in shaping an international discourse around the preparation of educators (particularly teachers) and the renewal of schools: His quotes here all come from John Goodlad, *Teachers for Our Nation's Schools* (Jossey-Bass, 1990), p. 22ff and 48ff.

1. **Enculturation into a political and social democracy:** Hardly anyone would challenge the notion that schools, at least in democratic countries, should enculturate the young into an understanding of the constitutional system and the nature of representative government. But in many schools, often the study of democracy is limited to descriptions of structures and processes of government situated in "majority rule." Social democracy, however, represents a more complex and difficult idea: that all citizens and institutions of a democracy must adhere to broad democratic principles—freedom, liberty, justice, equality, and fairness; one of balancing individual rights against the common good.

Several colleagues and I have argued in our writings that "democracy implies both a process and goal, that the two, while often contradictory, cannot be separated. Democratic processes cannot justify undemocratic ends. For example, we cannot justify racial and gender inequity on the basis that the majority voted for it. While this dual-referenced test for democracy is not simple or clean, and while it often requires us to choose between two incompatible choices, both in the name of democracy, we can conceive of no other way to approach it." Enculturating young people into the principles of this social and political democracy is at the heart of the civil society we value and at the heart of schools' moral responsibility to society. Only through the realization of both process and product can we secure a democratic way of life.

Quote from: Richard Quantz, Nelda Cambron-McCabe, and Michael Dantley, "Preparing School Administrators for Democratic Authority," *The Urban Review* Vol. 23 (1991), pp. 3–19.

2. **Access to knowledge:** "The school," Goodlad notes, "is the only institution in our society specifically charged with providing to the young a disciplined encounter with all the subject matters of the human conversation: the world as a physical and biological system; evaluative and belief systems; communication systems; the social, political, and economic systems that make up the global village; and the human species itself." Most people in our society would identify access and engagement with knowledge as the primary goal of education.

   Yet some of the greatest inequities in schooling occur around access to knowledge. Goodlad reminds us that "the educative processes advanced by schools must go far beyond the mere recapitulation of information…[Educators] must be diligent in ensuring that no attitudes, beliefs, or practices bar students from access to the necessary knowledge." When school practices result in maldistribution of knowledge with poor and minority students receiving less access, it is morally wrong "whatever the arguments regarding teachable classes, teachers' comfort, parents' preferences, and even achievement."

3. **Nurturing Pedagogy:** A nurturing pedagogy is the art and science of teaching that provides nourishment, support, and encouragement for all children to promote their learning at various stages of their development. "The epistemology of teaching," Goodlad asserts, "must encompass a pedagogy that goes far beyond the mechanics of teaching. It must combine generalizable principles of teaching, subject-specific instruction, sensitivity to the pervasive human qualities and potentials always involved, and full awareness of what it means to simultaneously 'draw out' and enculturate." A teacher's failure to create an intellectually reflective, engaging classroom for learning is not simply malpractice, it is immoral, particularly for students who do not have the option of withdrawing.

4. **Responsible stewardship of schools:** Who is responsible for creating high-quality schools that meet the needs of all students? Goodlad points to teachers as moral stewards along with principals. If the school site, as many argue, is the center of change for substantive renewal, it can be accomplished only if teachers are involved in creating and sustaining schoolwide change, not simply improving efforts in their own classrooms. Such involvement means teachers seeing the educational dynamics in all classrooms across the building as their responsibility. "Teachers," argues Goodlad, "must be critically inquiring stewards of schools."

Being a steward involves more than talking together about improving schools—it requires reflecting, studying, inventing, and rethinking, and always in a context that is morally explicit. In recent years, for example, technical rationalists have held sway in educational policy circles. They argue that pragmatic solutions work, no matter what the ideology, and that most methods of teaching are "value neutral." One has only to look at the vast number of publications addressing school improvement that are directed primarily at "how to fix schools" to see the impact of this thinking. States become preoccupied with establishing standards and measuring student outcomes through tests. Educators focus their attention on techniques and strategies to respond to the policymakers' mandates, often narrowing the curriculum and increasing the emphasis on rote learning.

Educators opposed to technical rationalism can argue that it is less effective in the long run—can, in effect, make technical arguments against it. But a steward would oppose it as inherently immoral. Students, who are already disadvantaged by the existing system, now see no possibility of passing proficiency tests or completing the more rigorous course work required for graduation. They are simply leaving the system in large numbers. High-poverty schools and school districts struggle to hire qualified teachers; teaching vacancies are difficult if not impossible to fill. Educational stewardship is necessary to raise these issues: to recognize that high standards are important to assure that students receive better opportunities for educational success, but to insist that standards be set in the context of the school's mission, vision, and capabilities. Without a complex curriculum, one that promotes thinking and reasoning and is taught by qualified teachers, rationalistic standards will penalize those students who have the greatest needs.

Goodlad sees the first two dimensions, enculturation and access to knowledge, as primarily the responsibility of schools, while nurturing pedagogy and stewardship represent arenas where teachers must excel in their individual practice. As stewards, teachers focus their work on the other three moral dimensions of schooling: enculturating children into a social and political democracy, ensuring all students access to knowledge, and practicing a nurturing pedagogy.

QUESTIONS FOR REFLECTION

As you engage this book and its exercises, raising explicit questions about the moral aspects of schooling will lay the groundwork for confronting deeply embedded mental models about possibilities for schools and for students. In his book *The Reflective Practitioner*, Donald Schön reminds us of the limits of our reliance on technical rationality when we deal with issues involving uncertainty, uniqueness, and value conflict. More often than not, problems encountered by educators involve conflicting frames and values that cannot be resolved by drawing on technical knowledge. Yet these indeterminate zones of practice are the most central to professional work.

See Donald Schön, *The Reflective Practitioner* (Basic Books, 1984).

- **How do I critique my teaching, my classroom, and my school?** The powerlessness we often experience comes from our own assumptions and beliefs about organizations. Instead of seeing our organizations as socially constructed, we view them as having a life of their own. "Schools have always looked this way; classrooms in every school system function this way." Yet we know kids fall through the cracks every year. We know we are not reaching all the kids in our own classroom, but we know other teachers aren't either. So we don't have to feel bad about it, because we're doing what we can and what is expected of us.

  If, however, you consider our ethical responsibility, what action do you take? In one school, the teachers said, "It doesn't have to be this way." They decided that, in spite of the fact that many students move in and out of that school in the course of a year, they would follow each child who remained through the elementary grades with a detailed history. For example, as a child moves from second grade to third grade, the teacher notes that even though the child is being passed to the next grade level, there are weaknesses that require special attention. The record includes a thorough analysis of all previous assessment results—not merely quantitative data but descriptive information noting strengths and weaknesses as well as instructional strategies that have been successful. This practice is not just a technique the teachers implemented; it is a process that grew out of their collective concern for all the students in the school. Today, these students no longer simply arrive at the next grade level with their new teacher trying to figure out during the first few weeks, or even months, of class what the specific academic needs are.

As individual teachers, often we do not look closely at the overall conditions of learning for students in our schools. "We teach different students different things," points out Kati Haycock, president of the Education Trust. Her nonprofit organization has amassed astounding data about disparities in schools: Low-income high school students are less likely to be enrolled in a college preparatory track (28 percent compared to 65 percent for high-income students); classes in high-poverty high schools are more often taught by under-qualified teachers; fewer African American high school graduates complete advanced math and science courses; and math and science classes with a high percentage of minority students are more often taught by under-qualified teachers. Her data includes extensive statistics but also many observations of high school classes. She tells of differences in two English classes in a high school. In one, a high-ability-track class, the students were reading complex books and writing in-depth critical analyses of the authors' imagery, writing style, and so on. In the other class, a lower-level section, students were drawing posters for book reports. The second group of students, without opportunities to develop their writing and thinking skills, has little chance of entering or succeeding in postsecondary education.

In bringing the language of critique, we ask, "Who benefits by the present structure? Who is harmed by it? What values does it affirm?" These questions challenge highly bureaucratic school structures that weaken the voices of all participants. Bringing such critique to school organizations enables us to see how certain practices are legitimated and maintained. It forces us to face the moral issues surrounding the uneven distribution of many privileges and rights. We come to understand the consequences of defining the curriculum in terms of specific performance objectives rather than in terms of student needs. Equity and social justice issues become evident.

You can begin this critique with some of the issues raised here or begin with your own. Consider what is the impact and whose interests are served by: current grading practices, student discipline policies, tracking of students, standardized testing, level of school funding, extracurricular opportunities?

⟩⟩ See "The Dignity of the Child," page 177, and "What Signals Are You Sending?," page 204.

■ **Do I work to alter the learning conditions of my school?** Critical to moral purpose is the way in which teachers define their role in the broader context of the school. As my coauthors and I have collaborated on this book, we continually return to the point that a teacher's commitment to students' learning plays out on the classroom, school, and community levels. This commitment means working actively to change policies and practices that may marginalize many students, whether they exist in your own classroom, in the school building, or in the community at large.

Where does one start? A high school English teacher moved to a highly respected, racially diverse urban high school. All freshmen were taught in teams of one hundred students and assigned to six different ability levels. Within the first few days, she became acutely aware that almost no African American students were assigned to the highest-ability team, and the lowest-ability team was almost entirely African American students. She asked her colleagues, "Don't you think something is wrong here?" Their response: "That is how it has always worked in this school." Her frustration increased when she realized that the best teachers taught only the brightest kids and had fewer students in their classes. "Morally and ethically," she argued, "we are obligated to place our best teachers with our neediest students. Smaller class size is absolutely necessary to address individual learning difficulties."

Following extended conversations over several years, the school reconfigured its team structure so that now all teachers teach all ability levels. "Most teams are still homogeneously structured," notes this teacher. "However, we are continuing to refine the team assignments, carefully matching teachers and students. A few teachers still lament that the new arrangements are not fair to the more senior teachers who have earned the right to teach the highest-level students. But we are moving beyond that concern; the most important point for us is that we no longer ignore the inequities we have created."

Taking no individual responsibility for schoolwide practices may permit many routine decisions to adversely affect some students. A high school counselor in a large East Coast high school described an incident where two students transferred in around midyear. The first, a Caucasian student who had flunked out of an elite prep school and had low test scores, was placed in the college preparatory track. The second, an African American student who had a high grade point average and high test scores was assigned to the general education track. When the counselor questioned these assignments, she was told the placements were necessary to keep the number of students somewhat evenly distributed across the levels and that the Caucasian student's parents would never tolerate the assignment of their son to the general level.

According to data from the Education Trust, such occurrences are not unusual. Even with the problems inherent in relying on performance and ability measures, these are not always used neutrally to make decisions about students' access to programs.

Both of these high school stories poignantly capture the moral dilemmas facing teachers today. We can either accept the system as it exists or exercise moral agency and actively protect the interests of all students.

■ **Do I inquire about the ends of schooling or just the means of schooling?** Peter Vaill talks about the importance of every organization knowing, understanding, and engaging its "purpose story." This story reminds us constantly what we are about and has profound meaning for our organization's learning. For educators, engaging in the purpose story represents a serious inquiry into "Why are students in school? For what purpose?" Neil Postman uses an interesting metaphor to distinguish means from ends. "We can make the trains run on time," Postman argues, "but if they do not go where we want them to go, why bother?" And, I would add, "Why bother unless we know where they are going or care deeply about where they might go?"

■ **Do I engage in continuous inquiry?** Inquiry is thoughtful, reflective, and informed deliberation about one's practice: Why do I structure interaction in my classroom as I do? How does it impact students? What data from my practice leads me to believe that this is the best way? What other alternatives might I consider? Who else can help me in this deliberation? How can I sustain collective inquiry with my colleagues? While the inquiry process can be informal or quite formal, it is always systematic and continuous.

Kenneth Sirotnik, who was on the educational leadership faculty at the University of Washington before he passed away, posed a few questions that educators can use to assess the depth and extent of their own inquiry. These questions provide a beginning point for your own reflection or for dialogue with colleagues.

■ To what extent does the organizational culture support you as inquirers into what you do and how you might do it better?

■ To what extent do you engage competently in discourse and action to improve the conditions, activities, and outcomes of schooling?

■ To what extent do you care about yourself and each other in the same way you care (or ought to care) about students?

This concept comes from Peter B. Vaill, "The Purposing of High-Performing Systems," in Thomas Sergiovanni and John Corbally (editors), *Leadership and Organizational Culture* (University of Illinois Press, 1986), pp. 93–101. The quote from Neil Postman comes from Neil Postman, *The End of Education: Redefining the Value of School* (Knopf, 1995), p. 61.

John Goodlad, Roger Soder, and Kenneth Sirotnik, *The Moral Dimensions of Teaching,* (Jossey-Bass, 1990), p. 312, 314.

- To what extent are you empowered to participate authentically in pedagogical matters of fundamental importance, such as what schools are for and how teaching and learning can be aligned with this vision?

In her book *Why Are All the Black Kids Sitting Together in the Cafeteria?* Beverly Tatum relates a powerful lesson of our individual ethical responsibilities. While she was traveling on a book tour, a white interviewer expressed despair at the lack of change and even the worsening conditions of race relations and economic inequality. The interviewer used his own racially mixed community as an example.

Tatum describes the exchange this way: "Here was a place, he said, where people of color and white people lived together as neighbors, and yet there was little meaningful interaction across racial lines; no dialogue took place. He lamented, 'We just don't have the leaders we used to have; we don't have the leaders we need.' I paused and then asked, 'Well, if you are interested in dialogue, have you invited anyone to your house to talk about these issues? You are a person who has a sphere of influence. How are you using it to make things different?'" Tatum concludes by quoting Gandhi: "[We need to] be the change we want to see happen."

As educators, we also must look at what we do as individuals to renew the schooling conditions around us. Are we waiting for others to lead the change?

Beverly Daniel Tatum, *Why Are All the Black Kids Sitting Together in the Cafeteria?* (Basic Books, 1999), p. xi.

IMAGES OF ORGANIZATION
by Gareth Morgan (Sage Publications, 1986, 1997)

We don't work for school systems, we work for our perceptions of them. York University professor Gareth Morgan portrays seven mental models that influence the ways people act in organizations: the organization as machine, living organism, brain, culture, political system, psychic prison, flux and transformation, and domination. When I teach organizational theory, I always assign this book. Students connect these metaphors to their lives, and they don't forget them. They create and re-create the metaphors as they move on to work in real school systems, and their increased facility in moving from metaphor to metaphor (which is the underlying purpose of the book) gives them a much stronger presence in whatever kind of organization they work for. Developing and thinking through images of organization is soul work. —Nelda Cambron-McCabe

CULTURAL PROFICIENCY AND
CULTURALLY PROFICIENT LEADERSHIP

Cultural Proficiency: A Manual for School Leaders, by Randall B. Lindsey, Kikanza Nuri Robins, Raymond D. Terrell (Corwin Press, 2nd Edition, 2003); *Culturally Proficient Leadership: The Personal Journey Begins Within,* by Raymond D. Terrell and Randall B. Lindsey (Corwin Press, 2009).

"Why do we have to read more textbooks about diversity?" asked the graduate student, in an almost defiant tone. It was one of those teachable moments that the authors of these books describe. I responded with another question, "Why do you think the texts are about diversity?" and we were off on a semester-long adventure of teaching and learning.

These books are not primarily about diversity, although that element is present in the examples. They are about helping school leaders, and future school leaders, effect individual and organizational change, and respond effectively to people who are different from us. As the authors remind us, we are all different from each other in fundamental, if not visible, ways. One of the tools, the "cultural continuum," teaches a common language to describe practice and behavior. I consistently find that this foundation of common language provides a structure to move beyond personal affronts to a deeper understanding of the transforming power of cultural mores and cultural difference. —Ellen Bueschel

IX. School Vision

1. A Shared Vision for Your School

Bryan Smith, Tim Lucas

The lights go down in a high school auditorium, the school orchestra stops playing, and the superintendent of schools steps onto the stage. "We've worked really hard," she says, "we've taken all of your concerns into account, and here it is: The vision for our school district for this year and into the future." A large cloth banner unfurls with a slogan sewn into it. The words seem to symbolize the concerns that members of this community have, and those of teachers as well. They were considered with great care by the superintendent and a carefully chosen team over the course of a two-day retreat.

SV

Everyone in the audience applauds. The superintendent looks with appreciation over the crowd, thinking, "Well, we've shared our vision. Now we'll show what we can do."

But it is highly unlikely that a brief process, such as a two-day retreat and a two-hour assembly, can lead to a true shared vision—a vision that draws out the commitment of people throughout a school or school system. In the year after that assembly, you might hear the superintendent say, "Once again, we've proved that people spend all their time complaining. They're obviously not interested in doing anything more. We'll just have to decide everything at the central office from now on." You also might hear teachers, parents, and staff members say, "It's obvious that the school district really has no interest in anything except its own ideas." Both of these attitudes are symptoms of the fact that no deliberate, strategic design of a shared visioning process occurred.

But now imagine that an assembly takes place—in the same auditorium, with the same audience, an identical banner, and the same orchestra playing. This time, however, the hour on stage represents the culmination of a year of intensive conversation and dialogue. Everyone in the audience has taken part in at least one related session, talking about their aspirations for the children of the district. The resulting vision is a creative synthesis of all that has emerged. It is like a diamond with many diverse facets, and each member of the audience sees his or her own aspirations reflected there.

Six months later the process continues. People throughout the school district continue to meet in small groups and teams, sometimes in school facilities and sometimes in one another's homes. Every group contains teachers, parents, staff, administrators, and outside community members. Many groups contain students. Conversations focus on what people can do, individually and as teams, to move toward the vision. The pride, energy, and commitment that people feel is even more evident than it had been in the auditorium six months before.

This is the power of a full-scale shared vision process for the school: a process of involving everyone together in deciding and developing the future of the school system. It doesn't mean taking people's input, selecting some of it, and discarding the rest. It means establishing a series of forums where people work together to forge the future direction of the school. None of the participants (including the superintendent) will get all the outcomes in the exact form desired; but all will get outcomes they respect and can make a commitment to. Moreover, in a well-designed process, the relevant choices are better than those that any individual, including the most capable superintendent, or school board could come up with on his or her own.

For more on Shared Vision processes, see pages 94–95 and 216.

THE OVERALL PROCESS DESIGN

A good shared vision process design has three separate but related purposes. First, it addresses pent-up tensions over current problems and concerns. People, both individually and collectively, experience enormous relief when the system finally gives voice to their problems and concerns. Second, a shared vision process must be generative: People must be able to talk about their deepest hopes and desires for their children and community. Only then can they recognize the source of each other's aspirations, enough to generate momentum and mutual trust.

Third, the process leads to action. People must have the inherent satisfaction of re-creating the school together, with one another's support— including the support of those whom they have mistrusted in the past.

Schools are partnerships, in effect, among teachers, legislators, parents, and community members—all of whom already act autonomously. Thus, a shared vision effort in school should begin by calling people to come together to think and act, with the power they already have, about the things that are important to them.

If you are a leader of this process, either a formal leader or a key participant, do whatever you can to encourage work on personal vision and personal mastery before the shared vision process begins. Look dispassionately at your own strengths and weaknesses as a leader of this process. How do you best communicate? What pressures are you under, and how do you respond to those pressures? What confidence do people have in you, and on what do they base that confidence? How much time do you have available for this effort? Will that be enough? Are you already aware of the visions, goals, and feelings of people throughout the school system, and how curious are you to find out what you don't already know? Most important of all: What is your personal vision for the school system? When you begin talking about generating a vision for the school, you will be called upon to speak authentically about its personal meaning for you and your commitment to it.

⟩⟩ See "Drawing Forth Personal Vision," page 81.

Three Images of School This Year Tim Lucas

Purpose:
To help open up conversations among parents, students, and educators in a shared vision process.

Before the exercise, the session leader needs to canvass a group of students (from the relevant grades) ahead of time: What would you like to learn in school this year? What kinds of things would make it a good school year? Then canvass a group of teachers: What would you like your class to accomplish this year? Record the answers as lists on chart pages, and keep the pages hidden during step 1.

STEP 1: PARENTS
Ask parents about their hopes: What would you like your children to learn this year in school? What would you like your children's experience to be?

STEP 2: STUDENTS
Now reveal the flip chart where you previously wrote down the children's expectations. This moment can be both fun and poignant. It often disarms the parents, because it shows how they and their children hold different mental models of school.

xamples of comments raised by this exercise:

PARENTS:

My child will: Get along with other children.

Get attention and recognition.

Be in a very good place to play.

Speak French like my nephew in another district.

Count and begin arithmetic.

Paint, draw, and make music.

Learn to love school.

STUDENTS:

I'm going to learn to read.

I'll get to play on the school playground.

I'll learn to go off the high dive.

I'll get to stay up later.

I'll learn to write like my sister does.

I'll get my driver's license.

I'll see my friend every day.

TEACHERS:

We get through a good curriculum.

We meet state standards and all students move up.

Children develop social competencies.

We get to know children and determine special needs.

We provide opportunities for parent involvement.

STEP 3: TEACHERS

Now reveal the third chart, also prepared ahead of time, of mental models held by teachers and staff. Here again you will see a different viewpoint (see examples in the margin). This view arises from the teachers' training, the structures of their schools and districts, and the goals set by the district and the state.

STEP 4: MAKING CONNECTIONS

Display all three mental models so they can be seen at the same time, with the differences and similarities sinking in as people recognize the three images of learning on the wall. Check off as many similarities as possible. These represent starting points for creating common goals.

Then talk through the differences. What might lead the children, or their teachers, to see a successful kindergarten year so differently? (You may be able to provide some insight here.)

The group will usually add new items to its own list. If each model is valid to the people who put them there, what does that suggest parents might do differently?

VARIATION: "THE TRUTH ABOUT KIDS IS…"

For parents who have already been through the previous exercise, this variation may be more interesting. In our district, this is usually conducted by a local social worker who works closely with us. She brings a series of cards on which "The truth about kids" has been printed, followed by a statement:

- "They want to argue about everything."
- "They understand more than you think they do."
- "They do what you do, not what you say."
- "They are natural systems thinkers."
- "They tell you 'yes' even when they mean 'no.'"
- "They do better when someone is watching."
- "They don't know how to share."

Distribute the cards, at random, to the parents and then say, "These are statements people have made about kids. Will you read yours aloud and make any statement you want about them?"

The first parent will read: "They don't like being singled out." And she will say, "Well, that's not true of my kid. He's always trying to get on stage somehow." But someone else will say, "But it is true of my kid."

And what, the facilitator then says, might that suggest about the needs of the school? As you go around the room, the conversation naturally turns to parents' attitudes about the way school ought to be based on their own school experience. One of the best ways to help them break free of this is to ask them to think about the different nature of children today. "Was your life as scheduled as your child's life? If you're like me, you used to play more on your own. They're more used to structure." And so on.

Community Vision Meetings   Tim Lucas, Bryan Smith

These meetings need a lot of planning and design, but the value—in building relationships among parents, school leaders, and the community—is immense. Assign seats in advance, arranging tables for heterogeneity—a kindergarten parent new to the building might sit next to a parent of a fifth grader whose oldest child is already in college. Each has something to learn from the other. The parents of older children can reassure the parents of younger children that everything will work out fine. The parents of younger children, in turn, remind the parents of older children of the way they saw their families several years earlier.

Each table works together. First, people introduce themselves and then go around the table, brainstorming every issue, concept, and concern that they have about the school and their children. Their list might include twenty to thirty ideas per table. Next, the table-team members select the five most critical concepts, writing each one on a separate card or large self-sticking note. Then, on another set of cards, they answer two questions for each of the five main ideas: What should be the role of the school in addressing this issue? What should be the role of parents?

After forty-five minutes of discussion, ask the table-teams to present their ideas to the whole, posting them for all to see. It will soon become clear that seven or eight concepts recur, table after table. Draw these out to be discussed by the full group. They might include concerns about curriculum, extracurricular activities, social standing ("My child is continually picked on"), safety, homework, teaching approach, or anything. Once the concerns are all posted, the interconnectedness of ideas and concerns can be looked for, moving cards together if they cover a similar theme or if they seem to contradict. While one group might have written a card on "increasing access to technology," another group might have written "our children should be global citizens." These ideas naturally lead to questions about the school's approach to social media like Facebook. If several groups have come up with a common theme, that con-

Purpose:

To build relationships and open the door to a shared vision process for a school and its community.

Overview:

A one- or two-day annual school community meeting.

Participants:

These large-scale dialogues can accommodate as many as eighty to one hundred parents along with a group of school leaders.

Environment:

A large meeting hall with enough space for breakout sessions at separate tables. The design for these sessions is derived from community vision meetings held at the Willard Elementary School in Ridgewood, New Jersey, during the 1990s.

cern has extra weight, and the cards should be embellished, grouped, and emphasized.

Now the group, as a whole, has a sense of one another's priorities around problems and crises. The leader can introduce other problems and issues that weren't generated from the tables but that emerged from process one. Having talked about current reality, people should feel some sense of closure. They don't know what's coming next, but they know that their critical concerns have been raised. They are ready to talk about a shared vision for the school system.

The session so far has probably taken a full day or evening. Now, in a separate session, return with the same group, once again broken into table-teams (preferably different teams), and ask each table's team members to imagine that they have created, three years from now, the school system they most want. Have them consider the questions below, one by one, painting an ever-clearer shared vision.

Describe the children who attend this ideal school. What kinds of things take place during a typical day? What range of subjects is taught? How are those subjects taught? What do children know at any particular age level? What knowledge do teachers have? What relationships do teachers and students have? How are parents involved? What is the relationship between the school and the community? What does the building look like? How does the school handle its children's academic and social needs? How does the school raise money? What happens to the graduates? What expectations and information are given to parents who come to the school? How is the student's achievement assessed?

Ask each table, once again, to prioritize. Groups should select five (to ten) of the components of greatest interest that they would most like to see in the school they envision. These concerns should be presented to the full group and consolidated with the ideas of the other tables.

Since this activity still represents only a midpoint in the process, the group does not need to reach agreement about the most desired components of the shared vision. People do need to feel, however, that their most desired aspirations for the district were heard (and ideally, were heard coming from others). From here, your goal is to establish alignment by bringing the vision process to the existing school teams and committees whose members now need to incorporate the new visions into the work they're already doing.

Refining and Implementing the Vision Tim Lucas

Every school has a team or committee, composed of administrators, teachers, parents, and sometimes students, responsible for overall school planning. (Some states, such as New Jersey, require them by law.) In this process, the "central vision team" becomes the visible fulcrum of the school's future. Its members think through and internalize the comments from the two previous exercises and develop key strategic priorities for the school.

For an alternative approach see "Parent to Parent," page 491.

The following checklist can help the central planning team make sure that it has considered every key aspect of a school's vision, current reality, and strategic priorities. It takes about a year for a committee to consider these issues, more or less in order; then it's time to start at the beginning again. The vision itself should stay strong and evocative of genuine aspiration during this stage—while the view of current reality remains clear and candid.

1. **Vision:** Based on the previous processes, what are the critical aspects of a school vision called for by the school's constituents? If the vision were realized, how would the curriculum, the design of the school system, the mix of classes and offerings, and all other factors fit together? Create a description—not as the final word, but as a starting point for further dialogue. If these components were in place, what would that get you? You may not reach the goals you set here, but you need them to help you, and others, chart your direction.

2. **Current reality:** How are student needs changing? Compare data on demographics: enrollment, attendance, drop-out rates, ethnicity of the student body, gender, grade level distribution, and language proficiency with that of previous years. What processes and programs work best today for different groups of students with respect to student learning? How have these assessments changed over time? How has student performance changed, year by year? How has the quality of instruction, overall, changed over time? Do students, parents, and teachers perceive the school as a learning environment? What observations do they make of the school and classrooms? Finally, look closely at the teacher training, school goals, educational philosophy, and school climate.

3. **Strategic priorities:** What are we going to do first to get closer to realizing our vision? How can staff and curriculum development be improved? How can the school environment be improved? Consider

This exercise is adapted in part from Victoria Bernhardt, "Multiple Measures," in *Data Analysis for Comprehensive Schoolwide Improvement* (Eye on Education Inc., 1998), p. 15.

security, community relationships, facilities, student needs, parking, and traffic. Where can parents drop off and pick up their children with less fear of traffic? What resources are available?

ACCOUNTABLE TEAMS

Having identified strategic priorities, the central committee now sets up "accountable teams" to develop them into new projects. These teams do not so much implement policies as develop a vision for one particular area of the school, establish a few critical first goals, and experiment with reaching those goals.

You might set up a technology committee, for instance, with parents, community members, teachers, students, and a member of the board of education. This group might oversee computer use and Internet access. There might also be a school climate committee ("What kind of intellectual environment do we want to create? How should we talk to each other?"); an assessment committee to look at portfolios, tests, and other forms of student assessment; and various program teams. Each team picks two measurable goals for every annual cycle, articulates their relationship to the overall emerging school vision, creates pilot projects to fulfill those goals, evaluates the pilots, and reports, at the end of the year, on their results (and their interpretation of the results).

REFLECTION AND REFINEMENT

Vision is more powerful in light of experience. Thus, convene a large reflective session, once again with eighty to 200 people, at the end of each school year. The purpose: to reconsider and refine the vision for the school, to hear reports about this year's pilot efforts, and to add new goals and bring new problems to the surface. As with previous stages, the meeting is divided into a session on current reality ("What is happening right now with the school system?"), a session on vision ("What do we want to create here?"), and a session on strategic priorities ("Where do we choose to put our attention?").

The shared vision initiative is powerful because it is continuous. Parents develop a deeper understanding of the forces that drive the school and the ways they might get involved with the school. Teachers broaden their awareness of the potential resources and opportunities that exist in the school outside their classroom. Most importantly, the old culture of cynicism begins to shift. In the past, people might come to the leader and, in effect, download their concerns and complaints. Now they are automatically invited into a process where they don't just look at problems but at their desired future; where they don't just talk but act; and where they don't run out of steam but continue in a constructive fashion, seeing the fruits of their efforts unfold, year after year.

Finding a Partner Janis Dutton, Tim Lucas, Nelda Cambron-McCabe, Bryan Smith

Teaching can be one of the most isolated professions. If you are a teacher, the bulk of your time may be spent separated from colleagues and peers. In many schools, if you want time for creative innovation with other teachers, you must schedule it yourself.

This is one reason that building shared vision is so difficult in schools. The structure of your schedule may tempt you to start innovating on your own, making changes in your classroom. But an innovative classroom without active links to the world around it is not sustainable. We know of creative teachers whose innovations didn't last long, even with passive encouragement from their principals and other teachers. Why? They couldn't invent everything they needed by themselves, and they had nobody to invent with. They operated in isolation.

Even in an educational system without time or resources to implement new programs, finding a partner can be one of the most beneficial things that an educator can do. The energy generated by one person who is willing to take risks and try something new needs to find a release, much like electricity seeking a ground. An innovator needs someone to talk with for encouragement and perspective—and someone to grow with as an innovator. The flow of partnership benefits both people involved.

Bringing educators together for learning, in itself, is not a new concept. Many schools have experimented with collaborative learning efforts involving two or more teachers or administrators. These include team teaching, mentoring, "critical friends" (deputized to provide constructive criticism to each other), and, more recently, professional learning communities.

What do all these partnerships have in common? The partners are not there to make each other feel better but to make each other more effective by inventing together and experimenting with their inventions. This is a different dynamic from finding a sympathetic fellow educator with whom you can "dump" your bad feelings about staff development, administrative rules, or a tough class day. It is about creating something new together.

Finding a partner may seem like an obvious move, but it's not always easy to find such opportunities unless you deliberately seek them out. In reading this, you may already have identified a potential partner. (It may or may not be another teacher, administrator, parent, or community member.) If not, there are many ways to test potential partners in a school. Find an article you resonate with (or perhaps a section of this book), and hand it to someone you've teamed with before. Ask what he or she thinks of it. Try a new activity with someone in your building or community. Start slowly and gently; you are, after all, asking someone to make a commitment to your future growth as a teacher and a person, and you are making a commitment to that person. Your future partner may or may not agree philosophically with your professional values or opinions, but he or she will be prepared to travel with you and learn along the way.

SV   MM

2. Renewing Educational Leadership

Re-creating a University Department Around Guiding Ideas for What it Means to be a School Leader

Nelda Cambron-McCabe

As I observe school districts and university departments attempting to accomplish change, I am always struck by the importance of organizations having a clear understanding of their fundamental purpose and a set of guiding ideas that govern them. Too often in curriculum re-design, the faculty starts by talking about the specific courses or "skills" that are needed. From these courses or skills, they find themselves backing into their core purpose at a later point in time. That means no matter how worthy, the program always will represent an incremental refinement of programs of the past. Yet the most fundamental and sustainable changes always seem to begin when the members of the faculty and the administration sit down together to ask each other: "Why do we exist? What do we want to accomplish? What do we stand for? What do we believe about teaching and learning?"

Peter Senge's quote is taken from *The Fifth Discipline Fieldbook*, p. 23.

}} See "Shared Vision," page 86, and "Are You Smarter Than a Thermostat?," page 151.

"Every organization, whether it deliberately creates them or not," says Peter Senge, "is governed according to some explicit principles." These principles are "guiding ideas"—concepts that define what an organization stands for and what its members desire to create.

Guiding ideas have philosophical depth and are never fixed and permanent. They do not result from single conversations, accreditation or curriculum reviews, or one-day retreats. Instead, they evolve from prolonged reflection and conversation and continue to evolve through the implementation of new programs and strategies. These guiding ideas represent much more than formal vision and mission statements; they are shared visions that shape and reshape the organization in fundamental ways and are intimately tied to the organization's identity and core purpose.

I experienced this evolution firsthand during the early 1990s, when I was part of an influential renewal effort at Miami University in Oxford, Ohio. The Department of Educational Leadership (where I am a faculty member and former department chair) achieved significant recognition for redesigning its graduate programs to produce more reflective, transformative school administrators—by helping them learn how to be leaders rather than managers. But we did not start with the idea of reinventing school leadership. Rather, we simply felt that our existing program in school administration did not prepare individuals to meet the complexity of the changing world in PK–12 schools. We were sure that if we looked we'd find notable programs at other universities that would provide us with a roadmap for preparing people as capable school leaders.

So we looked. Guess what? Other universities were doing essentially the same things we were doing. This fact did not comfort us. It meant we would have to create a new model on our own. With that position, we cleared the table and said, "Let's think from scratch about what today's PK–12 schools confront, what kids need, what school administrators can bring as creative leaders, and what we as a faculty can bring to foster the kind of leadership that is needed to change schools."

From our department of eighteen faculty members, we established a core group of five individuals for intensive, ongoing conversations. We started at the beginning: If we could do anything we wanted in education, what would we change and what did we really believe? We selected readings from people who were in the forefront of thinking differently about leadership and schools. These readings supported the conversation and pushed our thinking. We felt that schools were failing to meet the needs of society; yet most universities trained educational administrators to maintain the status quo. Future administrators were being handed skills and knowledge that had little meaning in helping them change their organizations. We began to develop a vision for our department of educating school leaders who could transform schools. We deliberately talked about "reconstructing" schools, to imply not just a revision of some policies, but a practice of challenging the fundamental assumptions under which they operated.

At the same time, it made no sense to educate leaders for a future that did not yet exist while failing to educate them to survive (and thrive) until that future arrived. We wanted the graduates of our program to be seen (and to see themselves) as successful from the moment they assumed leadership positions. That success, in turn, would give them the leverage they needed for change—as long as they continued to have the support they needed to keep raising questions about their fundamental assumptions.

The value of dialogue and skillful discussion as tools for team learning became increasingly evident. David Bohm has remarked that the closest thing to dialogue that many of us have had are late-night conversations in college dorms, where conversation moves from one topic to the other but without an announced purpose. As the core group continued to meet, we recognized the creative potential of first suspending our own assumptions and beliefs and having deep conversations around more global ideas, instead of trying to make quick decisions.

From time to time during our deliberations, we regularly convened the entire faculty to respond and create shared meaning. Initially, as ideas were introduced, we would sit around the table and say, "Well, yes, we believe that." Yet as we attempted to move to the next level of engagement, it became apparent that we held quite different conceptions of the same words or statements. In these early meetings, dialogue was not possible, but the tools of team learning were invaluable to unearth the mental models we each held about our work.

See "Team Learning," page 115, and "Balancing Advocacy and Inquiry," page 104.

We talked about the definition of leadership; the place of schools in society; the cultural, political, and moral contexts of schools; and school leadership as an intellectual, moral, and craft practice. Over time we went back and forth, sometimes with the help of outside facilitators, until we arrived at a set of core beliefs and principles that would help us achieve our shared vision: to produce transformative educational leaders.

Sometimes I speak or consult with groups at other universities trying to build a similar shared vision. They invariably ask how long it took to develop our guiding principles. When I say, "It took almost two years," the atmosphere in the room immediately changes. "That won't work for us," they say. "We've got to do this in the next six months. Our dean wants the program changed now." But I have to tell them: A shift of purpose in a graduate degree program is not like changing an academic course. It cannot be done in one semester, because everything in the program, including the people, must change together.

Making connections to people outside our department was critical to our effort. Funding from the Danforth Foundation linked us on a national scale with a few other university programs that were seeking change. Members of this national group critiqued our work and posed questions that deepened our thinking. The power of their questions forced us to think more deeply about our beliefs—our shared vision. The financial support also allowed us to persevere with an unusual project in the face of pressure on time and resources. This kind of soul-searching conversation cannot be rushed. Every person and every perspective must be given a chance to be heard and engaged. Mental models need to be surfaced, and deeply held beliefs need to be articulated and understood.

With our core beliefs developed, we moved into the creation of new curriculum. We began to talk about the alignment of our beliefs with the courses we wanted to develop. In proposing courses, we constantly came back to those core beliefs. As Gareth Morgan notes, the core beliefs become a referent for your work: They provide the "minimum critical specifications" that enable each aspect of the organization to evolve and at the same time be congruent with the vision for the overall organization. They're always there to help you gauge the value, importance, or significance of your decisions, particularly in chaotic times.

See Gareth Morgan, *Images of Organization* (Sage Publications, 1986, 1997), p. 110, reviewed on page 339.

Almost two decades later, the program still actively engages all members of the department. The process, in fact, has no end result—no stopping point. We regularly return to our core beliefs to check them against current reality and the current beliefs of "old" and newly hired faculty. Doing so is particularly vital because of faculty turnover. We also knew when we adopted the core principles that we could not just promote them for others to implement—we would have to model them in our own behavior and teaching as well. These core ideas have continued to evolve as new faculty joined, bringing significant new perspectives to our work.

Our process exemplifies the development of a shared vision through team learning. Without team learning, the department could not have embedded this new vision across the program. Without team learning, we would have had something that looked great on paper but with little or no meaningful changes in the program. After we created the principles and new curriculum, we did not return to our separate endeavors. We continued to learn together. During the first few years, many faculty members audited one another's courses. Our teaching is more powerful because we understand the ideas students are bringing in from other courses. We continue to have conversations about our guiding ideas and the ways they affect the content of our courses and our approaches to teaching.

In a sense, we all redesigned our lives to take part in building this program. (My decision to join in co-creating *Schools That Learn* was a natural outgrowth of that same commitment, because the work did not stop at the boundaries of my own organization.) Pedagogically, I teach differently now because of these principles and beliefs and my experience in developing and implementing them. I cannot imagine that I would ever go back to teaching the way I did before. The critical pedagogical issue for a faculty member, in my mind, is not the decision about whether to lecture or whether to facilitate interactive seminars. The critical point is: What kinds of issues and questions do you raise with students? Do you raise narrow, pragmatic questions, or do you invite them to consider the purpose of schools, to question school practices and structures that may disadvantage many students? If you do the latter, in the context of community, then you have opened the door to a pedagogy that can weave together the intellectual, moral, and craft dimensions of schooling. We would like to think that we have created that sort of pedagogy in our department, and to the extent it works, it works because we started by clearly defining our purpose and articulating guiding ideas.

Guiding Principles for School Leaders Facing Transformation   Nelda Cambron-McCabe, Richard Quantz

The transformation of the graduate programs in educational leadership at Miami University began with the development of some guiding ideas. The development of something as central as "guiding ideas" takes a lot of time and discussion. No organization can skip the investment of this time because part of the power of the development of guiding ideas results from the process of developing them. Because of our commitment to the process itself, we believe that no organization can merely import another's guiding ideas and be able to generate true commitment. Borrowed ideas and vision statements rarely have the power for another group that they do for the creators. But others' ideas can provide a place to begin one's own journey. They may be a good place to start.

The guiding principles that organized our reform efforts resulted from hours of conversation and consensus building. But while we repeatedly used the principles in our work, the guiding ideas were not formally written down until several of us began to publish pieces reflecting on our experiences. In those pieces, the guiding principles were presented as broad ideas influencing the direction of our program.

A few years after our program was launched, the two of us went back to our earlier writings and translated these works into a set of written principles. Although these principles were embedded in our original work and consciously engaged in our departmental conversations, we felt that explicitness and elaboration were necessary at that time. This process exposed the mental models behind our program and its structure. All departmental members, but particularly newer faculty and graduate students, needed the opportunity to engage the guiding ideas and make them their own. The principles needed to be examined against the current reality of our programs.

Some of the original guiding principles are briefly captured here.

- The field of educational leadership must be reconstructed so that the transformation of schools becomes its central focus. The schools we saw around us were failing to meet the needs of society, yet most educational administrators were trained to maintain the status quo. Administrators had been taught that organizations are rational, almost mechanistic, structures that operate in a bureaucratic manner. We believed that a shift needed to occur from thinking about the training of administrators to considering the education of leaders. This shift required a fundamental rethinking of schools and authority—a rethinking that recognized the centrality of culture, politics, and ethics in the everyday struggle of students, teachers, and administrators. Our vision shifted from administering schools to transforming them: from managing schools to challenging the fundamental assumptions under which they operate.

- The primary goal of public schools is to educate children for the responsibilities of citizenship in a democracy. In recent years, a plethora of private and individual interests have replaced the civic responsibilities of the schools. While recognizing that schools do have some responsibility to individual private goals, we believe that broader civic responsibilities must resume their place as the central mission of the public schools. As a result, we had to revisit our own curriculum and work practices and assure ourselves that these civic responsibilities held a central place.

- School leadership is an intellectual, moral, and craft practice. This principle is at the heart of our work; it shapes all other principles. We think the principle moves one from a management perspective to a leadership perspective. Leadership is more than a technical act emphasizing effectiveness and efficiency. Leadership is informed by multiple theoretical perspectives, drawing our attention to moral questions related to core purpose and values of our organizations.

At the same time, we felt that everyone involved in education, from university professors to educators in elementary and secondary schools, should be good practitioners. For this reason, our theory courses have a practice dimension to them. Originally we talked about the "technical" practice of education, but when we set out to capture what we meant by "technical," we realized the word was too narrow. We were talking about the craft of teaching and learning. Donald Schön, in criticizing the highly technical approach of professional schools, reminds us that many areas of our practice involve uncertainty, uniqueness, and value conflicts and cannot be resolved by drawing on technical theory and knowledge. According to Schön, we must look to the competence and artistry that is embedded in skillful practice. Gaining this craftlike wisdom involves a coaching dimension and a "learning by doing."

■ Educational practice must be informed by critical reflection—reflection situated in the cultural, political, and moral context of school. We wanted to teach people to be, as Schön put it, "reflective practitioners"—to reflect on their work and sort through the aftermath of their experiments in a systematic way but always within the context of culture, politics, and ethics. Most experienced teachers have tremendous knowledge of their craft, but they don't gain that knowledge in the classroom alone. It comes from systematic and informed reflection on their work—for example, thinking about how to modify practices or how to reach certain kids given our understanding of pedagogy or of cultural politics. Similarly, as leaders, we also learn from systematic and informed reflection—for example, thinking through the ways in which different groups can be engaged and connecting those ways to theories of organizational development. Critical reflection is more than just reflection. It is reflection that ties practice and theory together.

Critical reflection within the cultural, political, and moral context of schools is not simply taught in our program, but practiced. At one point, the university president called together a small group of faculty and asked, "What conversations do you have in your department about teaching?" Most of the faculty said they didn't talk about it at all—except when they had a program review or a new course, and then it was a formal committee exercise. But speaking for our department, I could say we had regular, fierce, and yet contemplative conversations where we said, "Here is the way we teach, and here are the reasons we believe in it."

■ Schools are sites of cultural politics. Thinking about schools as bureaucracies makes the political struggle around culture invisible. At best, such an approach places cultural politics outside the school organization and considers it an unnecessary intrusion on efficiency. But the politics of culture is not simply an external interference; it is the central activity of schooling itself. Becoming educated means learning culture. This fact becomes much clearer when we begin to think of schools not as bureaucracies but as arenas in which different ethnic or cultural groups struggle to get their culture (and, therefore, themselves) legitimated by the schools. If one is to be an effective school leader, one must understand the centrality of cultural politics to schools as organizations. Some people don't find this focus comfortable, and some prospective faculty members don't feel prepared to teach it. One candidate for a faculty position said, "I recognized, after the interview, that I should be entering your program as a student instead of as a faculty member!"

■ Leadership should not be equated with positions in a hierarchy. We deliberately challenged our own mental models about what it meant to be a leader. From our observations, most administrative programs taught leadership as a series of "best practices" to individuals who would be assuming administrative positions. Instead, we assumed that leaders could arise in any organizational position, and many people who were assigned to positions of authority might not be leaders. In that context, leadership became a quality of anyone's practice. To teach effective leadership, we would have to challenge people to think about what they did and what they created, instead of telling them what we thought was right. We also opened our program to different types of people seeking leadership roles in education—school administrators, teachers, social service workers, researchers, and other concerned citizens.

■ Diversity is not only a positive good; it is a necessary element of education. Diversity has become a catchword on university campuses as well as in PK–12 schools. Too often presented as an afterthought, diversity is typically advocated to achieve equity. While we believe that equity is an excellent reason for the pursuit of diversity, we also believe that there are other reasons central to the process of a good education that makes diversity a necessary, rather than just positive, characteristic. Like the well-known philosopher John Dewey, we recognized that all learning begins when our comfortable ideas are

Suggested readings for Educational Leadership Renewal: William Foster, *Paradigms and Promises: New Approaches to Educational Administration* (Prometheus Books, 1986); Ronald Heifetz, *Leadership Without Easy Answers* (Harvard University Press, 1994); Thomas Mulkeen, Nelda Cambron-McCabe, and Bruce Anderson (editors), *Democratic Leadership: The Changing Context of Administrative Preparation* (Ablex, 1994); Gareth Morgan, *Images of Organization* (Sage, 1997); Donald Schön, *Educating the Reflective Practitioner* (Jossey-Bass, 1987); Margaret Wheatley, *Turning to One Another: Simple Conversations to Restore Hope to the Future* (Berrett-Koehler Publishers, 2009).

found to be inadequate. And also like Dewey, we recognized that the diversity of ideas that comes with the diversity of people is one of the best ways to create this necessary condition of learning. We resolved to foster the diversity of ideas and to engage people who brought with them diverse personal and cultural histories. Doing that is absolutely necessary, we felt, for a vibrant intellectual education. Rather than a catchword or an afterthought, we wanted diversity to be a central guiding idea for our department.

■ A graduate program should be a "program," not a series of disparate courses. This principle implies a strong core purpose. When we embarked on our program reconstruction, we were asked by one of our facilitators, "What do you want from this process?" Without hesitation, we responded, "We want our program to have an identity. When people talk about our program, they will know what we stand for; they will know our commitment to school transformation, to issues of equity and social justice." To us, a program means that our guiding ideas will be evident throughout the course work and engagement among faculty and students.

■ Faculty and students must make a commitment to community. Community building is difficult in many schools because teachers tend to teach in isolation from one another, and their workday is scheduled tightly with little or no flexibility for conversation. In higher education, we teach our own specialties and conduct our own research with substantial autonomy and academic freedom. These conditions become barriers when trying to develop a culture where people take shared responsibility for the program as a whole and where courses are connected to each other.

The building and development of community, within the school and around it, must not be assumed but must be nurtured and supported continuously. We defined "community" as the dynamic set of relations among people, where each individual is invited to participate. We explicitly did not want people to mistake community for "thinking or looking alike," or as "everyone doing everything together." The community focus also meant that our vision would evolve continuously because we would need to welcome new people into the department. For example, when we consider changes in the doctoral program, we explicitly invite the recent additions to our community—faculty, staff, and graduate students—to talk about their understanding of the core principles and what they want to see happen.

■ While the primary focus of our department is on schooling at all levels, education should be considered broader than schooling. In ordinary life, people know the difference between education and schooling. Few adults confuse their education with merely what they learned in school. In fact, many people believe that schooling interfered with their education. Often those in the profession of schooling forget this distinction. The result is a defensiveness about school practices that may make for efficient schooling but poor education. We believed that keeping this distinction at the center of our conversation about school leadership would help us keep our eyes on what was important about schools—the education of young people.

While the development of these principles began our process of transformation, they continue to evolve with us. By having a set of guiding principles, we are able to focus our conversation as a community around some living ideas. As new members join our community, they are invited to engage and to reinterpret these ideas. In our discussions, those of us who have been here longer are able to use the principles as a vehicle to nurture institutional memory—not as an oppressive set of unmalleable traditions, but as a focus for reasoned, critical, and reflective conversation. In that way, we hope the principles work to encourage the continuous transformation of our own programs.

X. Current Reality

MM

1. Predetermined Uncertainty

How School Systems Can Use Scenario Planning to Prepare for the Turbulence of the Future

Art Kleiner

Thanks to Jay Ogilvy and Napier Collyns for their help, insight, and interest.

Like all organizations, schools continually suffer the temptation to guess what will happen in the future. Will enrollments rise or fall? Will the budget pass? Will standardized test scores rise or fall? Will state laws be more or less restrictive? Anyone who has tried to plan a budget knows that reality can easily shift in a way that makes all predictions moot; how many educators, for instance, foresaw the emergence of the Internet, social media, and the tablet, and the difference these would make to student reading, research, and conversation?

Scenario planning is a way to plan for the future without making a commitment to any particular prediction. Instead of guessing the most likely future, you imagine several futures simultaneously. All are plausible, and each has something important to tell you—some surprise that can help you see past your blind spots. You spend some time, as a school leadership team, imagining yourself in each of those future worlds and equip yourself to make decisions that will be robust no matter which future comes to pass.

Like many people practicing scenario planning today, I learned the craft from a small group of people closely tied to mainstream business. But the methods are even more appropriate to small, less business-oriented organizations, particularly schools. It doesn't cost a lot to conduct a scenario exercise; it requires very little advanced training; and while there's rigor to the method, a dedicated amateur facilitator can learn it very easily. (Indeed, I'd argue that it's better to have as facilitator an open-minded, flexible amateur with the skill of listening to people and summing up what they have to say on a flip chart than a seasoned scenario-planning veteran who doesn't listen well.) The point of the exercise is to take your uncertainty seriously: to give names to your fears and hopes; to recognize that there is something important to discern lurking in the distinctions between the facts you know for sure about the future and the facts you don't know at all.

One caveat: The practice is time-consuming. People often want to condense scenario work to a half-day or weekend session, but such efforts don't give people enough time to delve past their existing preconceptions. At Royal Dutch/Shell, planners generally take more than a year of intensive work to develop their scenarios. In schools, a scenario project could occupy a planning team for a semester or more, meeting once every few weeks; or it could make up the bulk of a week-long professional development session. I have seen it condensed into two one-day sessions, separated by a month, but only with a tightly knit group of educators, all administrators, who already were accustomed to working together.

STEP 1. THE SCENARIO QUESTION (HALF A DAY)

Scenarios provoke genuine learning only when they answer genuine concerns. Thus, you need at least three hours for this key step. If the participants are as diverse as most school constituents are, then articulating your focus will not be trivial. Ask one another: If we could ask an oracle only one or two facts about the future, what would those be?

Your "question for the oracle" will probably be more useful if it is aimed at a significant decision involving the investment of time, energy, and money—while facing an uncertain future. For example: How should you prepare for the special education needs of the next twenty years? The absolute right answer is unknowable right now. It depends on unpredictable changes in enrollment in your school system, evolving scientific understanding of conditions like autism and ADD, and budget restrictions that will rise or fall with the economy. You can't possibly know the conditions under which you'll have to operate, but you have to make a decision now, nonetheless. Similarly, when you face curriculum issues ("Should we change the math we teach?"), budget issues ("Should we expand the middle school?"), or strategy decisions ("How will we meet the new test requirements?"), you must commit yourself now without knowing exactly how each choice might fare. If you look back several years from now, your current options might seem prescient and others might seem ill-fated, and there's no way to tell for sure.

Pick the question that concerns you most regarding the decisions you have to make today. The exercise will help discern the patterns of forces at play and illuminate to your working group in a dispassionate way the hidden possibilities of each of your current options.

The "oracle question" was developed by Pierre Wack and adapted by Kees van der Heijden. For more on Pierre Wack and the history of scenario planning, see Art Kleiner, *The Age of Heretics* (Jossey-Bass, 2008), pp.121ff and 238ff.

Also pick the year in the future that the scenarios should look back from. How long a timeframe will the decisions you make now need to be concerned about? Scenarios for next year will be so close to current reality that they won't reveal much; scenarios for twenty years hence embody so many wildcard possibilities that it's difficult to learn from them. School scenarios often can be valuable by looking ten to fifteen years into the future, at least: long enough for many current students to move on into the next phase of their lives. By considering the world they might inhabit then, you can think about giving them what they need now.

2. DRIVING FORCES (TWO TO THREE DAYS)

Every year, we are affected by driving forces: factors in our external environment that shape our world, and over which we, as individuals, have little control. Some are relatively predictable. For twenty-five years, demographers have known that the global population would reach seven billion around 2010 (as it did, in 2011). Today, it's clear that the global middle class is expanding—people in emerging economies like China, India, Brazil, and Indonesia will be more prosperous than they were before. Other factors are prone to turbulent, rapid oscillation: the price of oil can rise or fall rapidly, and so can the tenor of the general economy. And while many factors seem to be trending slowly but surely, their implications are not clear. The increasing evolution of the Internet is an inexorable trend, with more people and more types of devices connected and the growing availability of online services such as "cloud computing." Will this introduce children in your district to highly enriching contact with other parts of the world and with your community itself? Or will it expose them to malevolent influences and cyberbullying? Or both?

In education, relevant driving forces include many diverse factors. Changes in healthcare affect students' interest and capability. Changes in technology provide challenges and opportunities for teaching. Changes in the economy can affect how many people with children move into your community, move out, or start to require public assistance. Some seemingly unrelated forces can have major impact on education. For instance, in the 1960s and 1970s in the U.S., the acceptance of women by professions and fields that had previously excluded them meant that the pool of prospective teachers, in many communities, declined. Another seemingly unrelated driving force, the increasing impact of global climate change, has in some cases revitalized curriculum around service learning and community engagement. The more clearly we can see these and other possible forces at play in our community, the more realistically we can understand our prospects.

Thus, in this stage, we list as many potential driving forces as we can, with the facilitator (or a recorder) taking them down on self-stick notes, checking the wording quickly, and posting them on the wall. Some driving forces will be self-evident; others will require discussion, to hone the description down to the heart of the matter. Some may pertain to your particular school population: What are the trends on real estate prices? What attitudes do community members have about schools? Others relate to broader nationwide or global forces.

Many of these forces will provoke counterforces. For instance, if there continues to be a movement toward standardized testing in your region, then opposing forces may grow stronger. These, in turn, might provoke a counterreaction on behalf of "accountability." Schools that are unprepared for the cross-currents might get caught up in them inadvertently.

Conversations about driving forces require intensive give-and-take within the group, often with bouts of outside research between sessions. In the sessions I facilitate, we follow the guidelines of skillful discussion—for example, no interrupting or gratuitously critical, deflating comments (such as, "That's stupid"). And we downplay our feelings about the forces—how much we like or hate the implications and how probable we think their coming true might be. Seemingly improbable—but plausible—forces can affect everything we do. For instance, many catastrophes are ignored as "improbable," when a scenario exercise might have drawn attention to the need to prepare for it.

As you consider each driving force, ask three questions:

1. Is this predetermined to happen? Or is it uncertain? Predetermined forces are reasonably predictable. Based on conceptions that have already occurred, we know, barring unforeseen calamity, how many ten-year-olds will exist in any region nine years from now. Based on technological research that has already taken place, we can assume that Moore's law (the continual doubling of computer power per dollar every eighteen months) will continue for at least five years: This means that $1,000 will buy roughly thirty-two times as much computing power in 2020 as it does today.

But there are always uncertainties. What will those ten-year-olds care about? Will Moore's law "hit a wall" after 2018 or accelerate? And how would kids use those powerful computers—or would they give up computers entirely for tablets, smartphones, or some other yet-unknown device? These, and the vast majority of driving forces around education, are uncertainties. Will qualified teachers be harder to find? Will "distance learning" find a market—or fall flat? Will laws be passed establishing vouchers for parochial schools? We can't know the answers, but we can become far more aware of the reasons why events might move in one direction or another and the implications of their movement.

Any member of the group can veto the designation of an item as "predetermined"; the group must unanimously agree that the predetermined elements are, indeed, predictable. In the end, there may only be a handful of predetermined elements that everyone accepts, but they will be powerful; they set the boundaries within which scenarios take place. For instance, in a scenario exercise with the principals and administrators of Pelham, a small suburban school district near New York City, we talked about the education programs at nearby universities. Most had changed during the past few years; they were graduating young teachers who were better prepared than they had been in the past and who wanted influence over school management and curriculum, instead of just having a job and an autonomous classroom. Second, because of the influx of immigrants to New York and the "baby boomlet" of young children—both of which had already taken place—the need for teachers in the region would keep rising. These trends might not last forever, but for three years or more they were predetermined to influence the relationship among the district, newly hired teachers, and the teacher's union.

2. What is most significant about this driving force? For example, the Pelham administrators wondered about the future of student achievement, but as we talked about our different mental models of the word "achievement," we realized there were at least four different driving forces at play:

- Scores on external tests (such as standardized state exams) could go up or down, partly depending on factors outside the school's control;
- Scores of measured improvement, such as classroom grades and other measures that students considered important, would rise or fall independent of standardized test scores;
- "External life" measures such as acceptances into college, starting job salaries, scholarships, awards, and other material indications of success might, more than any other factor, determine the town's perception of the school system's capability;
- Internal values, awareness, and genuine competence—unmeasurable and perhaps unnoticed in any formal way—could have the greatest impact on the students' ultimate success in life.

The most significant aspect of student achievement had to do with how these forces fit together. The ongoing reputation of the school depended on all four of them.

3. How might this change in our timeframe? It is sometimes helpful to plot the most significant driving forces in a "behavior-over-time" graph, showing how they might rise or fall between now and your target date. Alternatively, name a couple of ways in which the future might evolve. "Within ten years, the pool of teachers available to us might be much larger—or there might be a teacher shortage—and we need to be prepared for both possibilities."

STEP 3: CONVERGING INTO SCENARIOS (HALF A DAY)

By this point, typically, the room walls are papered with scribbled notes about potential things that might happen, and a wave of anxiety and gloom overtakes the group: "We'll never get anywhere." And, indeed, convergence must be forced. Of several possible ways to do this, the method I like best is to hold a brief election. I ask people to walk around the room and inscribe stars on the five most "critical" of the critical uncertainties: particularly those that seem farthest "upstream," with the broadest influence over most other factors. While they're at it, I ask them to check the five forces that personally interest them the most.

Then we tabulate the results, pick the three or four forces that seem most significant to most people, and imagine them each pushed to the furthest plausible extreme. For example, Pelham educators saw "volatility of the economy" as a crucial factor. What, then, was the greatest possible recession imaginable as plausible for our target year, five years hence? One subgroup volunteered to look at this future in detail. Another critical driving force was the trend of tests and standards and the correlating increase in education "winners and losers." What if that trend were driven to its farthest plausible expression? And then there was the potential drift of prevailing values in our culture: would it be toward greater community spirit, toward greater materialism and fragmentation, or would we oscillate between them? From the many possible scenarios, three important ones emerged: a "Perpetual Values Crisis," in which schools were called upon to replace the sense of worth and value missing from the rest of society; a "Culture of Learning," in which educators found widespread support for the idea that all children can learn; and a "New Recession," in which education was charged with filling some of the gaps of economic failure.

Then each subgroup meets during the hiatus between sessions to imagine its future. Don't be afraid to change details at will; as long as it's plausible, posit any conceivable factor or detail that will make your future come to life. Answer these questions:

■ How did we get here? What plausible chain of events, composed of actions and counterreactions, could lead to this future? Consider the future as if you were looking back on it, like a historian, choosing details to bring out the dramatic effect of your story: "When newly elected American president Kim Kardashian refused to appoint Ben Bernanke to a seventh term, this sent the precariously balanced global economy into a tailspin."

■ How diverse a future is it? Does this future play out differently in every part of this community? At every age level? Among different ethnic groups? Who are the "haves" and "have-nots" in this future? Who would need special attention (that they're not getting now)?

■ What does this future have to tell us? Look for the element of surprise. What unexpected convergences and barriers could arise in this future in ways that might not seem obvious now?

■ What is going on in critical arenas? Run through a checklist of significant driving forces: the economy, technological change, regional development, student population change, the political environment. What would have to take place, in each of those arenas, to make this scenario plausible?

■ What does it mean for our constituencies? What's it like to be a teacher in this future? An administrator? A parent? A student? A school board member? Is this future more or less pressured, fulfilling, and controlling than today? Are there more or fewer opportunities? Why would and wouldn't you want your children to go to school in such a future?

■ What will you call it? Look for a catchy name, ideally one that is sound-bite snappy and soulfully deep, to provide a resonant handle so that the scenario idea can enter into the school system's common vocabulary.

STEP 4: REHEARSING THE SCENARIOS (ONE TO TWO DAYS)

When the subgroups return, each one briefly presents its future to the others. We consider them as a whole together. Could any of them possibly be combined? It became clear, for example, that "Perpetual Values Crisis" and another future called "Winners and Losers" were so similar they had to be combined; if one came true, so would the other. Try to settle on three or four solid futures, all distinct from one another. Five or more will blur together.

As you talk, note when people start talking about the future they would like to create. Building shared vision is important, but it can cloud your perception of outside current reality, so note any desired options or strategies and put them aside for later use in step 5.

As a full group, for each future in turn, pretend that the year has come. You are living there. What is going on? What's it like? For example, in a "New Recession," what cost-cutting would be needed? What programs would be curtailed? How might public support for programs like special education change? Revisit the name—is it still appropriate? (We changed "Culture of Learning" to "Culture of Renewal" at this stage, to show that a change of values had taken place not just in schools but all throughout America.) Return to the questions from step 3. Challenge and resolve any contradictions that you find. (For instance, in "Culture of Renewal," what would happen to the influence of standardized testing? Would it disappear altogether? That seemed implausible. So how would the tests be reconciled with the new trends that we saw? Try to avoid wishful thinking; if kindergartners everywhere must be better prepared for school than they typically are now, or your future won't "fly," then you must find a plausible reason why that change would take place.

STAGE 5: STRATEGY AND CONSEQUENCES (HALF-DAY TO INFINITY)

You have now created a language in which these hard-to-see insights can be voiced. "Will our current building plan stand up in the 'New Recession'?" you may ask. Or, "If 'Perpetual Values Crisis' comes to pass, will we be prepared?" Regrettably, many scenario exercises stop here. But the real work, the work that yields real benefits, is just beginning. Having developed two, three, or four images of the future, consider the present in these ways:

■ What current policies or practices would be dangerous or shortsighted if one of these futures came to pass? Are you willing to "bet the school system" on that future not arising?

■ What strategies are you considering that would be robust in helping you prepare for all futures: effective ways to lay the groundwork for a better life, no matter which scenario came to pass? In Pelham, for instance, a comprehensive redesign of staff development and an apprenticeship program with local businesses were clearly advantageous in all three futures.

■ Look at the potential silver linings of pessimistic futures and the hidden downsides of optimistic ones. For example, listening to some educators rhapsodize about the "Culture of Learning," I found myself thinking "Be careful what you wish for. You might get it." In a world where everyone promoted more learning and fulfillment, public schools would no longer have a unique role to play, and they might

For a more in-depth guide to scenario practice (albeit with some outdated examples) see Peter Schwartz, *The Art of the Long View* (Doubleday, 1991).

become far less relevant in people's minds. What counterintuitive messages do these futures reveal?

- What "early warning" indicators would show you that a particular future is coming? For example, the Pelham educators talked about creating an open forum on the values of the next generation of children—what did the community want their children to learn? If this forum were popular and well attended, that would suggest a "Culture of Learning" future was more likely. If it felt like pulling teeth, that would indicate a looming "Perpetual Values Crisis."

Finally, remember your purpose in conducting this exercise: to raise better awareness of your own current reality and its implications going forward. When you look back, ten or fifteen years from now, will you be glad you made the decisions you are making—back then in what is now the present but will soon be the past?

THE SCHOOLS OUR CHILDREN DESERVE

Moving Beyond Traditional Classrooms and "Tougher Standards," by Alfie Kohn (Houghton Mifflin, 1999)

When I first heard writer Alfie Kohn speak, I half expected him to walk on stage in Dickensian garb, as his many books on education portray a passionate anger similar to those written about the devastating effects of child labor in the mid-1800s. But his twentieth-century clothing does not detract from the power of his advocacy for children.

Buttressed by research and clearly written, this book lays out five fatal flaws of the movement toward tougher standards that overemphasize achievement at the cost of learning. Kohn argues that most of what the pundits are arguing for just gets the whole idea of learning and motivation wrong, and that the harder people push to force others to learn, the more they limit that very possibility. This book should be required reading for people who think they have the answers to issues of student achievement. —Janis Dutton

ONE SIZE FITS FEW AND CAUGHT IN THE MIDDLE

One Size Fits Few: The Folly of Educational Standards and Caught in the Middle: Nonstandard Kids and a Killing Curriculum; both by Susan Ohanian (Heinemann, 1999 and 2001).

"The really scary thing about teaching," writes Susan Ohanian, "is that we teachers, particularly those of us in elementary school, teach who we are." Ohanian has the gift of expressing the invisible essence of a bureaucratic absurdity in full flight. *One Size Fits Few* is a polemic against the "Standardistos"—education officials in California (her state) and elsewhere. *Caught in the Middle* tells the story of the "nonstandard kids" who get overlooked or slammed by standardized tests, but who are otherwise brilliant, distinctive, and compelling in their learning and their lives. Unless we find contexts for them to succeed, many of these individuals could be lost. These books manage all at once to be sharp-tongued, empathetic, thoughtful, and immensely fun to read. —Art Kleiner

See also Alfie Kohn, *What Does it Mean to Be Well-Educated?* (Beacon Press, 2004) and the website www.alfiekohn.org.

2. The $19,000 Question
The Ladder of Inference in Practice

MM

As told to Micah Fierstein

Micah Fierstein is an assistant professor of educational leadership at the University of Alaska in Anchorage. He writes, "For more than two decades, I have engaged in co-learning projects with teachers and administrators. The groups I work with begin each session sharing their experiences in applying the learning organization tools in their work. One of the most powerful stories is this one, recounted by a director of curriculum at a suburban school district. She taught our group that it is possible to engage a system with information and knowledge, and it can lead to profound results. She taught us that the key themes in this work are courage and trust—the trust to learn from other people and the courage to believe you can impact the system. Courage also means the willingness to make yourself vulnerable and having a keen awareness of the vulnerability of others."

It all started when an elementary school administrator asked me to come and meet with his staff. They had some questions about the new math curriculum. I had no idea what I was walking into. The teachers' anger toward the district overflowed right at me. "Last year it was a new reading curriculum," they complained. "Next came the new report card,

The director of curriculum who tells this story is anonymous at her request but has checked and approved the story printed here.

They are afraid of change and ungrateful

They don't respect me and are out to attack me

They set me up deliberately

This is a recurring pattern

Teachers are complaining

state standards, and now the math series." The first thing I did was jump to a conclusion that this was a setup. They obviously didn't respect me enough to tell me in advance what the meeting was really about, they were clearly out to attack me, and they didn't have a clue how hard we had worked to get the money for the new materials. They were afraid of change, stuck in their ways, and ungrateful.

Thanks to the things we have been learning in this group, I recognized I had skipped a few rungs of my ladder of inference and decided to suspend my assumptions and practice some dialogue and inquiry. I decided to ask questions and listen with a beginner's mind. The teachers expressed a deep commitment to their students and a frustration over their inability to bring new curriculum alive as quickly as they desired. Their frustration centered on integrating new instruction strategies at several levels simultaneously. I began to understand better the unrelenting changes that we had been asking teachers to make these past three years. The new demands of state standards, a new report card, curricula, and more seemed to be triggering feelings of incompetence. No wonder they were angry.

See The Ladder of Inference, page 101.

"What do you want me to do?" I asked. This question seemed to catch them off guard. They took a big breath and sat back. "We don't want you to do anything," they said. "We just want you to listen."

Returning to my office, I reflected on what I heard. My initial conclusions regarding the teachers' anger were incorrect. Perhaps they were more flexible than I had been led to believe. I had never stepped back and looked at the total number of changes we were working on. The district had never acknowledged the complex and excellent work that teachers did. I sat down and wrote a letter to them, thanking them and acknowledging all their contributions to our new curriculum initiatives.

The teachers' union reprinted my letter (without my knowledge) in their newsletter. The response I got was interesting. A dozen teachers contacted me directly. They told me how meaningful the letter was for them and that it was the first time in a long time that anyone from central administration showed they were listening. But at the next administrative meeting with the principals, I was soundly criticized for kissing up to the union.

That was an uncomfortable experience. I could have backed down, yet for the students' sake I wanted to ensure the long-range success of the new math program. I knew this depended on the teachers harnessing the new learning opportunities that the curriculum provided. The questions that the teachers raised were significant—they came from their daily interaction with the curriculum and students. The teachers also would have to explain it to parents. I felt we had a unique window of opportunity to alleviate their frustration and strengthen student learning, by dealing directly and coherently with the inevitable questions that arise from any innovation.

I decided the teachers needed release time for an in-service opportunity to learn more about the program. The cost of hiring substitutes and other expenses was $19,000. The only problem was that I didn't have that money in my budget. I would have to go to the superintendent for it.

I knew I was putting myself in a vulnerable position. The superintendent was new to the district. He might think I was incapable of assessing the needs of the district or that I lacked budget-planning skills. I was also surfacing the undiscussable issue of teacher resentment toward the district. In other words, he could infer that I was a bad administrator. I was opening myself up for another round of criticism—this time from the boss.

When I had asked for money in the past, I had never had to talk through the assumptions underlying my reasoning. This time I knew if I didn't, the superintendent would have an easy time leaping up his own ladder of inference. With this in mind, I decided to walk him up the rungs one at a time.

I told him about the teacher meeting I had attended and the anger and frustration I observed. I told him about the response I had received to the letter I had written. Then I said, "I think this is a sign they are concerned, not inflexible. I am assuming that their concern arises from a desire to be successful teachers and a willingness to try new things in their classrooms, yet they have too many questions about the program. I think that too many curriculum innovations fail because frustration prevents teachers from taking ownership in implementing changes. I believe we have a unique window of opportunity here to alleviate their frustration by harvesting the inevitable questions that arise in any new program. Therefore I am requesting $19,000 for release time for an in-service opportunity."

I half expected him to be resistant and braced myself to suspend my "noble certainties" to listen with a beginner's mind. I thought I would have to listen to his concerns and engage in skillful discussion. Imagine my surprise when very quickly he told me my explanation was solid, the plan was responsible, and it was something the district needed to do.

The director is a bad administrator

The director was too lenient

The director did not stop the complaints

This is a recurring pattern

Teachers are complaining

Let's explore this in staff development

We need to address their concerns

They are concerned for a reason

This is a recurring pattern

Teachers are complaining

ST

3. Success to the Successful

Michael Goodman, Janis Dutton

Every year the administrators of a school resolve that all the students will be given equal opportunity to succeed. But every year, some students, often from the lower-income neighborhoods, seem to get caught in a vicious spiral of defeat. They come to school less prepared; some of the teachers see them as sullen. They don't seem to fit in with the prevailing school culture; they don't speak with the same diction or wear the right kind of clothes. Despite the educator's desire to help all children learn, the system itself seems to divide them into "good kids" and "problem kids." Eventually, there is too much strain on the system's limited resources, such as people's time and energy, to help all the "problem kids," so many of them are written off.

For an introduction to system archetypes, see page 143.

It's natural for teachers to focus their interest and attention on the "good kids." And the good kids, too, are caught up in a spiral—a virtuous spiral of success and approval. They win elections for student government; they get "tracked" into advanced placement courses; they do well on tests. Much is expected of them, and they fulfill those expectations.

The same thing happens at the districtwide level. Some schools are "bad schools," caught in a vicious spiral. No matter how much money is allocated to them, or so the perception goes, they continue to do worse. Eventually it feels too exhausting to help them, so they, too, are written off. In some cities, if a school's test scores don't improve, money is taken from that school and reallocated to schools that are already improving. They may not need the resources as much, but there is overwhelming temptation to stick with the winners.

What causes a child, or a school, to be assigned an intangible status of "winner" or "loser"? In the "Success to the Successful" dynamic, two reinforcing cycles come into conflict. One is indeed a virtuous spiral, where things get better and better for some. The other is a vicious spiral, getting worse and worse for others. At the beginning, both groups may be equally competent or promising; but the "virtuous" group shows its promise more quickly and visibly. The earlier that a student (or a school or a practice) is seen as "successful" compared to its peers, the more resources it gets, the fewer resources will go to other groups, and the faster its virtuous spiral of success will spin.

Dedicated teachers and administrators notice the dynamic when they try to balance work and family life. It's easier to keep working through dinner if you have an evening meeting than to go home and face the complaints: "Why do you have to go back to work again?" The more you ignore family time in favor of work time, the more rewarding your work time will be in comparison—you will be tempted to shift your attention there even more in the future. Another common example is the "Why-can't-you-be-more-like-Mary?" syndrome in parenting. The child (or colleague or associate) who is easier to get along with will gain more attention from you, at the expense of a child (or colleague or associate) who is much more irritating but who needs you much more fundamentally—and who may be just as capable.

This dynamic also illustrates the subtle but pervasive influence of "cultural capital" in education. In many schools, especially in the higher grades, the prevailing curriculum and the processes by which it is taught is geared to an upper-middle-class, white, male, Anglo-Saxon, verbal/analytical, and facile pattern of thinking and learning. Studies show, for example, that concise, direct, linear speech—so-called "masculine" speech—is considered to evoke higher status, whether it is spoken by women or

The diagram of a Success to the Successful dynamic—in this case, the impact of "cultural capital"—shows two reinforcing loops, linked by a common but limited resource (here, the allocation of opportunities and resources available at the school). On the left, a "virtuous reinforcing process" favors those who are favored, leading to more visibility for them and thus more opportunities. But on the right, a "vicious reinforcing process" is also at play. With opportunities and resources allocated elsewhere, the net effect is systemwide disfavor. Without anyone intending it, this situation leads to a greater sense of invisibility and ultimately fewer opportunities and resources for some of the people in the system.

See Deborah Tannen, *You Just Don't Understand: Men and Women in Conversation* (Ballantine Books, 1990).

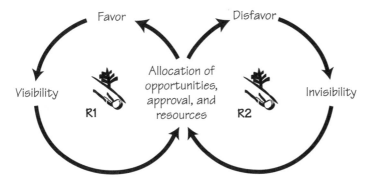

men. But many people, particularly many children, don't speak that way, particularly if they come from nonwhite backgrounds, have learning disabilities, or are female. Thus, they feel invisible. The more invisible they feel, the less they attract the approval, opportunities, and attention of the school (except as "problems"); the less of the school's approval and opportunities they attract, the more invisible they feel, the less they participate in the school's daily life, and the more invisible they become.

STRATEGIES FOR A SUCCESS-TO-THE-SUCCESSFUL SITUATION

The dynamic persists in Success to the Successful as long as the reinforcing loops are tied together—as long as the advances in the "virtuous spiral" group take place at the expense of the group caught up in the

The pattern of behavior over time for Success to the Successful, as with all reinforcing processes, involves a continually accelerating trend—or, in this case, four trends. Allocation of resources to the "virtuous" group goes up, and that group's visibility rises as well, while resources going to the "vicious" group get smaller, and that group's visibility goes down.

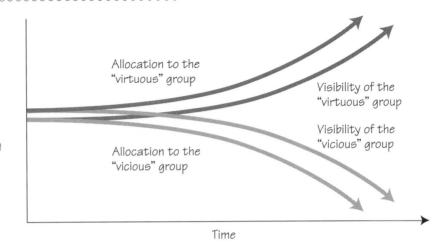

Allocation to the "virtuous" group

Visibility of the "virtuous" group

Visibility of the "vicious" group

Allocation to the "vicious" group

Time

"vicious spiral." Is there a way to decouple them? Does it have to be a zero-sum, winner-take-all game? What can be done to increase the resources? For example, is it possible to devote deliberate time and attention to the students who (for whatever reason) have never been considered part of the "high-achievement" group?

Another way out of the dilemma is to look for an overarching goal that will include the success of both groups. A shared vision exercise may show that the innate goal of the school has, in fact, been compromised over the years by the practice of favoring one group over another.

See "A Shared Vision for Your School," page 341, and "The Great Game of High School," page 380.

You may be tempted to reverse the cycle quickly and dramatically by setting in motion new policies that "compensate" the "vicious spiral" group by giving them privileges that previously belonged to the "virtuous spiral" group. But doing this can set the two groups against each other, with an oscillating pattern ensuing as they fight for a larger share of dominance over scarce resources. When the system finally settles into stability, things may be worse for the "vicious spiral" group than they were at the beginning.

Look into the mental models that underlie the archetype. Based on the people (students and teachers) who are tagged as high achievers, what are the values, attitudes, and characteristics of "successful" people at your school? Is this group representative of the population as a whole? What attitudes keep other people from being considered successful? If you did not have these attitudes—if you broadened your idea of success—then how might you use your school's resources to celebrate and foster the potential of a much larger group of successful people?

Reconsider the ways that success is measured. As systems writer Daniel Kim puts it, "We tend to think that we believe what we measure, but it's more likely that we measure what we believe." What measurable results contribute to the school's history of favoring some groups over others? How might those measurements be changed—and still be faithful to the school's overall vision of excellence?

Unfortunately, many individuals find themselves caught in the "vicious spiral" side of this dynamic. We know of three strategies that people use to escape. The first, accommodation, involve doing everything possible to join the "virtuous spiral" group, at whatever cost. This strategy often takes place at the expense of people's identity and relationships; it is a wrenching thing to ask of oneself (and it buys into the idea that the Success to the Successful pattern is inevitable). The second strategy is to "break the rules": to turn some aspect of the "vicious spiral" group into a pathway to success. Thus, for instance, when the prevailing culture looked down on rap and hip-hop music, the musicians turned it into an inventive and successful genre. This approach starts by learning to recognize your own strengths and talents, even if the prevailing system doesn't, and by building a network of people who will help one another develop and test their talents—ultimately to return to the system more on your own terms. The third approach is to raise awareness of the dynamic as a whole, perhaps using the Success to the Successful archetype to ask: "How many people are affected by this pattern? And does the school system, as a whole, really want to produce these results?"

4. Shifting the Burden

A Systems Archetype for Pernicious School Problems

Michael Goodman, Janis Dutton, Art Kleiner

Something must be done, and fast!" A "Shifting the Burden" story usually begins with an urgent problem symptom and two calls to action. One "quick fix" is obvious and immediate; it has the illusion of certainty and the reward of short-term efficiency. But it diverts attention away from the real or fundamental source of the problem, and ultimately it does not sustain itself. The other solution is more fundamental, but it takes longer and is much more uncertain; building support for it is more difficult. Torn between these two problematic approaches, people are naturally drawn to the quick fix.

⟩⟩ For an introduction to system archetypes, see page 143.

One continuous, and well-known, form of "shifting the burden" is high-stakes testing. By now, the pattern is familiar. Schools feel pressure from federal law, state legislatures, local businesses and real estate developers, and parents to "prove" their competence by improving scores with high-stakes testing. But state standards have nothing to say about the fundamental reasons why performance in some schools might be worse than others or how to close the gap in any sustainable way. So the quick fix plays out: From January through March, teachers review for the test. They convert their classrooms into preparatory courses for test-taking skills, and the initial results are indeed higher. The quick fix worked!

But once the test is over, nearly all students forget the material. Students who have difficulty with the tests, for whatever reason, find fewer channels in which to excel. They see no reason to try, and both the failure and dropout rates increase. In effect, the children who are not attuned to the test are punished. This situation leads to lower overall skill levels, which leads to lower overall performance. With the problem symptom reappearing, there is renewed demand for another "quick fix" —raising the bar again, for even tougher standards and tests.

Everyone in the system knows of the dangers of the standardized test "quick fix." Yet everyone feels forced into the pattern. Why? Because fundamental solutions require more investment, time, and care up front. They require more thoughtfulness and experimentation and more attentiveness to varied learning styles and in-depth staff development. Different constituents have different views about how to resolve problems, and there are a host of competing and contradictory school designs to consider. Most of all, fundamental solutions are slower to produce results, and one cannot be certain of them. It is very difficult to endure the delay before results improve, while the school district next door sees scores jump 20 percent.

There are many other "Shifting the Burden" structures in education. If there is a discipline problem, will you adopt a fundamental solution, which might involve family therapy or new teaching practices, or a "quick fix" such as medication or expulsion, which may lead to further discipline problems down the road? If teachers lack training, will you look for quick forms of staff development or in-depth systems that are codesigned by the teachers, parents, and administrators of each school? Sometimes the quick fix may indeed be the appropriate solution—if students threaten each other, they may well need to be separated—but rarely is it considered in light of long-term effects or fundamental alternatives. And in many "Shifting the Burden" structures, additional reinforcing processes occur that degrade the system further. For example:

VARIATION 1: ADDICTION (LOSING OUR CAPABILITY)

As educators in the school system lose their capability to move to the fundamental solution, the system can become "addicted" to solutions that don't really help and that don't even relieve the symptoms very well after a while. The addiction becomes worse than the original problem because of the devastation it wreaks on the fundamental ability to address the problem symptom. When school districts put all their time and money into helping students pass tests, often they are forced to limit other services and programs—counseling, physical education, art, music, special education, nutrition, and connecting with parents. Before long, capabilities in these areas atrophy. If they need to return to some of these more fundamental areas, they will no longer have the staff, the knowledge, or the capability to do so. They will be addicted to the quick fix and unable to escape it.

Like any addiction, this can lead to more serious difficulties. When the pressure to do well on tests increases, and the school's capacity to educate effectively erodes, people begin to feel that the ends justify the means. There may be great temptation to game the system—to manipulate the results in some way. Efforts to step back and find another approach are harder and harder to implement, because there isn't time. The quick fix, in the end, is not quick at all; it is all-consuming.

VARIATION 2: SHIFTING THE BURDEN TO THE INTERVENOR (THE INDISPENSABLE PROFESSIONALS)

Sometimes an organizational "addiction" occurs when an outside professional is called in to help solve a difficult problem. The role of the "intervenor" is meant to be temporary, but gradually the people with the problem become dependent on the intervention and never learn to solve problems themselves. This is not simply a matter of passing the buck. If the outsider could genuinely solve the problem, that would be acceptable. But in the long run, the insiders are the only people who can make and sustain the fundamental changes necessary to solve the problem.

This often occurs with education specialists—reading teachers, special education specialists, disciplinarian administrators, and school psychologists—who get more and more problems referred to them by teachers. If the specialists do not help the regular classroom teachers become more capable, the teachers will become less capable, because every time they refer a particular kind of child to a specialist, they lose

This causal loop diagram portrays a "shifting the burden" structure. Faced with pressure to improve measurable student performance (in the center), educators have a choice. The faster, "quick fix" approach (B1) focuses on improving standardized test scores. The "fundamental solution" (B2) requires in-depth investment in such measures as literacy and math improvement, curriculum revision, nutrition, and much more. Since this is more difficult and uncertain, and it might take years longer (note the delay), it is slower to show results—but there is more chance of fundamental gains. At the right is an "addictive" reinforcing process (R1), diminishing the school's capacity to return to the fundamental loop, and thus making it dependent on further quick fixes.

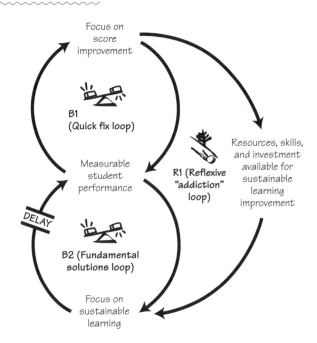

practice in dealing with that kind of child. They will grow more and more dependent on the professionals.

VARIATION 3: ERODING GOALS (ISOLATING THE POOR PERFORMER)

In this common form of shifting the burden, the gap between desired performance and real performance grows so great that instead of trying to improve performance (through fundamental improvement), people take the pressure out of the system by settling for a lower level of achievement. Many schools, for example, have a policy where students who get poor grades are prohibited from joining extracurricular activities, even if they are athletes (for instance) and even if the extra activity is one of the few things they love about school.

This is not punishment; in the minds of the educators, it represents a compassionate solution. Distractions must be eliminated. The student needs all available time to focus (for example) on math or science and not waste that time in the camera club, field hockey, or the marching band. When you force someone's attention, there often is a short-term gain—as the person initially goes along with the new restrictions. But it generally doesn't last. The student, sooner or later, internalizes the real message: "There is something wrong with me." One of the few connections that student has to the school is severed. The result often is either rebellion or passive-aggressive acquiescence and a sense of being ostracized and isolated that can even lead to violence.

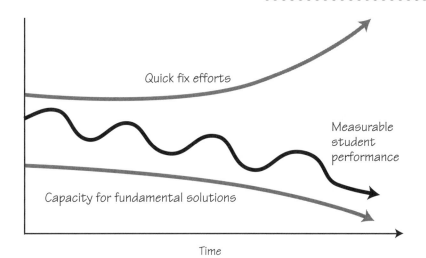

This behavior-over-time diagram shows the impact of shifting the burden structures. The effort and investment spent on quick-fix solutions continually rises. The problem symptom (measurable performance) oscillates—improving briefly at times but with gradual overall deterioration. And fundamental capabilities erode over the long term.

"I was learning to be a team player," one student in this situation told us. "In the hockey team, I finally found something I loved at school, and I was starting to connect with teachers better. Now, after this, why should I even bother anymore?"

A more fundamental solution would involve looking at the reasons for each student's problems in detail. In ways that might not be obvious, the student might need tutoring or evaluation for problems such as dyslexia or attention deficit disorder. Or it might be appropriate to involve all the kids on the team in helping one another gain competence in English and math, for the sake of the team as a whole.

Another common example of eroding goals often takes place after a school district decides on a guiding principle that "all kids can learn." After several enthusiastic months, it becomes clear exactly how difficult it will be to put this principle into practice (or how much of a change in attitude it will take). Gradually, without much fanfare, the aspirations of the district change—to "most kids will get better opportunities," and then to "we prepare more kids for the job market," and ultimately back to where it was when the initiative began.

STRATEGIES FOR A SHIFTING-THE-BURDEN SITUATION

If you find yourself in a shifting-the-burden structure, or one of its variations, start by trying to understand the situation better. What is the problem symptom that you tried to fix? What quick fix has tempted you? What were (or might be) the unexpected results, and how would they affect the original source or root cause of the problem?

Then comes the leap: What alternative solutions might you try if the quick-fix avenue were not available? How would these more fundamental actions address the causes of the problem? What kinds of investment, and timeframe, would you need to really make them work? How could you sustain these investments?

There is a temptation to assume that your preferred solution, whatever it may be, is the fundamental solution. Teachers may see one solution as "fundamental," while parents see another and administrators a third. That's why it's important to talk through the situation in teams that include all constituencies of the problem (perhaps including students) and to suspend preconceptions about which solution is best.

When you feel you have a shared sensibility of the long-term versus short-term solution, strengthen the long-term solution. If possible, go "cold turkey" on the addiction by denying access to the short-term solution entirely. See what happens then. If you must address a problem symptom with a quick fix, do so with restraint. Stay aware of your main purpose: to gain time to work on the fundamental solution. Sometimes, short-term solutions are available that can actually move you toward a long-term focus. For example, some forms of "teaching to the test" might be designed as aspects of curriculum that also pave the way for longer-term investments in student learning.

5. The Great Game of High School

Nathan Dutton, Rick Quantz, Nolan Dutton

To many adults it may seem that high school kids are not serious about school, but maybe it's because their attention is consumed by two simultaneous pressure-cooker systems—endlessly constricting, endlessly enervating. First, they must push constantly for performance in class and on tests. Second, they are caught in a social game. Popular books, movies, and TV shows about school across the decades—from S.E. Hinton's The Outsiders *to Tina Fey's* Mean Girls *to J.K. Rowling's* Harry Potter *series to the television series* Glee, *and many, many others—have games like this at the heart of their story lines. People carry the scars from these games for years, possibly for life. But few people see it the way it is seen by the kids caught up in it.*

This article began when a few teenagers we knew (the sons of coauthor Janis Dutton and correspondent Betty Quantz, since grown to adulthood) showed us the secret map they'd made of the great game of life in school. We believe that similar maps (with variations in the details of the categories) could be drawn in nearly every school around the world.

One fascinating aspect of this story is the way it resonates with the "dignity of the child" (page 177)—teenagers create for themselves the diversity and individuality that schools do not grant them.

If your high school experience is like ours, you spend seven hours every day at school. The half-hour lunch, and other time with friends, may compete for the most intellectually engaging moments, despite our teachers' best intentions. The other six-and-a-half hours, in class and out, are spent working your ass off—trying to find a girlfriend or boyfriend, flirting, dispelling rumors about yourself, starting rumors about other people, and all the other things you do to survive high school. The great game of high school is rooted in adult mating rituals and the social reproduction of class hierarchy. To a degree that very few parents, teachers, or administrators admit, the game determines your success at school. Parents, teachers, and administrators may claim that every student has the same opportunities, is accorded the same respect, or plays by the same rules, but we aren't, and don't. Adults may think they are stressing academics, but they're not. Instead, the adults of the system have colluded in setting up its hidden rules; and its practices mirror the game that they play out in the "real world."

It's not really a game, at least in the sense that people can simply opt to play it, like they might sit down to play Monopoly. It's invisible to most people, and most don't even recognize the extent to which it influences their choices and controls their behavior. It was pretty invisible to us as well until one night during a sleepover. We were talking about different groups and cliques at school. In our small town, a lot of families seem to stick around and many of us had been in school together since kindergarten, if not daycare. Some peer groups stayed intact throughout the years, but many shifted during middle school, and by high school some people who had been friends in third grade didn't even acknowledge each other's existence. Around 3 a.m., for some reason, we decided to map the school's social groups.

We had been discussing the way the media portrayed teenagers as forming cliques with clearly drawn distinctions and separations. We felt the separations were not all that clear and that the boundaries were diffused, much like a spectrum. We started mapping opposing interests and values and drew them like the ordinals on a compass. We had not even considered a social hierarchy. Like most teenagers, we had little nice to say about anyone who wasn't in the room at the time. And while we probably used a variety of terms to describe the groups during the mapping, we ended up with the names the groups tended to call themselves at the time: preps, Gs (for "gangstas"), hicks, and freaks. We know some people might find these names offensive, but we feel people should have the right to name themselves. People in different schools, with different populations, might put different labels on various positions. (Some schools might have a quadrant for "jocks" and no "hicks.")

Just as most of the points on a map are not perfect north or south, neither are people pure "prep" or "freak." Nearly every student would fit somewhere around this circle. Most people would gravitate not toward the purer poles (prep, freak, G, and hick), but somewhere between. We and our friends, for instance, hung out in the prep-freak quadrant. We knew very little about the G/hicks on the opposite side. And our diagram definitely represented a boy's vantage point; a group of girls might draw a very different arrangement. But we suspect every high school has similar circumstances.

Soon we had one of those intellectually engaging peer-group moments, and the implications of our map quickly became evident. While we had not originally been discussing hierarchy, clearly one had emerged. The preps were on top, and there was a social class-inspired "underclass" culture at the bottom. The quadrants represented the ideals that we all imitated, not necessarily our real identities. Many preps imitate a richer lifestyle than they have. The Gs imitate the black urban condition and imitate being poor and rebellious, even though they come from upper-middle-class suburbs. One's actual economic status or race, at least at our school, had little to do with these assumed social identities.

We showed the chart around school, just a little bit—in a fourth-year French class, for instance, or when friends came over to visit. A lot of the people agreed with it in principle, but then they asked us to place them on it. A few were terribly insulted with the way we placed them. We found that preps, in particular, did not recognize themselves as preps. They'd say, "I am just a person." But ask someone else to name a typical prep, and that "just a person" would be named.

Preps are the most successful players of the great game of school, and yet it's hard to talk to them about it. They've played the game so steadily, and so long, that their privilege and cultural capital is invisible to them, just as it is to dominant groups in the larger game.

These are the unwritten rules of the game at our school—and probably at any public secondary school in America (if not the world).

RULE 1: RESISTANCE IS FUTILE!

The game constitutes the shared experience of school. When you are in it, it is everything. It is the way to survive. Once you find your slot, the pressure to fit in is overwhelming; the way you dress, act, move is determined by your social group. You don't join a group because of how you look. You look the way you look because of the group you join. You can tell where kids stand on the circle by their haircuts, because they cut their hair based on the way their group looks. If you stop looking and acting "right," then your group reacts. "You dweeb, get out of here." And you have to find another place. That's one reason why the game takes so much energy, because the way you have to look and act continually changes.

One of our friends was angry with us for telling him about it. "I feel like the characters in the movie *The Matrix*. Once you break away from the matrix and understand how it controls everything you do, you can't go back. I play the game now because, if I didn't, I would be bored to tears."

The game is not really science fiction, but like the Borg, the alien race in Star Trek: *The Next Generation*, the game will try to assimilate you. Resistance is not necessarily futile, but if you do resist, there are consequences.

RULE 2: IF YOU WANT TO SCORE, YOU HAVE TO PLAY

The game is really a mating ritual and controls your social life. If you opt out (or get pushed out), you are no longer part of the school's social structure. "I don't want to play the game seriously," a friend of ours once said. "That's why I don't have girlfriends." People without a conventional love life—such as many geeks, gay kids, and special education students—don't have a spot on the circle. They're not playing the game.

RULE 3: YOU ARE WHO YOU KNOW

Your place on the circle is not determined by the way you dress, the way you act, or the way you think. Those are all determined by your place on the circle. Your place depends on the people you associate with. For example, you can be thoroughly disliked, but if your best friend is Joe Prep Smith, then people will say, "He's a jerk, but he's cool. He's got cool friends." Similarly, we've heard kids say, "I'd like to be a prep, but I don't like any of them—so I'm a freak instead."

How do you get to know the people on one part of a circle and not another? That depends, in part, on whom you've grown up with. The big transition comes in middle school, when you're thrown up in the air amid kids from different elementary schools. You no longer have a group defined by the classroom you attend, so you no longer have an obvious

The "Great Game" chart on page 384 was created in 2000, for the original edition of *Schools That Learn*. We chose not to update the topical references for the new edition because any specific references will go out of date, and the specifics may not apply everywhere. But at any point in time, every school with teenagers could have its own counterpart to a chart like this.

Preps

Organized sports.

Country clubs.

Abercrombie & Fitch, the Gap.

Homecoming kings and queens.

Student government; yearbook.

Top 40 music; Britney Spears, Ricky Martin.

Will Smith "Saved by the Bell."

Most of the characters in "Clueless" (including Murray, a prep playing at being a gangsta).

Absorb the "cool attitudes" from the rest of the circle.

The prep-freak quadrant

Most of the school valedictorians.

Tennis players; cross-country athletes.

School orchestra and band members.

Non-cigarette smokers.

The hick-prep quadrant

Most varsity athletes, especially football.

Most baseball and softball (which is why freaks don't play baseball, even if they like the game).

"Buffy, the Vampire Slayer."

Freaks

Daring to be different . . . like each other.

Videogamers & role playing gamers.

Tolerant of sexual ambiguity and homosexuality.

Alternative music: Pink Floyd, Grateful Dead, Phish.

Violin, cello, guitar.

Act like they don't care about the game (but they do).

The skateboarder in "Clueless."

Bicycle riders.

More respectable in recent years.

Idealism; communal property rights.

Hicks

Cowboy boots, tight, tight jeans.

Religious conservatives.

Garth Brooks, Shania Twain.

Pickup trucks.

Varsity Blues—the alltime teen-age hick movie

The only group without black students in our school.

The gangsta-hick quadrant

Cigarette smokers.

We don't know much about this quadrant (since we were on the opposite side).

Gangstas

Pick-up basketball.

Murray in "Clueless" was a prep pretending to be a G.

In our rural Midwest school, these are mostly white kids, imitating inner-city rap pop culture.

Rap, R&B.

The freak-gangsta quadrant

People who never touched a piece of sports equipment in their life.

Goths.

Grunge.

The "third girl" in "Clueless."

The vampires in "Buffy, the Vampire Slayer."

place to fit. You look up and see the categories of the high school. As a high school freshman, you start to take on a little of the identity: There are "freshman freaks" and "freshmen hicks." Slowly, over that ninth-grade year, you graduate up into your spot on the circle. You end up feeling a great deal of loyalty to your group, even if you don't like the game, because you chose your spot by choosing your friends, or they choose you. Some people are known as "prep wannabes" but never quite make it because the preps choose each other. Being a prep takes a lot more than a charge account at Abercrombie & Fitch. Like being a part of any group, it is a learned behavior, assimilated throughout the course of a lifetime. Though you may not like it, your parents were also part of that group.

RULE 4: INTELLIGENCE AND ABILITY DON'T COUNT

The circle doesn't show brains or academic capability at all—or, for that matter, talent of any sort. As it happens, most of the National Honor Society members in our school are preps. But that doesn't mean the preps are smarter; it is just easier for them to succeed. In our school, to get in the NHS, you have to submit an application and be selected by a panel of teachers; the result of this process favors preps. There are very smart and talented people all around the circle, and the highest academic achievers are often not so smart in many other ways. Intelligence can make it easier to play the game, but the game does not reward intelligence in itself. In fact, being able to think critically can work against you.

Some of the people who became Gs are so smart that the school doesn't know what to do with them. They and their friends gravitate toward the bottom as an act of resistance. We know one G kid who was a National Merit finalist. Any college would have taken him; he had scholarships waiting. But he dropped out before graduation. He stopped turning in his homework because he recognized the meaninglessness of busywork, which most homework is. Some teachers ridiculed him in class for it. And he lost interest.

RULE 5: OPPOSITES DO NOT ATTRACT

Wherever you are on the circle, there's one guarantee: The closer a person is to the opposite side of the circle, the less you know or care to know about that person. In our entire high school, we can't think of one boy-girl relationship that spans the circle. (The movie *Grease* represents a prep/G romance. So does *Pretty Woman.* Nice fairy tales.) The 1999 massacre at Columbine High School (a school with a student population much like ours) could be mapped as two kids from the freak/G quadrant trying to attack their enemies across the circle, who had taunted them as "fags." (Hick-preps hate and fear homosexuality above all other labels.)

We (the authors of this article) place ourselves at the upper right. We know we don't understand people at the lower left, in the "G/hick" quadrant, and they don't understand us. We've overheard some of them refer to the three of us as "hard-core preps," which shows how invisible we are to them. There are dozens of social incongruities that distinguish us "prep/freaks" from the preppiest preps. We know the prep distinctions intimately, but we miss dozens of cues that would help us read the nuances of the G/hick part of the continuum. They are as invisible to us as we are to them.

RULE 6: TO WIN POINTS YOU TAKE THEM FROM SOMEONE ELSE

The way to get more and more status within your group is to be the most popular prep among the preps, the most powerful hick among the hicks, the freak the other freaks admire, and so on. This game is getting much tougher year by year. Some of us in our "prep-freak" circle felt stronger and stronger pressure to stop associating with K., a geeky guy who is not part of the circle. Nobody said we'd lose status for hanging out with K.; the pressure might have been all in our imagination. But we felt it as real.

You can start to feel that if you slip up once, you will lose your standing forever. There's also a weird sense, particularly among the preps, that you can't really get ahead unless you destroy someone else in the process. Those who are ahead in the game harass people who get better grades or more recognition in class. They don't like sharing power.

RULE 7: THE GAME DETERMINES HOW WELL YOU DO IN SCHOOL

The game determines all sorts of aspects of a student's social life, but it is also intimately related to academic success. Teachers and administrators may not realize it, but they use the game as a guide to help them with everything from grades to discipline, favoring some students because of the group they are in and looking for excuses to expel members of groups that are out of favor. Sure, you can ask teachers if they are biased by their students' social status, and they will think the idea is preposterous; the game is just as invisible to them as it is to the students. The fact is that teachers and administrators not only let a student's group sway their actions, but they unconsciously encourage and sustain the game through school policy and informal interaction with students.

The official power structure of the school revolves around the preps. They are born with the deeds to Park Place and Boardwalk, and the school hands them the houses and hotels. Administrators favor them over other students. Student government is a prep popularity contest. Prep sports dominate the budget and the intramural schedules. Preps get most of the public praise from teachers and administrators, and everyone knows who they are. The school exists, on some level, to make them important in a way that doesn't exist to make the members of the other groups important. They also get away with more; they hold all the "Get Out of Jail Free" cards. In this way the schools, teachers, and administrators aid in reproducing the existing class/group hierarchy.

RULE 8: THE GAME NEVER ENDS, SO NO ONE WINS

When we first recognized the game, we looked at it as a phenomenon that ends with high school. We have begun to realize that the game never ends, it only changes form. By the time many students reach their senior year, they too have seen the game and try to distance themselves from it. This is one cause of the malady known as "senioritis." But most of those seniors only recognize the outer layer of the game, as we did at first. Even though they may not have recognized there was a game, they know the rules they've been comfortable with are going to change. Two of us are now in college, and we know our new schools have a similar game, but we haven't quite been able to identify it. One reason is that the college you choose is a process of self-selecting into your quadrant, so while the rules are the same, the food chain is less apparent. It may be even harder to notice those who are different when we leave school and join "the real world" that created our smaller worlds. The rules of gender, race, and class will be quite familiar by then. National elections, after all, are just a prep popularity contest.

We continue to share the map and the rules of the game with people. It seems as if the further away you get from high school, the more universal the game appears, because adults have had time to think back on their experiences. People fresh out of high school, or perhaps working in schools, have more difficulty seeing themselves, or they say, "That is so true of those other schools, but not ours." The ultimate irony is the game keeps students from learning and reaching their full potential, and the people inside it should be the first to resist it, because with these kinds of rules, no one wins.

The Great Game in Your Own School

Nelda Cambron-McCabe and Janis Dutton

We have used "The Great Game of High School" as a powerful tool for generating group conversations about school practices that may be detrimental to the learning of many students.

STEP 1: QUESTIONS IN BREAKOUT

In small groups, discuss the following questions (for about forty-five minutes):

1. What does the youth culture game look like in your school? How are different subgroups of students positioned? How do they see themselves? How do others see them?

Purpose:

To explore mental models that may classify students or limit their potential in your school; to examine ways to create a more inclusive culture to support all students.

Setting:

Tables for small groups of four to six people.

Time:

One and one-half hours. Participants should read "The Great Game of High School" beforehand, or at the start of the session.

2. What ladders of inference can be drawn about the ways each group is seen?

>> See the Ladder of Inference, page 101.

3. What are the implications of each subgroup's story for student learning?

4. What are the predominant mental models that drive this system?

5. What are the similarities from your own experiences as a high school student? What was the impact on your life? (Educators often remember their personal experiences with the "great game" of high school. Their stories speak to the lingering power of the categories.)

6. Does the story (system structure) operating in this school resemble any systems archetype?

>> See An Index to System Archetypes, page 144.

7. Identify some leverage points for changing the interaction, engagement, and communication in the classrooms. How, within the school, can you hear and validate more student voices?

Inevitably, in every school, some subgroups are treated more benevolently, and understood more readily, than others. These reflective questions can help educators become more aware of their own role in perpetuating these practices and of ways to support students who don't fit the school community's mental model of the ideal student.

STEP 2: REPORT BACK IN PLENARY

Invite each group to describe its perspective on the youth culture in this school and the mental models driving it.

STEP 3: NEXT STEPS IN SMALL GROUPS

Ask each group to refine and summarize its proposal to create a more inclusive culture for all students and then report back briefly. These suggestions can later be used to design specific plans for the school community.

OTHER OPTIONS FOR TEAM EXERCISES

School counselors can use "The Great Game of High School" with small groups of students to help them describe and understand their own school's social system.

Educators can conduct a similar session to examine their own social system. For example: How do different groups of teachers (such as, subject matter or grade level) fit into this model? Who receives the most or least attention in the school?

School leaders can also apply this model to the larger system around them. Which parents or community members does the school board pay the most attention to? Which groups get the least attention?

6. The Youth Leadership Forum

Joyce Bisso

At several points in this book, we speak to the importance of developing joint learning processes where students play a fully generative role in the learning of their schools and their communities. Dr. Joyce Bisso describes one such learning process, developed during her time as principal of the George W. Hewlett High School in Hewlett, New York, which gave students influence and opportunity to innovate and participate at both the school and community level.

Also see "The Systems Citizen," by Peter Senge, page 558; and "Creating a Core Learning Group," by Les Omotani, page 445.

Dr. Joyce Bisso is now the superintendent of schools at Hewlett-Woodmere Public Schools; Dr. Les Omotani, then the superintendent, is now retired.

In the mid-2000s, I began using organizational learning and systems thinking tools as a member of our school district's leadership team. This quickly led me to embed the concepts and tools into my day-to-day leadership efforts at the building level with teachers. As I watched the adults respond, I recognized the potential it could have for the learning of high school students. Thus, in November 2005, Dr. Les Omotani and I launched the first George W. Hewlett High School Youth Leadership Forum (YLF).

The Forum is now in its seventh year. With Tom Russo now serving as the high school principal, it continues to evolve and deepen our youth's commitment to the school system and community. There are from 50 to 100 students and about a dozen adults in each session; the goal is for participants to listen to all voices and engage in respectful, meaningful conversations. We developed guidelines called the "YLF Rules of Engagement," which we discuss at most sessions to remain mindful of our commitment to listening, inquiry, and being respectful.

When we designed YLF, we asked counselors and teachers to suggest students who represented the broad diversity of the high school popula-

The YLF Rules of Engagement

- *Leaders listen.* It is very difficult to engage in active listening. It takes practice.
- *Inquiry* means questions rather than opinions and advocacy for your position.
- *Embellish* means adding to, rather than taking away from, the comments, perceptions, and ideas of others.
- *Being respectful* communicates that ideas are at the center of the conversation, not personalities.
- *Demonstrating caring and empathy* makes conversation easier and less

threatening. Leaders make people feel safe in expressing ideas.

■ *Seeking to understand* requires patience, inquiry, respect, and genuine inquiry.

The adults participating in YLF are educators and leaders at the school and system level, who have the knowledge and decisionmaking ability to support student initiatives, resolve issues, and provide resources to allow student ideas to become successful. Sometimes the adults are people who have created the rules and structures that students want to change.

tion. We wanted more than the student leaders whom teachers typically tapped for recognition. From the nominated list, we selected twenty-five students from each grade (nine through twelve), chosen to cut across all categories: academics, sports, clubs, ethnicity, language, and extracurricular interests. For YLF to be successful, we needed a microcosm of the student body.

YLF meets on four or five full-day sessions each year (scheduled on Fridays). These sessions are built around the five disciplines as well as servant leadership. The students and adults learn about inquiry and advocacy and are given plenty of time to practice the skills together. They create their own ladder of inference stories (page 101) from their personal lives and school experiences, describing mental models that interfere with understanding situations. They use the iceberg exercise (page 126) to identify leverage points to change systems. The language they gain about systems gives them more confidence to participate in conversations elsewhere: about sustainability, local and global environmental issues, school culture issues, technology, intergenerational collaboration, how high school should be transformed, the preferred role of educational technology, student leadership in the system and the community, and community sustainability.

In addition to the formal YLF sessions, students participate in a range of student-led projects in the community. They choose the projects, collect data, develop strategies, and implement them. One effort involved designing and selling reusable bags to reduce the waste from plastic bags. In another, students "dreamed" about the ideal high school and directly influenced the development of our "one-to-one laptop" initiative, which provided each student in the high school with a laptop. In a third project, in collaboration with the Cornell Cooperative Extension, YLF sponsored a seedling booth at the community Harvest Festival. "We feel that as a group we can have an impact on our community," said one student. "We are the future and can make a difference."

A powerful way to begin YLF each year is to engage the students in a conversation about their own culture and practices in high school. We use "The Great Game of High School" exercise (page 338). After everyone reads the article (page 380), some students typically say that it does not represent our high school: "We don't have those groups—or any groups for that matter." But others assert that, in fact, we do have groups and that the dominant student groups think their experiences are the norm for all students.

On one level, many students have been aware that these differences exist, but they have not confronted what that means educationally and socially for the student body as a whole. When they engage in these conversations, they begin to "see" some other students for the first time. "Before Youth Leadership," remarked one student, "I saw kids based on their groups, which was a stereotype of what I thought they were like. Now that I know them from YLF, those barriers have been broken."

Using "The Great Game of High School" is risky because of its potential for strong emotions to be shared openly. Participants must develop skills associated with dialogue and thoughtful inquiry. Trust and team-building are prerequisites. Nonetheless, in our experience, this was the most compelling and meaningful learning experience initiated for students and adults.

An essential element in YLF is creating maximum opportunities for interaction among the participants. The students hold strong ideas and beliefs and need a space to practice engaging others. We use numerous conversational designs, such as jigsaw discussions, the World Café, gallery walks, and team projects to move the students out of their comfort zone. Students also serve as hosts for community conversations, generating great response, attendance, and participation from parents.

The students reported to us that all these experiences have given them confidence to express their ideas in class as well as at the dinner table with parents and siblings. This new confidence also extends to relationships with teachers. One student commented, "I love that teachers are learning together with students. For the first time, we feel we are on the same level—all learners at the same table. Teachers' perspectives rule the classroom. In Youth Leadership Forum, our ideas carry equal weight. They really listen to us; they make us feel that our opinions are legitimate."

Through the feedback that students provide us after they leave our high school, we know that YLF has been one of the significant ways we have helped them see themselves as taking on influential roles in shaping the future. We feel so strongly about this endeavor that we formed a YLF this year for middle school students, who have eagerly embraced it. Our school system welcomes its role in preparing youth for the leadership demands of the future. One of our students reminded us of why we do this work: "We see ourselves as being active participants in national and international change. If no one helps us think about ourselves as leaders, that is a missed opportunity for everyone." The voice and thoughtfulness of students—those who have experienced the PK–12 system firsthand—are vibrant and necessary for any transformation and improvement effort to be successful.

We found David Hutchens's series of learning fables highly effective in teaching systems thinking. The students connected with the stories and translated the systems thinking elements into their own experiences. See *Outlearning the Wolves: Surviving and Thriving in a Learning Organization* (1998); *Shadows of the Neanderthal: Illuminating the Beliefs That Limit Our Organizations* (1998); *The Lemming Dilemma: Living with Purpose, Leading with Vision* (2000); *The Tip of the Iceberg: Managing the Hidden Forces That Can Make or Break Your Organization* (2001); *Listening to the Volcano: Conversations That Open Our Minds to New Possibilities* (2005); all from Pegasus Communications. Also see Hutchen's website at: www.davidhutchens.com.

If policymakers at the state and national level, boards of education, administrators, and teachers are sincere in their desire to transform the public education system in our nation positively, they will actively support the use of strategies such as the Youth Leadership Forum in high schools throughout the United States.

Variation on the "Great Game" Exercise

Joyce Bisso

STEP 1: FIRST TABLE

Seat participants at tables for eight; assign each participant a color that corresponds to the color of one of the eight rules. Each person presents his or her rule, and the group discusses its meaning.

STEP 2: SECOND TABLE

Participants move to a new table. Each new group must have all eight colors and rules represented. Share your knowledge of each rule. Discuss whether the rules apply in your high school, and, if so, how.

Name and map the social groups for your high school. On a sheet of paper, draw and name the quadrants; fill in with other groups or combinations of groups. On a flip chart, map your table's grid for display.

STEP 3: GALLERY WALK

One person from each table remains as host to explain the flip chart. Others walk from table to table viewing the charts.

STEP 4: BACK TO TABLE 2

Upon your return, discuss:

- What are the noticeable similarities/differences among the tables?
- What does it take to be successful at your high school?
- Are some groups favored over others?

STEP 5: LARGE GROUP

In plenary, discuss: What can or should individuals do to unlock the "high school" grid?

Purpose:

The Great Game exercise helps to make visible what so often is invisible to many of our students.

Materials:

Assign each of the "rules of the game" a specific color.

Rules of the Great Game:

Resistance is futile.

If you want to score, you have to play.

You are who you know.

Intelligence and ability don't count.

Opposites do not attract.

To win points, you take them from someone else.

The game determines how well you do in school.

The game never ends, so no one wins.

Communities of Practice   Art Kleiner

The "Great Game of School" does not exist only in the imagination of students and television producers. Social groups act much like organizations anywhere. The "Communities of Practice" theory, developed by a group of collaborative researchers led by Etienne Wenger and Jean Lave, suggests that organizations tend to conduct their work less through a hierarchical chain of command and more through informal networks of people who pass on messages and values in thousands of subtle, small ways throughout the day. In schools, these informal networks, or social groups, are also where the bulk of the learning takes place.

"Students go to school," wrote Wenger, "and, as they come together to deal in their own fashion with the agenda of the imposing institution and the unsettling mysteries of youth, communities of practice sprout everywhere—in the classroom as well as on the playground, officially or in the cracks. And in spite of curriculum, discipline, and exhortation, the learning that is most personally transformative turns out to be the learning that involves membership in these communities of practice."

Penelope Eckert, a professor of linguistics and cultural anthropology at Stanford University, documented the ways in which communities of practice set the learning horizons for high school students. Her three years of field research at several Detroit-area high schools in the 1980s led to a book, *Jocks and Burnouts*, that echoes the "Great Game of School": She argues that social class determines the way that children choose their friends, their activities, and ultimately their future. The "Jocks" (equivalent to preps or the "socs" of S. I. Hinton's *The Outsiders*) she studied were middle class; the "Burnouts" were working class. (These names, like the labels in "The Great Game of School," were given by students to themselves.) Kids who wanted to escape a low-income future had to cross the boundary between the groups. Even if they were willing to try, they faced daunting challenges from within themselves and terrible discouragement from many teachers, administrators, and students.

"One of the biggest Burnouts in the class that I followed," Eckert said, "had been a cheerleader in junior high. She said it was really fun, but the other cheerleaders were friends with each other, and her own friends were not into that activity. Not only did being a cheerleader pull her away from her friends, but she was also excluded from other social activities related to the cheering squad. Eventually she backed out and remained a Burnout all through school."

In Eckert's field research, Burnouts often gave up trying to cross over when they discovered how much they would have to change about themselves. The most wrenching change was often the new, dispassionate attitude they would have to adopt about their old (and new) friends. Close loyalty to friends and family was one of the strongest cultural pulls in most Burnout cultures. Nor did they make friends easily on the other side. The scars created in transitions like this can linger for the rest of an individual's life. Even if they manage to develop a successful career for themselves, they often feel as if they don't fit in anywhere.

To Eckert, the school teachers and administrators subconsciously and consciously promoted the Jocks at the expense of the Burnouts. "There

See Etienne Wenger, *Communities of Practice: Learning, Meaning, and Identity*, (Cambridge University Press, 1998), p. 6.

Quotes are from an interview with Penelope Eckert. Also see Penelope Eckert, *Jocks and Burnouts: Social Categories and Identity in High School* (Teachers College Press, 1989). For her more recent work, see www.stanford.edu/~eckert.

are not enough resources for all the kids to participate and do the same things," she said. "So a lot of extracurricular activities, like access to the student council, are competitive, and a hierarchy develops that is made up of less than 5 percent of the kids in a class. This creates a status system in the school that allows certain kids to gain institutional control. They are the ones who decide what dances there are going to be, who will organize the fundraising for the prom and decide on the decoration for dances and so on."

No school change effort will be complete unless it brings to the surface the structure of its elite and the influence it has over the school. What, then, can someone who sees this damage do about it? Eckert's research had not uncovered any schools that had successfully gone against the grain to treat their "Burnouts," "Gs," or "Freaks" with the same respect and consideration that they offered to the "Preps" and "Jocks." But the literature of communities of practice, and people like Wenger and Eckert who have researched it, do have some theoretical ideas about measures that might make a difference.

- Hold extracurricular debates or dialogues for students who are interested in talking about the "great game" of their school. What does it take to be successful at this school? Are some groups favored over others? As in all dialogues, don't plan on (or expect) any outcome. Just talking about the issue, ideally with a teacher/facilitator who can help students suspend their assumptions, may start to make a difference. For some students, this will be the first time they've been able to talk about the great limiting factors in their lives.

- Set up a wider range of extracurricular activities, including some deliberately designed for "Burnouts," "G's," or whichever parts of the community are systematically ignored. These might include auto shop groups, for instance, where boys and girls can work on cars. It might include support for alternative theater or music groups that speak to "Burnout" culture. "I know a lot of the Burnouts in one school who got very involved in the Special Olympics," said Eckert, "because they spent a lot of time taking care of younger siblings and were very concerned about them."

- Recruit "Burnout" faculty. Where possible, hire and promote teachers who come from "Burnout" backgrounds (or whatever the non-privileged local backgrounds may be.)

- Set up representative elections for student council. Most student councils are elected by their grades as a whole or in other forms that establish one or two groups as dominant. When other students have a genuine concern (when, for example, they want to go off campus for lunch) they have no voice. But if student elections are representative of the social structure—if, for example, students could self-select into groups of thirty and elect a representative from within each group—then the student council becomes an official place where members of various student communities meet.

- Consider multigrade classrooms. Burnout students are often much more used to larger extended family-friendship networks, with friendships across grade lines. They are more used to being amid brothers, sisters, cousins, and neighbors of varied ages.

- If there is a shared vision process in the school, link it to shared vision efforts for the broader community.

- Involve everyone, not just the school elite. It can also revitalize the school to involve teachers in home or community visits. They often find that kids who seem listless or truant at school have an active, even exhausting life at home taking care of others. A sophomore boy may have to bring his two-year-old sister to daycare every morning before school. A junior girl may be highly involved in an after-school church or community group.

GEEKS

How Two Lost Boys Rode the Internet Out of Idaho, by Jon Katz (Broadway Books, 2000).

Jon Katz, a writer and contributor to such publications as Wired, Rolling Stone, and Slate.com, weaves a memorable tale about Jesse and Eric, two teenage boys fluent in technology who escape a small town in Idaho and make their way to Chicago, with the author's encouragement and remarkable belief in them. I think educators, wherever they teach, can gain tremendous insight into the lives of teenagers like Jesse and Eric—geeks, learning largely on their own, who live complex, isolated lives on the fringes of school and community life. When I read the book in 2001, I immediately recommended it to the graduate students I teach. These invisible, highly intelligent outcasts float under the radar of most adults, often noticed only rarely (for example, when they hack into the school's computer system). It is too easy to write off such students for whom the schools' curriculum cannot compete with the cyberworld where they hold the keys to open far more challenging doors. —Nelda Cambron-McCabe

XI. Development

1. No More "Drive-By Staff Development"

The Five Learning Disciplines as a Path Toward Comprehensive School Change

Edward T. Joyner

This article was adapted and updated from the first-edition version, which was written during Dr. Joyner's time at Yale. We thank James Comer for his influence, example, and support.

Ed Joyner has been a thought leader on improving staff development, particularly in inner cities, for the past 25 years. During the 1990s and 2000s, as an assistant professor of child and adolescent development at Yale, he was the executive director of the Yale University School Development Program (a school reform approach popularly known as the "Comer Process," after its founder James Comer). In founding the Comer Process teacher training program, he drew a continuing link between the effectiveness of schools and the learning orientation of staff development. He is also a former community activist (for Community Progress, Inc., the first antipoverty agency in the U.S.), a former high school teacher and middle school principal (in New Haven, Connecticut), and currently an associate professor of education at Sacred Heart University in Fairfield, Connecticut.

Much of the discussion around school reform takes place in a power-coercive framework. State legislatures announce that, in effect, "These children will achieve." Regardless of whether they've been fed well, live in safe neighborhoods, have parents at home, have good medical care, or live in a peaceful and tranquil environment, they will be judged against the children who have those things. Teachers, similarly, are told, "You will have high test scores, or we will close you down." The states, in effect, are like agriculture departments telling a farmer, "You will have a high crop yield this year. We want the corn to ripen in forty-five days where before it took sixty, and it had better be good corn." The results they want are laudable, but they show no awareness of the process that must occur naturally to produce those results.

That is the context of staff development today. All too often, it is "drive-by staff development:" external trainers parachute in to offer their new method for teaching math or reading. They don't know what the staff already knows, what challenges they face in educating the young people of this particular community, or anything else about the school or district. Nor do they try to find out. They merely offer their new method for, say, teaching math or reading. No time is allotted for reflection or active participation, by the educators or anyone else.

The result is a smorgasbord of "dog and pony shows," where the instructors don't listen to the participants or talk to each other, and they might even contradict each other. The content might be provocative or feel compelling, but nothing reinforces the techniques that are learned, so participants move immediately back to their previous approach and their previous comfort level. The trainers move on, and no coaching occurs to allow trainees to gain mastery of the skills or knowledge presented in the training event. Moreover, principals, central office staff, parents, and other stakeholders frequently are left out or elect not to participate. At its worst, the packaging of expertise sends a message that people can't solve their own problems; they shift the burden of school improvement and reform to outside professionals.

See Shifting the Burden, page 375.

THREE FUNCTIONS TO FULFILL

The alternative is a reflective, generative staff development process where training incorporates what educators already know and helps them improve what they can do based on the challenges they face now. I am currently working with Dr. William Lloyd, the superintendent of the Uniondale school system on Long Island, New York, to design such a program and put it into practice. Under this design, sessions are conducted by individuals who have studied the context of the district and who are willing to transfer their knowledge and skill. Instead of being consultant-dependent, teachers and administrators solve their own problems through a process that allows them to collaborate without fault or blame. This staff development model, instead of merely transmitting knowledge to educators as individuals, tries to improve the capability of the whole school, by consistently giving educators a way to learn from and work with each other.

At Uniondale, we have three basic principles at the core of our design:

1. **Looking at real challenges faced by the school.** Every session should be driven by problems that educators are trying to solve right now.

For example, in one part of the district, there has been a demographic shift; parents from El Salvador, recently arrived in the United States have moved in en masse with young children. Suddenly, the elementary school population contains many more students for whom English is a second language. The professional development program has thus been explicitly revamped to help the administrators and teachers look ahead, to anticipate how teaching and curricula might be affected, and to marshal local and state resources to help.

Elsewhere in the district, language is an issue. Children grow up speaking African American vernacular English (also known as ebonics), and schools need to help them learn the kind of standard language and critical thinking needed to be ready for college and the workforce. This is not just a responsibility for English, reading, and enrichment teachers; for example, science and health involve a large number of important words that may not be used frequently in daily life. Science teachers need training to provide ways, such as immersion and practice, that will increase the probability that students will read, speak, and write well in standard, science-oriented language. This is a priority for staff development.

2. **Action learning at the session and in follow-up.** In Yale's Comer Process, this is known as "back-home planning." Every staff development design should explicitly recognize that new skills atrophy when there is inadequate follow-through. There needs to be a planned strategy for bringing new insights back to the work site, trying them out consciously, assessing how they work, and comparing notes on their effectiveness—all actively supported by the administration. If a new idea is not worth that level of attention, it isn't worth introducing in the first place. A critical part of each session should be a "train the trainer" component, so that attendees can think about the implications of doing this new approach back in their school's context and bring others on board. Another critical form of follow-up is quantitative and qualitative, using data to assess whether the new approaches have made a difference. These experiences and results should then influence the next round of training.

3. **Leadership and community engagement.** Teaching is not a one-way process, in which teachers act alone. It is embedded in relationships with students, school system administrators, parents, and community leaders. Staff development at Uniondale is designed to bring out the active learner in all of those constituencies. It explicitly follows the priorities set at district retreats (where the school board and administrators attend) and selects external speakers to match those priorities.

Parents are invited into those staff development sessions, with ample time for dialogue and reflection with the outside speaker and each other. This form of staff development is fluid and responsive. For example, an expert on child development could be brought in to work with educators and parents together—helping parents understand more about the ways their children learn and develop and bringing everyone's understanding into harmony. Sessions also involve collaborative learning, sharing the kinds of tacit knowledge that teachers have about their students and methods that they typically don't share and that can't be captured in the pages of a book.

Learning Disciplines in Staff Development

In making the transition from "drive-by" staff development to a more generative development system, the five learning disciplines—systems thinking, personal mastery, mental models, shared vision, and team learning—are critical.

MENTAL MODELS

Thousands of teachers in public schools today unwittingly operate out of a deficit perspective when teaching poor children. Consciously or not, these teachers have adopted the "bell curve" mental model—that student performance should be distributed across a bell-shaped curve, with some students destined to be below average. After all, somebody's got to be in the first percentile, just as somebody has to be in the ninety-eighth. We generally expect wealthy children to perform better on the curve than poor children and white children to perform better than black, brown, and red children. Related to this model is the pervasive mental model that children's brains are separate from the rest of their lives; that, as my longtime friend and colleague Jack Gillette puts it, children are like "brains on a stick," and can either be educated or not, based on the innate academic capabilities of those brains, separate from any other aspect of the child's life.

These mental models all influence educators to expect less from some children, to provide fewer productive challenges for those children, and not to look for the leverage that might exist for them. For teachers who have grown up in poor neighborhoods, or who come from minority backgrounds, these mental models are doubly pernicious, because the adults feel stigmatized themselves. For example, an elementary school principal told me that based on their perception of the learning capabilities of that community, "We're trying to get the teachers to have the kids learn one

word per month." This extremely low set of internalized expectations—
only ten words a year—is likely to become a self-fulfilling prophecy.

A more accurate mental model, according to the current state of
cognitive science, would regard children as systems whose learning is
affected by a variety of interrelated factors. The ability to read, for example, depends directly on the nutrition, engagement, parenting, and
physical development that very young children receive. Social awareness (the ability to understand and engage other people), psycho-emo-
tional development (the development of temperament, age-appropriate
maturity, perseverance), linguistic ability (facility with expressive and
receptive language in both dialectical and standard form), and ethical
development (capacity for making fair and just decisions) all influence
one another. In the long run, academic performance and good citizenship depend on all of these abilities. Far too many educators spend time
blaming the kids, parents, teachers of previous grade levels, and themselves, when we could devote that energy and attention instead to try to
meet the full range of kids' needs and to support one another in doing so.

Mother Nature provides us with the best examples of development.
For example, the development of a tree depends on where it is planted.
Similarly, a child's potential is rooted in the kind of social, emotional, and
physical environment where he or she grows up and the examples set by
the adults who care for the child. While every human being should have
access to the basic necessities of life, nonmaterial factors play a large role
in shaping human behavior. People sometimes assume that if parents can
provide a nice home, car, and food in the refrigerator, then children will
thrive. But we see many children who do well in low-income families;
and we have seen wealthy children who have been deprived in other
ways and who never capitalize on their unearned advantages.

We can't change these mental models through logical analysis or argument; certainly not through "drive-by staff development." We can change
them only by holding conversations with colleagues, parents, and community members—where we openly examine our attitudes and the influences
that put those views in our mind in the first place. This is not an easy task.

A staff development process that addresses this challenge might have
four questions on the table for dialogue:

1. What are our beliefs about how children learn? What do we know
   about the ways in which performance is linked to both nature and
   nurture? What leads us to those conclusions, and what observable
   "data" can we point to?

   At one Comer school—Bowling Park Elementary in Norfolk, Virginia—a school custodian was concerned about the way some of the

sixth-grade boys were behaving, so he got the principal's permission to involve them in landscaping around the school and a little bit of money to pay them. Every weekend he and the boys worked, and then had lunch and talked about issues. Before long the teachers noticed a major difference in the way these boys acted. Their grades went up. And where they had been about to be written off, they became solid citizens. The custodian couldn't teach them algebra, but he could engage their social and ethical development—by setting a good example that showed how work, no matter what kind of work it is, has an innate dignity. When the principal received a national leadership award from our organization, the custodian was on the podium with him.

2. What skills and knowledge will students need to thrive in a society that is both technologically advanced and highly diverse?

Most staff development programs have dealt with standardized tests by isolating academic disciplines from each other. Reading improvement programs are targeted at reading teachers; math programs target math teachers. Such programs reinforce "teaching to the test" along with the tendency to focus on a few high achievers in each area and to demand less from the other students. By contrast, in our staff development, we look at all the course material together, across grade levels, trying to align the subjects we want to teach, the subjects we have to teach, and the subjects that will help children progress.

3. How is the material best taught? If we could do anything to educate kids well, what would we do?

Many people seem to think that to reach high standards teachers simply need to teach harder, in the same ways. But that idea ignores everything we know about human development. Teaching is the most complicated job of all the professions because children have been shaped by so many other factors. The teacher's work has to recognize, to fit with, and often to counter, what the child is learning at home or in the peer culture. That means applying any methods necessary to reach different kids in different ways. To paraphrase Malcolm X, we educate kids by "any means necessary," as long as those means are legal and ethical.

Teachers need training to do this; good intentions are not enough. Good intentions lead to the kind of teaching I often saw in the 1970s, where teachers talked readily about how disadvantaged the kids were and how they needed to be loved; so they gave them easy work and let them get away with not learning. Perhaps the greatest insult was to romanticize their low-income backgrounds or to try to forge solidarity by imitating their speech. Instead of helping these students blaze a path to mainstream America, these "well intentioned" teachers were reinforcing behaviors that kept low-income kids poor and uneducated. Good teachers help children overcome unearned disadvantages.

4. How is staff development best supported organizationally? What do we need from the school system and community? How does our thinking on this differ? And what will we do when we leave this session?

If you conduct staff development without asking people to plan for the return back home, you might as well not bother. In our experience, if nothing concrete happens within thirty days after a session, nothing will ever happen. The administration must support it, and experience with this new method must be taught to other teachers around the district. This can happen only if the teachers have thought about the support they need from the school system and community and what they intend to use that support for. The organizational support of desired changes is critical to effective staff development.

PERSONAL MASTERY

Highly effective staff development includes the central practice of personal mastery: learning to keep both a personal vision and a clear picture of current reality before us. If you're a teacher, your own personal mastery is closely tied to that of the children in your classes. If you put limits on your own aspirations, you will unconsciously influence your students to feel the same way about themselves.

⟩⟩ See "Drawing Forth Personal Vision," page 81.

When I was a principal at Jackie Robinson Middle School, I had some sixth graders in serious danger of not being promoted. They were not as serious about school as was necessary and had developed a peer culture that was anti-intellectual. I met with the teachers, parents, and students to develop a strategy to address the problem. When I met with the students I said: "Listen, you guys will have to work harder. If you don't know something, you're going to have to ask. You're going to have to follow through on homework." They were intellectually smart, but they needed to develop psychosocially—they had what many teachers call "emotional problems." And they were used to being promoted, even when they weren't qualified.

At the end of the year, I held a significant number of them back. The parents and teachers had agreed that we should not let kids go to the next grade if they were not ready, but we would change the schedule to accommodate the retentions. And we would design an instructional plan that would help low achievers reach grade level.

When they came back in September, still in sixth grade, some of them were a little more humble. At this point, many kids stopped trying. But

I said to them, "If you do well in the first quarter, we'll promote you to seventh grade at the beginning of the second quarter."

Most of the members of that group returned to the grade they had been bumped out of—essentially by doing twice as much work as their peers during the first quarter. The teachers began to change their perceptions of the kids and of themselves. They began to see the flex in the system that they could appropriate if they had to in order to make it work for kids.

TEAM LEARNING

In any human endeavor, the quality of relationships determines outcomes. For that reason, staff development and team learning should be synonymous. Ordinarily, teachers are taught to work as individuals, so staff development has to help them learn to work together. And it needs to be an ongoing process, with enough time to learn new ways of teaching, to develop esprit de corps, and to unlearn old habits.

SHARED VISION

Staff development design can and should include sessions where attendees co-create a view of how the school should evolve. I first saw the power of shared vision when I was a middle school principal. Once a month, I held a day of "family meetings," as we called them—just to give kids a place to talk, grade by grade, about anything that they wanted to talk about. The topics ranged from citizenship in a free society to racial stereotypes to dress codes to whether boys should wear earrings. But they always came back to the question of what they wanted from life and what they wanted from school.

We'd talk about what it meant to be cool or slick, and what it meant to have persistence or resilience; we'd talk about how you could get trapped by beliefs like "We don't play chess, we play checkers." Or "We don't play stringed instruments; we breakdance." And within a year of such meetings, we had kids in the school trying to do everything, including chess and playing the violin, because they now believed it was appropriate to try.

Teachers also get trapped by their beliefs. Like the children, they cannot step out of them on their own. They need deliberate conversations, supported by the community and the school, to do so. Staff development is the natural place.

SYSTEMS THINKING

There is too little communication in many schools across grade levels and fields of study. A child gets an experience in one year that might not relate to the next year's experience. This situation makes the school par-

Effective Learning Behaviors

In our staff development efforts, we use these articulated norms as a way for teachers and students to judge their own leadership and learning potential. The message to teachers is: Your behavior makes a difference to how well students learn. The message to students is: Your behavior also influences the teacher. Teachers go a lot further for students that are responsive to them, and it's fair to ask students to match or exceed the commitment of their best teachers. —*Edward T. Joyner*

Effective Teaching Behaviors
(for a "Premier teacher")
Adapting
Planning
Relating
Evaluating
Managing
Instructing
Expectancy
Resilience

Effective Student Behaviors
(for an "Active student")
Attention
Cooperation
Task-Orientation
Intention
Verbalization
Enthusiasm

ticularly vulnerable to tests, because each year's instructor feels that he or she alone must prepare the kids for the assessment. But aligning curriculum across levels requires using the skills and techniques of systems thinking; teachers must agree about where the starting level for students exists and how fast to carry them along the development path. Teachers in successive grades need to think of themselves as relay racers, passing a baton. Year after year, as students change and state requirements shift, teachers need to discuss openly the work that is going well, the work that is not, and the changes they need to make.

If you're a systems thinker in planning staff development, then you focus on building collaborative relationships and structures for change. You need a mechanism and a process that allows people to talk, across grade levels, departments, and schools within a system, about how they want kids to develop and what supports they need. You also need to involve the school board and local government in the conversation, instead of just receiving mandates from them—to create a network of support for children of which the school is just a part.

In general, the goal of staff development should be to institutionalize a systems understanding of the school district—as a knowledge-based organization that can continually revitalize itself. Educators don't have to be dependent on drive-by staff development. We can use staff development in the same way that farmers have used cooperative extension support: to share and augment our existing knowledge, bringing in new information and protocols bit by bit, testing them in practice and comparing notes, so that we can build our capacity for generations.

2. The Cognitive Studies Group

A Strategy for Teachers

Faith Florer

Faith Florer is a cognitive psychologist, learning coach, and faculty member at Mercy College, New York. We thank Daniel Schack for contributing to the original version of this article.

A significant amount of research during the last twenty years has brought new understanding of mental processes such as learning, intelligence, motivation, emotion, attention, and the interaction of those processes. Teachers who understand these processes can understand how students construct knowledge about academic disciplines, their social world, and their selves. This understanding can also help teachers construct more effective teaching techniques.

Consider memory. When people learn a new piece of information, it is stored in their long-term memory. The long-term memory functions in an associative pattern. Memories are linked to one another and when one memory is activated, the connecting memories are activated as well. The concept for eagle is linked to the concepts for bird, feathers, bald, and whatever else one's mind has associated with eagles. When the memory for eagle is activated, so are the memories for all the other concepts associated with it. Emotions and motivation add "valence"—psychological attraction—to those connections. It follows that the more concepts a memory is connected to, the more likely it will be easily retrievable from long-term memory.

Cognitive psychology also explains why the context of instruction is so important. Relating concepts to ourselves leads to some of the highest retention rates for learned materials. The research on associative learning suggests that every learner, whether an adult or a child, forms unique associative patterns in his or her memories, derived from his or her unique base of knowledge and experience. By connecting to those patterns, every person can learn to learn better. Therefore, material should be taught to all students in a way that relates this information to their experiences and leads to a better-connected associative network to take advantage of what we know about learning to learn.

It is not enough simply to relate material to students' existing knowledge and personal experience. Knowledge is created and exists in synapses—the spaces between neurons that are filled with chemicals. These synapses are affected by emotions and motivation, which can aid or hinder memory. Teachers can learn how to motivate students and how to identify and create an appropriate emotional learning environment—to stretch students' understanding, while not paralyzing them emotionally. Teachers who can explain why a topic is relevant and who can relate information to students on multiple topics, with just the right amount of stretch, will increase the likelihood of retention and easy retrieval from students' memory.

Other cognitive theories of associative learning demonstrate why students should be active participants in the classroom environment, not just passive recipients of information. They show why a teacher should encourage students to search out additional material relating to the subject, aside from class readings. And they show why peer tutoring is an excellent way to increase understanding of material for both the tutor and tutee.

Many teachers already have been exposed to these ideas—but despite their interest and enthusiasm, it's hard for the ideas of cognitive science to take hold. That's because few writers have translated insights into effective teaching practices. Arguably, no book can accomplish this on its own, because educators' learning is also subject to the same cognitive principles. Any recipe for changing teaching to "boost long-term memory," for example, will be relevant only for the teachers whom it fits—and it will be relevant to them only if they come up with the methods themselves. Only then can they associate the novel aspects of teaching practice, suggested by cognitive science, with their own experience.

Hence the value of cognitive science study groups, ideally organized by teachers themselves. In these groups, professionals can work together to explore basic knowledge about learning, memory, attention, and motivation in a practical manner, instead of focusing on technique without a sound theoretical basis. Teachers in a cognitive studies group can explore a principle, suggest some approaches, try them in class, and then return to talk through the results.

Start with one of these books. Read one chapter at a time and then meet. Ask one another: What does this imply about your teaching methods? What methods would be more in tune with the insights from this chapter? By designing and coaching your teaching methods collaboratively, you are participating yourself in a cognitive process.

THINKING FAST AND SLOW

by Daniel Kahneman (Farrar, Straus and Giroux, 2011)

Thinking Fast and Slow is a tour de force by Nobel prize winner Daniel Kahneman. It is about the two types of thinking that underlie decisionmaking—fast, intuitive, habit-based, somewhat emotional type 1 thinking; and slower, more logical, controlled type 2 thinking. This book includes descriptions of the author's seminal work with Amos Tversky that demonstrated how individual thinking is not logical. For example, when asked, most people will erroneously state that the letter "k" is more likely to appear in the first position of a word, (as in "kite") rather than in the third position ("cake"), because it's easier to think of words starting with "k." Similarly, people overestimate the importance of dangers that are easy to think of (like abduction by strangers) compared to dangers that are more likely to occur (like bicycle accidents without a helmet). The book covers the most influential findings in these cognitive areas and helps people to understand how to assess and modify the two types of thinking in an engaging and thought-provoking manner. Consider how useful it would be to help students navigate their responses to multiple choice and essay questions, to help students with their knee-jerk reactions to other people, and to help teachers understand their knee-jerk reactions to students. This book will help.

HUMAN: THE SCIENCE BEHIND WHAT MAKES US UNIQUE
by Michael Gazzaniga (Harper Collins, 2008)

In this book, one of the most prominent and influential neuroscientists and teachers of our time, Michael Gazzaniga, explores the biological and brain-related functions that make people uniquely human, as compared to the animal kingdom. He conveys a wide range of concepts easily: topics include language, art, consciousness, and social interactions. He covers these and others with compassion, fairness, and deep understanding. This book can provide teachers with the foundational concepts that are necessary for understanding the human mind, which in turn can help them understand how to create the best learning environment for students.

SYNAPTIC SELF
by Joesph LeDoux (Penguin Books, 2002)

Much current research on cognition, learning, and memory explores how systems of neurons in the brain constrain and create our perception of the world and our understanding of ourselves. That is the subject of this book, written by prominent neuroscientist Joseph LeDoux, of NYU's Center for Neural Science. LeDoux' work has centered on emotions—particularly fear and anxiety—and their interactions with thinking and behavior. This book is a must-read for people who want to understand how neurons and synapses (the space between the neurons) constrain and create our learning environments, our social interactions, and our selves. The book includes links to his webpage at NYU, which archives ongoing and original research, and links to his rock band, the Amygdaloids (named after the amygdala, one of the seats of anger and emotion in the brain). The band performs songs about the brain and its disorders; some of their music is based on his findings.

YOU ARE NOT YOUR BRAIN: THE 4-STEP SOLUTION
by Jeffrey Schwartz and Rebecca Gladding (Avery, 2011)

Are we victims who are controlled by our neural circuitry? Is medication the only solution to helping students who are diagnosed with ADHD and other psychiatric disorders? Prominent neuroscientist and UCLA researcher Jeffrey Schwartz and clinical psychiatrist Rebecca Gladding answer "no." This book explains how mindfulness can help people to gain control over maladaptive behaviors, without medication. This book will help readers to understand the principles behind programs such as PATHS (Promoting Alternative Thinking Strategies), as well as to develop new possible individual programs that can help children (and adults) modify their emotions and behavior to improve their learning and classroom behavior.

Also see Emotional Intelligence, by Daniel Goleman, page 207.

THE WISDOM OF THE BODY
Discovering the Human Spirit, by Sherwin B. Nuland (Knopf, 1997)

Where was this book when I was studying human physiology? It is one of the most profound and thorough treatments of the body and its functions in existence, but the book also has a spiritual dimension in that it shows how physical development impacts every aspect of our lives. Imagine what it would be like to be a kindergartner with medical problems that affect your hearing, but no one diagnoses you. How might that limit your academic performance? What kind of assumptions would you make about yourself? Or consider the possibility that dyslexia is genetic and curable through genetic therapy. Nuland, a Yale professor of surgery, describes the body's functions in the context of our development. He shows clearly and clinically the connections between what we are physically and what we do in the world. It's a fascinating book, and if I were teaching preservice education, it would be required reading. —Edward T. Joyner

3. Learning to Teach

Collaboration, Reflection, and Inquiry in the Student Teaching Experience

Nancy Hoffmann

In the early 1990s, John Goodlad brought national attention to a critical dilemma for schools: Which comes first, good schools or good teacher education programs? We are not likely to have good schools unless we prepare excellent teachers. Yet it is unlikely that we will send out excellent teachers unless they spend a great deal of time in exemplary schools during their preparation. Sustainable change cannot occur in schools without changes in student teaching.

Goodlad founded the National Network for Educational Renewal (NNER), which has been a valuable and influential source for partnerships between universities and public schools. They have prototyped and fostered new types of partnerships, with reflective, dialogic, and collaborative experiences, to improve educational opportunities for kids and future teachers. Many of these partnerships have been in place since the mid-1990s and are still experimenting and improving, as teachers and university faculty collaboratively work to strengthen their programs.

These two articles, written in 1999, still evoke the value of a reflective student teaching experience, based on experience at one of the NNER partnerships (with Miami University of Ohio). The first is written by Nancy Hoffman—then a teaching associate working with student teachers at the Madeira School District in suburban Cincinnati, and now a staff member with Lifelong Learning at Miami University of Ohio. The second is by Bernard Badiali, then chair of Miami's Department of Educational Leadership, now a professor in the Educational Leadership program at Penn State University.

Also see John Goodlad, *Educational Renewal: Better Teachers, Better Schools*, (Jossey-Bass, 1994), or the National Network for Educational Renewal website at www.nnerpartnerships.org.

I'm sure my experience in preparing to teach is not drastically different from that of other educators reading this book. Nearly all of us were submerged in a concentrated student teaching experience, the most universal component of teacher preparation and the generally accepted "most critical experience" for influencing those who teach. As student teachers, we worked with cooperating, experienced teachers who gradually and slowly turned over classroom responsibilities to us—the novices. I vividly recall sitting patiently in the back of the classroom for sev-

Landon Beyers and Kenneth Zeichner, "Teacher Education in Cultural Context: Beyond Reproduction," in Thomas S. Popkewitz (editor), *Critical Studies in Teacher Education* (The Falmer Press, 1987), pp. 298–335.

Seeing teachers as inquirers "assumes that research—or thinking critically about the process in which you are engaged—is not something you do after you have learned how to teach. It is something you do in order to learn to teach." — B. Bowen, "Response" in N. Amanda Branscombe, Dixie Goswami, and Jeffrey Schwartz (editors), *Students Teaching, Teachers Learning* (Boynton/ Cook-Heinemann, 1992), pp. 293–295.

eral weeks, watching and noting every move of the cooperating teacher, anxiously waiting for my turn. I admired and respected her, but not for a moment did I forget the power differential in this relationship. My task was clear: to mimic the master teacher, even if that meant thoughtless reproduction of her practices. Thinking deeply about challenging educational issues, or questioning the reasons for her approaches, was not required, and there was no time for it.

Like most student teachers, I focused on demonstrating the mastery of content and implementing specific methodology rather than on the processes teachers use to learn to teach or construct meaning from their practice. Too often teacher education programs offer "recipe-style" methods of instruction that students then must follow during student teaching. Instead of promoting a critically reflective practice, future teachers are effectively initiated into the status quo that sees teaching as an apolitical, technical, and procedural activity. Learning to teach, in this sense, is didactical and hierarchical. Learning about teaching is passive—something to be gotten or had rather than something engaged, constructed, and connected to the participants. These practices shape the beginning teacher's identity as "one who implements rather than produces knowledge."

Now, as a supervisor of university interns, I am part of the school-university partnership between the Madeira School District and Miami University directed toward changing these practices. A guiding principle of the partnership is that teaching is an ongoing, fluid process that unfolds and evolves throughout our professional life, rather than a static, fixed procedure one can master. Our interns are both receivers of knowledge and generators of knowledge during their learning-to-teach experience. We build in opportunities for reflection and inquiry as an integral part of their experience. Along with regular reflective writing about their experiences, the interns conduct an inquiry project (action research) through the entire semester to engage and question their own practices. They internalize what they are learning, reflect upon it, analyze it, and make meaning from it.

In the Miami/Madeira student teaching model, interns are placed with a mentor teacher (or team of mentor teachers) who remains in the classroom with the student teacher throughout his or her experience. Student teachers and mentors engage continuously in dialogue that brings to the surface some of the mental models that guide their practices. This conversation involves raising questions of substance relative to the specific classroom or school context as well as to the broader community. They reflect on the ways their experiences in schools and at the university have contributed to shaping their identity as well as the ways in which the cultural construction of the teacher through various forms of media have defined the teacher's role and image. They challenge these images and construct new identities that align more with the values and beliefs that undergird their specific context.

A primary component of our partnership approach is a team learning effort where mentor teachers and novices conduct research (inquiry projects) to gain a better understanding of their practices and their roles as teachers. This process communicates to prospective teachers that novices and experienced teachers alike are continually learning to teach. It also emphasizes that one of the best ways to link theory and practice is through a process of self-critical and systematic inquiry about teaching. Not only is knowledge generated through the inquiry project, but the personal and professional relationships of the interns and mentors are strengthened.

Learning from Student Teachers

Bernard Badiali

Perhaps one of the most interesting and powerful examples of inquiry was an investigation by Jenn Reid, who interned in senior English in 1999 with DJ Hammond, a high school teacher at Madeira. Jenn was interested in the issue of gender equity in high school; more specifically, she was interested in the way in which senior girls participated in their classes. She had read widely on the subject as part of a summer project, including books like *Reviving Ophelia* and *Schoolgirls*. Were young women more reluctant to speak in class than young men? And if so, what might help them change?

DJ was interested in this issue too, because she observed girls in her classes who were bright and articulate but unwilling to say much during class discussions. As part of their teaching together, Jenn, the intern, and DJ, the twenty-five-year veteran, devised a plan to collect information from the senior girls in several classes. They interviewed girls at regular intervals during the semester. They solicited journals and other writing asking how the girls felt about speaking out in class, about expressing their views, and about their "air time" compared to the boys in the room.

Instead of the typical superior/subordinate relationship, Jenn and DJ were partners in the research. The results of the inquiry were profound. The data Jenn and DJ collected surprised them both. Girls spoke and wrote about feeling inferior in discussions. They were afraid of the social consequences of saying something "dumb." They worried about what the boys might think about their comments. Jenn was confirming for herself what she had read the semester before. She and DJ began devis-

Mary Pipher, Reviving Ophelia (Grosset/Putnam, 1994); Peggy Orenstein, *Schoolgirls: Young Women, Self-Esteem, and the Confidence Gap* (Anchor Books/Doubleday, 1995); also see William Pollack, *Real Boys: Rescuing Our Sons from the Myths of Boyhood* (Owl Books, 1998) for the challenges and obstacles facing boys.

Jenn Reid became a full-time language arts teacher at Madeira in 1999, where she taught for seven years. She was also a director of a program called Young Women Writing for (a) Change in Cincinnati. She is now a language arts teacher for the Dayton, Ohio, Regional STEM School, where female students are outnumbered two to one.

ing strategies to encourage more active participation from the girls in their classes. They discussed the issue with the classes they researched. The two of them had deep and meaningful conversations about instruction, about curriculum, and about the nature of girls' socialization.

At the end of the semester there is a ritual at Madeira where all of the interns take twenty or thirty minutes to report their findings to the entire faculty. Jenn made her presentation to about twenty-five Madeira teachers, several Miami professors, and a few visitors from other schools. She presented data in the form of quotes from the interviews, girls' writing samples, and anecdotal accounts of classroom events. The teachers, especially those who had senior girls, listened intently. The presentation was powerful, sometimes tearful. At the end of her presentation, the head of the mathematics department at Madeira stood up and said, "That's it! Every girl in my class will participate tomorrow and from now on! I will find a way to make that happen."

Later the school superintendent, who had been in the audience, told me that she was stunned at the powerful response to Jenn's report. She said, "I could have spent thousands of dollars on a staff development program about gender equity and would never have gotten such a response from teachers. They have read the studies. They know what the national data shows. It's just that this report was about us. These girls are our girls. They have names and they have faces and we know their parents."

Jenn's inquiry project was the talk of the faculty for days, even weeks. Several teachers acknowledged that they saw senior girls in a new light. The wonderful thing about making these projects public is that they create discussion among staff. Interns enjoy a sort of political immunity with regard to their findings. Veteran teachers always can write them off as just superficial investigations of a neophyte discovering the craft of teaching, or they can learn from what they discover. But it is obvious by their questions, during and after the presentations, that teachers are willing to learn from interns who can provide them with observable data about the workplace. And interns feel pretty good about being able to give something back to the setting that hosted them for a semester.

EDUCATIONAL RENEWAL
Better Teachers, Better Schools, by John Goodlad (Jossey-Bass, 1994)

This is a book for redesigners of the teaching of teachers—and those who care about it. John Goodlad focuses not on improving reading scores or the debate over how to teach math but on the long-term questions of educational purpose. What civic identity will people have? How will they learn to think? How will they earn a living, look at the world, understand people, understand themselves, pursue knowledge? What kind of moral sense will they have? Goodlad argues that most schools (and university education departments) have lost that sense of purpose. He suggests creating "centers of pedagogy," closely connecting universities and local school systems, to revitalize schools. Educators who feel themselves ambivalent about the "industrial model of schools" (page 32) should look here for an alternative. —Nelda Cambron-McCabe

Also see the Learning Research and Development Center, page 206.

XII. Leadership

1. Leading Without Control
Moving Beyond the "Principal Do-Right" Model of Educational Leadership

Charlotte Roberts

Though she is not a coauthor of this book, Charlotte Roberts was a key figure in its evolution. A leading consultant in organizational learning and coauthor of The Fifth Discipline Fieldbook and The Dance of Change, she began to help the Danforth Foundation (page 421) in a project defining a new leadership model for public school superintendents in 1993 and has worked with educators and schools ever since.

The elementary school principal turned to me during the final session of an administrators' year-long course on organizational learning and said, "My ladies (meaning his teachers) want me to make all the decisions and tell them what to do. They don't want any part in decisionmaking or planning for our school." He was a young principal with a recent graduate degree, and his comment was extremely curious. He had just spent twelve months studying ways to develop authentic participation by his staff. Did he really believe that all this time had been wasted?

Several months later, another elementary school principal gave me the "aha!" I was looking for. She was a member of a school district team from the American Midwest, one of six teams that had agreed to use their own experience as a case study for learning-about-learning organizations. Each team included teachers, principals, and administrators; some even brought along their superintendent. We dug into the theories of Harvard Business School professor Chris Argyris, theories that provide the foundation of the discipline of mental models. Argyris had written:

> There seems to be a universal human tendency to design one's actions consistently according to four basic values:

The quote comes from Chris Argyris, "Teaching Smart People How To Learn," *Harvard Business Review* (May-June 1991), HRB Reprint #91301.

1. To remain in unilateral control;
2. To maximize "winning" and minimize "losing";
3. To suppress negative feelings; and
4. To be as "rational" as possible—by which people mean defining clear objectives and evaluating their behavior in terms of whether or not they have achieved them.

The purpose of all these values is to avoid embarrassment or threat, feeling vulnerable or incompetent.

In the article, Argyris points out that the net effect of these values is to block any kind of fruitful learning or change in an organization. Our conversation was lively and full of disclosure. People were "'fessing up" to their own transgressions. There was release and freedom in the air. Suddenly a principal named Becky Furlong called a halt to the conversation with her exclamation, "Hey, wait a minute! This is all backward! Those four values are the exact measurements of a good superintendent or principal!" She went on to lead the group in detailing the prevailing model of leadership in public education. In my own mind, I began to think of this as the "Principal Do-Right" model:

Rebecca (Becky) Furlong was then the principal of Mid-Prairie School of Kalona, Iowa; she is now assistant superintendent of the Iowa City Community School District.

1. A good leader gains and remains in control at all times. Never let them see you doubt or sweat. Take a stand and hold that position. No one else will defend the children (or policy, teacher, or curriculum) as well as you will.
2. A good leader "wins" all confrontations, regardless of the party with whom she or he is sparring—child, parent, teacher, administrator, board member, politician. Winning isn't always possible, so be able to recast the exchange as learning, planning, or negotiation. Above all, when pursuing a "win," wear your opponents down with rationality (point four). Another strategy for winning is to redefine the issue as a local situation that will be dealt with privately. By dividing a complex situation and initiating local "fixes" on the parts, the leader can declare a "win."
3. Negative feelings expressed by the principal indicate loss of control and maybe incompetence. If the building has an undertone of negative feelings, it's a sign that the principal has not been able to inspire or motivate the teachers. A display of anger, anxiety, or grief by the principal or superintendent poisons the air and ultimately spills over to the children. "If negative feelings have a hold in your building," said another principal, "it's like getting rid of roaches in an old apartment building."

4. Being rational is a sign of being educated—it's that simple. An educator, after all, develops the minds of our young people. To not appear rational is to appear incompetent. Even with emotional issues like unexpected violence, leaders are supposed to gain control, remain in control, and quickly come up with a rational plan for responding.

Becky's description reminded me of a doctoral program for educational administration that I attended several years before. (I left when I realized I didn't have the constitution to endure the treatment that public education leaders get.) There, too, we were presented with an implicit (and sometimes explicit) model of effective leadership: Advocate. Clarify the problem and take a position. Don't back down. Be strong. Be rational. Be convincing. Be right. This "Principal Do-Right" model, in itself, is a burden that many of our public educators are saddled with. It leads directly to the kinds of behavior that make it difficult to inquire and reflect at length or to draw people together to a common purpose.

Now I understood the reason why that principal from the year before had said, "My ladies want me to make the decisions." He meant: "They refrain from getting involved so that I can personally deal with all the school's conflicts." His job, as he espoused it, was to shield his staff from problems, so they could be free to teach. But in reality, his entire leadership approach was designed to funnel problems directly to him, before anyone else could get to them (a form of unilateral control on his part). In short, the "Principal Do-Right" model of leadership was the primary driving force behind his behavior.

For more about unilateral control and an exercise for helping people overcome their own tendency to "take charge" of conversations counterproductively, see *The Dance of Change*, pp. 252–54.

Since the leadership style itself was undiscussable and perhaps even subconscious, he could not recognize its power over his school. He had to see his "ladies" as not just tolerating but demanding control from him. Nor could he allow himself to see any of the negative consequences that came from this leadership style, such as the anxiety he felt about being wrong or the passivity and cynicism it engendered among the teachers. Imagine the trap in which he was caught. He could go to a hundred seminars on organizational learning, but if they clashed with the "Principal Do-Right" style, he would have to discard them—perhaps with regret, but with a sense of giving in to the inevitable. After all, what other model of educational leadership could there be?

A NEW MODEL OF EDUCATIONAL LEADERSHIP

For more than five years, I worked with a study group of school superintendents, sponsored by the Danforth Foundation, to draw forth a new leadership model for public education. We focused on four key competencies that allow people to lead without having to control.

1. **Engagement:** Ron Heifetz, director of the Leadership Education Project at Harvard's Kennedy School of Government (and one of the mentors of our project), defines leadership itself as the ability to mobilize people to tackle tough problems. To my mind, that is engagement, and it has two components. First is the capability to recognize an issue or situation that has no clear definition, no simple "cause," and no obvious answer. (Ron Heifetz calls these "adaptive problems"; the late systems theorist Russell Ackoff called them "messes.") When faced with such complexity, convening the appropriate people in the system and facilitating their conversations and learning is called for. This is the second part of engagement.

In his book *Leadership Without Easy Answers,* Heifetz provides twelve questions for reflection that, in themselves, represent a process of engagement. The first five questions are aimed at stepping back and dispassionately diagnosing the nature of a crisis or problem and the attitudes people hold about it:

- What's causing the distress (from the "mess" or "adaptive problem")?
- What internal contradictions does the distress represent?
- What are the histories of these contradictions?
- What perspectives and interests have I, and others, come to represent to various segments of the community that are now in conflict?
- In what ways are we in the organization or working group mirroring the problem dynamics in the community?

The next three questions reflect upon the tolerable levels of tension, distress, and learning that the community (in this case, the school system) can handle:

- What are the characteristic responses of the community to disequilibrium—to confusion about future direction, the presence of an external threat, disorientation in regard to role relationships, internal conflict, or the breaking up of norms?
- When in the past has the distress appeared to reach a breaking point—where the social system began to engage in self-destructive behavior, like civil war or political assassination?
- What actions by senior authorities have traditionally restored equilibrium? What mechanisms to regulate distress are currently within my control, given my authority?

Ronald Heifetz, *Leadership Without Easy Answers,* (Harvard University Press, 1994). The leadership definition occurs on p. 15 and the definition of adaptive systems on p. 72ff. The questions for what Heifetz calls the "balcony perspective," with a great deal of explanation, are found on p. 250ff. A longer review appears on page 427 of *Schools That Learn.*

The final four questions help identify the places to intervene:

- What are the work and work avoidance patterns particular to this community?
- What does the current pattern of work avoidance indicate about the nature and difficulty of the present adaptive challenge and the various work issues that it comprises?
- What clues do the authority figures provide?
- Which of these issues are ripe? What are the options for tackling the ripe issues, or for ripening an issue that has not fastened in people's minds?

Engagement is not as easy as it might seem. First, the complexity of the situations usually comes with a lot of emotion on the part of constituents. Creating a safe space for conversation and facilitating listening as well as speaking are not skills taught in graduate schools. With the lack of clarity and the high pitch of emotions, the temptation is to go back to Argyris's value number one: gain unilateral control and create temporary peace.

For those trying to engage others in working on adaptive problems, Ron Heifetz, Marty Linsky, and Alexander Grashow, *The Practice of Adaptive Leadership: Tools and Tactics for Changing Your Organization and the World* (Harvard Business Press, 2009) is an invaluable resource.

2. **Systems Thinking:** The ability to recognize the hidden dynamics of complex systems, and to find leverage, goes hand in hand with engagement. Ludwig von Bertalanffy, one of the grandparents of systems thinking, offered a critical question to reflect on before taking action on a complex problem: "Where are the boundaries to this situation?"

That's not a small question. If you think it is, raise it before a group and see how long it takes to gain consensus. The answer identifies (or begins to identify) the people who need to be included in the thinking and action. Bertalanffy suggested that when groups took their thinking one boundary larger than the place they set it, valuable insights often occurred. For example, if a group thought the situation involved only their middle school, they might look at the situation from the perspective of the next larger system, the school district. In other words, they could consider to what extent other schools in their district or elsewhere are part of the problem.

One compelling story that required a school administrator to use this kind of judgment was a case, developed at Harvard University's Kennedy School of Government, recounting an intervention in a community crisis at an elementary school: "Deciding Who Decides: The Debate Over a Gay Photo Exhibit in a Madison School," by Susan Rosegrant (Harvard Kennedy School of Government Case Study #1440.0, 1998).

After the boundaries are temporarily set, the next questions to ask (from Meg Wheatley's work) are: "Who belongs to the system? Do they know they belong?" Get their input. Work the social system.

Convene a group, for example, to consider the forces at play and the interaction of those forces. A sample scenario: A state legislature's decision to measure the performance of each school causes anxiety, which leads to over-supervision by administrators, which leads to fear by teachers, which leads them to do two things. They can "teach to the test," forgoing teachable moments and exciting tangents. They also can tell children who are expected to produce low scores to stay home for the next few days while the tests are being given. School scores go up, the legislature takes credit for good things, and schools go on gaming the testing process. The performance of the schools looks good; the performance of the children is lost.

A new superintendent comes into the system and discovers what's going on. Should she disclose the cover-up or bask in the artificially high performance? What is the vision for the system? Whose issue is this? Where are the boundaries? Who belongs in this situation, and do they know they belong?

3. **Leading Learning:** The ability to engage people and to study systems is not enough for dealing with complex issues in public education. To lead learning means to model a "learner-centered," as opposed to an "authority-centered," approach to all problems, inside and outside the classroom.

Most of us have experienced the authority-centered approach to problems in the way we were taught as we progressed through the educational system. Teaching in its authoritative form exposes the child to theories, techniques, and rules, and requires the child to prove the accurate reception of all this information through testing. Then teachers "grade" the quality of the child's reception. If the child receives poor grades over a course of time, he or she gets "remedial" teaching. Teaching, in short, is organized for the adults in the system—in the same way that "Principal Do-Right" leadership is organized for the sake of the administrator's self-image.

Authority-centered problem-solving is insidious and sometimes difficult to spot. Even if there is a plaque on a school wall saying "We're student centered," be suspicious. Look at the school policies. You may find the policies are designed to reinforce authority at the expense of learning and to make the life of the adult teachers safe and comfortable.

What, then, does learner-centered leadership, as a competence of educational leaders, look like? You see that learning—and the acceptance of uncertainty that is always part of learning—are part of the culture, or the genetic code, of the system. Teachers still teach, but probably in many different ways from how they were taught themselves, even during their professional education. When the child doesn't understand a concept, the teacher asks, "How did I contribute to this situation? What does this student need to succeed? What can I say or do to help this child take in and apply these concepts? Does the student feel a part of his or her learning? Who belongs in this conversation, and do they know they belong?"

In such a culture, all people in the system are seen as learners and act as learners. It is no longer as important to appear "learned"—to have several graduate degrees and authoritativeness as the primary credential of leadership. Instead, leaders expect themselves and others to be uncertain, inquiring, expectant of surprise, and perhaps a bit joyful about confronting the unknown. Leading learning gives principals and superintendents the freedom to say: "I don't know where we're going…and I'm still willing to dig into this mess with you to discover a way forward."

4. **Self-awareness:** This competence recalls, for me, one of the most painful and yet useful conclusions from our Danforth study group conversations. Leaders in public education come and go (voluntarily and involuntarily) at an alarming rate, as did the superintendents in our group. What had all of us missed seeing? What were the early warning signals that the superintendent no longer "fit" the organization and was about to be let go?

We concluded that leaders must be self-aware. They must know the impact they are having on people and the system and how that impact has changed over time. Perhaps the leadership model has changed since they've come to the job. The school board that hired the superintendent rarely has the same membership after two to four years. The new members may demand another leadership model. Then it's time to go.

Self-awareness is a position of strength. There are at least two components to the task of developing it: taking time away from the office to personally reflect and engaging a personal coach in the office for some period of time. Time away from the office may involve a personal mastery program or a good psychotherapist who understands the pressures of public leadership. A personal coach is someone who genuinely likes you and cares about your wholeness. The coach also must be committed to your journey into the dark of the decision: "Can I continue to offer value for this system?"

The pain of being fired or retired early, after being shredded in the local media, is horrible. There will, of course, always be pain (and joy) in any leadership position. Knowing one's strengths, personal vision and values, and where your personal "lines in the sand" are drawn will build a base of self-awareness that allows you to craft your career and leave on your own terms, satisfied with your contributions to the organization.

}} Also see Images of Organization, page 339.

2. Peer Partners

The Danforth Foundation Superintendent's Forum

For ten years, between 1993 and 2003, the Danforth Foundation (a nonprofit foundation based in St. Louis) regularly brought together a group of about sixty school superintendents to talk about their organizational learning efforts. Officially called the Forum for the American School Superintendent, these "Danforth Forums" (as we called them) were different from the usual professional meeting. Danforth provided some support for superintendents' travel expenses and for small-group learning initiatives, but there was much more to it than money. The superintendents came from urban, suburban, and rural districts; but all of them had at least half of their students at a high risk of failure. And all of them shared a common commitment to all children learning. Early in the development of the forum's agenda, the superintendents turned to organizational learning concepts as they developed their school renewal strategies; they all felt that they could not do it alone. They needed one another's help and support.

Even now, years after they concluded, the people who participated in these forums speak of them as a remarkable experience—a gift to all involved. The network that resulted still exists, and is still important to all of us who participated. When we put together the first edition of this book, I asked several members of this group to come together for a conversation about the design and value of the forum. We think there are powerful precepts here for peer groups of educators everywhere who are looking for support from their peers across the country or across their school. —Nelda Cambron-McCabe

Nine alumni of the Danforth Forum networks came together and formed a new network called the National Superintendents Roundtable that has created a powerful learning group of school superintendents, focused on designing twenty-first-century schools. See www.superintendentsforum.org.

LET THE PARTICIPANTS SET THE AGENDA

Lynn Beckwith, University City, Missouri: The forums have been focused around our concerns as superintendents. The topics we focused on—leadership, public engagement, principalship, early childhood, and race and class—came directly out of the questions we raised.

Peter Negroni, Springfield, Massachusetts: Because the forum was developed for and by the superintendents, we can be sure that it's relevant and that we will deal with the issues as they emerge: developing principals, creating responses to very young children, fostering achievement for all kids in the district, or engaging the public. Over the period of this forum, we've even predicted the major school issues before they received national attention. We've been able to work on these questions intensely

Lynn Beckwith is now an endowed professor of urban education at the University of Missouri, St. Louis.

Peter Negroni is now senior vice president for relationship development at the College Board. See page 428.

Paula Butterfield has retired.

in subgroups and then share our experiences across the broader group. That means, for any given issue, we have sixty people all working on strategies for providing better leadership for schools. By designing our own agendas, we view ourselves and each other as learners—learners who can sustain learning organizations back in our home school districts.

CULTIVATE RELATIONSHIPS AMONG THE PARTICIPANTS

Paula Butterfield, Bozeman, Montana: The Danforth Forum members are all people who have dedicated themselves to making lasting change in public education. We have developed friendships, not just with the people in our individual initiatives but across the entire group of superintendents and also with the consultants and academics who work with us. I don't know of another organization or group of people that has sustained an effort like this for so long. In the process, the web of relationships has become much bigger than the forum itself.

Do you remember the movie *Same Time Next Year* with Ellen Burstyn and Alan Alda? That's how I feel about this group. I personally dread when it ends, because I just think the relationships we have created are so powerful. In other meetings among superintendents, the goal seems to be to allow people to brag about how everything is going well. Facilitating brag sessions is not the goal of the Danforth network.

Peter Negroni: As a result of the Danforth experience, I don't feel alone. I feel supported. I feel energized. I feel we work on the right things, because we share the view that children are what really matters in a school. That energy comes from the network. Networking, to me, means drawing on the energy of other people to construct your own energy to respond to problems. That is what has happened here, and it is why we are so successful in sustaining our relationships.

Lynn Beckwith: I come because I know I can get help here. I can learn here. I can share my inner feelings here, because we are in the same fraternity or sorority. Very few people have been able to walk this walk. I know that we will understand each other, although we come from very different school districts—some large, some small. When I have an intractable problem, I know that there's somebody here who can help me. For example, when I first became superintendent, I was having a difficult time dealing with a micromanaging board. I needed help from someone to find a way to thwart that, and I found the help here.

BRING THE INSIGHTS AND RESOURCES BACK HOME

Paula Butterfield: I have been trying to develop the same types of relationships at home that I found at Danforth: places to talk openly about problems, not just progress. We have brought outsiders, whom we met through the Danforth Forum, back to our district to work with us, to talk, to ask questions, and to point out good things. That has been very powerful for people working in our district, and it has helped the school board recognize the importance of the program. I guess that also makes it different from some of the other kinds of experiences that we have as superintendents. We're always going off to some conference elsewhere. But with this group, we sometimes stay home and people come to us.

Vern Cunningham, Danforth Facilitator: One day I unexpectedly crossed paths with a Danforth superintendent at the airport in Washington. He was there with one of his school principals. As we were talking, I remarked that I had appreciated the superintendent's gift for teaching, which I had seen in a recent Forum workshop. The principal accompanying him said to him, "I wish you would do that back home." That was startling to me. It made me recognize how superintendents' behavior at the national level can differ so much from their behavior in their own districts. That superintendent has since become intensely engaged in such activities with his staff.

Vern Cunningham, former Dean of Education at Ohio State University, continues as a facilitator with the National Superintendents Roundtable.

ENCOURAGE BOLD INITIATIVES THAT MIGHT INFLUENCE CHANGES AT HOME

Lynn Beckwith: The impact of the Danforth Foundation programs ripples through the entire community of your home school system. The result is often a systemic shift in the way the community addresses education and children's issues. In our "Success For All Children" initiative, early care and education have been raised to a new level, not only in the school district of University City but in the entire community. We focus on uplifting the readiness of all children, whether they are in our school district, in home care, or in daycare.

At one time, some members of the community felt that it was not the job of the superintendent's office to worry about children who were not part of the school district. Our success was measured exclusively on how well we handled PK–12 issues and problems. The community now understands that if we address the developmental concerns and needs of young people earlier, we might be able to avoid some of the remedial work required later. As a result, there's an infrastructure now in place that unites all the key community actors in early childhood care and education to carry on this work. This systemic shift started with the Danforth Forum. Fragmented at one time, the community is now united.

Paula Butterfield: In Bozeman, the Success for All Children Initiative had a dramatic impact on the relationships that existed among members of the community. In our first local meeting convened by Danforth, I was able to pull together people who hadn't been talking to each other or who hadn't been working collegially with the school district. Traditional barriers had long existed between some of these people, and often for no good reason other than habit. That meeting started to break down those barriers.

Instead of not talking to one another, the different forces in the community began eventually to co-fund projects. A process for grant applications was set up so that no grant received competing applications from someone else in Bozeman. Instead, a team of people would apply for the grant under the umbrella of the Danforth group. That was an amazing step, and it didn't come easily—or quickly. We joked about needing to learn how to spell "collaboration."

In fact, membership in the local Danforth steering committee became highly desirable. Even people who weren't directly involved in the early childhood field wanted to be on that team; they knew that if one of you went for a grant, the whole group supported it. But it wasn't just the Danforth board that had representatives from all parts of the community. Everyone began serving on each other's boards. For example, I was asked to be on the County Health Board, which wrote a grant with the Kellogg Foundation and became part of a national health initiative. The new county health officer didn't have other administrators on her board. It helped her to have someone with administrative experience— and who knew how the work of the county health department affected children.

You could say that we were "cross-pollinating" each other's boards with both support and with thinking. The mentality of independence, which is particularly strong in a place like Montana, is evolving into a mentality of interdependence and openness.

SET EXAMPLES FOR EACH OTHER

Lynn Beckwith: When the superintendents from the various participating districts get together at the national level, you can quickly tell—just through their conversations—in which school districts the superintendents have been full participants in change projects. A few of the superintendents clearly gave the project their blessing but never really became involved.

Those who make it succeed learn: You have to take off your superintendent's hat when you're a part of the leadership team in your district. Your comments and thoughts technically do not count for any more than the comments and thoughts of others. It's not easy, however. I sometimes have to restrain myself from giving directions when I feel that I have the answers. But I let the committee take the lead.

In one committee meeting, a community-based early childhood director told the committee, "I'm not here to be Dr. Beckwith's PR director or to make him look better. He's only a member of this committee." I took that to heart. That speaker was exactly right.

Of course, relinquishing a leadership role is not an excuse for relinquishing the responsibility of fully participating in the program. I have always felt that the work that grew out of this forum was not something that I could delegate to somebody else. It was incumbent upon me to attend and participate in the team meetings, even though this participation was sometimes difficult with my busy schedule. In their evaluation of the program, some of the team members specifically noted that the superintendent's attendance and participation in the meetings raised the initiative to a new level.

Nelda Cambron-McCabe: I have noticed a shift in roles among many superintendents. For example, many superintendents have changed their way of leadership as a result. In Providence, Rhode Island, Diana Lam's participation in a principals' workshop led one principal to comment that he had never seen a superintendent take part that way before. "Typically," he said, "a superintendent comes in, introduces the outside expert, and walks out as the person starts to talk. But Diana is there taking notes, asking questions, and engaging with her principals, struggling with the ideas." This provides a great example of Ronald Heifetz's concept of adaptive leadership, which we've used in the leadership initiative. Heifetz argues that leadership effectiveness depends not merely on how you set up the circumstances for people to learn together but on how you learn with them.

GIVE CHANGE TIME

Paula Butterfield: One key characteristic of the Danforth initiative work is that it didn't require a product right away—a radical approach in this age of instant gratification. The foundation's wise patience creates a whole different perspective on the way change occurs. Each of us has been dealing mostly with a "We want it now!" attitude in others—if not in ourselves. Because of the work with this initiative, I have shifted gears away from that stance.

Lynn Beckwith: For some of us, it didn't seem as if we were making progress. But I think the Danforth Foundation showed wisdom in not requiring a product right away. The program eventually began getting results and achieving its goals.

CREATE A SAFE PLACE TO TALK ABOUT DANGEROUS THINGS

Lynn Beckwith: The forum's race and class meetings were really helpful to me as I worked with my board of education. Race and class are sensitive issues in University City, as in many other communities. Sometimes there's the feeling that too much is made of them. But I remember one forum meeting in which a white woman made a presentation on white privilege. I took the paper she presented back and shared it with the school board members at home. One board member asked for an appointment with me and said, "Lynn, I never thought about it before; there is such a thing as white privilege."

This was quite a breakthrough. My concerns were no longer greeted with the dismissive comment, "There you go again, Beckwith, you're always talking about race and class."

And I've even noticed a difference in the forum sessions. In the beginning, we were very closed-mouth about race issues. Frankly, when I heard some African Americans loudly and passionately talking about race, I felt that it turned some white superintendents off. So we approached [the African American superintendents] to urge them to take a less aggressive approach. We told them that if we wanted to have a discussion on these topics—and we did—they could not issue indictments. They had to listen.

In one meeting, a superintendent, who was white and came from a very poor background, said that it was the problems of class, not race, that had to be overcome. That really affected me. This person's comments opened up a whole new world for me. I finally realized that whatever your color, if you're poor in America, you've got a problem.

Paula Butterfield: That meeting was powerful for me because I had made some assumptions about the backgrounds of my colleagues in the superintendency. I'm intimidated by wealthy people, because I grew up poor. After that meeting, I recognized that most of us shared similar backgrounds—ranging from poor to far less than affluent. Sharing that common bond reinforced the powerful relationships that I've developed with the other superintendents.

If we had tried to tackle these subjects earlier, before we knew each other as well as we did, it wouldn't have worked at all. But we had worked long enough together. We had developed strong bonds with one another. It was uncomfortable at first, but we all knew that we wanted to do it. And we all knew that if we couldn't do it, who else in America could?

Often, when people ask me "What is it you do in that group?" I say, "You know, in my mind, it's a very spiritual group."

THE SUPERINTENDENT'S FIELDBOOK

A Guide for Leaders of Learning,
by Nelda Cambron-McCabe, Luvern Cunningham, James Harvey, and Robert Koff (Corwin Press, 2005)

Convened from the conversations and experiments sponsored by the Danforth Foundation, and organized in a format like *Schools That Learn,* this compendium of tools, exercises, field research, and stories is very valuable for leaders on the ground. It's sort of like a peer group on paper—or the first step toward one. As one superintendent puts it, "Much of what we know about how to be successful is learned the hard way." This book makes it easier. —Art Kleiner

LEADERSHIP WITHOUT EASY ANSWERS

By Ron Heifetz (Harvard University Press, 1998)

To Ron Heifetz, "adaptive challenges" are the difficult issues that demand changes in attitudes, behaviors, and values. They include complex social and political challenges, like riots and economic crises, where the causes are not clear and the fixes not obvious. And they include many of the problems that school leaders encounter. Heifetz asserts that leaders can deal with adaptive issues, not by providing authoritative answers, but by asking hard questions that spur the entire community to rethink its assumptions. He illustrates this through precepts and carefully interpreted stories of leaders asking people to make difficult choices (ranging from Gandhi to Ronald Reagan to a doctor informing a patient's family that he has cancer) and through the twelve questions that Charlotte Roberts cites on page 417 of *Schools That Learn.* These questions will help you identify adaptive challenges, create a holding environment for talking about them, direct disciplined attention to the issues (and to the reasons why people avoid the issues), and give the work of dealing with them back to the people. —Nelda Cambron-McCabe

lso see Ronald A. Heifetz and Marty Linsky, *Leadership on the Line: Staying Alive Through the Dangers of Leading,* (Harvard Business Press, 2002), for more on making a difference without getting pushed aside.

3. "Lone Ranger" to Lead Learner: One Superintendent's Journey

How Leaders of "Learning"-Oriented School Districts Can Think About Their Own Personal and Professional Development

Peter Negroni

In 1989, Peter Negroni, formerly a principal and superintendent in the New York City system, took on the superintendency of the small, economically struggling city of Springfield, Massachusetts, about eighty miles west of Boston. Negroni was committed to the idea that all children could learn. He came in with a mandate to make a difference. But things weren't so simple. He had to learn to develop not just relationships and humility, but also a learning orientation that was more personal and respectful. The four phases described here represent a developmental path that few "reforming" superintendents can avoid—if they want their reforms to survive their tenure. Dr. Negroni went from Springfield to the College Board, where he is now senior vice president for relationship development.

This article was adapted from a previously published version in Nelda Cambron-McCabe, Luvern Cunningham, James Harvey, and Robert Koff, *The Superintendents Fieldbook: A Guide for Leaders of Learning* (Corwin Press, 2005), pp. 42–48. That was adapted from an earlier version in the first edition of *Schools That Learn*, which had been written while Peter Negroni was still superintendent in Springfield. For a review of *The Superintendent's Fieldbook*, see page 427.

When I retired in 2001 as superintendent of the public school system in Springfield, Massachusetts, a leading national newspaper put the advertisement for my successor in the wrong place. They listed it under "S" for superintendent rather than "E" for education. Applications from managers of buildings and grounds came pouring in. Well-meaning applicants paraded their experience overseeing water heaters, cleaning buildings, and collecting rents in apartment buildings.

It was comical but not really amusing. The mistake reflected an unsettling trend in school administration. For the past several decades, superintendents and principals have become increasingly focused on the machinery and structures of education and on driving up test scores. These issues are more easily comprehended by the public than the messy and often hidden work of teaching and learning.

In today's environment, successful leadership is animated by the will to educate all children to high standards. Such leadership depends, first and foremost, on the example set by the district superintendent. This requires a radical change in the superintendency itself. We cannot manage systems if that means we neglect teaching and learning, leaving the business of instruction to others. We cannot lead learning if we leave the core of instruction unquestioned, unexamined, and essentially mysterious. If we truly intend to educate all students to high standards, then superintendents must become head teachers again.

THE SUPERINTENDENT'S JOURNEY

Most superintendents come to their position after moving up steadily through the teaching and administrative ranks. They are unprepared for the leadership role that faces them. Their careers in the classroom are usually distant memories; their leadership training usually occurred on the fly. An effective superintendent has to relearn what it means to be an educator.

I know this from my own experience. When I became superintendent in Springfield, the system was desperately in need of educational leadership. The staff was insular. There was no overall curriculum. Schools were set up with haphazard grade levels; some elementary schools were K–4, while others were K–6. Some youngsters had to go to as many as four different schools before starting high school.

Most critically, Springfield had very rapidly changed from a basically white and black community to an increasingly Hispanic city. Many civic leaders, including school leaders, had not acknowledged that change. Our high school dropout rate was 51 percent and showed no signs of improving. I came to the district with an overriding personal goal of changing this static, inbred system.

As I look back, I realize that I had embarked on a journey that sometimes quite literally kills people. If one takes on this position as I did—with conventional ideas about the kind of leadership required—he or she might be lucky to last three years. I lasted eleven. I credit this longevity to a particular type of good fortune. As I tried to "make change happen," I was lucky to be confronted by the community in a way that forced me to make some painful but essential discoveries. If my experience is typical, successful superintendents go through a four-part journey. They go from being Lone Rangers to being Lead Learners.

PHASE ONE: THE LONE RANGER

Many new superintendents coming into a district are tempted to do it all. Often, they bring a lot of experience from other systems, but they're not familiar with the new environment, and they're typically alone. Even if they bring trusted colleagues with them, the colleagues are also new to the district. The new superintendent is tempted to act like the Lone Ranger. I know I was.

Convinced that I knew what was wrong with the system, I also assumed I knew how to fix it. Instead of trying to build relationships with the union or the board, I worked around them. Most of the time, I felt that I was way ahead of them. I could change things on my own. And I could change them to suit my preferences.

Take my word for it: you can enjoy some exciting successes as a Lone Ranger. Early on, I managed to develop a clearly defined set of district standards and assessments. I adjusted all the schools into a coherent K–5 elementary, 6–8 middle, and 9–12 high school structure. Beyond that, I committed to build some badly needed new schools, in the process breaking a political deadlock that had blocked all new school construction. And I took on Springfield as a racist city, opining that if we wanted to create conditions where all children could learn, we would need to do plenty of work on ourselves first.

But they were three brutal years. I found myself confronting people on an ongoing basis. At public meetings, I would dress down school committee members who didn't agree with me. I would yell: "Well, if you don't see it my way, I can go somewhere else." I knew I might be riding for a fall, but I didn't know how to slow down.

I now realize I needed to learn three lessons during this phase. They should be part of the developmental roadmap for any superintendent. First, I had to articulate the goals more effectively, not just what I wanted to achieve but the motivation behind my goals. Second, I needed to learn how to engage people in genuine dialogue. My version of "public engagement" was really a vehicle for pushing people to buy into the changes that I had already agreed to. Third, I needed to search beneath the surface of the discrimination problem to discover its root cause. It wasn't rooted in racism; it was rooted in a dearth of quality educational alternatives and people's anxiety about the future.

A "Lone Ranger" cannot implement the necessary changes. Implementation requires something else—a deeper, stronger web of relationships, on which the superintendent and everyone else can rely.

PHASE TWO: REEXAMINING RELATIONSHIPS

In my fourth year, I started to realize that I would never be able to accomplish lasting change by being a loner. Yet I still saw myself as the central character in Springfield's story. Everyone else was a minor character.

I recognized that I couldn't go it alone after two crises hit at virtually the same time. The first had to do with teachers' contract negotiations. I still didn't understand that the critical issue wasn't getting the union members to recognize *me*. I had to learn to recognize *them*. This became abundantly clear when the membership voted the contract down. Even the union representatives were shocked. After the vote, they sat down with me, and we agreed that the rejection of the contract was a signal that we were all out of touch.

I also needed to pay more attention to relationships with the school committee. I'd established a reputation as an arrogant stranger from New York. In my fifth year, I cemented this reputation by restructuring the central office—eliminating all of the positions that existed and saving a lot of money. Soon, a candidate for the school committee ran on a platform based on throwing me out of office—and won. Some people in the school system regarded me as a symbol—not of the solutions that would save the system but of the problems that had to be eradicated.

Soon after, I talked with Harvard's Ron Heifetz about these stresses in Springfield. He asked what the people who supported the candidate had to lose. He pointed out that the candidate who had triumphed had received 18,000 votes. "Who does she represent?" he asked. "Once you find out what she stands for, you may find out that you represent the same principles."

Typical, my first response was, "Here is a woman with an axe to grind. I'm right and she's wrong." Then, as I began to listen more closely, I realized that Heifetz had offered me a genuine insight. My opponent wasn't anti-school. She wasn't a racist. She didn't oppose high achievement. On the contrary, she cared deeply about the students. She wasn't an opponent at all; she represented a point of view that could be incorporated into the drive for excellence.

I began to change. I made new attempts to get parents genuinely involved, trying to make sure I really heard and was willing to be persuaded by them and wasn't just trying to make them feel good. I made dramatic adjustments in the way I negotiated with the union. Instead of sitting down at the table with the goal of winning, I sat down with the goal of letting the union win something as well. My approach to the school committee began to shift. Instead of giving half-hour presentations about what I wanted to do next, I began to solicit its opinion about the best way to proceed.

PHASE THREE: COACHING INSTRUCTION

My role began to evolve quite naturally from that of boss to that of coach. I began to create opportunities for others to reflect and act together. This meant trying things on their own and accepting the occasional failure. Rather than micromanaging, I helped principals, staff, and teachers find their own way.

A good coach raises awareness by asking questions. The best place to start that questioning and creating of opportunities is the classroom. And the best topics revolve around core matters of teaching and learning. My visits, and the nature of the visits, sent a powerful message to the entire system. This is what matters, my visits said. My job is to coach improvement. So I started to visit classrooms and never stopped. By this phase, I was making 150 classroom visits a year.

These school visits became learning experiences, a much more intensive process than simply visiting classrooms as a critical observer. The most tangible aspect was the "walkthroughs." In every classroom I visited, I looked for evidence that the children were learning something. I saw it in the ways they dealt with the teacher, in the work they produced, and in their interactions with their classmates.

Some teachers reacted badly to my visits. They questioned how I dared come into their classroom and interrupt their lesson. I always explained that the point was not to judge teachers but to open up conversations with them about how to meet students' learning needs.

We encouraged principals to do the same with teachers at their schools. To support and model this, at the beginning of the year three or four central office administrators and I conducted forty-six school visits in forty-six days, with the principals of each school alongside us. Then the administrators and all forty-six principals met to summarize what we had seen.

In the beginning, nobody would critique anything at our meetings. But people grew more capable of identifying issues and areas for improvement, without shutting down discussion. Principals also began to realize that some of their assumptions about who was a good teacher and who wasn't were cockeyed. I recall one principal saying, "I've always called that teacher my best because I don't see many kids from his classes for discipline." But of course the academic growth of the students was what was important, not the teacher's ability to make life easy for the principal.

During this phase, I made a presentation to superintendents in Texas. They were fascinated to discover that a superintendent of a 28,000-student district with forty-six campuses could spend almost every day in the schools. Yet, I know they had trouble believing me. They asked how I did it. I told them I delegated everything else. It was more important for me to be in the schools. The staff would tell callers: "He's visiting schools. That's what he's supposed to be doing." At last, I had stopped managing the machinery and was focused on our core enterprise.

PHASE FOUR: COACHING COMMUNITY

Once you get principals and teachers to sustain their own dialogue, engage critically in their own growth and development, and delegate the management of machinery, what should you be doing? In this final phase, which overlaps with Phase Three, you turn from coaching classrooms to coaching the community.

We all know that what we do in schools is only part of what educates children in our communities. In 2003, a new Commission on Children at Risk confirmed what I knew in my gut. For students to be successful in schools, they need to be supported by what this commission called an "authoritative community"—one that respects the students and that the students can respect.

While my initial efforts at community engagement in Springfield yielded few real-world results, it set a precedent and pattern upon which to build. We continued to structure a series of interactions whereby we could examine, make explicit—and change, when needed—the views of education held in the community. We engaged parents, businesses, religious groups, and social service agencies so that we could all define an explicit covenant with one another. That covenant, which was most visible in our curriculum, then could drive our common enterprise.

A genuine personal transformation takes place for many superintendents as they go through this final phase. They move from being advocates—experts with answers to convey—to conveners of dialogue, in which the right answer might emerge from anyone in the room. In this phase, the superintendent stops managing the machinery altogether and takes the lead in establishing opportunities for people to experiment, innovate, and stretch themselves and the school system.

Part of me still holds on to the view that I internalized for most of my life—that I should give focus and direction to the people who report to me; tell them what to do, and they should do it. You may feel that way too. But my experience convinces me that genuine leadership means enhancing the opportunity for people to think, act, grow, and develop on their own. It is a journey from discovering personal motivations to engaging one's colleagues and then the larger community. It is a journey you must be willing to make if you want to advance equitable student learning.

4. No Throw-Away Children

Mary Leiker

Demographics can change rapidly in urban areas, especially when relatively prosperous (often white) families flee communities they perceive as declining. Minority and lower-income urban residents then migrate in. During the 1980s, 1990s, and early 2000s, this happened to many "first-ring" or "inner-ring" suburbs near cities like Memphis, Detroit, and New Orleans. These towns lost more than half of their white population, with their schools becoming predominantly minority and experiencing substantial declines in educational quality and student achievement. Ironically, an opposite trend started after the economic crisis of the late 2000s, with relatively prosperous families moving back toward the inner ring to reduce their commute and exurban neighborhoods filling with foreclosures.

When communities change through migration and economic stress, the school districts face significant challenges—but also major opportunities. In the early 1990's, Superintendent Mary Leiker and the school board of the Kentwood Public Schools in Michigan recognized that the influx of students from nearby Grand Rapids was changing the demographics of the traditionally Caucasian school district and community. Rather than focus on the increasing diversity as a deficit, they saw it as a way to strengthen the educational opportunities for all students. In their shared vision with the community, diversity became a tremendous asset for everyone's learning.

Shortly after my appointment as Kentwood superintendent of schools in 1991, a racial issue set in motion a series of defining events that led us to clarify what we wanted to become as a school community. Two African American male students attacked a Caucasian student in the high school hallway. The boy's injuries were so severe he required life support. The hearing that followed the incident involved thirty-three hours of testimony and four attorneys—one representing the white student, one the two black students, one the superintendent, and one the school board—with standing room only. At this time, the Ku Klux Klan actively recruited in the local newspaper. So for those thirty-three hours, middle-aged white men sat in the back of the school board room watching and waiting, and an African American community skeptically watched what we would do. It truly looked like we were headed for a crisis in the community. Ultimately, the two black students were expelled, which failed to completely satisfy the white community and intensified the furor of the black community.

When I was appointed superintendent of schools in 1991, the student population was 9 percent minority and 10 percent at risk (based on low family income). At the elementary level, test scores were at 45 percent in meeting standards. I believe there's a seed of truth in every complaint; something was happening in the schools, and I needed to get to the bottom line. But when I first tried to investigate, the tension in the community increased even more. My family and I received threats on our lives from both whites and blacks. African Americans marched to my office with signs: "We want justice." Because I wasn't taking sides, neither group felt it could count on me.

It soon became clear that minority students weren't receiving the same opportunities. In the high school, few were enrolled in upper-level classes. Between September and March, in any given year, between eighty and 125 students were routinely kicked out of school—mostly minority students. Only two black students had been on the basketball team in ten years. In response to my questions, people said, "This is Kentwood, and that's the way we do things."

HOLDING DIFFICULT CONVERSATIONS

During this tense time, representatives from the NAACP and several other groups asked if we would be willing to work with the U.S. Department of Justice. I said, "Absolutely!" We needed someone with a different set of eyes to look at the situation, and I did not feel that a learning organization should have anything to hide. Whatever was discovered would be good.

For two years, the Department of Justice representative and I met once a month with a small group representing high school students and parents within the community. If we were going to make progress on the issues, we could not rush the process. Two years prevented premature closure and gave the community time to reflect.

We had long, difficult conversations that required all of us to set aside ingrained assumptions about each other. Listening was critical in moving to new understandings. The Department of Justice had stipulated "no media coverage," which allowed us to be frank and honest about our situation. We recognized that a lot of attitudes had to change among the staff. We needed more minority teachers; our numbers were abysmal. We had to challenge some prevailing assumptions that certain children could not learn. We set goals in purchasing and bidding contracts, plant services, business areas, and the interviewing process to ensure repre-

After sixteen years, Dr. Mary Leiker retired from the Kentwood School District in June 2007. The systems approach established during her tenure continues under the leadership of Dr. Scott Palczewski.

See Glenn Singleton and Curtis Linton, *Courageous Conversations About Race: A Field Guide for Achieving Equity in Schools* (Corwin Press, 2006) for strategies to break the silence about racial inequities in schools.

sentation of diverse groups. We committed to continuous monitoring of our system to gauge how well we were achieving the new goals.

⟩⟩ Also see "Public Engagement" by Ellen Bueschel, page 527.

Nothing is more difficult in a community than cultural change, because it shakes the very foundation of privilege and security. Our struggle in Kentwood exemplifies Ronald Heifetz's writings on adaptive issues. The demographic changes and what they brought us could not be treated with technical fixes from the school superintendent. The school board had to be willing to let the community wrestle with the issue, and the superintendent could not try to cover it up or quietly make it go away to avoid disturbing people. You must disturb people; engage them in conversations that may be unpleasant in order for them to reach a higher level of learning and understanding. When I look at other superintendents, I can see that many are fearful of community conversations about diversity. And, when you're fearful, you try to fix the problem rather than engage in adaptive work. We can celebrate this diversity if we look at it as a strength, not as a burden. We can make it a gift for our students, schools, and community.

⟩⟩ See Ron Heifetz' twelve questions, page 417; and his book, page 427.

RATCHETING UP EXPECTATIONS AND PERFORMANCE

I came away from the racial incident and our two years of intense deliberations with a number of questions. What was the lesson here? What was the opportunity? What might take the students and school district to a higher level of performance and a better reputation? The school board and I felt that we could show the rest of the country how to create a school district that did not simply accept differences but valued those differences for the strength they brought. We could become a district that attracted diverse students because of the excellent education they would receive. We *needed* the diversity to ensure that Kentwood students would be prepared for our global society. Students are handicapped if they are educated in an exclusive system.

During the years since then, Kentwood has demonstrated its belief in diversity. Back in 1991, at the time of the attack, the student population was 9 percent minority and 10 percent at risk (a measure based on family income). At the elementary level, test scores were at 45 percent in meeting state standards. In 2007, the year I retired, Kentwood had 40 percent minority students, with 42 percent at risk—and test scores at 89 percent. Of that 40 percent minority, African American students consti-

Our demographic diversity has strengthened the schools and community. Coming from a science background, I appreciate the importance of biodiversity and the interconnectivity in living systems. The more diversity you have, the stronger an ecosystem is.

Our district was talking about being customer-focused long before charter schools appeared on the scene. Now with so many schools of choice, parents can pull their kids out and send them to another school down the street or to a nearby district. The more diversity we have in school systems the stronger we can be in responding to rapidly changing conditions and the more flexible we can be in problem solving. —Scott Palczewski, Kentwood superintendent (2007–present).

tuted 28 percent and refugees and immigrants from over fifty countries worldwide the other 12 percent. This demographic shift and increased academic performance of our students defies any predictions that might have been made in the 1990s.

How did we do it? We achieved it through a deeply held shared vision of excellence and equity for *all* students created by the school board, school staff, and community. The Board of Education's vision set the context for our commitment: "Kentwood Public Schools will be a place of excitement and enthusiasm for education and an appreciation for diversity. Everyone will be encouraged to be a creative force in the development of an educational system for the future." Too often such words are only rhetoric. Not here. This vision was lived out every day in the work we did.

Systems thinking became pivotal in moving us from seeing diversity as a deficit to seeing diversity as a tremendous asset. Instrumental in the work was a book called *The Key Work of School Boards*, developed by the National School Boards Association (NSBA). It focuses on student achievement and community engagement to promote student achievement, emphasizing that no action is taken in isolation. School boards must understand the interconnectedness of every decision, exploring possible reactions as well as the unintended consequences. There are eight action areas, but they are not distinct steps to be checked off. Rather they represent the whole that must be considered as the school board acts. The most critical aspect in our work involved the creation of a vision with the community, followed by setting high standards for every student. This positioned the professional staff to develop the necessary curriculum and instructional strategies to meet the needs of all students.

Making progress toward our vision and reaching the new standards required significant learning for everyone. My role shifted to one of facilitating the learning of others. I've worked with tremendous scholars, practitioners, and researchers over the years, and the learning I gained, I shared. I taught board members, central office administrators, and principals on a regular basis. During my time in Kentwood, we purchased and studied together about twenty-five books, and I led monthly sessions to promote the growth of the entire system. When I say the administrators were involved, I mean all the support administrators, too— Director of Food Services, Director of Transportation, Director of Plant Services. Everyone has a role in educating students. For instance, I tell custodians, "If you're cleaning a floor and a child is having difficulty, I expect you to stop what you're doing and attend to that child; a child is much more important than the floors."

The NSBA framework involves eight key action areas:

- Vision (a shared statement on the desired future, often starting with student achievement)
- Standards (educational expectations)
- Assessment (tools and processes for measuring educational outcomes against the standards)
- Accountability (assigned responsibility for those outcomes)
- Alignment (resources, communication, planning, and program implementation all work together)
- Climate (the conditions for successful teaching and learning)
- Collaboration and community engagement (trust and confidence among all educational stakeholders, including educators, parents, business leaders, media, and other citizens)
- Continuous improvement (constantly seeking and planning new ways to improve the system).

For more in-depth information on the Key Work of School Boards, see http://www.nsba.org/keywork or Katheryn Gemberling, Carl Smith, and Joseph Villani, *The Key Work of School Boards Guidebook* (National School Boards Association, 2000).

In our systemic school improvement efforts, we became data driven, focused on our customers and on continuous improvement. This is particularly evident in instruction. With stringent state curriculum mandates, little flexibility exists in what to teach, but how to teach becomes an opportunity to really blossom. With constant monitoring of the data on our students' needs, we're always looking for instructional approaches that can make significant differences in student learning. However, as well as we were doing with student achievement, I could see us hitting a ceiling.

The biggest breakthrough resulted from taking advantage of the significant research in neuroplasticity. I'm convinced that's the missing link—the absolute hidden link—to breaking down barriers for non-readers. For many students, everything tells us that they should be functioning normally—yet they just can't read fluently no matter what we do. They may be students with learning disabilities, students with emotional impairments, bilingual students, students with attention deficit, or just students who seem unable to hear phonetic sounds. Two programs grounded in neuroplasticity provided the missing link for us: Scientific Learnings' Fast ForWord programs and the work of the Lindamood-Bell group. With these programs, the elementary teachers now can pinpoint the specific problems non-readers are experiencing and provide direct intervention to develop and strengthen the cognitive skills of memory, attention, processing, and sequencing.

For Scientific Learnings' Fast ForWords program, see www.scilearn.com.

For Lindamood-Bell learning centers, see www.lindamoodbell.com.

See, for example, Jeffrey Schwartz and Rebecca Gladding, *You Are Not Your Brain* (Penguin, 2011); and David Rock and Jeffrey Schwartz, "The Neuroscience of Leadership," *strategy+business*, Spring 2006; http://www.strategy-business.com/article/06207.

NEUROPLASTICITY

The basic principles of neuroplasticity, which were stated long ago by the psychologist Donald Hebb, can be summarized with the phrase, "cells that fire together, wire together." It has long been known and well documented in neuroscience that when cells can be made to fire together, they will literally wire together and form new neural networks. There is increasing evidence that focus of attention—related to mindfulness, or the deliberate awareness of the process of thinking and the flow of one's own impulses—can accelerate this process by which the cells fire together. This is extremely important because it means that systematic changes can be made in brain circuitry and the formation of new neural networks through attention density: The continued, repeated, conscious act of thinking in deliberate ways. —Art Kleiner

 Also see The Cognitive Studies Group, page 404.

Even with our high percentage of minority students and students at risk, every year in every school we've made the adequate yearly progress (AYP) demanded by both the federal No Child Left Behind law and by the State of Michigan. Meeting this under Michigan's subgroup requirements is difficult, because we have a tremendous number of transient, refugee, and immigrant students. We are expected to reduce the gap between subgroup populations and show growth within each group on a yearly basis, a goal we strongly support. However, when students arrive who have attended three or four schools in a given year or who have never been enrolled in a school or even seen running water, the odds are stacked against us. We're one of the Kent County school districts selected for settling refugees, more than 500 students from more than fifty countries. Yet, we make AYP every year.

LEARNING COMMUNITY SUPPORT

We conduct a community survey every other year. When we had problems with diversity, people told us they had concerns and issues. Now they are more likely to say that one of the strengths of Kentwood is its diversity. Community members are not as fearful that the system will be weakened academically as the students become more diverse with a greater proportion of them at risk, because they've seen just the opposite as achievement results continue to climb. A 2007 high school graduating class of 599 received more than $2.5 million in scholarships—667 scholarships in all.

I worked regularly with parents from the middle school through high school years to help them through the college maze process. We wanted them to know that their children had options; that support could be found for college expenses. When they saw our high expectations for their children, they could also set high expectations. When you believe, as we do, that there are no throw-away children, teachers and administrators expect nothing but the best.

The community's pride in its schools could be seen with its strong financial support. People consistently voted for bond elections and building and site renewals. When they supported the bond election in 2003, Kentwood had the highest unemployment rate of any area in Kent County. With major manufacturers cutting workforces by as much as 50 percent, we suffered tremendously in this state. And yet, in the 2003 election, we needed money to build out our system to make sure that our facilities could keep up with the demands. The $85.5 million bond issue passed two to one.

Because of this tremendous community support, our school facilities are first class—from the buildings themselves to the technology in the

Among the books discussed by Mary Leiker and the Kentwood staff administrators and board members were:

The Fifth Discipline Fieldbook (p. 5)

Ronald Heifetz, *Leadership Without Easy Answers* (p.427)

Daniel Goleman, *Emotional Intelligence* (p. 207)

Martin Seligman, *The Optimistic Child* (Harper, 1996)

Patricia Hersch, *A Tribe Apart* (Ballantine, 1999)

Ruby Payne, *A Framework for Understanding Poverty*, third edition, (Aha Process Inc, 2003)

Judith Bardwick, *Danger in the Comfort Zone* (Amacom, 1995)

Jim Collins, *Good to Great* (HarperBusiness, 2001)

Jim Collins, *Good to Great and the Social Sectors: A Monograph to Accompany Good to Great*, (HarperCollins, 2005)

Norman Doidge, *The Brain That Changes Itself* (Viking, 2007)

George Lakoff, Howard Dean, and Don Hazen, *Don't Think of an Elephant!* (Chelsea Green, 2004)

For her story on how these books made a difference, see "Positive Change and Perpetual Motion," by Mary Leiker, *The School Administrator*, April 2008 www.aasa.org/SchoolAdministratorArticle.aspx?id=5730.

Adequate Yearly Progress (AYP), as defined by the No Child Left Behind Act of 2001, represents annual academic proficiency targets, established by each state, in reading and math. The federal law requires school districts and schools to reach these targets to be considered on track with the federally mandated goal of 100 percent proficiency by school year 2014.

classrooms to the quality artificial turf on the football and soccer fields to the quality sound systems in the band rooms. From fourth grade up, more than 3,000 students participate in after-school activities. If someone cannot afford football cleats or a trombone, we find support. We want kids involved with us; if they're involved, they stay connected and out of trouble.

One sign of the value of diversity for us came in July 2005, when *Grand Rapids* magazine published the rankings of the twenty-nine area school districts across Kent County based on 2003 and 2004 data. Kentwood Public Schools tied for the rank of fifth overall; we were ranked with school systems with very different profiles. Our diversity percentage (number of nonwhite students) was 40.1 percent; the districts above us ranged from 2.6 percent to 5.8 percent. Kentwood's economic disadvantage was 35.8 percent; above us the range was 4.2 percent to 9.0 percent. Interestingly, our community and school staff perceive that we are comparable in quality to those wealthier suburban communities.

We aspired to be a model for other school districts facing sweeping demographic changes. I think we are. Through our commitment to a systems approach and to learning together, we have defied the odds. We can say" "Look it's not true that as you become more at risk and more minority that your school district is going fall apart. It's absolutely not true. If you buy into that thinking, it will happen. But shame on you if you do; you will be shortchanging the future of our most valuable asset, our children."

〉〉 Mary Leiker was a member of the Danforth Group described in Peer Partners, page 421.

View from the Kentwood School Board

Bill Joseph, Kentwood School Board Member from 1995 to 2011

Kentwood is a microcosm of the nation in our ethnic and socioeconomic makeup. Our long-term vision has been to show that students at risk—whether African American, Bosnian, Hispanic, Ethiopian, Asian, or the poor and disadvantaged—will be able to achieve. As an African American board member, I take pride in the fact that as we became more diverse, we did not lose ground. We continued to improve as well as to gain a very rich culture that benefits everyone. Our vision gave us focus—you must know what you aspire to achieve if you're going to achieve it.

And you must also be a risk taker. Kentwood has led the way with significant changes, such as the standards-based report cards for K-12 students (one of the first in the U.S.) and most recently the programs based on neuroplasticity research.

Professional development has been a major part of the board members' work. Too often, educators forget that we need our own development. We attend state school board meetings, but far more is needed. With our learning, I think we are ahead of other school board members. In fact, they're often surprised in state meetings with what we know. We had a deep understanding of poverty issues and the achievement gap long before No Child Left Behind.

Partnership with the city cannot be ignored in school transformation. As the school system goes, so goes the city. The mayor and city commissioners understand this relationship. We have a regular City School Meeting consisting of the mayor, a few commissioners, school board members, and the school superintendent. Sometimes we hold these sessions in school buildings so the city representatives can visit classes. Recently, we did a "walk and talk" on two Saturday mornings; leaders from the school and city government visited several areas of the community together, asking residents how we were doing. We've collaborated on a number of projects, such as summer school, to meet the needs of students. The city is quick to say that because of the schools we have more businesses locating in Kentwood. They understand that our futures are tied together.

A Family Embraces Diversity

Sandi Talbott, parent, former member of the Kentwood School Board

As both a parent and a school board member, I was clear about our school system vision. That's one reason my family and I stayed. We could have lived in any community we wanted; we chose to be here because we wanted to be part of this multicultural community where every child was learning. After they left high school, both my daughters thanked us for living in Kentwood, because things didn't intimidate them—they were confident, and they had empathy from their experiences here. A lot of what they learned can't be taught; it has to be lived.

It is always amazing to watch our seniors at their graduation ceremony. As you look across the group, it looks like the United Nations. They are successful, praising each other, hugging each other. You know these kids are going to make it—that every single child is going to learn and succeed—and this school system has been an important part of making it happen for them. One of our student speakers commented one year that labels don't exist here. "We're leaving here now, and we'll be labeled," she said, "but we know who we are because we come from this school and this community."

Kentwood is one of the very few communities that will ask hard questions and stare them right in the face. I remember when I was first elected to the board; we were sending a survey to our high school students, including some tough questions about race and identity. I said I wasn't sure if we should be asking them. A parent sitting across the table said, "Well, if we don't ask them, who will?"

People work so hard here; it's an uphill battle and will continue to be. Sometimes you hear people say, "We're at a crossroads now." But we're always going to be there; that's where we belong, asking tough questions and staring down the things that can defeat us. High educational and behavioral expectations for all students works here because it has to work. Too many lives are at stake, and students depend on us to help them become successful, productive adults.

View from the School Kitchens

Chef Mo Shamali, Director of Food Services, Kentwood School District

My job is not only to feed the students but to educate them. We understand our role in food service and how we fit in. We must educate the students about food and make sure they eat well to do well in the classroom. A student with a hungry stomach cannot focus. We try to give them food they will enjoy.

All students are our challenge, regardless of ethnicity, race, religion. We want them to know about healthy diets and nutrition; we see it as our job to create patterns of eating that will influence their choices later. Otherwise, they will eat what's cool. That translates into eating food that is not good for them.

To have an impact on eating habits, we started in the early elementary grades. We set up salad bars with lots of fresh vegetables and fruits. The students liked it. Then when they came to middle school and high school they were eating these fruits and vegetables. Before, almost no one at those levels ate fruits and vegetables. Our other strategy was to hide things. In stir fry dishes, we mixed in carrots, celery, and bok choy. Through great-tasting dishes, we gained acceptance for healthy choices. When we switched from ranch dressing to light ranch dressing and other low-fat options, they asked, "Why do these taste different?" Once they changed their eating habits, they didn't like the higher fat versions.

We don't draw attention to students who receive free meals. We set up a system so no one, including the cashier, knows. Following that change, more students who qualified started eating because no one would know.

We also involve parents in the child's eating. Each child has an account number. When the students use their ID cards to purchase food, all items are registered. Parents can go online, or check with us, to see everything their child eats. Also, if there are certain items those parents don't want their child to eat, or that they can't eat, it pops up on the screen, and the child cannot purchase it.

We educate students to make healthy food choices while they are with us and hope that after they leave they continue to make such choices.

View from the School Leader's Desk

Kari Anama, Principal, Southwood Elementary School

Kentwood Public Schools' vision is the clearest I've seen. Everyone is held to high standards—students, teachers, and administrators. We're about continuous improvement, and we're data driven and customer focused. This clear focus is what drew me to Kentwood; I knew I would be challenged as a leader and learn a lot from Mary Leiker and others.

Mary's mentoring was powerful. She met with all administrators at least once a month to focus on our learning, not the technical side of running schools. Assistant superintendents handled the managerial details during those times. Kentwood is the only district I've ever worked at where that time is held sacred. Things became hectic when we faced a bond issue or during contract negotiations, but this learning time was never used to take care of business.

I arrived in the late 1990s to be principal at Southwood Elementary School, where the diversity is amazing. The student body included almost equal proportions (10 to 20 percent) of African American, Hispanic, Vietnamese, and Caucasian students, along with many other ethnic groups. Southwood had a high number of children on free and reduced-cost lunch and one of the highest transient populations in the district. And it was in danger of being taken over by the State of Michigan because of low test scores.

Over the next six years, we progressed at Southwood from barely 20 percent of our kids passing the standardized tests to 99 percent across the board in math, science, reading, and social studies. We changed the atmosphere and the expectations and transformed into a learning school and a learning staff.

The first thing we did to bring about this change was to teach reading and writing better. Many teachers told me that it took so long to do reading lessons that they rarely got to writing. We adopted a completely new reading program called the Four Blocks Literacy Model: a framework that held everyone accountable to teach writing every day. In this program, kids self-select reading materials, receive guided reading, write, and work on phonics. Our students have become better thinkers.

Recently, I moved to another school within the Kentwood district, Glenwood Elementary School. There are similar challenges, and the same principles apply. All teachers believe that all kids can learn and will learn—no matter their background. There are no excuses here; just high expectations.

To learn more about the Four Blocks Literacy program see their website: http://www.four-blocks.com/

GOOD TO GREAT

Why Some Companies Make the Leap…and Others Do Not, by Jim Collins (HarperCollins, 2001)

We made significant gains in the Kentwood Public Schools during my time as superintendent. As I neared retirement, I began studying the specifics of how a school system makes the transition to a new superintendent and sustains its hard-won gains. Collins, in his book, examined companies that had been able to maintain their greatness over the years. The transition at the top was one key factor. Over decades, the companies that maintained their greatness fostered leadership within the existing organization so there would always be someone to take over.

Although Collins' book is addressed to business, you can adapt the ideas to education. Unfortunately, I don't see school superintendents looking at transitions as part of their job responsibility. Too often, new superintendents are hired from outside the school system and become focused on ways to establish their own legacy. Collins recommends "growing your own." I accepted that as a key responsibility of my job as I trained people to sustain and keep our school district moving forward. When I made the transition, I recommended internal people to replace my own and several other critical positions. —Mary Leiker

5. Creating a Core Learning Group

Les Omotani

Few school leaders are as experienced as Dr. Les Omotani in using the five disciplines in schools. With the community and schools (serving 9,000 students) of West Des Moines, Iowa, he brought together a districtwide learning community, engaging not just school and parent group leaders but local government and business leaders around a compelling shared vision of how the schools could be better. In 2004, he was recruited as superintendent for Hewlett-Woodmere Public Schools in New York. He brought a deep commitment to facilitating the learning of all individuals—students, teachers, administrators, parents, and citizens—through a high-performing school system. Hewlett-Woodmere, located on Long Island, serves about 3,500 students from both affluent and lower socioeconomic families who hold high aspirations for their children. The community expects and embraces a wide breadth of experiences and educational opportunities for their children and takes pride in a 99 percent graduation rate. This section provides a glimpse of how Dr. Omotani and his administrative team have changed the way they work together.

This article was written before Dr. Omotani retired in 2009. Dr. Joyce Bisso, then Assistant Superintendent for Curriculum and Instruction, is now superintendent and is continuing to expand the systems thinking work in the district. Dr. Bisso was appointed by the Board of Education as part of a deliberate long-range succession plan to continue implementing the learning community work at Hewlett-Woodmere.

I've frequently been asked why I (or anyone) would want to be a school superintendent. At this point in my life, I'm quite clear about why I'm here. It's about building a community of learners who can create an organizational structure and culture to maximize the opportunities for students. As such, the most important thing that I do as superintendent is to place a high priority on setting aside time on the job for learning together. It's definitely the key; there's no way people can learn new ways of thinking, new ways of doing things, or new habits if they're just trying to fit a discussion in on top of everything else they've got to do.

The move to valuing collective learning represents a fundamental change for me. During the first half of my administrative career, others expected me to know what was going on, to have answers, and to make decisions. I was comfortable with those expectations, thinking that was what I was supposed to do. Quite frankly, I gained a lot of recognition and reward for doing that well. But, that leadership role was more about winning compliance than commitment. Many people did things because

Dr. Omotani believes that the prevailing "Race to the Top" strategy with its emphasis on misusing standardized test scores is an ill-advised top-down effort. It gets compliance by using a big carrot (dollars) and an even bigger stick (negative sanctions). He characterizes it as another example of the archetype "Fixes that Fail" (page 144).

"Trust that meaningful conversations can change your world." From Margaret Wheatley, *Turning to One Another: Simple Conversations to Restore Hope to the Future* (Berrett-Koehler Publishers, 2002), p. 145.

they were told to do them, by me or other administrators in our district. It wasn't that we were telling them to do bad stuff; the stuff made sense, but it wasn't their own. That was the way things worked in traditional organizations.

In the current stage of my career, leading is about learning with others, serving and caring for people, and ensuring the best possible learning environment for both kids and adults. I have found this to be a more powerful way of leading, resulting in more impressive outcomes. The school system is everyone's work, their learning, their creation; and you can't predict where it's going. Wherever it goes, it'll go there because we've struggled as a group with it and believe it's the right direction. We rely on the strengths and the experiences of one another; we make better decisions by pulling in multiple perspectives on the system.

As I moved into the superintendency in the Hewlett-Woodmere Public Schools, I felt that developing a community of learners with a group of administrators had to be my top priority. As a core learning group, we could not only make better decisions but also create the conditions for everyone else in the school community to learn. Our learning would ripple through the system opening up opportunities for faculty and students. We would trust, as Meg Wheatley puts it, that meaningful conversations could change our world. A community of learners, however, doesn't just form on its own. It requires deliberate work to create the right conditions; its members must acquire new skills. In my experience, people think that they know how to talk with each other, but they do not. Traditional ways of interacting in meetings do not lead to thoughtful, productive dialogue. If we want to build collective intelligence and action, we must learn new rules for engagement.

CONVENING THE CORE LEARNING GROUP

There already was a "district leadership team," known as the DLT, where principals and selected central office administrators regularly met. But, according to several members and to no one's fault, over the years the DLT had become a dreaded two-hour meeting with talking heads giving out information. Agendas could consist of fifteen or more items with minimal time for speakers to get their points across. If you were at the bottom of the agenda, forget it; maybe next time. Few, if any, opportunities existed for individuals to learn from each other.

So we expanded the DLT into our core learning group. It consists of twenty-eight individuals, including central office administrators, building principals, and assistant principals. We have invested significant resources in preparing them with sophisticated skills to lead organizational learning. Many of the members have said that for the first time they feel they've been given permission to bring their whole selves into our interactions. Through the processes we use, even little warm-up activities like check-ins, we've unlocked a yearning to know one another better, to build stronger relationships, to be able to trust more, and to depend upon one another more. As a group, we find our interactions rewarding, energizing, and reinforcing.

When we first started down this path, the administrators couldn't envision a two-hour meeting, let alone a full day on the learning disciplines and dialogue. That was too much time away from their offices or buildings. But they soon reached a point where they wanted more time to interact with each other. This is typical in systems where leaders come together in this way: Even if they've been traditionally focused on their unit, school, or department, they begin to see the interrelationships and bring their own energy to the process.

THE SYSTEM HOLDS THE PLAN

In my previous position in Iowa, I had been regarded as a leader with a plan; I had mapped out our direction, based on assumptions about what each group should learn and how they should learn it. We had put an impressive systems approach into place, and we had accomplished some major goals. This time, however, it was clear that deeper learning and changes could be made if driven by other individuals in the organization besides myself. The core learning group would be critical to this approach, because the individuals in the group connected to all aspects of the school system. They were in positions to model their learning and to "teach" others. In Hewlett-Woodmere, the core learning group would guide the learning. I had no other end point in mind—other than the development of an influential community of learners to support students.

In our first conversation, we decided that the core group would be ongoing and embedded in our practice. We set aside one day a month during the school year to learn together; individually, we would practice our learning every day. Conducting this development and learning right here in the district, as opposed to in an external setting, would turn out to be critical to our success. I've never seen an organization change leadership habits by sending a few people away to specialized training or bringing someone in for a day or two.

Typical staff development programs have specified content and a fixed timeline with progression planned in advance. Not this one. We simply said, "Let's learn and practice together." We moved along an evolutionary path where the learning in each session set up the next. As we talked and thought about leadership, the initiative to move our learning along came directly from the core group.

⟩⟩ See "No More Drive-by Staff Development," page 396.

A small planning group, led by Kathy Anderson, Assistant Superintendent for Human Resources, laid out a proposal for our first semester. Because of my work in systems and frequent use of the "fifth discipline" language, the group proposed five sessions—one session dealing with each learning discipline—even though I had encouraged them not to build the agenda around what they thought I wanted. But they convinced me that if the five learning disciplines were so integral to my thinking, they needed to understand the underlying theories and practices.

Though I had led numerous sessions about the fifth discipline concepts elsewhere, I felt that I could not be both the teacher and the learner in this core group. That was a pivotal decision. I convinced Nelda Cambron-McCabe, a coauthor of this book and former associate of mine in the Danforth Foundation Superintendents Forum, to be our facilitator and guide. Being present as a learner has given me a feel for how the other individuals in the group experience the learning; I don't think you can understand that unless you are in the sessions as a participant. It requires deliberate patience and restraint, so that I don't dominate or others don't get in the habit of looking to me for guidance. There are times when I'm sitting in a session thinking, "Oh, I'd love to comment on that." But I don't. It's more important that the members of the core group hear from one another than from the superintendent. Most superintendents tell themselves and others they are good listeners. Feedback from others tells us we are not as good as we like to think we are at listening. I took our sessions as an opportunity to practice listening and reflection. These were skills that I was relatively (compared to my peers) good at doing but needed to make into a permanent habit. I truly believe that the core group sees this as *our* work, not *my* work.

⟩⟩ See "Peer Partners" on the Danforth Superintendents Forum, page 421.

The ladder of inference has become a prominent visual in every core group learning session. There is a stepladder in the room with each step labeled, like the illustration on page 102.

Rather than follow a linear path of spending one day on each discipline, Nelda proposed that we integrate them. We began with an all-day session examining the five learning disciplines together. We decided then to spend our second session on what it meant to learn together, focusing heavily on team learning and mental models. In that session, we learned about and practiced many of the tools in *Schools That Learn*, including the ladder of inference, inquiry and advocacy, and double-loop learning from the wheels of learning, now "Are You Smarter Than a

Thermostat." We were introduced to concepts; equally importantly we engaged in practice exercises that forced us to use each idea or skill. We made them our own by applying them.

⟩⟩ These practices are described in "Mental Models," starting page 97; and in "Are You Smarter Than A Thermostat?," page 151.

In the third session, at the core learning group members' request, Nelda introduced systems thinking. We created examples from within the school district to illustrate the archetypes. The group found the concept of the iceberg to be so powerful that they decided that the next session would be devoted to it. For that session, small groups of administrators prepared by developing a real case problem in their specific areas of responsibility. We then analyzed these using the iceberg. Each group presented its case and analysis as everyone else listened and engaged in conversation about the issues. This activity promoted team learning in multiple ways. Individuals gained a better appreciation for dilemmas facing other administrators; everyone received valuable feedback about their issue; and people had an opportunity to practice their listening and inquiry skills.

⟩⟩ See The Iceberg, page 126; and Systems Archetypes, page 143.

This evolutionary approach became the model for our planning. Shortly after each session, we scheduled a conference call with Nelda, Kathy, and several core group members. We talked about the last session, what team members are experiencing in their work, and where they need further assistance. From that conversation, the group agreed on the focus for the next session. The power of this format is its evolving nature. Although we focus on learning processes, the sessions are also rich in content. No one sees this as in-service or professional development; rather, it's the way we come together to do our work. We trust that our conversations about systems and our own work will lead us to the disciplines and processes we need; and the disciplines and processes will lead us to the topics we need to cover. That's what happens when you create a high-functioning community of learners, emphasizing communication, dialogue, collaboration, and servant leadership.

Sessions have included the development of a vision for the district; creation of a significantly different format and structure for DLT meetings; practicing listening skills and productive conversations; using the World Café format (facilitating a larger group) to take up critical questions facing the district, with core members developing their own large-scale meetings with teachers, students, parents, and other groups; working with personal vision; distinguishing the difference between technical and adaptive problems as Ron Heifetz describes them; using archetypes to tell our stories; and engaging in a decisionmaking model using the context of the five learning disciplines. Our outside facilitator does not come with any agenda. She spends substantial time on monitoring where we are, gauging how fast we can move, simply listening to us, and designing the sessions accordingly.

⟩⟩ For more on the World Café, see page 122.

WHAT WE'VE LEARNED

The dreaded DLT meeting has become a substantive learning space. We moved from a dozen agenda items per session, with three or four people reporting and everybody else listening, to sessions with a few key items where the group controls the direction. This has been such a profound change that people comment about it frequently. DLT members don't want to miss the meetings. We've also created space on the district website for all information related to DLT meetings; we no longer need to use meeting time to read information. Our meetings are for interaction.

The interactions have changed substantially. Individuals listen closely to each other, raising questions for clarification and wanting to understand. In the meetings, almost everyone talks. Our extensive work on holding meaningful conversation has given us a language to support each other. Someone will say, "We need to hear from everybody because we can't read minds." Saying simple things such as, "There's a reason why everybody's around the table," makes a difference.

To embed this work organizationally, we work on a lot of fronts at once. That goes against the traditional change theory that emphasizes "strategic focus." But a school organization must always be aware that it is a system. Actions in one place affect others; intended and unintended consequences are always present. Within the core learning group, we have recognized this complexity by bringing the learning organization work to new people, without predicting or planning where in the school system it will move next.

Each member of the team is comfortable with different approaches—some modeling the thinking and ideas, others modeling the application of the tools and strategies. In general, when they are back in the schools, team members listen more. They don't tell people what to do as much. They ask more questions. The impact has been noticeable; staff members in the schools are asking, "What's going on with the DLT?"

For me personally, the greatest lesson has been the importance of letting go of the need to offer rapid solutions. I've learned to say to people,

"Confusion is okay; it's normal; it's to be expected. Just trust the process because we're going to be fine." I watch people who are frustrated with this hang in there a while; then, all of a sudden they get it. It's hard to describe the energy that this generates within the group. At first, because of members' concerns about the time taken, we agreed to limit most sessions to four hours. But by the second session, the core group members said, "That's simply not enough time; we need full days."

Maybe the most important lesson I've learned is not to set our purpose as creating a learning organization; it is to support individuals as they learn how to collaborate. The learning community emerges out of that work.

For school leaders who want to follow this path, you must always keep the focus on trust. I stay mindful that trust is fragile, and I have to be aware that if I'm not living out the principles we have established then I risk the trust of those around me. If I fail to listen and hear all team members, I lose trust. As a leader, I cannot expect others to engage in inquiry unless I model it in my interactions. A safe, trusting relationship does not mean that we must agree on everything. It does mean, however, a safe place to express our differences and to engage those differences to make better decisions for our schools.

As the work progressed, I saw more of a shift from a problem-solving orientation to one of creating, as Robert Fritz defines it. Leaders can be consumed with reacting to events around them rather than being proactive. But, our core learning group talks more about what we want to create. This is an important place to be. We need to be able to say to our students, our faculty, and our community: This is what we're trying to achieve for the future. Yes, we know we've got to deal with conditions and problems right now, but we're going to spend less time putting out fires and managing crises and more time thinking about the strategies, resources, and effort needed to create what we want for our kids.

〉〉 See "Teaching Structural Tension" by Robert Fritz, page 209.

Our next challenge is to talk more about current reality and to identify the variety of things we can do to close the gap. That will lead us more deeply into work on personal mastery, which can more intensely inform our team learning agendas for the future as we form our own individual professional development plans.

Also see Robert Fritz, *The Path of Least Resistance: Learning to Become the Creative Force in Your Own Life* (Fawcett Columbine, 1989).

To do this work, school leaders must take a long-term view of *time*. This type of fundamental transformation takes more than one superintendent's career to successfully implement and sustain. Consequently, the Board of Education must support and endorse a succession plan for

What is needed to do this work?

Allow the learning journey to evolve; traditional professional development doesn't work.

Develop trust within the team and continuously build on it.

Conduct development and learning *within* the district with the entire team; sending a few people away for training does not help the team.

Learn and practice together the skills to hold meaningful conversations.

Use school system issues as a practice field.

Establish a culture that says it's okay for school administrators to take time away from their buildings for their own learning and development.

Bring the school board along on the journey through sharing the team's methods of reflection and inquiry (mental models, the ladder of inference, and others).

leadership. We were fortunate to have our board embrace the learning community concept, goals, and vision, and they appointed Joyce Bisso, a key member of the core team, to continue the culture of learning.

No Longer a Meeting But a Team

Kathleen Anderson, Kevin Bayen, Joan Birringer-Haig, Joyce Bisso, Joseph DiBartollo, Jeff Malis, and Peter Weber

This conversation took place in 2009 among a few members of both the core learning group and the District Leadership Team (DLT) in the Hewlett-Woodmere School District. Kathleen Anderson is Assistant Superintendent for Human Resources and Student Services; Kevin Bayen is Director of Music; Joan Birringer-Haig is Principal of the Ogden Elementary School; Dr. Joyce Bisso, now superintendent, was then the Assistant Superintendent for Curriculum and Instruction (before that, she had been the principal of the district's high school); Joseph DiBartollo is Business Administrator; Jeff Malis is Director of Health, Physical Education and Athletics; and Dr. Peter Weber is Assistant Superintendent for Business.

DEVELOPING A COMMON LANGUAGE

Peter: Gaining a shared vocabulary has eliminated a lot of misunderstandings in our team conversations. Maybe we're using the language correctly or maybe not, but at least we're doing it consistently with a shared meaning. It provides us with shortcuts in the conversation. If we're having difficulty with an issue, a reference to the iceberg can get us back on track. If someone thinks we're not examining an issue deeply enough, they'll ask if we're doing single-loop rather than double-loop analysis. The ladder of inference becomes a shorthand phrase to push us to look more closely at the data and assumptions driving specific observations.

Joyce: When someone has an unexpected or extreme reaction to something I say that I immediately see them as running to the top of the ladder, skipping any number of rungs, making assumptions not grounded in data, and then jumping to conclusions. Instead of jumping to my own conclusions, I can raise questions to move the person back down the ladder and also learn something that maybe I'm missing.

Joan: In the last budget meeting, I reacted to a comment that someone made. Les [Omotani] was sitting across the table and raised a question about my assumptions. I knew exactly what he meant; I was jumping up the ladder. The way we interact now makes us more thoughtful when we're in a meeting. The vocabulary and tools give us permission to feel comfortable with saying certain things as well as responding to others.

Peter: The language gives us a way to explore our own weaknesses in a safe way. I know I'm a poor listener. Before you're half way through making your point, I've formulated not only that response but also the two or three after that one. Many of us work with colleagues who don't just run up the ladder, but jump off the ladder repeatedly. The common language lets us remind each other of what we're doing in a way that's constructive rather than destructive.

Joan: We're moving toward bringing the vocabulary to those that we interact with outside the DLT. Kathy has worked directly with the clerical staff, and Les has conducted sessions with the school board about team learning, inquiry and advocacy, and the iceberg. Although the formal training has been limited, we use the vocabulary and we're modeling the behavior, so people see it. That may be the most important thing we've done.

FORMING RELATIONSHIPS

Kathy: Previously, no space or time existed for us to make connections. Now I know people in such a different way. Someone at a recent meeting said that she had learned to enjoy and respect every member of the leadership team through this process. I think that sums it up.

Joe: We trust each other, and leadership trusts us. These relationships make everything possible. When we are invited to be part of the process, then we feel a responsibility. It would be easier to be told what to do, but we've moved beyond that kind of thinking.

Jeff: With trusting relationships, you don't feel that you will be judged when you speak up. I know my opinion will be heard and valued before someone jumps to a conclusion.

Kathy: All of us believe we're making better, higher-quality decisions through the relationships we've created. It shows up in my sessions with the other assistant superintendents. In the past, I thought it was a waste of my time to sit through those meetings and listen to others talk about finance and curriculum issues. Now I find that when I have a decision, I think to myself, I wonder what Peter or Joyce would say? If a meeting is cancelled, we clamor to reschedule it as soon as possible instead of being relieved that we've gained a few hours. Together we've made decisions that we never would have made individually.

Kevin: Because of the relationships we've created, we spend more time explaining what we do rather than defending our turf. I know our team members see music, art, and athletics as essential for developing our students.

Kathy: I knew we had arrived—the "aha" moment—when somebody pointed out that we were trying to write a vision statement for the District Leadership Team (DLT) *meeting*, but that the DLT is not a meeting—it's a team.

MAKING OUR WORK A PRACTICE FIELD

Kathy: We are incorporating the organizational learning skills into the ongoing work in the district. Our work must be our practice field if the learning is to be sustained. Our recent budgeting exercise to identify possible cuts was an interesting test. We weren't sure people were ready to take the responsibility for making budget decisions across the system. As in the past, they might rather defer to those of us in the central office, so we could shoulder the blame. But that didn't happen! Peter Weber did a beautiful job of orchestrating a systems meeting, a very long day, the first of many such sessions. Participants could not look at their own schools in isolation, but at the priorities across the district.

In the past, we would have said, "Every school will reduce its budget by $250,000. You tell us where the cuts are going to be." Now people are saying, "There might be a need to save a high school science teacher with a genetics background or make pre-kindergarten class size a priority, and I am prepared to give up some of my school's budget to support it." This is new thinking and a big step for us. And it's scary. Once you go there, you can never go back.

Joyce: At the high school, the assistant principals and I applied many of the concepts that we've learned. We had a quite serious communication issue last year involving technology. We looked at it as an iceberg and solved it! We still revisit the issue to make sure the ice isn't building up. We've used the World Café model in our Youth Leadership Forum and at a faculty meeting. The results were astounding in the inclusive and expansive conversations that took place.

Joan: I was thrilled with the outcome of the World Café I led in my building. I reminded the staff that this will be an ongoing conversation. We're starting to see teachers use it in their classrooms.

Joyce: One of the most exciting things we've done at the high school is the creation of the Youth Leadership Forum, in which we are training about a hundred kids in systems thinking. Through regular meetings every four or five weeks, they are beginning to solve problems in a different way. We're preparing them to think about the world beyond high school. Membership in the Forum cuts across all four grade levels

Karen Osterman and Robert Kottkamp, *Reflective Practice for Educators*, second edition, (Corwin Press, 2004) provides excellent illustrations of how the five disciplines can be used in the classroom and school.

and across socioeconomic levels, race, ethnicity, and interest groups. We see this as building capacity, and we expect it to carry over to the classroom—and to life.

⟩⟩ See "The Youth Leadership Forum," page 389.

A MUTUAL STAKE IN THE OUTCOME

Peter: When I arrived here, information was hoarded, and knowledge, whether about the budget or other areas, was power. Now, with the evolution of DLT, knowledge is opportunity rather than power.

   Kathy: Previously, most decisions had already been made before the DLT meetings. If I had something that required a decision, I'd make the decision, bring the information to DLT, tell the group what had been decided, and ask if anyone wanted to comment. And, of course, nobody ever did. Now, if we make a decision about something that doesn't require group input, we send out a memo. We're not going to waste everybody's time. If an item appears on the DLT agenda, it is complex and requires everyone's best thinking.

   Joan: It's much more meaningful to participate in the decisionmaking and understand the impact across the system.

   Peter: One pleasant surprise has been watching a group of highly motivated, results-oriented people suspending their own judgments, willing to embark on an unknown process, and sticking with it.

   Kathy: We're all suffering from fewer resources, but there is no longer the feeling that someone is doing this to us; it is what's happening to us together.

   Joe: We raise lots more questions as opposed to engaging in confrontation. Can you tell me why we do this? What's its purpose? Help me understand. Inquiry lets us place issues on the table when in the past we would have avoided them. We've moved from our own individual concerns to systems considerations.

   Joan: I think an important part of this process was the reflective piece. I had to look back on what I was doing and think about what type of a leader I wanted to be. It also gave me the opportunity to speak regularly with Les as a mentor, and I've learned so much from the feedback that I've gotten from him and from the trusting relationship. I'm able to talk with him and others about what is happening in my school and talk about different approaches in handling issues.

   Kathy: In fact, all members of the DLT have expressed their comfort in initiating, scheduling and participating in completely optional one-to-one support conversations with the superintendent in which they discussed their personal struggles and successes with this learning and leadership work.

Joyce: As the new superintendent, I have found that the DLT has made a successful and effective transition as key members of the team have left and been replaced by new leaders. The learning and the use of systems thinking continue to be a core competency and strategy for our highly effective leadership team.

INSTRUCTIONAL ROUNDS IN EDUCATION

A Network Approach to Improving Teaching and Learning,
by Elizabeth City, Richard Elmore, Sarah Fiarman, and Lee Teitel (Harvard Education Press, 2009).

As the Chief Administrator at Northwest Area Education Agency, a regional agency that supports thirty-six school districts in ten counties in northwest Iowa, I have been facilitating instructional rounds with a network of superintendents for the last four years. Like medical rounds, the practice of instructional rounds tries to improve teaching and learning by having educators observe and analyze teaching. I have found that this book and the rounds process provide a balance of school improvement and leadership principles. The process allows school leadership teams to be connected with the work in the classroom. It reminds us that we can't focus on just the content, or just the teacher, or just the student; we must focus on how the teacher and the student interact with content.

In Iowa, we have used instructional rounds as a cultural building process, through professional learning communities. One-third of the superintendents in nine regions of the state come together on a monthly basis to observe instructional practices in classrooms. There is also an organizational learning component; at the host school, we review a problem of practice and then help them get to their next level. Participants learn from each other and the rounds become an example of how the collective intelligence of the staff far outweighs the intelligence of any individual educator. —Timothy Grieves, Chief Administrator, Northwest Area Education Agency, Sioux City, Iowa.

6. "You Can't Do That!"

Treating Physical Education as a Subject Worth Caring About

Ann Marie Gallo

Years after they leave school, a startlingly large number of people re-member their "gym class" as frustrating, as brutal, even as torture. Could the heart of the problem simply be the fact that physical educa-tion is treated as a "dumping ground" and not as a place to learn? Dr. Ann Marie Gallo is currently an associate professor of physical educa-tion at Salem State College in Massachusetts. This story recounts an episode during her time as a physical education instructor at Minute-man Regional High School in Lexington in the 1990s. She started with a seemingly simple point of leverage and ended up contributing to the growth of the entire school as a learning organization. Could teachers do the same in your school? Or would they feel too vulnerable?

It was a typical autumn day during the first month of school. On the tennis courts, a class of thirty-four students restlessly waited their turn to participate in a forehand drill. Twice that day, students approached me with a piece of paper, informing me that they had been switched into this class. As a first-year teacher in a public high school, I was grateful to have the job, but I wondered how effective I could be with this many students. I couldn't work with them personally; I could only put them into drill teams, forgoing the feedback they needed. Often they had to wait for equipment or space to practice. They then misbehaved and dis-tracted the other students.

I had learned in my teacher training that classes became less effective when the magic number of twenty-four students is exceeded. Moreover, after Christmas break I ventured out of my small office in the women's locker room and explored the school. In the science and English wings, I noticed teachers instructing classes of eighteen and twenty students. I wondered if maybe there was a high rate of absenteeism, but a few weeks later, on a return trip, I noticed that the class sizes still seemed small.

Finally I approached the school physical education director and asked her why our classes were so much larger. "We are a dumping ground," she said, looking at her work. I stood and waited for more information. She glanced at me and said, "It has always been that way."

The simplicity of the statement stunned me! Clearly, we were a system with a learning disability that had deteriorated into a mode of learned helplessness. As I left the director's office, yet another student approached the secretary with a course change form and said, "I need to change my PE class." The secretary signed the form without even looking at a class list to see if there was room. Evidently, the process of admitting kids indiscriminately into physical education classes had become an unconscious habit. So I turned back to the director. "What would happen if we didn't sign that schedule change? What if we said there was no room?"

"We can't," she replied. "It will cause too many problems, and guidance has nowhere to put the students."

The following year, heartened by a new physical education curriculum that emphasized grade-specific and student-centered classes, I began to try to learn more about the problem. Whenever a student attempted to enter a large class, I called the guidance counselor to tell them the class was closed. "You can't do that!" they replied. But I persevered. Ultimately, frustration levels on both sides escalated. The director of guidance contacted the principal, who decided to meet with the physical education director, the director of guidance, the guidance department, and me.

The principal opened the meeting by stating the problem, again with startling simplicity: "Guidance has no place to put students, and PE has too many students." The guidance counselors voiced their concerns and the constraints of the master schedule. We presented our new curriculum and discussed teacher effectiveness, personalizing a student's learning experience, and safety. Each side defended its stance; it was like watching a tennis match.

Finally, I volunteered to act as a liaison between physical education and the guidance department. I suggested that the guidance counselors direct students with schedule changes to me, and I would find them a class that could accept them. Skeptical, but lacking a better solution, the guidance department agreed to try the new procedure. For my part, I had no idea what I had gotten into. For the rest of the year, a clipboard filled with class lists and yellow sticky notes accompanied me everywhere I went. I continued trying to limit physical education classes to twenty-four students. When I walked into the guidance office, counselors dispersed so they would not have to confer with me on rescheduling students.

As the years passed, our mental models about each other began to change. I learned more about the guidance counselors' constraints. They grew to respect our quest for smaller classes. Eventually, guidance counselors began calling me on the phone before making a change in a student schedule. They would ask "I have to change a student's math class; what PE classes are still open?"

Today the average physical education class size is twenty-two. We occasionally rise above twenty-four, but everyone recognizes that thirty students in a class is unacceptable. As a result of our commitment to teach, we have developed a significant collegial relationship with the guidance department. When I walk into their office, I am welcomed and greeted. Admittedly, there is some extra work, and I now sometimes find myself taking the side of the guidance department, arguing that a PE instructor should accept another student. Each year the department head asks if anyone else would like to volunteer for the liaison position, and so far, no one else wants the "extra burden." I now believe that liaison positions like this should rotate, not so much to relieve "burdens," but so that every teacher can learn about the complexities of the school as a whole.

Altogether, this has been one of two highly significant experiences in my teaching career. The other is the change in my classes. My students no longer have to waste their time waiting to learn; there's reason to think that many more of them will carry away enough knowledge to become lifelong participants in golf, tennis, swimming, strength training, and other physical activities.

Community

XIII. Moving Into Community

1. Fostering Communities That Learn

Former Superintendent Roland Chevalier of St. Martin Parish, Louisiana, tells the story of an elementary school principal who upon arriving at school one early morning found a six-year-old boy sitting on the steps, waiting for the building to open. When the principal asked, "How long have you been here?" the boy said he didn't know. He didn't know how to tell time yet. He was only in kindergarten. His mother was a single parent who worked the 5 a.m. shift at a factory and left an alarm clock set to wake him up for school. That morning, before the alarm went off, he had woken up without knowing what time it was, had dressed himself, walked to school, and sat and waited for everyone else to show up.

How far does the school's responsibility for that child extend? Has the school done enough when it teaches the boy to tell time? Does it need to help the mother find or build a support network of people who can help rouse the boy and take him to school? Should the school offer early morning childcare for all working parents? Does it need to get involved somehow in addressing the reasons why a single mother would have to take a job that starts at 5 a.m.? Or should the school's responsibility focus forward, on the boy's future, as opposed to his immediate needs?

These kinds of questions are taking on importance in every locale today, both in the United States and in the rest of the world. In turn, they are symptoms of a deeper question: What do people need communities to be? Even in these times of change for communities—of globe-spanning information technologies, diverging family forms, mobile corporations, shifting urban populations, fragmenting political structures, and increased interest in lifelong learning for everyone—the answer is always tied to the needs of children. Communities always exist, at least in part, because children need them as a place to grow to adulthood. Thus, a "school that learns," wherever it is located and whatever form it takes, requires a community that fosters learning all around it.

There are a surprisingly large number of evocative examples of communities that, in one way or another, have broken down the barrier between school and the rest of a child's life. In these cases, the community takes a strong stand in favor of learning, the school embraces its connections to the community, and both sides recognize that the school is not the only organization with responsibilities for children.

In 1997, a local community-service coalition called the Partnership for Children proposed a guiding idea to the Greater Kansas City area: The "#1 Question" campaign: "Is It Good for the Children?" The premise embodied in the question was simple: Whenever any business, government agency, school, or individual made a decision, they should ask themselves first: Would that decision be good for children?

The Partnership for Children still exists, still with the same campaign. The conversations and activities associated with it (including an annual policy agenda report) have broadened over the years including establishing a public park, promoting nutrition, providing funding for foster care, financing after-school activities, allocating money among schools, and a wide variety of legislative issues. By asking, "Is it good for the children?" people essentially ask, "Will this add civility, tolerance, and nurturance into the fabric of life here?"

Similar stories take place in many communities. In some cities, there are family resource centers on school premises run by local health and social service agencies under the guiding idea that a child's ability to learn is deeply related to the learning capability of the child's family and to the resources available to that family. Other efforts bring the school and classroom into the community, setting up in-depth projects off school grounds or by establishing "service learning" opportunities, where students can apply their knowledge on behalf of others. And there are some efforts that take responsibility for learning out of the hands of the school and put it into the hands of parents—involving them in surveying one another and interpreting the results or in developing their own places for children to study amid severe poverty and opposition (as the Rainmakers community group did in Miami Beach, Florida).

Believing that "all communities can learn" is a starting point to developing a capability that may start with children and transform all of human society—not from the top down but from the inside out. A comprehensive guide to building a learning community would require a full

For more on the "#1 Question: Is It Good for the Children?" campaign, and the Partnership for Children that sponsors it, see www.pfc.org. A few other locations, including Rock Hill, South Carolina, and Memphis, Tennessee, have put in place campaigns with the same slogan.

fieldbook in itself; here we offer the theories, tools, methods, and stories that we have found powerful for the communities' role with children. In this part of the book, you will read about reclaiming community centers in Cincinnati, Ohio (page 473); standing up to civil war in Colombia (page 549); and setting up student-run sustainability-oriented enterprises in many locales (page 537).

COMMUNITY

Two Indo-European roots (*kom*, meaning "everyone," and *moin*, meaning "exchange") came together before recorded history to mean "shared by all." This word evolved into the Latin *communis*, meaning "a source" (of water used by many). The French adapted this to *communer*, meaning "to make available to everyone." The original meaning of "community," in other words, is not a place defined by boundaries but by shared resources. We would like to think that a community that learns carries forth that tradition.

In this part of the book, we do not use the term "community" to mean a group of people within an organization—as in a "learning community" inside a school. A community of people is a place, rooted in the biosphere, rife with activity and mutual respect, and the recognition that everyone in that place is responsible for and accountable to one another, because the lives of all are interdependent.

A community that learns, in our view, shares a mutual commitment with its schools. The community is a nurturing, supportive, sometimes challenging, but always caring container wrapped around the school and the development of children. Community institutions would be included (local government, media, police, health, and business) as would larger-scale institutions: larger-scale government, academic research, global media and business. All of these institutions affect the interplay between residents of a community and its schools, and children depend on the continual improvement—the continual learning—of that interplay.

From the experience that exists so far among "communities that learn," there seem to be three strong guiding ideas that anchor community leaders in developing a common learning approach to their shared future: identity, connections, and sustainability.

IDENTITY

The lines of a town or city may be charted and inscribed on a map, but different community members have different attitudes about the boundaries of their community and the extent to which they are responsible for one another. People who live in a country club community may not explicitly register the fact that, just across a river or a railroad track, there is a trailer park with 300 or 400 children attending the same schools, using the same recreation facilities (or requesting them from a town government that doesn't provide them). Aging people, people with disabilities, and people who are homeless may be present but unseen. Residents may choose to draw boundaries around themselves, to avoid associating with other people, and to avoid responsibility for them. That may well be a part of their conception of community identity.

But, as became clear in Greater Kansas City, the needs of children often seem to transcend that isolated view. Children do not stay within the boundaries of a gated community, at least not after they have started school. If we are members of a community together, simply because we have chosen to live near one another, we have entered into an implicit covenant for the mutual development of all the children of the community. Just as we assure the mutual support of our health by funding hospitals, we assure the presence of a viable and vibrant future by funding and supporting the presence of learning schools and other resources for children.

Schools play a larger role than many people may think in defining the nature of a community. It starts when people choose their homes. The first question often asked of real estate and rental agents is: "How are the schools?" In some places (such as New Jersey), laws establish the boundary of the school as "portal-to-portal"—from the child's home into the school building—so that insurance can cover them for bus transportation. This means that the school superintendent is literally responsible for children's safety throughout the local community. No matter where the legal definition stops, there is always some ambiguity about the place the school stops and the community begins.

For example, to what extent are educators who live elsewhere, but who are intimately aware of the needs of the children in their schools, part of their school's community? We know a junior high school teacher who gave up Friday nights for years to chaperone PTA-sponsored dances. He finally asked to be paid a few dollars per night and was told, "Shouldn't you do this out of the kindness of your heart?" He said, "I have three small children at home. And I'm not there with them." Teachers often buy supplies that the school is lacking, or gifts of other sorts, with their own money. The community that expects this kind of commitment from its teachers also must exhibit commitment to those same teachers and the education system.

All of these are fundamentally issues of identity. What kind of community do we want to live in? What is the nature of this community right now? In short, defining identity is a practice of building shared vision for the community, with the school system as an active and valued player, but hardly the only player.

CONNECTIONS

Members of a community draw their paychecks from different sources, work in different locations (some of which may be relatively far away), attend different churches, have different demands on their time, and have different affiliations. Given all of these varied loyalties, the need to build regular connections often gets short shrift. Yet this capability is one of the highest-leverage ways to establish a pattern of learning in a community.

A rare kind of energy and electricity is present when a new community connection is made between players in the system who have been previously isolated from one another. A social worker and a teacher, a business executive and a curriculum coordinator, or a hospital administrator and a student have far more leverage to change the community together than they would have on their own.

If a school system is not a prominent and deliberate actor in its community—if the superintendent does not have good relationships with other community leaders, if the teachers don't see themselves as connected to the community, and if residents don't see the schools as vibrant contributors to the community—then that in itself indicates a diminished capacity for connections. Conversely, when schools learn to see the value of other groups that affect children's lives, and other groups learn to see the value and connections of schools, then new possibilities emerge. Support groups that work with children in poverty suddenly hook up not just with social services but with educators. Educational experiences occur across numerous community institutions: museums, symphonies, public libraries, Scouts, theaters, conservation groups, public services, religious organizations, local law enforcement, Head Start, and businesses. Intergenerational connections begin to hook children up (for example) with tutors and role models in their retirement. Community leaders regularly mention the resources provided by the school. School leaders discover that they can't do it alone…but they don't have to do it all alone.

The building of connections has increased in recent years as the Internet has taken hold. Schools can now become information centers for the communities in which they exist. Students in many schools have begun to research, write, and publish online community histories, interviewing everyone from the mayor to the oldest citizen to the most recent person to move in. These histories then link the town and school more closely together. The school doesn't just "see" the community—it helps the community find a voice. In short, making connections can amplify the disciplines of mental models and team learning and institutionalize those disciplines at a broad level.

SUSTAINABILITY

Sustainability involves an awareness, akin to the awareness in systems thinking, of the long-term implications of the actions taken today. When educators get involved in early childhood education, for example, they exhibit the kind of time sense involved in sustainability. "The child has just been born? My gosh, he or she will enter school only five or six years from now. That's a very short horizon." We know of an urban superintendent, deeply involved with systems thinking, who set a school goal of raising the birth weight of babies born to teenage mothers in his school system. He set up welfare offices and clinics in each of his ten high schools and made sure that within a two-block radius of each school there was a grocery store that carried infant formula and vitamins for pregnant women. He understood that one of the highest-leverage ways to ensure that "all children in a school can learn" is to invest in early childhood nutrition.

Another example of community-oriented sustainability occurred during a scenario exercise with a school district. District members thought that they might have to build new schools quickly, but they weren't sure when. State law prohibited them from putting too much money aside for a rainy day. One of the people in the room suggested that they focus on raising their communications skills to get tax levies passed more easily. That way, if there were a need for a budget increase, no matter what happened to the economy, the school could raise the money it needed.

Then the assistant superintendent for finance spoke up. "I think we should not do that. If the community is flush and wants to invest in the school, then we'll pass the levy. If the community has hard times, then we need to match its frugality. Our job is not to improve our ability to raise money, but to do more for children and thus to improve our relationship with the community. If we have a genuine need for the money, they'll know and appreciate why." In other words, she argued, instead of thinking about their town as composed of pro- and anti-tax factions, they should start by assuming a high level of mutual trust between the school system and the community, and design their budget campaigns accordingly.

Sustainable communities hold a long-term perspective and thus understand their interdependence with education. Community members understand, as individuals, that the evolution of each young child depends on the individual attention that he or she receives. They invest their time with children because that is what they want to do.

A professional mother we know tells the story of taking her two children to their local school playground on a cherished day off. They came across an injured cat by the swing set. Together, they summoned Charlie, the school custodian, who happened to own a small farm and was good with animals. He picked up the cat and said, "Yes, it looks like its leg is broken," and made a home for it in a small box.

The boy's mother offered to take the cat to the vet, and she started to walk off with her two children. Then she looked at Charlie and said, "What am I doing? The last thing I need right now is another errand. We'll be in the vet's office for a half hour or more."

"You've just shown your children," said Charlie, "what you want them to be like when they are adults."

XIV. Identity

1. Taking Stock of Community Connections

Tim Lucas, Janis Dutton, Nelda Cambron-McCabe, Bryan Smith

You are about to innovate—to try something new for the children in your community. Or you want to conduct an ongoing conversation about the future of the community's children. You are thinking big, and you know you cannot do it alone. Whom do you involve outside the school? This exercise can open you up to possibilities you might never have considered.

STEP 1: LISTING YOUR COMMUNITY CONNECTIONS

In a small group, brainstorm about the people and organizations in the community around the school, drawing on the informal and formal knowledge of everyone in the room.

- Who represents the "support community" for your school or organization? Whom do you draw upon regularly for time, advice, collaboration, or financial support? Who in the community is involved with setting the school vision or with school planning? Who are the people you would like to reach out to?
- Who are the people that your school's (or organization's) children draw on for support? These may include people who have no formal or informal relationship with the school but who are important in children's lives. If your school is in the United States, and a child calls a grandparent in Costa Rica or the Philippines once a week to talk about school, that grandparent is part of your community.
- Whom do the children correspond with by text, email, or social network?

Purpose:

For school leaders (or other community leaders) to come to a better understanding of the community around them and the resources available in that community for children.

Participants:

A group prepared to make connections. This may include educators, parents, government officials, business owners, clergy, and nonprofit and service groups.

Time:

*Two hours or more,
possibly divided among
two or more meetings.*

■ Who's in the school's neighborhood? Which storekeepers depend on the school for their business? Who is legally responsible for traffic, student safety, and crime in the immediate area? What does that accountability actually mean?

■ Where does learning take place in this community outside the school? Once, if you asked this question in a school, the answer would be: "On the farm or in the home." Now there is a vast number of other places, some in cyberspace. Where do kids hang out? In a park? At a mall? On streets? At clubs, youth centers, or religion-affiliated groups? What other organized activities for students—public, private, and not-for-profit; athletic and academic; seasonal and year-round—exist in your community? What are children learning at each of them? And is there anyone associated with any of them who should be added to this list?

STEP 2: EXPANDING THE LIST OF COMMUNITY CONNECTIONS

Inevitably, your list has left out important people, because you don't know who they are. So expand the list, first, by imagining individuals or groups who are not currently in the room. Select four or five of them based on their breadth of knowledge and experience, so that if you had them in the room, they would represent among them a fairly large percentage of the school population. How would they answer the questions in step 1? Whom would they list?

Optionally, call a break here so you can ask other people directly to help you expand the list, by interviewing them singly or together. Continue adding names to the list until you meet again and pick up with step 3.

STEP 3: PRIORITIZING

Looking at all the community connections from steps 1 and 2—both individuals and groups—which five are most important to you? Make three separate lists according to three separate criteria:

1. List them by the quality of shared experience with any member of your group. The more closely someone has worked with them in the past, the more likely you are to create a successful project with them now.
2. List them by the importance of their efforts to children. A child welfare worker can be of more benefit to most schools than the purchasing department head at a local corporation.
3. List them according to the access you have to them. If you know them personally or can make a personal connection, that is valuable, even if you haven't worked with them in the past.

Now make a new list of the five to ten key potential community connections most visible on all three lists. This list becomes your starting point.

STEP 4: "WHERE ARE THEY COMING FROM?"

Stand in the shoes of the key potential community connections listed in step 3. What does each of them see as their primary mission or purpose? What do they want most? What leads them to want it?

You might conclude, for example, that local business leaders want your school to produce cooperative workers with basic literacy skills; that the city council wants a visible decrease in the "Saturday night scene" downtown; that a parents' group feels that the school district has singled them out unfairly; or that a family resource center wants both facilities and referrals.

What observable data led you to these conclusions? If you cannot identify any direct, observable reason, on what do you base them?

You may find it helpful to role-play this part of the exercise. Taking on the persona of, say, a religious leader or a government official, address the rest of the group about "your" concerns as that person. Be judicious; make sure that you believe that if those people were listening, they would feel their perspectives were treated fairly.

STEP 5: MOVING TOWARD A RELATIONSHIP

Pick several of these community connections as starting points for initial contact. Ask three more sets of questions about them:

- What is it you want from them? What do you see as their existing contribution—both to the community and the school?
- How do they see your school (or, if it's not a school, your organization)? Are they aware of the resources you provide the community? What is it that they want from you—and are they getting it? Why do they want these things?
- How *could* they see your school or organization, if they looked closely? How have you addressed community initiatives for children in the past? What partnerships have you formed? What progress did you make? What did you learn from that experience that you have communicated with others?

For example, you may have created a family resource center in your school. Now look at it with the eyes of a community connection from your list. They might have very different criteria for judging its value. For example: Can parents borrow books from the center? Is information about social service agencies available? Does it provide access to information that families might need about alcoholism, sexually transmitted diseases, or other sensitive topics? Is the room separate from other school activities? Is it accessible to people with disabilities? Is it in a part of town close to the people who need it most? At the same time, is it accessible to everyone else and set up in a way that allows all people, no matter how wealthy or poor, to feel welcome?

STEP 6: CONTACT

We have seen this exercise used as a starting point for meetings with community members. Open by showing the lists you have made and using them for inquiry: "We thought we recorded your concerns, but we don't think we were precise enough. How would you rephrase the wording we have here? What other key individuals have we left out?"

COMMON FIRE

Leading Lives of Commitment in a Complex World,
by Laurent A. Parks Daloz, Cheryl H. Keen, James P. Keen, and Sharon Daloz Parks (Beacon Press, 1996)

We really have only three choices when it comes to living in our communities: do nothing, become discouraged and/or cynical about the complexity of participation and give up, or commit ourselves to making them better places to live. If you are like me, you may alternate among all three depending on your energy level. And that's why I like this book. It communicates the power of personal and shared vision through the experiences of more than a hundred people in many walks of life who have sustained a commitment to the common good of their communities when all too many people give up. The authors, who are educators and researchers, write from their shared concern that as the world becomes increasingly more complex, and as previous certainties become more ambiguous, people will seek comfort in trying to control the complexity rather than engaging it. If you are interested in tapping deeper into your own commitment, this book identifies a number of key patterns in how commitment to a common good is formed and how it can be sustained in the face of discouragement and cynicism. —Janis Dutton

2. "Expression Is the First Step Out of Oppression"

Building Grassroots Capacity for Local Education at Cincinnati's Peaslee Neighborhood Center

Bonnie Neumeier

The exterior walls of the Peaslee Neighborhood Center, a former elementary school, are painted with a quilt of squares depicting the programs inside (which include tutoring, music, child care, and women's support). The quilt provides a splash of color in the inner-city neighborhood of Over-the-Rhine, just north of the central business district of Cincinnati, Ohio.

The Over-the-Rhine neighborhood is a highly contested part of the city. It is marked by extremes of gentrification and homelessness. Upscale commercial development competes with neighborhood-serving businesses for poor residents. There is an alliance of corporate and city interests promoting market-based initiatives and a poor people's movement resisting that alliance and calling for fairness and equality. In short, the community represents a classic story of many American inner-city neighborhoods.

Peaslee is an integral part of the grassroots aspect of the neighborhood. Since its founding in 1984, it has been a center of advocacy for poor people's rights, in such areas as social service, community education, sheltering the homeless, landlord/tenant relations, religion, and affordable housing development. The history of Peaslee, recounted here, shows how a community organization, especially when linked to children, can become more vibrant, inclusive, creative, and influential over the years—the Center's motto, from the beginning, has been "Dream Big." Bonnie Neumeier, a neighborhood leader and one of the founders of Peaslee, shares the story of the powerful vision that developed when a group of women tried to prevent the closing of a neighborhood school. This story shows how leaders may appear when you least expect it.

For more information about Peaslee and other community groups in this area, see www.peasleecenter.org.

Peaslee School was one of the best schools we had in Cincinnati in 1981. Peaslee kids did great academically, and their high test scores were rare for an inner-city school. The teachers were dedicated and sensitive to the social issues that the children faced. They worked well with parents and provided as much support as they could—including a clothes closet with coats and sweaters for children who needed them. It was close by and easy for the children, ages five to eight, to walk to. When the school board announced the decision to close it and relocate our children, we were angry.

The neighborhood was already actively engaged in a struggle to survive. For much of Cincinnati and the local media, the name Over-the-Rhine meant stereotypical poverty, homelessness, and the crimes common to inner-city America. To us, the name identified a neighborhood with a growing grassroots movement of people empowering themselves to work together to shelter the homeless, create jobs, provide substance-abuse counseling, establish food and clothing banks, and organize extensive efforts to rehabilitate abandoned buildings into affordable housing. We used the name with pride. We were more than just a collection of streets and buildings. We were a true neighborhood of poor Appalachians and people of color with supportive networks who would not be ignored. And our children were very important.

With our history of organizing grassroots efforts, we naturally tried to save Peaslee School. Our losses have been many, but in any grassroots movement, the byproducts of those efforts can be just as important as the original goal. Women led this particular struggle and, in the process, discovered new friends, support systems, and the strength to become neighborhood leaders. We built a dream together. Holding on tight to that dream got us where we are. I hope that if we can remember and share that dream, other folks in the neighborhood, especially young girls, can discover their own strengths and commitment.

THE DREAM

Cincinnati Public Schools were facing court-ordered integration, and many of the district's buildings were old and crumbling, but we didn't understand why the school board would close a modern, racially integrated school that received high academic ratings. They told us the school was "under-enrolled." We felt they had created that problem by not enforcing the policies determining where kids went to school and by eliminating special programs and moving those students to other buildings. Now they were asking us to pay for their decisions.

Many of the parents had attended Peaslee School when they were children. At least, they had attended the institution named Peaslee. In 1974, the school board had torn down the historic one-hundred-year-old building that had been Peaslee and promised to build a new one. The current school had originally been the annex. The site of the old

W hy is this neighborhood called "Over-the-Rhine"? Originally settled in the mid-1800s by Germans who immigrated to work in the growing city of Cincinnati, it is located north of downtown, across what was once a canal in the Ohio-Erie Canal system. This location and the strong German identity earned the neighborhood the name Over-the- Rhine. Appalachians seeking work moved here during the Great Depression and were joined by African Americans after World War II.
—Bonnie Neumeier

school was still an empty lot when we asked the board to meet with us and listen to our concerns. Among these concerns was the fact that the children would be transferred to another neighborhood school—the one ranked last in district test scores—and that these very young children would have to walk much farther and cross a busy four-lane street. We couldn't understand why they would close a school that worked so well and had such a good working relationship between educators and parents. The board members seemed to understand, because, at that meeting, they said they would keep the school open. We thought we had won a victory.

That was December 1981. In March 1982, without us knowing ahead of time, board members broke their promise and voted to close the school. We were pretty upset. We had already lost six neighborhood schools. There were no plans to rebuild any. Two of the mothers, Kathleen Prudence and Everlene Leary, talked about it on the playground one day when they were picking up their children and said, "We can't let them do this without objecting to it." The three of us held a meeting and said, "What can we do?" The Peaslee Women's Movement was born.

We started attending every school board meeting and asked the board to reconsider. We passed out flyers and put up signs and banners because a lot of people didn't have phones. We marched to the meetings downtown instead of taking the bus. And we got smarter along the way. We wanted to know why this school at this particular time? We documented all of the school closings in the previous ten years and placed colored pins on a map of the city. It was obvious that most of the closings were in poor neighborhoods, Appalachian and African American neighborhoods like ours. We didn't like what we saw.

We also learned that this wasn't just about education; it was also a struggle over land. The areas to the east and south of the school were becoming gentrified. Housing that had for years been crumbling, due to the neglect of absentee landlords, was being restored for the upper and middle class. A lot of our families lived in those buildings; closing the schools, whether deliberately or not, would help force them out of the neighborhood. In that context, the fight for Peaslee was part of a larger struggle for neighborhood identity and for the basic human right of low-income people to self-determination.

Gradually the number of people involved grew. Each board meeting had a period of time set aside called Hearing the Public. Each meeting we brought new speakers. Board members let us vent our frustrations, but they felt no need to respond, or even listen. We tried to get a temporary injunction to keep the school open on the basis of discrimination against poor people and the African American and Appalachian cultures.

Three African American and three Appalachian mothers filed the claim. At a preliminary hearing, the court said there is no such thing as discrimination against poor Appalachian people, and if we wanted to pursue racial discrimination we would have to join in a suit that had already been filed in District Court in Dayton, Ohio. We could not afford the legal costs to challenge the decision and pulled back. By then the school had closed and the kids just got scattered.

We lost the battle, but we really didn't lose. We rebounded with a new strength and a new realization of the power of women's voices. Some of these women had never been involved in our movement before. We were amazed we could organize such a massive grassroots campaign. They discovered they could be leaders. We continued to meet and support each other and refused to give up on the importance of an educational neighborhood resource. I had been involved in an earlier effort to raise money to buy the Drop Inn Center, a building that housed a homeless shelter, and then in raising money to expand the shelter to accommodate the increasing numbers of women and children. I said, "Hey, maybe we can do the same thing."

We started calling friends and others who had supported our women's effort to raise some earnest money to buy the school building. We had the building appraised. We went to the school board meeting and offered them $15,000 as a down payment toward the appraised price of $125,000 and asked for a year to raise the remainder. They said no. Now, our local school board has been known to give buildings away for $1 to developers and other groups, both before and since we made the offer, but not to low-income women. We didn't give up. We lobbied the board for six months, and eventually they agreed to sell us the building. But they changed the price tag. The new price was $240,000.

That's a big undertaking: raising $240,000. I don't think they thought we'd ever do it. But they underestimated the determination and the energy of people who felt strongly that Peaslee had been an educational resource for more than one hundred years and deserved to stay in the hands of the neighborhood. We started raising money, five dollars, ten dollars at a time. We sold "Bricks for Peaslee" at ten dollars apiece. We sold balloons at neighborhood festivals. The Cincinnati Women's Muse held a benefit concert. At that rate, we wondered if we would ever raise the money, and we did not yet have the credibility to get the larger grants.

Our vision kept the effort going, and once again a woman made the difference. We made a presentation to the Greater Cincinnati Foundation, and a woman on the foundation staff, who seemed to connect with us as women, helped us get a $25,000 grant. That credibility helped us get a few more grants, including a Community Development Block Grant from the city. But the year was ending, and we were $40,000 short. We pleaded with the school board to drop their price. Eventually they agreed to $200,000 for the building, but they charged us another $9,000 for "maintenance costs" they had had while the building sat vacant. Since we were not incorporated, a local neighborhood development corporation held the deed in trust for the Peaslee Women's group. Neighbors and volunteers started cleaning, painting, repairing, and decorating the building. Peaslee came alive again.

THE HUB OF A WHEEL

We had come a long way, but some of the biggest struggles were still ahead. During the fundraising year, we organized a development committee that conducted community surveys and held meetings to determine what the neighborhood needed. First came the Homework Room, which has become our longest-running program. In collaboration with the schools, it provides tutoring; basic reading, writing, and math skills; and other after-school help. We offered women's educational programs, art and music programs for children, and space for community meetings.

To help pay operating costs and keep our doors open, we needed to rent a certain amount of space to other programs, such as daycare, that fit into our vision. Over the years, different organizations have rented spaces in the building. Ironically, in the early 1990s, Cincinnati Public Schools was one of our tenants. They rented space for a daycare center for children of the young mothers who were finishing their education.

We had been up and running for four years when suddenly events threatened Peaslee's survival. One of our biggest paying tenants pulled out, due to its own internal problems. Worse still, the development corporation that held our deed and trust, without telling us, put the building up for sale. Potential buyers started coming into the building looking at it for office space, and we ended up marching and protesting around our own building, saying, "Peaslee is not for sale!"

We couldn't convince the development corporation not to sell the building out from under us. So the Peaslee Women formed a corporation—Peaslee Neighborhood Center, Inc.—and went through mediation in court. The mediator ruled in our favor, and Peaslee was ours. Free and clear.

We have had to learn to create and manage budgets and programs, write grants, and coordinate the many volunteers who work here. Each year our budget has grown because of different programs, but I think we've spent our money wisely. When you live on very little, you learn how to make do. Still, it is difficult. We rely mostly on small grants from private foundations and donations, yet people seem more willing to give money to homeless issues than to education. It shouldn't be so difficult to raise money for the kids. We operate under the belief that if we focus early on their education, we can prevent other problems from developing.

We have remained participatory and community-based, even as we have expanded and changed. In the early 2000s, we added to the building to extend our daycare facilities. Women who have left welfare are desperate to find safe and adequate care for their children while they are at work. They need before- and after-school care, as well as infant and preschool care. There is a countywide shortage of spaces for these children. The center has always provided some spaces for homeless children so their mothers can seek jobs and housing and have support to get their lives back together. The dream of saving Peaslee and buying it for a community-based educational resource center is connected to a larger vision for the people in the neighborhood. The Over-the-Rhine People's Movement is dedicated to defending the basic human right of low-income people to self-determination.

I like to think of this movement as the hub of a wheel, with our grassroots movements being the spokes that stand for the right to have a roof over your head at night, access to services, and affordable housing. Peaslee is a spoke dedicated to culture and education. The programs at Peaslee that provide learning opportunities for children and support for women will help us build a stronger, healthier neighborhood, because the strength of the neighborhood depends on the individual development of each person. And that can only happen with strong community support.

We have a slogan: "Expression is the first step out of oppression." If you can express what you are angry or upset about, whether it is an addiction, an abusive spouse, or facing eviction from your home, you will eventually say it enough to enable you to act. When you can do that in your personal life, you can also act against injustice on the collective level. Peaslee tries to facilitate expression, helping people use their voice in any medium: writing, poetry, art, or music.

From the beginning, women's support groups met regularly to provide a sense of solidarity and empowerment to women in the community. Then we asked ourselves: "If we have always been about individual development and the empowerment of women, why don't we start a girls group to help them discover the power of their own voices?" This group continues to meet; it is a place to talk about the pressures of being a young girl in the inner city. We talk about self-esteem and how to say no to drugs or sex. We write stories and poetry, and we talk about how important they are. Like the women who founded the Peaslee Neighborhood Center, these girls rely on one another. Progress is slow; it takes time to build up self-esteem. It's not like you can have it tomorrow.

⁑ Also see "The Over-the-Rhine Residency Program," page 497.

3. Reclaiming Citizenship through Conversations

Peter Block

What if your school district or city isn't interested in conversations about community issues or creating change—or can't afford to sponsor them? What if they hold conversations, but the same small group of people are the only ones ever invited or heard? Then you have to start different conversations, where the leaders are not necessarily those in authority. Peter Block is an author, consultant, and citizen of Cincinnati, Ohio. In the 1980s and early 1990s, as an active organizational development consultant, he wrote influential, best-selling, learning-oriented business books. Then he moved increasingly into the public and volunteer sectors, where his primary themes—empowerment, stewardship, chosen accountability, and the reconciliation of community—resonated even more. His goal is to bring change into the world through consent and connectedness rather than through mandate and force.

Peter Block's book Community: The Structure of Belonging (Berrett-Koehler, 2008) focuses on how community can emerge from fragmentation. Also see John McKnight and Peter Block, *The Abundant Community: Awakening the Power of Families and Neighborhoods* (Berrett-Koehler, 2010). Block's earlier business books include *Flawless Consulting* (Third Edition, Jossey-Bass, 2010), *The Empowered Manager* (Jossey-Bass, 1987), and *Stewardship: Choosing Service Over Self-Interest* (Berrett-Koehler, 1993). His publication and work website is www.designedlearning.com. Finally, Peter Block and John McKnight maintain a joint website on restoring community at http://www.abundantcommunity.com.

During the first twenty years of my career, I just followed the money, much like the bank robber Willie Sutton. I worked in the private sector because it was easier to make a living there.

Then, in 1995, I had the opportunity to work with a group of city managers, and I loved it. I became fascinated with how they balanced the jobs of managing utilities and streets with a broad view of community and civic engagement; how they coped with having all the wounds of the community dumped on their desks. I accepted their invitations to facilitate meetings in their cities. I felt that the methodology I had spent my life making sense of and using in the private setting had something to offer that setting.

I also worked with the government in the Philippines right after the Velvet Revolution in the early 1990s. I worked with people there who had given up their lives to overthrow Marcos and ended up governing. The new cabinet members were amazing in their energy and commitment. At the sessions I facilitated, they jumped into assigned tasks before I had finished assigning them. These people stood for something larger than themselves; they sought to bring democracy to their country and economic well-being to poor people. I tasted what it was like to be with people who really cared about something. This was in sharp contrast to the private sector, where the commitment is to a career and the economic well-being of one institution.

In the community work, I began to understand the distinction between operating from mandate and operating from choice. I began seeking out places where people cared from the heart. These were places such as schools, fire departments, and community activist organizations. They were willing to explore the ideas of civic engagement and its meanings. Community work was so much more value-driven, people showed up because they cared. I loved it. Still do.

Then I moved to Cincinnati. It dawned on me that I should live out all the things that I'd been talking about. When living in other communities, I'd always been a guest. I should become a citizen. I volunteered myself, declared my availability, and found a new focus in having conversations with other citizens seeking to create positive change in their communities.

THE PUBLIC CONVERSATION AND SCHOOLS

Not just any conversation in the public sector has the power to create a distinct future. For example, conversations about problem solving do not create real change; they just make things a little better. Authentic change comes from a shift in thinking about community and in the way of being in community. It comes from a new language oriented toward creating possible new futures. Transformation focuses on gifts rather than deficits and puts choice in people's own hands instead of waiting for the transformation of others. A healthy public conversation is the act that precedes other actions. Re-creating the nature of the public conversation will change the direction of communities.

Healthy public conversations include conversations in large or small settings, conversations with oneself, and conversations in the media. Contrary to popular opinion, the media does not create or control the public debate. The media reflects the conversation people have chosen. It exploits the wounds of community by over-reporting fear, dramatizing opposition, and headlining retribution. Citizen silence and passivity creates the space for the media to profit from people's wounds.

A SMALL GROUP

I have been working with a group of other citizens in my community to facilitate conversations among small groups and associations, to break through the passivity and change the nature of the public conversation. We named our organization "A Small Group." Our work focuses on direct efforts to bring into the conversation those groups of people who are not in relationship with each other. This is an alternative to like-mindedness, which leads to no change.

Another limitation with most traditional public conversations is people's desire to talk about those *not* in the room. Many people think that change must come from others, as if changing others will help them reach their own goals. This does not produce power; it consumes it.

We also believe that healthy democratic communities grow out of high civic engagement, with a strong focus on the gifts and strengths of the communities and their citizens. Our intention is to create the possibility of an alternative future by creating a healthy public conversation based on communal accountability and commitment. With all the efforts aimed at changing schools, it is easy to miss the fact that educating our children is a community function. As much education takes place outside the school building as in it. If a community cannot demonstrate a willingness to invest, show up, engage, and care for its children, on its own, in its neighborhood, what does the future hold for those communities? Public schools are the litmus test of a community's strength and commitment and its capacity to care for itself.

Within the schools world, the dominant public conversation on changing schools stems from a set of beliefs that retribution, incentives, competition, legislation, new standards, and tough talk will force accountability and higher student performance. After all my years in the private sector, I am convinced that these beliefs are really myths and bring about little change.

For example, why push for competition when business is getting rid of it as fast as it can? Competition in business is disappearing. There are fewer choices. Exxon and Mobil merged because their leaders felt they weren't large enough. I saw Lee Raymond, President of Exxon, explain that they had to merge to generate economies of scale. If you are already one of the largest companies in the world, and you still don't think you are large enough, scale is not the real issue. Something else is going on. That something else is empire.

More information about A Small Group and its work on reconciling and restoring community through conversations, can be found at www.asmallgroup.net. The site also contains a social network devoted to restoration and reconciliation in Cincinnati. The group cites the work of Robert Putnam and John McKnight as strong influences in their work. You can learn more about their work, respectively, at these links: http://www.bowlingalone.com and http://www.abcdinstitute.org.

For more on restoring community and the joint effort between Peter Block and John McKnight see http://www.abundantcommunity.com

In schools, no one would argue against the need for more attention to poor performance and more transparency around expectations and achievement. However, competition is set up to separate the winners from the losers. It's very difficult to understand why a community would want to relegate any child to loser status or to set up a structure that produces more losers than winners.

Why promote pay for performance in schools when it has never worked in business? There is no evidence that anybody's performance goes up with variable payment. In fact, there is evidence to the contrary. Why have we lost faith in our teachers? There's no question there are some lousy teachers and school administrators, but there are lousy employees and CEOs in business and other organizations too.

If you believe, as I do, that public education is a cornerstone of opportunity, democracy, and equal access, then the belief that more competition is good is not only unhelpful; it is an assault on all things public.

RESTORING COMMUNITY ACCOUNTABILITY

The dominant public conversation around most public issues (not just schools) claims to be tough on accountability, but it lacks the very characteristic it demands. Accountability is the willingness to acknowledge that you have participated in creating, through commission or omission, the conditions that you wish to see changed. To be accountable is choosing to care for the well-being of the whole, not just your segment of the community. Commitment involves the willingness to make promises on behalf of the common good with no expectation of return; promises that are not conditioned on another's action.

Healthy, powerful, transformative conversations occur when invitation replaces mandate, policy, and alignment; possibility replaces problem solving; ownership and cause replace explanation and denial; dissent and refusal replace resignation and lip service; and gifts replace deficiencies.

The role of leader also shifts. Citizens lead. Being in a position of formal authority is no longer required. The dominant, conventional assumption is that the task of leadership is to set a vision; enroll others in it; and hold people accountable through measurements and reward. But in a healthy public conversation, the task of leadership is to convene and create opportunities for engagement. Leaders name the debate, issue the invitation, and provide the space for those who choose to show up. Leaders reject lip service and insist on authentic commitment; they ask people to say no and pass rather than speak without that commitment. Leaders help surface doubts and dissent without having an answer to every question. One primary task of leadership and citizenship is to bring the gifts of those on the margin into the center.

See "We Dance Together," by Candee Basford, page 195.

Facilitating conversations in the civic sector is ten times more complex than facilitating in the private sector. The biggest barriers in the public sector are not the lack of leadership, funding, expertise, or good programs. All of these exist in abundance. Communities are hurt by profoundly deep fragmentation and the lack of social fabric. In addition, most people can only volunteer part time; when you call a meeting, no matter how great your cause, you don't know who will show up.

The dominant existing public conversation drives us apart; it does not bring us together. It cannot restore community because it nurtures entitlement and individuality and not accountability and commitment. Efforts to solve fragmentation through that dominant conversation will only yield more fragmentation; it leads communities to work against themselves as vigorously as they are trying to move forward. The real work of building community is to keep creating healthy public conversations that build social fabric, that weave together all who have a stake in it. This type of work is slow and vague; it is hard to see immediate results. But it is the type of work that will make a difference.

Purpose:

If you want to create change in your community, start a conversation. If you want to change the conversation, change the questions. Each of these six conversations sets up a context for problem solving and personal accountability.

Six Conversations That Make a Difference

Peter Block

Here are the specific conversations I use with people seeking greater engagement in their communities. All of us want action and to create a future we believe in. The nature of the questions people ask is critical. It can either keep the existing system in place or bring an alternative future into the room. Many conventionally asked questions have little power to create an alternative future.

Powerful questions are ambiguous. Don't try to precisely define what is meant by the question. The ambiguity allows each person to bring their own, personal meaning into the room.

Powerful questions are personal. All passion, commitment, and connection grow out of what is most personal. Create space for the personal.

Powerful questions provoke anxiety. All that matters makes us anxious. The wish to escape from anxiety steals liveliness away. If there is no edge to the question, there is no power.

Substitute curiosity for advice. Trying to be helpful and giving advice are ways to control others. Advice is a conversation stopper. Create a context which is more likely to provide surprises when people talk.

CONVERSATION #1: INVITATION

Transformation occurs through choice. An invitation offers a possibility to choose to participate. It also warns people that if they do come, something will be required of them. They will be asked to explore ways to deepen their learning and commitment.

When people show up at the gathering, refer back to the invitation and then connect with these questions:

- What led you to accept the invitation?
- What would it take for you to be fully present in this room?
- What price (in money, time, attention, etc.) are others paying for you to be here?

CONVERSATION #2: POSSIBILITY

This conversation is framed as a choice to enter a new possibility for the future, as opposed to negotiating from interests and problem solving the past.

Questions for individual reflection:

- What is the crossroads at which you find yourself at this stage of your life or work, or at this stage of the project around which we are assembled?
- What declaration of possibility can you make that has the power to transform the community and inspire you?

Collective questions for possibility:

- What do you all want to create together that would make a difference?
- What can you all create together that you cannot create alone?

CONVERSATION #3: OWNERSHIP

This conversation takes the stance that we are the creator of our world as well as the product of it. It asks us how we have contributed to creating the current reality.

- How valuable an experience (or project, or community) do you plan this to be?
- How much risk are you willing to take?
- How participative do you plan to be?

- To what extent are you invested in the well-being of the whole?
- What have you done to contribute to the very thing you complain about or want to change?

CONVERSATION #4: DISSENT

This conversation begins by allowing people the space to say no. If we cannot say no, then our yes has no meaning. Each person needs the chance to express his or her doubts and reservations, without having to justify them or move quickly into problem solving. Saying no is the beginning of a conversation for commitment.

- What doubts and reservations do you have?
- What do you want to say no to or refuse that you keep postponing?
- What have you said yes to that you do not really mean?
- What is a commitment or decision that you have changed your mind about?
- What forgiveness are you withholding?
- What resentment do you hold that no one knows about?

CONVERSATION #5: COMMITMENT

Wholehearted commitment makes a promise to peers about your contribution to the success of the whole. It is a promise for the sake of a larger purpose, not for the sake of personal return. The commitment of only a few people may be needed to create the future you have in mind.

- What promise are you willing to make?
- What measures have meaning to you?
- What price are you willing to pay for the success of the whole?
- What is the cost to others for you to keep your commitments?
- What is the cost if you do not keep your commitments?

CONVERSATION #6: GIFTS

Every exercise ends with this conversation.

People rarely talk about gifts. They tend to be obsessed with deficiency. Rather than focus on weaknesses, which will most likely not go away, you gain more leverage by focusing on the gifts you all bring and how to capitalize on those. What you focus on, you strengthen.

Pay special attention to the setup for this conversation. Sit in a circle. One person at a time receives statements from others of what they have appreciated from that person. The person receiving these statements says, simply, "Thank you, I like hearing that." Don't deflect the appreciations. Maintain a ban on discussing weaknesses and what is missing, even if people want this feedback; otherwise you risk diluting this part of the exercise.

- What gift have you received from another in this room? Tell the person in specific terms.
- What is the gift you continue to hold in exile?
- What gift do you hold that no one knows about?
- What are you grateful for that goes unspoken?

Also see Art Kleiner, "The Thought Leader Interview: Meg Wheatley," *strategy+business*, Winter 2011, http://www.strategy-business.com/article/11406?gko=15f1d; and the Alia Institute of Nova Scotia, where Wheatley and Frieze have taught the concepts in Walk Out Walk On, along with leaders of several of the communities they write about: www.aliainstitute.org.

WALK OUT WALK ON

A Learning Journey Into Communities Daring to Live the Future Now,
by Margaret Wheatley and Deborah Frieze (Berrett-Koehler, 2011)

Walk Out Walk On, by two former co-presidents of the Berkana Institute, describes seven innovative community-building initiatives: a self-organizing university in a highland Mexican village, where students build small-scale technologies such as bicycle-powered water pumps as a means of local empowerment; a Brazilian institute that sets up "thirty-day games" in which players come together to improve conditions in debilitated neighborhoods; a Zimbabwean village dedicated to self-sustaining agriculture in the midst of politically created famine; a remarkable network of people transforming healthcare, education, and social service institutions in Columbus, Ohio; and similarly groundbreaking initiatives in South Africa, India, and Greece. The organizers of all these endeavors walked out of restrictive or confining ways of thinking, and Wheatley and Frieze show that anyone can do the same—which might mean changing jobs in some cases, but always means shifting perspective within one's current situation. —Art Kleiner

4. Sharing a Vision, Nationwide

The Thinking Schools, Learning Nation Initiative of Singapore

Tan Soon Yong

Many people feel it is overwhelmingly audacious to propose a shared vision for a community. In that light, consider this shared vision story: 23,000 educators taking part in a process to shape the evolution of the national education system. Much of this process was influenced by the five learning disciplines, in part through the participation of Daniel Kim and Diane Cory, noted learning organization researchers and practitioners who brought this story to our attention.

Singapore is a small nation, known for its unusual history (a former British colony turned independent in 1965, then managed into modernity by the forward-looking but non-democratic government of former prime minister Lee Kuan Yew), its wealth as a financial and trading center, and its attention to education—with high emphasis on exams and rote learning. Before the "Thinking Schools, Learning Nation" (TSLN) initiative described here, its young graduates were seen as highly skilled in science and math but less creative and capable of critical thinking than they needed to be. When the first edition of this book appeared in 2000, TSLN had just started; by 2005, some signs of change were apparent. School children were running parts of schools; junior college students were tackling major systems problems (like planning for the demographic effect of the country's declining birth rate); young entrepreneurs were making and selling their own products (including a health-quality chocolate) or running their own businesses.

This article, written at the beginning of the initiative, doesn't just apply to Singapore. It shows that large-scale efforts toward schools that learn can exist. Consider the questions raised by this article. What if a similar initiative started, say, in Illinois, Texas, Italy, India, or Brazil? How far would it get? Would it be just a publicity exercise? Could it ripple out, as it has here, to nationwide and schoolwide dialogues? If the quality of implementation is important, then would an initiative like this have a deeper long-term effect on public schools than a mere decree, policy, voucher plan, or standardized test?

These results were listed in Seah Chiang Nee's "Singapore's Changing Schools: Stepping Up Gear to Produce a Thinking Workforce," *Sunday Star*, September 25, 2005; reposted on the Little Speck blog, http://www.littlespeck.com/content/education/CTrendsEdu-050926.htm. Also see educator Bill Jackson's series on "The Creativity Initiative in Singapore," in *The Daily Riff Blog*, www.thedailyriff.com/articles/thinking-schools-learning-nation-singapores-education-initiative-409.php.

Any national education system is only as good as its schools. Since 1997, the schools of Singapore have been following the course of a shared vision to which they contributed. This vision, encapsulated in the phrase "Thinking Schools, Learning Nation" (TSLN), envisages *every* school in Singapore to be a "thinking school": a crucible of critical, creative thinking and active, self-directed learning, where staff and students continually challenge assumptions, ask good questions, learn from past mistakes (their own and others'), and survey best practices globally and adapt them locally. In our view, "thinking schools" form the foundation of a "learning nation"—a people dedicated to lifelong learning and thriving in a knowledge society and economy.

TSLN emerged from a strategic review of education, motivated by a preoccupation with the future. The challenge, as we saw it, was not just to be forward-looking and prepare our children to be in step with the future, but to prepare them so that they could be continually prepared for the future. We started by bringing together a committee of educators and policymakers (called the TSLN Committee) and using a scenario planning method to identify driving forces, emerging trends, and critical uncertainties around Singapore that might influence the needs for education. For example, it became clear that the nature of knowledge in the future would be faster changing; knowledge would be larger in breadth, more available worldwide through electronic communication and more dependent on "global" languages, particularly English. Later, this led us to cut curriculum content across the board by 10 to 30 percent to free up time for imparting higher-order thinking skills.

⟩⟩ For more about scenario planning, see page 360.

The next step concerned the delineation of end objectives. A group of about 300 teachers and officials gathered for a residential program to discuss emerging social and global trends and the desired educational outcomes for the Singapore of the future. Through the discussions, a general consensus surfaced. In a curious paradox, the secret to preparing our young for an unpredictable, rapidly changing future lay in a return to education fundamentals: the holistic development of our young in the moral, cognitive, physical, social, and aesthetic spheres.

The discussions and brainstorming sessions yielded many ideas, and these were boiled down to a manageable series of eight desired outcomes, both in the milestone stages of education (the primary, secondary, and pre-university years) and at the end of formal education. This list was then forwarded to all teachers and principals in all schools for comments. The role of the ministry's leaders in this exercise was to let go of their traditional attitudes about leadership and to acknowledge that good ideas would come from anyone and anywhere. Our job was to encapsulate a vision that expressed the aspirations of the people we had heard from in a form suitable for dissemination. At first, it was difficult to articulate this, but over time, it came together—not so much as jigsaw puzzle pieces fitting together but as faint images coalescing into crisper pictures with clear details.

Singapore Prime Minister Goh Chok Tong first introduced the idea of Thinking Schools, Learning Nation at the Seventh International Conference on Thinking in 1997. Since then, TSLN has been continually refined and reshaped by the stakeholders in our education system. Any vision, if it is to have any chance of actualization tomorrow, must be a vision of the people who are involved.

WAVES OF IMPLEMENTATION

The TSLN Committee then turned its attention to positioning schools—and the entire education system—to achieve these desired outcomes. The immediate challenge was to identify problems on the ground. In the first wave of discussion, a practitioners' review group was commissioned to gather extensive feedback from people in schools. Some 300 teachers and officials were organized into more than thirty project teams to identify the policies and practices that hindered the realization of our desired outcomes. The teams were given a free hand to raise issues and even propose solutions.

The reports of the project teams made it clear that Singapore was at the threshold of a major paradigm shift in education. The solution to many problems lay in consciously moving education from being efficiency-driven to being ability-driven and from being school-centered to being student-centered. But what would that mean? The concept, at first raw and incomplete, was put through much debate.

We started our second wave with a strategic imperative that we called "ability-driven education." This had two components. First, we would meet the learning needs of individuals. The scope and scale of talent differs from one student to another, but everyone should excel according to his or her combination of talents and abilities. To excel would not mean rising to the top of a competitive ranking; it would mean being the best that one can be. Second, we would inculcate in our young people the national values and social instincts that would foster commitment to the nation and lead them to actively contribute their talents for the good of the society.

In the third wave, we translated these broad policy recommendations into specific programs and practices at the executive level of the

Ministry of Education and integrated them into the processes and plans of various divisions. We put together a coordinated work plan for the ministry and published it as a document available to all schools, so they could do the same. We set in place monitoring processes and feedback channels to ensure that new ideas and initiatives could be easily communicated from the ministry to schools, or in the other direction. We understood that the main feature of this wave was internal communications. Schools will embrace only what they believe in. The TSLN was feasible because, having developed as a shared vision, it was entirely consistent with teachers' sense of professional calling to develop young people. It was critical that teachers understand the rationale and intent of what we were doing in the entire education system. We are still in the midst of the third wave, but preliminary feedback has been encouraging. There has been strong agreement at the school leader level, and we believe teachers on the ground will respond positively to the TSLN vision as well. The challenge is to maintain our effective two-way communication between schools and the ministry. In the meantime, people at the ministry's headquarters (and some people in schools) are looking ahead to the challenges we will face when we have an entire system of Thinking Schools in a Learning Nation.

XV. Connections

1. Parent to Parent

The Community Engagement Process at St. Martin Parish

Roland Chevalier

Here is a method for tackling community problems that has worked numerous times in practice. School leaders can use it to help develop an entire community's ability to learn. Parents survey each other, but this is not your typical community survey—it brings people together to learn together. Every neighborhood is distinct and unique; its people need to be involved in designing the way they help themselves. We asked Roland Chevalier, then the superintendent of St. Martin Parish school district in Louisiana's bayou country (about a hundred miles west of New Orleans), to reflect on his experience with the community engagement process. St. Martin Parish (Louisiana's counties are called parishes) is a rural district (9,000 students total), with more than 70 percent of the families below the poverty line. This technique helped the parish solve a pernicious problem with early childhood reading, but it also gave the people of the parish a sense of identity they never had before, with a raft of significant effects. Chevalier, as you'll see, was in the thick of it, learning to lead the process without controlling it.

Roland Chevalier is now a senior associate with the Schlecty Center www.schlechtycenter.org.

Around 1993, we identified a serious problem in our district: In some elementary schools, 30 percent of the students were being held back each year. That atrocious record was the good news. The bad news was: Many parents, teachers, and principals thought we were doing the right thing, especially for our slow learners in reading, by giving them an "extra shot" of second- or third-grade medicine. They didn't know that when children are retained in the early grades even once, their chances of graduating from high school are cut in half. Retain them twice, and you might as well write them off right there; almost none of those students

The "steps" in the margin of this article are adapted from material written by Susan Philliber and Sharon Lovick Edwards, the two consultants mentioned by Roland Chevalier, based on this and similar projects. We put their steps side-by-side with the story so you can see the way in which a generic method translates into the specific demands of the community. For more information about the community engagement process, see Philliber Research Associates' website, www.philliberresearch.com.

Step 1: Preliminary meetings are held to define precisely what is meant by "community" and to design a strategy for interviewing individuals most easily.

graduate, either in our district or anywhere. Different children develop in different ways, and measuring them all at a one-year milestone is an unfair way to assess them. Some children do a small amount of reading development in second grade, a normal amount in third grade, and then they catch up in fourth. By holding back the late developers at the end of second grade, you send the message: "We don't think you can do it," and you disconnect them from their age group.

Conversely, you can spark a great deal of forward movement by giving them the right kinds of incentives. In our junior high, for example, we told some of the formerly "left-back" kids that we would move them up to their original grade if they could do two years' worth of work in one. They attended a special intensive program, and many have regained a lost grade level. These children will graduate. But that solution would not be effective unless we could address the reading problem where it started, with the youngest children of the parish. And we could not do that in isolation from the parents of these children.

PHASE 1: DEFINING THE COMMUNITY AND ASSEMBLING THE CORE GROUP

Over the years, my philosophy has been: if you focus on getting things done, you can do a great deal with very little money. That's one reason why we were willing to try everything and anything. When the Danforth Foundation looked for districts to try the community engagement process, it knew we would volunteer. We always did. It gave us a small amount of money, the services of two consultants, and a method. We had asked parents questions in the past, but on a superficial level—sending a note home with their kids. Very few had responded, almost none with any candor. We didn't know how they really felt about the schools, their children, or reading. We needed to find out.

The first step was to find volunteers from the community in the areas that most needed help. We listed all the kids who had been retained, from grades K through eight, found their home addresses, and stuck pins in a map accordingly. Wherever the pins clustered, we looked for key volunteers—people who would join our core group and make a long-term commitment to us. Fortunately, I grew up here and knew some parts of the parish very well.

We started with a core committee of six volunteers, all key stakeholders who had credibility and knew the community's needs. It was vital to make sure that not all of them were from the school district administration. Some, like the local director of Head Start and a private daycare center owner, had been traditionally seen as our rivals. (In fact, the Head Start director knew much of the parish I didn't know; his involvement was key to starting off on the right track.) Two key central office administrators (the director of curriculum and the supervisor of early childhood) were indispensable to the overall process. They were responsible for the work actually getting done. We later added the personnel director of Fruit of the Loom, our biggest employer in the district; someone from social services in child protection; some principals of primary schools; and someone from the sheriff's office. This group became our advisory council, and they organized the process.

We needed the community to bare their souls and talk about their needs—which meant talking about their shortcomings and weaknesses. That's why it was so critical for community people, not school officials or outside consultants, to create our survey. We brought together about forty people from every segment of the population, all invited by word of mouth, for several all-day sessions to create a questionnaire. We included business leaders, elected officials, and people in the sheriff's department.

We brought them together in a room for several hours and asked, "What do you want to know from the community?" The consultants facilitated the meeting and then took the questions and refined them. They brought the final draft back to us so the group of forty could approve it.

The result was several pages of questions about the things people cared about in their community and schools. What kinds of support did they need for their children? What did they think about homework? What did they want for their children's futures? What were they afraid might happen to their kids? What were they afraid their kids would do? We didn't restrict the content to education; we included a page of their questions about safety in their neighborhoods, on the streets, as well as in the entire community. Several of the questions were written by the sheriff's department. This ultimately led to a lot of innovations in community policing, including the placement of "school resource deputies" in our three high schools. Even before we got any answers, the questions themselves were eye-openers for me and other community leaders; we would not have thought to ask many of them.

PHASE 2: COMMUNITY MAPPING

The "question design" group then suggested another fifty or so people as "foot soldiers"—to be trained in the interview process and go door to door, like the Census Bureau did in the old days. They would interview their neighbors or conduct coffee get-togethers in their houses. We avoided using teachers or students for this. If a teacher holds the key to your child's future, you will say what you think he or she wants to hear. You're more apt to tell a neighbor how you really feel. Some of our parent-to-parent interviewers had never graduated from high school. Many

Step 2: A discussion is held with a committee of community residents to determine the nature and content of the survey instrument and how best to recruit interviewers.

Step 3: The researcher/evaluator drafts the survey instrument from committee responses.

Step 4: The community group reviews the questionnaire and makes recommendations for the final version.

Step 5: The community group recruits interviewers and introduces them to the objectives and purposes of the community engagement process.

Step 6: The researcher/evaluator trains the interviewers and supervises the survey work.

of them weren't very confident at first, until we trained them: "This is how you introduce yourself," and so on. The sheriff, who was getting more and more involved, provided food for the training session.

We also inserted a survey in the payroll checks at the local Fruit of the Loom plant, which had 2,000 employees, and we got a tremendous response from that. Since many of those people lived outside the parish, we had comments from them asking when we would conduct a survey in their school districts.

Step 7: At the completion of the surveying, a focus group is held with the interviewing team to discuss what they heard.

Finally, we conducted a companion survey, with questions on the same themes, for the teachers and administrators. Doing this brought us into dangerous territory. It turned out that teachers and parents disagreed on several key issues. Parents, for example, had much higher expectations for their children than their teachers did. Many teachers believed that parents didn't care much about schools or didn't want to get involved. But 98 to 99 percent of the parents wanted to be involved. They felt shut out.

One question asked: "Do you believe all children can learn?" Most of the parents said yes. Sixty-two teachers said no. That was eye-opening for me; I wouldn't want my own child in the class of a teacher who doesn't believe all kids can learn. That raised some issues in terms of staff development needs for our faculty. The most chilling part was that parents correctly understood the teachers' attitudes; they knew that many teachers did not expect their children to graduate. In all of our planning sessions, we had never considered this.

PHASE 3: ENGAGING THE COMMUNITY

Step 8: The researcher/evaluator prepares a computer database from the questionnaires and develops a report for the community drawing from the questionnaires and the interviewers' perceptions.

Sharon Edwards and Susan Philliber, the consultants, analyzed the data and wrote up a report. We were supposed to hold a focus group for the "foot soldiers," and we made it part of a celebration. We gave them copies of the report, because it was their report. We had awards for the youngest interviewer, the oldest interviewer (Mrs. Patin, a lady in her seventies), and the person with the most interviews. And we talked about what we had found and what we might do about it.

Step 9: The researcher/evaluator reconvenes the group to review the data and report.

For example, one complaint was a lack of quality child care at 5 a.m. for people who work factory shifts. People on late shifts had no one to help their kids with homework. Hearing about this, people volunteered solutions. One foot soldier started a homework club in one of the subsidized low-income housing projects. All the kids ended up in a common room in the building after school, with older kids helping younger kids, and parents, on a rotating basis, supervising. The school had nothing to do with organizing it; the childcare professionals had never imagined it. All of that came out of the residents' sense of efficacy: They could do something significant and make a difference.

The interaction with the community expanded our focus and direction. It made us take a hard look at what the community expected of us; our task was much more complex than we had realized. We addressed the area of reading by researching programs that work, and we zeroed in on Success For All—the Johns Hopkins reading program—in part because that's what the parents wanted. We expanded our health services for children; there are now three school-based health clinics, serving sixteen of our seventeen schools. We reconsidered our family center concept. The previous year, to address the issue of teenage pregnancy, we had planned a facility where teenage parents could finish their education, have access to daycare, learn parenting and nursing skills, and eventually pay back the costs by working at the center themselves. We had a $65,000 grant and an abandoned building that we could renovate, and we were ready to go—except that our local private daycare centers saw this as an attempt to take customers away from them. That had influenced the school board to veto the project. Consequently, communication with private daycare providers was increased, and a partnership was developed with the Head Start program, building on the new relationship we had cultivated with the Head Start director on the questionnaire planning team. At the urging of parents, the center opened in the spring of 2000 with grant funding from Head Start.

Other benefits of community engagement went far beyond our original intent. A group of people from the low-income housing development, trained in our method, were contracted to conduct surveys for other towns and corporations in the area. They also started a tutoring program, using a vacant apartment in their own buildings. We had offered tutoring at school, and nobody came. This project was so successful that they eventually came to us asking for teachers who could help but continued to direct and manage it themselves.

In response to the survey needs, we began running courses for parents of kids convicted in juvenile court. The judges, one of whom was part of our survey team, began requiring the parents to attend these meetings. Many parents continue meeting even after their time is up, because it gives them a support group. The judges also decided to assign all the juvenile cases to one judge so that he could provide some continuity and follow up on the kids over time. He happened to have grown up in St. Martin Parish and had been one of my student workers when I was principal here. He came from one of the toughest neighborhoods that we had targeted, and he was now a positive role model that kids could look up to.

Step 10: The community team plans the dissemination process and the strategies for engaging all stakeholders in dialogue.

Other groups of people, having met or rekindled relationships through this project, continued to meet on their own. We started holding interdenominational lunch meetings, once a year at Thanksgiving, for all the church ministers in the district. They had never communicated with one another, and now we had Catholic priests and Baptist preachers breaking bread in the same room. There was no agenda the first year—just a chance to meet and talk. The second year we began looking for common problems that we could work on together, such as helping children manage their anger or discouraging foul language.

Then I took a risk. I invited the ministers to come in for lunch once a month at the school. Two of them had their own parochial schools; none of them had any close contact with public school. This visit changed their perception of what we were trying to do. Some of them had heard false reports—for instance, that we gave out birth control pills and condoms at the health clinic. Now we had the kind of relationship where we could invite them to visit and see what we actually were doing. We went from being competitors to allies, and we began collaborating on some projects, including some of our staff development.

MAKING IT WORK IN YOUR COMMUNITY

Doing all this was very difficult for me at first, because I had to listen and not speak. That is a tough skill for a superintendent to acquire. I had to learn to be open to suggestions and prepared for criticism, because the community might not necessarily think that my answer would be the right answer. And I had to realize that I could not be the one to do everything. As with the daycare center, which has been successfully managed by Head Start, sometimes I had to learn to support projects that other people were running.

I also learned, all over again, the value of close relationships with other members of the community. The sheriff and I have a strong personal relationship. This past year, he received a grant to build a juvenile detention facility, and on that site he built a gymnasium and classrooms. We now combine our efforts, and run our alternative program for expelled students from that facility. He provided the building and two full-time deputies; we provide the teachers and desks. Similarly, he used the data from the survey process to generate hundreds of thousands in grant money for community policing—and to organize his police deployment more effectively. We have also set up a program where some of the prison inmates, those with carpentry and building skills, work for us on building maintenance when school is out of session. That represents an in-kind contribution of about $250,000 a year. And we pay for the salary of the deputy who supervises them.

This doesn't cost him or us anything extra. But the community benefits. Each institution has half of what the community needs. He jokes that the other sheriffs are complaining to him: "Now their superintendents are asking for the same things."

We have similar relationships with other community and business leaders. The meetings run well, I think, in part because we came together over this community inquiry. One committee member is Fay Tucker, the Fruit of the Loom personnel director. At one of our community engagement meetings five years ago, she said, "You know, I like these meetings. This is the first group I've worked with that actually gets things done."

2. The Over-the-Rhine Residency Program

Thomas A. Dutton

Thomas A. Dutton, an architect and professor of architecture and interior design at Miami University in Oxford, Ohio, has been involved in a social justice movement in Cincinnati's Over-the-Rhine neighborhood (the contested neighborhood described in Bonnie Neumeier's essay "Expression is the First Step Out of Oppression," page 473) for more than thirty years. He is the founder and director of the Miami University Center for Community Engagement in Over-the-Rhine and (as of 2009) holds the endowed position of Cincinnati Professor of Community Engagement.

In June 2009, as a result of the innovations described here, Thomas Dutton was awarded the National Thomas Ehrlich Civically Engaged Faculty Award by Campus Compact for "outstanding contributions to service-learning, engaged scholarship, and institutional and community change through collaborative engagement." Also in 2009, the Center was awarded the inaugural "Partner in Building the Beloved Community" award by Over-the-Rhine Community Housing, a nonprofit housing development corporation dedicated to housing for low- and moderate-income citizens. Dutton is married to *Schools That Learn* coauthor Janis Dutton.

As comfortable as I personally feel in Cincinnati, Ohio's inner-city neighborhood of Over-the-Rhine—Cincinnati's oldest and poorest neighborhood, predominately of color and listed on the National Register of Historic Places because of its Italianate architecture—it is difficult to shake the media perceptions on the nightly news or in the morning newspaper. "Another shooting on 18th Street" may be the headline that arrives with my morning coffee. I know the media get it mostly wrong, but it still takes a toll.

And any uneasiness on my part is no match for the reaction the neighborhood provokes on people who visit it with me from out of town: for example, the parents of the college students who sign up for the program

I founded. The parents try to act nonchalant when they help their son or daughter move into the residency program in this urban locale, but their faces show that they are struggling with vetoing that decision. I have to admit, I have also been worried at times. There were nights I awoke abruptly at 4 a.m. for no reason. The program was a big experiment, and I wasn't always certain how it would turn out.

My involvement with Over-the-Rhine dates back to 1981, when I began taking architecture students there and assigning them hypothetical urban design studio projects back on campus. From the beginning, I was involved in movements to alleviate the barriers and stigma of poverty, and over time I carefully built a network of relationships and trust with individuals and community groups.

An audio interview with Dutton about this work is available as an American Institute of Architects "Citizen Architect on the Move" podcast at http://www.aia.org/advocacy/local/AIAB051119.

In 1996, three university students asked to take on a more hands-on studio, where they would design and physically rehab a unit for low-income residents. Another student asked to work with me on a design-build project, based in the neighborhood, for his graduate thesis. So we were off and running, more or less, working on a series of projects to design and rehabilitate livable spaces. Miami University is fifty minutes away from Over-the-Rhine in the next county. We would load students into cars at 1 p.m., drive to the neighborhood, work until five, and drive back, three times a week.

In the late 1990s, my students pushed me again. They had taken the time to talk to children and other residents. "We are learning a lot about design, materials, and construction," they said, "but we want to know more about the neighborhood." Like any urban area, Over-the-Rhine embodied a dynamic range of issues such as poverty, racial unrest, disinvestment in housing and jobs, and struggling schools. An interdisciplinary approach would be needed. With support from university colleagues and neighborhood organizers, we created what came to be called the Miami University Center for Community Engagement in Over-the-Rhine (MUCCE), a storefront center on a major street running through the neighborhood. We opened our doors in February 2002.

Starting this was not a simple task. At the university, we had to conduct multiple dialogues with faculty across academic disciplines, write multiple drafts of the mission and goals of the Center, seek approval of the university administration and the board of trustees, and submit grant proposals for start-up funding. That was the easy part. I knew that people in the community would resist the university helicoptering in a center and treating the neighborhood as a laboratory and the people as subjects to study. They were sick of being studied by academics from the colleges and universities in the area, and they were tired of taking time out of their busy days to advance other people's work and getting nothing in return. I knew they deserved the courtesy and respect to be included in developing the shared vision of the center, and that ultimately we would not move in until they invited us. I also knew that the invitation would include the adage attributed to Australian Aboriginal activists and often heard in the community: "If you have come to help me, you are wasting your time. But if you have come because your liberation is bound up with mine, then let us work together."

Our vision involves creating genuine opportunities for collaboration among university students, faculty, and neighborhood groups for interdisciplinary and cross-cultural learning that would intersect with the goals of the social movement that already existed there. Unlike many joint university-community initiatives that partner with establishment institutions such as city hall and the chamber of commerce, our MUCCE engages with the Over-the-Rhine People's Movement and other groups struggling for human and racial rights and social justice. Our mission places human and ecological needs as priorities in community development, and challenges the profit motive as the dominant arbiter in urban social policy. This distinguishes us from programs that are based on charity and noblesse oblige—unlike those models, we challenge students' self-awareness and sense of why charity may be needed in the first place.

We also challenge those student/faculty motivations that too often result in university programs that "do it to" or "do it for" community members, rather than working with them. We resist the word "help," as it too often comes from the mental models that "to help is to fix," that the people in Over-the-Rhine need saving, and that "experts" have all the answers.

}} See "We Dance Together," page 195, and "Public Engagement," page 527.

According to Bonnie Neumeier (page 473), the neighborhood has benefited from our collaboration: "The Center has proven to be a wonderful space for learning. It is a space for dynamic dialogue where people of varying backgrounds, racial and class mix, and with different perspectives can meet and discover our common ground. This prominent place on Vine Street has its doors open to the community. We have dialogued with people we would never have met if it wasn't for [the Center] sharing its connections and resources with us to bring prominent guests to the neighborhood. Our world expanded."

All of this was present from the beginning, but it wasn't enough. The architecture students were still commuting only three afternoons a week for the design-build projects. Some of our larger projects, such as a two-story, four-bedroom apartment, took years to complete. We were thankful for the patience and trust of Over-the-Rhine Community Housing,

For another account of advocating for people that others don't (or won't) see or hear, see *Horton Hears a Who*, by Dr. Seuss, (Random House, 1954).

The author of this chapter and Bonnie Neumeier were listed as role models in the book: Peter Block, *Community: The Structure of Belonging* (Berrett-Koehler, 2008) and the Center listed as a community resource.

the nonprofit housing agency that owned the units, but they deserved more. The students also wanted more. I had always wanted to create a full-semester immersion program, a school of social life, in which the students would live in the neighborhood. They would combine a minimum of fifteen hours a week working with neighborhood organizations that serve the underserved with a course of interdisciplinary study that presented them with the academic tools needed to analyze and understand the current reality of the neighborhood they lived in every day.

Again, this was not just a matter of getting university approval. For that, we had to engage in dialogue with Miami University's faculty and administrators to create a curriculum of new and existing courses that would meet the parameters of the program and graduation requirements, determine the departmental capacity to cover the classes, find the necessary funding mechanism to make it work, and get final approval from upper-level administrators. We also had to go back to the community and ask for more of their time and commitment. We worked together to set up and supervise service and internship opportunities in their organizations, to involve community members in the program's administrative and teaching team to have them be responsible for the students' orientation and weekly reflective journal writing, and to set up the project so that the students would be thoroughly involved in community-based campaigns.

LIVING AND LEARNING IN OVER-THE-RHINE

The Residency Program began in fall 2006, and the first cohort consisted of twelve students. They were mostly white, from upper middle class suburbs and small towns. Six were majors in architecture and interior design. Others came from psychology, philosophy, teacher education, and interdisciplinary studies. Students enrolled in four courses: Service Learning, the History of the American City, Family Poverty, and a Community Engagement Practicum. Subsequent cohorts have included students from business, anthropology, art education, speech pathology, family studies and social work, and geography and urban planning.

This program has allowed us to deepen four ongoing initiatives that benefit both the university and the community:

■ Design/Build: In collaboration with Over-the-Rhine Community Housing—a nonprofit, affordable housing development corporation—students in the Design/Build Studio have been working with staff and end users for more than fifteen years to rehabilitate livable spaces for low- and moderate-income residents. With architecture students now spending twenty-five hours per week on the projects, our completion rate increased dramatically. Completed projects include two single-family homes; a laundromat/meeting space; five apartments ranging from one to three bedrooms; a social worker's office and conference room, and the Center's own location. One project that I'm especially proud of is Venice on Vine, a pizzeria and food catering business run by Dominican Nuns who train "hard-to-employ" persons.

- Agit-Props: In this initiative, students and faculty join community artists and leaders, at their request and guidance, to build installations that "agitate" and "propagate" points of view regarding the neighborhood's history and political awareness. Since 1999 we have completed twelve installations, seven in exterior settings. Placing art-making within a strategy of social change articulated by the People's Movement, Agit-Prop projects create opportunities for community residents to share stories about their lives and history with the broader public. For example, students from Miami and Northern Kentucky University conducted oral histories and collaborated with community leaders to produce the Over-the-Rhine People's Movement Timeline, documenting nearly forty years of history.

- Community Assistance: Students in majors other than architecture spend their community engagement practicum working in neighborhood organizations. They might work in a homeless shelter, with women's entrepreneurial efforts, early childhood programs, tenant advocacy groups, medical clinics, or other organizations that serve the underserved. Teacher education majors work full-time in neighborhood schools. All students attend meetings of various community groups, perform community service on the weekends, and host weekly dinners with community guests.

- Community Advocacy: Students spend an additional fifteen hours a week assisting the community organizing that is already in motion. They might design posters and paint banners for neighborhood events, help plan marches, organize community meetings, or conduct petition campaigns. One semester, community members, students, and children painted a football field, baseball diamond, and four-square courts at a temporary school site so that the pupils had a place to play while their historic school building was being renovated.

For more information on the design-build projects see: http://arts.muohio.edu/otr/.

Venice on Vine was awarded a Cincinnati Chapter of the American Institute of Architects Merit Award in 2006. The project was a collaborative effort among eight architects, multiple contractors, and also included students from the architecture program of the University of Cincinnati.

For more on the Agit-Prop projects see: http://arts.muohio.edu/cce/engagement.html.

GUIDING PRINCIPLES

We have learned much about student, faculty, and community learning through the Over-the-Rhine Residency Program. This has enabled us to hone the guiding principles that are integral to our work:

■ **Critical Community Pedagogy.** The Over-the-Rhine Residency Program organizes learning that explores the intersection of community life and critical pedagogy to reveal the social construction of society. We examine the dominant ideologies, interests, and institutions in the neighborhood that are instrumental in reproducing current reality.

■ **Power and Knowledge.** Social knowledge is always produced according to particular voices, for particular ends, and situated within relations of power. We identify the ways privilege and internalized oppression are learning disabilities that create barriers to achieving a vision of just and equitable communities.

■ **The School of Social Life.** Creating community requires that people engage meaningfully with otherness to learn to recognize their own partiality and question their deeply held assumptions about themselves and others.

■ **Creative Inquiry.** Inspired by the Peaslee Neighborhood Center motto that "Expression is the first step out of oppression" (page 473), we maintain that when tied to an analysis of oppression, expression becomes a more creative and liberating practice.

■ **Political Exposure.** As we study the systemic structures that reinforce oppressor-oppressed relationships—especially how class and race struggles take specific form in Over-the-Rhine and Cincinnati—we seek ways to act upon those structures and relationships with the community.

〉〉 See "Knowledge and Power," page 250.

Janis Dutton's master's thesis, "Learning to Unlearn: Organizational Learning, Popular Education, and Intersecting Stories of Community, Leadership, and Democracy," (2006) and her ongoing participatory action research have taught me the power of the concept "privilege is a learning disability."
—Thomas Dutton

TRANSFORMATION AND KNOWLEDGE

From the beginning, I was certain that the students would gain a deeper understanding of the issues facing Over-the-Rhine and cities across the country through the residency program. However, I did not foresee the strong bonds they would forge with community members and how deeply the experience would transform them. One student told me she had to pull over to the side of the road on her trip home at the end of the first semester because she couldn't stop crying—from grief at leaving the neighborhood and the relationships she had forged.

Their assignment at the end of the semester is to write a reflection of their experiences in light of the course readings. Each year I am overwhelmed with powerful, personal testimonies about how they wrestled with their privilege, their fears, and their anger at the recognition that little is done by city officials, corporations, and state and federal governments to address the conditions prevalent in Over-the-Rhine. Many of them came to see life differently. Poverty became real. Voting became relevant. They were amazed at how the daily lives of ordinary people affected them. They learned from those who are homeless and their neighbors. They opened their hearts and minds and developed compassion and empathy. They saw community and realized both its strong bonds and its responsibilities. And they saw through the stereotypes of their middle-class biases.

〉〉 See "Intelligent Behaviors," page 240.

As they struggle to make sense of their new relationships and knowledge, they begin to recognize a dissonance between the mental models they have held and their current experiences. They come to realize that the dissonance requires disassembling their middle class consciousness and constructing a new one that allows them to experience life in new ways. Make no mistake: going through a change like this is very hard work, and the change can be profound. As one student wrote:

"Before setting foot in Over-the-Rhine, poverty didn't exist. Secluded by the picket fences, cul-de-sacs, half-acre lawns, and strip malls, my perception was that everyone had the resources and money necessary to live in America. I also believed in the idea of economic opportunity for everyone. However, Over-the-Rhine hit me like a bat hitting an apple. Everything that made sense crumbled. The experience has transitioned me from a passive, accepting, and narrow-minded idiot into a questioning, revolting, and active participant in this corrupt [society]."

Another student who struggled with certainty in the first weeks wrote: "Coming to Over-the-Rhine I was confident in the permanency of my beliefs, beliefs that had never been thoroughly challenged. Thankfully I was not unwilling to be altered, I just didn't think that it would happen…Every single day provided me with something to ponder…I am the different person I never thought I needed to be. Now the real challenge will be returning to Oxford."

Many students find it difficult to make the transition back to life on campus. They repeatedly tell me that they had never lived in neighborhoods as friendly as Over-the-Rhine, or experienced such a strong sense of community. They see that poor people and their advocates are not a problem, as the media and politicians claim, but an asset. One student, who had struggled with missing her close friends and the campus when she was in Over-the-Rhine, discovered that when she returned to campus she missed the neighborhood even more. She chose to remain in the neighborhood and commute to campus to finish her degree. She wrote: "[The residency program] overwhelmed my mind and senses and I can't

See the residency program website for links to student reflections, videos, interviews, and media coverage: http://arts.muohio.edu/cce/residency_program.html.

get away from it. I think about issues like gentrification, city life, urban education, business development, racial tension, class conflict, police presence, and community activism all of the time…The best part about it is that I want to be thinking about these issues all of the time. Unlike so many classes at Miami, I don't shut off the material when I leave the class. I can't shut it off here, and I don't want to."

Community members also recognize and talk about the value of the relationships and the shared understandings they build with students. Acting as mentors and teachers, community residents are able to share their histories. In the process, they often undergo personal transformation and deepen their understanding of their own experiences. Mike Rogers, a former staff member of Over-the-Rhine Community Housing who worked with students for three years renovating a vacant storefront for a nonprofit coffee shop, said: "Those kids have changed my life dramatically. They have no idea. They allow me to mentor them."

Community activist Bonnie Neumeier is the program's community liaison and takes on the roles of neighborhood guide, advisor, team teacher, and also shepherds the students through their weekly journal reflections. "As our future architects, city planners, social workers, advocates, journalists, teachers, entrepreneurs, and politicians," says Bonnie, "[the students] can bring much deeper wisdom into our world so that equality for all is not just a dream, but can be a reality." At the end of the semester she tells the students, "You are now part of this place. When you leave you will leave something of yourself here, as I know you will take something of us with you."

3. The "Systems Basketball Coach"

Nancy W. Lippe

Program Officer for the Los Altos Community Foundation, mother of four, longstanding girls basketball coach, and former member of the U.S. Olympic Field Hockey team (1980), Nancy Lippe describes how community members involved with children can use systems thinking to improve their involvement—not just in sports, but in any kind of coaching or mentoring.

Every year I receive the roster in the mail: ten fifth- and sixth-grade girls on my basketball team. I know a few of them really well; others by name only; most not at all. We will practice twice before an eight-week playing season and then once a week—so we'll have ten practices in all. In that time, my charge is to teach the game of basketball, to coach games, and to finish the season with each girl—I hope—understanding and liking the game and feeling good about herself.

Because this team is not a select team, the players bring to the game a host of motivations—and sometimes a desire to play competitively is not among them. So the more of a holistic systems view I take, the more "successful" we will be. I have learned that I will better achieve my goals if I focus on three things:

1. **Treating our team as a system** by stepping back and remaining aware of all the factors that affect us. The team's performance is more than just the sum of efforts by ten individual girls whose parents signed them up to play ball. The team is a network of interrelationships— among the players and also with the game of basketball, which is itself a system.

     I have coached several girls in more than one sport, which helps me understand team dynamics. Although any player's essence re-mains stable, her skills will manifest differently on different teams. Each player exists simultaneously in many environments: school, family, and extracurricular activities, such as basketball. For example, my team is a subset to the developing women's sports culture world-wide, to the YMCA sports programs in our community, to the milieu of developing social ethics, and to other "suprasets" that I may not even be aware of. An event in any one of these associated systems will affect other parts of our team. Every season, I draw a map of my team as a system. As I become more aware of the variables in my system (such as the needs of the individual players), I can better an-ticipate problems, make structural changes, and successfully achieve my goals.

2. **Developing our shared vision and mission.** At the beginning of the season, I give the girls blank puzzle pieces on which they write their goals for the season, something they do well, and something they don't do well. The girls put together the pieces, and I frame the puz-zle. We talk about our vision for the season and agree on team goals. These goals typically include: having fun, learning and playing bas-ketball, and becoming better individual and team players. At the end of the season, we all enjoy looking at the puzzle and noting how each

of the players has changed—and surprised themselves. Some who wrote "dribbling and running at the same time" as something they couldn't do laugh as they now see themselves as fast-break experts. I always offer to return the pieces to the girls, but they always say, "You can't take it apart—that's our team!"

3. **Developing a responsive, open system** that thrives on feedback (reinforcing and balancing processes, discussed on page 134ff.) My best players have quick physiological feedback systems—their bodies and minds work well together and respond quickly. When the team performance begins to move away from our goals, and we play too poorly (or unexpectedly well), then "negative feedback" returns us to our expected performance. This feedback often takes the form of physiological signals—players losing their balance, missing shots, and so on—or the form of criticism from other teammates.

We regularly revisit our goals according to the way the team handles feedback. Maybe a previously noncompetitive team has developed confidence and wants me to coach it to play more competitively, or maybe it needs a less intensive form of coaching. This focus on team objectives and goals keeps the team together instead of fragmenting into smaller units of unhappy players. When conflicts among players arise, revisiting our goals reminds us of the purpose and context of the team as a whole.

Sometimes I map the flow of energy and relationships to illustrate for myself how different aspects of the system of our team interact and affect one another. Let's say I have a player who seems lazy at first glance. She sets herself up to fail, afraid to put herself on the line and try her best. She also spends a lot of time in the bathroom working on her hair. Her attitude and performance affect the whole team, because they respond to her in a negative way, which creates frustration on the court and breaks the team's flow. And that, of course, sets up a vicious reinforcing spiral. As other team members get mad at her, she retreats and makes excuses for her playing. This generates more negative response from her teammates, which makes her continue to grow more self-conscious and afraid of taking risks. Soon she is not only getting negative feedback from her teammates, but from her body, her mind, and even me. I have to stop myself to break that cycle of feedback.

There is, in fact, a generic reinforcing loop at play. It happens to be running viciously for this player, but it can also be a virtuous cycle—I call it the "self-esteem loop" (shown in the diagram as "R1"). Individual attitudes can lead to higher performance, which generates better team performance, which leads to better responses from others, which affects the individual's attitude.

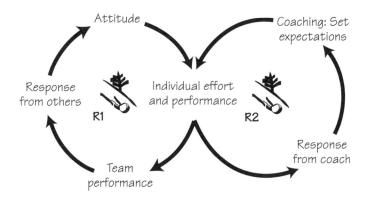

This feedback loop was adapted from Virginia Anderson and Lauren Johnson, *Systems Thinking Basics: From Concepts to Causal Loops* (Pegasus, 1997).

Where, then, can I intervene to change this spiral from vicious to virtuous? I can't change her attitude directly; nor can I expect the other team members to pretend that they aren't frustrated with her. Nor can I affect the team's performance "around her." My point of highest leverage is to add a second reinforcing loop (R2), to focus directly on her individual performance through one-on-one coaching. We identify goals and expectations; that influences her performance; I respond to the performance with encouragement and constructive help; she responds in turn.

I take research sociologist Ida Hoos's criticism of systems diagrams and maps to heart—they are like a piece of artwork that I create to suit my needs. They may not accurately portray my team or my difficult player. But these maps make me step back and look for factors affecting my team that I might not otherwise think of. Systems maps are but a beginning to systems thinking. No matter how complex the map I construct, no matter how many causal loops I draw, I will always be reducing a complex situation to something manageable. As a coach, I can only do my best to see as much as I can and to teach my players that they are not alone but part of an exciting, dynamic, interrelated world.

4. Improving Business-Education Partnerships

First, Do No Harm

Andrea Gabor

Andrea Gabor, the Bloomberg Professor of Business Journalism at Baruch College at the City University of New York, is also a biographer of W. Edwards Deming (a leading figure in quality management and organizational learning) and the author of several books, including The Capitalist Philosophers: The Geniuses of Modern Business—Their Lives, Times, and Ideas *(Three Rivers Press, 2002). She is also a contributing editor at* strategy+business, *where she has regularly covered the nexus between business and education. Here she looks at the best and worst ways for business to get involved in educational change.*

In the midst of a great unemployment crisis, there is also a yawning talent gap: From the factory to the oil field to white-collar jobs in the global marketplace, companies are searching for applicants with the scientific knowledge, communications skills, and technological acumen that many high school graduates (and even some college graduates) lack. That's why business leaders are pushing for school reform with such urgency; they see public schools as both suppliers of talent and incubators of the future.

Most of these reformers, whether in the public, private, or philanthropic sectors, share a core set of ideas derived from conventional business practice. These include school choice (setting in place a competitive market for schools, including new charter operations), management training for school administrators, incentive pay for teachers, and the intensive use of digital technology.

The basic concept underlying these reforms is that schools need to be run more "like businesses"—adopting the highly competitive management style that seeks to identify high performers, root out waste in all its forms, measure performance, impose numerical goals, blame teachers' unions for poor performance, and force each individual to prove his or her value every day. In other words, they seek to impose on schools the same top-down, carrot-and-stick, compliance-driven management ideas that have proven unreliable and, in many cases, counterproductive even in business. The quality movement leader W. Edwards Deming referred to their approach as the "prevailing system of management" in the West and correctly regarded it as the source of most business and economic ills. It does not help anyone to transfer this type of command-and-control-driven management approach to schools.

Moreover, virtually all the studies on key reform initiatives, including the charter movement and merit pay for teachers, suggest that these measures have been disappointing and have failed to improve educational outcomes. For example, a 2009 study by Stanford's Center for Research on Education Outcomes found that only 17 percent of charter schools had better test scores than traditional schools, while 37 percent were significantly worse. A major 2010 study by Vanderbilt University found that teachers who were offered a $15,000 bonus for improving student test scores over a three-year period performed no differently than teachers who weren't included in the offer.

"[The effort] to improve the quality of education turned into an accounting strategy: Measure, then punish or reward," writes Diane Ravitch in *Death and Life of the American School System.* "The strategy produced fear and obedience among educators; it often generated higher test scores. But it had nothing to do with education."

⟩⟩ See the review of *Death and Life of the Great American School System*, page 329.

As for educational technology, there is still virtually no research on what works and what doesn't in PK–12 education. While no one doubts that technology is likely to play an important role in education in the coming years, assessments of how and why to apply new electronic tools have been distorted by the potential size of the educational technology industry—which could be as much as $500 billion. Many companies interested in educational reform—from Apple, Microsoft, Cisco Systems, and NewsCorp to many smaller media and software companies—also have interests in this business, which makes it difficult to tell which assessments are disinterested and reliable.

All of this is unfortunate, because business leaders have a great deal to offer education—if they could offer the most collaborative, generative aspects of business thinking and action instead of management by fear, control, and measurement. These companies (including Whole Foods, HCL, and Container Corp.) argue that profit maximization is not their central goal. They have learned from experience that by doing well for their employees, their community and their customers, the profits will follow. Many educators recognize and appreciate this. "If you are trying to run a system as large as a small city, you need a diverse set of skills," says Shael Polakow-Suransky, Senior Deputy Chancellor for the New

York City Department of Education, noting that the city's education system when it was controlled almost entirely by educators was "incredibly poorly run." When the district began to draw talent from the business sector in the 1990s, he adds, there were some false starts where MBAs clashed with educators. "But we learned that we need both."

How, then, should businesspeople who are genuinely interested in school reform take on this challenge? They could start by bringing to bear on the challenges facing schools the kinds of collaborative, systems- and improvement-oriented management ideas that have helped to transform some businesses. A more participative system is ideal for financially strapped schools that can't afford hierarchy; moreover, digital technology has made the work rules that govern many school systems obsolete. A stakeholder-oriented culture—in which decisions are made on behalf of all the organization's constituents, not just to boost shareholder return (for business) or standardized test results (for schools)—also suits many individual educators, who are motivated by a range of factors besides money, including job security and the desire to make a contribution. Most importantly, a stakeholder focus that also includes parents and community members promotes the sort of collaborative, improvement-oriented culture necessary for education reform.

On the ground, this often means providing new training for teachers and principals, fostering innovative education opportunities in which both students and parents can participate, and creating bridges between schools and the outside world, including potential employers.

The following stories demonstrate some of the attitudes and actions that can lead to better business-education partnerships. As always in this arena, these collaborations were not without problems. But what distinguishes them from many failed efforts is that business leaders and school leaders have come together in genuine collaboration. Businesses did more than donate funds and technology; rather, schools and businesses learned from each other.

EMBEDDING LEADERSHIP TRAINING

See Andrea Gabor, "Leadership Principles for Public School Principals," *strategy+business*, Summer 2005 www.strategy-business.com/article/05207.

In 2003 in New York City, business-executive-turned-mayor Michael Bloomberg and executive-and-lawyer-turned-schools chancellor Joel Klein created the New York City Principals Leadership Academy. Modeled on GE's John F. Welch Leadership Center at Crotonville, N.Y., it was intended to fill a shortage of qualified principal candidates in a system with more than 1,200 schools. The Academy was originally set up as a public-private partnership with a $69 million budget for its first three years of operation, much of it coming from foundations and corporate donations.

In the early years, The Academy struggled to strike the right balance between private-sector management sensibilities (for example, a great deal of emphasis was put on recruiting principal candidates who had work experience *outside* education) and the very different culture of schools.

But following the departure in 2005 of founding CEO Robert E. Knowling Jr. (who had previously been a corporate change consultant and CEO of Covad, a telecommunications company), leadership of the academy was taken over by Sandra J. Stein, who had previously served as its academic dean. Today, the Academy operates under contract with the New York City Department of Education (NYCDOE), which funds nearly all its activities—and it seems to have found a sustainable balance between business and education cultures, in part through an emphasis on learning disciplines such as systems thinking.

The structure of the Leadership Academy curriculum has been much the same since 2003. It is focused on a six-week summer intensive built around a school management simulation, in which aspiring principals are asked to do everything from oversee a school budget to come up with a professional development plan for teachers. The simulation also forces them to confront some of the unexpected curveballs that real principals field every day, such as sudden budget cuts and crises involving problem kids and angry parents. Then there are follow-up sessions throughout the school year in which principals can talk about issues that they are experiencing in their schools.

Under Stein, the tone and culture of the Academy shifted, and some traditional business ideas were replaced by a more explicitly systems-oriented approach. Jack Welch, the former GE CEO, no longer lectured there, as he did in the early years, and most of the instructors were now education experts. Stein introduced the use of the "iceberg" (page 126); and *Schools that Learn* became a core text.

One of the major business concepts that was reinforced and expanded under Stein was a focus on the value of data as one of five core leadership competencies. Aspiring principals are expected to capture qualitative and quantitative information about students and learning from multiple sources and to think through their implications for improving student achievement. George Foley—the former math teacher and principal who leads the team that teaches analysis and the use of educational data at the academy—is quick to point out that "one piece of data" is never sufficient. He concentrates on helping principals go beyond a punitive approach (judging students and schools based on test scores) to using data to recognize patterns, including potential problems, high points, and opportunities for improvement.

Sandra Stein resigned in 2011 for personal reasons. The current head of the Leadership Academy is Irma Zardoya, former superintendent of New York's District One in the Bronx.

In January 2012, the Leadership Academy launched a strategic plan that includes new accountability metrics and bonus-based incentives, de-emphasizing the collaborative learning that had made the Academy effective. If this plan takes hold, it would be an example of the way pressures for accountability can divert or co-opt learning-oriented business-education partnerships if the partners are not careful.

Some critical lessons from the Academy's experience:

■ Make sure educators oversee the training so it remains relevant;

■ Use guidance from businesspeople where it is most relevant; for example, in learning to use data to identify problems and opportunities for improvement;

■ Use peer training, participative team efforts, and other means of sharing insights;

■ Focus on follow-through, with projects that involve teachers, business volunteers, and students together.

In one recent example, Foley pulled together the English test scores from one school to show how the high performance of a single teacher, an outlier among a group of eight fourth-grade English teachers, had lifted the school's overall grade. By looking more closely at the practices of that one outlier—her work materials, lesson planning, conference notes, and feedback to students—her colleagues could learn to improve their own teaching. Data is a "powerful tool, a motivator," says Foley. "People raise their game after they see it." Mining data in this way also makes it possible to change the tenor of the conversation between principals and teachers, by focusing on problem-solving rather than on blaming teachers individually or as a group.

》》 Also see "Peer Partners," page 421, and "No More Drive-By Staff Development," page 396.

FOSTERING TECHNOLOGICAL EXPERIMENTS

Many education reformers have begun to focus on the potential for educational technology to open the classroom to outside expertise and opportunities for innovation. So far, much of the education technology and software on the market has been geared to consumer and home-schooling markets; it is not well-suited to the needs of inner-city kids or for use within the public school classroom. Now a series of experiments that have taken place in New York, Louisiana, and other locales—fostered in part by partnerships between school districts and technology firms, such as the large computer networking company Cisco Systems—are attempting to use technology to enrich education in public schools.

The New York project known as the iZone (for "innovation zone"), demonstrates both the promise and the pitfalls of this type of partnership. Funded by local business leaders as well as Cisco, it was formed in 2009 with the idea of helping schools not just put new computer technology in place, but to become seedbeds of freewheeling, learning-oriented activity, with students, teachers, and school administrators all encouraged to tap real-world expertise and integrate it with the school's curriculum.

"Equipping Every Learner for the 21st Century," by Tae Yoo (Cisco Senior Vice President for Corporate Affairs), et al. (Cisco Systems, 2008), http://newsroom.cisco.com/dlls/2008/ekits/Equipping_Every_Learner_for_21st_Century_White_Paper.pdf.

In its planning stages, the project drew inspiration from a 2008 Cisco white paper, "Equipping Every Learner for the 21st Century." The white paper argued that a changing and global workforce puts a premium on diverse skills and knowledge, including cross-cultural insight, multilingualism, problem-solving, decisionmaking, and creative and critical thinking. Company and district leaders explicitly spoke of each other as "thought partners," with a mutual respect grounded in recognition of each other's expertise.

"Cisco is not an education technology company, it's a networking IT company," explains Mary Anne Petrillo, Cisco's Global Campaign Manager. "We bring our core competencies to help [school districts] think through their processes…and to build their capacity to manage technology."

During the iZone's first year, Cisco provided professional training in digital technology, along with funding. Teachers came to Cisco offices near Penn Station in Manhattan for several all-day training sessions on a variety of classroom technologies—including teleconferences with outside experts, PowerPoints, and video. Cisco also sought to learn from the schools, sending teams of engineers into their classrooms to see how teachers and students used digital technology.

To be sure, there was a commercial motive; Cisco was developing a full-scale technology portal for commercial sale to other school systems, with a number of features designed to give students, parents, and educators better access to coursework and collaborative learning opportunities. As part of its arrangement with the NYCDOE, Cisco planned to give the iZone schools free access to the portal beginning in the fall of 2010.

However, in August 2010, Cisco's role was abruptly reduced, and the technology was replaced by a much more limited portal of off-the-shelf software. The reasons for the shift were never entirely explained; the NYCDOE said that Cisco had fallen behind schedule. But iZone principals and teachers, who were counting on working with Cisco, were disappointed. For its part, the company still officially supports the iZone project in New York. Growing pains like these illustrate the complex political, organizational, and commercial issues that can make a business-education partnership difficult, especially when it is brought to scale in a large school system. And it highlights how ongoing dialogue is needed, especially among leaders of initiatives that span the business and education sectors.

Recently, the iZone has undergone its third reorganization in as many years. It is now a two-tiered experiment with more than a hundred schools taking part in a limited way via access to education software offerings on the NYCDOE portal. About twenty-five schools participate in a more involved initiative called iZone360, which is phasing in a program where each student will eventually receive one laptop for use in school, providing so-called "innovation coaches" to advise schools on technology and other reform ideas, as well as offering other supports

Another visible Cisco partnership, called the 21st Century Schools Initiative, was established with eight school districts in Louisiana and Mississippi in 2005, in the wake of Hurricane Katrina. Here, too, donations of equipment and the testing of new technologies were balanced with opportunities for entrepreneurship and new types of training. One school system that has participated fully is Jefferson Parish, Louisiana. This is a large suburban school system with eighty-eight schools, located just outside New Orleans, with a mix of incomes and ethnic backgrounds among its students, many of whom live in the Mississippi delta lowlands. After the storm and flooding destroyed many of the district's school buildings, Cisco was one of the first companies to offer help.

As in New York, Cisco donated equipment, including white boards and laptops (Jefferson Parish has a one-laptop-per-student policy), as well as professional-development training. The company was also instrumental in the district's decision to hire a Chief Technology Officer. A 2009 study by the Center for Children and Technology found that Cisco's partnership with the local school district, in which the majority of students are poor, black, and Latino, helped to "launch a dramatic educational transformation." (In neighboring New Orleans, by contrast, much of the school system has been taken over by charter organizations.)

Cisco insists that it maintains a "Chinese wall" between its business and philanthropic interests. However, the company has clearly benefited from the partnership. It has sold routers, switching systems, video conferencing technology, and much more to the school district. Cisco argues that its partnership with Jefferson Parish represents a virtuous cycle in which the company's corporate responsibility programs help local districts develop priorities, strategies, and expertise even as they give the company new insight into how technology is used on the ground and enabling them to develop more useful products.

COLLABORATING FOR INNOVATIVE CHANGE

One of the earliest schools to join the iZone was the Global Technology Preparatory, one of the city's new middle schools in Harlem. As it happened, the school's first principal, Chrystina Russell, was also an alumnus of the Leadership Academy. A former special-education teacher, Russell took to heart the concept of systems thinking; she also has sought to leverage the school's resources by collaborating with outsiders, including philanthropies and businesses.

Teamwork was an explicit aim, even before the school formally opened, when Russell began recruiting teachers. During the summer of 2009, she corralled prospective faculty members for regular Sunday brunches at the home of her friend and colleague Jacqueline Pryce-Harvey, a veteran special-education teacher who would become Global Tech's assistant-principal-in-training. Pryce-Harvey, a Jamaican immigrant who holds a Ph.D. in geography, is also a master cook who had once worked as a personal chef for New York socialite Brooke Astor. Over gourmet meals,

L*essons from experience so far:*

■ Set up partnerships so that while corporations may profit from the R&D, all aspects of the project are transparent to outsiders;

■ Foster experimentation; it is not always clear in advance which ideas and projects will work best;

■ For every new technology, establish in-depth training with businesspeople and educators learning together and learning from each other.

the teachers brainstormed Global Tech's curriculum, ways to recruit kids, criteria for new hires, and a strategy for introducing technology into the classroom. The brunches underscored the collaboration and flexibility that Russell would expect from her staff—and that she insists is crucial to a successful school—as well as an implicit understanding that their teaching responsibilities do not end when school officially lets out at 3:30.

Russell developed a collaborative culture that relies on partnerships inside and outside the school—but she insists on keeping the focus on what she and her staff have identified as core values, rather than following donor agendas. For example, every student received a laptop to work with at school, courtesy of the iZone and corporate donations. But Russell and her staff were clear that technology was not to become an end in itself; thus, in most cases, software is used to reinforce—not replace—traditional instruction. And unlike some other schools, Global Tech did not hire outside technology experts for training. Instead, Russell chose to rely on a few tech-savvy teachers from within the school to help coach the staff and students, reinforcing the school's collaborative culture. She also sent her teachers to the training sessions offered by Cisco in the 2009/10 school year.

In addition, Russell enlisted Computers for Youth, a program that provides free desktop computers, loaded with educational software, and training for poor families; the program is designed to teach parents how to help their children with schoolwork. And she teamed up with Citizen Schools, a not-for-profit after-school learning program that extended Global Tech's school day to 6 p.m. Students get homework help and academic enrichment and participate in hands-on apprenticeship programs that are run by local professionals and businesses, including engineers from Google who taught programming. Significantly, Russell arranged for the school's own teachers to mentor the Citizen School volunteers, most of whom are still in graduate school, ensuring that kids get the help they need. All of these companies and organizations formed a collaborative network that was stronger than any of them would have been separately.

Another way that Russell has tried to leverage teamwork and systems thinking is in mainstreaming "special education" kids. Thirty-one percent of Global Tech students are certified as needing special education. Russell has moved almost all of them into so-called ICT (Integrated Co-Teaching) classes that are team taught and include a range of other students. There is a clear expectation that by the time these students graduate eighth grade, most will be able to function in a regular class.

The role collaboration has played in this effort was highlighted in 2011 when Josniel Martinez, a Global Tech seventh grader, was selected to introduce U.S. Education Secretary Arne Duncan at the White House launch of Digital Promise, a national center founded to spur development of breakthrough educational technologies. Standing at the podium in front of more than a hundred dignitaries, the eleven-year-old Dominican émigré explained how he had started out failing sixth grade until the school put together "a whole team to help" him. The team, he explained, included teachers who helped him with his "nightmarish" organization skills and checked his backpack every day for the pencils, assignment sheets, and other items he needed to succeed in class; Computers for Youth, which provided extra software for the home computer they had given him; and his mother, who insisted he work on the educational software three times a week and cut back on TV. "In ten years, I'm going to college," he concluded. "And maybe one day Secretary Duncan will be working for me."

Global Tech's collaborative approach has produced impressive results in a short time. Many students start school fifteen minutes early to take advantage of free computer time. The school got an "A" on its 2011 progress report and was ranked in the top 95 percent of all middle schools in New York City. To be sure, there are challenges: The school made less progress with English language arts (ELA) than math and has struggled to reach students with severe personal or family problems. But virtually everyone involved with the school seems to love its approach; on a 2011 Learning Environment Survey, Global Tech scored well over 90 percent in parent, teacher, and student satisfaction. Global Tech is also one of only two schools—out of the original cohort of ten iZone schools—that remains in the program today.

Another telling indicator is the number of people who have succeeded at Global Tech after being written off in other schools. This includes some teachers. For example, math teacher David Baez has been identified as a possible future administrator. He was recruited from a dysfunctional school in the Bronx where, as a young teacher, he was rated unsatisfactory by a supervisor. But a colleague (at the time, Pryce-Harvey was working as a special-education teacher at the same school) happened to teach a class with him, saw his potential, mentored him, and eventually brought him to Global Tech. Today, visitors flock to Baez's math classes, which combine old-fashioned instruction and online math games and visuals. Baez also has won Global Tech thousands of dollars in grants. This type of collaborative, entrepreneurial culture is usually associated with business startups, not with schools (or, for that matter, with many corporations). To keep it going will depend on how well the school continues to foster a culture of collaboration both inside the school and with partners in the outside world.

Implications of Global Tech's experience:

■ Set up informal gatherings, including school leaders, teachers, and business collaborators, to plan innovative efforts;

■ Focus attention on the problems that school leaders identify as important;

■ Use collaborative teams that bring together multiple outside organizations, including businesses and nonprofits;

■ Foster a participative staff and student culture that echoes the best of the business culture you see around you.

THE PETROLEUM ACADEMY

In Houston, Texas, another public-private partnership is emerging between the school systems and the energy industry. It was deliberately set up to bridge a growing shortage of energy workers. The average age of industry employees is fifty, and every year there are fewer young applicants graduating local schools with the science and math skills required for entry-level jobs. In 2005, the Independent Producers Association of America (IPAA) sought to address this problem by establishing the Petroleum Academy: a program within selected public schools designed to give young people the requisite math and science education to fill entry-level jobs in the oil patch.

The IPAA has opened petroleum academies in four public schools so far in the Houston area. These include Milby High School, which has a student body that is largely poor and Latino, and the Young Women's College Preparatory Academy, an all-girls school. The academies offer industry-tailored advanced placement-level courses, as well as special programs. Teachers receive training to help tailor courses across the curriculum to the academy's energy focus. For example, in addition to teaching standard literature courses, Milby offers lessons in "technical English," which are designed to help students focus on reading and comprehending nonfiction texts. A typical assignment might include writing a persuasive essay on the value of renewable versus nonrenewable energy. Similarly, an algebra course focuses on data analysis in the petroleum industry.

The IPAA's education advisory committee includes many local companies from the oil and gas industry; the companies provide funding, internships, as well as speakers to the schools. For example, Milby, the IPAA's first petroleum academy, received $115,000 worth of laptops from Shell. And Halliburton has donated $27 million of geoscience and engineering software to enable Milby to teach elective courses in those fields.

Milby graduated its first Petroleum Academy class last year. Of eighty students in the starting cohort, sixty-two are going to four-year colleges, almost all on scholarships. Most of those who didn't make it to a four-year college are going to community college. By contrast, among the equivalent Milby students who did not attend the petroleum academy, only 37 percent enrolled in a four-year college, and 46 percent entered a community college.

Experience from the Petroleum Academy suggests:

■ Integrate business reform efforts into the established curriculum and design recruiting efforts accordingly;

■ Come up to scale slowly, starting with just a few schools and learning from the experience of the early group.

GAINING BETTER EXPERIENCE

Business-education partnerships are likely to proliferate as schools and school districts struggle to improve PK–12 education. The more successful examples, from New York to Texas and elsewhere, are ones in which innovation becomes, almost literally, everyone's job. Just as schools can learn from business, so business leaders interested in education reform would do well to learn from the schools they want to help. The challenges they face, as well as the remedies that work best, might surprise them.

Media Literacy for Educators and Parents

Art Kleiner, Tim Lucas, Bryan Smith, Janis Dutton

Purpose:

To develop a deeper awareness of the messages, influence, and values of media, among educators, parents, students, and community members.

One of the great ironies of education in our time is the fact that the two great influencers of children—teachers and TV producers—rarely, if ever, communicate with each other. They don't speak the same language or appreciate each other's priorities. The following questions prompt you to look with an open mind at various forms of media—TV, films, newspapers and magazines, music, advertising, mobile devices, online games, social media, and anything on the Internet—and the implicit theories about the world held by producers and consumers.

VISION

1. What image of education do we aspire to see portrayed in the media? What do we aspire to see in print, text, and Internet publications? What do we aspire to see in television and film? What do we aspire to see in blogs and videos—either those by adults or by children?

2. What aspects of the world do we aspire to see reflected in the media that the children we teach pay attention to—news media, fiction, films, television shows?

3. What types of themes and conversations do we aspire to see reflected in the media that children produce—their conversations, videos, photographs, blogs, tweets, and art?

4. What kinds of protections do we aspire to see for children—from intruders, cyber-bullies, commercial interests, strangers, or anyone. What protection should be provided for children by parents? What protection by the school or community? And what protection should they learn to provide for themselves and each other?

CURRENT REALITY

1. What images of reality (in sound, text, video, interactive media, or film, including advertisements and uploaded videos) do the children in a classroom or school talk about most?

2. Where do these images come from? Who has made them? Why have they been created? (To make money? To make a name for oneself? To persuade others? To express an idea or an image? Or for other reasons?)

3. What do the people who make these images seem to think about schools? About children? About life?

4. Why do kids like them? Why are they popular? What do kids and/or adults get from them?

5. How accurate or reliable are these images? How well (or poorly) do they express what actually happens in life?

6. What observable details (as shown at the bottom of the ladder of inference, page 101) lead you to your conclusions in this exercise?

COMPARATIVE VIEWS

Having answered these questions yourself, compare the answers with those of someone else—such as your own child or the children in your class.

How are your answers the same? How are they different?

CONVERSATIONS WITH MEDIA

Using social media like Facebook, Twitter, and Linked-In, and public online forums (including some sponsored by your community's local media), it is easier to hold fruitful conversations with journalists and writers than ever before, especially since many local writers come to prominence now through the Internet. If you develop interesting answers to the questions in the first two sections of this exercise, for example, email a summary of them to the creators of the media that you consider. They may or may not reply. But you may find that broadcast and website producers, in particular, are keen to get in-depth critiques of their programs. They may be aware of their audience through statistics and surveys, but they may have lost their visceral sense of their audiences. And they may be grateful to you for reminding them—especially if you can show them that you appreciate what they are looking for: a way to connect, concisely and fruitfully, with the people they are trying to reach.

XVI. Sustainability

1. The Rainmakers

Katharine Briar-Lawson

Katharine Briar-Lawson is the dean of the School of Social Welfare at the University at Albany, State University of New York. She has built a nationwide practice of fostering educational renewal, working with her colleague Hal Lawson. In contrast to the prevailing mental model of a school as a standalone organization in which educators are expected to do it all alone, Briar-Lawson's model emphasizes interdependence. Families and community agencies are key resources for school improvement; and schools become key resources for families, social and health service professionals, and community leaders. Families and children, in effect, become key partners in and joint leaders of this comprehensive process.

The "Rainmakers" is probably the best-known project that Katharine has been involved with. While the South Florida program described here is no longer in operation, it has become a national model for other similar projects. Katharine, a leader in organizing the project from the beginning, tells its story from her own perspective.

In 1990 I began to work, through the Danforth Foundation, in South Florida in an elementary school in Miami Beach, considered one of the most challenged schools in Dade County. The neighborhood was also challenged. More than 90 percent of the children were on free or reduced-cost school lunches. Their parents were mainly undocumented workers. They were immigrants facing impediments that kept them from being integrated into the rest of the community. Residents spoke forty-six different languages. They were crowded into abandoned apartments, ignored by their landlords and the rest of the city; indeed, some political and real estate interests that wanted to gentrify Miami Beach continually threatened to displace them. But there was nowhere else for them to go. All of this took its toll. Children were often absent from school; there were regular "police sweeps" where police pushed the children off the street back into school. And a tragic child abuse death drew media attention to the area as a vulnerable community.

We had about $60,000 to work with. These funds allowed us to start a project called Healthy Learners, with a social worker helping parents help their children do better in school. We moved slowly at first, unsure how we could best help. Then there was a head lice crisis, so severe it threatened to close down the school. We started in a conventional way— by attempting to get a legal waiver, all the way from the White House, so that teachers could distribute Medicaid-funded lice shampoo that was ordinarily available only by prescription. With the help of a community consortium, we arranged for free shampoo bottles from the pharmaceutical companies. But the crisis continued.

Finally the family advocate in our program, a social worker with empowering skills, knocked on the doors of some of the parents with the most lice episodes. She asked if they would serve as consultants to us. She told them that they were the experts and that we could not solve this problem without them.

A small group of parents arranged to meet. They called themselves the Lice Busters. The problem, they said, was not waivers or shampoo, but housing. Some homes were one-room apartments in abandoned buildings with no running water, with eighteen mattresses on the floor. To solve the crisis, they needed vacuum cleaners. They needed coins for laundry, scissors to cut children's hair with, and—by the way—a place for the children to do homework.

As I had seen in other initiatives around the country, the parents— who were seen as "challenged" with "problems" by some of the teachers and other professional service providers—turned out to be the real experts. They alone knew how to solve the problem. They also understood the barriers that kept their children from learning. And their expert knowledge had not been tapped. The family advocate worked with them on the fundamental problems—coins for the laundry, and fumigating services—rather than just shampoo. You could tell which children had contact with the Rainmakers, because of their haircuts.

They weren't called the Rainmakers yet, and the most fundamental needs of all—the economic pressures that kept these families in this kind of housing—were not addressed. But it was obvious that these parents were not a "problem." They were a treasure and a resource for

For more in-depth stories of the impact of poverty on education and the dilemmas it raises, we suggest Jonathan Kozol, *Savage Inequalities* (Harper Collins, 1991), and Jonathan Kozol, *Rachel and Her Children: Homeless Families in America* (Crown, 2006).

the school and the community: a potentially extremely powerful and capable group. They simply lacked supports, such as an advocate, training, stipends, and occupational ladders. The family advocate put on a forty-hour training for these parents, mostly mothers, so that they could become paraprofessional social service aides, health aides, tutor aides, teacher aides, and resource supports to one another. They called themselves "Rain Mothers," after an acronym for Referral and Information Network. They had come to the United States from Central and South America, and they liked the image of rain as a cleansing, purifying, spiriting reality.

Almost immediately, the Rain Mothers opened a homework club to provide a place for the children to do homework after school. Then, as now, there is a perception in many schools that poor children aren't motivated to learn. But apartments crowded with people, with no running water, offer no place to learn. The day the homework room opened, we expected perhaps twenty kids to show up. We were flooded with many more children than any teacher or the principal had expected.

The Danforth Foundation provided a small stipend, about $40 per week, for the mothers who worked at the school and in their own school-based family resource center called the RAIN Room. But the benefits went far beyond that. Every day the students saw their parents having hope. Parents were not just playing important roles but learning how to manage their own family support and social service program.

Next, the Rain Mothers worked on the problem of absenteeism. When a child missed a day of school, two or three Rain Mothers brought the day's homework to the child's house. This wasn't called a truancy intervention. Rather, it was a neighbor's visit. Rain Mothers would say to the child that they had been missed and wondered what could be done to help them get back to school. They would emphasize to the parent that it was really important that the child go to school, because without school, children would have trouble ever getting ahead. This strategy was so effective that the school suddenly developed the lowest absenteeism statistics of any of the schools in its part of the school feeder system. Around this time, the mothers acquired the name "Rainmakers" from a journalist writing feature stories about them.

The Rainmakers tackled social services next. In the beginning we had assumed we knew the kinds of services the parents and community needed...but we had not asked them. We had brought Medicaid and other social service agencies to the school's family resource center, but they were underused. It turned out that the parents wanted Legal Aid and support groups to deal with gender and violence issues. Thereafter, they chose the services. One major need was real estate support for help finding homes and Legal Aid for people who had been evicted.

JUDGING THE RAINMAKERS' SUCCESS

With the Rainmakers jointly leading the work of improvement, our attention turned to evaluation. In this public school with very few resources, test scores had improved dramatically. Absenteeism problems had declined. These figures were made public. But what was the cause? As often happens in poor neighborhoods when residents gain power and jointly determine what will happen, some observers questioned the results. For example, some suggested that there must have been cheating given the rise in test scores. A few observers assumed that somehow there was "a better breed of parents here now." Some teachers and administrators attributed the increase to the Comer philosophy and design (the School Development Program) that the school had recently adopted. Others pointed to other professional interventions made possible by service providers linked to the school.

It was especially hard for some to attribute success to the work of the parents. But the observable, undeniable data were there, and these data made the impact of the Rainmakers clear. For example, a few months after the "homework visits" started, the rate of absenteeism dropped so low that everyone assumed the problem was solved. Then the Rain Mothers turned their attention elsewhere. When their visits tapered off, the absenteeism rates quickly rose again.

We also had the benefit of a comparison school. One mile away, a corporation had underwritten a highly public change initiative in another public elementary school. It was a beautiful school with a great deal of student and teacher enthusiasm, and far more money than our $60,000. This new school served the same kinds of children. But the achievement measures in the Rainmakers' school were at least as good, if not better.

Some teachers recognized the differences that the Rainmakers had made. "When you look at a kid in the classroom who's problematic," one teacher told me, "all you see is the problem. But when there's a staff meeting with a Rainmaker advocate, then we can see the pressures that the kid is having. And we now see the child in a different way." For example, a child who had been up all night because her mother was a victim of domestic violence might not have to act out the pain in the classroom if the teacher and her Rainmaker advocate were sensitive to this child's needs.

A NATION OF RAINMAKERS

In 1993, on the one-hundredth day of the Clinton administration, then Vice President Al Gore visited this school to honor and recognize the achievements of the Rainmakers. That same year, the Rainmakers initiated the steps to incorporate as a nonprofit organization, so they could get their own grants and contracts. Already, they had in mind a childcare center, their own microenterprise. They also had the vision of establishing some practices and guidelines that others could learn from—just as they had learned from the examples of other self-determining groups, like the Grace Hill Settlement House in East St. Louis, Missouri.

For example, they developed a Bill of Rights addressing the maltreatment of poor children and parents. They felt that some organizations on Miami Beach mistreated them. Their Bill of Rights asserted that a family had a right to a second opinion, for instance, or to aid from a culturally competent provider. Agencies and service providers aligned their practices with this Bill of Rights and adopted missions that fostered family-friendly helping stations.

The school-community consortium—consisting of service providers, the mayor, the media, teachers, administrators, and the Rainmakers—continued to solve problems throughout the Miami Beach area. And the Rainmakers were known as a force in the school and the community. After welfare reform, they established internships; people on welfare could start working through Rainmakers and feel they had some control over the transition. They helped people deal with hurricanes, evictions, and the general stresses of poverty, along with family-friendly school issues.

Rainmaker projects have been replicated in different parts of the country for almost two decades, so now we can see the impact over time on local families. We've seen tough, violent kids, who had already been in jail, return to school wholeheartedly and do community service. We've also seen, once again, that when the Rainmaker attention stops—when they no longer have the help and guidance of people from their own community—they may return to their older, less constructive ways of life, because the pressures that put them there no longer have a counterbalance.

The basic Rainmaker technique—training people to care for their own community, creating occupational and educational ladders for them, and getting out of the way—has had success with some of the most pernicious challenges in poor American neighborhoods. I've worked with professional service providers to deal with the problem of substance-exposed newborns by offering substantial resources to support parents' help-seeking and abstinence. Few parents signed up. But in the same neighborhood, we trained parents who were in recovery from crack cocaine as paraprofessionals. They would knock on apartment doors at 2 a.m. and say: "Open the door. You and I have shared the same crack dealer. We've shared the same needles. I'm HIV positive, and I've lost

An in-depth manual exists, including exercises and resources, for developing your own Rainmaker-style practice. See Katharine Briar-Lawson, Hal Lawson, Bobbie J. Rooney, Vicki Hansen, Lisa G. White, M. Elise Radina, and Karen L. Herzog, *From Parent Involvement to Parent Empowerment and Family Support: A Resource Guide for School* Community Leaders (Danforth Foundation and Institute for Educational Renewal at Miami University, 1997). Also see K. Briar-Lawson, H. Lawson, C. Collier, and A. Joseph, "School-linked Comprehensive Services: Promising Beginnings, Selected Lessons Learned, and Future Challenges," *Social Work in Education*, vol. 19, (1997), pp. 136–148.

my children to adoption. There's still hope for you." And we were flood-ed with referrals.

Graduates of the Rainmaker training carved out careers for themselves. Their success was based, paradoxically, on the opposite of what profession-als would prescribe. Most challenges facing communities and schools today are multisystemic and tied to poverty. The solutions must be similarly mul-tisystemic: economically and occupationally enfranchising, guided by the indigenous leadership of the neighborhoods, and based on residents' ex-pertise. When you treat individuals and families as dependent clients, view them as hopeless, or condemn them as failures, you block their ability to help themselves. When you see their capability and honor their expertise, creating economic and occupational supports for them, you gain a power-ful resource that enables powerful learning and important improvements.

Questions for Designing a Rainmaker-Style Initiative Katharine Briar-Lawson

1. What is the dominant mental model—of the needs of children and the reasons for their academic and behavioral issues in the class-room—held by parents and families in your school district?
2. Do these mental models impede student learning and success in the classroom?
3. What mental models must educators change to mobilize parents and family support?
4. What systems structures must be put in place for teachers to access rapid services and responses for the high-need youth in their classrooms?
5. What new norms are needed to build and enforce high-quality re-sponses for the most challenging children, youth, and families?

Purpose:

To lay the groundwork for a community-based effort by educators, parents, and citizens.

ROCA, INC.

Truth, Trust & Transformation, www.rocainc.org

Roca is a nationally recognized community organization focused on helping disengaged and disenfranchised young people move out of poverty and violence. Started in Chelsea, Massachusetts, it is based on strategies developed over more than twenty-five years for how to reach those "that nobody else will work with"—and a context that differs radically from the conventional industrial-age school. Roca has almost a hundred "youth workers," many of whom are themselves former gang members, who engage young people on the streets. Their programs embrace a variety of life and academic skills and include sophisticated early-employment programs for young people with little employability capacity. Many of the teenagers and young adults who work with Roca would otherwise be in jails or dead by the time they are twenty; yet they end up in community and four-year colleges, take jobs, and become economically independent. As importantly, they become powerful contributors to a healthier community, as the Chelsea police and social service departments can attest.

Underlying Roca's approach is an evolving theory of engagement and change for high-risk youth. "When they are reengaged through positive and intensive relationships," says the group's website, "they can gain competencies in life skills, education, and employment that move them toward living out of harm's way and toward economic independence." To accomplish this, the organization is dedicated to three main principles:

- Truth—"We are truthful about everything that is going on with young people, the challenges in their lives, and that change is hard but possible."
- Trust—"We are committed to building trust through relationships and staying in them over long periods of time."
- Transformation—"We provide opportunities for participation in life skills, education, and employment. Most importantly, we are hopeful no matter what."

Finally: "How we do our work is about loving people, believing they are equals and that they can succeed."

It makes a major difference that Roca is grounded in systems thinking and organizational learning principles and that its staff, led by executive director Molly Baldwin, continues to refine and test their approach. As of 2010, they were working with about 900 young people, aged fourteen to twenty-four, per year. Their website is a valuable source of insight, data, and evidence about their theory and methods and confirmation that all people can learn, including those who have been written off by most of society.

—Peter Senge

2. Public Engagement

Breaking Out of Traditional Ways of Thinking and Interacting with Each Other

Ellen Bueschel

Dr. Ellen Bueschel has the rare experience of having served as superintendent of rural, suburban, and urban school districts. She currently teaches in the Department of Educational Leadership at Miami University in Ohio. She has cycled through her superintendencies with stints in higher education, and she has brought the spirit and tools of the five disciplines into both her administrative work and her university work in profound ways. Here Ellen describes her experience with public engagement in Rockford, Illinois, an industrial city of about 150,000 people that suffered in the 1980s and 1990s from a loss of manufacturing jobs and a bitter desegregation case that lasted decades. In this effort, she and the other leaders learned to move from "telling" the community what they had decided to regenerating both schools and community through public engagement.

During the seventeen years since it had been ordered by a district court to desegregate the schools, the Rockford School District "has committed such open acts of discrimination as to be cruel, and committed others with such subtlety as to raise discrimination to an art form." So wrote the district court judge, mandating federal oversight of the district in a 1993 decision on a civil rights case raised by a parent group. It would take eight more years before the courts fully released the district from federal oversight in one of the most contentious desegregation cases in the country. During this time of judicial oversight, the district would also experience a series of divisive school board elections; rapid shifts in policies around busing, school closings, and school reopenings; a tax rate mandated by a magistrate judge rather than approved by voters; millions of dollars in legal fees and court-mandated operational expenses that the district had to pay; the nonrenewal of the contract of the first African American superintendent; and the firing of his white successor.

You can imagine what the hostility was like in the community—fury, resentment, aggression, and race and class prejudices. There were school board and community meetings where people in anger jumped across the table at each other. A lot of good-hearted people wanted it to stop, but the structure was so dysfunctional it was difficult to change.

The judge's quote comes from: People Who Care, et al. v. Rockford Board of Education, 851 F. Supp. 905 (N.D. Ill 1993). For an overview and timeline of the story, see Jeff Kolkey, "Discrimination Lawsuit Haunts City, Schools," *Rockford Register Star*, September 12, 2009, http://www.rrstar.com/news/x1420198361/Discrimination-lawsuit-haunts-city-schools-20-years-later.

People Who Care, et al. v. Rockford Board of Education, 246 F. 3d 1073 (7th Cir. 2001).

Though the court would release the school district from federal oversight in 2001, this decision came with a dire warning: "It should go without saying that if the board takes advantage of its new freedom from federal judicial control to discriminate against minority students in violation of federal law, it will expose itself to a new and draconian round of litigation. We trust that $238 million later, it has learned its lesson."

By 2003, when I took a position of interim superintendent for one year at the Rockford school district, nearly thirty years of court-ordered desegregation had taken a tremendous toll on the community's ability to come to agreement about even small things. People hadn't talked to each other civilly for years. Many of them didn't think they had to be civil, because the school issues were no longer community issues; they belonged to the federal court. Yet the very real possibility of the schools becoming resegregated loomed on the horizon if they couldn't find a way to resolve decisions about the future of the schools.

But Rockford had no capacity to deal with the issues. And its issues weren't just school issues. During the prolonged desegregation era, Rockford had also lost its manufacturing base, and the community's longstanding identity as a strong, blue-collar, and middle-class town disappeared with it. Together, the schools and community faced tremendous challenges. It was time to bring these issues back to the community where they belonged; the people of the city could no longer "shift the burden" to the courts as an excuse not to become involved in their community's schools. They would have to struggle with these difficult decisions themselves.

⧏ See "Shifting the Burden," page 375.

As interim superintendent, I had one year. I knew we would need a lot of help.

CHALLENGING OUR OWN ASSUMPTIONS

When the Rockford School Board asked me to return for one year as interim superintendent, I was teaching in the educational leadership department of Miami University in Ohio. I knew the Rockford community well; I had been the deputy superintendent there for four years in the 1990s and had served briefly as the interim superintendent. The school board agreed that if I returned for a year I could continue my research on public engagement, with the Rockford school community as a testing ground. I felt that the public engagement strategies I was studying and teaching school administrators might help stimulate positive dialogue within the community.

At other times in my administrative career, I had been a superintendent in a small rural district in the Midwest and assistant superintendent and then superintendent of a suburban district in Massachusetts. I had come to an appreciation of the importance of a community's involvement in schools. With 29,000 students, Rockford was much larger and more urban than the other districts where I had worked. However, whatever their differences in demographics, all school districts and their communities share a common characteristic. They are a product of the way their citizens think and interact with each other.

I had seen this first-hand starting with my very first appointment as superintendent at the rural Midwestern district. One month into my tenure, the school board told me that we were going to place a $14.9 million operating levy on the ballot. Having recently finished my doctoral program in educational administration, with courses on school finance, I thought, "This is crazy; no one does this." I asked the board members if they had thought through what this election would mean for the taxpayers. They obviously knew the community better than I did and responded, "We won't know if we don't try." This meant a board member and me visiting every home in the community prior to the election. We talked about why the money was needed and answered questions. I not only met everyone in the community, I also went to every event in town. (I took vacation time in minutes and hours so I wouldn't violate state laws on campaigning.) On Election Day, the operating levy passed the first time out, which even at that time was unusual. I thought, "Well, so much for the experts." I realized then that as a school administrator, you've got to know the community. That was an important lesson for me.

Years later in Massachusetts, I arrived with the impression that we needed to close at least one, and maybe two, of the community's four elementary schools. After all, they were located within six densely populated square miles, and one of the schools was almost a hundred years old. Once again the expert (me) didn't know what she was talking about. In this community, the principal of each school knew every child, every parent, and every family. Instead of closing schools, we came up with a bold plan to ask voters to approve funding for four new schools on one ballot initiative. The architect thought it would never happen and asked about our back-up plan when the levy failed. I told him we didn't have a back-up plan; it was going to pass on the first ballot, and it did. The reason that it passed was because we listened to the community. The vision of four new schools was their vision, not mine or the school board's.

Sometimes expertise can deafen school leaders to the voices in the community. We are trained to master the arts of public relations and marketing. We write reports and newsletters and prepare budgets and action plans to *tell* the public about the schools and the leadership goals that drive operations. We campaign for more tax revenues and *sell* community members on the idea of giving us more money. Unfortunately, in public relations and marketing, communication moves in only one direction; it is intended to influence the public and manage the flow of ideas. By contrast, in a democracy, it is critical that leaders engage with citizens and community institutions. Through engagement, communication moves in cycles. This builds the capacity of the community to develop its own vision; it also builds the capacity of leaders to serve the public.

Public engagement requires a shift in the traditional way school systems function. Reliance on experts gives way to greater self-governance—the foundation on which this country was built and on which the compact between the public and its public schools was forged. Public engagement also requires a shift in perspective from seeing the children only as students to seeing them as part of the larger community. Authentic public engagement, in schools and elsewhere, requires that people develop strategies that involve all sectors of a community in ongoing deliberation to build common ground.

Public engagement for schools involves several questions: "What do we want for our children? How can we collaborate to help them achieve as students and as citizens? How do we increase student learning and achievement for *all* of the district's children?"

I had one year to get this type of process started in Rockford. Fortunately, the city was home to a liberal arts college, Rockford College, with a strong emphasis on civic engagement. When I approached the college president with my idea, he was eager to be involved. The mayor joined our effort, and the three of us became partners in planning a process to involve the community in its schools. We spoke often in various public formats and arenas about the imperative to focus on the improvement of the public schools and the need to serve all the students. Each of us had some experience with public engagement, but we agreed that ultimately this contentious and unstable environment required the skills and oversight of an experienced facilitator with no ties to the community. Because I had been working with Public Agenda's seven-stage model for coming to public judgment developed by Daniel Yankelovich, we invited Will Friedman of Public Agenda to help us plan our public forums.

See Cambron-McCabe, Cunningham, Harvey, and Koff, *The Superintendent's Fieldbook: A Guide for Leaders of Learning* (Corwin Press, 2005), pp. 261, 305) for these and other powerful engagement questions.

Public Agenda is a nonpartisan opinion research and civic engagement organization. See http://www.publicagenda.org. Their seven-stage model is described in Daniel Yankelovich, *Coming to Public Judgment: Making Democracy Work in a Complex World* (Syracuse University Press, 1991).

The Public Judgment Process

Public judgment involves a community deliberating on an issue sufficiently to produce a working consensus on how to move forward. Yankelovich's seven stages can be grouped into three major clusters:

CLUSTER 1: CONSCIOUSNESS RAISING

- Dawning Awareness: People acknowledge the problem but do not yet feel a pressing need to take action.
- Greater Urgency: People move to a greater sense that something must be done, often triggered by anxiety.

During these stages, media and traditional PR strategies can help bring issues to public attention. If the issues are complex and arcane, then it helps to connect them to a strong top-of-mind concern (for example, how does the budget relate to school safety?). Remember the "first things first" principle: people must know you understand their priorities if you want them to pay attention to yours.

CLUSTER 2: WORKING THROUGH

- Reaching for Solutions: Converting free-floating concern into calls for action.
- Wishful Thinking: The public's resistance to trade-offs is manifest as people assume they can "have it all."
- Weighing the Choices: The public does "choice work:" the hard work of considering the pros and cons of each alternative way of dealing with the issues.

Avoid forcing a single solution on people—particularly your preferred one. Help people understand the pros and cons of different approaches. That provides an opportunity to develop mature views. Nonpartisan, user-friendly issue guides can help people deliberate effectively; work with those journalists, particularly in local media, who can provide nonpartisan, in-depth, user-friendly treatments of issues.

Be wary, especially during the "reaching for solutions" stage, of poll results before the public has had a chance to deliberate in depth. Resistance to the hard work of deliberation and decisionmaking is a natural part of the process. As a leader, your job is to understand resistance and help the public get past it. Sometimes providing the right piece of information does the trick; sometimes confronting people's wishful thinking is required.

Community conversations are an excellent strategy for helping significant cross sections of the community work through their thinking.

CLUSTER 3: INTEGRATION AND RESOLUTION

- Intellectual Acceptance: People accept an idea in their minds.

Some of this language is adapted from "The Seven Stages of Public Opinion," by Daniel Yankelovich, Public Agenda website: www.publicagenda.org/pages/seven-stages-public-opinion.

■ Moral Commitment: After sufficient time and dialogue, people integrate new ideas and solutions enough to act on them.

As the community resolves its future, don't mistake initial acceptance as whole-hearted commitment. Give people opportunities to play an active role devising and implementing solutions. This deepens the sense of ownership and helps ensure success as all community assets are brought to bear on the problem.

Resolution in Rockford

For our work in Rockford, Will Friedman recommended that we establish two committees to direct the process. One, the Steering Committee, would deal with the "big picture" processes and the other, the Operations Committee, would handle the details of the first forum. This structure was central to our success.

For another example of public engagement, see "Community Conversations in San Jose" by Linda Murray and Thomas S. Poetter, in *The Superintendent's Fieldbook*, p. 275.

Committee members and forum participants were chosen carefully to include voices from all segments of the community and voices that would, by design, represent different perspectives. We specifically sought racial and class diversity. Friedman trained the facilitators for the forum, individuals who were recruited from churches and other community groups. We sought out people who had not typically been involved in the past.

The forum, called "Our Schools: A Community Discussion," was held at one of the new schools built under a federal court order. For many of the participants, it was the first time they had been in the school to see some tangible benefit from their tax dollars. One of the high school Booster Clubs in the community provided a picnic dinner. Participants were asked to discuss four topics: Areas of Common Ground, Areas of Disagreement, Questions and Concerns, and Actionable Ideas.

Rockford College's civic engagement work takes place at the Jane Addams Center for Civic Engagement, named after the college's Nobel laureate alumnus. See www.rockford.edu/?page=JACCE.

The forum had several explicit purposes. First, we would demonstrate that community members were capable of having a thoughtful, civil discussion about their schools. We would also give fresh voices an opportunity to be heard—and, further, establish a model for ongoing discussions that involve these additional voices. Finally, we would provide school administrators and the elected school board with a direct line of communication to and from the community at large. This type of engagement was unfamiliar, but also compelling. By the time the small groups finished their conversations, people started asking about getting together again. They had not realized how much they had in common, even though they had been chosen for their diverse perspectives. Engaging in these conversations began to break down some long-held mental models that existed among various groups.

Additional forums followed during the school year. Each was held in a different venue, but the process and outcomes were similar. They provided an opportunity for people to articulate their feelings of isolation and frustration, and the structure provided a way to take the conversation beyond griping. This set the stage for next steps.

The local media attended the forums and assumed some responsibility for improving the communication about school issues to the public. The local paper initiated a new column in which the next incoming superintendent, my successor, answered questions that were submitted.

But the most significant outcome was internalizing the importance of conversation in building community. The participants left the forums knowing there was considerable agreement within and among the groups, even though they came together as strangers representing multiple constituencies. They had found common ground in a deeply divided community and could begin the long process of re-creating a shared vision based on the commonalities.

From my experiences, the seven stages of coming to public judgment is a useful model for understanding the processes of public engagement. People find it easy to identify the stages, and they recognize where they, and others, are at a particular point in time. They come to understand that it is not lock step, and people don't have to be in the same stage at the same time. It also helps everyone recognize how long it takes to build community. I work with educators from a variety of districts, and I have come to realize that re-creating community is an important project—even if it feels like we're trying to re-create it in a vacuum. There are always significant pockets of community to draw upon, even in a locale that seems fragmented beyond repair.

For the story of another community dealing with similar issues, see "No Throw-Away Children," by Mary Leiker, page 434.

AMERICAN FAMILY: THINGS RACIAL

by Stacy Cusulos and Barbara Waugh (CreateSpace, 2010, published by the authors) www.thingsracial.com

Barbara Waugh and Stacy Cusulos, two white middle-class professionals, adopted two black children and raised them in a prosperous suburb (Palo Alto) in one of the most supposedly enlightened

regions of the world, Northern California. This became a story of love and grief, raising awareness in any reader about the divides between black and white people, rich and poor schools, tolerant and intolerant people, adored and defamed children, neighborhoods of prosperity and neighborhoods at risk (including the very real risk of drive-by murder), "normal" and learning-disabled children, hope and despair and hope again. This book is a quiet, lingering, compelling wake-up call for anyone who cares about healing the fractures of a diverse society. Some of those fractures are surprisingly easy to heal, and others may never be resolved—except through experiences like those in this book. —Art Kleiner

IS THERE A PUBLIC FOR PUBLIC SCHOOLS?

by David Mathews (Kettering Foundation, 1997)

Public engagement for schools is not really about schools. It is the first step in coming to a public judgment about values. Together with other community leaders, school leaders raise questions: What should community life be like? Where will kids fit into that community? How do we get from here to there? Very few school administrators take on this role; as David Matthews notes, the mantle of expertise that many educators put on prevents us from taking part as community members. We don't go to city council meetings; we let other people handle other services. This book shows the alternative. —Nelda Cambron-McCabe

RECLAIMING PUBLIC EDUCATION BY RECLAIMING OUR DEMOCRACY

by David Mathews (Kettering Foundation Press, 2006)

This second book by David Matthews, President of the Kettering Foundation, looks more closely at the perceived chasm between the public and its schools. He offers ways to reframe attitudes and conversations by reclaiming democratic principles. —Nelda Cambron-McCabe

3. Vision Escalation, Position De-Escalation

An Exercise for Impasses

Bryan Smith

Acting at the level of community often leads to conflict, and accelerated conflict can overload people. Participants can walk away feeling that "I can't work with those people," simply because they don't understand one another. This exercise can break the barrier by helping each group come to a more complete understanding of itself and of the other group before they all sit down together.

The exercise depends on a style of "shuttle diplomacy" that was developed by the Harvard Negotiation Project, with which I worked closely in a series of meetings on the Canadian constitution. Groups favoring Quebec secession, groups favoring Native American secession, and groups favoring national unity all mistrusted each other; after years of meeting primarily in highly legalistic and oppositional settings, they never revealed their true concerns. Instead, they operated from negotiating positions, and they relinquished each element of their position only after a fight, for fear that they (and their constituencies) would otherwise be taken advantage of. This situation, of course, escalates the mistrust even further and encourages everyone to buttress their positions even further, until their original aspirations are long since forgotten.

School leaders may find themselves caught in similar positions. "We will not take accountability for children outside our building," they might say. "Absolutely not. We have too much of a workload as it is. The union wouldn't let us." That is a position, not an aspiration, and it immediately provokes a positional response from the other side: "You will, or we will fight you." When the impasse reaches this point, it takes an independent negotiator to defuse the situation, to help people on each side see the deeper issues at stake, and to create an environment where those aspirations can emerge.

STEP 1: VISION ESCALATION

As an independent "shuttle diplomat," you visit each group separately. You conduct two stages of inquiry. First, you try to raise creative tension by making the vision clearer. A clearer vision draws people toward it.

Purpose:

To increase creative tension as a constructive force in a situation of conflict.

Overview:

Using "shuttle diplomacy" to bring to the surface underlying aspirations and fears that shape the boundaries of an impasse.

Participants:

Two (or more) oppositional groups and a "reflective diplomat" (or pair of diplomats) who can talk candidly, if privately, with each.

Time:

This process can take months.

For more information about the highly effective, skill-building work of the Harvard Negotiation Project, see their website at www.pon.harvard.edu/research. We particularly recommend Douglas Stone, Bruce Patton, and Shelia Heen, *Difficult Conversations* (Viking Penguin Putnam, 1999). As educator/writer Jim Evers notes, "It is a helpful tool for teachers and administrators who want to avoid the blame or advocacy game in their interactions with each other, with students, and with their community. It's also valuable material to teach to students."

You ask about the ongoing confrontation: "What is it you hope to achieve out of this episode?"

When they tell you, you escalate the vision. "That would be wonderful. But if you had that, what would it bring you? What would it feel like to obtain this?"

Continue drawing them out until you have a sense that they are talking about the authentic vision that they most care about. Be supportive: Don't challenge or question them or ask them how the other groups might see their vision. Work to see their whole array of visions, goals, and results articulated to the fullest extent possible, in a way that rings true to them and explains why they feel so passionate.

Even if their vision includes hatred for the other side ("We would basically like to see them moved away, even forcibly, if we could"), you also can shift that to a stance of vision. If they had that, what would it get them? Often, there is something unarticulated that they are trying to protect, or they see the other group as threatening. You do not need to see it as rational, or worthy. But you do need to understand why it exists, and why it compels them.

STEP 2: POSITION DE-ESCALATION

Creative tension pulls toward resolution. For that reason, it is not enough to talk about vision. You need to see current reality more clearly. A critical part of these groups' current reality is the extent to which their position is constraining them. Thus, again in a spirit of inquiry, look at the constraints.

"What are your concerns? What keeps you awake at night? What are you grappling with?" By using forgiving language, you legitimize people to talk about the fears and doubts that have led them to stake out a position. "We don't really want to be stuck here," they may say. "But if we give an inch, we'll find ourselves in this kind of trouble…"

As in step 1, take the time to draw people out. "But what is it that concerns you about that kind of trouble? Why would that be a problem for you?" You are trying to understand the most basic fears that are driving their behavior.

STEP 3: FOUNDATION FOR PARTNERSHIP

A shuttle diplomat may make many visits before he or she is trusted enough to really understand the fears and concerns. Now comes the most challenging part. Without breaking the trust from any side, the deepest issues on all sides must be brought to a common table. The process may start by the diplomat raising one subissue that everyone feels strongly about, where agreement is possible. The purpose of this initial session is to give them an experience of coming to a mutual agreement about something they care about.

Gradually you and the groups can gain the capability to move to the deeper issues that have divided you. This exercise is based on the premise that underneath the hostility and the anger that is felt over recent events, there is in fact a way to provide all groups with the things they most want and a way to avoid their deepest fears. After all, everyone wants the impasse to end.

4. It Takes a Child to Raise a Village

Education for Sustainability and Its Implications for Schools That Learn

Jaimie P. Cloud

The Cloud Institute for Sustainability Education was founded in 1995 to promote healthier communities by helping students—in schools from pre-kindergarten through the twelfth grade—learn how to contribute to sustainable community development. Jaimie Cloud, the founder, explicitly set out to work with schools to design courses and practices that would inspire young people to think about the world, their relationships to it, and their ability to influence it in an entirely new way. The Institute starts from the assumption that the best way to reach young people is by working directly with their entire community—educators, government officials, community members, and the business community. Cloud, who is writing a book with the same name as this article, lays out some of the experiences of the Cloud Institute and what she and her colleagues there have learned.

For more about the Cloud Institute and its work see the website: http://www.cloudinstitute.org. Among the resources on the website is the "EfS Reality Check," a tool to assess the degree to which schools and communities are learning together for a sustainable future.

You are a tenth-grade student in an urban neighborhood—in this case, it's Bushwick, Brooklyn, New York, but it could be many places where drug dealers congregate near a high school campus. You are taking a class called Inventing the Future, which replaced an older Participation in Government course (that, frankly, never had enough participation.) In learning about systems, you cover some of the ways to distinguish symptoms from root causes, and you realize that the presence of drug dealers on campus is only a symptom. If you report the drug dealers to the police, they will at best be removed temporarily, and others will take their place. So you start looking for root causes. The gangs who import drugs are way outside your sphere of influence. But there is a root cause closer to home: the tolerance in your neighborhood. A crack house on the corner serves as a home base for the drug trade near your school and a symbol that the neighborhood is vulnerable. So you and your classmates decide that, as a class project, you are going to shut it down.

The teachers, though impressed that you have come this far, are nervous and skeptical that you can do any good, but you and your classmates won't take no for an answer. So you visit your city council representative. She tells you that some residents had tried to shut it down; the business community had also tried. But they didn't succeed. Maybe with your involvement, she says, they could get the attention of the media and higher city officials. Sure enough, within two weeks, the house is leveled—literally bulldozed. The city fines the owner, and you and the other tenth graders make plans with the city to build a park on that site.

Now imagine that you're a fifth grader, in a smaller school district: Burlington, Vermont. As part of your science class, you set up research teams to monitor indicators of sustainability all around your school, including air quality. You discover that when the cars pull up to pick up children at 3 p.m. outside the school exit, the carbon monoxide levels go way up. So you and your classmates start a campaign against idling. Parents pay attention, and the pollution levels drop.

Or perhaps you're one of the fourth-grade students at the Marin Country Day School, across the country in California, who are trying to distinguish among the indigenous and invasive species in your locale. Finding that no book exists on the subject, you write and self-publish one. The local library carries three copies, which are almost always checked out.

You could be any of thousands of school children in hundreds of classes who are working on projects of this sort. You're still the regular kid you always were; you do your homework, spend time with friends, and watch TV just as you used to do. But you have learned that when a system isn't healthy—when there are social problems, environmental damage, or even economic breakdowns—you make a difference and you get involved to make positive change. Project by project, move by move, you take responsibility for making things better. You recognize how people and living systems are interdependent, and you see how a healthy and sustainable future is possible. That's what education for sustainability (or, as we refer to it, EfS) has done for you.

EDUCATION FOR SUSTAINABILITY

At heart, sustainability means living well within the means of nature. It refers to the kind of world that many of us aspire to: where human activity increases rather than diminishes environmental quality, shared prosperity, and social equity, and where most people can live well, without imposing a burden from that lifestyle on future generations. The idea of sustainability recognizes the interdependence among environmental, economic, and social health; they all reinforce each other. Finally, EfS recognizes that the natural systems of our time are vulnerable; the prevailing practices of industrial society are destroying or harming them. Not only does that have to stop, but we have to put into practice what we know about generating better systems—in our ecology, economy, and society—and continue to learn more in the process.

Schools are important to sustainability for two reasons. First, our current system of education has been part of the problem, and that needs to change. Environmental literacy pioneer David W. Orr notes that the unsustainable practices inherent in industrial society to date were "not the work of ignorant people," but were developed by well-educated people with advanced degrees. As Orr puts it, any educational system that emphasizes theories, abstractions, neat answers and efficiency instead of values, consciousness, questions, and conscience will lead people to similarly mechanistic and unsustainable results. Since the prevailing system of education contributed to these ways of thinking, a different kind of education is required. EfS can make a difference.

David Orr, *Earth In Mind: On Education, Environment, and the Human Prospect*, 10th Anniversary Edition (Island Press, 2004), pp. 7–8.

Second, the people who learn to think and act in school today will be decisionmakers tomorrow—not just "when they grow up" in the future, but literally tomorrow. As the examples of the crack house, the idling campaign, and the invasive species book show, they can make enormous, practical contributions from the moment they start to think about sustainability. Schools can be one of the most fertile grounds for shaping a society committed to sustainable development. To make the shift toward a healthy and sustainable future, we will need to design education accordingly.

The movement known as "education for sustainability" began after 1987, when the United Nations-sponsored World Commission on Environment and Development released its report *Our Common Future*. Led by former Norwegian prime minister Gro Harlem Brundtland, the commission coined the phrase "sustainable development" with the definition "meeting the needs of the present without compromising the ability of future generations to meet their own needs." A few years later, at the UN Conference on Environment and Development in Rio de Janeiro, an in-

The nine content areas in the Cloud Institute's Education for Sustainability are accompanied by a set of measurable performance indicators. The areas are:

Cultural Preservation and Transformation: Students develop the ability to discern with others what to preserve and what to change in order for future generations to thrive.

Responsible Local/Global Citizenship: Students learn about the rights, responsibilities, and actions associated with leadership and participation.

The Dynamics of Systems & Change: Students apply the tools and concepts of system dynamics and systems thinking.

Sustainable Economics: Students learn twenty-first century economic practices and how to produce and consume in ways that contribute to the health of the financial, social, and natural capital.

Healthy Commons: Students recognize and value the vital importance of (and the means of caring for) air, trust, our collective future, water, libraries, public health, heritage sites, topsoil, and other shared resources.

Natural Laws and Ecological Principles: Students learn the cycles of nature and the underlying science of sustainability. They see themselves as interdependent

depth action plan called Agenda 21 included a chapter (chapter 36) on "promoting education, public awareness, and training."

A network sprang up of people who took this idea to heart. We saw that the conventional ecological, economic, and social systems of the present were unsustainable—they were destructive to natural and human life. As Chapter 36 made clear, there was real leverage in schools: If teachers could lead students to recognize sustainability as a natural goal, and students could pick their projects and engage wholeheartedly, then education could be part of the solution.

We have found that EfS engenders a new type of commitment on the part of individuals. Our goal is thus to develop in young people, their teachers, and other adults around them the new knowledge and new ways of thinking needed to achieve economic prosperity, participate democratically, and secure justice and equity—all the while regenerating the health of the ecosystems, the gift upon which all life and all production depend. We can teach this way of thinking; we can learn it; we can assess for it; and we can produce student work as evidence of it.

THE EFS CLASSROOM

Much of the work of EfS builds upon and expands regular classroom activity. We've identified at least forty fields of study that are closely related, including biology and health, earth science, psychology, history, economics, cultural anthropology, mathematics, probability and game theory, future studies, statistics, and neuroscience. Actually, it's hard to think of a subject that doesn't have something to contribute to our ability to educate for a sustainable future. The Cloud Institute's EfS Framework, which we developed by evaluating the work of educators for sustainability around the world, is organized around nine core content areas. They can be embedded within existing curricula or serve as inspiration for new curricula.

But while the subjects may overlap, the way of thinking tends to be more participative and constructivist than that of many conventional classrooms. The goal of instruction is to engender a way of thinking—a framework of knowledge, skills, attitudes, organizational learning, practices, pedagogical practices, and practices between schools and their communities that all operate in the service of a sustainable future.

Students may spend time, for example, playing and debriefing the "fish game": a simulation of fishing strategies and their individual and collective impact on the common resource of ocean life, based on experience with real-world over-fishing trends. Players who maximize their own short-term profits in the game tend to accelerate the collapse of the ecosystem; only those who come together to manage the "commons" sustainably can thrive. Once they've internalized the experience, students can then look for similarly endangered commons in their own communities: parkland, shared highways with traffic congestion, funding for community projects, and many more. How can these shared resources be managed most effectively? How can the entire system avoid collapse?

In these efforts, we try to avoid the direct problem-solving approach that many "practical" or environmental courses apply. Before you can solve a problem—for example, by fining a local polluter or insisting that they use filters on their emissions—you need to learn to distinguish the underlying problem from the symptom. For example, could a high level of emissions represent a waste stream that could have application elsewhere, or that might not have to be created at all? Students in these courses learn to look as far upstream as they can in the chains of causal relationships and to seek solutions that solve more than one problem at a time and minimize the creation of new problems. As we know from brain science, thinking repeatedly about the vision of a goal and solution, rather than ruminating on problems and crises, changes the patterns of neural flow and can promote more creative, long-term thinking.

See "The Cognitive Studies Group," page 404.

Our survey research to date on the impact of these classroom activities suggests definite improvements in student achievement and student engagement. EfS consistently reduces the number of students who say, "I think I can succeed" (from almost 30 percent to 6 percent in one study) and who see low grades as a barrier to success (from more than 38 percent to about 16 percent). Surveyed teachers also report an increased ability to achieve stronger academic outcomes. We've also seen a higher level of civic engagement among students and teachers, and a stronger sense of love for the places in which they live. Attendance rates go up; measures of student health and nutrition show improvement, in part because of rising air quality and more attention to better food consumption. And as with many curricula involving engagement, scores on standardized test scores tend to rise, even though the time spent directly "teaching to the test" goes down.

SCHOOLS FOR SUSTAINABILITY

Most leaders of sustainability initiatives don't typically invest much time trying to engage school systems. When asked about it, they say they don't believe schools are interested in leading in this area—or that they don't believe that schools can change. But in fact, many educators are

with each other, all living things, and natural systems.

Inventing and Affecting the Future: Students design, implement, and assess actions in the service of their vision.

Multiple Perspectives: Students learn about, value, and draw from the life experiences and cultures of others, as well as their own.

A Sense of Place: Students build a connection to the place in which they live, recognizing and valuing the interrelationships between the social, economic, ecological, and architectural history of that place and its continuous health.

The author thnaks David Rock for these insights about brain science.

The Cloud Institute's Fish Game, designed for use by PK–12 school students, is available at www.cloudinstitute.org/curricula-units-courses. It was adapted (with many changes) from another fish banks simulation, developed by John Sterman and Dennis Meadows; that one is available through the MIT Sloan School. See http://forio.com/simulate/mit/fishbanks/simulation/login.html.

More PK–12 examples can be found at http://www.cloudinstitute.org/model-programs/.

predisposed to teaching and fostering sustainability, and we have seen dramatic effects when entire schools, or school systems, get involved.

For example, in a statewide certification program called Sustainable Jersey, communities form a "green team," composed of people that can include both the school district and local businesses, community-based organizations and governments. Municipalities develop strategic plans and take actions that contribute to community sustainability. Several districts (notably Cranford and Cherry Hill) have formally aligned with their municipalities, signed resolutions to educate for sustainability, and are improving physical plant attributes and developing partnerships with their communities. Staff development is involved, so that everyone gains a shared understanding of sustainability. Subgroups take on curriculum innovation: making changes, providing criteria to measure student and class performance, and analyzing student work as evidence of progress.

There are many initiatives at the school level. The Denver Green School, in its first year of educating for sustainability, started its own garden and small farm. Its sixth grade students, with no special training, facilitated a session of the Cloud Institute's Fish Game for seventy-five adults in the U.S. Green Building Council.

For more about Sustainable Jersey, see www.sustainablejersey.com.

A schoolwide sustainability initiative can remind educators of the idealism that brought them into teaching originally. Their aspiration for a better future can trump all the doubts and concerns they may have about change. And as the school begins to produce results, they are drawn in.

THE PHYSICAL PLANT

Some of the most visible—and important—results take place in the architecture and land use of the school. Ecological awareness is manifest in any physical structure. Many schools start an education for sustainability initiative by improving their physical plant procedures: reducing energy, eliminating waste, and getting more of their cafeteria food from local farms or gardens. They put gardens on their roofs or in their fields. They rethink the use of busses to reduce air emissions.

One pioneering school is the Ethical Culture Fieldston Middle School, in Riverdale, NY, where the "green dean" Howard Waldman has stated that "the school is our curriculum." Fieldston had always concerned itself with environmental issues, particularly in its ethics classes—but in recent years, it has encouraged people to bring forth their ideas for changes in school procurement and infrastructure management. The school carries only Fair Trade coffee in its cafeteria, with about eighty-five percent of it organic and shade grown. They've eliminated paper and plastic cups, purchasing washable mugs for every teacher. Emulating some colleges, they gave up lunchroom trays in 2011—which saves water and reduces the waste of food. "There were all sorts of predictions of disaster," recalls Waldman, "but there were no disasters; it was clean, safe and fine." They also stopped serving meat on Mondays.

Fieldston's environmental club began a composting program at the school, working with the facilities managers to compost weeds and leaves; they are planning to compost food waste from the kitchen as well. The environmental club, at the urging of teacher Kenny Styer, conducted an energy audit of the school, measuring how much energy could be saved by turning off lights and computers at times they weren't needed. Cost savings added up potentially to $325,000 per year. Each September, they announce how much has been saved, making everyone more and more conscious of the potential gain from turning off lights and computers. Perhaps most impressively, the middle school building, opened in 2008, won a difficult-to-get silver rating from the Leadership in Energy and Environmental Design (LEED) process, set up by the U.S. Green Building Council to certify buildings on environmental impact. Among the features was a green roof comprised of native plants, with consultation from Columbia University.

One fascinating aspect of work on infrastructure is the human connection. Every hands-on initiative attracts people—whether it's to a day spent working on the green roof or abandoning the cafeteria trays. Students, educators, and parents all become more aware of the effect that the things they do (and don't do) have when the school building and grounds become tangible, living symbols of change.

THE COMMUNITY CONNECTION

Making more explicit links with the external community is a critical component of education for sustainability—in large part because of its importance outside the school. When teachers and children raise their awareness and act according to sustainability-oriented principles, the entire community becomes healthier. In other words—it takes a child to raise a village.

EfS efforts tend to diffuse tension between schools and communities. They may have been fighting for years over taxes, but now they come together with a shared goal, with each side having a role to play. In several districts (examples include Byram Hills and Ossining), we've had world cafés where formal educators and community members have sat shoulder to shoulder to talk about the future of their community and the role of education. That never happened before. And the kids, who aptly recognized that *they* were the commons, were the facilitators at each of the tables.

}} For more about the World Café method, see page 122.

Community progress is also one of the major ways to assess our progress. While learning and behavioral outcomes are visible at the school level, it's only at the community level that an EfS effort can demonstrate how well it has fulfilled its original intention. We use several sustainable community indicators: increase in renewable energy, conservation of existing energy, waste patterns, the state of the commons, the ecological footprint, and children's health. We set a baseline for these at the start and then watch to what extent they change over time.

Every so often, people question the premise of EfS. They say that sustainability is a politicized topic and should not be an educational objective. Student achievement should be the only goal. But school is always operating on behalf of some outcome, even if it isn't expressed explicitly. Even student achievement is a means to other ends—including the development of a workforce and a more responsible citizenry. An effective EfS process raises these questions explicitly. People have an opportunity to ask: "What are schools for?" Or, to put it another way, "What kind of world are we trying to create with the next generation?"

In their book *Hope's Edge*, Anna Lappé and Frances Moore Lappé tell the story of Belo Horizonte, Brazil, where a mayor named Adriana Aranha led an effort to give everyone in the city access to nutritious food, thereby ending the hunger and much of the poverty that constrains many cities in emerging economies. At the end of their interview with her, the authors complimented her on her city's remarkable achievement, and the mayor—who was in the last months of her term of office—found her eyes filling with tears. "I knew we had so much hunger in the world," says the mayor. "But what is so upsetting, what I didn't know when I started this, is it's so easy. It's so easy to end it."

That's similar to our experience with Education for Sustainability. People expect it to be extremely difficult to bring schools and communities together for sustainability. But when you start, and you give people transformative learning experiences and they participate in meaningful dialogue, and you prototype solutions with curriculum innovation and community engagement, it all becomes feasible. There's very little pushback. The kids, parents, educators, and community members are all on fire. It reinforces all the best aspects of school: It's fun, intellectually stimulating, and nourishing in a variety of ways. Thinking about it may be daunting, but doing it is joyful work.

Educators may feel that they're in a system that is innately fixed and resistant to change, but they are positioned to be the change agents in their community. Kids may feel that they will have everything handed to them until they become adults, but they and we are responsible now

See Frances Moore Lappé and Anna Lappé, *Hope's Edge: The Next Diet for a Small Planet* (Jeremy Tarcher/Putnam, 2002), pp. 93ff and 100.

for the health and sustainability of our collective future. Everything we do and everything we don't do makes a difference. We need to figure out what our unique contribution is and make it.

5. The Tragedy of the Commons

Michael Goodman, Janis Dutton, Art Kleiner

Commons are the places and things we all share, upon which we all depend, and for which we are all responsible. Examples include public spaces, fish and other marine wildlife, our shared future, the atmosphere, the top soil, and human trust. Sometimes a commons is considered limited, because it can be depleted more rapidly than it is replenished. When that happens, it's known as the Tragedy of the Commons, the archetype of systems where the benefit to individuals is unintentionally placed at odds with the benefit to the whole.

⟩⟩ For an introduction to archetypes, see page 143.

Not all commons are tragic; shared ownership can be a very powerful way to manage a resource. But this archetype shows what happens when that commonality is stressed. Within a few blocks in some cities, for example, you might find a public elementary school, a charter school for grades K–3, a Head Start center, and several daycare centers. All draw on the same "commons"—in this case, the local budget from city government and foundations. If the budget is finite and difficult to replenish, then each group will feel pressure to get its share. Each group will apply its ingenuity and skill to draw grants and city contracts to its organization before the others, instead of looking for ways to save money by cooperating. The result, to everyone's detriment, is that money available for preschool child care is depleted over time. Other examples include:

■ The underlying drain caused by many voucher and charter plans. They are created under the premise that competition will force schools to become more innovative and efficient at serving "customers"—the area's students. Unfortunately, when resources are finite and shared, the new schools tend to focus not on providing better service but on taking more resources away (including the highest-scoring students) from their competitors.

■ Volunteer programs, which often burn brightly for a year or two but gradually get "overgrazed" as volunteers burn out. Volunteers might feel appreciated at first when several different organizations, plus the local schools, Boy's Club, and YMCA, independently seek their participation. But a volunteer will feel the Tragedy of the Commons in full force when he or she decides to drop back a little bit—and every one of the organizations pushes hard for "just one more effort."

■ The community's willingness to invest in schools at all. Especially during inflationary times, local property taxes do not keep pace with inflation, so schools must return to propose new bond and tax increases. This can deplete not just the tax resources but the goodwill that a community feels toward its institutions of learning.

The concept behind this archetype was described by Garrett Hardin in "The Tragedy of the Commons," *Science*, December 13, 1968.

Unlike Success to the Successful (page 372), where eventually the re sources all wind up in the "winner's circle," and there are clear winners and losers, "Tragedy" eventually makes everybody a loser. A Tragedy of the Commons often involves a catastrophic crash—the destruction or degeneration of a limited Commons' ability to regenerate itself. This is what makes the "Tragedy" tragic. When resources are depleted past a certain point, they cannot be replenished or regenerated. Yet every individual group is constrained by its own perspective; its leaders see resources dwindling, so they push harder to get their share. Doing so stresses the overall system capacity even more, making a crash more likely and more dangerous.

Over-depletion can affect every aspect of educational resources, from pencils to staff development to technology, in wealthy areas as well as poor ones. Tim Lucas recalls a principal who made a plea to his staff: "Folks, I need your help. The photocopier is on its last legs. We can't afford a new one until July, when the new budget comes in. Would you all take it easy and photocopy as little as possible until then?" The next day, everyone was lined up at the photocopier, to get their individual needs met before the crash. The machine broke down in two days.

STRATEGIES FOR A TRAGEDY OF THE COMMONS

Tragedy of the Commons poses a difficult governance challenge, in part because it often puts well-intentioned groups at odds with each other unnecessarily. Can you anticipate the dynamic before it goes so far that a crisis is inevitable? And can you find the appropriate way to intervene? Here are four potential ways to intervene, depending on the situation:

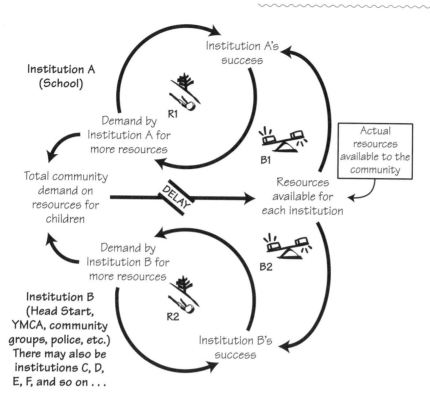

Institution A's
success

Institution A
(School)

R1

Demand by
Institution A for
more resources

B1

Actual
resources
available to the
community

Total community
demand on
resources for
children

DELAY

Resources
available for
each institution

Demand by
Institution B for
more resources

B2

Institution B
(Head Start,
YMCA, community
groups, police, etc.)
There may also be
institutions C, D,
E, F, and so on . . .

R2

Institution B's
success

This diagram shows the underlying structure of a Tragedy of the Commons dynamic. In the rectangle is the implicit limit of the system: the finite or difficult-to-replenish total resources of the community. This limit might include appreciation, time, space, money, knowledge, and volunteer capacity for children. Divided among the various institutions, these resources boost individual institutions' successes. As their individual success improves, more demand for their services is generated, and more demand for resources by each of them is created (shown for each institution in the reinforcing processes R1 and R2). This demand places added pressure (shown as the balancing processes B1 and B2) on the common resource. The more successful each individual institution is, the more it drains the resources available to all. The delay allows the demand to accumulate, unnoticed by many individuals, until it can lead to collapse.

1. **Collaboration:** In some cases, such as many situations involving rival agencies, individual organizations work together to pool resources rather than compete for them.

2. **Quarantine:** As in the photocopier budget (which everyone knows will be renewed after a time), a limited common resource is closed off until it has time to be replenished.

3. **Replenishment:** Sometimes it is possible to replenish a limited commons actively, by seeking greater degrees of funding or other reserves on which to draw. The earlier the replenishment takes place, the easier it tends to be, and often that means replenishment must begin before some people realize that there is a problem at all.

4. **Regeneration:** You can whole-heartedly take on the common aspiration of tending the commons, so that instead of being depleted it continually regenerates. For example, you can set up a common staff development process among all the agencies and schools so that the capabilities of everyone in the community keeps rising.

   All four of these strategies depend on being able to step back and see the big picture. Sometimes doing so may mean dictating a "whole-systems" answer: "We're going to ration everyone's use of the photocopier for the next four weeks." It is difficult for any individual to manage the Tragedy of the Commons alone, because each individual actor faces overwhelming pressure to keep using up the resource. In fact, it's generally in their individual best interests to do so.

But when you educate people about the value of the commons and their shared responsibility in tending it, you can also interest them in replenishment and regeneration. As Jaimie Cloud notes, the "tragedy" of the commons can turn into a "joy of common endeavor." A highly beneficial way of life can evolve if the individual actors understand the regeneration rate and trust each other enough to give each other time to act on behalf of the whole. So long as they feel they are not running a risk of being exploited themselves, they will develop their own ways to build back the resource base, simply by regenerating the resource base faster than they harvest it. This can then become a reinforcing cycle, which accelerates the speed of regeneration over time.

One such regeneration story, as recounted by ecologist Gerald Marten, is the marine sanctuary of Apo Island in the Philippines. In the mid-1960s, after new destructive fishing methods such as dynamite fishing, small-mesh nets, and cyanide were introduced, conditions in the island's coral reefs deteriorated, almost past the point of no return. Desperate for catches, fishermen resorted to destructive methods even when they knew it would ultimately destroy their livelihood. Then in 1979, the fishermen themselves (with the advice and support of a marine biologist named Angel Alcala) set up their own rules against destructive fishing, turning the island's entire fishing grounds into a safe zone, patrolled by village volunteers. The catch-per-effort improved dramatically, and without the need to travel so far, fishermen enjoy more time for either leisure or other ways to generate income—including tourism prompted by the revival of the coral reef ecology. One interesting side effect: the villagers now recognize the ecological impact of their own population and have instituted family planning efforts.

In your community, how many times do various community groups get together and talk about their common problems? Do they work together to set priorities, so that each agency and group can do what is most important to it? They may not want to act in a coordinated fashion, but are they willing to talk about it? If so, their ability to deal with the Tragedy of the Commons probably will be much greater.

For more of the story on Apo Island, see Gerald G. Marten, "Environmental Tipping Points: A New Paradigm for Restoring Ecological Security," *Journal of Policy Studies* (Japan) No. 20 (July 2005), p. 75–87, http://gerrymarten.com/publicatons.html.

6. Children as Leaders

The Lessons from Colombia's Children's Movement for Peace

Sara Cameron

In our Fieldbook series, we generally tell stories in the words of protagonists. That was impossible for this article, which was originally published in 2000 and is still highly relevant today. The protagonists were too much at risk to tell their story alone. They were children, ages six through eighteen; there were thousands of them, and they ultimately transformed their country.

Novelist/journalist Sara Cameron was invited by the United Nations Children's Fund (UNICEF) to chronicle Colombia's children-led peace movement. That assignment led to a book (Out of War), a CNN documentary, and an ongoing role in helping children in a variety of countries tell similar stories about war, famine, and health crises—and about their efforts to create peace where adults could not and to survive where adults did not help them. The children of Colombia made the adults more aware of the system they created—and changed the system in the process.

Also see Sara Cameron, *Out of War: True Stories from the Front Lines of the Children's Movement for Peace in Colombia,* (Scholastic, 2001); and stories about women's and children's leadership in Kenya, Bangladesh, Senegal, Sudan, Tanzania, India, Papua New Guinea, Iraq, and elsewhere at www.saracameron.org.

For more than forty years, Colombia was caught up in a brutal conflict between political opponents. On the left, the Revolutionary Armed Forces of Colombia—known by their initials in Spanish as FARC—and other groups conducted guerrilla warfare against the government, starting in the mid-1960s. They funded themselves through kidnap ransoms, extortion, and taxes on coca growers. On the right, a confederation of paramilitary groups had close links to drug traffickers and some units of the Colombian army. The paramilitaries were responsible for most of the worst human rights violations. Moving from village to village to drive out guerrillas, they murdered, mutilated, and rendered homeless hundreds of thousands of people.

By the late 1990s, the country was caught in a seemingly unresolvable, unendurable crisis. Both the FARC and the paramilitary groups routinely committed massacres. Adults who tried to make peace or who were merely suspected of aiding the wrong side (such as grocers selling them groceries) were systematically exterminated or displaced. Husbands were slaughtered in front of wives, parents in front of children, and community

One day the guerrillas came to our home in Santander and killed both my parents. I was four years old at the time. Fortunately, I was at my grandmother's house and did not see it happen, but my sisters were at home. They were five and six years old, and they saw everything. They have never forgotten. —Twelve-year-old child.

I work as a volunteer play therapist with children who have been forced to leave their homes because of the war. Some of the children have seen terrible things, like their father tortured and killed. They find it very difficult to understand what happened. We play together with the trucks, boats, and rag dolls, and sometimes after that you can figure out what went on. Some of the children are very shy, but I give them the parrot puppet, and sometimes they tell him things. They often talk about the goats and chickens and cows they left behind when they left their homes. They worry about the animals. —Wilfrido, age 16.

leaders in front of entire villages. For all these reasons, Colombia would have become a country essentially without hope—except for one thing: the desperate, loving, truth-telling leadership of its children.

In a sense, children had no choice but to assume that role. More than 850,000 Colombian children were forced out of their homes by violence between 1988 and 2000. Sixty percent of those displaced children dropped out of school. At least 2,000 children under the age of fifteen were enlisted in guerrilla or paramilitary groups in 1999, some as young as eight years old. More than 4,000 children were murdered in 1996 alone, with the number continuing to rise each year; and impunity was widespread. Rarely, if ever, was a murderer arrested. Many children lived in fear of losing their families. As one fifteen-year-old put it, "Sometimes, [the soldiers] kill only your father, but when they kill your father they kill a part of your life."

Many of the Colombian children had to come to terms with the fact that adults could not or would not protect them against the incredible violence of their society. They had to learn to be responsible for themselves, for each other, and for the community around them.

The Children's Peace Movement was organized in 1996. Within three years, it led to a political shift in the national government, and the leaders of the movement, all under twenty years old, were nominated for a Nobel Peace Prize in 1998, 1999, and 2000. At the same time, the war in Colombia grew more intense and deadly, only gradually wearing out its intensity during the decade of the 2000s. The experience of the Children's Peace Movement, meanwhile, showed that children play an important role in any troubled community. They can lead.

THE CREATION OF A CHILDREN'S MOVEMENT

The Urabá region, close to the Panama border, had been a virtual fiefdom of the guerrillas for decades. They dominated the banana workers' unions and gave shelter for illegal trade in drugs and arms. Then, in the 1990s, right-wing paramilitaries moved in. Many schools became battlegrounds between the armed groups, even while class was in session.

In April 1996, the internationally known children's advocate Graça Machel (the former minister of education of Mozambique, who was to marry Nelson Mandela in 1997) visited Apartadó, a city in Urabá, conducting research for a United Nations report on the impact of armed conflict on children. The mayor summoned a few students to talk about their experience; before long, 5,000 children had volunteered for a Week of Reflection backed by the church, the Red Cross, and UNICEF. They wrote stories, poems, letters, painted pictures, and constructed sculptures; the combined student council of the nearby communities also drew up a "Declaration of the Children of Apartadó."

The declaration was direct and wrenching: "We ask the warring factions for peace in our homes, for them not to make orphans of children, to allow us to play freely in the streets, and for no harm to come to our small brothers and sisters…we ask for these things so our own children do not suffer as we have done."

Things did not end there. The students researched their nation's constitution, which had been rewritten in 1991 to guarantee extensive rights and democratic freedoms, including rights to children. They decided this gave them a constitutional right to form a local "government of children." The students sent notices to schools in the municipality, and soon up to 200 children were pouring out to peace meetings three times a week, gathering in football fields and in parks. There was considerable chaos at first and argument about what children could and could not do to make peace.

"To have peace you need to solve poverty, and children cannot do that," recalled Farliz Calle, one of the leaders, who was fifteen that year. "But we found other things that children could do." They set up "peace carnivals" that encouraged children from feuding communities to play together, because they believed that children having fun was a good way to help peace. Other children worked with the municipality and the Red Cross on dental and health campaigns. Later, hundreds trained as counselors in play therapy and went on to help thousands of other children who had been displaced by violence.

Meanwhile, a group of twenty-seven children from around the country, aged nine to fifteen years, gathered at a May 1996 workshop organized by UNICEF. There were thirty adults in the room as well, representing peace and children's organizations, but the young people did most of the talking. They took turns describing the impact of the country's violence on the children in their communities. Some spoke of gangs roaming the streets, terrorizing children on their way to school. Many of the children were amazed to find out that they were not alone. They had not realized until then that so many other children lived under such conditions of violence.

Three main realizations emerged from the workshop. First, most Colombians were unaware of the impact of the war on children. Second, no one would be more effective at getting that message across than children themselves. Third, they needed a bigger platform to reach a wider and more influential audience.

Thus, the participants—both adults and children—began planning a special election for children only—the Children's Mandate for Peace and

The activities described in this article were sometimes organized by children, sometimes by adults, sometimes by adults and children together. They were generally made possible through the support of UNICEF, the Colombian National Network for Peace (Redepaz), the Scouts, the Red Cross, the Catholic Church, the YMCA, the Christian Children's Fund, World Vision, Defense of Children International, and other organizations.

Some of the facts in this article came from the following sources: Sara Cameron, "The Role of Children as Peace Makers in Colombia," Development, vol. 43 no. 1, (March, 2000); Jorge Enrique Rojas Rodriguez and Marco Alberto Romero Silva, "Un pais que huye…" (Bogotá, Consultoría para los Derechos Humanos y el Desplazamiento, 1999), www.codhes. org; "¿Que hay detras del maltrato infantil?" (Bogotá, Conferencia

Episcopal de Colombia, 1999);
"Defensoría del Pueblo, La niñez y sus
derechos," Boletin 1–4 (1996–7);
"En cuatro años, 4.925 secuestrados," *El
Espectador*, (May 5 1999), p.6A; Graça
Machel, "Impact of Armed Conflict
on Children," (UNICEF, 1996) and
"Children and Conflict in a Changing
World" (UNICEF, 2007), both at http://
www.un.org/children/conflict/machel/
english/; "Informe sobre el 'Mandato
Nacional de los Niños por la paz'"
(Bogotá, UNICEF, 1996); and Reuters
news coverage of the Colombian Civil
War in August, 1999.

I dream that one day I will wake up
and my father will go to work and I
will not have the fear that he will be in
danger, that he will be shot. This is the
dream that we are all trying to build.
If I am killed, at least it will be over
something worth dying for. It is better to
die for something than for nothing, isn't
it? —Farliz Calle

Results of the assemblies were
formally presented to the
government and led to a national
peace project between the Children's
Movement, UNICEF, the Scouts, and
the Colombian High Commissioner for
Peace, Victor G. Ricardo.

Rights. Children were deeply involved in organizing and planning it. The colorful ballot listed twelve rights summarized from the Colombian constitution and the Convention on the Rights of the Child—including the right to education, to justice, to a safe environment, to peace, to freedom of expression—and invited children to vote on what they wanted most, for themselves and their communities. The young organizers devised child-rights games and taught them in schools and public meetings. They designed and starred in advertisements and ran press conferences and town meetings, talking publicly about the war, peace, and their rights. Even the guerrillas and paramilitary groups observed the occasion; for one day, there was an impromptu cease-fire across the nation.

The organizers hoped that perhaps 500,000 children would vote. But on election day (October 25, 1996), more than 2.7 million children—about a third of all people aged seven to eighteen years—packed the polls. At some locations children ran out of voting cards, but they copied the ballot onto paper napkins and still cast their votes. In Bogotá voting had to be held on two consecutive Saturdays to meet the demand.

Before the children's vote, the peace movement in Colombia had been weak and fragmented. Thousands of human rights activists had been assassinated or forced to flee the country. Plans to hold a national referendum on peace had been put on hold because it seemed too difficult and dangerous. Now the children had moved onto adult turf—they had proved, for the first time, that neither the guerrillas nor the paramilitaries had the kind of broad popular support they claimed. This represented a profound wake-up call for the nation. As one human rights activist explained, "Until the Children's Mandate came along, we really had no idea that children understood."

The following year, a coalition called the Citizen's Mandate for Peace, Life, and Liberty went before Colombians asking them to back the children and reject the war. More than ten million Colombians pledged their support. As a result, peace was catapulted to center stage and became the basis on which the presidential elections were fought and won in May 1998 by Andres Pastrana. Still, the massacres, kidnappings, assassinations, and unofficial emigration continued at all-time high levels. Against this backdrop of unremitting violence, the Children's Movement for Peace continues to define itself. A core group of about twenty-five children drawn from different institutions and municipalities form the Children's Council in Bogotá. Since 1996, several Children's Assemblies, involving between 100 and 200 children from across the country, have met to discuss child rights and peacemaking. The last assembly, in 1998, led to the development of Children's Councils for Peace in other municipalities.

BUILDING A VISION FROM THE CHILDREN'S HOPES AND DREAMS

One of the legacies of the Children's Movement is the way in which it shows how children can make a difference. This idea brought together people from across Colombia's rigid class boundaries. One wealthy teenager joined the movement after seeing a video report on it: "Look at what these children are doing, and they have nothing. What are we doing, when we have so much?"

The Children's Mandate took on no enemies, no matter what the provocation. This was a principled stand and a highly pragmatic one as well. "We never accuse any of the armed groups," said Farliz Calle. "If we did we could become targets. We will always denounce these terrible events, but we never know who is responsible. We simply do not know." The strategy not only protected children individually but helped the movement retain the neutrality that was crucial for its survival and growth. Children did not join any gang; they worked for peace instead.

The level on which most children "understood" this complex situation was different from that of adults. They thought less about political and economic concerns and more about justice and fairness. Perhaps as a result, their definition of peacemaking was very broad—it included any activity that improved the quality of life in a community affected by violence. The Children's Movement stated that making peace in homes and on the streets was just as important as making peace in the war. After all, domestic and neighborhood violence was much more prevalent. While approximately 6,000 people died every year as a result of the war, another 25,000 were murdered in domestic, street, or other criminal violence.

Through extensive networks of supporting organizations, thousands of adolescents became "peace constructors" who worked with other children promoting conflict resolution, tolerance, and nondiscrimination. More than 10,000 children received training and helped others, for example, learn how to avoid accidents with landmines. Hundreds of children were trained as volunteer counselors to thousands of displaced children.

This approach gave children a different model to follow, besides joining one of the armies or a street gang. "I sometimes take part in workshops of the Children's Movement for Peace," said thirteen-year-old Lelis. "There are so many children who come there from different places. They seem so strong, so well organized and well trained. They know what they are doing. They talk well. They have good ideas. I am so impressed. That is what I want to be like. I want to join in like them."

The estimated 100,000 children in the movement knew that they would eventually grow up into adults. And they would be needed more

People never used to care about the war unless they were directly affected by it. But when children talk about pain and sorrow, we make adults feel the pain as if it was their own. Children are the seeds of the new Colombia. We are the seeds that will stop the war. —Mayerly, a movement leader, age 14

At first, when my father was murdered, I thought that all the work I was doing for peace was worth nothing because it had not saved him. Yet my father had always wanted me to work for peace, and I did not want other children to share the nightmare of losing someone they loved so much. In the end, my father's death pushed me harder and gave me a more realistic attitude toward peace. I know this work can be dangerous, but if they did not stop me when my father was alive, they can do nothing to stop me now. —Juan Elias, a movement leader whose father was shot July 1996.

than ever. As peace activist Ana Teresa Bernal noted, "Colombia has been at war for so long that its people don't know how to live in peace. That is why the things these children are doing are so important, especially if peace comes." They had the experience of living in one of the most dangerous situations imaginable; of articulating their hopes, galvanizing a national movement, learning through teaching each other, and taking responsibility for their lives. This gave them the first step toward a shared vision for their country.

"My mother sometimes tells me that there is a lot more to life than all this peace and rights stuff," said sixteen-year-old Elena. "She thinks it takes up too much of my time, but I cannot think of anything else that is more important."

EPILOGUE: WRITTEN IN 2011

Children in Colombia continue to be active participants promoting peace within a wide range of organizations, many of which were part of the Children's Movement for Peace in Colombia from the start. Yet today the Children's Movement does not exist any longer as the overarching national body it once was. The decline of the Movement as a coherent force happened for several reasons.

First, it was feared that the Movement was giving too much publicity to individual children and had exposed them to risk. Some of the child peace leaders received threats; a few even fled from Colombia and found political asylum in the United States or Canada.

Second, there were concerns that ethical principles for child participation were not being followed. Children from the Movement for Peace were in high demand at international conferences. They were featured in glossy magazines and TV documentaries. Often children were selected for participation in these events without enabling the broader constituency of children to fully debate the issues, decide on their position, and elect their own representatives to participate.

Third, there was no clear shared overarching vision for the Movement, and this sometimes exacerbated misunderstandings among the participants. For example, there was occasional disagreement among the organizations engaged in the Movement about the relative publicity each organization should receive. Some organizations had greater international exposure.

Finally, changes in the way people communicated had an effect. In 1995, when the first workshops were held that led to the creation of the Movement, children had to physically travel from their towns and cities to meet and hear about the experience of others. One young participant,

Every day I hear people fighting—husbands and wives, parents and children, and even in my own home there is violence. It makes me very sad and sometimes afraid. I beg my father to stop, but still he fights my mother. But he did not like to see me unhappy. He heard about children who were training to be peace constructors, and he took me to a meeting. I felt much happier after I joined the group. We talk about making peace with each other, with our friends, with anyone who will listen. I talk to my parents about it. They told me that they don't want to fight, but sometimes they cannot help it. —Isabel, age 14

Juan Elias, told me that it was only at that meeting that he realized his experience was not unique—that other children in Colombia suffered just as much. Today, through social networking, children have the possibility to listen and learn from each other without having to leave their communities.

There is still a place for the Movement, not as an organization but as a commitment that children across the country, and beyond, can make to work together for peace. The involvement of children as peace activists is still important in Colombia—a society that continues to experience high levels of domestic and street violence. As Mayerly Sanchez told me in her Soacha house in 1998, "Peace that begins in the heart of a child can cover the whole world"—but only if it is amplified and heard.

Children's Workshops for Community

Sara Cameron

Every weekday in the Colombian cities of Bogota, Medellín, and Cali, the Rafael Pombo Foundation held creative workshops in literacy, video, fine arts, and drama for hundreds of disadvantaged children. In addition to expanding the horizons of these children, the institute worked with teachers in order to influence the otherwise formal atmosphere of most Colombian classrooms. The Rafael Pombo staff also ran workshops in guerrilla-controlled territory, with a focus on conflict resolution and peace building. This design is based on those workshops.

First, conduct a series of warm-up exercises to make the students feel comfortable with one another and act as a link to a new way of working and learning. These may include movement and mirroring exercises, trust exercises, bridge building, and so on. In bridge building, for example, the students work in groups, and using their bodies, try to construct the strongest bridge they can. They are then asked to decide whether they could improve the design and make appropriate changes. Afterward the students are asked to comment on how they changed their minds about the design. How easy or hard was it for one or two members of the group to persuade the others to change? How did they feel about it? Was the result an improvement? What was the best way to work? And so on.

Next the students work in groups of five or six to create their own community or town. To support the task they have paper, pens, felt-tip pens, cardboard boxes, rolls of paper, tape, glue, and any scrap materials useful for creating the physical buildings of the community. They are also asked to work together to decide all or some of the following:

Overview:

This exercise is based on the belief that in order for adults to achieve peace, they first need to imagine it, and that there is no better place to begin than with children.

Participants:

The exercise works well with many different age groups and with mixed age groups.

A group of us constructed a town during one of the Rafael Pombo workshops. We decided we needed a church, but what kind of church? How could we choose? In the end we decided on a multipurpose building where anyone could worship any God, and we had priestesses as well as priests. We said that everyone had the right to freedom of religious belief, and this should never be a source of conflict. —Marcela, age 17

1. Explain the history of the town: Where is it located? Why was it established? By whom? Where did the people come from who founded the place?
2. Name the town and explain why and how this name was chosen by the founders. (This actually may be preceded by a discussion of the origin of the name of the town that the students currently inhabit.)
3. List the laws of the town. (These can include national laws, such as freedom of speech, as well as local laws such as recycling.)
4. Name the most important/impressive buildings in the community and explain their significance.
5. Describe the economic base of the community: What sort of work do people have? What is the quality of life? (Often the students take on specific roles and explain the economy by referring to themselves as residents of the community.)
6. Describe how schooling, religion, the legal system, health service, refuse collection, and other activities are carried out.
7. What does the future hold in store for this community?
8. The students also may be asked to create a coat of arms for their town and to explain the meaning and historical significance of the various symbols they employ. (The coat of arms exercise can work as a stand-alone activity.)

After about an hour, the groups present their towns or communities to one another. The group as a whole discusses ideas that seem especially useful and interesting. The exercise could be extended over a longer period, but the rapidity with which the children have to work often increases the spontaneity and fun. The exercise also bears repetition and can be set in specific time periods or with certain geographical or political limitations.

7. How Do You Know Your Organization Is Learning?

Janis Dutton

What does it mean for an organization to learn? In practice, it means developing a clear and honest understanding of current reality that is accessible to the whole organization; is used to produce new, equally accessible knowledge; and that helps people take effective action toward their desired future.

Picture your group or organization: It can be a classroom, a curriculum team, a site-based team, a group of administrators, or your community—whatever group you choose. Ask the following questions about it—either by yourself or with the group as a whole.

- Does the organization have a clear and honest understanding of its current reality? How much truth can your organization tolerate? Do you seek out data or wait for the government, parents, or newspapers to require it? Whom do you include in surveys? Are you balancing inquiry and advocacy? Do you avoid data that is potentially embarrassing? Do you test your experiences? Are you challenging your underlying assumptions? How many messengers have you shot lately? Do you rely solely on numbers, or are you talking to people, asking them how they feel, what they think, what they desire personally and for the organization?

- Is the understanding of current reality shared throughout the organization, and from there do you create new knowledge that is also shared? Does everyone have support to be a "learner" as opposed to a "knower"? Does the environment support continual learning, or is it just coincidental? What do you do with information? Is it privileged? Do people have to have a title or a degree to see it? Do you develop a shared understanding and build knowledge from the data? Do you accept only the data that supports your assumptions, or do you ask "What if we looked at this from another viewpoint?" Who builds shared understanding? Who's at the table? Is all of the school data available to parents? To staff? Are you developing staff? How is that development shared throughout the organization? Are you creating new knowledge? Does your organization show capabilities it didn't have before? How does that new knowledge change current reality?

- Is knowledge translated into effective action toward your desired future? Can people make use of new knowledge? Is it relevant? Are they applying it? Or are people quoting articles and books but never getting anywhere? What is your strategy? What are your priorities? Who is involved in designing staff development programs? How much time do people have for sharing professional practice? Are your energies focused toward your desired future, or are you chasing a hundred different priorities? Can you tell a story of how you are closing the gap between current reality and your vision? Can you identify

Purpose:

To assess your organization's learning process.

Overview:

A series of questions based on a definition of organizational learning.

What does it mean for an organization to learn? In practice, it means developing a clear and honest understanding of current reality that is accessible to the whole organization; is used to produce new, equally accessible knowledge; and that helps people take effective action toward their desired future.

We are grateful to Charlotte Roberts for helping to conceive of this exercise.

the benchmarks in your progress? Does your organization show capabilities it didn't have before?

PERSEVERANCE

by Margaret Wheatley (Berrett-Koehler, 2010)

Since the early 1990s, Meg Wheatley's views on communities and her experience with innovative management practice have made her a central figure in a worldwide network of pioneers in organizational learning and change. Starting in the mid-2000s and accelerating with the economic crisis of 2008, Wheatley focused on the anxiety she saw among her friends, clients, and business acquaintances. Even the most organizational learning-oriented leaders when confronted with the harshness of business pressure felt compelled to cut back their most enlightened practices. She responded with *Perseverance*, a personal meditation on tenacity in the face of adversity. It is written explicitly for people dedicated to organizational change (including education reform), who find their work growing more difficult for whatever reason and who are looking for ways to sustain their effort and their peace of mind. —Art Kleiner

8. The Systems Citizen

Education for an Interdependent World

Peter Senge

What if we viewed schools as a vehicle for shifting society? What if we saw education as a leadership development laboratory where students learn what it takes to bring about the sorts of changes that need to occur, within the school and beyond, for a healthy future?

Over the years I have taken part in many cross-generational dialogue circles, often with young children present. In one such gathering, a school superintendent (who was also a leading figure in a national school association) sat across from two eleven-year-olds. Larry, the superintendent, asked the children what they thought about the world today. With little hesitation, the eleven-year-old girl said, "We sort of think that you drank your juice and then you drank ours."

Several years later, at a large community gathering in St Louis, there was another small-circle "check-in," where mixed groups of adults and children, speaking in turn, reflected on why they were there. A teacher said that she was concerned about sustainability issues, like the food and water supply. Another adult commented about the gap between the rich and poor in their community. Then it was time for a young girl, probably nine or ten years old, to offer her comment. She simply said, "I want to live."

The directness of these statements often startles adults. But we should not be surprised. Young people today are growing up in an unprecedented way. They have an awareness of the state of the world that greatly surpasses that of previous generations. They know about climate change and about our addiction to fossil fuels. They know about the persistent gap between rich and poor. They are often in direct communication with friends in other countries, and they know about the struggles of the world's cultures to live respectfully with one another. Much of what they hear is negative: ecological collapse, terrorism, economic anxiety, ineffective leaders, and untrustworthy institutions. But all these negative messages do nothing to undermine their deep desire to contribute.

Later that day in St Louis, the audience of 250 people heard a series of presentations by students about their own sustainability projects. Few who were there will forget Annalise, a twelve-year-old who spoke about the wind turbine she and her classmates had gotten built at their middle school. The project started in science class, where their teacher talked about the need to move to alternative sources of energy not based on fossil fuels. Annalise and four of her classmates (she gave each of their names) talked with the teacher after class, asking what they could personally do. The wind turbine idea was born right then. They got different parents involved—engineers, businesspeople, and others—to help sort out the options and develop a proposal. Then they presented their idea to the school principal and then the mayor of their local town.

"I was worried that our presentation did not go very well with the mayor," recalled Annalise before the assembly. "She really didn't say anything when we presented our ideas." Nonetheless, they had later been called back for a second presentation to the mayor and members of the town council, and from there the project took off. Annalise closed her remarkable story, which took all of three minutes to relate, with a photograph of the vertical wind turbine that now provides power for the school.

Having by now the undivided attention of the mostly adult audience, many of whom were stunned at what the young children had accomplished, Annalise then set down her notes and looked directly at audience, some seventy-five pounds of fierce determination, and said, "We kids often hear that 'You children are the future.' We don't agree with that. We don't have that much time. We need to make changes now. We kids are ready. Are you?"

I believe that children today are not only aware of the conditions in the world in which they are growing up, they are concerned—and many more than we think are fully prepared to get involved. Of course, it's impossible to know, because as adults we have a lot to do with their opportunities for engagement. All too easily, adults can develop self-reinforcing mental models about children. "The kids don't care about the world. They just care about video games, texting, and Facebook." When we adults believe this, we don't create any space for children to step forward. Given few opportunities to make a difference, it is no surprise that many disengage and become apathetic, feeling that there is no place to raise questions and that no one really cares what they have to say.

But time and again I have seen that when the space is created, young people like Annalise do step forward. I have come to believe that a core purpose of school today should be to create that kind of space. Kids will respond. Some will step forward to speak, others to build, and still others to demonstrate, through example, a more systems-conscious way to live. They will become—many are already becoming—the systems citizens of their future. Because they know that this is exactly what is needed.

〉〉 See "The Youth Leadership Forum," page 389.

The Systems Citizenship Gap

As we have noted elsewhere, the industrial-age education system that has spread around the world in the past 150 years is likely to change dramatically in the coming decades. This will not happen because it is easy. Indeed, as most educators know only too well, few institutions are more resistant to innovation and change than primary and secondary schools. But fundamental change in education will happen nonetheless because it is necessary if human society is to survive and thrive. The Industrial Age—the Age of the Machine—is ending, and it will not be possible to transition to what is coming without rethinking and reshaping the educational system. After all, it has been and continues to be one of the primary propagators (with business) of the Industrial Age worldview and skillset.

)) See "The Industrial Age System of Education," page 32.

The current moment in history is a time of profound crosscurrents. On the one hand, global industrial expansion has brought extraordinary material benefits and opportunities for quality of life. For the first time in human history, billions of people share a material standard of living previously unimaginable, just as more share reasonable expectations of long life, democratic processes, and formal education than at any previous time. For all these reasons, virtually every society in the world continues to pursue the goal of industrial, material expansion.

But continued business-as-usual industrial expansion is also leading to unimaginable dangers. Human beings are destroying other species and ecosystems at unprecedented rates and altering their ecological environment locally and globally as never before. According to the World Wildlife Fund, to support today's global economy takes the resources of one and one-third Earths. If China ever reached the material level of consumption and waste of the U.S, we would need two Earths. If India does the same, we would need three. But we have only one Earth, and the inevitable adjustment to living within the scope of nature's generosity grows more severe every year that humanity continues down the current "take-make-waste" path of our present industrial, materialistic form of existence.

The challenges created by this tension are social, economic, and cultural as well as ecological. Indeed, all of these challenges are interdependent. The rapid acceleration of international mobility, migration, and business activity has caused a collision of cultures as well as economic systems, with many around the world fighting to preserve their traditional cultural identities against the spread of western-style consumerism, while competition over wages and opportunity leads to widespread joblessness and social upheaval. For many people, there is a clear sense that we (humanity) don't quite know how to live with the forces that our own society has unleashed, and we have only just begun to suffer the unintended consequences.

A student of systems thinking might present this situation in a simple behavior-over-time graph showing the growing gap between the level of interdependence of modern society and the ability to understand that interdependence:

From "Education for an Interdependent World: Developing Systems Citizens," by Peter M. Senge, in Joy Richmond, Lees Stuntz, Kathy Richmond, and Joanne Egner (editors), *Tracing Connections: Voices of Systems Thinkers* (iSee Systems and Creative Learning Exchange, 2010).

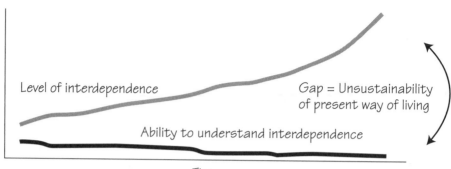

For more on behavior-over-time graphs, see page 139.

What does this rising "interdependence" curve mean? Simply that global industrial expansion has woven a web of interdependence the likes of which has never before existed. Simple activities like producing goods and services, growing food, and living our daily lives are inter-twined as never before, both locally and globally. The average pound of food travels almost 2,000 miles prior to its purchase by an American consumer. Many everyday goods travel much farther. The waste byprod-ucts of our way of life travel equally far. For example, the United States generates 20 percent of global greenhouse gases with less than 5 percent of the world's population by virtue of the cars and SUVs we drive, the buildings we live in, and our video games, flat panel TVs, and web surf-ing—the electricity for which mostly comes from burning coal. These emissions contribute to shrinking glaciers, reduced spring runoffs, and hundreds of millions of chronically dehydrated people in northern In-dia. Weather instability, flooding, and rising sea levels affect a great many more. Soon, the same statement will be valid in reverse: China's and India's surging greenhouse emissions are eclipsing those of the U.S. and contribute directly to weather instability and severe storms in North America. Never before in human history have people's daily choices on opposite sides of the globe been so entangled.

But while this web of interdependence has been growing, human capacity to understand interdependence has not. Indeed you could ar-gue that it has steadily deteriorated over centuries. As humans have moved from tribal to agrarian societies and more recently to the modern industrial society, our sense of connection to the larger living world has progressively become more tenuous. For example, some American chil-dren believe that their food *comes* from the grocery store, and most kids and adults in the U.S. have no visceral concept of seasonality in food, since all foods are available at all times.

In 2010, Oxfam estimated that the costs to the world's poor of adapting to global climate change (including costs due to loss of crops, spread of tropical diseases, and migration camps, which are becoming an increasingly permanent feature on the landscape of many developing countries) exceeded $50 billion (see www.oxfam.org) This figure is expected to rise sharply in the coming years.

As this gap grows, our way of living becomes increasingly unsustainable. Very few adults today understand the global economy, let alone where the products they buy come from, or the social and environmental side effects of the global supply chains through which they move. Few appreciate, for example, that the worldwide expansion of industrial agriculture, driven mostly to serve middle class consumers in Europe and North America, displaces tens of millions of rural residents per year due to falling farmer incomes. It is a major source of greenhouse gases (including CO_2 from shipping food around the world and methane from the expansion of livestock to meet growing demands for meat), drives deforestation for growing livestock or cash crops, and has caused the loss of over a billion hectares of topsoil in the past fifty years, more than the size of India and China combined.

Like a financial bubble, where seeming profits actually come from betting that the expansion can continue indefinitely, the Industrial Age seems from the inside like it will go on forever. But it cannot last. The contradictions between how nature works and how modern society works simply cannot continue indefinitely. Just as with a financial bubble, the collapse of the Industrial Age bubble could be devastating—even threatening all of humanity. We could also be on the verge of a transition to a "life beyond the bubble": a regenerative or restorative economy and society that mimics nature and strikes a different balance between material needs and the non-material qualities that human beings value. But this sort of survivable transition will not take place on its own. To accomplish this will require real change in the energy we use, the products we make and buy and the associated waste generated, the way land is used, the relationships between humanity and other species, and many, many other aspects of institutional and individual life.

While there are many facets to the malaise of global industrial society, it is hard to imagine much real change without addressing the fundamental gap between our growing interdependence and our ability to understand that interdependence. No technological fixes are likely to solve climate change alone. No global government will suddenly appear to deal with the growing stresses of food and water. No enlightened corporate responsibility movement will miraculously change the prevailing operating model of global business so that short-term profit comes into balance with long-term contribution to people and planet.

All of these changes, and more, *will only happen as our thinking changes*. The institutions of the modern world work as they do because of how we work—as managers and employees, financiers and regulators, consumers and citizens. How we think and interact shapes their policies and

The idea that the industrial age is a bubble that has run its course is developed in Peter Senge, Bryan Smith, Nina Kruschwitz, Joe Laur, and Sara Schley, *The Necessary Revolution: How Individuals and Organizations are Working Together to Create a Sustainable World* (Doubleday, 2008).

practices, none of which will change without a deeper understanding of interdependence—not just by formal "leaders," but by all of us who shape those expectations, norms, and daily ways of operating of those institutions.

Closing the systems citizenship gap constitutes the core mandate for an education system if it is to serve society's genuine needs. Developing systems citizens—people who understand and can act proactively to address the profound imbalances of the industrial era—is a very unusual way to think about the purpose of education right now. It is far from the mainstream view. But it is exactly what Annalise, and millions like her, are asking for. As she said, the real question is: "Are we ready?"

A Blind Spot: The Purpose of Education

While it might sound grandiose, I believe the kids in school today sense the significance of the current moment of transition. Though they express it in a variety of ways, they all know the same thing: that the only citizenship that matters today is citizenship for the whole. They sense that people everywhere will have to work together to, in the words of Buckminster Fuller, "create a world that works for everyone." This is why they are disengaged when traditional schooling does not address the imbalances that will shape their future, and why they thrive when it does.

How can institutions of learning overcome their own inertia to recognize the stake that young people have in the future and to help give them the skills and perspective they need most? The task at hand is not to re-create the best of yesterday's cultures, but to foster the interrelated culture of tomorrow.

To accomplish this, we must build a meaningful consensus about the scope and substance of education for the twenty-first century and how it differs from education in the past. Without clear aims, there is no real energy for innovation. Without clear aims, all efforts at "reform" will end up circling back to the only goals people know how to work toward—the operational goals of the past: basic skills in math, science, and literacy, and ultimately better test scores. These are crucial but not sufficient. They have built our modern industrial world. They will not be sufficient to build the regenerative economies of the future.

The absence of an operational consensus on aims is the first reason why we have no real ecosystem for innovation in education today. Innovation for what? There will be no answer until we come together to articulate a compelling and consensual answer to the question, *"What are our basic aims for education in today's world?"* If this can be done thoughtfully and in a way that engages a meaningful cross section of key stakeholders—students, teachers, parents, local businesses, and community leaders—it will create the focus that is tragically absent today.

This will neither be quick nor easy. It will need to be done in ways that respect the inherent localness of schools and in a way that serves to connect them to the communities they serve. But there will also be areas where broad consensus is needed. What are the critical skills and areas of knowledge students will need to be effective workers as well as citizens? How do these skills build on the goals of traditional education? What are the basic innovations in instruction and pedagogy that will be needed? How do we make teaching an attractor as a profession to the best and brightest? And lastly, are schools here to "teach kids" what we as adults already know? Or, is the purpose of education now to provide a way for everyone to learn together the capabilities we all need to create a healthy and sustainable way of living?

Young people long for the latter. But most adults, consciously or not, assume the former. If ever there was a time to question this assumption, it is now. One hundred fifty years ago, society needed workers in factories, so school was designed to produce them. Today, by contrast, society needs engineers, entrepreneurs, designers, architects, teachers, doctors and nurses, managers and workers who can help create a workable, sustainable, and prosperous global civilization. This is no small change.

Education is the one social institution with a built-in time horizon of fifty years or more: the lifetime of today's students. Business, government, and the media do not have this perspective, but education, by its very nature, does. That is why attitudes about school always indicate the future direction of a society—and why schools should be primary sources, key institutions, for the fundamental long-term changes that humanity needs. "Education is the most powerful weapon, which you can use to change the world," said Nelson Mandela. No other institution has this potential in the same way.

There are precedents—some going far back in human history—for seeing education this way. In a recent series of talks in China, Nan Huai-Chin, famous in China as a master of traditional (Taoist, Confucian, and Buddhist) Chinese culture, pointed out that the modern term "education" did not exist until recently in the Chinese language. It entered China from the West. The traditional Chinese term that would be closest was *jiao hua*, which would be literally translated as, "to teach in order to transform." This was the job of everyone who sought to improve society, all the way up to the Emperor, whose job in traditional Chinese culture was to help people transform through teaching.

The characters for *jiao hua*, "to teach in order to transform"— the closest traditional Chinese term for "education."

For example, the famous Yellow Emperor, an archetypal Chinese leader, organized existing knowledge about medicine into a canon that has served China for almost five thousand years. He also taught in other domains like astronomy, meteorology, art, and poetry. His basic job, it is said, was to convey knowledge for the people's well-being.

Educating to create global systems citizens takes us into unfamiliar territory. It's unfamiliar to everyone. No one knows how to do it. There is no set curriculum, any more than there is agreement on the processes of learning that will be needed. Moreover, it is not a job for educators alone. The resistance to change that is inherent in schools (especially in locally governed public schools) will continue to thwart innovation until communities of leaders from schools, business, civil society (including social service, healthcare, other local organizations), and local government start working together to create an environment for ongoing innovation in education.

⟩⟩ See "Three Nested Systems of Activity," page 16.

In this context, our overarching aim should not be educational reform but recontextualizing the whole process of education: starting with young children learning how to be more responsible for their own school environment and gradually moving to interconnecting diverse stakeholders as they tackle complex real-life community issues. Students would stop being passive recipients of someone else's curriculum and become active agents in developing a sense of responsibility and efficacy for an interdependent world—a start on the road to systems citizens.

Qualities of Education

In the rest of this essay, I would like to describe some of the qualities that a school for systems citizens could have. The specifics would vary, of course, by locale, but the broad outlines are clear from experience with diverse schools that are already committed to developing systems citizens. Here is what we have learned.

⟩⟩ Also see articles by Jay Forrester (page 269) and Linda Booth Sweeney (page 301).

WHERE CHILDREN AND ADULTS LEARN

The traditional school is a place where adults seek to cause children to learn. By contrast, educating systems citizens demands learning from everyone. Teachers invite inquiry in subjects that they have not mastered, because no one has mastered them. Children come to insights of genuine value to their teachers. Teachers learn with and from one another. Administrators create an environment that fosters trust, vulnerability, and shared vision, and along the way, they too become more open to seeing how their own behaviors must often change. Parents and community members get lured into the excitement and energy of a human community connecting with itself. As has happened for millennia, when we genuinely value and listen to children, their enthusiasm to learn and grow permeates our encrusted attitudes. Even in the microcosm of a single school, we discover the wisdom of the old Chinese adage, "The mark of every golden age is that the children are the most important members of the society and teaching the most revered profession."

For teachers, especially, this means opening up to the tremendous challenges of transforming pedagogy and classroom instructional strategies, and letting go of established norms of "stand and deliver." How to deal with the remarkable diversity of learners? How to support children in their own process of learning how to think for themselves and to create that space for reflection for one another? How to apply deep knowledge of human development as the underpinning for all education? How to blend a developmental orientation with diverse subject material, so that the one supports the other? And how can everyone continually learn how to work better together in accomplishing these changes?

A PLACE FOR PEOPLE TO FIND THEIR VOICE

Schools for systems citizens embody above all else a relentless commitment to growing human beings, to nurturing the distinctive inborn sense of purpose and responsibility in each of us. Each child's vision, like their persona, is unique. Each will see ways to make a difference that others do not. Systems citizens will not be rolled off an assembly line by teaching everyone a standard set of "systems tools." They must be grown by helping each child grow their distinctive sensibilities for an interdependent reality.

"Human nature is the core question for education," says Nan. "Why are all babies born so different?" For him, to grasp the depth of our uniqueness, you must look at the innate qualities of the karma that infants bring with them into this life. If we are blind to the differences each person embodies, teachers may "accomplish the reverse of the intent to nurture." While Westerners are not used to thinking of qualities of a soul developed through many reincarnations, the idea that each person is unique is not foreign to us. Indeed, it is a cornerstone of Western enlightenment and democracy—that each person is entitled to "life, liberty, and the pursuit of happiness," with each defining the meaning of those terms for him- or herself.

One of the oldest functions of school has been to help young people find their vocation, their unique path of developing as valued and self-sufficient contributors to society. The essence of this undertaking, like the etymological root of the word "vocation," is all about finding your voice.

VOCATION

The word vocation literally means, "calling," and it comes from the Latin *vocare*, "to call," which is descended from the same root, *vox*, that produced the English word "voice."

Remember Annalise—the young girl who spoke so confidently in St. Louis about the wind turbine? Her self-confidence, clarity, and concise articulateness mesmerized the people in the audience. There seemed not to be a wasted word, quite in contrast to a few of the adults who proceeded her on the program.

It was only afterwards, in a touching conversation with her father, that I learned that this had not always been so. He came up to me during the break after her presentation, in tears. "I just can't believe it," he said. "You have to understand that I and Annalise's mom have been concerned for so long that she was so shy. So quiet. We worried a lot about that. I guess she's found her voice."

Later, reflecting on his comment, I wondered: Had she found her voice? Or had we found our ear? Only a few educators believe deeply in the power of youth leadership on issues like food, energy, water, and poverty. Many young people get stuck in self-fulfilling prophecies that preclude them from expressing this potential. Moreover, many adults are fatalistic about the immense and growing imbalances that characterize our present society; the problems so outweigh the solutions that it is easy to believe that nothing can be done. Kids don't have that fatalism or pessimism. And once they get involved, they stay involved. It's their future, and they know instinctively that this is what real education is all about, even when the adults have forgotten.

AN INCUBATOR FOR HIGHER-ORDER SKILLS

Educators have many frameworks for higher-order skills. Our experience returns again and again to—

■ Systems thinking and understanding complexity

See Barry Richmond's systems thinking skills, page 296.

- Reflection
- Collaboration and building learning partnerships
- Communication & listening
- Design thinking: how to create systems that are more likely to produce the outcomes we desire
- Sense of self: aspiration, self-motivation, self-control
- Sense of efficacy: how we can influence the problems we care about.

These are all thinking and interacting skills that a systems citizen needs to have in hand. They incorporate not just awareness of systems, nonlinear feedback, and leverage, but other thinking and learning skills that are almost completely ignored by many schools today. In many ways, these parallel the "core capabilities" in building learning organizations, what it takes to continually develop individual and collective capacity to learn, for children and adults.

⧓ See the Three Legs of the Stool, page 74.

Educators have tended to think of these as "higher-order skills." But they are the skills involved in solving complex real-life problems at whatever age we confront them—that are complex in a very different way than, say, a complex math or physics problem. Long regarded as the purview of graduate education, twenty years of evidence now exists to show that, with the right kind of instruction and overall learning environment, these skills can be nurtured in primary education and developed to remarkably advanced levels in secondary education, not just for an elite but for the majority of students.

⧓ See, for example, Linda Booth Sweeney's essay, page 301.

A PRACTICE FIELD FOR REFLECTIVE AND COLLABORATIVE LEARNING

One critical dimension in fostering the skills of systems citizens of all ages is the ability to reflect on what we are learning, often in "real time."

In pioneering systems thinking schools, such as the Borton Primary Magnet school in Tucson, it is common for kindergartners to end their day by sharing their "behavior-over-time" graphs where they have charted their learning for the day. With their graphs posted on the wall, they stand in a circle and talk about what they have learned, hour by hour. For those hours where they learned a lot, they stand very tall. For those where they learned little, they get down close to the ground. If they were in between, they stand in between. Then each child talks about what was happening that shaped their experience each hour: when they were fresh and full of energy, when they were tired or distracted, when they were hungry. In this simple matter-of-fact practice, reflection becomes part of each child's school day. Just as importantly, they become aware of the uniqueness of each other's experience. There are no right and wrong answers to "How did you feel?" There is not standardized curve that defines a correct day. Each is honored.

》》 For systems thinking in the classroom, see page 268ff.

As they get even a bit older, children in this type of school move from seeing patterns in their school day to exploring systemic forces at work in their lives. One of the more widely watched videos among educational innovators shows three first-graders sitting and examining a reinforcing feedback loop they have drawn to understand why they are having fights on the playground.

"First we have mean words," says one six-year-old, pointing to their loop. "Then there are hurt feelings and then more mean words." The fights, he says, start after that. What is especially amazing to adults who see the video is the spontaneous conversation that ensues about "different ways we can intervene in this system."

"We tried saying 'I'm sorry,'" says another boy, also six years old. It sort of worked, he continues, but they decided there were other things to try that would work better—his way of saying that he understood where to find leverage in the system.

In simple, everyday ways like this, students learn to move beyond blame and hopelessness. They become engaged in the timeless challenge to better understand their own lives and the intrinsic pursuit to accomplish things that matter to them (like not having flights on the playground). Their curiosity is cultivated, and their innate sense of responsibility develops. These are two foundations for systems citizenship. Gradually a third falls into place: learning how to solve difficult problems together. Once they stop blaming each other or feeling guilty about their fights, they can start working together to change things. Last summer, when I met one of the boys— now all of seven years old—and asked him how things were going, he said that he and the two other former combatants were now "best friends."

With a foundation of curiosity, hopefulness, and knowledge about how to collaborate about complex issues, it is natural that students mature to dealing with larger community issues. The key is to continue to keep their learning focused on what is real and relevant to them, *and* to give them the space to tackle non-trivial problems, especially ones that the adults do not know how to solve, like: "How we can get renewable energy for our school?"

The video is at the Waters Foundation website: http://www.watersfoundation.org/webed/examples/playground/playground.html. It is also available on YouTube: http://www.youtube.com/watch?v=OWFDivyk7gI&safety_mode=true&persist_safety_mode=1.

Adults have no less need for regular practices of reflection and collaboration. Unfortunately, most educators don't provide space for their own reflection and learning as part of the day-to-day work environment, and most principals don't recognize their crucial role in creating that space. Non-reflective practice is re-enforced by funding systems that pay teachers for face time in the classroom only, professional development "clumped" into summer recess sessions, and a culture of individual, not collective, competence. This is reinforced even further by popular efforts to drive change today: when teachers' individual competence is rated publicly, it has more or less the same impact as when members of a sports team compete with one another to be the star player: team success suffers.

}} See "No More Drive-by Staff Development," by Ed Joyner, page 396.

It takes time and deep commitment to go beyond platitudes about collaboration and create an environment of ongoing collaboration and collective innovation. "Of all the changes I tried to lead as principal, helping teachers learn how to team was probably the most difficult," says Mary Scheetz, former principal of the Orange Grove Middle School in Tucson, Arizona, where many of the systems thinking practices described in the book were pioneered. Scheetz personally led several day-long retreats where teachers learned to reflect and listen to one another and to build their mutual capacity for dealing with the inevitable conflicts that arise (for example, between different teachers' lesson plans or strategies with particular kids). "There is so much more potential for collaborative solutions than normally gets realized given the professional isolation common to most schools," says Scheetz.

}} See "Context and Engagement," page 293.

But, just as innovative businesses have learned, the reflection and collaboration needs to occur regularly, not just in intermittent training sessions. Building teams must be ongoing, and the moments of greatest learning often arise in dealing with breakdowns and crises. Determined to create this space as part of the everyday routine of the school, Scheetz and then assistant principal Tracy Benson (who later succeeded Scheetz as principal), eventually redesigned the schedule so that each day, all teachers had forty-five to sixty minutes set aside to "clinic" with one another. "Collaboration only starts to make a difference when teachers can practice coordinating in real time," says Benson. "They need to know what Billy's teacher found out in his first period class or how a new systems idea that is supposed to integrate across civics and science is actually playing out for the kids. This actually helps teachers feel like a team."

Gradually, Orange Grove's teachers began to build a larger vision of the type of school culture they wanted to create, and they found that the ongoing work in developing themselves as a learning community started to reshape the way they interacted. "We have to lead by example," said math teacher Kelly O'Connor. "If we show respect to the kids and to one another, the kids see that." "Any topic we talk about is a process of building a community," said Jay Barwell, English teacher. "Dealing with all our differences is the key to building our shared vision."

As the teachers developed as a team, so did their understanding of how to improve the overall school environment. In the end, their vision for the school came down to one idea: respect. With this as their guiding rule, they were able to create trust among themselves as well as with their students.

A LABORATORY FOR FOSTERING CONNECTEDNESS AND BUILDING HEALTHIER COMMUNITIES

The isolation of teachers from one another within schools is sadly mirrored by the way schools see themselves—as isolated institutional entities sitting apart from the larger communities in which they are embedded. This tragically also often becomes a self-fulfilling prophesy: isolated schools contribute little to their communities and in turn fail to tap the potential engagement and support from those communities. As this happens, the reciprocal benefits from interdependence between school and community are lost.

The value of recognizing interdependency is starting to be understood among innovative businesses in ways that are transforming their strategies and practices. "If I reflect on what many organizations have been going through, the awareness of sustainability has been growing," says Andre van Heemstra, a retired member of the management board of Unilever (one of the world's largest consumer goods companies). "Systems thinking, in different forms, is enabling us to see many more interdependencies than we have seen in the past." He adds, "It is those interdependencies which make you conclude that it is more than stupid, it is reckless to think of commercial sustainability in isolation of either social or environmental sustainability."

How could a similar awakening to the strategic significance of interdependence occur in education? One way could be through the growing movement of education for sustainability—a recognition among educators and community leaders that schools could be a far more proactive force in helping our communities evolve beyond the industrial-age bubble. This is starting to become a new strategic imperative for some schools; the Portland, Oregon, school system, for example, has made it an explicit districtwide priority for students, administrators, and operations staff.

⟩⟩ Also see "It Takes a Child to Raise a Village," page 537.

The Orange Grove journey and the long-term effects on the students are captured in a fascinating video, "That School in Tucson," available from the Creative Learning Exchange clexchange.org. The video contains compelling footage of former middle schoolers as students and fifteen years later as young adults.

The van Heemstra quote is from Senge et al., *The Necessary Revolution*, p. 217.

Over the last decade, Unilever has developed bold sustainability goals for 2020 and shown how embracing the core challenges of an interdependent world can to transform a formerly non-innovative business into a world leader—for example, sourcing all inputs to all products sustainably, integrating half a million "small holders" into their global value chains, and reducing their environmental footprint in absolute terms while they grow the business. See their "Sustainable Living Plan" at www.unilever.com.

As these ideas take further root, we will see that education for systems citizenship—and especially the systems thinking tools and collaborative learning skills—can provide young people with the intellectual and developmental foundation they need to be prepared for the host of core sustainability challenges they will face: food, water, energy, waste and toxicity, growing gaps between rich and poor, building restorative businesses and economies—starting here and now, in the communities where they live.

Unfortunately, what passes for sustainability education is often reworked environmental science curricula. At worse, it becomes an extra burden for teachers and added cost for schools. Schools could do much more. As Jamie Cloud's work has shown, teaching sustainability is, at heart, a practice of crossing boundaries—across fields of study, across age groups, across the boundary between school and the outside, and across the artificial boundary separating "book learning" from practice.

Connecting school with the larger community can start simply. For example, The Monte del Sol charter school in Santa Fe, New Mexico, came up with a simple first step: the school's innovative "community learning project" requirement. Here's how it works.

Every tenth grader can identify something she or he wants to learn that someone in the community can teach. The resulting project then constitutes one of their required courses for the year. I have met students at Monte del Sol who have learned carpentry, consulting, and community organizing. As important as what they learn is how they learn it. Freed from the classroom, they re-create the oldest form of education: apprenticeship. Not only does this lead toward learning that has real meaning to them, it connects many adults with students and makes them meaningful contributors in the school, paving the way for both to work together to build healthier and more sustainable communities

Another example, one that is a bit more focused, has been so compelling that many educators are trying to extend and replicate it. Middle school science teacher Scott Beall transformed his science class into the "DoRight Leadership Corps" by teaching sixth and eighth graders how to conduct energy audits and then engaging local businesspeople as their clients. Not only do the students learn how to apply science to practical analysis and develop entrepreneurial skills in the process, local businesses start to reduce their energy (and carbon) footprint. Along the way, the students discover the difference they can make to their community.

The difference for student learning, even as defined traditionally, is dramatic. "There is no doubt that the kids in the DoRight course learn as

Jaimie Cloud of the Cloud Institute, a national leader in education for sustainability for over a decade, identifies seven primary "habits of mind" to be cultivated in education for sustainability:

Understanding of Systems as the Context for Decision Making. The extent to which one sees both the whole system and its parts, as well as the extent to which an individual can place one's self within the system.

Intergenerational Responsibility. The extent to which one takes responsibility for the effect(s) of her/his actions on future generations.

Mindful of and Skillful with Implications and Consequences. The extent to which one consciously makes choices and plans actions to achieve positive systemic impact.

Protecting and Enhancing the Commons. The extent to which one works to reconcile the conflicts between individual rights and the responsibilities of citizenship to tend to the commons.

Awareness of Driving Forces and Their Impacts. The extent to which one recognizes and can act strategically and responsibly in the context of the driving forces that influence our lives.

Assumption of Strategic Responsibility. The extent to which one assumes responsibility for one's self and others by designing, planning, and acting with whole systems in mind.

Paradigm Shifting. The extent to which one recognizes mental models and paradigms as guiding constructs that change over time with new knowledge and applied insight.

See www.cloudinstitute.org, and C. Federico, J. Cloud, J. Byrne, K. Wheeler, "Kindergarten through Twelfth-Grade Education for Sustainability," *The Environmental Law Reporter News and Analysis.* 33(2) (February 2003).

Murphy School District's Learning Communities, by Dennis Sandow, Virginia Piper (Charitable Trust research paper, 2006).

much science content as counterparts in more traditional science classes," says Beall. In fact, their New York Regents science exam results tend to be as high or higher than counterparts in more traditional classrooms. "There are many ways you can design meaningful service learning sustainability projects with particular curricular content in mind," says Beall. "The big payoff is student motivation and a completely different understanding of what it means to do science rather than do schoolroom exercises." Today, a half dozen school systems in The Society for Organizational Learning (SoL) Education Partnership network are collaborating on the "kids footprint project" inspired by Beall's example.

For more on the SoL Education Partnership network, see page 31.

One of the highest leverage strategies for reconnecting school and community can be simply starting to "see" the connections that already exist. The Murphy School District in Phoenix, Arizona, is located in one of the poorest neighborhoods in America. A recent study by SoL researcher Dennis Sandow showed how members of that community have created networks of mutual support that have delivered food and clothing to those in need; fostered a decrease in youth violence, domestic abuse, and substance abuse; and helped generate an increase in student achievement over a five-year period. Sandow found that the "students and their families, as well as the neighborhoods within Murphy School District, all benefit from a large, collaborative social system whose members include, but are not limited to, not-for-profit, government, faith-based, and business organizations; teachers; counselors; parents; and Murphy School District graduates. There is a single (although unstated) purpose to this social system: to generate health and well-being for Murphy School District students, families, and neighbors."

Sandow's similar studies in businesses like Hewlett-Packard have shown that making visible these previously invisible collaborative networks has strengthened them. "Once people start to legitimate the networks of collaboration, people naturally become more aware of them and how they operate, and how important they are. When they are invisible, it is easy to neglect them." Sandow specifically links the strengthening of these networks of engagement over the past five years with student performance, noting that "the larger social system (is) supporting the Murphy School District student's academic achievements."

District superintendent Paul Mohr, a founding member of the SoL Education Partnership, puts it this way: "Maybe it is the harsh circumstances of Murphy, but it has always been obvious that if school here is to succeed, it must become a hub for community building. When that happens, the benefits for students as well as adults can go well beyond what educators can do on their own."

Connecting schools and communities more consciously also creates important opportunities for youth leadership development. "We tend to greatly underestimate young people's capacities as leaders," says Les Omotani, recently retired superintendent of the Hewlett-Woodmere district in Long Island, New York.

For the past several years, Omotani has invited high school students to serve as facilitators for numerous community dialogues hosted by the schools. "The young people learn that they can help adults have meaningful conversations about how to make the community, including the schools, more healthy," says Omotani. "The adults learn to accept the young people as thoughtful and committed community members. It is a huge win-win for everyone." For example, out of a recent dialogue, students started a "bag it" project to introduce reusable shopping bags throughout the community with the goal of eliminating many of the plastic bags that inevitably end up in landfills.

}} See the "Youth Leadership Forum," page 389.

All this goes beyond changes in curriculum, or even pedagogy, though both are also foundational. It requires a radical shift in conceptualizing schools as a locus for both student and community learning and how the content and process of education can be interwoven with *real-life contexts* to create opportunities for young people to learn and to lead in building sustainable communities and societies. In such contexts, education is no longer something that adults do to kids. Education becomes a joint learning process for growing healthier and more sustainable ways of living together.

What if the prevailing view of school was defined not by institutional geography but by the geography of students' lives? What if not just teachers were the professional educators, but all the adults (and the older youth) with whom a student interacts? What if we assumed that sustaining innovation in education will only occur to the extent we develop collaborative networks linking local business, local social services, government organizations, and families who share a common vision of supporting kids in their development? What if we realized that whatever shortage in teachers we perceive is but an artifact of the fragmentation of school from the larger community—that in fact there are vast numbers of potential teachers waiting to be asked to help?

A CENTER OF REAL INNOVATION

Lastly, developing systems citizenship could place schools as natural centers of innovation—particularly the kinds of innovations that will help society make the transition out of the industrial age.

"Public education has no research and development (R&D) capability," observes Tony Wagner, the first innovation education fellow at the Technology and Entrepreneurship Center at Harvard. "What if school districts each had an R&D school site? What if education was afforded the opportunity to invest a similar proportion of their budget and time into R&D as do their business counterparts?"

Most businesspeople live in a world where they must innovate or their company will die. They understand how to manage the risks that comes with experimentation, how to focus on testing new ideas in local ways before they are extended prematurely to broad application, how to finance, and how to assess innovation. Increasingly, the most innovative firms are looking to nature and harmony with nature as the guiding beacon for the innovation needed in the future—in renewable energy, material selection and product design (the "biomimicry" movement), in "closed loop product cycles" that eliminate waste (like Starbucks' aim to eliminate disposable cups), and business models that address embedded poverty (like Unilever's aim to source food products around the world from a half million innovating "small holders"). Competitive strategy expert Michael Porter has observed that successful businesses of the future will focus on creating "shared value" with society, a radical shift from the self-centered competition traditionally thought to drive innovation.

Michael Porter and Mark R. Kramer, "Creating Shared Value," *Harvard Business Review* (January 2011).

Educating systems citizens presumes that, sooner or later, the same shifts in thinking must come to education—and that this is already starting to happen. As people committed to innovation in education further understand the historic shift in economic priorities, it will become natural for schools to shift their educational priorities as well. Then, questions of basic aims will come center stage, along with a host of practical imperatives around specific goals and metrics and processes, starting with development processes for educators. As in all change, much of the effort will center on the practical question: Who will lead the change? For my money, the leaders will come from everywhere, and especially from the students themselves.

Life in a World of Systems Citizens

In 2010, I spent time with a group of students making the transition from middle to upper school in one of the systems-thinking-oriented school systems in Tucson, Arizona. They were just finishing their end-of-year assignment: to pick any complex subject of their choosing and then immerse themselves trying to understand it from different points of view. At this time in Arizona, a law had just been passed requiring non-U.S. citizens to carry identification; in practice, this meant Hispanics (whether U.S. citizens or not) would continually be asked to show ID cards. Several picked this subject. Others picked topics with equally contentious public debates: topics like abortion rights or narcotics legalization.

I was especially struck by their common observation that they had all picked topics where they had a strong point of view. They thought they knew what was right. But as they got into it, they realized it was more complicated than they had expected, and, to a person, they found themselves questioning their own views. One kid said, "Even the people with whom I strongly disagree, like on the identity card issue, have a point of view that's legitimate. I now understand that." Some kids said that, when all was said and done, they were no longer sure what they thought about the issue; others said that they still had a strong opinion, but they saw other points of view as also legitimate.

As I listened, I thought: "This is education." It's easy to have an emotional conviction about an issue, until you immerse yourself in another person's reality and see more facets of the system. Then you can see how other people can come to a different point of view.

I left pondering something I had heard Deborah Meier, the legendary New York City principal once say, "If kids do not learn democracy in school, where will they learn it?" There was a subtle poignancy hanging in the air that afternoon. It was clear how crucial this sort of openness is for an effective democracy, and how much it is missing in today's mainstream politics of polarization, anger, and distrust. Without this sort of capacity for empathetic engagement, how can we truly understand complex issues in a non-trivializing way? I left accompanied by a simple answer: We can't, so we don't.

Look again at the video of those three six-year-old boys reflecting on the system they created that produces fights on the playground. Almost anyone would characterize their thinking as higher-order skills. They reflect together on how their own thinking and actions shape their reality. You can actually see them solving their problem and testing hypotheses: If saying "I'm sorry" didn't work, they'll try something else. Many people would think that six-year-olds are incapable of such analysis.

But such limiting assumptions hold us all back, adults and children. For example, conventional theories of learning development profess that children must first master basic skills—like reading and arithmetic—and then get to higher-order skills when they are older. But experience in schools like this suggests a more complex and far more exciting picture: a more

See Deborah Meier, *Keeping School: Letters to Families from Principals of Two Small Schools* (Beacon Press, 2005); *In Schools We Trust: Creating Communities of Learning in an Era of Testing and Standardization* (Beacon Press, 2003); and *The Power of Their Ideas: Lessons for America from a Small School in Harlem* (Beacon Press, 2002).

spiral-like progression. Developmentally, a six-year-old is at a very different level than a fifteen-year-old. But the six-year-old can clearly master some sophisticated ways of thinking. This then motivates and gives meaning to more basic skills like writing. That six-year-old now has something to write about that has meaning, and someone else to write for—his or her co-learners. This can also affect developing language skills.

In schools like Borton, with a high percentage of "English as second language learners," evidence is growing that systems thinking skills accelerate their learning of English. By giving them a visual language of graphs and diagrams where they can express their thinking in sophisticated ways without having to have high English language proficiency, their communication skills and confidence grow. This, then, accelerates their development of language skills because they have come to value their own thinking. They have something of value to say, and they want to say it!

Time will tell the effectiveness of these particular ideas and approaches, as they get further tested. But, for me, these first steps represent the beginning of a big idea that could be transformative in education: that by laying a foundation of higher-order skills early in life, mastery of basic skills will occur faster and deeper—and for more and more diverse learners. There is no rigid ladder governing a fixed ascent from basic to higher-order skills. Rather, we ascend a braided rope, where we continually deepen our sense of who we are and our innate abilities to connect and think, and in tandem we build our verbal and logic skills—an ongoing weave of intuition and reason, self and subject, aesthetic and analytic, emotional and objective.

Who knows how far this braid extends? But, I for one have seen enough examples of extraordinary student insight to believe that education for systems citizenship will reveal far greater human capacities than we can imagine. It will also reveal just how much the industrial-age school model is, in fact, a massive system of dumbing down. Direct experience with small children suggests that they are ready to start. Five-year-olds everywhere know what matters to them. When exposed to the reality of human systems, they see that their needs and sense of self are also entangled with those of others. If they are going to create things that matter to them, like not having fights, they have to do it together, mindful of one another's needs and perceptions.

Schools that foster systems citizens may foster a return to a more basic, human-centered form of education, for young and older children, teenagers, and adults. In so doing, we will be all learning the real lesson of our times: that building a more sustainable world is building a more meaningful and interconnected world in human terms. As the kids show us again and again, it is a world where we actually would like to live.

XVII. End Notes

1. Acknowledgments

Schools That Learn was developed over more than fifteen years, through two editions, with a large number of people offering help, guidance, and inspiration. The impetus came originally from the authors of the original *Fifth Discipline Fieldbook*. Rick Ross, George Roth, and Charlotte Roberts have lent this book significant help and goodwill.

Nina Kruschwitz, the managing editor of the original *Fieldbook* series, shepherded the first edition of the book through development and production. For the second edition, she served as a contributing writer and co-developed (with Lees Stuntz) the section on systems thinking in the classroom. All the books in the *Fieldbook* series have benefited from her skill and commitment.

Ellen Henrie was the second edition's copyeditor, proofreader, and indexer; her efforts immeasurably helped the book's quality and allowed us to keep our promises. John Hair designed many of the images and icons and produced the graphics for the second edition pages, providing consummate elegance on a very tight deadline. He worked from a format originally designed by Chris Welch in the early 1990s—a format that has stood the test of time. Joe Spieler, literary agent, was an active advocate of this book from the beginning and a vital link in its contractual and thematic evolution. Josie Ford has consistently and cheerfully served as the book project's business manager, making it possible for the book to exist. Tape transcription, always a critical part of the *Fieldbook* process, came from Sharon Harkey, Purple Shark Transcriptions, Brooklyn, NY. At Random House/Doubleday, editors Talia Krohn, Roger Scholl, and Michael Palgon provided counsel, comments, and support.

Others whom we wish to acknowledge for their guidance and help include Margaret Arbuckle, Warren Bennis, Sara Cameron, Angela Cox, Jim Evers, Diana Fisher, Michael Goodman, Nan Lux, Paul Mack, Maggie Piper, Betty Quantz, Lewis Rhodes, and many others. We particularly thank a group of people who helped us put together an article on the Innovation Academy Charter School that we could not include for space reasons: Laura Hagopian, Melissa Kapeckas, Stephanie Kelly, Walter Landberg, Darin Leedberg, Greg Orpen, Mairead Orpen, and Freddie Pereyra.

This book benefited from association with the following organizations: The Society for Organizational Learning, Cambridge, Massachusetts; The Department of Educational Leadership at Miami University, Oxford, Ohio; The National Superintendents Roundtable, Seattle, Washington; *strategy+business*, published by Booz & Company, New York, NY; The Creative Learning Exchange, Concord, Massachusetts; and The Systems Thinking in the Classroom Project at the Sloan School of Management, Massachusetts Institute of Technology, Cambridge. We would also like to thank all of the school, classroom, and community practitioners whom we have worked with, who have had the courage to stick with it, and from whom we have learned. Though we can not list them by name, we also wish to thank the attendees at various conferences and working sessions that have influenced this book.

We produced *Schools That Learn* as camera-ready copy, using Apple Macintosh computers, Microsoft Word, Adobe Illustrator, and InDesign. Our "lexicon" etymologies derive from two primary sources: John Ayto, *Dictionary of Word Origins* (Arcade, 1990) and Eric Partridge, *Origins: A Short Etymological Dictionary of Modern English* (Greenwich House, 1958).

Creating a book of this size and scope inevitably involves the support and attention of the people with whom we are closest in our lives. Therefore, we particularly wish to acknowledge, with love and appreciation: Harry McCabe and Patrick McCabe; Thomas Dutton, Nathan Dutton, Nolan Dutton, Jennie Dutton, and Ariel Dutton; Faith Florer, Frances Kleiner, Elizabeth Kleiner, and Constance Kleiner; Emily Lucas and Maggie Lucas; Diane Senge, Nathan Senge, and Ian Senge; Susan Simington, Anthony Smith, and Michael Smith.

2. About the Authors

Peter Senge is a Senior Lecturer at the Sloan School of Management, Massachusetts Institute of Technology, and the Founding Chair of the Society of Organizational Learning (SoL), a global network of people and institutions working together for systemic change (http://www.solonline.org). His work centers on promoting shared understanding of complex issues and shared leadership for creating healthier human systems. Today, this involves major cross-sector collaborative projects focused on global food systems, climate change, circular (zero waste) business models and regenerative economies, and youth leadership and the future of education. Peter is the author of *The Fifth Discipline: The Art and Practice of the Learning Organization* (Doubleday, 1990 and 2006). More than two million copies of this book have been sold worldwide, and it was recognized by *Harvard Business Review* as "one of the seminal management books of the past 75 years," and by the *Financial Times* as one of five "most important" management books. He is also coauthor of the three Fieldbooks: *The Fifth Discipline Fieldbook: Strategies and Tools for Building a Learning Organization* (Doubleday, 1994); *The Dance of Change: The Challenges to Sustaining Momentum in Learning Organizations* (Doubleday, 1999), and this volume. Peter's other books include *The Necessary Revolution: How Individuals and Organizations are Working Together to Create a Sustainable World* (with Bryan Smith, Nina Kruschwitz, Joe Laur, and Sara Schley) (Doubleday, 2008); and *Presence: Human Purpose and the Field of the Future* (with C. Otto Scharmer, Joseph Jaworski, and Betty Sue Flowers) (SoL, 2004). The *Journal of Business Strategy* named him as one of the twenty-four people who had the greatest influence on business strategy in the twentieth century. He has a bachelor's degree from Stanford University (where he received the F.E. Terman senior engineering award) and a master's and Ph.D. from MIT. He lives in central Massachusetts.

Nelda Cambron-McCabe is a professor in the Department of Educational Leadership and Chair, Department of Educational Psychology at Miami University (Ohio) (http://www.units.muohio.edu/eap/edl/). As an advisory board member and a facilitator of the National Superintendents Roundtable, she works closely with Roundtable superintendents in planning programs to support them as they pursue educational change in their school systems. At Miami University, she teaches courses in school leadership and public school law and is coauthor, with Martha McCarthy and Stephen Thomas, of *Public School Law: Teacher's and Student's Rights*, sixth edition, (Allyn & Bacon, 2009). Professor Cambron-Mc-Cabe has focused significant attention on the professional development of school superintendents; her ten-year work with the Danforth Forum for the American School Superintendent resulted in the publication of *The Superintendent's Fieldbook*, by Cambron-McCabe, Luvern Cunningham, James Harvey, and Robert Koff (Corwin Press, 2005). She was president of the Education Law Association and the American Education Finance Association and has served as editor of the *Journal of Education Finance*. She lives in southwestern Ohio.

Timothy Lucas has been a teacher and administrator in public education for the past four decades. He has taught at the elementary, middle school, high school, and college levels. He has experience at the district level as a Director of Curriculum and Instruction, Assistant Superintendent, and Superintendent of Schools. He has worked with school leaders and departments of education across the U.S., Canada, and Europe. Tim is a practitioner, focusing his research and work on integrating the concepts of the five disciplines into curriculum development, sustainable school improvement, and school leadership. He is a recognized innovator for developing systems thinking tools in classrooms and school administration work. He is currently teaching at Wilkes University and is on the board of the Institute for the Future of Learning, a nonprofit group, supporting schools and their communities as they develop twenty-first century learning environments (www.instituteforthefutureoflearning.org). He lives in the Lehigh Valley of Pennsylvania and is an avid sportsman.

Janis Dutton is a freelance editor, writer, educational consultant, and community activist. She was the managing editor of *The Fifth Discipline Fieldbook*. She used the learning organization principles in her community to build individual and collective capacities as change agents when she served on the city council, planning and environmental commissions, adult education committees, and chamber of commerce community leadership initiatives. She continues to practice the disciplines in a variety of community conversations and grassroots initiatives in her work for democratic social justice. After completing work on the first edition of this book, her interest in social movements led her to earn a master's degree from Antioch University, where she explored the intersection between organizational learning and popular education. She also managed production for and copyedited two anthologies that link architectural and educational theory and practice. She has coordinated production projects for the Miami University of Ohio Department of Architecture, the Cincinnati Environmental Awareness Center, and Catalyst, a magazine for children. Her writing has appeared in *Garbage Magazine*, *The Burbank Daily Review*, *The Cincinnati Enquirer*, and *The Superintendents Fieldbook*. She lives in southwestern Ohio.

Bryan Smith is an internationally recognized author, speaker, and consultant on leadership development, vision-based planning, and organizational learning, with a strategic focus on leadership for sustainability. Prior to founding Broad Reach Innovations, Bryan was a Senior Partner for eighteen years at Innovation Associates, the firm that pioneered the field of organizational learning. Bryan has been a central contributor to the creation of innovative tools, methods, and strategies for building inspired learning organizations. He has worked with the UN Foundation, the UN Office of the Secretary-General, and many other education, governmental, nonprofit, and business organizations worldwide. He is a founding faculty member for the Sustainable Enterprise Academy at York University in Toronto and a coauthor of all three *Fifth Discipline Fieldbooks*, plus *The Necessary Revolution*. Bryan is committed to supporting the growth of leadership and broad community capabilities in developing countries. As part of his doctoral research, he carried out the first empirical study of charismatic leadership in organizations, which has informed his work with leaders on six continents. He received his MBA and Ph.D. in Organizational Behavior from the University of Toronto and lives in Toronto, Canada.

Art Kleiner is a writer, editor, educator, and the editorial director for the Fieldbook Projects; he was a consulting editor on the first edition of *The Fifth Discipline* and a coauthor of all three associated *Fifth Discipline Fieldbooks*. Since 2005, he has been the editor-in-chief of *strategy+business*, the award-winning management magazine published by the management consulting firm Booz & Company (www.strategy-business.com). Among the subjects that *strategy+business* introduced is neuroleadership, the evolving application of neuroscience to organizational effectiveness. Kleiner is the author of *The Age of Heretics: A History of the Radical Thinkers Who Reinvented Corporate Management* (second edition, Jossey-Bass, 2008), which was praised by Warren Bennis as "that rarest of books, one that is both important and a pleasure to read." He is also the author of *Who Really Matters: The Core Group Theory of Power, Privilege and Success* (Doubleday, 2003), about which Jim Collins wrote: "Art Kleiner has uncovered a central truth about the way organizations work…Like any deep insight, it makes explicable what had previously been mysterious." Writing on technological, cultural, management, and environmental topics, Kleiner has contributed to *Wired*, the *New York Times Magazine*, *Fast Company*, the *Harvard Business Review*, and many other publications. He is a scenario-planning consultant and a developer, with George Roth and Nina Kruschwitz, of the "learning history" form of organizational storytelling and evaluation. He is also a former editor of the *Whole Earth Catalog and CoEvolution Quarterly*. Kleiner is on the faculty of the ALIA (Authentic Leadership in Action) Institute of Halifax, Nova Scotia, and the Interactive Telecommunications Program at the Tisch School of the Arts at New York University. He has a master's of journalism from the University of California at Berkeley. He lives outside New York City.

Index